The Writings of Frithjof Schuon
Series

World Wisdom
The Library of Perennial Philosophy

The Library of Perennial Philosophy is dedicated to the exposition of the timeless Truth underlying the diverse religions. This Truth, often referred to as the *Sophia Perennis*—or Perennial Wisdom—finds its expression in the revealed Scriptures as well as in the writings of the great sages and the artistic creations of the traditional worlds.

The Perennial Philosophy provides the intellectual principles capable of explaining both the formal contradictions and the transcendent unity of the great religions.

Ranging from the writings of the great sages of the past to the perennialist authors of our time, each series of our Library has a different focus. As a whole, they express the inner unanimity, transforming radiance, and irreplaceable values of the great spiritual traditions.

The Essential Frithjof Schuon appears as one of our selections in the Writings of Frithjof Schuon series.

The Writings of Frithjof Schuon

The Writings of Frithjof Schuon form the foundation of our library because he is the pre-eminent exponent of the Perennial Philosophy. His work illuminates this perspective in both an essential and comprehensive manner like none other.

Books by Frithjof Schuon

The Transcendent Unity of Religions
Spiritual Perspectives and Human Facts
Gnosis: Divine Wisdom
Language of the Self
Stations of Wisdom
Understanding Islam
Light on the Ancient Worlds
In the Tracks of Buddhism
Treasures of Buddhism
Logic and Transcendence
Esoterism as Principle and as Way
Castes and Races
Sufism: Veil and Quintessence
From the Divine to the Human
Christianity/Islam: Essays on Esoteric Ecumenicism
Survey of Metaphysics and Esoterism
In the Face of the Absolute
The Feathered Sun: Plains Indians in Art and Philosophy
To Have a Center
Roots of the Human Condition
Images of Primordial and Mystic Beauty: Paintings by Frithjof Schuon
Echoes of Perennial Wisdom
The Play of Masks
Road to the Heart: Poems
The Transfiguration of Man
The Eye of the Heart
Songs for a Spiritual Traveler: Selected Poems
Form and Substance in the Religions
Adastra and Stella Maris: Poems by Frithjof Schuon

Edited Writings of Frithjof Schuon

The Essential Writings of Frithjof Schuon, ed. Seyyed Hossein Nasr
The Fullness of God: Frithjof Schuon on Christianity,
ed. James S. Cutsinger
Prayer Fashions Man: Frithjof Schuon on the Spiritual Life,
ed. James S. Cutsinger

The Essential
Frithjof Schuon

Edited by
Seyyed Hossein Nasr

The Essential Frithjof Schuon
© 2005 World Wisdom

Library of Congress Cataloging-in-Publication Data

Schuon, Frithjof, 1907-
  [Selections. English. 2005]
  The essential Frithjof Schuon / edited by Seyyed Hossein Nasr.
     p. cm. – (The library of perennial philosophy) (The writings of Frithjof Schuon)
  Includes bibliographical references.
  ISBN-13: 978-0-941532-92-1 (pbk. : alk. paper)
  ISBN-10: 0-941532-92-5 (pbk. : alk. paper) 1. Religion–Philosophy. 2. Religions. 3.
Philosophy. I. Nasr, Seyyed Hossein. II. Title. III. Series.
  BL51.S463213 2005
  200–dc22
                                        2005014071

Cover Picture: Frithjof Schuon in 1974

Printed on acid-free paper in Canada.
For information address World Wisdom, Inc.
P.O. Box 2682,
Bloomington, Indiana 47402-2682
www.worldwisdom.com

Contents

Preface to the 2005 Edition

THIS ANTHOLOGY OF THE WRITINGS of Frithjof Schuon was prepared in the mid 1980s over a decade before his death in 1998. With the remarkable creativity that he possessed, he continued to write up to nearly the very end of his earthly existence. One might, therefore, think that a new version of *The Essential Writings of Frithjof Schuon* should include new selections from his later works written during the last dozen years of his life. But there are several reasons why we have decided to preserve the original selections.

First of all, the present anthology was sent to Schuon himself and after several discussions and exchanges, was finalized in its present form with his own definitive approval. He mentioned to us that what we had selected did indeed represent the "essential" Schuon, even if because of limitations of space one could not have included all that we ourselves considered to be essential. In any case both the selections and the introduction to this work had his firm confirmation and *imprimatur*.

Secondly, the wonderful prose works that Schuon produced during the last years of his life were mostly syntheses, reformulations, and summaries of what he had expounded in his magisterial writings over a fifty-year period preceding the publication of our anthology. When we discussed this matter with the author himself, he confirmed this appraisal, adding that there were a few works such as the essay "To Have a Center" in which he had embarked upon a new subject, but that for the most part his later works had the function of further clarifying and synthesizing his earlier writings. As for the large amount of poems written by Schuon at the end of his life, they in a

sense summarize in poetic medium the whole corpus of his teachings. Already, a selection of those poems has been published and one
hopes that others will follow. But in any case there is such a large
body of this later poetry that one cannot do justice to it by simply
adding a few of these poems to this volume.

The few poems originally included in this volume represent
something quite different: they are selections from two small volumes of poetry written by Schuon in his earlier years and they were
included with Schuon's approval to demonstrate his poetic gifts and
the spiritual nature of those early poems. These early volumes of
poetry are like brooks of clear running water flowing from some
mountain spring. The late poems are vast in number and more like
an ocean of which an anthology could not be made by including just
a few examples. One hopes that, first of all, the whole collection of
these later poems—almost all of which are in German—will be published in the original language; secondly, that the whole corpus will
then be translated and published in English; and, thirdly, that a separate anthology will be made of these late poems in their English
translation, along with samples of the few poems Schuon wrote in
English during the last years of his life.

Finally, it is necessary to remember that the present anthology
was in print for many years and is seen by many readers interested in
the works of Schuon to be a good place of entry into that vast intellectual and spiritual world. We therefore thought it best to preserve
it in its present form rather than creating basically a new anthology
by incorporating material written by Schuon after *The Essential
Writings of Frithjof Schuon* appeared. Our hope is that others will come
forward to publish new anthologies of his writings in general. As for
anthologies concerned with specific subjects, that project is in fact
fortunately proceeding forth already under the auspices of World
Wisdom.

In conclusion, we wish to thank World Wisdom for making *The
Essential Frithjof Schuon*—which has been out of print for some time—
accessible once again for those who are seeking an introduction to
the luminous writings of one of the most significant spiritual and
intellectual figures of the twentieth century.

Seyyed Hossein Nasr
Bethesda, Maryland
November 2004

Frithjof Schuon in 1968

Introducing The Writings of Frithjof Schuon

On Some of the Features of His Works

THE WRITINGS OF FRITHJOF SCHUON are characterized by essentiality, universality and comprehensiveness. They have the quality of essentiality in the sense that they always go to the heart and are concerned with the essence of whatever they deal with. Schuon possesses the gift of reaching the very core of the subject he is treating, of going beyond forms to the essential formless Center of forms whether they be religious, artistic or related to certain features and traits of the cosmic or human orders. To read his works is to be transplanted from the shell to the kernel, to be carried on a journey that is at once intellectual and spiritual from the circumference to the Center.

His writings are universal, not only because the formless Essence *is* universal, but also because even on the level of forms he does not confine himself solely to a particular world, period or region. His perspective is truly universal in the sense of embracing all orders of reality from the Divine to the human and on the human level worlds as far apart as that of Abrahamic monotheism and the Shamanic heritage of Shintoism and the North American Indian religions. It is also of course universal in the metaphysical sense of always being concerned with either the meaning of the Universal as such or the particular in the light of the Universal. For him the particular at once veils and manifests the Universal as form hides and reveals the Essence and as the phenomenon, while opaque in

1

itself, is, as symbol, the gate to the noumenal world which is none other than the universal order.

Schuon's works are also comprehensive and all-embracing in the sense that they include practically the whole mountain of knowledge understood in the traditional sense, ranging from its metaphysical peak which touches the infinite expanse of the heavens to particular fields such as formal theology, anthropology and psychology, which are the foothills along with the trails which lead from these foothills to the exalted peak. Amidst this century of the segmentation of particular branches of knowledge and the proliferation of usually unrelated bodies of information which have made the vision of the whole well nigh impossible for those who begin from the parts rather than the whole and who remain rooted only in a knowledge of an empirical order, Schuon demonstrates with blinding evidence the possibility of an all-embracing knowledge. This knowledge is rooted, however, not in the scattered multiplicity of the world of the senses but in the unity of the intellect which Schuon understands in its traditional sense and as it has been used by a Meister Eckhart. Schuon is at once metaphysician, theologian, traditional philosopher and logician, master of the discipline of comparative religion, expositor of traditional art and civilization, authority in the science of man and society, spiritual guide and a critic of the modern world in not only its practical but also philosophical and scientific aspects. His knowledge, moreover, embraces East and West, the ancient medieval civilizations as well as the modern world, German literature as well as Hindu sculpture. From the point of view of sheer scholarly knowledge combined with metaphysical penetrations, it is hardly possible to find a contemporary corpus of writings with the same all-embracing and comprehensive nature combined with incredible depth. As a result of this quality in addition to the essentiality and universality which characterize Schuon's works, it can be said that these writings demonstrate in a unique fashion not only the unity of the Divine Principle but also the unity within diversity of the multiple recipients of the messages which have issued from the Divine Principle in the form of religions and civilizations and cultures which the manifestations of that Principle have brought into being. His works depict upon a vast canvas the descent of all that exists from the One, the multiplicity and richness within the human order as a result of this descent, and finally the reintegration of this multiplicity back into the One. In achieving this enormous task across religious, theological, philosophical and cultural borders, Schuon has accomplished a synthesis which could in fact have been brought about only in this day and age when the normal barriers between human collectivities are becoming weakened or even falling apart. His synthesis is an antidote, issuing from the fountainhead of grace, for the ills of chaos, confusion, relativism, skepticism and nihilism which have befallen many people in the modern world precisely as a result of the erosion and in many places collapse of the traditional structures which have, over the ages, provided meaning for human beings during their earthly journey.

The Study of Religion

The vast writings of Schuon are concerned most of all with religion. But for him religion is not reduced to that truncated reality with which so many modern authors who treat the subject called religion are concerned. For him religion is still related to *religio*, to all that binds man to God, to the Ultimate Principle. Religion for Schuon is not reducible to the limited category of modern thought bearing that name and not even to much of what passes for theology in the West today, divorced as religion in this sense has become from the other domains of human thought and action, alienated from both the cosmos and human society, and exiled to a corner of man's life in a world which is being secularized to an ever greater degree. Schuon, needless to say, is perfectly aware of this process and the sad state into which religion and religious studies have fallen in the modern West, but he does not accept this state as the norm or "reality" with which he must grapple as a theologian like so many modern religious thinkers who have conceded defeat even before beginning the battle against all that threatens religion today.

Nor is Schuon satisfied with the study of religion in terms of any other category of thought or discipline. While being fully aware of the unfolding of each religion in history, he is strongly opposed to historicism or the reducing of the reality of a religion simply to its history. While emphasizing the central role and importance of faith, he refuses to reduce religion to only faith with total disregard for the element of doctrine or truth seen as an objective reality. While being aware of the significance of every phenomenon in the traditional universe, he does not limit the study of religions to mere phenomena divorced from their universal reality and the total sacred universe within which religious phenomena reveal their meaning *qua* religious phenomena. While being fully aware of the role of a religiously structured society, its stratifications and ethnic elements in religion, he stands totally opposed to reducing religion to its sociological component. While being a master of religious psychology and having written some of the most illuminating pages on the transformations which the religious and spiritual life bring about in the psyche of those who follow such a life, he distinguishes clearly and categorically between the spiritual and the psychic and criticizes severely those who would reduce religion to religious psychology.

One can summarize his approach to the study of religion by saying that for Schuon religion is the principle reality of human existence not to be reduced to any other category although it is related to all other categories and domains of human thought and action. One of the main reasons in fact why Schuon has been so much neglected in circles concerned with religious studies in the modern world is that for most of them he takes religion too seriously while many modern religious thinkers and theologians, although purporting either to study religion or to think in theological categories, function in a world in which the light of religion has already become dim. To face an intellectual and spiritual universe in which religion shines once again as the central sun which illuminates and orders all things is too daring and awesome an experience which few are willing to face. The glare appears too blinding to those accustomed to semi-darkness. Better to act as if such a universe did not exist while studying religion in terms of non-religious categories. Better to discuss religion in terms of abstract concepts depleted of all sacred content to the extent possible than to enter a fire which consumes the whole of one's being.

The singular neglect of Schuon's writings in both academic and nonacademic circles concerned with religion, there being some notable exceptions, is precisely because these writings are so seriously concerned with religion that one cannot even take cognizance of their presence and take their challenge seriously without having to change one's own halfhearted engagement with the religious world, without questioning the skeptical and secularized world of modern man and replacing it with one based on religious certitude while possessing the greatest intellectual rigor. If finally today after such long neglect of Schuon's writings, there is a much greater interest in his works, it is because many people who possess the necessary perspicacity are finally tired of halfway solutions and are willing to face the challenge of his writings whatever might be the consequence for their own intellectual and spiritual life. It is because many an intelligent person who is attracted to the study of religion is no longer satisfied with the reduction of the study of religion to its history, or phenomenology, or sociology. One cannot study the writings of Schuon on religion without taking religion and man's religious nature seriously and thereby without developing an attitude toward the whole reality of religion and religious studies different from what most modern men are presented with today not only in their course of education, but also in many cases by theologians and religious philosophers and thinkers of their religious community.

Schuon is concerned with both the study of religion and religions, with the reality of religion as such and with the relation between the many religions which exist and have existed on the global scale. These two concerns are in fact related together in his perspective for he writes for a world in which the journey across religious frontiers has already become a profound reality and where for many people the study of religions affects in one way or another their own participation in and understanding of religion in itself. Schuon, while accepting and in fact honoring and respecting in the profoundest sense the diversity of religions which is willed by Heaven, emphasizes both the inner unity within this diversity and the religious significance of this diversity itself. He has written over and over again on how each religion is *the* religion, how to have lived any religion fully is to have lived religion as such and therefore in a sense all religions, how each religious universe is absolute for those who live within that universe and yet only the Absolute Reality which stands above all manifestation and particularization is the Absolute as such, how the sun of each religious cosmos is for that cosmos *the* sun while being a star in that spiritual firmament which symbolizes the Divine Infinity.

Schuon emphasizes the spiritual genius and originality — in the etymological sense of the word as being related to the Origin — of each religion along with the civilization, social structure, art and culture which it brings into being. He also emphasizes perennial religion, or *religio perennis*, that he also calls the religion of the heart, which resides at the center of every particular religion and also at the center and in the very substance from which man is made. If man were able to penetrate to the center of his own being, to enter the inner kingdom, he would reach that *religio perennis* or *religio cordis* which lies at the center of revealed religions. But because of the fall of man and its effects upon his soul, it is in fact not possible to enter the heart save with the aid of the grace which issues from those objective manifestations of the Divine Logos which are the revealed religions. The emphasis upon the perennial and universal religion of the heart, far from destroying or diminishing the significance of the religious traditions of mankind, accentuates their Divine Origin, sacred character, absolute necessity for the human order and indispensable nature in making possible access to that *religio perennis* which lies at the center of all religions.

The usage of the term religion by Schuon and his expansion of the boundaries of its meaning far beyond the confines that modern readers are accustomed to associating with it can be better understood by turning to the word "tradition", another key concept which Schuon uses very often in his works usually in close conjunction with the term religion. The writings of Schuon can in fact be characterized as being before anything else traditional. He considers himself a traditional metaphysician and religious "thinker", if such a singularly modern term can be transposed into the traditional context. Therefore, if we were able to understand what is meant by tradition as used by him and other writers of this school, we would be able to gain a profound insight into the nature of his writings and world view.

Tradition, as used by Schuon and before him by such masters as René Guénon and Ananda K. Coomaraswamy, is neither custom nor habit. Nor is it simply what has been believed or practiced for a certain period of time during the history of a particular civilization. Rather, it is a supraformal reality, hence impossible to define completely through delimitation. It is all that has its origin in Heaven, in revelation in its most universal sense, along with its unfolding in a particular spatio-temporal setting determined by the Source from which the tradition originates. It applies not only to this truth of celestial origin, but to the application of the principles contained therein to realms as disparate as law and art, as methods of meditation and the manner of cultivating a garden. There is therefore not only such a usage of this term in relation to metaphysics and religion, but there is traditional art, traditional social structure and the traditional sciences. In the words of a well-known expositor of the traditional perspective, Marco Pallis,

It will already be apparent to the reader that by tradition more is meant than just custom long established, even if current usage has tended to restrict it in this way. Here the word will always be given its transcendent, which is also its normal, connotation without any attempt being made, however, to pin it down to a particular set of concepts, if only because tradition, being formless and supra-personal in its essence, escapes exact definition in terms of human speech or thought. All that can usefully be said of it at the moment is that wherever a complete tradition exists this will entail the presence of four things, namely: a source of inspiration or, to use a more concrete term, of Revelation; a current of influence or Grace issuing forth from that source and transmitted without interruption through a variety of channels; a way of "verification" which, when faithfully followed, will lead the human subject to successive positions where he is able to "actualise" the truths that Revelation communicates; finally there is the formal embodiment of tradition in the doctrines, arts, sciences and other elements that together go to determine the character of a normal civilization. (*The Way and the Mountain*, London, 1960, pp. 9-10).

The full impact of the term "tradition" becomes evident when it is contrasted to all that lies outside of its embrace, namely the modern world which is at once modern in the temporal sense and antitraditional in nature. The traditional writers distinguish between the traditional and the modern not because of the particular period of history in which certain patterns of thought or forms of art happen to have been prevalent but because of the nature of those patterns and forms. Traditional therefore does not mean simply ancient and medieval or old and modern postmedieval and new. Not all that is old is traditional, late Graeco-Roman art and philosophy being an example. Nor is all that is new or postmedieval modern as the poetry of Angelus Silesius or present day Navaho sand paintings exemplify. That is why within this perspective a clear distinction is made between modern and contemporary. One can be contemporary yet opposed to all that characterizes the modern world as such and distinguishes it from all the traditional, and from the perspective of Schuon and those who share his perspective, normal civilizations of East or West. To stress the crucial term tradition is to provide the means with which one can discern between truth and error, between all that comes from Heaven and that is in conformity with the spiritual nature of man, and all that is simply of human origin, based on the negation of the supra-human, and because of this limitation ultimately sub-human. To neglect the meaning of tradition is to lose sight of the centrality of the concern for Truth as such in the writings of Schuon and those who belong to the traditional school. To lay aside this basic concept in order to avoid causing an affront to various proponents of modernism is to be forced to face the dangerous forest of confusion and chaos which characterizes the modern world without the light of discernment that alone can save man from becoming lost and finally devoured by the beasts lurking in this forest. The result of the negation of tradition cannot but be the weakening of the will to know the truth and become attached to that truth. It cannot but lead to half-truths if not pure error and the penetration of the secular into the precinct of the sacred itself. To refuse to accept the category of tradition and significance of the traditional, is to be disarmed against the dangers of the antitraditional which has withered away the religious life and thought of Western man since the Renaissance and of Oriental man since the last century and now threatens to undo religion from within.

To comprehend the message of Schuon, therefore, it is essential to gain a clear understanding of the meaning of the term tradition and its applications. Perhaps no other concept is so crucial for the understanding of his writings. Schuon is first and foremost an expositor of traditional teachings and wants to be known as such. Both his expounding of religion, metaphysics, art, etc. and his criticism of the modern world and its aberrations are based on the meaning of tradition. Not only does Schuon write about aspects of things human and divine in the light of tradition, but he also criticizes philosophy, art, science, social structures and other thoughts and activities related to human existence in the light of that truth of which all traditions are embodiments. Schuon is traditional in all that he writes as both expounder of the truth and critic of error.

A second basic characteristic of the writings of Schuon, especially as it concerns religion, is orthodoxy. Schuon considers himself strictly orthodox and the defender of orthodoxy. It might therefore appear as some what strange for those who identify orthodoxy with limitation and narrowness that under the umbrella of orthodoxy, Schuon should defend not only a Meister Eckhart within the Christian tradition but also both the exoteric and esoteric dimensions of other religions, while in the name of the same principle criticizing pseudo-yogis and other syncretic modernists within Hinduism. For Schuon orthodoxy is related at once to Truth and the formal homogeneity of a particular traditional universe. To speak of the Truth is also to speak of the possibility of error. To be orthodox is to be on the side of the Truth. But since the Truth has revealed itself not once and in only one formal language but many times in different 'worlds' possessing their own formal homogeneity and language of discourse, the question of being on the side of the truth involves also the formal world in question. Schuon therefore defends Christianity as orthodox in itself while being heterodox from the point of view of Jewish orthodoxy and he explains why Buddhism is an orthodox relgion, that is an embodiment of the Truth and means "provided" by that Truth to attain the Truth, while it is considered as heterodox from the perspective of Brahmanism.

Within a single religion also, he explains why an esoteric school such as Sufism in Islam is strictly orthodox in itself while being sometimes misunderstood as a heterodox phenomenon by the exoteric authorities and why also within Sufism there have been those who have deviated from orthodoxy. He also points out the significance of the criterion of orthodoxy even on the esoteric level for the evaluation of certain individualistic or aberrant manifestations which can take place and in fact have taken place even in traditional worlds as far apart as medieval Japan and Europe. For Schuon orthodoxy does not mean limitation. Rather, it is like form which is not opposed to the illimitable expanses of the Formless but is the indispensable gate which opens inwardly unto the Formless. The limitations imposed by orthodoxy are there to prevent man's falling into error. They are rails on the two sides of the straight path of correct doctrine (*orthodoxa*) and correct practice (*ortho-praxis*) which prevent the seeker from falling into the abyss of ignorance, error and finally disintegration. They are not to prevent him from marching upon the path which leads ultimately to complete freedom and liberation from all limitation and constraint either in this life or the next. For Schuon orthodoxy is not only not opposed to the loftiest metaphysical knowledge or spiritual realization but is a necessary condition for their attainment, the exceptions being there only to prove the rule and to re-affirm the truth that, "The Spirit bloweth where it listeth." In his study of religion, as of other domains, Schuon must be characterized as being orthodox as he is traditional, if both of these terms are understood in the universal sense which he himself, along with other expositors of the traditional perspective, have given to them.

Schuon's works are concerned at once with the elements which constitute a religion and the relation between religions. He deals with the components of religion in itself such as the meaning of revelation, hermeneutics, theology, ethics and mysticism and also with different religions as they are related to each other and the problems which the multiplicity of religions poses for the reality and significance of religion in itself. He does not deal so much with the history of religions as currently understood which means the reduction of the reality of religion to its history and temporal unfolding. He is also not concerned with the sociology or philosophy of religion if these terms are understood in their usual academic sense which reduces religion to a social phenomenon or introduces the categories of a profane philosophy to understand and explain the verities of religion. Nor is he concerned with the psychology of religion if again one understands by this term the psychologization of religion and its reduction to simply a psychic phenomenon. But he is interested in all of these aspects of religion from the point of view of the primal and principial reality of religion. He deals extensively with the manner whereby the reality of a particular religion manifests itself in different times and places. He has devoted many studies to the applications of the teachings of religion to the social order. His studies are replete with the exposition of the intellectual dimension of religion and are concerned with the "philosophy of religion" in the profoundest sense of this term if only philosophy were to be understood in the traditional sense. Likewise some of the most far-reaching discussions of the effect of the reality of religion upon the human psyche are to be found in his writings for Schuon is a master of the traditional science of psychology which in order not to be confused with the modern field bearing the same name should perhaps be called pneumatology for it is concerned not so much with the psyche as with the pneuma and with the psyche itself to the extent that it becomes wed to the pneuma in that sacred union from which is born the gold of spiritual alchemy.

In any case there is hardly a branch of religious studies with which the contemporary discipline bearing this name is concerned that is not treated amply in the writings of Schuon with both amazing metaphysical and religious insight and science and scholarship. Only the point of view is radically different from what is found in most modern works on various aspects of religion. That is precisely why without being a historian, philosopher, sociologist or psychologist of religion, Schuon brings the profoundest insight into all these fields, namely, the history, philosophy, sociology and psychology of religion. His works are like the morning wind, which breathes new life into a stifling, closed space wherein religion is imprisoned in the modern world and especially within the academic disciplines which are supposed to be concerned with it. He deals with religion in a manner which brings out the primacy of religion and demonstrates its relation to facets and aspects of human thought or experience without subordinating it to these facets and aspects.

Schuon is also a theologian of great import without being just a theologian for he is concerned most of all with a metaphysics or *scientia sacra* which stands above theology as this term is usually understood in Christianity. But he does concern himself with theology as such and displays amazing knowledge of not only the major traditional Christian schools of theology such as the Augustinian, Thomistic, Palamite and also Lutheran but also of the various schools of Islamic theology or *kalām*. His discussion of the Trinity or the question of the two natures of Christ within the context of Christian theology, or of free will and determinism in Ash'arite *kalām* as found in such a work as *Logic and Transcendence,* reveal his mastery in the treatment of classical theological issues with intellectual rigor and at the same time on the basis of certitude. In studying his theological expositions one realizes how little theology is actually left in the works of some of the most famous modern theologians who, in their desire to placate what they consider to be the imperative demands of modern rationalism and empiricism, have practically depleted theology of its theological nature and thereby destroyed its very *raison d'être.*

Being the outstanding metaphysician and expounder of the intellectual aspects of religions that he is, Schuon is nevertheless also deeply concerned with the practical aspects of religion as it is crystallized in ethics. Although he has not written a separate opus on ethics any more than he has on theology, his works on religion, such as *Esoterism as Principle and as Way* and *Spiritual Perspectives and Human Fact* , are replete with passages which concern ethics. He deals with morality in its relation to the principles of each religion and also to the spiritual virtues which are inward embellishments of the soul but related in an inextricable manner to the domain of morality. Schuon seeks to demonstrate at once the necessity of morality for the religious life, the relativity of moral injunctions within each religion in relation to other religions, and at the same time the absoluteness of the inner content of these injunctions as they concern the spiritual virtues and their effect upon the human soul.

Speaking from the metaphysical perspective, from the Center of the circle of existence which is at once above forms and at the heart of things, Schuon is of course concerned with inwardness without which there is no spirituality. The essentiality characteristic of his works to which we have already referred necessitates dealing also with the essential or inward aspect of religion which is usually called mysticism. In order to avoid the ambiguities and ambivalence surrounding the term "mysticism" which many equate with vagueness rather than clarity and passivity rather than activity, Schuon has been very careful in the way in which he has used this term. Rather, he has based his treatment of the whole subject of mysticism upon the fundamental traditional distinction between the exoteric and esoteric dimensions or aspects of religion and has written numerous works to elucidate their fundamental nature and rapport, as well as complementarity and opposition.

Religion issues from the Source or the Ultimate Reality which is at once transcendent and immanent, completely beyond and here at the center of things. But man lives in the world of forms, of multiplicity and of opacity which is a subjectivization if the Ultimate Reality is considered as the Supreme Object, the Transcendent One; or an objectivization and superimposition if that Reality is considered as the Supreme Subject, the Immanent Self. In either case the very principle of manifestation requires the acceptance of the distinction between Essence and form, between the inward and outward, between the noumenon and phenomenon, religion being no exception since like the cosmos itself, it issues from and is created by that Ultimate Reality which is the source of all that is. Moreover, being the direct revelation to man, religion is itself the key for the understanding of the inner reality of the cosmos as well as man seen as the microcosm.

Religion is like a walnut, to use the Sufi image, with both a shell and the core or fruit which can grow and possess existence only within the shell. The purpose of the shell is to protect the fruit but without the shell there would be no fruit. Likewise, the final end of religion is to guide man to God, to enable man to be delivered from the bondage of limitation which is the goal of esoterism here in this life and which even exoterism aspires to in future life. Exoterism is, however, absolutely necessary to make the attainment of this end through esoterism possible even when man lives in this world. Without the exoteric, no esoterism could survive and be efficacious. But also without esoterism religion would be reduced to only its external aspects without means of providing a way for those whose nature is such that they must follow the esoteric path in order to follow religion. Such a situation would also leave religion without the means of responding to certain challenges of an intellectual order which only the esoteric is capable of answering with the result that cracks would appear in the wall of even the exoteric aspect of religion and threaten the very existence of the religion in question.

Schuon has gone to great pains not only to distinguish exoterism from esoterism and to show their necessity and Divine Origin within each tradition, but also to make a clear distinction between esoterism and occultism, individualistic mysticism and especially all the pseudo-esoteric movements of modern times which claim authenticity without recourse to exoterism or to traditional orthodoxy and which would seek to open the gates of Heaven without the aid of those plenary manifestations of the Universal Logos to whom alone such a key has been given. In this context Schuon provides not only an unrivaled exposition of the various aspects, elements and manifestations of esoterism in itself and within different religions but also a chart with which one can navigate upon the dangerous waters of the present day scene where on the one hand man is faced with so many religious institutions and teachings shorn of their esoteric dimensions and on the other hand with so many pseudo-esoteric cults and groups. Schuon's aim is to substantiate the reality of esoterism not as a vaguely defined reality by itself, but within each orthodox religion, thereby strengthening religion as such and even exoterism as considered in itself and independent of the esoteric. Schuon always defends the most outward and limited exoterist who has faith in God and His revelation against any pseudo-esoterist with the wildest metaphysical and esoteric claims who in the name of a supposedly "higher truth" rejects the traditions which have guided men over the ages.

Within the context of the Christian tradition where the term mysticism has gained a rather special meaning, Schuon has turned over and over again to the elucidation of the message of those concerned with mysticism, whether these mystics be Catholic or Orthodox and including also certain Protestant mystics. He has distinguished between the three fundamental types of Christian mysticism, namely Christian gnosis as represented by a Clement of Alexandria or Meister Eckhart, Christian love mysticism of a St. Bernard or St. Francis and finally the passionate mysticism of the Renaissance and later periods represented by such figures as St. John of the Cross and St. Teresa of Avila. With the discernment and lucidity which are characteristic of his works, Schuon clarifies the differences between not only the ways of knowledge and love within the Christian mystical tradition, but also the intrusion of the passionate and individualistic elements characteristic of the Renaissance into Christian mysticism thereby creating a mode different from traditional Christian mysticism yet nevertheless capable of producing saints because it still remained within the orthodox Christian tradition.

Schuon's treatment of the modes and forms of esoterism in other traditions which could also be called mysticism, if this term were to be understood as that which is concerned with the Divine Mysteries, is imbued with the same profundity, subtlety and lucidity. He has a direct sense of the sacred and the understanding of the meaning of sanctity which can only issue from experience and which enables him to discern the presence of sanctity wherever and whenever it is to be found. In the complex domain of esoterism in general and mysticism in the more particular sense given to it in the Christian tradition, he provides guidance of unparalleled luminosity and universality. To experience the perfume of his writings is to experience something of the presence of sanctity itself. That is why a contemporary traditional Catholic could write, "If in the *Transcendent Unity* he [Schuon] speaks of the way of Grace as one who understands that Divine economy in relation to the esoteric and exoteric paths of Islam, and in principle, in relation to exotericism and esotericism as such, in *Spiritual Perspectives* he speaks of Grace as one in whom it is in operation and as it were in virtue of that operation. The book has a fullness of light which we have no right to find in the twentieth century, or perhaps in any other century." (*Dominican Studies*, vol. 7, 1954, 265.)

The Multiplicity of Religions and the Method of their Study

As already mentioned, the study of religion for Schuon is almost always carried out in the light of the multiplicity of religious forms which has become an undeniable reality for the life of modern man.

In fact if there is one really new element in the religious life of men and women today to the extent that they and their society are touched by the forces and influences of the modern world, it is the presence of other religions which pose a most profound challenge to one's own religious faith and threaten that faith if they are not taken seriously. The reality of other religions may not be of "existential" concern for those who still live in what remains of traditional worlds, whether this be a Moroccan town, an Indian village or even some faraway hamlet in the countryside in Spain or Italy. But the multiplicity of religious forms cannot but be of crucial concern for men who no longer live in a homogeneous traditional ambience and yet thirst for the certitude of faith and the beatitude of the spiritual life. It is to this category of human beings that Schuon addresses his studies of the multiple religious universes within which humanity lives today, providing an indispensable key for the understanding of these worlds in religious terms without relativizing or weakening one's own religion. In fact his exposition of the inner or transcendent unity of religions as contained in such works as *The Transcendent Unity of Religions* and *Formes et substance dans les religions*, not only does not place a tool in the hands of the materialists and relativizers who want to destroy the absoluteness of religion by pointing to the multiplicity and relativity of religious forms and external practices, but provides an indispensable support for the protection of religion itself. As depicted and described by Schuon, other religious worlds become a divine compensation for the loss suffered by religion in the modern world as the result of the incessant attacks made against the very structure of religion in the West since the Renaissance by such forces as humanism, rationalism, empiricism, materialism, Marxism and the like.

The use of the term transcendent unity of religions by Schuon emphasizes the fact that this unity is not to be sought on the level of external forms. Each religion lives within a world of forms and yet is based upon and issues from the formless Essence. It also possesses an esoteric dimension which is in fact concerned with the inner reality above forms and an exoteric dimension which governs, orients and sanctifies the domain of multiplicity and forms within which human beings live and act. The unity of religions can only be found on the level of the formless, the inward, the esoteric. On the exoteric level there can be polite conversation and diplomatic harmony but not unity. As he has said, it is only in the divine stratosphere and not in the human atmosphere that the real harmony and ultimate unity of religions can be sought.

Each religion comes from the Absolute and possesses an archetype which determines its earthly reality. Within the universe created by each religion the manifestation of the Supreme Logos is central and "absolute" whereas metaphysically only the Absolute as such is absolute. Nevertheless, the concept of the "relatively absolute", a term often used by Schuon, is indispensable for the understanding of the absoluteness of a religion even in its formal order within its own universe while in reality only the One is Absolute in Itself. Each religion contains within itself the absolute truth and at the same time is a method and means, or *upaya*, to use the Buddhist term, for the attainment of that truth. As an *upaya* it is based on opportuneness to save human souls rather than on the Truth as such. To move from the level of religion as opportune truth to the Truth which resides at its heart, to penetrate into the meaning of forms and to reach their Essence, to see beyond the multiplicity of religious forms which come from Heaven and are most precious precisely because they are willed by God to the unity which transcends these forms without destroying them requires a dimension of inwardness, a profound spirituality and a metaphysical knowledge which belong to the esoteric domain properly speaking. As Schuon has written more than once, if ecumenism about which there is so much discourse today is to become anything more than either a tool for diplomacy or an aid to the forces of modernism to secularize religion even further, it must be based on the esoteric perspective. The only legitimate ecumenism is esoteric ecumenism. In fact ideally speaking, only saintly men and women possessing wisdom should and can engage in a serious manner in that enterprise which has come to be known as comparative religion. The works of Schuon are like a gift from Heaven in this crucial enterprise for they have carried out this esoteric ecumenism with a depth and also expansion in the geographic sense to embrace all the major religions of the world providing those who are of a religious nature but who cannot carry out such an enterprise themselves indispensable keys for the understanding in depth of these religions without doing any injustice to any particular religion. Schuon has both elucidated the various religious traditions with unparalleled spiritual sensitivity and metaphysical insight and provided a vision of that perennial religion, the *religio perennis*, which lies at the heart of each religion.

Schuon's study of what has come to be known as comparative religion has not involved only the analysis, description and penetration into the meaning of the messages or the manifestations of the Absolute but also the human receptacles which color and condition the Heavenly messages. In a number of essays he has dealt with the ethnic, linguistic and temperamental characteristics of various human collectivities, characteristics which alongside the primary archetypal realities of different religions are responsible for the diversity to be observed among religions and even within a single religion. With his mastery of the science of man in its many aspects, he has dealt with the human margin which is responsible for certain ambiguities and even apparent contradictions which one sees not only in the perspective of comparative studies but even within the traditional structure of each religion. In dealing with the human margin in religion and more generally speaking the veil in the metaphysical sense (the Arabic *al-ḥijāb* and the Sanskirt *māyā*) which conditions all cosmic manifestation, he has for the first time brought a crucial element to bear upon the study of religion in the contemporary context, an act which can only be called ingenious.

It is indeed amazing that in the modern West and especially in the English speaking world where there is so much interest in comparative religion and endless debates about the theological significance of the presence of other religions, the traditional point of view as expounded by Guénon and Coomaraswamy and especially in its most perfect and complete form by Schuon is not considered more seriously. If there had been satisfaction with the prevalent methodologies and philosophies revolving around historicism, phenomenology and the like, one would understand this almost total neglect. But seeing how dissatisfied are in fact some of the most perceptive religious thinkers today with prevalent theories and practices of ecumenism and the study of comparative religion, one would think that at least a serious attempt would be made to make an in-depth study of Schuon's point of view. Of course it is true that the understanding of this perspective requires much more metaphysical knowledge and also devotion to religion itself than the other methods and schools prevalent in academic and religious circles these days.

It can be said with certainty, however, that the desert of desolation which characterizes the religious scene today, especially as it pertains to comparative studies, is forcing many to search more desperately and with greater effort for that oasis which contains the salutary spring of life. In such a situation despite deliberate neglect on the part of some scholars in the field and unintentional neglect on the part of others, the traditional approach to the studies of religion in general and that of Schuon which crowns the traditional school in particular are bound to find finally their way as at least one of the recognized paths of charting a course in the turbulent waters of contemporary religious studies. As for those who fully understand his message, the way provided by him cannot in fact but be the only way which can present the dazzling beauty and majesty of other religions without in any way belittling or relativizing one's own so that the very study of comparative religion becomes a religious study which abets one's own religious and spiritual life rather than becoming a detriment to the intellectual understanding and even practice of religion itself.

Schuon has of course not only written about how to study diverse religions but also carried out in practice such a study in the case of the major religions of present day humanity as well as many religions of historic significance whose light has ceased to shine upon the earthly plane.

Of the major families of religions it is the Abrahamic one consisting of Judaism, Christianity and Islam that has received, along with Hinduism, the greatest attention in Schuon's works. He has dealt with the reverential love for God reflected in the Psalms, with the dazzling peaks of Kabbalistic esoterism as well as with Talmudic Law and the *Mischna*. He has written of the covenant of the people of Israel with God, of the sacred nature of the Torah and the reasons for the rejection of Christianity by orthodox Judaism. His treatment of the Old Testament has turned on many occasions to the Songs of Solomon whose esoteric significance he has sought to resuscitate. Although he has not devoted a separate book to Judaism, the significance of the first of the Abrahamic religions in the whole history of the monotheistic faiths as well as its relation both exoterically and esoterically to Christianity and Islam appear in many of his works starting with *The Transcendent Unity of Religions* wherein he dealt for the first time in a systematic fashion with the relation between exoterism and esoterism within the Abrahamic traditions. There is a kind of concrete presence of the spirituality of the traditional Semitic world in Schuon's writings which give a particular flavor to his study of Judaism as seen in relation to the universal Abrahamic monotheism before its particularization or "Israelization" in historic Judaism while at the same time he reveals the profound significance of this particularization for the religious history of later humanity.

Although only his book *Christianisme/Islam* contains the name Christianity in its title, Schuon has been concerned with nearly every aspect of the Christian tradition in practically all of his works some of which, like *Gnosis — Divine Wisdom*, contain major sections devoted to Christian spirituality. Schuon has tried to defend the integral Christian tradition from the attack of skeptics from without and modernists from within and to resuscitate the esoteric and metaphysical teachings of the Christian tradition which have been eclipsed or forgotten during the past few centuries. He has also sought to distinguish between Christianity and modern European civilization with which certain Christian thinkers have been only too anxious to identify themselves with catastrophic consequences for the Christian religion.

On the doctrinal level Schuon has sought to resurrect sapiential teachings of Christianity as contained in the works of such figures as Origen and Clement of Alexandria as well as Dante and Meister Eckhart. He has been especially keen to emphasize that although Christianity is an esoterism which became an exoterism when called upon to save a whole civilization, that although Christianity is essentially a way of love and that even if Christianity did incorporate such pre-Christian esoteric doctrines as Platonism and Hermeticism into its structure, Christian esoterism in general and Christian gnosis (which is used by Schuon as principial knowledge which liberates and not in its sectarian sense) in particular is Christian in the most basic sense of this term in that it comes from Christ and the Christic message.

Schuon also defends the various schools of traditional Christian theology, whether they be Augustinian, Bonaventurian, or Thomist. He defends these schools rigorously against those modern critics who reject them because they simply fail to understand them, while he points to the limitation of these theological formulations, especially the medieval Scholastic syntheses, in the light of that pure wisdom or *sapientia* which lies at the heart of the revelation. For obvious reasons Schuon rejects strongly such modernistic "theologies" as Teilhardism while pointing to the reason for the reaction against the Church in the Reformation and the existence of a certain type of Christian spirituality within Evangelism and especially among certain Protestant mystics.

There are also many pages devoted by Schuon to Orthodox theology and spirituality, especially works such as the *Philokalia* concerned with quintessential prayer. There is something of the "Oriental" doctrine of the saving grace of beauty, of the mystery of icons, of the Hesychast prayer of the heart, of the apophatic theology of a St. Gregory of Palamas and of the luminous skies above Mt. Athos in the writings of Schuon. Many have, in fact, been led to the discovery of Orthodoxy through his works, as others have been guided by them to the rediscovery of Catholicism or even traditional Lutheranism.

The concern of Schuon with the study of the Christian tradition has not been only doctrinal. Nor has it been only to situate it within the Abrahamic family of religions or to compare it with Hinduism and Buddhism. Rather, Schuon has also written extensively on the Christian rites, on prayer and litanies, and on Christian art. He has defended the traditional Christian rites, especially the liturgy, vigorously. He has written on the possibility of inward prayer, meditation and contemplation as Christian disciplines in the contemporary world where access to contemplative methods has become very difficult for most Christians, and he has composed some of the most illuminating pages on Christian sacred art distinguishing it rigorously from the worldly religious art of the Renaissance and the Baroque and demonstrating the crucial role of Christian sacred art for the Christian tradition.

Finally within the Abrahamic family of religions it is especially Islam with which Schuon has been concerned and to which he has devoted numerous studies. Already in *The Transcendent Unity of Religions*, there is a sense of the presence of the grace or what in Arabic is called *barakah* of Islamic spirituality which could only come from intimate contact with the very essence of this tradition. It must be remembered that Schuon has journeyed extensively in the Islamic world and that he knows both the Arabic language and Arabic literature, especially as it has received the imprint of Sufism. One cannot read this work without taking seriously the reality of Islam as a religion willed by Heaven and seeing Islamic spirituality as one which possesses powerful and efficacious means that can aid contemporary man wherever he happens to live. Many a half-Westernized Muslim has returned to the practice of Islam as a result of the study of this treatise not to speak of Schuon's major opus on Islam entitled *Understanding Islam*. This latter work is his best known book in the West and is as well known in the Islamic world from Senegal to Malaysia as any work on Islam in a European language. It is in the view of many leading Muslim thinkers the best book written to introduce Islam to the Western world.

While in *Understanding Islam* Schuon has explained the significance of the fundamental aspects of the Islamic tradition itself, namely the religion of Islam, the Quran, the Prophet and the Way or Sufism, in such other works as *Dimensions of Islam* and *Islam and the Perennial Philosophy*, he has dealt with some of the most difficult issues of Islamic metaphysics and cosmology such as God being both the Inward and the Outward or man being able to realize Divine Unity while remaining the "slave of God". He has also confronted such complex issues as the question of free will and determinism as discussed by the Ash'arites and other schools of *kalām*. He has, moreover, delved into the very spiritual substance of the Prophet to discover the roots of that dichotomy between Sunnism and Shi'ism which has marked all later Islamic history. He has also compared Islam extensively not only with Judaism and Christianity in nearly every one of his works on comparative religion but also with Hinduism. The chapter on Sufism and Vedanta in *Spiritual Perspectives and Human Facts* is one of the masterpieces of comparative religion across that difficult-to-traverse boundary which separates the Abrahamic religions from the Indian ones.

As can be expected, since Schuon speaks from the point of view of the *sophia perennis*, it is especially Sufism that has occupied him more than any other subject in his studies on Islam. His intimate experience of Sufism and grandeur of vision has made him the foremost expositor of the verities of Sufism in the contemporary world. His knowledge of not only Sufi doctrine and practice but also the various schools of Sufism and the multifarious manifestations of Sufism within Islamic history are simply a source of wonder. While many of those who call themselves "traditionalists" in France and who claim to follow Guénon have gravitated around the teachings of Ibn 'Arabī as the sole and supreme authority of Sufism, Schuon has insisted on the presence, in Sufism, of many peaks and many major figures such as Jalāl al-Dīn Rūmī, pointing over and over again to the wealth of diversity manifested within the Sufi tradition. In his *Sufism, Veil and Quintessence*, which is a unique work in the annals of Sufism, he has penetrated into the writings of even the greatest masters of Sufism such as al-Ghazzālī and Ibn 'Arabī to reveal within them a quintessential Sufism based on Unity (*al-tawḥīd*) and invocation of the Divine Name (*al-dhikr*) to be distinguished from a more peripheral manifestation of Sufism which displays certain characteristics most difficult for Westerners with the best of intentions to comprehend. In writing with incomparable lucidity and depth about Divine Unity, the esoteric meaning of the Quran, the spirituality of the Prophet, the early saints of Islam, the inner life of prayer, the theophanies to be contemplated in virgin nature and art, the alchemical effect of love, poetry and music, Schuon has produced a corpus of writings on Sufism which are themselves among the most important and precious works of Sufism.

Altogether the works of Schuon on Islam are unique in the contemporary Western world. Not only do they reveal for the first time for the Western audience the depth and amplitude of the Islamic tradition in a way which cannot be found elsewhere and which force those scholars of religion who are serious to take a new look at the Islamic tradition long neglected by most of the scholars in comparative religion; but they also provide an indispensable intellectual weapon with which Muslims can defend themselves against the onslaught of modernism in its various forms as it threatens the very existence of the Islamic world, weapons without which they are faced with the tragic alternatives of some form of secularization or a blind fanaticism which paradoxically enough is simply the other side of the coin of modernism. His works are therefore as important for the Muslim intelligentsia in need of discovering intellectual means of preserving the identity of the Islamic world and of responding to various modern challenges as they are for Westerners to understand Islam.

Before departing from the Abrahamic world, it is important to mention the central role that the one female prophetic being in this world, namely the Virgin Mary, plays in the spiritual universe of Schuon. He has written eloquently about her role not only in Christianity and even in Judaism through the house of Aaron, but also in Islam where she is called the woman chosen by God among all other women of the world. Schuon speaks of the Virgin's inviolable purity and receptivity to the Divine Message, her primordial sanctity, her never-failing mercy, her embodiment of Divine Wisdom and her beauty which saves and infuses the soul with paradisal joy and beatitude as one who has himself experienced the Marian grace. It is in any case impossible to understand his spiritual universe without considering the importance of that feminine element of the Universal Logos of which Mary is the embodiment in the Abrahamic universe, casting a merciful and beatific presence within both the Christian and the Islamic worlds.

If one travels East from the lands which gave birth to the Abrahamic family of religions, one first traverses the Iranian plateau, the home of the Iranian religions such as Zoroastrianism and Manichaeism. Schuon has been less concerned with this group of religions than those born east and west of Persia, but he has mentioned in several of his works the significance of the ethical dualism of Zoroastrianism in the light of religious monotheism which is metaphysically satisfying but has difficulties, theologically speaking, in explaining the famous question of theodicy or the presence of evil in a world created by God who is absolute goodness. As far as the Iranian world is concerned, it is mostly with the Islamic culture of Persia, especially Sufism, that Schuon has been concerned rather than those ancient Iranian religions only one of which — namely Zoroastrianism — survives to this day.

The spirit of Schuon was drawn from his youth to the majestic peaks and rolling plains of India, to the battlefield where Kṛṣṇa taught Arjuna the truth of life and death, to the forests where the Ṛṣis received those metaphysical revelations known as the Upanishads. This interest has been preserved throughout his life, and he has referred often to the "miracle of India" about whose religions, art and society he has written so extensively. While *The Language of the Self* devoted mostly to Hinduism was published in India, and highly appreciated by some of the most important traditional authorities of Hinduism, Schuon has written many other studies devoted to various aspects of Hinduism ranging from yoga to Hindu art. In fact he considers Hinduism as a kind of religious museum wherein is to be found nearly every mode of religious teaching and path of initiation, of which the well-known division into the ways of knowledge (*jñana*), love (*bhakti*) and work (*karma*) is only the most obvious.

Schuon finds in Hindu metaphysics, especially as expounded by Śankara in the form that is known as Advaita Vedanta, one of the most complete and perfect expressions of metaphysics and therefore willingly uses some of its terminology in his own metaphysical expositions while also expounding the meaning of these teachings themselves with a firm mastery of Sanskrit religious and metaphysical terminology. An example is the term *māyā* which is not only used in a very central and crucial manner by Schuon in his numerous studies on manifestation and the principle of "veiling" which accompanies it, but is also explained in a magisterial manner in several studies as both veil and divine creativity.

Schuon discusses both Hindu metaphysics and its social structure, rites and art. While being concerned mostly with the Vedanta, he strongly opposes those pseudo-Vedantists who separate the Vedanta from the traditional Hindu cadre within which it belongs. He is also a staunch defender of the traditional Hindu doctrine of caste within the particular traditional structure which Hinduism represents while recognizing many of the misdeeds and malpractices which are prevalent in India today. He defends the Hindu tradition in principle against all modernist deviations and deformations without neglecting, to say the least, that in this Age of Darkness or Kali Yuga Hinduism is certainly not in that state of perfection and vigor characteristic of the Golden Age. The result is the appearance of certain cracks within its structure without which in fact Islam could not have spread in India to the degree that it did.

As for the other major religion to have issued from India, namely Buddhism, it has been mostly with the northern or Mahayana school that Schuon's works have been concerned. Touched deeply by the manifestation of the Void in Buddhism and by the beauty of Buddhist art and spirituality, Schuon has set about in numerous essays and the major opus *In the Tracks of Buddhism* to explain the significance of this particular tradition based on silence concerning the nature of Ultimate Reality and the metaphysics of the Void and yet possessing an extremely elaborate cosmology and eschatology. He has also sought to remove misunderstandings concerning Buddhism in the West, such incredible misjudgements which cause some people to call Buddhism atheistic or even to claim that the Buddhists have no religion. He has also explained some of the most difficult elements of Buddhist doctrine such as the "mystery of the Bodhi sattva" and the presence of grace in Mahayana Buddhism.

It is especially Japanese Buddhism and in fact all things Japanese that have always been of great interest to Schuon. He sees in Japan a perfection of artistic forms, an awareness of beauty and a power of creativity related to wisdom and closely tied to the ethnic genius of a more or less homogeneous and secluded people that has made of Japanese civilization a unique and remarkable witness to the truth and beauty of tradition. He has in fact written a great deal more on things Japanese, including Buddhism, than on China whose religions — not only Buddhism but also Confucianism and Taoism — he treats in a more summary fashion. On the basis of the belief that the Japanese tradition has survived more intact into the modern world than the Chinese, it is especially to Japanese religious and artistic forms that he has turned over and over again in his study of the religions of the Far East as living realities.

In the Japanese Buddhist world he deals with many aspects of Zen Buddhism whose very popularity in the West has caused numerous fads and pseudo-esoteric cults to be created around its name. While trying to save the Western reader from being attracted to Zen for the wrong reasons, Schuon explains the causes for the iconoclastic attitudes of certain Zen patriarchs and clarifies such major Zen practices as the use of the *koan* and various artistic activities connected with the perfecting of inner discipline. But he also deals with the much more neglected Jodo-Shin school and the practice of the *nembutsu*. In fact he considers this form of Japanese Buddhism to be more appropriate for most Westerners who are at present drawn to Zen.

As in India so in Japan, some of the greatest traditional authorities have found in Schuon's writings a masterly exposition of Buddhism and have espoused his works warmly. They have seen in his words the traces of the presence of the Void and the power of a mind which having stilled the waves of *samsāra* is finally able to affirm the identity of *nirvāṇa* and *samsāra*, of a mind which without falling into a crude mixing of tongues, can assert that the affirmation of such an identity in Buddhist terms means, for those breathing in the universe of Abrahamic revelation, "seeing God everywhere".

The interest of Schuon in Japan has caused him to delve also into the national religion of Japan, namely Shintoism, which complements Buddhism in the Land of the Rising Sun. In studying its complex cosmogony and mythology in *In the Tracks of Buddhism*, he has also dealt with the meaning of mythology and mythological language in general while providing what is perhaps the most accessible account of Shintoism in a Western language. He has also dealt through Shintoism with some of the general characteristics of the Shamanic family of religions to which Shintoism belongs, such characteristics as the apparent refusal to deal extensively with questions of eschatology.

The other branch of Shamanism which spread into America in the form of the North American Indian religions has also been amply treated by Schuon. In fact it can be said that as far as the religion of the nomads of the Plains in North America is concerned, no one has presented the heart of the cosmological and metaphysical teachings of these Indians with the same light and lucidity as has Schuon. Drawn from early childhood to the courage, virility, nobility and beauty of the American Indians, he made a profound study of their religion and art and during two journeys to their homeland encountered some of the most important representatives of the tribes who still possessed a knowledge of their traditions. Schuon has been in fact received into one of the tribes and been actually present during the performance of the Sun Dance. The experience is reflected in his remarkable study of this central rite of the Indians while his intimate knowledge of the Indians is reflected in both his exposition of their teachings and his own painting of the traditional Indians and their religion. His descriptions of the majesty of mountains and contemplative calm of lakes, of the traceless flight of the eagle in the infinite expanse of the sky and the dispersing of the leaves of a flower in the morning breeze are reminiscent also and even reflect something of this American Indian spirituality which sees in the forms of nature the direct reflections of the Divine Presence, preserving something of the paradisal vision of primordial man.

This introduction does not permit a complete analysis of all the facets of Schuon's study of religion and religions. Suffice it to say that he has dealt not only with religion as such and the major religions which govern the life of humanity today but also with the art, social structures and thought patterns created and molded by religion. He has sought the ultimate meaning of events in religious history in the light of the Ultimate Itself while exposing religions in themselves as means of attaining the Ultimate. With an encyclopedic knowledge of many religions and metaphysical penetration into the heart of each religion, Schuon has provided an unparalleled knowledge of the religions of the world while providing keys for the understanding of religion in its essence. But at the center of his concern has always lain that perennial religion which lies at the core of all religions and which can only be attained by a person who lives one of God's religions fully and realizes the meaning of religion as such. One can say that the works of Schuon have been written to cast light upon the path of religion in general and perennial religion in particular which lies at its heart and that his writings in their totality can in a sense be called by the title of one of his latest works, namely, *On the Trace of Perennial Religion.*

Metaphysics

Whether it be the domain of religion, art, theology or epistemology, the perspective of Schuon remains always metaphysical. He
is first and foremost a metaphysician concerned with the reality of
religion, art, human society or the cosmic order. To understand the
meaning of metaphysics as used by him, however, requires a new,
and at the same time age old, appreciation of the connotation of this
term. For Schuon, metaphysics is not a branch of philosophy concerned with what lies beyond physics. Nor is it in fact a purely human
knowledge bound by the context and categories of the human mind.
Rather, metaphysics, which some of his translators render as metaphysic in order to emphasize its non-multiple but unitary nature,
is the science of Ultimate Reality, attainable through the intellect
and not reason, of an essentially suprahuman character and including
in its fullness the whole of man's being. It is a sacred science or *scientia sacra*, a wisdom which liberates and which requires not only certain mental capacities but also moral and spiritual qualifications.
It is gnosis in the original non-sectarian meaning of the term, the
sophia of the ancient sages and the *sapientia* of medieval ones. It is
the *jñana* of the Hindus and *al-maʿrifah* or *al-ḥikmah* of Muslims. It
is light and presence and issues from the seat of the intelligence which
is the heart while its elaboration is carried out by the mind. Its conceptual understanding, however, although of great importance, is
one thing and its realization quite another.

Metaphysics as thus understood is therefore not at all a branch
of philosophy. Rather, philosophy when it was still of a traditional
character, corresponded to the theoretical and conceptual aspect of
metaphysical knowledge as distinct from the operative methods for
the realization of this principial knowledge. As stated in some of
Schuon's earliest works such as *Spiritual Perspectives and Human Facts*,
metaphysics is of a sacred character and therefore accessible in its
fullness only within a traditional cadre which provides the appropriate
means for the transmission of this knowledge much of which has in
fact been kept in an oral form to this day. Schuon has mentioned
often that if this knowledge is now being written in books, it is only
because the modern world is in every way an anomaly when com-

pared the millennial civilizations which have guided mankind over the ages and one anomaly deserves another. For him metaphysics is inseparable from tradition, from traditional transmission, from spiritual realization. It lies at the heart of religion and even of the *religio perennis* and also at the heart of man himself where resides the Divine Intellect. Being of a sacred character, it requires of man all that he is. That is why in traditional worlds it is taught only after a long period of moral and intellectual preparation of those qualified to receive such knowledge.

Nevertheless, the modern world being what it is, namely a world in which normal channels for the transmission of such knowledge are no longer available for many who would be qualified to receive it, it is necessary to present this knowledge in the manner done by Schuon. There are always those with sufficient intellectual intuition to grasp its import. There are those whose minds and souls are in such a state that the spark of such type of knowledge even if contained in books can set them on fire, burning the obstacles which exist within them and which prevent them from seeking and attaining what Christ has called the one thing necessary.

Man's intelligence was made to know the Absolute and as Schuon has written often it is only the Absolute that man *can* know absolutely. Metaphysics, which is none other than this knowledge of the Absolute, resides in the very substance of the intelligence. Its fountainhead is to be found at the center of man's being himself. But this spring will not gush forth and the inner Logos will not be attained save with the help of that objective manifestation of the Logos which is revelation. That is why in normal civilizations where the tradition molds all things according to the principles contained in the celestial message ruling each civilization, metaphysics is always formed within the inward or esoteric dimension of the religion in question, in the Orphic mysteries, in the Kabbala, in the Dionysiuses, Erigenas and Eckharts of Western Christianity, in the writings of Sufis within the Islamic world. In the Oriental traditions also where the esoteric teachings are present often in a more open and direct fashion in the works of such men as Nāgārjuna and Śankara, of Lao-Tzū and Chuang-Tzū, they are nevertheless found within certain circles of adepts qualified to receive them. To grasp the significance of metaphysics as expounded by Schuon, it is this traditional understanding of this supreme science, its content and significance that must be understood fully.

Schuon is not only a metaphysician of the highest order to be compared to the foremost metaphysicians of history, but he also possesses a knowledge of the metaphysical schools of many traditions. His studies of comparative religion nearly always reflect at their center a study of comparative metaphysics. He not only speaks of metaphysics as the science of the Real, but also juxtaposes, compares and contrasts the views of the metaphysicians of both East and West. Those who share the current interest in what is coming to be known as comparative philosophy—but most of which should be called, properly speaking, comparative metaphysics—will find an almost inexhaustible wealth in his writings wherein he brings his characteristic essentiality and universality to bear upon the discussions of the major themes and issues of this domain of comparative studies.

The metaphysical doctrine expounded by Schuon exposes for the contemporary reader the full range of metaphysics in a manner which has not been available in the West since the end of the medieval period save for the works of Guénon and Coomaraswamy whose metaphysical expositions might in fact serve as a basis for some, but not necessarily all, readers for the comprehension of the more all-embracing and spiritually vivid presentations of Schuon.

To gain a complete knowledge of Schuon's metaphysical expositions, it would be necessary to read over all his books and most articles because he returns to various metaphysical questions in nearly every study. Already in *The Transcendent Unity of Religions* and *Spiritual Perspectives and Human Facts* one sees the clear distinction made between metaphysics and profane philosophy and comes to understand what is the nature of metaphysical knowledge, while in such later works as *Gnosis—Divine Wisdom* and *Stations of Wisdom*, many chapters deal with purely metaphysical subjects, as does his more recent *Logic and Transcendence*. But it is especially in *Esoterism as Principle and as Way* that he deals most directly with esoteric knowledge which is inseparable from metaphysics. The most important work of all in this field, however, is *From the Divine to the Human* which can be said to summarize Schuon's metaphysical teachings.

Metaphysics, as expounded by Schuon, does not begin with Being but with that Ultimate Reality which is at once the Absolute, the Infinite and the Perfect Good and which contains all the possibilities of manifestation. Beyond being in Itself, It is the Principle of Pure Being which is the first determination of the Beyond-Being in the direction of manifestation and creation. Inasmuch as it is infinite, the Ultimate Reality must possess all possibilities including the possibility of the negation of Itself which is the world or manifestation. There is therefore a projection towards nothingness which constitutes the cosmogonic act and brings all things into existence. The Beyond-Being generates Pure Being, Pure Being generates Universal Existence and Universal Existence actualizes and externalizes the latent possibilities in the world of existence as usually understood. In a hierarchic fashion there is a descent in the direction of nothingness or non-existence without this limit ever being reached.

In a language which draws from the technical vocabulary and symbolic imagery of several traditions including not only the Platonic and Christian but also the Islamic, Hindu and Buddhist, Schuon depicts in a dazzling fashion and with a freshness which can result only from vision and realization, the traditional doctrine of the nature of the One, the descent through the cosmogonic act of the various levels of existence, the question of theodicy and the presence of evil, the role of the Logos in creation, the nature of eternity and the generation of time, causality and numerous other questions of a metaphysical nature turning at every moment to answer criticisms brought by various types of modern philosophy against traditional metaphysics and drawing from different traditions to both strengthen his metaphysical presentation and to accentuate the remarkable harmony which exists in various traditions once the symbolic language used for the presentation of such knowledge is fully grasped.

Cosmology

Cosmology, as traditionally understood, is the application of metaphysical principles to the cosmic domain. It is not a generalization of an empirical physics as one finds in the modern world. It is a knowledge of the cosmos on all its levels of existence and not only the material. Although he has not written separate treatises on cosmology itself or on the cosmological sciences such as alchemy, as have some of the followers of his thought and teachings, Schuon has devoted many pages to the study of cosmology and its spiritual significance. He has devoted in-depth studies to Islamic cosmology and angelology to which it is closely related in his *L'Oeil du coeur* and to the cosmology of the American Indians in *Language of the Self*. On several occasions he has dealt with the complexities of Buddhist cosmology and has referred to the main tenets of Hindu cosmology whose doctrine of cosmic cycles he has turned to on many occasions in order both to criticize the linear and quantitative conception of time of modern science and to clarify certain misunderstandings that can be observed in modern Western interpretation of the Hindu doctrine of these cycles.

Although not as concerned with traditional mathematics and the symbolic science of letters which is closely related to it as was Guénon, Schuon has also dealt in more than one instance with traditional mathematics. His mastery of the subject can be seen in *Esoterism as Principle and as Way* where, as in his earlier references to the subject, he is particularly keen to point out the qualitative nature of traditional mathematics, the Pythagorean number and geometric form. He has emphasized the archetypal nature of both number and geometric form as traditionally understood and the role they play in art as means of bringing about recollection in the Platonic sense of the celestial essences and in metaphysical and cosmological sciences in providing a powerful intelligible language for the exposition of such forms of knowledge which, however, are not bound to this type of language alone and which can be expressed through non-mathematical means as well.

Epistemology

When confronted with the writings of Schuon, one is faced with the question, "How does he know?" How can one gain the kind of knowledge of which Schuon speaks? Besides writing on initiation, spiritual practice and the development of inner faculties which enable man to have a new mode of consciousness and awareness, Schuon has spoken explicitly about the faculty of the intellect which exists within man and which can be made operative through spiritual practice and of course by the grace of Heaven. For Schuon man can know through a hierarchy of means which range from the senses, through the various powers of the psyche and the mind including imagination and reason, to the intellect which is a supranaturally natural faculty within man and which can know God and suprasensible realities directly provided it is not prevented from being operative by the passions and veils that hide man from himself. The intellect resides in the heart whereas reason which is its reflection on the mental plane is associated with the brain and the head.

Moreover, the inner Intellect is the subjective pole of the Word, the Logos, the Universal Intellect by which all things were made and which is the source of revelation in its objective mode, in the mode which established formal religion. That is why revealed truth is the highest source of knowledge when compared to reason, the sentiments and the senses which for the vast majority of men constitute their only sources of knowledge. For the sage, however, the eye of whose heart has opened and who is able to receive this inner and subjective "revelation" which issues from the Intellect residing at the Center of his being, the objective revelation is the complement of this inner source of knowledge. The objective revelation also provides the cadre for the actualization of this knowledge and places at the disposal of man the indispensable means of attaining to this source of inner knowledge. That is why there is such a profound nexus in Schuon's writings between faith and knowledge and also orthodoxy and intellectuality as seen in such work as *Stations of Wisdom*.

For Schuon ultimate knowledge lies in the very substance of human intelligence which was made to know the Absolute. There is for him no legitimate right to absurdity in the name of religious mystery. If the Divine is a mystery, it is so because of the limitation of our knowledge and not because of an obstacle which cannot be surmounted in principle. If all men could be taught metaphysics, if they were able to use their intelligence without the impediments of the passions and individualistic aberrations, they could know God. Moreover, there would be no atheists and agnostics, the existence of intelligence, like that of human consciousness, itself being the proof of the existence of God.

For Schuon even the categories of logic are of a divine nature and come ultimately from the Spirit. What is the origin of logical or mathematical certitude if not ultimately the Divine Intellect? Schuon stands always on the side of logic against illogicism which does not mean that he stands on the side of rationalism. Logic is one thing and rationalism quite another. In fact in *Logic and Transcendence* he criticizes modern rationalism not through fideist appeals but through the use of logic. Also in the same work he resuscitates the classical proofs for the existence of God and demonstrates that they are still meaningful and efficacious by appealing to logic and logical demonstration rather than solely to faith. For him logic is inseparable from intelligence, hence from the Transcendent. Reason is not the rebellious agent which having declared its independence runs havoc through the world of faith and as the progenitor of an inhuman technology creates chaos in the world of nature. Rather, once illuminated by the Intellect, it becomes the complement of faith and the instrument of man as the vicegerent of God on earth. In this age of positivism on the one hand and irrationalism on the other, Schuon's epistemology, based upon the hierarchy of faculties leading to the intellect through which revealed and inner knowledge are united and the positive appreciation of logic in its wedding to transcendence and the most intense form of spirituality, is a salutary alternative of the greatest import for not only theology but also philosophy and science if only his message were to be fully understood.

Philosophy

To comprehend Schuon's views toward philosophy, it is necessary to distinguish philosophy in its current sense from the meaning it had for a Pythagoras or a Plato or even a Cicero. Schuon is strongly critical of postmedieval European philosophy based firstly upon rationalism and empiricism and finally, because of the very limitations of these approaches, upon the irrationalism which characterizes so much of twentieth century philosophy. Schuon sees this kind of profane philosophy as a caricature of traditional metaphysics and philosophy and asserts that profane philosophy, even when it does express certain correct intuitions as one sees among a number of nineteenth century German philosophers, does not possess efficacy as far as the realization of this truth thus discerned is concerned. As he has said in his early criticism of profane philosophy in *Spiritual Perspectives and Human Facts*, such a philosophy cannot engender sanctity.

In contrast to this profane understanding of philosophy, however, there is traditional philosophy to be distinguished from the pure metaphysics or *sophia* already mentioned. This traditional philosophy whether found in an Aristotle, Ibn Sīnā or St. Thomas, is given its full positive appreciation in the traditional intellectual universe where, as Schuon asserts, there are not two but three intellectual disciplines which are concerned with knowledge of principles: theology, philosophy, and metaphysics which can also be called gnosis or theosophy if this term is understood in its traditional sense. He also mentions that every great theologian is also to some extent a philosopher and metaphysician, as every great traditional philosopher is also a theologian and metaphysician and every metaphysician a theologian and philosopher. This assertion holds true very much in the case of Schuon himself who is not only a metaphysician of incredible breadth and depth but also a theologian and philosopher who is a master of logical discourse and philosophical dialectic.

Schuon defends schools of traditional philosophy against both their theological and mystical opponents. He demonstrates the validity of certain theses of the Islamic philosophers against the attacks of both the scholars of *kalām* and even those Sufis who in emphasizing intuition have denigrated the works of the Islamic philosophers based upon demonstration. He has likewise defended the sapiential strand of Greek philosophy against the attacks of certain of the early Church Fathers showing how in the dialogue between the Hellenists and Christians, it was not simply a question of debate between truth and error, but contention between two perspectives whose unity can only be grasped by metaphysics as it was in fact by the Christian Platonists and Neoplatonists.

Schuon renders the greatest service to the correct understanding of both the Western and the Islamic and Jewish intellectual traditions by reevaluating Platonism and especially Neoplatonism as an authentic metaphysical doctrine of an ultimately Divine Origin destined providentially to provide a suitable metaphysical language for the expression of principial knowledge by the sages and metaphysicans of Judaism, Christianity and Islam rather than a harmless and "inoffensive" philosophy in the modern sense with the help of which one simply removes the claim of seriousness on behalf of any metaphysical doctrine. How often have such sapiential doctrines of the profoundest depth as those of an Erigena or Ibn 'Arabī been dismissed simply by calling them the result of Neoplatonic influence? The works of Schuon cast light upon a subject which cannot but be of central concern for those who are now in the process of reappraising the meaning of the Western intellectual tradition. His discussion helps especially to grasp anew the spiritual and intellectual import of Platonism and Neoplatonism which have served in the hands of modern historians of philosophy and religion to veil the true nature of the doctrine of those called Jewish, Christian, or Islamic Platonists and Neoplatonists and to draw a wall between the world of faith and essential knowledge, a wall which certainly did not exist in the traditional universes of Islam and Judaism and even Christianity.

Before leaving the discussion of philosophy, it is essential to mention perennial philosophy or *philosophia perennis* to which Schuon has referred on several occasions in his works including his latest opus *Sur la trace de la religion pérenne*. As that perennial and universal wisdom which lies at the heart of all traditions, *philosophia perennis* can in fact be identified with metaphysics and its multifarious applications. Since this knowledge is related to spiritual practice and is not limited to theory — even *theoria* in its traditional sense — it can also be called *sophia perennis* in order to emphasize more the operative element related to realization. It is not accidental that Schuon has summarized his whole message in an essay entitled *"Sophia perennis"*. Certainly he is the foremost living expositor of this perennial wisdom, the *philosophia perennis*, interest in which has been resuscitated during this century, and which has seen its most powerful and eloquent contemporary spokesman in Schuon.

Art and Beauty

Schuon is not only a metaphysician but also an artist, at once poet and painter. Moreover, as metaphysician he has always emphasized the importance of forms on their own level and the necessity to "possess" form in order to be able to pass beyond it. Therefore, he has been concerned from the beginning with the significance of art and beauty and has written extensively on what could be called traditional aesthetics in such works as *The Transcendent Unity of Religions, Spiritual Perspectives and Human Facts, Language of the Self*, and *Esoterism as Principle and as Way*, while making numerous references to the subject in his other books and essays.

Beauty plays a central role in spirituality as expounded and described by Schuon for, as he has written more than once, beauty is to the contemplative person not the cause of worldly dissipation and diversion, but the occasion for recollection, in the Platonic sense, of the spiritual world. Beauty is an extension, a reflection of Divine Infinitude and as such melts the hardness of the heart and removes the obstacles before the mind leading to liberation and deliverance.

There is for Schuon first of all a fundamental distinction to be made between traditional and profane art which can include an art whose subject might be religious such as post-medieval European religious art, but whose language is not symbolic nor is its inspiration suprahuman. Then he distinguishes within the domain of traditional art between sacred art which is directly concerned with the sacred rites and practices of the tradition in question and other types of art in a traditional civilization which, although not directly concerned with cultic and ritual elements of the tradition, reflect its principles through the symbolic language, methods and techniques provided by that tradition. With an incredible knowledge of various types of traditional art, he provides a universal key for the understanding of the spiritual significance of art in different traditional civilizations. In fact his explanation of traditional art complements his study of different religions. In both cases he acts as guide for the journey across frontiers which, until modern times, have separated humanity into several humanities. He seems to have been blessed with the gift of the "language of the birds", to use the well-known Islamic symbol, in penetrating into not only the inner meaning of different religious forms but also diverse worlds of artistic form which are always profoundly related to the inner dimensions of the religion dominant in the civilization that gives birth to the artistic forms in question.

It is this inner nexus between spirituality and art that causes Schuon not only to devote so many studies to questions of traditional art and aesthetics, but also to criticize in a relentless manner post-medieval European art which at once reflects and has abetted the gradual fall of modern man from the state which tradition considers as normal and which European man shared with other members of the human race before beginning on that perilous adventure identified with the Renaissance and the age of rationalism and humanism. Schuon traces the stages of this fall in European art which after the Middle Ages first becomes humanistic rather than hieratic while preserving certain human and natural characteristics in the hands of the greater artists of that age. Then, this early period of rebellion against the medieval artistic norms and in fact the whole medieval philosophy of art as expounded by a St. Thomas or Meister Eckhart is followed by an even greater degree of naturalism corresponding to the spread of rationalism on the philosophical level. Finally, the naturalistic forms in a sense crack under their own weight leading to that dissolution of forms which should properly be called sub-realism rather than surrealism for it is the level below the world of forms with which such an art deals rather than with the level above it. This dissolution, morever, has its counterpart in anti-rational philosophies such as existentialism which appear on the European philosophical scene at almost the same time as the breakdown of artistic naturalism.

While emphasizing the catastrophic consequences of a titanic and Promethean art and its later dissolution from below for man seen as *imago Dei* and the role of such an art in aiding in man's rebellion against Heaven and in fact against his own theomorphic nature, Schuon nevertheless points out some positive qualities to be found among certain artists even amidst this non-traditional climate of European art.

One can find in the works of Schuon both a metaphysics and theology of art of the highest order and a universal criterion for the judgment of the spiritual significance of art in both East and West. Moreover, like all plenary messages of gnosis which originate in a fresh vision of the Truth rather than simple repetition of another source, the writings of Schuon are themselves clothed in a language of highly artistic quality with a resonance of beauty which only confirms once again the veracity of the saying that beauty is the splendor of the truth. One cannot read his works without becoming aware that metaphysical knowledge once realized and lived rather than merely thought cannot but express itself in vehicles which possess beauty and that this wisdom is inseparable from art. This is a truth to which the Sacred Scriptures and the earthly manifestations of the Logos in various traditions bear witness at the highest level for they save not only through the content of their message but also through the beauty of the container which is itself determined by the content.

Nature

Schuon's concern for beauty is not limited to art as created by man but embraces the work of the Supreme Artisan, that is, virgin nature. Besides writing of the cosmological sciences, Schuon has devoted many pages to the spiritual significance of nature which has its own metaphysics and spiritual life. The pages of the cosmic book bear a gnostic message of the highest order which can in fact be deciphered only by a person of high spiritual realization. When reading the works of Schuon, one feels as if they were not written in some closed room but in the bosom of nature. There is something in the very substance of his works of the crystalline majesty of the Alps, the inviolable purity of the North African desert, the inner mystery of the forests of North America, all of which he has experienced and which he loves. He stands always on the side of the grandeur of God's handiwork as seen in virgin nature against the pettiness of the works of fallen man and especially the stifling ugliness of the modern urban environment created by Promethean man to enable him to forget the absence of God.

Schuon not only defends the rights of nature against the incessant encroachment of the modern industrial world, but also asserts the primacy of the rhythms of the life of nature over those of modern man and its final victory over that type of man who sees himself as nature's conqueror rather than the bridge between Heaven and earth. He also has written extensively of the spiritual significance of nature not only in particular cases such as Taoism, Shintoism or the North American Indian religion where its forms play a specific cultic role but in general as a most powerful support for the spiritual life and gift from Heaven at a time when much of the earthly environment is so desolated. There is something of the prayers of the birds in the early morning hours, of the luminosity of the rising Sun upon mountain peaks and of the glittering stars of a desert night in Schuon's writings which are reminiscent of classical Sufi poetry and also certain types of German nature poetry and which remind man of the great spiritual significance of nature and the central role that virgin nature can play in the spiritual life without man falling into any form of naturalism of which so many Christian theologians have been fearful. In defending the spiritual rights of nature and the metaphysical significance of virgin nature and her forms and rhythms, Schuon has resuscitated an aspect of spirituality of which the Western world is in direst need and which in fact many have been seeking since the existence of the ecological crisis has become a reality for them. He has described nature as one who sees all things in God and God in all things, as one who has realized the goal of seeing God everywhere.

Man

Among all the traditional sciences such as alchemy, arithmetic, geometry, music and astronomy with which other expositors of traditional doctrine such as René Guénon and Titus Buckhardt have dealt, it is the science of man or anthropology, if only the *anthropos* were to be understood in its traditional sense, that has been of particular concern to Schuon. He has always been interested with the insight and keenness of intelligence which characterize all aspects of his thought in the human phenomenon and while attacking strongly humanism has defended man staunchly against all that seeks to debase and degrade him. He has insisted that if anyone wishes to speak for man, he should speak of the whole of man and not just his animal part, for to leave the spiritual dimension and spiritual needs of man aside while claiming to speak for him is to reduce him to a level that is not just animal but below the animals. Schuon has confirmed on many occasions the Augustinian dictum that to be human is to seek to be suprahuman. Man can in fact be defined as the being created to transcend himself and to seek the Transcendent as such.

Schuon's exposition of the science of man appears in many of his writings but is summarized in a very condensed and concentrated form in his *From the Divine to the Human*. He sees man as a theomorphic being with an intelligence made to know the Absolute and a will created to attach the whole of man's being to the Origin. He also deals with all the intermediate human faculties such as the sentiments and imagination and discusses their role in the spiritual life. He has analyzed the microcosmic structure of man in *L'Oeil du coeur* and *Gnosis — Divine Wisdom* and has returned over and over again to point to the remarkable mystery of human subjectivity which itself is direct proof of the Divine "I" and to the power of objectivity which is direct witness to the Absolute. To understand the meaning of human consciousness and the nature of intelligence is to be convinced of the reality of God for to say man is to say God. The need for religion and in fact the fountainhead of religious truth lie in the nature of man himself, at the center of his heart. If man were able to penetrate to the center of his being by himself, he would discover God within himself and in all things. He would be like Adam in paradise before the fall.

The theomorphic nature of man is not reflected only in man's intelligence and will nor even in the intelligence alone together with the sentiments which can be transmuted through the alchemy of Divine Love. This nature is also reflected in the human body, both the male and the female bodies possessing an innate perfection which could not possibly have been the result of some kind of evolution by chance or struggle. Schuon in fact rejects with arguments which are at once metaphysical, theological, philosophical and logical the theory of evolution as currently understood and reveals its absurdity with a clarity and vigor which is unique. Schuon also deals directly in *From the Divine to the Human* with the metaphysical and cosmological symbolism of various parts of the human body, unveiling an esoteric teaching in a manner which is not possible to find in other contemporary sources.

In speaking of man Schuon also of course speaks of woman for he uses man in its broad sense as embracing both sexes like the Greek *anthropos,* the Latin *homo,* the German *Mensch* and the Arabic *al-insān.* There is certainly a strong awareness of the feminine dimension of spirituality and the spiritual significance of femininity in his writings. While dealing on the metaphysical level with the Divine Infinity as the feminine hypostasis of the One and creative act or *māyā* as the feminine consort of the creating word or Logos, he has also written some of the most beautiful pages of living spirituality concerning the Virgin Mary in both Christianity and Islam and even explained the reason for the presence of a feminine element in Mahayana Buddhism, a tradition which appears to be so masculine in both its doctrinal and operative aspects. His paintings are also replete with feminine American Indian figures or the Virgin who is the subject of all his non-Indian paintings.

Schuon is fully aware of the feminine element in an integral spiritual way and even of the positive role which sexuality can play in the spiritual life while accepting the possibility and efficacy of that type of ascetic and sacrificial attitude found among classical Christian theologians. His essay on sexuality in *Esoterism as Principle and as Way* is a masterly treatment of a central aspect of human experience with which contemporary Christian theologians, heir to the age old manner of envisaging sexuality as a sin in itself and yet living amidst one of the most sexually permissive societies in human history, are confronted as a crucial moral and religious problem.

Schuon displays the grandeur of the human state while opposing strongly that Promethean and titanesque expansion of an earthly kind which, in the name of the greatness of man, sought to obliterate the seal of Divinity upon his nature, thereby condemning him to the subhuman world in which humanity finds itself today. Schuon also depicts man as a being at the center of the wheel of existence, destined for immortality, as a being presented with the precious gift of a state which is central and which can therefore lead to the spiritual empyrean beyond all cosmic becoming. He shows the great opportunity and also danger of human life precisely because man *is* the *imago Dei* and therefore bears a responsibility towards Heaven and earth, towards God, other human beings and in fact the whole order of nature, a responsibility which he cannot avoid under any pretext. To refuse to accept such a responsibility is to damn himself while to accept and to fulfill his responsibilities at the summit of which rests knowing and loving the Truth is to attain that goal for the sake of which all things were brought into being and, to use a Sufi image, all the wheels of the heavens were made to rotate.

The Spiritual Life

Far from being an expositor of doctrine alone, Schuon always writes from the point of view of realized knowledge and presents a teaching which itself has the operative power of transforming the reader. His concern is of course to present the Truth but in the context of the spiritual life and not just as theory. He has therefore devoted numerous studies to the spiritual life, to prayer, meditation, contemplation, modes of spiritual realization, the spiritual virtues and the states upon the spiritual path which he calls the stations of wisdom. Nearly all of his works contain some chapter or section dealing with the spiritual life starting with *The Transcendent Unity of Religions* which includes a most remarkable discussion of the prayer of the heart to *Esoterism as Principle and as Way* which in a long section summarizes his teachings on the spiritual life.

Schuon first of all emphasizes the absolute necessity of actually practicing the religious and spiritual life within the context of an orthodox tradition in order to attain the kind of knowledge of which he speaks. To understand the traditional point of view is to understand the necessity of the participation of one's whole being in the practice of a tradition and the inadequacy of only its theoretical understanding, for man is not just a disembodied and floating mind. In fact man's participation in the truth comes through the attainment of spiritual virtues by means of spiritual practice and not in mental concepts of the truth.

In the complex domain of religious and spiritual practices where Schuon describes the significance of rites as different as the Christian Mass, the Islamic benediction upon the Prophet and the American Indian rite of smoking the calumet, he emphasizes over and over again the centrality of prayer to which he has devoted many pages in his works, among the most complete being the chapter on prayer in *Stations of Wisdom*. It is, however, invocation and quintessential prayer or the prayer of the heart as it has survived in Orthodox Christianity to this day and of course as it is found in the *dhikr* of the Sufis, the *japa yoga* of the Hindus and *nembutsu* of the Buddhists that is his special concern. He has made reference to the central role of this mode of spiritual practice in the latter days of human history and its power to save those who invoke the Divine Name with faith, fervor and sincerity. He has also emphasized the indispensability of initiatic transmission, spiritual guidance and also the traditional moral and aesthetic cadre and ambience which alone enable the practice of the invocation of the Divine Name to be efficacious and without which such a practice becomes dangerous and at best without efficacy. Schuon writes about prayer as one in whom it is operative, as one whose being has been transformed by its grace. When he writes of the prayer of the saint and nature praying with him, he writes as one who has not simply read about or observed such a participation from afar. Some of the most moving pages on prayer written in this century are to be found in his works side by side with that penetrating metaphysical exposition which too often in the modern world has become divorced in the minds of people from the possibility of prayer and ritual practice as faith has become divorced from intelligence which is then seen as the progenitor of a knowledge according to the flesh and divorced from grace. In Schuon one discovers that theophanic prayer which both leads to the One and issues from the One in that Sacred Name wherein the Invoked, invocation and invoker are ultimately united.

Prayer of a quintessential order requires meditation and the control of the mind and is closely related to contemplation. Schuon has therefore also discussed both meditation and contemplation in many different contexts, showing what they are and what they are not and emphasizing their importance while criticizing all those peddlers of instant realization who seek to present Oriental methods of meditation and contemplation shorn of their traditional context and also of the protective presence of the "angelic" forces which guard the gates against the onslaught of the titans or *aśuras* in the traditional cosmos so as to provide protection for the hero who through meditation, contemplation and invocation seeks to journey beyond the cosmic crypt.

Not only different forms of Hindu and Buddhist techniques such as yoga are discussed with great mastery by Schuon, but he also presents in his works a vast canvas upon which is depicted the various modes of spiritual realization and different types of spiritual temperaments. The major paths of knowledge, love and action added to different human types and spiritual temperaments cause the spiritual life to possess many modes and modalities which Schuon explains in worlds as far apart as the Hindu and the Christian, pointing to the necessity of the diversity of spiritual paths within an integral living tradition in order to be able to cater to the needs of all the different spiritual types living within its embrace.

Schuon is especially insistent in pointing out the different features and characteristics of the path of love and of knowledge. Since he speaks from the perspective of realized knowledge, one might think that he belittles the significance of the way of love. But in reading his works, especially such an essay as "Concerning the Love of God" in *Logic and Transcendence*, one realizes how deeply he has experienced such a love and how he is so keenly aware of its importance. What Schuon seeks to achieve is not to criticize the path of love or *bhakta* in itself. Rather, he wishes to answer the arguments presented by representatives of this way against those who follow the path of knowledge. Furthermore, he shows how the path of knowledge or *jñana*, when realized, and not just discussed cerebrally as is the case with the modern pseudo-Vedantists, in one way or another embraces the path of love, this being especially true of Sufism which is essentially a path of knowledge but almost always wed to the path of love. But even in Hinduism in the case of a Śankara, the supreme *jñani*, there are devotional hymns composed by him and expressing something of a *bhaktic* character. One can hardly over-emphasize the concern of Schuon for the reality and significance of the love of God and faith in Him especially since in the contemporary world only too often discussions of metaphysics are divorced from that love which according to Dante "moves the heavens and the stars".

Spiritual realization is inseparable from the attainment of spiritual virtues which man must acquire before he becomes worthy of being burned in the fire of Divine Unity. Schuon has devoted an extensive study to the spiritual virtues in his *Spiritual Perspectives and Human Facts* and again in *Esoterism as Principle and as Way* in both of which he has projected a luminosity issuing from the world of the Spirit upon the whole domain of virtues thereby removing the opacity of sentimental virtue considered only in its moralistic sense and revealing its metaphysical basis. Far from opposing virtue to intelligence, he has shown how the virtues are in fact inextricably related to intelligence and the principial knowledge which is attained through the intelligence. Reducing all the virtues to the three fundamental virtues of humility, charity and truthfulness, he has commenced with humility and shown why one must be humble not because of sentimentality but because before God we are nothing and He is everything while before the neighbor we possess some kind of limitation or infirmity which he does not have and which should cause us to have a sense of humility towards him. Yet, we should not disdain the truth in the name of humility by denying honor and pride, in the positive sense of the term, in the gifts that God has bestowed upon us. Most of all Schuon criticizes that kind of pietistic humility which denigrates the intelligence and ultimately commits a sin against the Holy Ghost. He likewise redefines charity, this most maligned of virtues in modern times, in the name of which so much transgression has been committed against religion itself, by returning to the ontological reality which makes of charity ultimately an expansion of our own being. Most of all he reminds modern man of that most forgotten saying of Christ, "Seek ye first the kingdom of God and all else shall be added unto you," and discusses the futility and even demonic character of that type of charity which would put the love of the neighbor above the love of God and ultimately in its place leading to that idolatry of man's earthly life which characterizes the modern world. Finally, Schuon reveals how, on the basis of humility and charity, man can attain to the virtue of truthfulness which implies seeing things as they are and not through our subjective prejudices. The attainment of such a virtue thus leads to seeing things as God sees them and also realizing the Truth as such. It leads to the spiritual station of certitude after which man craves because of the very nature of his intelligence.

Schuon has summarized the stages of the spiritual life in a masterly and brilliant fashion in his *Stations of Wisdom* in the chapter which has given its name to the title of the book itself. Man participates in the truth passively and actively and on the three levels of action, love and knowledge. Hence there are six stations of wisdom. There is a passive station associated with action which is identified with inviolable purity and withdrawal from the vicissitudes and turmoils of the world. There is an active participation on this level which is spiritual action, combat and vigilance, the spiritual war against the laziness and sloth of the unrealized soul and its negligence of the Divine through a slumber that it considers ordinary life. There is a passive station of love which is repose in the peace and beauty which characterizes the Divine Presence and collectedness and inwardness against the externality and fragmentation of the profane world. There is an active station of love where man participates with perfect confidence in the love of God which saves and consumes him. There is a passive station of knowledge in which man realizes that he is nothing and the transcendent One everything. It corresponds to what the Sufis call annihilation (*al-fanā'*). Finally there is the active station of knowledge in which man realizes that only in the Divine "I" can he utter "I" and that at the center of his self resides the Supreme Self. It corresponds to the Sufi station of subsistence in God (*al-baqā'*).

Through this remarkable synthesis Schuon points to the major stages of spiritual realization and through their numerous combinations depicts not only the different types of spirituality but also the dominating form of spirituality within each religion such as Christianity. The stations of wisdom are like a map of the spiritual universe and also the ladder with the help of which man climbs until he reaches that roof that stands above the world of separative existence and in the Divine Presence. He thereby fulfills his entelechy and the final end for which he was placed upon the earth.

Eschatology

In speaking of man and his final end, Schuon has also written many essays on various questions of eschatology starting with his study of man's posthumous states in *L'Oeil du coeur,* continuing with essays on various eschatological problems and different modes and degrees of paradise in his *Islam and the Perennial Philosophy* and *Formes et substance dans les religions* and synthesizing his whole exposition in the final chapter of *Sur les traces de la religion pérenne.* In this difficult domain which even many of the traditional metaphysicians have passed over in silence, Schuon has delved into the complex nature of the intermediate states, the difference between the Abrahamic paradises which are permanent and certain Hindu paradises which are temporary, the apocatastasis in relation to the final consumption of all states of being including the infernal ones in the Divine Principle, the "freezing of the fires of hell" mentioned by Ibn 'Arabī and many other issues of the greatest theological and also personal importance for those who have faith in the immortality of the soul. Schuon deals particularly in detail with the grades of paradise as described in Sufism and the paradisal symbolism of the Quran which has been so often misconstrued in Western sources.

Against those pseudo-esoterists who belittle paradise as if they were a Sufi in union with God or a *jīvan-mukta*, Schuon emphasizes how precious is the paradisal state and how difficult it is to enter paradise upon the moment of death. But as one for whom the imponderables of Divine Grace are more than just theory, he refuses to be overschematic in his eschatological discussions, casting his usual light upon these issues while reminding the reader that the Divine Grace can operate as God wills and that as the Bible states "with God all things are possible."

Critic of the Modern World

The very first book of Schuon, *Leitgedanken zur Urbesinnung* contains some of the most relentless and scathing criticisms of the modern world to be found anywhere, a theme to which Schuon, like other expositors of the traditional perspective, has returned again and again. Both *The Transcendent Unity of Religions* and *Spiritual Perspectives and Human Facts* treat this theme in its various dimensions while *Light on the Ancient Worlds*, in addition to contrasting the traditional worlds and the modern one, traces the stages of the fall of theomorphic man which the optical illusion resulting from the subversion of the Truth in the modern world has caused to appear as progress.

To speak of truth is also to be forced to face the question of the presence of error. Moreover, to defend the truth is ultimately the highest form of charity while to overlook error in the name of charity is to destroy the very foundation of charity and its spiritual significance. Schuon's criticism of the modern world does not result from a lack of charity as some of his sentimental critics have claimed. It results from the love for truth. One cannot love God without rejecting that which would deny Him. Schuon criticizes the modern world not because of a lack of concern for modern man but precisely because of its concern for only a limited aspect of man who is a being born for immortality but stifled by a civiliization which is contrary to his real nature and ultimate end. In seeking to destroy the premises upon which the modern world is based, Schuon seeks to save man from this world before it devours and destroys him.

Today, criticism of modern civilization based on the horrors of war, pollution of the environment, scarcity of food and natural resources and other obvious maladies has become common-place. One no longer has to be a seer to predict what is finally going to happen to a civilization based on disequilibrium not only vis-à-vis Heaven which it has long denied, but also because of this denial, with the earth itself for whose conquest modern man has sacrificed his spiritual heritage and in fact his own spirit. Current criticisms, however, usually deal with effects rather than causes. They observe the symptoms without being able to discover the deeply rooted causes of the illness. Usually lacking metaphysical knowledge of an integral nature, most critics cannot distinguish between partial truths embedded in a cadre of error and Truth as such.

For Schuon modern civilization which began in Europe during the Renaissance and which after destroying traditional Christian civilization has been spreading into other parts of the globe, is false not only in its results but in its very premises. It has created hospitals and roads to be sure, but whatever partial good it has achieved fails utterly to save or legitimize it because of the falsehood of its very foundations and dominating ideals. It is based on earthly man as an end in himself. It reduces man to his rational and animal aspects and denies the central role of the spiritual life and final end of man as determining the character and purpose of his earthly life. It has lost the vision of primordial and paradisal human perfection which it places in some ambiguous future in time substituting the pseudo-dogma of evolution for the traditional doctrine of the descent of man and progress with its earthly paradise of the perfect human society in some future period for the gradual fall of man and his society taught by traditional doctrines. It cuts off the hands of God from nature and society even if belief in the Divinity continues among certain people and substitutes earthly and Promethean man as the Divinity on earth with ultimate rights over nature, society, and even religion. The result is that debilitating secularism which has led at once to the destruction of the inner man and the desecration of the natural environment.

Schuon does not of course identify the whole of the contemporary world with the modern one. There still survives something of the premodern and the traditional in the West which gave birth to modernism and within the soul of Western man. Were this not the case, it would be futile either to criticize the modern world or present the traditional doctrines to that world. Therefore, the criticism of Schuon is not against the West as such for he defends the Western tradition whether it be in the domain of religion, art or literature in the strongest terms while criticizing in the most categorical terms the modern West.

Nor is Schuon the kind of sentimental admirer of the East who extols all that is Oriental without distinguishing between the authentic and living traditions of the East and their decadent forms not to speak of the subversion of some of these forms in modern times. If Schuon admires the East, it is because of its millennial traditional civilizations and the fact that despite the vicissitudes of time, the traditional life still survives to a greater extent there than in the West and also because the sapiential sources of religion are more available in the Oriental traditions. In Schuon's writings one can discover a new chapter in the dialogue between East and West, one which bases itself on the Truth as such rather than on geographical prejudices and which speaks, one might say, from the vantage point of that Blessed Olive Tree, to use the Quranic image, which is neither of the East nor of the West but whose light illuminates the whole cosmos.

The criticism of the modern world by Schuon involves at once philosophy, science, art, everyday life and even religion wherever modernism has succeeded in penetrating into its structure. While certain chapters of his books and some of the essays deal in their entirety directly with such types of criticism, an example being his "Letter on Existentialism," it is often amidst the discussion of other subjects that he opens up parentheses and presents some of his most profound and direct attacks upon various aspects of modernism. Remarkable examples of such cases can be found in *Understanding Islam* and *In the Tracks of Buddhism* while such works as *Logic and Transcendence* contain not only whole chapters on the refutation of such modern philosophical ideas as rationalism and relativism, but return to these themes in later chapters treating of theology and religion. One could in fact publish a book on Schuon's criticisms of the modern world composed of the parenthetical comments he has made in those writings which deal mainly with various metaphysical and religious subjects.

In the realm of philosophy Schuon attacks the whole of modern philosophy starting with Descartes who in reducing ontology to epistemology and reality to the two substances of mind and extension prepared the stage for the impoverishment of philosophy in modern Europe. This "most intelligent manner of being unintelligent" prepared the ground for that agnosticism which characterizes Kant and which refuses to the intellect its innate power to know the essence of things in themselves, this refusal being the result of the confusion between intellect and reason. Likewise, Schuon criticizes those post-Kantian schools based on either rationalism or empiricism which cannot grasp the meaning of the intellect as source of knowledge and usually end up with one or another type of sensual empiricism. Schuon is even more relentless against the antirationalistic philosophies which follow Hegel and which result in various kinds of modern existentialism based on the total destruction of the functioning of the intellect and even its mental image, reason, and which in the attempt to go beyond Hegelian rationalism fall below it, preparing the way for that loss of the very coherence of thought which is a characteristic of much that passes for philosophy today.

As for science, Schuon's criticism is not of what science has discovered but of what is claimed as scientific knowledge while being only hypothesis and conjecture and of what is left aside by modern science. Had this science been integrated into a higher form of knowledge, it could have been legitimate to the extent that it corresponds to some aspect of physical reality. But Schuon asks by what right a science can study the whole of creation abstracted from God and His Wisdom. Moreover, science is totally ignorant of other dimensions of reality, of the rhythms of the cosmos, of the qualitative nature of time, of the inward nexus of matter with the subtle states and many other cosmic realities. Yet, it generalizes its particular vision of a part of the Universe as if it were the knowledge of the whole supported by the prestige that results from its material and technological feats. The result of its generalized perspective is a cosmos in which the existence of man has no meaning, where both life and intelligence are added realities to be explained away by some kind of evolutionary process rather than fundamental realities constituting the very substance of the Universe.

There is no scientific idea that is criticized with more vehemence by Schuon than the theory of evolution which in fact does not play only the role of scientific theory but also a pseudo-religious dogma which is upheld by its scientific supporters with a kind of religious zeal rather than scientific detachment and is defended in such a way that the very manner of its defense reveals how it has replaced religion for so many modern men. Schuon is especially critical of the intrusion of this pseudo-scientific dogma into the domain of religion itself in the writings of such figures as Śri Aurobindo and especially Teilhard de Chardin. He sees the spread of such types of modernistic theology as a very significant sign of our days for they bear witness to the penetration of the antitraditional forces into the very citadel of religion itself. If until modern times the forces of modernism secularized art, philosophy, science and the social patterns of life, they opposed religion from the outside and at least one knew where one stood. It has remained for the middle and end of this century to bear witness to the penetration of these forces into religion itself to subvert it from within, Christianity in fact not being the only religion confronted with such a phenomenon.

In criticizing the modern world Schuon clears the ground in order to make possible the presentation of the truth, for as the Quran states, "When Truth comes, error disappears." He has had to sweep the intellectual and religious ground clean and to break the idols of modernism in order to present that teaching which can rekindle the lamp of the spirit and provide the key for religion itself to defend its teachings from the array of forces before which the enfeebled army of modernized theology is helpless. Only tradition can provide the weapon necessary to carry out that vital battle for the preservation of the things of the spirit in a world which would completely devour man as a spiritual being if it could, and the verities of tradition cannot be made accessible save through that type of criticism of the modern world carried out by Schuon. This basic aspect of his writings must therefore be seen not only as a result of his concern for the truth but also his love and charity, in the profoundest sense of the term, towards man in his totality and all that makes him worthy of being loved and respected as God's vicegerent on earth, as the *imago Dei*.

Who is Frithjof Schuon?

Considering the grandeur and depth of his metaphysical expositions and the fact that he is the premier living expositor of that *sophia perennis* which lies at the heart of all revelations, it might appear strange that so little is known about Schuon. But it is in his character and also as a part of his intellectual and spiritual function to remain personally secluded, keeping at a distance from the sound and fury which characterize the lives of so many great and less than great men of this century. His works have caused echoes in East and West while he himself has refused to teach or lecture publicly in contrast to most of the well-known religious and spiritual teachers of this age.

Frithjof Schuon was born of German parents in Basle, Switzerland in 1907. His father was a musician and the household was one in which, in addition to music, other arts were prevalent, including the literature of the East as well as of Europe. Schuon lived in Basle and attended school in that city until the death of his father after which his Alsatian mother moved to Mulhouse, where Schuon was obliged to become a French citizen. Having received his earliest education in German, he was now exposed to a French education and hence gained perfect knowledge of both languages early in life. At the age of sixteen he left school to support himself as a textile designer, beginning his first steps in the field of art which he had always loved as a child but in which he never received formal training.

Also as a child, Schuon had been drawn to the Orient, to the lofty songs of the *Bhagavad-Gītā* which was his favorite work as well as to *The Thousand and One Nights*. He had also a natural propensity for metaphysics and read Plato even when he was of a tender age. While still in Mulhouse he discovered the works of René Guénon which only confirmed his intellectual intuitions and provided support for the metaphysical principles he had begun to discover.

Schuon journeyed to Paris after serving for a year and a half in the French army. In Paris not only did he work as a designer but also began his study of Arabic in the Paris mosque school. He was also exposed in a much greater degree than before to various forms of traditional art especially those of Asia which he had always loved even as a child. This period marked therefore on a more extensive scale than before both an intellectual and an artistic familiarity with the traditional world and was followed by Schuon's first visit to Algeria in 1932. North Africa was still witness to a more or less intact traditional pattern of life. This journey therefore marked Schuon's first actual experience of a traditional civilization and also his first immediate contact with the Islamic world, resulting in his gaining firsthand knowledge and intimacy with the Islamic tradition including Sufism some of whose greatest representatives such as Shaykh al-

'Alawi he encountered. In a second journey to North Africa in 1935, he was to visit not only Algeria but also Morocco, while in 1938 he journeyed to Cairo where he finally met Guénon with whom he had been corresponding for years.

In 1939 he stopped in Egypt again while on a journey to India, a land which he had always loved and whose spirituality had attracted him since his childhood days. Shortly upon his arrival in India, however, the Second World War broke out forcing him to return to France where he began to serve in the army. After several months, he was captured by the Germans and imprisoned. When he discovered that the Germans were planning to induct him into their army because of his Alsatian background, he fled to Switzerland where he settled and whose nationality he finally accepted.

For some forty years Switzerland became Schuon's home. Here in 1949 he married a German Swiss with a French education who, besides having interests in religion and metaphysics, is also a gifted painter. It was also here that he wrote most of his works and was visited by many well-known religious scholars and thinkers of East and West. Besides traveling from time to time to the majestic mountains of this land to breathe the fresh air of the morning of creation, he also journeyed occasionally to other countries. These voyages included regular visits to Morocco, and a visit in 1968 to Turkey where he spent some time at the House of the Holy Virgin in Kuśadasi near Ephesus.

In 1959 and again in 1963, Schuon journeyed to America to visit some of the American Indian tribes for whom he had had a special love and affinity since childhood and some of whose members he had met before in Europe. He and Mrs. Schuon visited the Sioux and Crow reservations in South Dakota and Montana and were received into the Sioux tribe. The paintings of haunting beauty of the life of Indians as well as the exposition of their traditional teachings by Schuon attest to his particular relation with the spiritual universe of the American Indians, a relation which was especially fortified and extended during these journeys.

Schuon as Poet and Artist

Schuon's concern with beauty is not only intellectual but also operative and practical in the sense that he not only writes about art and beauty but has himself produced remarkable poems and paintings. In addition to the aesthetic quality which characterizes all of his writings, one finds among the published works of the author two collections of poetry in German entitled *Tage-und Nächtebuch* and *Sulamith* while he has also composed poems which have never been published. His poetry combines the romantic musicality of the best German lyrics with a kind of mystical profoundness and nostalgia.

One might expect the author of such major religious and metaphysical works to be also a poet but one would hardly expect him to be a painter. Rarely does genius in the veritable sense of the term manifest itself within a single human being in both metaphysics and the plastic arts. But for Schuon these domains complement each other. His sense of beauty is an occasion for the recollection of the profoundest metaphysical truths while his spiritual message shines through his artistic works which reflect the same qualities as his teachings, qualities of grandeur combined with a childlike innocence, beauty enhanced with the sense of the presence of the sacred.

Some of Schuon's paintings have been exhibited in this country in the Colorado Springs Fine Arts Center and are now becoming gradually known, this fact being true especially of those paintings dealing with the Indians. To quote from the catalogue of this exhibition which was held in 1981, "Fundamentally, what he [Schuon] portrays are higher realities as lived through the medium of his own soul, and he does so by means of human portraits and scenes taken for the most part from the life of the Plains Indians. But he also has painted a number of pictures of the Virgin Mother, not in the style of Christian icons but in the form of the Biblical Shulamite or the Hindu *Shakti*." As for his style he combines the rules of traditional painting with certain techniques of Western art. To quote the catalogue again, "In short, he combines the positive features of Western art with the rigor and symbolism of the Egyptian wall painting or the Hindu miniature. Perhaps one could say that Schuon's work, as regards its technical aspects, lies somewhere between the Hindu miniature and expressionism, while at the same time being flavored with a certain influence from Japan." Through his art as through his writings Schuon portrays a message from the world of the Spirit clothed in forms of beauty which characterize that world and all that is concerned with the Truth.

The Language and Style of Schuon's Writings

Schuon does not only write in order to transmit a message but also to teach contemporary man to think and carry out intellectual discourse once again without becoming imprisoned in either the limitations of reason or the knots of his own subjectivism. He wishes to create an intellectual world and to forge a language of thought wherein the traditional teachings regain their reality and vitality. Through a rhythm comprised of oscillation between analysis and synthesis, punctuated not only by the assertion of metaphysical principles but often by their repetition as the subject at hand demands, Schuon has created a pattern of thought in which intuitive grasp of the truth is combined with intellectual rigor and logical acumen. He resuscitates the traditional styles and methods of thought and intellection in a language which is contemporary and which he has created for this purpose. The role of the language used by him is therefore of great importance.

In his writings, Schuon has made full use of the geometric clarity of French but also has brought into his French style something of the genius of the German language, its archaic nature and architectonic structure. There is also present in this language of discourse something of the intuitive depth of Arabic, a Semitic language, combined with the speculative and didactic possibilities of the Indo-European languages, the genius of whose sages for metaphysical speculation Schuon has discussed often.

Making full use of the possibilities of the French and German languages and employing occasionally technical metaphysical terms of Sanskrit and Arabic origin, Schuon has produced a language and style which is almost miraculous in its ability to express metaphysical knowledge. His language and style are as unique in the contemporary world as is the content of his message.

The style of Schuon possesses what one commentator upon his works has called a spherical quality in the sense that the sphere contains the greatest volume for a given area. Schuon's style likewise contains the maximum amount of meaning for a given expression. His language, at once symbolic and dialectical, always possesses a dimension of depth and is not exhausted by its surface. His writings are difficult for those not prepared intellectually and also spiritually to receive them and in fact open their embrace only for those for whom they are meant. But whatever one does grasp of his works even if it be only a part of some page, is heavily laden with meaning. To understand even a passage is to understand a great deal. His language and style reflect in themsleves the inner rapport between content and container which characterize all expressions of the Spirit and on the highest level those plenary expressions of the Logos, the prophets and *avatārs*, who are the founders of the traditions governing the human collectivity.

The Influence of Schuon

Schuon's writings have caused profound echoes and also reactions among many outstanding figures of this past half century. T.S. Eliot wrote of Schuon's first book, *The Transcendent Unity of Religions*, "I have met with no more impressive work in the comparative study of Oriental and Occidental religion." A.K. Coomaraswamy considered him as one of the very few Westerners qualified to interpret the teachings of the East to the contemporary world. Huston Smith, who is one of the leading philosophers of religion in America today, writes of Schuon, "The man is a living wonder; intellectually *à propos* religion, equally in depth and breadth, the paragon of our time. I know of no living thinker who begins to rival him." Of his *Transcendent Unity of Religions*, Smith writes, "At once the most powerful statement of the grand, or better, primordial tradition to appear in modern times and a statement of that tradition that is original in incorporating what our age for the first time demands; that religion be treated in global terms."

Schuon's writings have attracted leading authorities in different religious traditions. Such Japanese masters as D.T. Suzuki, Chikao Eujisawa, Kenji Ueda, Sohaku Ogata, Shin-ishi Hisamatsu and Shojun Bando have been in close contact with him. In India such revered authorities of Hinduism as Ananda Moyi Ma, the Maharshi, the Shankaracharya of Kanchi, Swami Ramdas, Hari Prasad Shastri, Ramaswami Aiyar, T.M.P. Mahadevan, K.V. Rangaswami Aiyangar, R. Raghavan and A.K. Saran have appreciated highly his exposition of Hinduism. In the Islamic world his writings on Islam and Sufism have been much praised and his *Understanding Islam* which is so widely known in that world exists in Arabic and is even taught in many places. His works have been acclaimed and have influenced many Muslim scholars and authorities including the late Shaykh 'Abd al-Halīm Mahmūd, the former rector of Al-Azhar, Uthman Yahya, A.K. Brohi, Muhammed Ajmal, Yusuf Ibish, and others.

In the Jewish world, the most lucid contemporary work on the Kabbala, by L. Schaya, is deeply indebted to Schuon. As for Christianity, some of the most notable figures of Christian theology, such as Jean Daniélou and Henri de Lubac, have been interested in Schuon's works. Thomas Merton had become deeply attracted to the writings of Schuon through Marco Pallis, the friend of Schuon with whom Merton corresponded regularly during the years preceding his death. Such traditional Catholic writers as Bernard Kelly, Jean Borela and Elémire Zolla have also highly appreciated his works.

The influence of the works of Schuon among scholars in both East and West is too extensive to record here. Suffice it to say that besides such figures as Titus Burckhardt, Martin Lings, Marco Pallis, Jean-Louis Michon, Victor Danner, Joseph E. Brown, William Stoddart, Lord Northbourne, Gai Eaton, W.N. Perry and Jean Canteins, who have been personally connected with the intellectual universe of Schuon over the years, such well-known scholars as H. Corbin, G. Durand, H. Smith, E.F. Schumacher, J. Needleman and many others have drawn deeply from his writings. J. Needleman has in fact edited a volume, *The Sword of Gnosis* (published by Penguin books), which is centered around the writings of Schuon and a group of scholars closely associated with his thought and works. There are also numerous scholars in whose writings one can detect the presence of Schuon's teachings without formal reference to his name and of course many who are not writers but whose thought patterns and even lives have been entirely remolded and transformed as a result of exposure to his books and articles. Schuon's influence, therefore, is much more extensive than external signs would reveal. He is a sun whose rays are not only directly manifested through his writings but which also shines upon the night of this world in spiritual eclipse through the reflected light of many a moon.

The Message of Schuon

If we were asked what are the main characteristics of Schuon's works, we would say that while from one point of view they possess essentiality, universality and comprehensiveness, from another they possess three spiritual characteristics which complement those already mentioned, these three being inwardness, the light of intelligence or a *scientia sacra* which penetrates into all things and the awareness of the sacred in the realm of the multiplicity of forms. Schuon's writings possess a dimension of interiority and inwardness that characterizes whatever he discusses whether it be an idea, a virtue or a form. His perspective has a penetrating quality like the rays of the sun, as if the cosmic intelligence itself were shining upon the manifold order. Finally, Schuon casts his vision upon the world of diverse religious and artistic forms, upon the world of man and virgin nature and reveals within them a spiritual and sacred quality which issues from the realization of the exalted state of seeing God everywhere and from the spiritual perspective based on the sacralization of the domain of multiplicity with the view of integrating it into the One. May the pages which follow and which have been chosen carefully from the vast corpus of his rich writings present, within the space alloted, the main aspects of his teachings as well as his intellectual style and manner of discourse. Above all may they aid the reader in discovering both the many facets of his work and his crucial message to the modern world and open a door into the religious and intellectual universe of one of the most remarkable spiritual figures of the contemporary period.

An Annotated Description of the Writings of Frithjof Schuon

Over the span of half a century, Schuon has composed a remarkable number of articles and books written mostly in French but also some in German and translated over the years into several languages especially English.[1] It must be emphasized, however, that the definitive presentation of the teachings of Schuon are to be found in his French books into which he has incorporated many of the essays written earlier in article form.[2] It must be pointed out also that not all the books have been composed in this manner, some having been written in their entirety solely in book form first. It is therefore particularly important to mention a few words about each of these books. A detailed discussion of all his writings would require a separate study.

De l'Unité transcendente des religions

The first major, doctrinal work of the author in which he sets out for the first time his method and approach to the study of religions, discussing the meaning of exoterism and esoterism and their relation especially within the Abrahamic family. There are also important sections devoted to traditional art, the particular nature of the Christian tradition and quintessential prayer.

L'Oeil du coeur

This work consists of three sections dealing with metaphysics and cosmology, forms of the Spirit and spiritual life. In the first section the author commences with the symbolism of the eye of the heart, which has given its name to the book, in order to discuss principial knowledge and the nature of knowledge as such, then turning to an extensive discussion of Islamic cosmology based on the symbolism of light (*al-nūr*), then to the Buddhist *nirvāna* and the posthumous states of man.

The second section deals with various themes drawn from different traditions in a comparative setting but including also studies devoted to a specific tradition such as those on the Buddhist *koan* and the Islamic ternary of *īmān, islām, ihsān*. The final section treats the various modes of spiritual realization, prayers, purification, sacrifice, meditation and other elements of the spiritual life.

Perspectives spirituelles et faits humains

The second book of the author to be written mostly in the form of aphorisms and short comments (following the German *Leit-gedanken*), this work represents a series of meditations upon tradition and modern civilization, art, the spiritual life, metaphysics and the virtues. Of special importance in this volume is Schuon's extensive discussion of the spiritual virtues as well as a masterly comparison between the perspectives of Sufism and the Vedanta.

Sentiers de gnose

Again consisting of three parts, the first section, entitled "Controversies", deals with specifically religious questions such as the sense of the Absolute within religions, the diversity of revelation, the question of "natural mysticism," and the different types of spiritual temperament. It also includes a metaphysical discussion of the doctrine of illusion. The second section entitled "Gnosis" discusses both the means of attaining gnosis and the nature of what is attained including a chaper on "Seeing God Everywhere." The final section entitled "Christianity" contains perhaps the most important synthesis of the views of the author concerning the Christian tradition.

Castes et races

This short work contains the author's most important study of human society based on the two concepts of caste and race which are applied in the traditional context while modern misconceptions of them are discussed and refuted. The work also contains an extensive essay on the "Principles and Criteria of Universal Art" which is one of Schuon's most important studies on art.

Les stations de la sagesse

One of the author's major works on religion itself, the work deals in six chapters with the relation of orthodoxy to intellectuality, the nature of faith and arguments for its defense, the various manifestations of the Divine Principle, the notion of charity with all the complexity it possesses and the misunderstandings which have grown around it in the modern world, prayer and finally the "stations of wisdom" which recapitulate and summarize the stages of the spiritual life.

Images de l'Esprit

Starting with a key essay on the "symbolist spirit" which characterizes traditional man, the author turns in three sections to the study of Shintoism, Buddhism and Yoga, the latter considered both as a technique and in relation to the question of operative grace and regularity of transmission.

Comprendre l'Islam

The author's most important work on Islam and among the books written by a Westerner on Islam the one most universally accepted by Muslims. This most widely read of Schuon's works deals in four chapters entitled, "Islam," "The Quran," "the Prophet," and "the Way" with the major dimensions of the Islamic tradition including Sufism. This book also seeks to answer many of the questions Christians have posed concerning Islam.

Regards sur les mondes anciens

In a sense an appraisal of the history of man seen from the traditional point of view, the work casts metaphysical light upon the ancient civilizations and their significance and traces the gradual fall of man to the modern period and the revolt of European man against the Christian tradition. It also deals with the crucial debate between Hellenists and Christians, the Shamanic character of North American Indian religions and the significance of monasticism. It concludes with the essay *"Religio Perennis"* which summarizes what lies at the heart of all religions and which may be considered to be the essence of religion as such.

Logique et transcendence

This long work is Schuon's most important philosophical opus in the sense of containing long chapters devoted to specifically philosophical questions such as relativism, the notion of concrete and abstract and rationalism. But the book also contains some of his most succinct theological discussions concerning both Christian and Islamic theology. The last part of the book turns again to diverse questions of the spiritual life including a discussion of the function of the spiritual master and concludes with a study of man and certitude.

Forme et substance dans les religions

This is the second work of Schuon (following *The Transcendent Unity*) which is devoted primarily to comparative religion. Beginning with two essays on the distinction between truth and presence and form and substance in religions, the author then turns to several major metaphysical studies of the most subtle nature concerning the distinction between *Ātma* and *māyā* and subject and object. He then devotes several studies to specifically Islamic themes including the Islamic understanding of Christ and Mary and two essays on Buddhism. The work concludes with another set of chapters which treat some of the most difficult theological and religious problems such as the question of theodicy, difficulties in sacred texts, paradoxes of spiritual expression, the effect of the human margin in revelation and certain eschatological issues.

L' Esotérisme comme principe et comme voie

This work is one of the major syntheses of Schuon in that it recapitulates his teachings on the meaning of esoterism, on the moral and spiritual life and on art and sacred forms concluding with two condensed studies on Sufism. The section on the moral and spiritual life is especially extensive containing nine chapters which treat of the most important questions and problems of the moral and spiritual life considered in a practical and operative manner.

Le soufisme, voile et quintessence

This unique work on Sufism commences with the elipses and hyperboles which characterize the Arabic language and which color the formal expression of Sufism in that language. Then the author discusses how elements of exoterism have penetrated into the domain of Sufism itself causing certain formulations and statements difficult to understand. To this symbiosis he contrasts quintessential Sufism based on the supreme doctrine of Unity whose hypostatic dimensions he examines in a final chapter. This book also contains Schuon's most important discussion of the meaning of the notion of philosophy.

Du divin à l'humain

This synthesis of the whole metaphysical message of Schuon, summarizes in three sections his teachings concerning epistemology, metaphysics and the science of man. Beginning with the discussion of the human subjectivity, consciousness and intelligence, he turns in the second section to present the most succinct and complete study he has ever made on the nature of the Divine Principle, the hypostases, principial possibility and the conditions of existence. Finally he turns to man to discuss what it means to have a spiritual anthropology, the message of the human body, man's sense of the sacred and the question of accepting or refusing God's message.

Christianisme / Islam — Visions d'oeucuménisme ésotérique

This work brings to its peak the author's comparative studies of Christianity and Islam and demonstrates what ecumenism can be if taken seriously. The first part devoted to Christianity discusses certain liturgical, ritual and theological questions as well as the significance of evangelism within the Christian tradition. The second part contains two very basic comparative studies in succession on the Semitic monotheisms and divergeñt moralities of Christianity and Islam. The last and longest part contains several studies on Islam including the dilemmas of Islamic theology and such problems as atomism and the Divine Will.

Sur les traces de la religion pérenne

One of the last works to have appeared so far from the pen of Schuon is another synthesis, mostly of his views on religion; but since his point of view is that of the *sophia perennis*, it is also a work of a highly metaphysical nature. In seven chapters the author deals again with the question of epistemology and the dimensions and degrees of the Divine Order. Then he deals with more specifically religious questions such as confessional speculation, the problems engendered by the language of faith, religious typology and certain enigmas present within Sufism. It concludes with a synthesis of eschatological teachings which he calls "universal eschatology".

Approaches du phénomènes religieux

Schuon's latest opus is once again concerned with the central issues of religion. In the first section of this work he deals with general traits of religions including certain complexities of religious language found in various revelations, the problem of exoterism, the question of evil and the meaning of eternity. The next two sections turn again to Christianity and Islam discussing some of the most difficult aspects of the theology of the two religions and ending with one of the most important essays of the author on Islamic esoterism dealing with the mystery of the spiritual substance of the Prophet and its significance in Sufism.

Besides these works in French, there are the following English books of Schuon which do not have a French original in the form in which they have been published but which must nevertheless be briefly mentioned here:

Language of the Self

A special arrangement of some of the essays of Schuon collected particularly with the view of the Indian audience for which it was prepared, the book having been printed in India and dedicated to the Shankara charya of Kanchipuram.

In the Tracks of Buddhism
A collection of Schuon's major studies on Buddhism to which his study of Shintoism has been added.

Dimensions of Islam
A collection of a number of Schuon's most metaphysical and esoteric works on Islam embracing the fields of metaphysics, cosmology and commentaries upon the Quran and *Hadīth*.

Islam and the Perennial Philosophy
Another collection of essays on various Islamic themes dealing with metaphysical, theological and eschatological questions.

The four works in English mentioned above were all assembled with permission and under the supervision of the author, the first two being prepared with the Indian and Buddhist worlds specifically in view, while the last two are more *"pièces d'occasion"*, prepared on particular occasions to make the author's works on Islamic subjects, especially certain articles which were not readily accessible, more easily available to the English speaking audience.

We must mention here also a German book written by Schuon in his youth and which has never been translated into any other language:

Leitgedanken zur Urbesinnung
A series of meditations on the nature of things, on God and man, on tradition and the modern world written mostly in the form of aphorisms and sayings in a very pure and traditional German which reminds us of Meister Eckhart's and Boehme's style. This work consists of four books written partly in Europe and partly in Algeria, the last book having been dedicated to the celebrated Algerian Sufi Shaykh al-'Alawī.

NOTES

An Annotated Description of the Writings of Frithjof Schuon

1. The English translations of the works of Schuon have been carried out by a group of men who are themselves accomplished scholars, devoted to his writings, completely familiar with his language and teachings and themselves masters of both English and French. The English works are therefore in a sense an extension of the French texts and possess an authenticity and literary quality rarely found in a body of translation of works of such a nature.

2. See the appendix to this volume for a list of his books and their translators.

PART I

RELIGION AND REVELATION

The Nature of Religion

Religio Perennis*

ONE OF THE KEYS to the understanding of our true nature and of our ultimate destiny is the fact that the things of this world never measure up to the real range of our intelligence. Our intelligence is made for the Absolute, or it is nothing. Among all the intelligences of this world the human spirit alone is capable of objectivity, and this implies — or proves — that what confers on our intelligence the power to accomplish to the full what it can accomplish, and what makes it wholly what it is, is the Absolute alone. If it were necessary or useful to prove the Absolute, the objective and transpersonal character of the human intellect would be sufficient as evidence, for that same intellect testifies irrecusably to a purely spiritual first Cause, to a Unity infinitely central but containing all things, to an Essence at once immanent and transcendent. It has been said more than once that total Truth is inscribed, in an immortal script, in the very substance of our spirit; what the different Revelations do is to "crystallize" and "actualize", in different degrees according to the case, a nucleus of certitudes which not only abides forever in the divine Omniscience, but also sleeps by refraction in the "naturally supernatural" kernel of the individual, as well as in that of each ethnic or historical collectivity or of the human species as a whole.

*From *LAW,* Chapter 11

67

Similarly, in the case of the will, which is no more than a prolongation or a complement of the intelligence: the objects which it
commonly sets out to achieve, or those which life imposes on it, do
not match up to the fulness of its range; the "divine dimension" alone
can satisfy the thirst for plenitude of our willing, or of our love. What
makes our will human, and therefore free, is the fact that it is proportioned to God; in God alone it is kept free from all constraint,
and thus from everything that limits its nature.

The essential function of human intelligence is discernment
between the Real and the illusory, or between the Permanent and
the impermanent, and the essential function of the will is attachment to the Permanent or to the Real. This discernment and this
attachment are the quintessence of all spirituality. Carried to their
highest level, or reduced to their purest substance, they constitute
the underlying universality in every great spiritual patrimony of
humanity, or what may be called the *religio perennis*. This and nothing
else is the religion of the sages, but always and necessarily on a foundation of divinely instituted formal elements. . .

The *religio perennis* is fundamentally this, to paraphrase the well-
known saying of St. Irenaeus: the Real entered into the illusory so
that the illusory might be able to return unto the Real. It is this
mystery, together with the metaphysical discernment and contemplative concentration that are its complement, which alone is important in an absolute sense from the point of view of gnosis. For
the gnostic (in the etymological and rightful sense of that word) there
is in the last analysis no other religion. It is what Ibn Arabi called
the "religion of love", putting the accent on the element of "realization".

The two-fold definition of the *religio perennis* — discernment between the Real and the illusory, and a unifying and permanent concentration on the Real — implies in addition the criteria of intrinsic
orthodoxy for every religion and all spirituality. In order to be orthodox a religion must possess a mythological or doctrinal symbolism
establishing the essential distinction in question, and must offer a
way that secures both the perfection of concentration and also its
continuity. In other words a religion is orthodox on condition that
it offers a sufficient, if not always exhaustive, idea of the absolute
and the relative and therewith an idea of their reciprocal relationships, and also a spiritual activity that is contemplative in its nature
and effectual as concerns our ultimate destiny. It is notorious that
hetero doxies always tend to adulterate either the idea of the divine

Principle or the manner of our attachment to it; they offer either a worldly, profane or, if you like, "humanist" counterfeit of religion, or else a mysticism with a content of nothing but the *ego* and its illusions . . .

The Sense of the Absolute in Religions*

Religions are cut off from one another by barriers of mutual incomprehension; one of the principal causes of this appears to be that the sense of the absolute stands on a different plane in each of them, so that what would seem to be points of comparison often prove not to be. Elements resembling one another in form appear in such diverse contexts that their function and their nature too changes, at any rate to some extent; and this is so because of the infinitude of the All-Possible, which excludes precise repetition. In short, the sufficient reason of a 'new' phenomenon is, from the point of view of the manifestation of possibilities, its difference in relation to 'antecedent' phenomena . . .

The 'sense of the absolute' is not grafted exactly on the same organic element, as between one religion and another — whence the impossibility of making comparisons between the elements of religions simply from the outside — and this fact is shown clearly by the differing natures of conversions to Christianity and Islam: while conversion to Christianity seems in certain respects like the beginning of a great love, which makes all a man's past life look vain and trivial — it is a 'rebirth' after a 'death'— conversion to Islam is on the contrary like awakening from an unhappy love, or like sobriety after drunkenness, or again like the freshness of morning after a troubled night. In Christianity, the soul is 'freezing to death' in its congenital egoism, and Christ is the central fire which warms and restores it to life; in Islam, on the other hand, the soul is 'suffocating' in the constriction of the same egoism, and Islam appears as the cool immensity of space which allows it to 'breath' and to 'expand' towards the boundless. The 'central fire' is denoted by the cross; the 'immen-

*From *GDW*, Chapter 1.

sity of space' by the Kaaba, the prayer-rug, the abstract interlacings of Islamic art.

There is, in every religion, not only a choice for the will between the beyond and the here-below, but also a choice for the intelligence between truth and error; there are however differences of correlation, in the sense that Christ is true because He is the Saviour — whence the importance that the phenomenal element assumes here — whilst when Islam has salvation in view it starts from a discrimination which is in the last analysis metaphysical (*lâ ilâha illâ 'Llâh*), and it is this Truth which saves; but whether it is a question of Christianity or of Islam or of any other traditional form, it is indeed the metaphysical truth which, thanks to its universality, determines the values of things. And as this truth envelops and penetrates all, there is in it neither 'here-below' nor 'beyond', nor any choice by the will; only the universal essences count, and these are 'everywhere and nowhere'; there is, on this plane, no choice for the will to make, for, as Aristotle says, 'the soul is all that it knows'. This contemplative serenity appears in the abstract freshness of mosques as also in many Romanesque churches and in certain elements of the best Gothic, particularly in the rose windows, which are like 'mirrors of gnosis' in these sanctuaries of love. . .

A question which inevitably arises here is that of the historicity of the great phenomena of the religions: ought more confidence to be placed in that radiation which presents a maximum of historical evidence? To this the reply must be that there is no metaphysical or spiritual difference between a truth manifested by temporal facts and a truth expressed by other symbols, under a mythological form for example; the modes of manifestation correspond to the mental requirements of the different groups of humanity. If certain mentalities prefer marvels that are empirically 'improbable' to historical 'reality', that is precisely because the marvellous — with which in any case no religion could dispense — indicates transcendence in relation to terrestrial facts; we are tempted to say that the aspect of improbability is the sufficient reason for the marvellous, and it is this unconscious need for feeling the essence of things which explains the tendency to exaggerate found among certain peoples; it is a trace of nostalgia for the Infinite. Miracles denote an interference of the marvellous in the sensory realm; whoever admits miracles must also admit the principle of the marvellous as such, and even tolerate pious exaggeration on a certain plane. The opportuneness of 'mythological' marvels on the one hand and the existence of contradictions between religions on the other — which do not imply any intrinsic absurdity within the bounds of a given religion, any more than the internal contradictions found in all religions are absurd — these factors, we say, show in their own way that, with God, the truth is above all in the symbol's effective power of illumination and not in its literalness, and that is all the more evident since God, whose wisdom goes beyond all words, puts multiple meanings into a single expression; [1] an obscurity in expression — whether elliptical or contradictory — often indicates a richness or a depth in meaning, and this it is which explains the apparent incoherences to be found in the sacred Scriptures. God manifests in this way His transcendence in relation to the limitations of human logic; human language can be divine only in an indirect way, neither our words nor our logic being at the height of the divine purpose. The uncreated Word shatters created speech, whilst at the same time directing it towards concrete and saving truth.

Must the conclusion of all this then be that from the point of view of spirituality an historical basis has in itself less value than a mythological or purely metaphysical basis, on the grounds that principles are more important than phenomena? Assuredly not, insofar as it is a question of symbolism; what has less value is an attribution to this historical basis of a significance greater than it should have, a substituting of it for the symbolic truth and the metaphysical reality it expresses; none the less the importance of historical fact remains intact in respect of sacred institutions. From another point of view, it should be noted that a traditional narrative is always true; the more or less mythical features which are imposed on the historical life of the Buddha, for instance, are so many ways of expressing spiritual realities which it would be difficult to express otherwise.[2] In cases where Revelation is most expressly founded on history, and to the extent that this is so, the historical mode is no doubt necessary: in a world which was heir to Jewish 'historicism' and to Aristotelian empiricism, Revelation could not fail to take wholly the form of an earthly event, without the adjunction of any non-historical symbolism; but we must observe that a too great insistence on historicity — not historicity as such — may somewhat obscure the metaphysical content of sacred facts, or their spiritual 'translucency' and can even end, in the form of abusive criticism, by 'eroding' history itself and by belittling what is too big for man's powers of conception.

Those who favour rigorous historicity against the mythologies of Asia will doubtless object that the historical truth furnishes proofs of the validity of the means of grace: in this context, it is necessary to point out, firstly that historical proofs, precisely, could not be quite rigorous in this realm, and secondly that tradition as such, with all that it comprises in the way of symbolism, doctrine and sanctity — not to mention other more or less indeterminate criteria — furnishes much more unexceptionable proofs of the divine origin and the validity of rites; in a sense, the acceptance by tradition — and the development in sanctity — of a means of grace is a criterion far more convincing than historicity, not to mention the intrinsic value of the Scriptures. History is often incapable of verification; it is tradition, not criticism, which guarantees it, but it guarantees at the same time the validity of non-historical symbolisms. It is the actual and permanent miracle of tradition which nullifies the objection that no man living has been a witness of sacred history; the saints are its witnesses in quite other fashion than the historians; to deny tradition as the guarantee of truth amounts in the end to asserting that there are effects without causes.

There is, doubtless, no truth more 'exact' than that of history; but what must be stressed is that there is a truth more 'real' than that of facts; the higher reality embraces the 'exactness', but the latter, on the contrary, is far from presupposing the former. Historical reality is less 'real' than the profound truth it expresses and which myths likewise express; a mythological symbolism is infinitely more 'true' than a fact deprived of symbolism. And that brings us back to what we were saying above, namely that the mythological or historical opportuneness of the marvellous, as also the existence of dogmatic antinomies, go to show that for God truth is above all in the efficacy of the symbol and not in the 'bare fact'.

From the point of view of historicity or of its absence, three degrees must be distinguished: mythology, qualified historicity and exact historicity. We find the first degree in all mythology properly so called, as also in the monotheistic accounts of the creation, and the second degree in the other 'prehistoric' narratives, whether they concern Noah or Jonah or the human *avatâras* of Vishnu.[3] In Judaism, rigorous historicity starts perhaps at Sinai; in Christianity, it appears in the whole of the New Testament,[4] but not in the Apocrypha or the Golden Legend, which moreover are not canonical works, a fact that has earned them a quite undeserved disregard, since symbolism is an essential vehicle of truth; lastly, in Islam, exact historicity attaches to the life of the Prophet and of his Companions, as well as to those of their sayings (*ahâdîth*) recognised by the tradition,[5] but not to the stories concerning the pre-Islamic Prophets and events, which are woven of symbols certainly 'exact' but more or less 'mythical'; to take them literally however is always to let oneself be inspired by their 'alchemical' virtue, even when a real understanding is lacking.

The historical perspective, with all its importance for a certain level of Christian doctrine, is however legitimate only insofar as it can be included in Platonic non-historicity. Christian 'personalism' derives from the fact of the Incarnation, and then from the 'bhaktic' character of Christianity, a character which in no way prevents this religion from 'containing' metaphysics and gnosis, for Christ is 'Light of the world'; but gnosis is not for everyone, and a religion cannot be metaphysical in its actual form; on the other hand, Platonism, which is not a religion, can be so. Christian 'historicity', which is conjoint with Jewish 'historicity', implies then no superiority in relation to other perspectives, nor any inferiority so long as the characteristic in question is situated at the level to which it rightfully belongs.

To Refuse or to Accept Revelation*

The foundation of the "logical subjectivism" of believers lies in what we call "religious solipsism"; and this is inevitable for two main reasons. Firstly, every religious message is a Message of the Absolute; this character of Absoluteness penetrates the entire Message and confers upon it its quality of uniqueness. God speaks for the Inward and is not preoccupied with the outward as such; He proclaims "the Religion" in a form adapted to given human possibilities; He does not engage in "comparative religion". Secondly, the average man is not disposed to grasp this character of Absoluteness if it is not suggested by the uniqueness of its expression; and God will not compromise this understanding by specifications stressing what is outward and relative, thus foreign to that which is the reason for the

*From *FDH*, Chapter 10.

existence of the Message. But this could in no way bind esoterism: on the one hand because it is not a religious Message and derives from the Intellect more than from Revelation, and on the other hand because it is addressed to men who have no need of a suggestion of uniqueness and exclusivity at the level of expression in order to grasp the character of Absoluteness in sacred enunciations.

All of this should serve to make it clear that we are as far as can be from approving a gratuitous and sentimentalist "ecumenism" which does not distinguish between truth and error and which results in religious indifference and the cult of man. What one has to understand, in reality, is that the undeniable presence of the transcendent truth of the sacred and supernatural in forms other than that of our religion of birth, should lead us not to doubt in the least the character of Absoluteness proper to our religion, but simply to admit the inherence of the Absolute in all doctrinal and sacramental symbolisms which by definition manifest It and communicate It, but which also by definition — since they are of the formal order — are relative and limited despite their quality of uniqueness. This latter is necessary, as we have said, inasmuch as it testifies to the Absolute, but is merely indicative from the point of view of the Absolute in Itself, which manifests Itself necessarily by uniqueness yet just as necessarily — in virtue of Its Infinitude — by the diversity of forms.

All of these considerations raise the following questions: how can a man, who observes that his religion of birth or adoption is visibly incapable of saving the whole of humanity, still believe that it is the only saving religion? And how can a man, who moreover observes the existence of other religions which are powerfully established and having the same claim, persist in believing that God, sincerely desirous of saving the world, should have found no other means of doing so than by instituting one single religion, strongly colored by specific ethnic and historical features — as it must necessarily be — and doomed in advance to failure as regards the goal in question? Finally, why is it that in the vast majority of cases the adherent of a given religion or denomination remains unmoved by the arguments of another given religion or denomination even when he has studied it as much as it can be studied?

Doubtless, these questions do not arise *a priori* but in the end they arise with the experience of centuries. And the fact that these questions arise and that they compromise to a great extent the religion which clearly has no adequate means of answering them — this fact, we say, shows precisely that they arise legitimately and providentially, and that in the religions there is, to the very extent of their exclusivism, an aspect of insufficiency, normal, no doubt, but nonetheless detrimental in the final analysis.

The divine origin and the majesty of the religions implies that they must contain all truth and all answers; and there, precisely, lies the mystery and the role of esoterism. When the religious phenomenon, hard-pressed as it were by a badly interpreted experience, appears to be at the end of its resources, esoterism springs forth from the very depths of this phenomenon to show that Heaven cannot contradict itself; that a given religion in reality sums up all religions and that all religion is to be found in a given religion, because Truth is one. In other words: the contrast between the absolute character of Revelation and its aspect of relativity constitutes indirectly one more proof — along with the direct and historical proofs — of both the reality and the necessity of the esoteric dimension proper to all religion; so much so that the religions, at the very moment when they seem to be defeated by experience, affirm themselves victoriously on every level by their very essence.

•   •   •

A proof which is often advanced in favor of religion, but which is rarely understood to its full extent, is the argument of the moral efficaciousness of Divine Legislation: indeed, what does human society become if it is deprived of a Law founded upon the authority of God? The unbelievers, who as a general rule have but a highly restricted and partially false idea of human nature — otherwise they would not be unbelievers — will answer that it suffices to replace the religious Law with a civil Law founded upon the common interest; now the opinion of the "free thinkers" concerning the public good depends upon their scale of values, hence upon their idea of man and therefore of the meaning of life. But what has been instituted by an individual can always be abolished by another individual; philosophies change with tastes, they follow the downward slope of history, because as soon as man is detached from his reason for existence, rooted in God, he can only slide downwards, in conformity with the law of gravity which is valid for the human order as well as for the physical order, notwithstanding the periodic renewal effected by the religions, the sages and the saints.[1]

Now the fact that the Divine Law, insofar as it is fundamental and thereby universal,[2] is definitively the only efficacious one — to the degree that a Law can and must be so — this fact shows that it is a Message of Truth; it alone is incontestable and irreplaceable. To be sure the contemporary world still possesses codes and civil laws, but even so for the general mentality there is less and less an authority which is such "by right", and not merely "in fact".[3] Moreover, the Law is made to protect not only society, but also the individual prone to offense; if the "secular arm" inspires fear to the degree that badly-intentioned men feel threatened by it, on the other hand these same men have no intrinsic motive not to follow their inclinations, outside the fear of God. The threat of human justice is uncertain, hence relative; that of the divine Justice is absolute; for it is possible to escape men, but certainly not God.

In summary: one indirect proof of God is that without Divinity there is no authority, and without authority there is no efficacy; that is to say that the religious Message imposes itself — apart from its other imperatives — because no moral and social life is possible without it, except for a brief period which, without admitting it, is still living off the residues of a disavowed heritage. And this brings us to another extrinsic proof *a contrario* of God, although it is fundamentally the same: it is a fact of experience that the common man, on the whole, who is not disciplined by social necessity and who precisely is only disciplined by religion and piety, decays in his behaviour as soon as he has no more religion containing and penetrating him; and experience proves that the disappearance of faith and of morals brings about that of personal dignity and of private life, which in fact only have meaning and value if man possesses an immortal soul. It is hardly necessary to recall here that believing peasants and artisans are often of an aristocratic nature, and that they are so through religion; without forgetting that aristocracy in itself, namely nobility of sentiment and comportment and the tendency to control and transcend oneself, derives from spirituality and draws its principles from it, consciously or unconsciously.

What the people need in order to find a meaning in life, hence a possibility of earthly happiness, is religion and the crafts: religion because every man has need of it, and the crafts because they allow man to manifest his personality and to realize his vocation in the framework of a sapiential symbolism; every man loves intelligible work and work well done.[4] Now industrialism has robbed the people of both things: on the one hand of religion, denied by scientism from which industry derives, and rendered unlikely by the inhuman character of the mechanistic ambience, and on the other hand the crafts, replaced precisely by machinism; so much so that in spite of all the "social doctrines" of the Church and the nationalistic bourgeoisie, there is nothing left for the people which can give a meaning to their life and make them happy. The classic contradiction of traditional Catholicism is to want to maintain the social hierarchy, in which it is theoretically right, even while accepting whole-heartedly — as an acquisition of the "Christian civilization" which in fact has long been abolished — the scientism and the machinism which precisely compromise this hierarchy by cutting the people off, in fact, from humankind. The inverse error is founded on the same cult of technology, with the difference that it is detrimental to the bourgeoisie rather than to the common people and that it aims at reducing the entire society to mechanistic inhumanity while on the other hand presenting it with an "opium" made of bitterness and frigidity which kills the very organ of happiness; for to be happy it is necessary to be a child, happiness being made of gratitude and confidence, humanly speaking. The machine is opposed to man, consequently it is also opposed to God; in a world where it poses as norm, it abolishes both the human and the divine. The logical solution to the problem would be the return — which in fact has become impossible without a divine intervention — to the crafts and at the same time to religion[5] — and thereby to an ambience which, by not falsifying our sense of the real, does not make unlikely what is evident. One of the greatest successes of the devil was to create around man surroundings in which God and immortality appear unbelievable.[6]

· · ·

There are attenuating circumstances for doubt when man finds himself torn between the bad examples given in the name of religion and his own instinct for the primordial religion — torn without having a discernment that is sufficient to put everything in its proper place. A workman once told us that he felt close to God in virgin nature and not in a church, and one of Tolstoy's characters said in a story: "Where are there baptismal fonts as great as the ocean?" There is here a sensibility both for the universality of truth and for the sacred character of nature, but it should not make us lose sight of the fact that persistence in such simplifications, which easily turn into narcissism, have no excuse in the final analysis; for man is made to transcend himself, and he ought to have this impulse even as a plant that turns towards the sun. One sensibility calls forth another, one must not stop halfway.

There is in the man of a "believing" or elect nature a legacy of the lost Paradise, and that is the instinct for the transcendent and the sense of the sacred; it is on the one hand the disposition to believe in the miraculous, and on the other hand the need to venerate and to adore. To this two-fold predisposition must normally be added a two-fold detachment, one with respect to the world and earthly life, and the other with respect to the ego, its dreams and its pretensions. The problem of the credibility of the religious Messages can be resolved only by starting from those facts which are normative because they are a function of man's deiformity.

"Abram believed in Yahweh; and Yahweh counted it to him for righteousness" (Genesis, 15:6): that is to say that Abraham's faith here was a merit because its object was something humanly impossible; the same is true for Mary's faith at the time of the Annunciation. The unbeliever by nature is not inclined to consider possible what is contrary to nature and consequently to reason; not to reason in itself but to reason inasmuch as it does not possess the information which would allow it to understand the laws of the supernatural. There are three possible attitudes or reactions with regard to the supernatural: refusal, acceptance and perplexity; the classic image of the latter being the attitude of the Apostle Thomas. "Blessed are those who have not seen, and yet have believed" (John, 20:29): those who, before seeing, are predisposed to believe. The unbeliever, on earth, believes only what he sees; the believer, in Heaven, sees all that he believes.

We are always astonished by the fact that unbelievers and even certain believers are strangely insensitive to the direct language of the sacred Messages: that they do not perceive from the very first that the Psalms, the Gospel, the Upanishads, the Bhagavad-gītā could only come from Heaven, and that the spiritual perfume of these books dispenses — from the point of view of credibility — with all theological analysis as well as with all historical research.[7] Personally, even if we were neither metaphysician nor esoterist, we would be a believer without the least difficulty; we would be convinced at the outset upon contact with the sacred in all its forms. We would believe in God and immortality because their evidence appears in the very form of the Message; since, to learn what God is is to recall what we are.

A point of view which is readily lost sight of—if one has even thought of it—when defending those who refuse the celestial Messages, is precisely the very appearance of the Messengers; now, to paraphrase or to cite some well-known formulas, "he who has seen the Prophet has seen God"; "God became man in order that man might become God". One has to have a very hardened heart not to be able to see this upon contact with such beings; and it is above all this hardness of heart that is culpable, far more than ideological scruples.

The combination of holiness and beauty which characterizes the Messengers of Heaven is, so to speak, transmitted from the human theophanies to the sacred art which perpetuates it: the essentially intelligent and profound beauty of this art testifies to the truth which inspires it; it could not in any case be reduced to a human invention as regards the essential of its message. Sacred art is Heaven descended to earth, rather than earth reaching towards Heaven.

A line of thought close to this one which we have just presented is the following, and we have made note of it more than once: if men were stupid enough to believe for millenia in the divine, the supernatural, immortality—assuming these are illusions—it is impossible that one fine day they became intelligent enough to be aware of their errors; that they became intelligent, no one knowing why, and without any decisive moral acquisition to corroborate this miracle. And likewise: if men like the Christ believed in the supernatural, it is impossible that men like the Encyclopedists were right not to believe in it.

Sceptical rationalism and titanesque naturalism are the two great abuses of intelligence, which violate pure intellectuality as well as a sense of the sacred; it is through this propensity that thinkers "are wise in their own eyes" and end by "calling evil good, and good evil" and by "putting darkness for light, and light for darkness" (Isaiah 5:20 and 21); they are also the ones who, on the plane of life or experience, "put bitter for sweet", namely the love of the eternal God, and "sweet for bitter", namely the illusion of the evanescent world.

•   •   •

One cannot understand the meaning of the divine Message without knowing the nature of the human receptacle; he who understands man, understands all the supernatural and cannot help but accept it. Now man is made to contemplate the Absolute starting from contingency; the Absolute is conscious of Itself in Itself, but It also wishes to be conscious of Itself starting from another than Itself; this indirect vision is a possibility necessarily included in the Infinitude belonging to the Absolute. In consequence it could not not be realized; it is necessary that there be a world, beings, men. To contemplate the Absolute starting from the contingent is correlatively to see things in God and to see God in things, in such a manner that they do not take us away from God and that on the contrary they bring us near to Him; this is the reason for the existence of man, and from it ensue existential rights as well as spiritual duties. Man in principle has the right to the satisfaction of his elementary needs and to the enjoyment of a congenial ambience, but he has this right only in view of his vocation of knowing God, whence derives his duty to practice the disciplines that contribute directly or indirectly to this knowledge.

The worth of man lies in his consciousness of the Absolute, and consequently in the integrality and the depth of this consciousness; having lost sight of it by plunging himself into the world of phenomena viewed as such — this is prefigured by the fall of the first couple — man needs to be reminded of it by the celestial Message. Fundamentally, this Message comes from "himself," not of course from his empirical "I" but from his immanent Ipseity, which is that of God and without which there would be no "I", whether human, angelic, or any other; the credibility of the Message results from the fact that it is what we are, both within ourselves and beyond ourselves. In the depths of transcendence is immanence, and in the depths of immanence, transcendence.

•   •   •

It has been said that, if nothing can logically oblige a people to believe what a Prophet preaches to them, nothing can oblige the Prophet himself to believe what God reveals or seems to reveal to him; the lack of credibility would be the same in the one case as in the other. Now, apart from the fact that in order to be able to assess the matter it would be necessary either to be a Prophet or to hear a Prophet preach, the opinion in question sins through a flagrant ignorance concerning the phenomenon of Revelation and that of faith, then through begging the question by positing that there is no God; for if God is real, He is bound to find a way to make Himself heard and make Himself accepted.

The fundamental solution to the problem of the credibility of the religious axioms, and in consequence the quintessence of the proofs of God, is in the ontological correspondence between the macrocosm and microcosm, that is to say in the fact that the microcosm necessarily repeats the macrocosm; in other words the subjective dimension, taken in its totality, coincides with the objective dimension, to which precisely the religious and metaphysical truths pertain. What counts is to actualize this coincidence, and that is done precisely, in principle or *de facto*, by Revelation, which awakens if not always direct Intellection, at least that indirect Intellection which is Faith; *credo ut intelligam*.

All that we know, we bear within ourselves, hence that is what we are; and that is why we can know it. We could symbolize this mystery by a circle comprising four poles: the lower pole would represent the human subject insofar as it is cut off from the object; the upper pole on the contrary would present absolute In-Itselfness which is neither subject nor object or which is both at once, or the one in the other. The right half of the circle would be the objective world, and the left half, subjective depth; in the center of each half, thus halfway towards Selfhood, would be situated respectively the absolute Object and the absolute Subject, or in other words In-Itselfness indirectly perceived or lived either as object or as subject. Now the circle is always the same Real; and that is why it is equally absurd to say that God does not exist since we have no objective perception of Him, or to say that He is absolutely unknowable because He is absolutely transcendent. For this transcendence, in the final analysis, is our own Essence and the foundation of our immortality.

●　●　●

The religious phenomenon is reducible in the final analysis to a manifestation at once intellective and volitive of the relationship between the divine Substance and cosmic accidentality or between

Atmā and *Samsāra*; and as this relationship comprises diverse aspects, the religious phenomenon is diversified in function of these aspects or these possibilities.

Every religion in effect presents itself as a "myth" referring to a given "archetype", and thereby, but secondarily, to all archetypes; all these aspects are linked, but one alone determines the very form of the myth. If the Amidist perspective recalls the Christian perspective, that is because within the framework of Buddhism it refers more particularly to the archetype which determines Christianity; it is not because it was influenced by the latter, apart from the historical impossibility of the hypothesis. The average man is incapable, not of conceiving of the archetypes no doubt, but of being interested in them; he has need of a myth which humanizes and dramatizes the archetype and which triggers the corresponding reactions of the will and sensibility; that is to say that the average man, or collective man, has need of a god who resembles him.[8]

The Taoist *Yin-Yang* is an adequate image of the fundamental relationship between the Absolute and the contingent, God and the world, or God and man: the white part of the figure represents God and the black part, man. The black dot in the white part is "man in God"— man principially prefigured in the divine Order — or the relative in the Absolute, if this paradox is permitted — or the divine Word which in effect prefigures the human phenomenon; if cosmic manifestation were not anticipated within the principial order, no world would be possible, nor any relationship between the world and God. Inversely and complementarily, the white dot in the black part of the *Yin-Yang* is the "human God," the "Man-God," which refers to the mystery of Immanence and to that of Theophany, hence also to that of Intercession and Redemption, or of the as it were "respiratory" reciprocity between earth and Heaven; if Heaven were not present in earth, existence would vanish into nothingness, it would be impossible *a priori*. Herein is the whole play of *Māyā* with its modes, its degrees, its cycles, its diversity and its alternations.

On the one hand the Principle alone is, manifestation — the world — is not; on the other hand manifestation is real — or "not unreal"— by the fact precisely that it manifests, projects, or prolongs the Principle; the latter being absolute, hence infinite for that very reason, It requires in virtue of this infinitude, the projection of Itself in the "other than Itself." On the one hand the Principle has a tendency to "punish" or to "destroy" manifestation because the latter as contingency is not the Principle, or because it tries to be the Principle illusorily and with a luciferian intention, in short because "It alone is"; on the other hand, the Principle "loves" manifestation and "remembers" that it is Its own, that manifestation is not "other than It," and within this ontological perspective the mystery of Revelation, Intercession, Redemption, is to be found. It is thus that the relationships between the Principle and manifestation give rise to diverse archetypes of which the religions are the mythical crystallizations and which are predisposed to set in motion the will and sensibility of particular men and of particular human collectivities.

But the archetypes of the objective, macrocosmic and transcendent order are also those of the subjective, microcosmic and immanent order, the human Intellect coinciding, beyond the individuality, with the universal Intellect; so much so that the revealed myth, even while coming in fact from the exterior and from the "Lord," comes in principle also from "our selves," from the interior and from the "Self." That is to say that the acceptance of the religious Message coincides, in principle and in depth, with the acceptance of what we are, in ourselves yet at the same time beyond ourselves; for there where immanence is, there is also the transcendence of the Immanent.

To believe in God is to become again what we are; to become it again to the very extent that we believe, and the believing becomes being.

NOTES

The Sense of the Absolute in Religions

1 Just as the blow of a hammer produces a multitude of sparks, so, say the Kabbalists, a single word of the Torah comprises multiple meanings.

2. The fact that the life of Buddha, which is historical in its main features, including certain miracles, retraces the myth of Indra, in no way means that it is itself a myth, any more than the prophecies concerning Christ invalidate His historical reality. On the contrary, if the first steps of the Buddha after the Illumination were marked by lotuses, this fact belongs to the subtle order, it is not in any way 'unreal'.

3. The non-human *avatâras* belong, in our opinion, to mythological symbolism; all the same it is necessary to avoid putting into this category all the phenomena which contradict the experience of our millennium. On this score we should like to remark that we see no logical reason for denying historicity to the loves of the *gopis*, for if such a symbolism be possible, it has also the right to exist on the plane of facts; there is something analogous in the case of the 'Song of Songs', where the literal meaning keeps all its rights, since it exists; moral interest must not be confused with the truth which runs through all levels of Existence.

4. Let us notice all the same the existence of a certain variability, for example on the subject of the 'three Mary Magdalenes', as also some contradictory features in the Gospel stories, which seem to us to indicate that sacred things, while being situated here in time, are beyond history; such 'irregularities' are in no way contrary to the divine Will, and they are moreover to be found also in sacred art, where they are like 'openings' safeguarding the indefinite flux of 'life'; this amounts to saying that every form is inadequate in the eyes of Heaven. There is something of this also in the extreme freedom of scriptural quotations in the New Testament: the divine Utterance, in crystallizing itself, rejects at the same time certain 'fixations'. Simply to read the Gospels is enough, from our point of view, to reduce to nothing all the artificial arguments aimed at ruining the authenticity of the texts. Those who, contrary to tradition, extol the value of 'criticism' or of 'objective analysis', forget the essential, namely intelligence, without which the best of methods is futile; though indeed intelligence is often identified with a critical attitude, as if to doubt evidence were a sufficient proof of being intelligent.

5. According to a very widespread opinion, almost all the sayings and gestures of the Prophet recorded by the *Sunna* are falsifications produced by certain interested theologians. The psychological improbability of such an hypothesis is ignored, and it seems to be forgotten that the supposed falsifiers were men who believed in Islam and feared hell; no weight is given to tradition or to orthodox unanimity, of course, and this shows ignorance of what is possible in a tradition and what is not; basically it shows ignorance of what tradition is.

To Refuse or to Accept Revelation

1. The dreamers of the XVIIIth century, unaware of being hereditarily influenced by Christianity and imbued with ancient civism and with freemasonic idealism, imagined that man is reasonable and that human reason coincides with their ideology; the latter being, to say the least, fragmentary and rendered inoperative in advance by the subversive cult of man. What they did not foresee is that once man is detached from divine Authority he does not in any way feel obliged to submit to a human authority; as soon as he knows himself to be independent of all morals other than his own, nothing prevents him from inventing morals conformed to his errors and his vices and completely bedecked with a veil of rationality, at least to the extent that euphemisms still seem useful to him.

2. There are revealed prescriptions which have in view not the nature of man — as does the Decalogue, notably — but given particular conditions or circumstances.

3. For this same mentality, morals are something merely subjective, and in consequence transgression is an entirely relative thing; now a judiciary apparatus is as it were reduced to impotence in a society which no longer believes that a crime is a crime, and which in this way contributes to the psychoanalization of justice and the abolition of public security.

4. Along with work, and the religion which sanctifies it, the people also have need of a wisdom; this is what Richelieu did not understand when he set himself against the guilds.

5. This is what a Gandhi tried to realize, heroically but without results other than a good example and all sorts of initiatives that remained partial and local. As for the Church, it will undoubtedly be objected that it could not compromise itself by opposing that "irreversible" phenomenon which is industrialism; we would reply first of all that the truth has precedence over any consideration of opportuneness or of "irreversibility", and then that the Church could always have affirmed its doctrinal position, to all intents and purposes, without having to be unrealistic on the level of facts; it could moreover have opted, with perfect logic and in accord with its entire past, for the monarchist and traditional right-wing which upheld it by definition, without having to compromise itself in the eyes of some, with the ambiguous "right" born in the XIXth century in the shadow of the machine.

6. And this certainly is not, in spite of all illusions, "Christian civilization".

7. How, in reading the life and writings of a Honen Shonin, could one doubt the validity of the Amidist tradition and the sanctity of this personage? A tradition and a faith which produce such fruits, generously and for centuries, can only be supernatural.

8. Personal and dramatic in the case of Christianity; impersonal and serene in the case of Buddhism; the one being reflected sporadically in the other. We cite these two examples be cause of their disparity. Let us add that Arianism is a kind of interference within Christianity of the possibility-archetype of Islam, whereas inversely Shi'ism appears within Islam as an archetypal interference of Christian dramatism.

Esoterism and Mysticism

Understanding Esoterism*

... ESOTERISM, BY ITS INTERPRETATIONS, its revelations and its interiorizing and essentializing operations, tends to realize pure and direct objectivity; this is the reason for its existence. Objectivity takes account of both immanence and transcendence; it is both extinction and reintegration. It is not other than the Truth, in which subject and object coincide, and in which the essential takes precedence over the accidental — or in which the principle takes precedence over its manifestation — either by extinguishing it, or by reintegrating it, depending on the various aspects of relativity itself.[1]

To say objectivity is to say totality, and this on all levels: esoteric doctrines realize totality to the same extent that they realize objectivity; what distinguishes the teaching of a Shankara from that of a Ramanuja is precisely totality. On the one hand, partial or indirect truth can save, and in this respect it can suffice us; on the other hand, if God has judged it good to give us an understanding which transcends the necessary minimum, we can do nothing about this and we would be highly ungracious to complain about it. Man certainly is free to close his eyes to particular data — and he may do so either from ignorance or as a matter of con venience — but at least nothing forces him to do so.

*From *EPW*, pp. 15-42.

86

All the same, the difference between the two perspectives in question lies not only in the manner of envisaging a particular object, but also in the objects envisaged; that is to say one does not only speak differently about the same thing, one also speaks of different things, which indeed is perfectly obvious.

Nevertheless, if on the one hand the world of gnosis and that of belief are distinct, on the other hand and in another respect they meet and interpenetrate each other. We may be told that one or other of the points we make has nothing specifically esoteric or gnostic about it; we would readily agree and are the first to recognize it. The two perspectives in question may or must coincide at many points, and at different levels, for the obvious reason that the underlying truth is one, and also because man is one.

On the exoterist side, the argument is advanced against universalist esoterism that Revelation said such and such a thing and consequently this must be accepted in an unconditional manner; on the esoterist side, it will be said that Revelation is intrinsically absolute and extrinsically relative and that this relativity derives from a combination of two factors, namely intellection and experience. For example, the axiom that a form cannot be absolutely unique of its kind — any more than the sun, though intrinsically representing the unique centre, cannot exclude the existence of other fixed stars — is an axiom of intellection, but *a priori* has only an abstract import; it becomes concrete, however, through the experience which, should the occasion arise, puts us intimately into relationship with other solar systems of the religious cosmos, and which precisely compels us to distinguish, within Revelation, between an absolute and intrinsic sense and a relative and extrinsic sense. According to the first sense, Christ is unique, and he told us so; according to the second sense, he said this as Logos, and the Logos, which is unique, comprises in fact other possible manifestations.

It is true that experience alone, in the absence of pure intellection, can give rise to completely opposite conclusions: one might well believe that the plurality of the religions proved their falseness or at least their subjectiveness, since they differ. Most paradoxically, but fatally — civilizationism having prepared the ground — the official stratum of Catholic thought has let itself be carried away by the conclusions of profane experience by voluntarily ignoring those of intellection; this leads these ideologists into accepting certain extrinsic postulates of esoterism — in particular that of the validity of the other religions—but at the cost of ruining their own religion and without understanding in depth that of the others.[2]

• • •

The esoterist sees things, not as they appear according to a certain perspective, but as they are: he takes account of what is essential and consequently invariable under the veil of different religious formulations, while necessarily taking his own starting point in a given formulation. This at least is the position in principle and the justification for esoterism; in fact it is far from always being consistent with itself, inasmuch as intermediary solutions are humanly inevitable.

Everything which, in metaphysics or in spirituality, is universally true, becomes "esoteric" in so far as it does not agree, or does not seem to agree, with a given formalistic system or "exoterism;" yet every truth is present by right in every religion, given that every religion is made of truth. This amounts to saying that esoterism is possible and even necessary; the whole question is to know at what level and in what context it is manifested, for relative and limited truth has its rights, as does the total truth; it has these rights in the context assigned to it by the nature of things, which is that of psychological and moral opportuneness and of traditional equilibrium.

The paradox of esoterism is that on the one hand "men do not light a candle and put it under a bushel", while on the other hand "give not what is sacred to dogs"; between these two expressions lies the "light that shineth in the darkness, but the darkness comprehended it not". There are fluctuations here which no one can prevent and which are the ransom of contingency.

Exoterism is a precarious thing by reason of its limits or its exclusions; there arrives a moment in history when all kinds of experience oblige it to modify its claims to exclusiveness, and it is then driven to a choice: escape from these limitations by the upward path, in esoterism, or by the downward path, in a worldly and suicidal liberalism. As one might have expected, the civilizationist exoterism of the West has chosen the downward path, while combining this incidentally with a few esoteric notions which in such conditions remain inoperative.

Fallen man, and thus the average man, is as it were poisoned by the passional element, either grossly or subtly; from this results an obscuring of the Intellect and the necessity of a Revelation coming from the outside. Remove the passional element from the soul and the intelligence — remove "the rust from the mirror" or "from the heart"— and the Intellect will be released; it will reveal from within what religion reveals from without.[3] This brings us to an important point: in order to make itself understood by souls impregnated with passion, religion must itself adopt a so to speak passional language, whence dogmatism, which excludes, and moralism, which schematizes; if the average man or collective man were not passional, Revelation would speak the language of the Intellect and there would be no exoterism, nor for that matter esoterism considered as an occult complement. There are here three possibilities: firstly, men dominate the passional element, everyone lives spiritually by his inward Revelation; this is the golden age, in which everyone is born an initiate. Second possibility: men are affected by the passional element to the point of forgetting certain aspects of the Truth, whence the necessity — or the opportuneness — of Revelations that while being outward are metaphysical in spirit, such as the *Upanishads*.[4] Thirdly: the majority of men are dominated by passions, whence the formalistic, exclusive and combative religions, which communicate to them on the one hand the means of channelling the passional element with a view to salvation, and on the other hand the means of overcoming it in view of the total Truth, and of thereby transcending the religious formalism which veils it while suggesting it in an indirect manner. Religious revelation is both a veil of light and a light veiled.

* * *

In those who accept esoterism or, what amounts to the same, the *philosophia perennis*, while feeling themselves emotionally linked to a given religious climate, the temptation is great to confuse the sublime with the esoteric and to believe that everything that they venerate pertains *ipso facto* to esoterism, starting with theology and sanctity. To escape all confusion of this kind, it is important to have a precise, not a vague, idea of what is in question; we shall choose as point of reference the example of the impersonalistic and unitive non-dualism of Shankara and shall contrast it with the personalistic and separative monism of Ramanuja. On the one hand, the perspective of the latter is substantially similar to the Semitic monotheisms, and on the other hand, the perspective of Shankara is one of the most adequate expressions possible of the *philosophia perennis* or sapiential esoterism . . .

It would be completely false to believe that gnosis within a given religion presents itself as a foreign and superadded doctrine; on the contrary, that which in each religion provides the key for total or non-dualist esoterism, is not some secret concept of a heterogeneous character, but is the very presiding idea of the religion; and this is necessarily so, since religion, which presents itself with an absolute exigency —*"extra ecclesiam nulla salus"*— thereby vouches for the totality of the message and consequently cannot exclude any essential possibility of the human spirit. Christian gnosis doubtless finds support in Thomas Aquinas as well as in Gregory Palamas, but these supports are in fact neutralized by the general bhaktism of Christianity, unless, precisely, they are isolated from the context; in any case they are not the basis of sapience. Christian gnosis finds its support *a priori*, and of necessity, in the mysteries of the Incarnation and the Redemption, and thus in the Christly Phenomenon as such, just as Moslem gnosis for its part finds its support above all in the mysteries of Transcendence and Immanence, and thus in the Koranic or Muhammedan Truth; furthermore, the gnosis of the two religions is founded on the mystery of Divine Love, envisaged in each case in conformity with the characteristic accentuation: love of the theophany that is both human and divine, in Christianity, and love of the Principle that is both transcendent and immanent, in Islam.

•   •   •

As regards esoterism in itself—and this is nothing else but gnosis—we must recall two things, although we have already spoken of them on other occasions. Firstly, it is necessary to distinguish between absolute esoterism and relative esoterism; secondly, it is necessary to know that esoterism on the one hand prolongs exoterism—by harmoniously plumbing its depth—because the form expresses the essence and because in this respect the two enjoy solidarity, while on the other hand esoterism opposes exoterism—by transcending it abruptly—because essence by virtue of its unlimitedness is of necessity not reducible to form, or in other words, because form, inasmuch as it constitutes a limit, is opposed to whatever is totality and liberty. These two aspects are easily discernible in Sufism;[5] it is true that here they are most often intermixed, without it being possible to say, as far as the authors are concerned, whether it is a case of pious unawareness, or simply of prudence, or of spiritual discretion; such a mixture, moreover, is entirely natural, as long as it does not give rise to absurdities and denials. The example of the Sufis in any case shows that it is possible to be a Moslem without being an 'Asharite; for the same reasons and with equal right, it is possible to be a Christian without being either a Scholastic or a Palamite, or let us say rather that it is possible to be a Thomist without accepting the Aristotelian sensationalism of Aquinas, just as it is possible to be a Palamite without sharing the errors of a Palamas regarding the Greek philosophers and their doctrines. In other words, one can be a Christian and at the same time a Platonist, given that there is no competition between mystical voluntarism and metaphysical intellectuality, leaving aside the Semitic concept of the *creatio ex nihilo* .

Finally, we must insist on the following point: the fact that transcendent truths should be inaccessible to the logic of a given individual or human group, cannot mean that they are intrinsically and *de jure* contrary to all logic; for the efficacy of logic always depends, on the one hand on the intellectual stature of the thinker, and on the other hand on the adequacy of the information or the knowledge of the indispensable data. Metaphysics is not held to be true — by those who understand it — because it is expressed in a logical manner, but it can be expressed in a logical manner because it is true, without — obviously — its truth ever being compromised by the possible shortcomings of human reason.

In their zeal to defend the rights of divine supra-rationality against the — *de facto* fragmentary — logic of the rationalists, some go so far as to claim for the divine or even the simply spiritual order a right to irrationality, and so to illogicality, as if there could be a right to intrinsic absurdity. To assert that Christ walked on water is in no wise contrary to logic or reason — although one cannot know the basis of the miracle[6] — for the law of gravity is a conditional thing, and thus relative, whether we know it or not; and even without knowing it, we can at least guess it or hold it as possible, given the level of the phenomenon. But to assert that Christ walked on water without walking on water, or that he walked on water by rising towards the sky, would assuredly be contrary to reason, since a phenomenon or possibility cannot be in one and the same respect another phenomenon or possibility or the absence of what they are: God may require acquiescence in a miracle or mystery, but He cannot require acquiescence in intrinsic absurdity, that is, an absurdity that is both logical and ontological.[7]

When one speaks of Christian esoterism, it can only be one of three things: firstly, it can be Christly gnosis, founded on the person, the teaching and the gifts of Christ, and profiting in certain eventualities from Platonic concepts, a process which in metaphysics has nothing irregular about it;[8] this gnosis was manifested in particular, although in a very uneven way, in writings such as those of Clement of Alexandria, Origen, Denis the Areopagite — or the Theologian or the Mystic, if one prefers — Scotus Erigena, Meister Eckhart, Nicholas of Cusa, Jakob Boehme and Angelus Silesius.[9] Secondly, it can be something completely different, namely the Graeco-Latin — or Near Eastern — esoterism incorporated in Christianity: here we are thinking above all of Hermeticism and the craft initiations. In this case the esoterism is more or less limited or even fragmentary, it resides more in the sapiential character of the method — now lost — than in the doctrine and the objective; the doctrine was principally cosmological, and consequently the objective did not transcend the "lesser mysteries" or horizontal perfection, or "primordial" perfection, if one is referring to the ideal conditions of the "Golden Age". Be that as it may, this Christianized cosmological or alchemical esoterism —"humanist" in a still legitimate sense, since it was a question of restoring to the microcosm the perfection of a macrocosm still in conformity with God — was essentially vocational, given that neither a science nor an art can be imposed on everyone; man chooses a science or an art for reasons of affinity and qualification, and not *a priori* to save his soul. Salvation being guaranteed by religion, man may, *a posteriori*, and on this very basis, exploit his gifts and professional occupations, and it is even normal or necessary that he should do so when an occupation linked with an alchemical or craft esoterism imposes itself on him for any reason.

Thirdly, and above all, and aside from any historical or literary consideration, one can and must understand by "Christian esoterism" the truth pure and simple — metaphysical and spiritual truth — insofar as it is expressed or manifested through the dogma, ritual and other forms of Christianity. Formulated in an inverse sense, this esoterism is the sum total of Christian symbols to the extent that they express or manifest pure metaphysics and the one and universal spirituality. And this is independent of the question of knowing up to what point an Origen or a Clement of Alexandria may have been aware of what is involved; a question which in any case is superfluous since it is obvious that, for more or less extrinsic reasons, they could not be aware of all aspects of the problem, inasmuch as they were broadly tied to the *bhakti* that determines the specific perspective of Christianity. At all events, it is important not to confuse esoterism in principle with esoterism in fact; or a virtual doctrine, which has all the rights of truth, with an effective doctrine which may not live up to the promise implied in its point of view.

In relation to Jewish legalism, Christianity is esoteric by reason of the fact that it is a message of inwardness: for Christianity inward virtue takes precedence over outward observance to the point of abolishing the latter. But its point of view being voluntaristic, it can be transcended by a new inwardness, that of pure intellection which reduces particular forms to their universal essences and replaces the point of view of penitence by that of purifying and liberating knowledge. Gnosis is of Christly nature in the sense that, on the one hand, it pertains to the Logos — the Intellect both transcendent and immanent — and because on the other hand it is a message of inwardness, and thus of interiorization.

* * *

We must reply here to the objection that the attitude of the esoterist entails a kind of duplicity towards the religion which he claims to practise while giving things a different meaning; this is a suspicion which does not take into account the actual perspective of gnosis or its assimilation by the soul, by virtue of which the intelligence and the sensibility spontaneously combine different points of view without betraying either their particular reality or their natural demands;[10] the concrete understanding of cosmic and spiritual levels excludes any secret falsehood. To speak to God while knowing that His necessarily anthropomorphic personality is an effect of *Maya*, is not less sincere than to speak to a man while knowing that he too, and *a fortiori* is only an effect of *Maya*, just as we all are;

likewise, it is not a lack of sincerity to ask a man a favour while knowing that the author of the gift is of necessity God. The Divine Personality, as we have said, is anthropomorphic; apart from the fact that in reality it is man who resembles God and not inversely, God necessarily makes Himself man in His contacts with human nature.

Religious loyalty is nothing else than the sincerity of our human relations with God, on the basis of the means which He has put at our disposal; these means, being of the formal order, *ipso facto* exclude other forms without for all that lacking anything whatsoever from the point of view of our relationship with Heaven; in this intrinsic sense, form is really unique and irreplaceable, precisely because our relationship with God is so. Nevertheless, this uniqueness of the intrinsic support and the sincerity of our worship within the framework of this support do not authorize for us what we might call "religious nationalism"; if we condemn this attitude — inevitable for the average man, but this is not the question — it is because it implies opinions contrary to the truth, which are all the more contradictory when the believer lays claim to an esoteric wisdom and claims that he possesses knowledge that permits him to take note of the limits of the religious formalism with which he sentimentally and abusively identifies himself.

In order clearly to understand the normal relationship between the common religion and sapience, or between *bhakti* and *jñana*, it is necessary to know that in man there is, in principle, a double subjectivity, that of the "soul" and that of the "spirit". One of two things is possible: either the spirit is reduced to the acceptance of revealed dogmas so that the individual soul is the only subject in the way towards God, or else the spirit is aware of its nature and tends towards the end for which it is made, so that it is the spirit, and not the 'I', that is the subject of the way, without nevertheless the needs and rights of ordinary subjectivity being abolished, the subjectivity, that is, of the sensible and individual soul. The equilibrium of the two subjectivities, one affective and the other intellective — which, moreover, necessarily coincide at a certain point — gives rises to the serenity whose perfume is transmitted to us by the Vedantic writings; an erroneous mixture of these subjectivities — in partial or imperfectly elucidated esoterisms — produces on the contrary the contradiction which we might call, paradoxically, "metaphysical individualism": namely a tormented mysticism often with irritating manifestations, but nevertheless heroic and open to Mercy; Sufism provides examples of this.

The ego as such cannot logically seek the experience of what lies beyond egoity; man is man and the Self is the Self. One must take care not to transfer the voluntaristic and sentimental individualism of religious zeal onto the plane of transpersonal awareness; one cannot wish for gnosis with a will which is contrary to the nature of gnosis. It is not we who know God, it is God who knows Himself in us. . .

. . .

The human individual has one great concern that exceeds all others: to save his soul; to do this,·he must adhere to a religion, and to be able to adhere to it, he must believe in it; but since, with the best will in the world, one can only believe what is credible, the man who knows to a sufficient degree two or more religions, and in addition has some imagination, may feel himself prevented from adhering to one of them by the fact that it presents itself dogmatically as the only legitimate and the only saving religion; that it presents itself, that is to say, with an absolute exigency, and possibly without offering in its characteristic formulation certain convincing and appeasing elements that one may have found in other religions. That the Psalms and the Gospel are sublime can be accepted without the least hesitation; but to believe that they contain in their very literalness, or in their psychological climate, everything that is offered by the Upanishads or the Bhagavadgita, is a completely different question. In fact sapiential esoterism — total and universal, not formalistic — can alone satisfy every legitimate mental need, its province being that of profound intentions and not that of expressions charged with prejudice; it alone can reply to all the questions raised by religious divergences and limitations, which amounts to saying that in the objective and subjective conditions that we have here in mind, it constitutes the only key that lets us understand a religion, leaving aside every question of esoteric realization. By the same token, integral esoterism can indicate what, in a given religion, is really fundamental from the metaphysical and mystical point of view — for mystical one may read alchemical or operative if one wishes — and consequently what permits it to rejoin the *religio perennis* .

While accepting that the religions must take account of psychological and social contingencies and are in certain respects limited, not by what they include but by what they exclude, while nevertheless necessarily presenting themselves with an absolute demand for adherence, they do not so to speak have the right to close themselves to every argument that transcends their dogmatist perspective; and in fact Providence, which operates in them by the fact of their divine origin, takes account of the situation that results from the very special circumstances of our time,[11] as in all periods it has taken account, in one form or another, of certain exceptional situations.

The religions take account, from diverse points of view, of the Divine Principle and of eternal life; but they cannot take account, as does esoterism, of the religious phenomenon as such and of the nature of the angles of vision. It would be absurd to ask them to do so, and this for two reasons: firstly, for the obvious reason that by definition every religion has to present itself as the only possible one, since its point of view is dependent on the Truth and consequently must exclude any danger of relativism, and secondly because in their intrinsic and essential content, which precisely transcends the relativity of formulation or symbolism, the religions fully keep the promise implied in the total character of their demands — fully, that is, in taking account of what can be demanded by the most profound possibility of man . . .

We could say, simplifying a little, that exoterism puts the form — the *credo* — above the essence — Universal Truth — and accepts the latter only as a function of the former; the form, through its divine origin, is here the criterion of the essence. Esoterism, on the contrary, puts the essence above the form and only accepts the latter as a function of the former; for esoterism, and in accordance with the real hierarchy of values, the essence is the criterion of the form; the one and universal Truth is the criterion of the various religious forms of the Truth. If the relationship is inverse in exoterism, this is obviously not as the result of a subversion, but because form, as a crystallization of essence, is the guarantor of Truth; the latter is judged inaccessible apart from form — or more precisely: apart from a form that makes an absolute demand — and rightly so, as far as the average man is concerned, otherwise the phenomenon of dogmatic revelation would be inexplicable.

What characterizes esoterism to the very extent that it is absolute, is that on contact with a dogmatic system, it universalizes the symbol or the religious concept on the one hand, and interiorizes it on the other; the particular or the limited is recognized as the manifestation of the principial and the transcendent, and this in its turn reveals itself as immanent. Christianity universalizes the nòtion of "Israel" while interiorizing the divine Law; it replaces circumcision of the flesh by that of the heart, the "Chosen People" by a Church that includes men of every provenance, and outward prescriptions by virtues, all of this having in view, not obedience to the Law, but the love of God and, in the last analysis, mystical union. These principles or these transpositions could hardly have been unknown to the Essenes, and possibly to the other Jewish initiates, but the originality of Christianity is that it made a religion of them and sacrificed to them Mosaic formalism . . .

•   •   •

It is a fundamental error to confuse the *jñani* with the rationalist, although in fact rationalism is a deviation from the intellective perspective; for the *jñani*, or let us say one who is intellective by nature, neither desires nor claims *a priori* to know the root of things; he takes note of the fact that he sees what he sees, that is, he knows what his "naturally supernatural" discernment reveals to him, whether he wishes it or not, and he thus finds himself in the situation of a man who, let us say, is the only one to see our solar system from a point in space and who is thereby enabled to know the causes of the seasons, the days and the nights, and the seeming movement of the stars, starting with the sun. The general dogmatic and formalistic religion is bound up — analogically speaking — with the viewpoint of a given human subjectivity; esoterism, on the contrary while accepting this system of appearances as a symbolism and at the level of a concomitant *bhakti*, is aware of the relativity of what we might paradoxically call "metaphysical phenomena". The rationalist, who lays claim to an intellection of which he may well conceive the principle, but which in fact he does not possess and who confuses the reason with the intellect, exemplifies a deviation comparable to the false inspirationism of heretical sects; but since "the corruption of the best is the worst", rationalism is much more harmful than false mysticism, which at least is not tempted to deny God and the future life. It is opportune to recall here something we have said on other occasions, namely that there are two sources of certainty, one outward and one inward,

namely Revelation and Intellection, sentimentalism readily usurp-
ing the first, and rationalism the second; in fact Intellection must
be combined with Revelation, just as Revelation must be illumined
by Intellection . . .

Here we must explain two paradoxes, that of the craft initiations and that of the emperor. The craft initiations pertain to *jñana*
but have been reduced to a cosmology and an alchemy, as we remarked above: it is a question of bringing man back to the primordial norm, not by sentimental heroism but simply by basing oneself
on the nature of things and with the help of a craft symbolism; it
seems likely that, in the case of masonry, this perspective has sur-
rendered the field to a humanistic universalism which is merely the
caricature of the intellective point of view, the distant cause of this
being the Renaissance, and the proximate cause being the "Enlightenment". As for the case of the emperor, it is paradoxical inasmuch
as the function of this monarch on the one hand, concerns the world
and not religion, and on the other hand continues the role of the
pontifex maximus of the Roman religion, which was jñanic in type
through its Aryan origin and in spite of the degeneration of the
general form it took for the majority; it is this pontifical and so to
speak "gnostic" quality, or this direct investiture by Heaven — of which
Dante and other Ghibellines seem to have been fully conscious —
that explains by what right, and without encountering any opposition, Constantine could convoke the Council of Nicaea; this same
quality, however blurred it may have been in fact, explains the tolerance and realism of the emperors with regard to non-Christian
minorities, whom they sometimes had to protect against the priests,
and of which one of the most striking examples was the understanding between Christians and Moslems in Sicily under the emperor
Fredrick II . . .

• • •

One of the modes of the esoteric dimension is what has come
to be called quietism, of which we wish to give a short account here.
For most people there is an association of ideas between quietism
and spiritualized sexuality, in the sense that they believe that these
two positions can both be reduced to temptations of "ease"; as if the
easy were synonymous with the false and the difficult with the true,
and as if true quietism and spiritualized sexuality did not comprise

aspects which, if not penitential, are at least demanding and serious. In reality quietism is founded on the ideas of existential substance and divine immanence and on the experience of the Presence of God: it consists of "resting in one's own being" or, in other words, resting in the Divine Peace; this attitude essentially demands, firstly a sufficient understanding of the mystery and then an active and operative attitude, namely perpetual prayer, or the "prayer of the heart", which implies a profound ascesis if it is not to be restricted to a completely profane and ephemeral improvisation that is more harmful than useful. Be that as it may, the fact that there has been a sentimental quietism unaware of the rigorous and active aspects of holy quietude, does not authorize the anathematizing of quietism as such, any more than a sectarian and intrinsically heretical gnosticism authorizes the condemnation of true gnosis; or any more than debauchery authorizes the calumniation of tantrism.

Apart from the reproach of "ease", there is also that of "immorality"; a spirituality that makes use of the sexual element seems compromised in advance by its apparent search for "pleasure", as if pleasure deprived a symbol of its value, and as if the experience of the senses was not more than compensated by the concomitant contemplative and interiorizing experience; and finally, as if pain were a criterion of spiritual value. Quietism is also accused of being immoral owing to the fact that it envisages a state in which man is above sin, an idea which refers to a sanctity — obviously misunderstood — in which the acts of man are golden because his substance is golden, and because everything that he touches is golden; this obviously excludes intrinsically bad actions, whether in regard to God or in regard to one's neighbour. In fact, quietism has often been ascetical, but by its nature it accepts without reticence the spiritual integration of sexuality, inasmuch as it is so to speak existentially in consonance with beauty, and so with love, or more precisely with the contemplative and peace-giving aspect of love. But this love is also a death (*amor / mors*) otherwise it would be spiritual; "I am black, but beautiful".[12]

•   •   •

The man of gnosis is always aware, at least this is his predisposition and intention, of the ontological roots of things: for him accidence is not only this or that, it is above all the diversified and inexhaustible manifestation of Substance, an intuition which, to the extent that it is concrete and lived, demands and favours not only discernment and contemplativity, but also nobility of character, for knowledge of the All engages the whole man. This nobility is moreover largely comprised in contemplativity itself, given that man is only disposed to contemplate what he already is himself in a certain fashion and to a certain degree.

Accidence is the contingent subject and object; it is contingency, for only Substance is necessary Being. Accidence is the world that surrounds us and the life that involves us; it is the aspect — or the phase — of the object and the point of view — or the presence — of the subject; it is our heredity, our character, our tendencies, our capacities, our destiny; the fact of being born in a given form, in a given place, at a given moment, and of undergoing given sensations, influences and experiences. All this is accidence, and all this is nothing; for accidence is not necessary Being; accidents are limited on the one hand and transient on the other. And the content of all this, in the last analysis, is Felicity; it is this that attracts us through a thousand reverberations and in a thousand guises; it is this that we seek in all our desires, without knowing it. In compressive and dispersing accidence, we are not truly ourselves; we are so only in the sacramental and liberating prolongation of Substance, for the true being of every creature is in the last analysis the Self.[13]

If we compare the Divine Substance with water, accidents may be likened to waves, drops, snow, or ice; phenomena of the world or phenomena of the soul. Substance is pure Power, pure Spirit, pure Felicity; accidence transcribes these dimensions in limitative or even privative mode; on the one hand, it "is not", and on the other hand, it "is not other" than Substance. Esoterically speaking, there are only two relationships to take into consideration, that of transcendence and that of immanence: according to the first, the reality of Substance annihilates that of the accident; according to the second, the qualities of the accident — starting with their reality — cannot but be those of Substance. Exoterically speaking, the first point of view is absurd, since things exist; and the second is impious, it is pantheism, since things cannot be God. That on the one hand things exist and that on the other hand they are not God is taken fully into account by esoterism, but to these two initial observations it adds a dimension of depth which contradicts their superficial and as it were two dimensional exclusivism. Whereas exoterism is enclosed in the world of accidence and readily derives glory from this when it seeks to demonstrate its sense of reality vis-à-vis what appears to it as shadows, esoterism is aware of the transparency of things and of underlying Substance, whose manifestations are Revelation, the Man-Logos, the doctrinal and sacramental symbol, and also, in the human microcosm, Intellection, the Heart Intellect, the lived Symbol. To "manifest" is to "be"; the Name and the Named are mysteriously identical. The saint and a *a fortiori* the Man-Logos are on the one hand, Manifestation of Substance in accidence, and on the other hand, Reintegration of the accident in Substance.

NOTES

Esoterism and Mysticism

1. It results from all this that by "objectivity" must be understood not a knowledge that is limited to a purely empirical recording of data received from outside, but a perfect adequation of the knowing subject to the known object, which indeed is in keeping with the current meaning of the term. An intelligence or a knowledge is "objective" when it is capable of grasping the object as it is and not as it may be deformed by the subject.

2. The modernists think they were the first to know how to combine extrinsic relativity with intrinsic absoluteness, but their demarcation line between the extrinsic and the intrinsic is completely false, precisely owing to the fact that they immediately reduce the inward to the outward or the Absolute to the relative. Every question of civilizationism aside, it is necessary to state clearly here that modernism cannot derive from Catholicism in itself but on the contrary has taken possession of it and makes use of it like an occupying power. The law of gravity does the rest.

3. This release is strictly impossible — we must insist upon it — without the cooperation of a religion, an orthodoxy, a traditional esoterism with all that this implies.

4. Such a Revelation has a function that is both conservative and preventive, it expresses the Truth in view of the risk of its being forgotten; it consequently also has the aim of protecting the "pure" from contamination by the "impure", of recalling the Truth to those who run the risk of going astray by carelessness.

5. The first aspect is manifested, as is well known, in Ghazali, who obtained recognition for Sufism within the official religion, while the second — a Koranic trace of which appears in the story of Moses and the unknown (=Al-Khidr) — is found for example in Niffari, who stated that the exoteric revelation does not support the esoteric revelation, namely gnosis, and that the common religion sees things according to plurality and not according to unity as the inward revelation does. Likewise Ibn 'Arabī: "God the Omnipotent is not limited by any belief because He has said (in the Koran): 'Wheresoever ye turn, there is the face of God.'"

6. By this we mean that miracles also have their mechanism, but in such a case the causal link is "vertical" and not "horizontal": the ray of causal development crosses several existential planes instead of being operative on one alone.

7. According to St. Thomas Aquinas, the principles of logic reside in God, and it is according to them that we must think; which means that a contradiction between our intelligence and the truth founded in God is impossible. Certainly, extrinsic absurdities exist, but in their case there is contradiction only through our ignorance or dullness of mind. "Right reason is the temple of God," said St. John of the Cross.

8. In a general manner, intertraditional influences are always possible under certain conditions, but without any syncretism. Unquestionably Buddhism and Islam had an influence on Hinduism, not of course by adding new elements to it, but by favouring or determining the blossoming of pre-existing elements.

9. In other words, one finds elements of esoterism in orthodox gnosticism — which is prolonged in the theosophy of Boehme and his successors — then in the Dionysian mysticism of the Rhinelanders, and of course in Hesychasm; without forgetting that partial element of methodic esoterism constituted by the quietism of Molinos, traces of which can be found in St. Francis of Sales.

10. As one knows, for the Hindu contemplative this sort of metaphysical flexibility is second nature and causes no difficulty; this means that the Hindu is particularly sensitive to what we have called on more than one occasion the "metaphysical transparency of phenomena". — Doubtless, *bilinguis maledictus*: language with a double meaning is accursed; but, precisely, it is situated on one and the same plane and not, as is esoterism, on two different planes; if this duodimensionality were illegitimate, it would be impossible to interpret the Song of Solomon in a sense other than the literal, and a large part of patristic and mystical exegesis would have to be disavowed. Christ used parables and metaphors.

11. The fact that in our age everything is read and everything is known, has the consequence, in religious circles, not that foreign spiritualities are accepted without question, but that a modified and often tolerant attitude is adopted towards them — except in certain circles which confuse traditional orthodoxy with the right to calumny, and which thus harm the cause that they strive to defend. To reject Islam is one thing, to allege that it excludes women from Paradise, or that Moslems have no virtue, is quite another.

12 "Who loves not women, wine and song, remains a fool his whole life long" (*Wer liebt nicht Wein, Weib und Gesang, der bleibt ein Narr sein Lebenlang*): this old German saying may well have had an esoteric origin which would relate it to analogous expressions found in Omar Khayyam and others. "Wine" is in fact "love", according to the most varied traditions: on the one hand it is esoteric doctrine, inasmuch as this is liberating and essentializing even though ambiguous and dangerous, and on the other hand it is contemplative drunkenness, either transient (*hal*) or permanent (*maqam*); "women" is beauty, or the attractive and liberating vision of God in forms that manifest Him or that manifest His radiant Goodness; the "eternal feminine" also represents this Goodness in itself, inasmuch as it forgives, welcomes and unifies, by freeing us from formal and other hardenings; "song" is the quintessential prayer of the heart, the "praise" which makes the heart "melt" and reintegrates it into the Essence. It is very unlikely — let it be said in passing — not that Luther said these words, as is believed, but that he is their author, for they also exist in an Italian form whose origin is likewise apparently unknown (*Chi non ama il vino, la donna ed il canto, un pazzo egli sarà e mai un santo*); in this form, the esoteric intention is in fact strengthened by the allusion to "sanctity": he will never be a saint — according to esoterism — who has not known these three things (vino, donna and canto). Likewise, Omar ibn Al-Farid in his *Khamriyah*: "He has not lived here below, who has lived without drunkenness, and he has no intelligence who has not died from his drunkenness"; the man "without intelligence" being precisely the "fool" (Narr or pazzo), that is to say, the profane or worldly man.

13. Exoterically it would be said that we are unfaithful to ourselves in sin, which is true but insufficient; we are unfaithful also in these dream caverns which seduce and imprison us, and which for most men constitute "real life"; it is these caverns that nourish the poison market that is worldly "culture". The earthly dream is an indirect sin: doubtless it does not exclude the practice of religion, but it compromises the love of God; except when it is of such a nature that it may attach itself transiently to this love, thanks to an opening upwards which transmits a perfume that is already heavenly and is an invitation to rise above ourselves.

Faith, Love, and Knowledge

The Nature and Arguments of Faith*

FAITH IS THE CONFORMITY of the intelligence and the will to revealed truths. This conformity is either formal alone or else essential, in the sense that the object of faith is a dogmatic form, and behind this an essence of Truth. Faith is belief when the volitive element predominates over the intellectual; it is knowledge or gnosis when the intellectual element predominates over the volitive. But there are also certitude and fervour, the latter being volitive and the former intellectual: fervour gives belief its spiritual quality; certitude is an intrinsic quality of gnosis. The term 'faith' could not mean exclusively belief or fervour, nor exclusively knowledge or certitude; it cannot be said of belief that it is all that is possible in the way of faith, nor of knowledge that it is not faith at all.

In other words, faith, on whatever level it is envisaged, has an aspect of participation and an aspect of separation: of participation because its subject is intelligence which as such participates 'vertically' in the Truth, and of separation because intelligence is limited 'horizontally' by its plane of existence, which separates it from the divine Intellect. In the first respect faith is 'certitude', whether its object compels acceptance through material or rational proofs, or whether it reveals its nature in pure intellection; in the second respect,

*From *SW*, Chapter 2.

104

faith is 'obscurity' because the believing subject is existentially separated from the object of belief. Neither crude reason — that is reason
deprived of supra-rational illuminations through our fall — nor *a fortiori* the body, can behold the celestial mysteries.

Intellection appears to the exoteric outlook to be an act of the
reason wrongly claiming freedom from obscurity and falsely asserting independence in respect of Revelation. In reality, obscurity in
intellective knowledge differs from obscurity in the reason by the
fact that it is linked, not to intelligence itself, but to the *ego* in so far
as it has not been transmuted by spiritual realization; intellective
vision, in fact, does not imply a prior integration of the whole of
our being in the Truth. As for Revelation, intellection lives by it,
for it receives thence its whole formal armoury; intellection then cannot be taken to replace the objective, prophetic, lawgiving and traditional manifestation of the divine Intellect. One can neither conceive a St. Augustine without the Gospel, nor a Shankaracharya
without the Veda.[1]

This leads us to reflect that there is a faith which can increase,
just as there is one which is immutable: faith is immutable thanks
to the content and number of its dogmas, as also through the metaphysical immutability of the truth, or again, it may be that immutability lies in the firmness of personal belief or in the incorruptibility of knowledge; as for the faith which may increase, it can be
confidence in the absolute veracity of Revelation, or fervent trust
in it; but according to the point of view, this faith can also be the
spiritual penetration of dogmas, that is gnosis.

Some people will doubtless point out that to use the word 'faith'
as a synonym for 'gnosis' is to rob it of all meaning, since 'seeing'
is opposed to 'believing', that is to say that faith requires both obscurity
of understanding and the merit of free adherence: but this distinction, which is legitimate on its own level, where it reflects a real situation, involves the disadvantage of limiting scriptural terminology
to the exoteric point of view. The exoteric point of view cannot,
however, determine the scope of the divine Word, although, inversely,
the divine Word is crystallized with a view to the necessities of exotericism, whence its universality. Faith, as we have said, is the
adherence of the intelligence to Revelation; it is true that exotericism
limits intelligence to reason alone, while replacing the Intellect —
the supra-rational nature of which it cannot conceive — by grace,
which it sees as the sole element that is supernatural; none the less

this restriction, though opportune, cannot change the nature of things nor abolish the intellective faculty where it exists; the concept of 'faith' then of necessity keeps its inner limitlessness and its polyvalence, for there can be no question, in a religious civilization, of denying faith to those whose intelligence surpasses the ordinary limits of human understanding. . .

Understanding and Believing*

It is generally recognized that man is capable of believing without understanding; one is much less aware of the inverse possibility, that of understanding without believing, and it even appears as a contradiction, since faith does not seem to be incumbent except on those who do not understand. Yet hypocrisy is not only the dissimulation of a person who pretends to be better than he is; it also manifests itself in a disproportion between certainty and behaviour, and in this respect most men are more or less hypocritical since they claim to admit truths which they put no more than feebly in practice. On the plane of simple belief, to believe without acting in accordance with the dictates of one's belief corresponds, on the intellectual plane, to an understanding without faith and without life; for real belief means identifying oneself with the truth that one accepts, whatever may be the level of this adherence. Piety is to religious belief what operative faith is to doctrinal understanding or, we may add, what sainthood is to truth.

If we take as a starting point the idea that spirituality has essentially two factors, namely discernment between the Real and the illusory and permanent concentration on the Real, the *conditio sine qua non* being the observance of traditional rules and the practice of the virtues that go with them, we shall see that there is a relationship between discernment and understanding, on the one hand, and between concentration and faith, on the other; faith, whatever its degree, always means a quasiexistential participation in Being or in Reality; it is, to take a basic *hadīth*, "to worship God as if thou

*From *LT*, Chapter 13.

sawest Him, and if thou seest Him not, yet He seeth thee". In other terms, faith is the participation of the will in the intelligence; just as on the physical plane man adapts his action to the physical facts which determine its nature, so also, on the spiritual plane, he should act in accordance with his convictions, by inward activity even more than by outward activity, for "before acting one must first be", and our being is nothing else but our inward activity. The soul must be to the intelligence what beauty is to truth, and this is what we have called the "moral qualification" that should accompany the "intellectual qualification".

There is a relationship between faith and the symbol; there is also one between faith and miracles. In the symbolic image as in the miraculous fact, it is the language of being, not of reasoning, which speaks; to a manifestation of being on the part of Heaven, man must respond with his own being, and he does so through faith or through love, which are the two faces of one and the same reality, without thereby ceasing to be a creature endowed with thought. In plain terms, one might wonder what basis or justification there can be for an elementary faith which is disdainful, or almost so, of any attempt at comprehension; the answer has just been given, namely that such faith is based on the illuminating power which belongs in principle to the symbols, phenomena and arguments of Revelation;[1] the "obscure merit" of this faith consists in our not being closed to a grace for which our nature is made. . .

Attention has already been drawn to the relationship between faith and miracles; perfect faith consists in being aware of the metaphysically miraculous character of natural phenomena and in seeing in them, by way of consequence, the trace of God.

The demerit of unbelief or lack of faith does not therefore lie in a natural lack of special aptitudes, nor is it due to the unintelligibility of the Message, for then there would be no demerit; it lies in the passionate stiffening of the will and in the worldly tendencies which bring about this stiffening. The merit of faith is fidelity to the supernaturally natural receptivity of primordial man; it means remaining as God made us and remaining at His disposition with regard to a message from Heaven which might be contrary to earthly experience, while being incontestable in view of subjective as well as objective criteria. . .

Faith as a quality of the soul is the stabilizing complement of the discerning and as it were explosive intelligence; without this complement, intellectual activity lets itself be carried away by its own movement and is like a devouring fire; it loses its balance and ends either by devouring itself in a restlessness without issue or else simply by wearing itself out to the point of sclerosis. Faith implies all the static and gentle qualities such as patience, gratitude, confidence, generosity; it offers the mercurial intelligence a fixative element and thus realizes, together with discernment, an equilibrium which is like an anticipation of sainthood. It is to this polarity, at its highest level, that the complementary terms "blessing" (or " prayer", *salāh*) and "peace" (or "greeting", *salām*) are applied in Islam.

It must be stressed again that an intellectual qualification is not fully valid unless it be accompanied by an equivalent moral qualification; herein lies the explanation of all the fideist attitudes which seem bent on limiting the impetus of the intelligence. The upholders of tradition pure and simple (*naql*) in the first centuries of Islam were deeply conscious of this, and Ash'arī himself must have sensed it (although it took him in the opposite direction since he ventured on to the plane of theological reasoning) when he attributed to God an unintelligibility which, in the last analysis, could only signify the precariousness of man's intellectual means in the face of the dimension of absoluteness.

One can meditate or speculate indefinitely on transcendent truths and their applications (that is moreover what the author of this book does, but he has valid reasons for doing it, nor does he do it for himself). One can spend a whole lifetime speculating on the suprasensorial and the transcendent, but all that matters is the "leap into the void" which is the fixation of spirit and soul in an unthinkable dimension of the Real; this leap, which cuts short and completes in itself the endless chain of formulations, depends on a direct understanding and on a grace, not on having reached a certain phase in the unfolding of the doctrine, for this unfolding, we repeat, has logically no end. This "leap into the void" we can call "faith"; it is the negation of this reality that is the source of all philosophy of the type that may be described as "art for art's sake", and of all thought that believes it can attain to an absolute contact with Reality by means of analyses, syntheses, arrangements, filtrations, and polishings — thought that is mundane by the very fact of this ignorance and because it is a vicious circle which not merely provides no escape from illusion, but even reinforces it through the lure of a progressive knowledge which in fact is inexistent.[2]

In view of the harm that the prejudices and tendencies of ordinary piety can sometimes do to metaphysical speculations, we might be tempted to conclude that piety should be abandoned on the threshold of pure knowledge, but this would be a false and highly pernicious conclusion; in reality, piety, or faith, must never be absent from the soul, but it is only too clear that it must be on a level with the truths that it accompanies, which implies that such an extension is perfectly in its nature, as is proved by the Vedantic hymns, to take just one particularly conclusive example. . . .

The sense of the sacred: this word felicitously expresses a dimension which should never be absent either in metaphysical thought or in everyday life; it is this which gives birth to the liturgies, and without it there is no faith. The sense of the sacred, with its concomitances of dignity, incorruptibility, patience, and generosity is the key to integral faith and to the supernatural virtues which are inherent in it.

• • •

If one adopts the distinction made by the alchemists between a "dry path" and a "moist path", the former corresponding to "knowledge" and the latter to "love", one should also be aware that the two poles "fire" and "water", which these paths represent respectively, are both reflected in each path, so that "knowledge" has necessarily an aspect of "moisture", and "love" an aspect of "dryness". Within the framework of a path of love, this aspect of "dryness" or of "fire" is doctrinal orthodoxy, for it is well known that no spirituality is possible without the implacable and immutable bulwark of a Divine expression of the saving Truth; analogously and inversely, the aspect of "moisture" or of "water" which, being feminine, is derived from the Divine Substance (*Prakriti*, the *Shakti*), is indispensable to the path of "knowledge" for the evident and already mentioned reasons of equilibrium, stability and effectiveness.

The two principles "fire" and "water" come together in "wine", which is both "liquid fire", and "igneous water";[3] liberating intoxication proceeds precisely from this alchemical and as it were miraculous combination of opposite elements. It is thus wine, and not fire, which is the most perfect image of liberating gnosis, envisaged not only in its total amplitude but also in the equilibrium of its virtual modes, for the equilibrium between discernment and contemplation can be conceived at every level. Another image of this equilibrium or of this concordance is oil; it is more over through oil that fire is stabilized and that it becomes the calm and contemplative flame of the lamps in sanctuaries. Like wine, oil is an igneous liquid, which "shineth even though the fire have not touched it", according to the famous *Verse of Light (Āyat an-Nūr)*...

It follows from all that has been said so far that faith and intelligence can each be conceived at two different levels: faith as a quasi-ontological and premental certitude ranks higher than the discerning and speculative aspects of intelligence,[4] but intelligence as pure Intellection ranks higher than that faith which is no more than an adherence of the sentiments; it is this ambivalence which is the source of numerous misunderstandings, but which makes possible at the same time an exo-esoteric language that is both simple and complex. Faith in its higher aspect is what we might call *religio cordis*: it is the "inward religion" which is supernaturally natural to man and which coincides with *religio caeli*, or *perennis*, that is, with universal truth, which is beyond the contingencies of form and time. This faith can be satisfied with little. Unlike an intelligence which is all for exactness but never satisfied in its play of formulations, and which passes from concept to concept, from symbol to symbol, without being able to make up its mind for this or for that, the faith of the heart is capable of being satisfied by the first symbol that providentially comes its way,[5] and of living on it until the supreme Meeting.

On Faith and Its Object*

Does the object of faith have precedence over faith itself, or does faith have precedence over its object? Normally, it is the object which has precedence over faith, since it is what determines faith and provides it with sufficient reason; but from a certain point of view and in certain cases, faith can be more important than its content and can 'force' the gates of Heaven despite the insufficiency of some immediate object of belief. Faith comprises two 'poles', one objective

*From *GDW*, pp. 25-26.

and dogmatic and the other subjective and mystical; the ideal is a perfect faith in an orthodox truth. It is idea which engenders faith, and the quality of the first determines the quality of the second, but the often paradoxical and unforeseeable play of universal Possibility can allow the predominance of the pole 'faith' over the pole 'idea', so that the Tibetans have been able to say that a dog's tooth which is mistaken for a relic and becomes the object of a sincere and ardent faith actually begins to shine. There can in fact be a faith which, in its very substance, carries the imprint of a truth of which ordinary consciousness is more or less unaware, provided no intrinsic error compromises the quality of its ardour, which must be of such purity and nobility as will safeguard it from serious errors; faith is like an 'existential' intuition of its 'intellectual' object. This possibility of a faith which excels the 'ideological' element and which 'compels' it, as it were, to surrender the truth in the end, presupposes a highly contemplative mentality, already freed from many obstacles; futhermore, if the quality of the faith can thus compensate for the precariousness of the idea, this idea must appear like a light, however feeble, and not like a darkness; on this plane there are many imponderables.

Earthly Concomitances of the Love of God*

The notion of the "love of God" evokes rightly or wrongly the image of a sentiment directed towards a human person. Such an image seems to contradict both the formless and transcendent character of the Divinity and the spiritual and supernatural character of contemplative love, but in reality there is no contradiction, in the first place because God effectively assumes, in regard to man, a human aspect,[1] and further because spirituality, insofar as it is human, necessarily includes the affective element of the soul, whatever be the place or the function accorded to it. But when we leave aside this humanization of the Divine, which is both law-giving and merciful, and also this spiritual canalization of human sensibility, we shall see that the "love of God" in itself has nothing limitative as

*From *DI*, Chapter 9.

regards the object nor specifically sentimental as regards the subject; it amounts in the last analysis to our choice of the "inward dimension", in conformity with the words of the Gospel: "The Kingdom of Heaven is within you." Fundamentally it is a question of a choice between the "outward" and the "inward", or between the world and God:[2] the "outward dimension" is the domain of multiple things, of dispersion and impermanence, and also, correlatively, the domain of limitation, of egoistic compression and "hardness of heart"; the "inward dimension", on the contrary, is the domain of unity, synthesis and permanence, and also, correlatively, the domain of unlimitedness, spiritual dilatation and "melting of the heart". Love of God thus appears as a fundamental change of emphasis or tendency, or as a reversing of an initial and natural movement — a movement which is inverted by reason of the perversion of our fallen nature; more over this reversal or conversion must constantly be renewed even within the framework of stabilized spiritual love, for the power of the ego is always there, and the movement towards the Inward always demands a certain separation from phenomena.

The man who "loves God" — whether he be Monotheist or Buddhist — is thus basically one who dwells in or is orientated towards the "inward dimension". In this attitude there is both immobility and movement: spiritual immobility is opposed to the endless movement of things situated in duration, while spiritual movement, on the contrary, is opposed to the natural passivity of the soul, which is but an aspect of "hardness of heart". . .

Love of God is essentially a function of faith; without the intrinsic integrity of the latter, love could not be real. There are many possible kinds of concentration — pride too involves a contraction — but there is no spiritual interiorization without this objective and intellectual element which is truth.

To conclude: interiorization is essentially connected with metaphysical discernment and with the idea of the absolute and the infinite; and it is obviously better to have only this idea, without adding the least effort thereto, than to seek a counterfeit inwardness and so fall into a trap a thousand times worse than distraction pure and simple. It is truth which ensures that every false satisfaction turns back on itself; it is truth again which neutralizes the natural egotism of the heart by introducing into contemplative alchemy a savour of death, in conformity with the saying: "Whosoever will save his life, shall lose it." *Amor Dei* is at the same time *mors Deo*; the analogy

between love and death is nowhere more real than in the presence
of God.

Love and Knowledge*

Metaphysical certainty is not God, though it contains something
of Him. This is why Sufis accompany even their certainties with this
formula: "And God is more wise" (*wa-'Llâhu a 'lam*).

A cult of the intelligence and mental passion take man further
from truth. Intelligence withdraws as soon as man puts his trust in
it alone. Mental passion pursuing intellectual intuition is like the
wind which blows out the light of a candle.

Monomania of the spirit, with the unconsious pretension, the
prejudice, the insatiability and the haste which are its concomitants,
is incompatible with sanctity. Sanctity introduces in the flux of
thoughts an element of humility and of charity, and so of calm and
of generosity. This element, far from being hurtful to the spiritual
impetus or the sometimes violent force of truth, delivers the spirit
from the vexations of passions and thus guarantees both the integrity
of thought and the purity of inspiration.

According to the Sufis mental passion must be ranked as one
of the "associations" with Satan, like other forms of "idolatry" of the
passions. It could not directly have God for its object, for, were God
its direct object, it would lose its specifically negative characteristics.
And it also contains in itself no principle of rest, for it excludes all
consciousness of its own destitution.

Man must beware of two things: first of replacing God, in practice if not in theory, by the functions and products of the intellect,
or of considering Him only in connection with this faculty; and,
secondly, of putting the "mechanical" factors of spirituality in the
place of the human values — the virtues — or only considering virtues in relation to their "technical" utility and not in relation to their
beauty.[1]

Intelligence has only one nature, that of being luminous. But

*From *SPHF*, Part Five, Chapter 2

it has diverse functions and different modes of working and these appear as so many particular intelligences. Intelligence with a "logical", "mathematical" or — one might say —"abstract" quality is not enough for attaining all aspects of the real. It would be impossible to insist too often on the importance of the "visual" or "aesthetic" function of the intellective faculty. Everything is in reality like a play of alternations between what is determined in advance — starting from principles — and what is incalculable and in some way unforeseeable, of which we have to get to know by concrete identification and not by abstract "discernment".[2]

In speculations about formal elements it would be a handicap to lack this aesthetic function of intellect. A religion is revealed, not only by its doctrine, but also by its general form, and this has its own characteristic beauty, which is reflected in its every aspect from its "mythology" to its art. Sacred art expresses Reality in relation to a particular spiritual vision. And aesthetic intelligence sees the manifestations of the Spirit even as the eye sees flowers or playthings. Thus, for example, in order to understand Buddhism profoundly, if one is not a Buddhist born, it is not enough to study its doctrine; it is also necessary to penetrate into the language of Buddhist beauty as it appears in the sacramental image of the Buddha or in such features as the "sermon on the flower".[3]

The aesthetic function of the intelligence — if you may call it that for lack of a better term — enters not only into the form of every spiritual manifestation but also into the process of its manifestation. Truth must be enunciated, not only in conformity with certain proportions, but also according to a certain rhythm. One cannot speak of sacred things "just anyhow", nor can one speak of them without limitations.

Every manifestation has laws and these intelligence must observe in manifesting itself, or otherwise truth will suffer.

Intellect is not something cerebral, nor is it specifically human or angelic. All beings "possess" it. If gold is not lead, that is because it "knows" the Divine better. Its "knowledge" is in its very form, and this amounts to saying that it does not belong to it itself, for matter could not know. None the less one can say that the rose differs from the water-lily by its intellectual particularity, by its "way of knowing" and so by its mode of intelligence. Beings possess intelligence in their form to the extent that they are "peripheric" or "passive" and in their essence to the extent that they are "central", "active" and "conscious".

A noble animal or a lovely flower is "intellectually" superior to a base man.

God reveals himself to the plant in the form of the light of the sun. The plant irresistibly turns itself towards the light; it could not be atheistical or impious.

The infallible "instinct" of animals is a lesser "intellect", and man's intellect may be called a higher "instinct". Between instinct and intellect there stands in some sense the reason, which owes its troubles to the fact that it constitutes a sort of "luciferian" duplication of the Divine Intelligence — the only intelligence there is.

Knowledge of facts depends on contingencies which could not enter into principial knowledge. The level of facts is, in certain respects, inverse in relation to that of principles in the sense that it includes modes and imponderables that are the extreme opposite of the wholly mathematical rigour of universal laws. At least this is so in appearance, for it goes without saying that universal principles are not contradicted. Even beneath the veil of the inexhaustible diversity of what is possible their immutability can always be discerned, provided that the intelligence is in the requisite condition for being able to discern it.

If the intellect is, so to speak, sovereign and infallible on its own ground, it cannot exercise its discernment on the level of facts otherwise than conditionally. Moreover God may intervene on the level of facts with particular things willed by Himself that are at times unpredictable, and of such things principial knowledge could only take account *a posteriori*.

Hidden causes — whether cosmic or human — must be admitted where their intervention results from the nature of things, but not for the sake of satisfying a postulate of which one has lost sight as to both its metaphysical basis and its practical bearing. When we see a waterfall we have no reason for saying that it moves by a magical force, even when a saint is drowned in it. The fact that there are some men who produce evil more consciously than do others does not authorize us to say that every human ill is a conscious product, both in its scope and in its repercussions. Still less does it authorize us to say that every work which has a negative aspect was undertaken with this aspect as its object. Human evil is intentional as to its immediate object, but not as to its cosmic bearing. Were it not so it would finish by being dissolved in knowledge. If Voltaire had foreseen the ills of the twentieth century, he would have become a Carthusian...

Strictly speaking doctrinal knowledge is independent of the individual. But its actualization is not independent of the human capacity to act as a vehicle for it. He who possesses truth must none the less merit it although it is a free gift. Truth is immutable in itself, but in us it lives, because we live.

If we want truth to live in us we must live in it.

Knowledge only saves us on condition that it enlists all that we are, only when it is a way and when it works and transforms and wounds our nature even as the plough wounds the soil.

To say this is to say that intelligence and metaphysical certainty alone do not save; of themselves they do not prevent titans from falling. This is what explains the psychological and other precautions with which every tradition surrounds the gift of the doctrine.

When metaphysical knowledge is effective it produces love and destroys presumption. It produces love, that is to say the spontaneous directing of the will towards God and the perception of "myself"— and of God—in one's neighbour.

It destroys presumption, for knowledge does not allow a man to overestimate himself or to underestimate others. By reducing to ashes all that is not God it orders all things.

All St. Paul says of charity concerns effective knowledge, for the latter is love, and he opposes it to theory inasmuch as theory is human concept. The Apostle desires that truth should be contemplated with our whole being and he calls this totality of contemplation "love".

Metaphysical knowledge is sacred. It is the right of sacred things to require of man all that he is.

Intelligence, since it distinguishes, perceives, as one might put it, proportions. The spiritual man integrates these proportions into his will, into his soul and into his life.

All defects are defects of proportion; they are errors that are lived. To be spiritual means not denying at any point with one's "being" what one affirms with one's knowledge, that is, what one accepts with the intelligence.

Truth lived: incorruptibility and generosity.

Since ignorance is all that we are and not merely our thinking, knowledge will also be all that we are to the extent to which our existential modalities are by their nature able to participate in truth.

Human nature contains dark elements which no intellectual certainty could, *ipso facto*, eliminate...

Pure intellectuality is as serene as a summer sky—serene with a serenity that is at once infinitely incorruptible and infinitely generous.

Intellectualism which "dries up the heart" has no connection with intellectuality.

The incorruptibility—or inviolability—of truth is bound up neither with contempt nor with avarice.

What is man's certainty? On the level of ideas it may be perfect, but on the level of life it but rarely pierces through illusion.

Everything is ephemeral and every man must die. No man is ignorant of this and no one knows it.

Man may have an interest that is quite illusory in accepting the most transcendent ideas and will readily believe himself to be superior to some other who, not having this interest—perhaps because he is too intelligent or too noble to have it—is sincere enough not to accept them, though he may all the same be more able to understand them than the other who accepts them. Man does not always accept truth because he understands it; often he believes he understands it because he is anxious to accept it.

People often discuss truths whereas they should limit themselves to discussing tastes and tendencies. . .

Acuteness of intelligence is only a blessing when it is compensated by greatness and sweetness of the soul. It should not appear as a rupture of the equilibrium or as an excess which splits man in two. A gift of nature requires complementary qualities which allow of its harmonious manifestation; otherwise there is a risk of the lights becoming mingled with darkness.

"The Four Jewels" of Human Life*

We have seen that the world, life and human existence show themselves to be in practice a complex hierarchy of certainties and uncertainties. To the question of what are the foremost things a man should do, situated as he is in this world of enigmas and fluctuations, the reply must be made that there are four things to be done

*From *LT,* pp. 256-66.

or four jewels never to be lost sight of: firstly, he should accept the truth; secondly, bear it continually in mind; thirdly, avoid whatever is contrary to truth and the permanent consciousness of truth; and fourthly, accomplish whatever is in conformity therewith. All religion and all wisdom is reducible, extrinsically and from the human standpoint, to these four laws: enshrined in every tradition is to be observed an immutable truth, then a law of "attachment to the Real", of "remembrance" of "love" of God, and finally prohibitions and injunctions; and these make up a fabric of elementary certainties which encompasses and resolves human uncertainty, and thus reduces the whole problem of terrestrial existence to a geometry that is at once simple and primordial.

NOTES

Faith, Love, and Knowledge

1. It is this *a priori* — and not *a posteriori* — dependence of intellection with regard to Revelation which is so well expressed by St. Anselm's saying *Credo ut intelligam*.

Understanding and Believing

1. The "signs" (āyāt) of which the Koran speaks, and which may even be natural phenomena envisaged in the light of the revealed doctrine. A remark which should be made in this context is that the insensibility of the believers of any intrinsically orthodox religion to the arguments of another religion does not in any sense come into question here, since the motive for refusal is in that case a positive factor, namely an already existing faith which is in itself valid.

2. A valid doctrine is a "description" which is based on direct, supramental knowledge, and the author is therefore under no illusion as to its inevitable formal limitations; on the other hand, a philosophy which claims to be a "research" is a mere nothing and its apparent modesty is no more than a pretentious negation of true wisdom, which is absurdly called "metaphysical dogmatism." There is clearly no humility in saying that one is ignorant because everyone is ignorant.

3. When the Red Indians called alcohol "fire-water", they were expressing, without knowing it, a profound truth: the alchemical and almost supernatural coincidence of liquidity and ignition.

4. This higher faith is something altogether different from the irresponsible and arrogant taking of liberties so characteristic of the profane improvisors of *Zen* or of *Jnāna*, who seek to "take a short cut" by stripping themselves of the essential human context of all realization, whereas in the East, and in the normal conditions of ethical and liturgical ambience, this context is largely supplied in advance. One does not enter the presence of a king by the back door.

5. In the lives of the saints, the spiritual career is often inaugurated by an outward or inward incident which throws the soul into a particular and definitive attitude with regard to Heaven; the symbol here is not the incident itself, but the positive spiritual factor that the incident serves to bring out.

Earthly Concomitances of the Love of God

1. The same applies even in Buddhism, in which the Buddhas and the great Bodhisattvas assume, in practice and according to need, the function of the personal Divinity.

2. Or *Nirvāna*, for what counts here is not the aspect of personality, but that of absoluity, infinitude and salvation.

Love and Knowledge

1. According to Eckhart's conception the sufficient reason for the virtues is not in the first place their extrinsic utility but their beauty.

2. This is the perspective of a Chaitanya or a Ramakrishna. It happened to them to fall into ecstasy (*samadhi*) on seeing a beautiful animal. In Sufism analogous examples of "spiritual aesthetic" are to be found in such cases as those of Omar ibn Al-Farid or Jalal ed-Din Rumi.

3. Without saying a word the Buddha lifted a flower and this gesture was the origin of *Zen*. Let us recall here that the Buddhas save, not only by their teaching, but also by their superhuman beauty, which is perpetuated — in a more or less "abstract" fashion — in the sacramental images.

Theology and Philosophy

Man and Certainty*

HUMAN LIFE IS STUDDED with uncertainties; man loses himself in what is uncertain instead of holding on to what is absolutely certain in his destiny, namely death, Judgement and Eternity. But besides these there is a fourth certainty, immediately accessible moreover to human experience, and this is the present moment, in which man is free to choose either the Real or the illusory, and thus to ascertain for himself the value of the three great eschatological certainties. The consciousness of the sage is founded upon these three points of reference, whether directly or in an indirect and implicit manner through "remembrance of God".

Besides the dimension of succession, however, one must also consider that of simultaneity, which is based on spatial symbolism: the world around us is full of possibilities presented to our choice, whether we wish it or not; thus it is full of uncertainties, not successive as in the flux of life, but simultaneous like the things offered to us by space. Here too whoever wishes to resolve these uncertainties must hold on to what is absolutely certain and this is what stands above us, namely God and our immortality in God. But even here below there is something which is absolutely certain when we are confronted with the multitudinous and bewildering possibilities of the world, something of which sacred forms represent so many ex-

*From *SCR*, Spring 1972, p. 70.

teriorizations, and this is metaphysical truth and the "remembrance of God", that center which is within us and which places us, to the extent that we participate in it, beneath the "vertical" axis of Heaven, of God, of the Self.

Man finds himself in space and in time, in the world and in life, and these two situations imply two eschatological and spiritual axes, the one static and "vertical", the other dynamic and "horizontal" and more or less temporal; thus it is that contingency, in the mind of the contemplative man, is conceived in terms of the Absolute, is attached to it and leads back to it. But these various points of reference, in effect, only enter into consideration to the extent that the sage is necessarily conscious of contingent situations; they characterize his manner of taking account of his own relativity. Within this whole context, but completely independent of it and not in any sense "localized", resides that mystery where knowing is being and being is knowing; in other words, these certainties of "succession" and "simultaneity", of "life" and "world", form the necessary framework of contemplation, representing points of reference which serve to free us from the world and from life, or which facilitate that liberation. Indeed exoterism, which is the necessary basis of esoterism, is in the last analysis centered upon these elements which concern our final ends, namely Heaven and God, or death, Judgement and Eternity, and our own terrestrial attitudes as conforming to these realities.

The important thing to grasp here is that actualization of the consciousness of the Absolute — the "remembrance of God" or "prayer" in so far as it brings about a fundamental confrontation of creature and Creator — anticipates every station on the two axes: it is already a death and a meeting with God and it places us already in Eternity; it is already something of Paradise and even, in its mysterious and "uncreated" quintessence, something of God. Quintessential prayer brings about an escape from the world and from life, and thereby confers a new and Divine sap upon the veil of appearances and the current of forms, and a fresh meaning to our presence amidst the play of phenomena.

Whatever is not here is nowhere, and whatever is not now will never be. As is this moment in which I am free to choose God, so will be death, Judgement and Eternity. Likewise in this center, this Divine point which I am free to choose in the face of this boundless and multiple world, I am already in invisible Reality.

On Miracles as Proofs of God*

Of quite a different order from the intellectual proofs of God and of the beyond is a type of proof which in the first place is purely phenomenal, namely the miracle. Quite contrary to what most people suppose, miracles, without being in the least degree contrary to reason, do not carry conviction in the manner of physical effects which may prove such and such causes, for then the certainty offered would be only an approximation, miraculous causation being unverifiable; this, moreover, is the objection most commonly raised against the conviction in question, quite apart from the habitual denial of the phenomenon as such. What a miracle seeks to produce, and what it does indeed produce, is the rending of a veil; it operates like a surgical intervention which, far from consisting merely of an abstract discussion, removes the obstacle in a concrete way. A miracle breaks down the wall separating outward and fallible consciousness from inward and infallible consciousness, which is omniscient and blissful. By means of a "therapeutic shock" it delivers the soul from its shell of ignorance, but it would amount to nothing if it sought to convince merely by a demonstration of phenomena, for then as we have seen, many doubts might be permissible as to the level and significance of the prodigy.

The miraculous phenomenon cannot help but exist given that one has the supernatural, on the one hand, and the natural, on the other. The supernatural, moreover, is not the contra-natural; it is itself "natural" on the universal scale. If the Divine Principle is transcendent in relation to the world while at the same time embracing it within Its unique substance, then miracles must occur; the celestial must sometimes break through into the terrestrial, the Center must appear like a flash of lightning on the periphery. To take an example in the physical realm, inert matter is of little worth, but gold and diamonds cannot fail to appear therein. Metaphysically the miracle is a possibility which, as such, must necessarily be manifested in view of the hierarchical structure of the whole Universe.

*From *LT*, pp. 72-73.

Evidence and Mystery*

God created the world out of nothing; this is the teaching of the Semitic theologies, and by it they answer the following difficulty: if God had made the world out of a preexisting substance, that substance must be either itself created, or else Divine. The creation is not God, it cannot therefore emanate from Him; there is an unbridgeable hiatus between God and the world, neither can become the other; the orders of magnitude or of reality, or of perfection, are incommensurable.

The main concern of this reasoning is not a disinterested perception of the nature of things, but the safeguarding of a simple and unalterable notion of God, while making allowance for a mentality that is more active than contemplative. The aim is therefore to provide, not a metaphysical statement that does not engage the will or does not appear to do so, but a key notion calculated to win over souls rooted in willing and acting rather than in knowing and contemplating; the metaphysical limitation is here a consequence of the priority accorded to what is effective for the governing and saving of souls. That being so, one is justified in saying that Semitic religious thought is by force of circumstances a kind of dynamic thought with moral overtones, and not a static thought in the style of the Greek or Hindu wisdom.

From the point of view of the latter, the idea of emanation, in place of *creatio ex nihilo*, in no way compromises either the transcendence or the immutability of God; between the world and God there is at once discontinuity and continuity, depending on whether our conception of the Universe is based on a scheme of concentric circles or on one of radii extending outward from the center to the periphery: according to the first mode of vision, which proceeds from the created to the Uncreated, there is no common measure between the contingent and the Absolute; according to the second mode of vision, which proceeds from the Principle to its manifestation, there is but one Real, which includes everything and excludes only nothingness,

*From *LT*, Chapter 6

precisely because the latter has no reality whatsoever. The world is either a production drawn from the void and totally other than God, or else it is a manifestation "freely necessary" and "necessarily free" of Divinity or of Its Infinitude, liberty as well as necessity being Divine perfections.

As for the contention that the creationist concept is superior to the so-called emanationist or pantheistic concepts because it is Biblical and Christ-given, and that the Platonic doctrine cannot be right because Plato cannot be superior either to Christ or the Bible, this has the fault of leaving on one side the real fundamentals of the problem. First, what is rightly or wrongly called "emanationism"[1] is not an invention of Plato, it can be found in the most diverse sacred texts; second, Christ, while being traditionally at one with the creationist thesis, nevertheless did not teach it explicitly and did not deny the apparently opposed thesis. The message of Christ, like that of the Bible, is not *a priori* a teaching of metaphysical science; it is above all a message of salvation, but one that necessarily contains, in an indirect way and under cover of an appropriate symbolism, metaphysics in its entirety. The opposition between the Divine Bible and human philosophy, or between Christ and Plato, therefore has no meaning so far as the metaphysical truths in question are concerned; that the Platonic perspective should go farther than the Biblical perspective brings no discredit on the Bible, which teaches what is useful or indispensable from the point of view of the moral or spiritual good of a particular humanity, nor does it confer any human superiority on the Platonists, who may be mere thinkers just as they may be saints, according to how much they assimilate of the Truth they proclaim.

For the Platonists it is perfectly logical that the world should be the necessary manifestation of God and that it should be without origin; if the monotheistic Semites believe in a creation out of nothing and in time, it is evidently not, as some have suggested, because they think that they have the right or the privilege of accepting a "supralogical" thesis that is humanly absurd; for the idea of creation appears to them on the contrary as being the only one that is reasonable and therefore the only one that is capable of logical demonstration, as is proved precisely by the method of argumentation used in theology. Starting from the axiom that God created the world out of nothing, the Semites reason thus, *grosso modo*: since God alone has Being, the world could not share it with Him; there had therefore to be a time when the world did not exist; it is God alone who could give it existence. On the religious plane, which so far as cosmology is concerned demands no more than the minimum necessary or useful for salvation, this idea of creation is fully sufficient, and the logical considerations which support it are perfectly plausible within the framework of their limitation; for they at least convey a key truth that allows a fuller understanding of the nature of God, as it is pleased to reveal itself in the monotheistic religions.

More than once we have had occasion to mention the following erroneous argument: if God creates the world in response to an inward necessity, as is affirmed by the Platonists, this must mean that He is obliged to create it, and that therefore He is not free; since this is impossible, the creation can only be a gratuitous act. One might as well say that if God is One, or if He is a Trinity, or if He is all-powerful, or if He is good, He must be obliged to be so, and His nature is thus the result of a constraint, *quod absit*. It is always a case of the same incapacity to conceive of antinomic realities, and to understand that if liberty, the absence of constraint, is a perfection, necessity, the absence of arbitrariness, is another.

If, in opposition to the Pythagorean-Platonic perspective, the concept is put forward of an Absolute which is threefold in its very essence, therefore devoid of the degrees of reality that alone can explain the hypostatic polarizations — an Absolute which creates without metaphysical necessity and which in addition acts without cause or motive — and if at the same time the right is claimed to a sacred illogicality in the name of an exclusive "Christian supernaturalism", then an explanation is due of what logic is and what human reason is; for if our intelligence, in its very structure, is foreign or even opposed to Divine Truth, what then is it, and why did God give it to us? Or to put it the other way round, what sort of Divine message is it that is opposed to the laws of an intelligence to which it is essentially addressed, and what does it signify that man was created "in the image of God"?[2] And what motive could induce us to accept a message that was contrary, not to our earthly materialism or to our passion, but to the very substance of our spirit? For the "wisdom according to the flesh" of Saint Paul does not embrace every form of metaphysics that does not know the Gospels, nor is it logic as such, for the Apostle was logical; what it denotes is the reasonings whereby worldly men seek to prop up their passions and their pride, such as Sophism and Epicureanism and, in our days, the current philos-

ophy of the world. "Wisdom according to the flesh" is also the gratuitous philosophy that does not lead us inwards and which contains
no door opening on to spiritual realization; it is philosophy of the
type of "art for art's sake," which commits one to nothing and is vain
and pernicious for that very reason.

The incomprehension by theologians of Platonic and Oriental
emanationism arises from the fact that monotheism puts in parenthesis the notion, essential metaphysically, of Divine Relativity or
Māyā;[3] it is this parenthesis, or in practice this ignorance, which in-
hibits an understanding of the fact that there is no incompatability
whatever between the "absolute Absolute", Beyond-Being, and the
"relative Absolute", creative Being, and that this distinction is even
crucial. The Divine *Māyā*, Relativity, is the necessary consequence
of the very Infinitude of the Principle: it is because God is infinite
that He comprises the dimension of relativity, and it is because He
comprises that dimension that He manifests the world. To which it
should be added: it is because the world is manifestation and not
Principle that relativity, which at first was only determination, limitation and manifestation, gives rise to that particular modality constituting "evil". It is neither in the existence of evil things that evil
lies nor in their existential properties nor in their faculties of sensation and of action, if it be a question of animate beings, nor even
in the act insofar as it is the manifestation of a power; evil resides
only in whatever is privative or negative with respect to good, and
its function is to manifest in the world its aspect of separation from
the Principle, and to play its part in an equilibrium and a rhythm
necessitated by the economy of the created Universe. In this way
evil, wholly evil though it be when looked at in isolation, attaches
itself to a good and is dissolved *qua* evil when one looks at it in its
cosmic context and in its universal function.

Platonists feel no need whatever to try to fill the gap which might
seem to exist between the pure Absolute and the determination and
creative Absolute; it is precisely because they are aware of relativity
in divinis and of the Divine cause of that relativity that they are emana-
tionists. In other words, the Hellenists, if they did not have a word
to express it, nevertheless possessed in their own way the concept
of *Māyā*, and it is their doctrine of emanation that proves it...

·   ·   ·

The theology of "transubstantiation" provides an example of the passage from a revealed premise into the sphere of a particular logic.[4] A logic is particular, not in its functioning, for two and two everywhere make four, but in its natural presuppositions, which among the Romans have the characteristics of physical empiricism and juridicism whence the tendency toward trenchant equations and simplistic and irreducible alternatives. When Jesus, who was an Oriental, expresses himself thus: "This is my body, this is my blood," that means, in Oriental parlance that the bread and the wine are equivalent to the body and the blood of Jesus in the context of Divine inherence and saving power, it being these, precisely, that confer on the body and the blood their sufficient reason and their value; in Western parlance, however, the words of Christ can only carry the meaning of a rigorous and massive physical equation, as if any such equation comprised the smallest metaphysical or sacramental advantage.[5] It may nevertheless be acknowledged that the dogmatism is inevitable in a climate of emotional totalitarianism, and that in this climate it consequently represents the most effective solution from the point of view of safeguarding the mystery. It may also be acknowledged, all question of expediency apart, that the Lateran Council was right in the sense that the Eucharistic elements, even while remaining what they are, quite plainly cannot be what they are in the same way that they were before, given that bread penetrated by a Divine Presence or Power must thereby change its substance in a certain respect. However, this consideration leads us into the realm of the indefinite and the inexpressible and cannot wholly justify the logic of the theory of transubstantiation; in any case, the words of Christ which are regarded as necessitating this formulation, do not in reality necessitate it at all, for an Oriental ellipsis is not a mathematical or physical equation; "to be equivalent in a certain respect" does not necessarily mean "to be the same thing in every respect."

The problem could be approached in the following way: if in truth the Eucharistic species have literally become the flesh and blood of Jesus, how much better off are we for this so to say "magical" operation, given that the value of this flesh and this blood lies in Divine content, and that this same content can itself penetrate the bread and the wine without any "transubstantiation"? For we can neither desire nor obtain anything greater than the Divine Presence; if that

Presence were in a tree, the tree would then be equivalent to the body of Christ, and there would be no need to ask oneself whether the wood was something other than wood, or to conclude that it was a tree without being one or that it was a "form" that contradicted its substance, and so forth. It is not the body of Jesus that sanctifies God, it is God who sanctifies it.

Let there be no misunderstandings: we have no preconceived opinion about the idea of transubstantiation, but if anyone says that the proof of this idea is in the words of Christ, we have no choice but to reply that these words in themselves do not imply the meaning attributed to them. It, however, can be admitted, discounting any questions of intrinsic truth, that the idea of transubstantiation has the value of an impelling argument, well fitted to forestall any naturalistic or psychologistic interpretation of the mystery in a society all too easily led into that kind of betrayal.

•   •   •

Trinitarian theology gives rise to a comparable hiatus between a very subtle and complex transcendent reality, described as "inexhaustible" by Saint Augustine himself, and a logic that is dogmatically coagulative and piously unilateral, that is to say, determined by the necessity of adapting the mystery to a mentality more volitive than contemplative. The theology of the Trinity does not constitute an explicit and homogeneous revelation; it results, on the one hand, like the concept of transubstantiation, from a literalistic and quasi-mathematical interpretation of certain words in the Scriptures, and on the other hand from a summation of different points of view, deriving from different dimensions of the Real.

The first paradox of the Trinitarian concept is the affirmation that God is at the same time absolutely one and absolutely three. Now the number one alone manifests absoluteness; the number three is necessarily relative, unless one accepts that it subsists in unity in an undifferentiated and potential manner only, but then the fact of considering it distinctively represents a relative point of view, exactly as in the case of the Vedantine *Sat* (Being), *Chit* (Intelligence), and *Ananda* (Bliss). The second paradox of the Trinitarian concept is the affirmation that the Divine Persons are distinct one from another but that each is equal to the Essence, which is something that no explanation of relationships can attenuate, since no theologian can admit that in one connection the Persons are inferior to the Essence and that in another the Persons are indistinguishable. Finally, the third paradox is in the affirmation that the Persons are only relationships, and that outside those relationships they are the Essence, which amounts to saying that they are nothing, for a pure and simple relationship is nothing concrete. One cannot have it both ways: either the relationship confers on the Person a certain substance, and then it is by that substance that the Person is distinguished from the other Persons; or else the relationship confers no substance, and then the Person is a pure abstraction about which it is useless to speak, unless one attributes it to the Essence and says that the Essence comprises relationships that render explicit the nature of the Person, which would lead us to the modalism of the Sabellians.[6]

However, there is still a fourth difficulty in Trinitarianism, which is its exclusiveness from a numerical point of view, if so inadequate a term be permitted. For if God incontestably comprises the Trinity which the Christian perspective discerns in Him, He also comprises other aspects that are in a manner of speaking numerical and that are taken into account by other traditional perspectives. It is precisely this diversity that indicates in its own way the relativity, in the most exalted sense possible, of the Trinitarian conception and above all of the "Divine dimension" that conditions that conception.

Christianity is founded on the idea and the reality of Divine Manifestation. If it were not a religion but a sapiential doctrine it might rest content with describing why and how the Absolute manifests itself; but, being a religion, it must enclose everything within its fundamental idea of Manifestation; the Absolute must therefore be envisaged exclusively in connection therewith and it is just this that gives rise to the Trinitarian doctrine, not only in itself but also in its theological and therefore totalitarian and exclusive form.

• • •

According to a first possible interpretation of the Holy Trinity, the Father is the Absolute while the Son and the Holy Ghost belong to Relativity and are as it were its foundations. This interpretation is irrefutable, because if the Son were the Absolute, he could not be called "Son," and he could not even have been incarnated; and if the Holy Ghost were the Absolute, it could neither proceed nor be sent nor delegated. The fact of the incarnation proves the relativity of the Son with respect to the Father, but not with respect to men, for whom the Son is the manifestation of the Absolute. It is true that the words of Christ announcing his subordination are attributed to his human nature alone, but this delimitation is arbitrary and interested, for the human nature is bound by its Divine content; if it is a part of the Son, it must manifest that content. The fact that this human nature exists and that its expressions manifest its subordination, and by the same token the hypostatic subordination of the Son, shows that the interpretation of the Son as the first Relativity confronting the purely Absolute Father is not contrary to Scripture and is inherently irrefutable.

But there is another interpretation of the Trinity, horizontal this time, and conforming to another real aspect of the mystery: God is the Absolute, He is the single Essence, while the three Persons are the first Relativities in the sense that on a plane that is already relative they actualize the indivisible characteristics of the Essence. This interpretation is also irrefutable and Scriptural, in the sense that there are Scriptural expressions which can be explained only with its help; and it is this interpretation that justifies the affirmation that the Divine Persons are equal, while being necessarily unequal in a different context. And what makes it possible to concede that they are equal to the single Essence is precisely the fact that the Essence comprises, principially, synthetically and without differentiation, the three Qualities or Powers that are called "Persons" *a posteriori* on the plane of diversifying Relativity; from this standpoint it is evident that each "Person" is the Essence in a total and direct sense; the relative, on pain of being impossible, has its root in the Absolute, of which it is a dimension that is either intrinsic or extrinsic according to whether it is considered in its pure possibility or as a projection.

What has just been said implies that the Trinity affirms itself on three planes which exoterism confuses, and cannot do otherwise than confuse in view of its concern for a simplifying synthesis and for what is psychologically opportune with reference to certain human tendencies or weaknesses. The first plane, as we have seen, is that of the Essence itself, where the Trinity is real, because the Essence admits of no privation, but undifferentiated, because the Essence admits of no diversity; from this standpoint one may say that each

Person or each Quality-Principle is the other, which is just what one cannot say from the standpoint of diversifying relativity. The second plane is that of the Divine Relativity, of the creative Being, of the personal God: here the three Quality-Principles are differentiated into Persons; one is not the other, and to affirm without metaphysical reservation that they are the Essence is to pass without transition, either by virtue of a purely dialectical ellipsis or through lack of discernment and out of mystical emotion, on to the plane of absoluteness and nondifferentiation. One may envisage also a third plane, already cosmic but nevertheless still Divine from the human point of view, which is the point of view that determines theology, and this is the luminous Center of the cosmos, the "Triple Manifestation" (*Trimurti*) of the Hindu doctrine and the "Spirit" (*Rūh*) of the Islamic doctrine; here also the Trinity is present, radiating and acting. To repeat: the first metaphysical plane is that of the Essence or the Absolute; the second is that of the diversified Personality or metacosmic Relativity; and the third is that of the diversified and manifested Personality, or cosmic Relativity, nevertheless still Divine and thus principial and central. It will have been noticed that these three planes themselves also correspond respectively to the three hypostases, with each plane in turn and in its own way comprising the Ternary.

On the Divine Will*

The enigma of the expression "God doeth what He will" becomes clear with the help of the following argument: Exodus teaches us that "the heart of Pharaoh hardened" or that "Pharaoh hardened his heart;" but it also teaches, on many occasions, that "Yahweh hardened the heart of Pharaoh," and has God uttering the following saying: "I have burdened his heart and the heart of his servants"; which shows that both apparently contradictory expressions are in reality synonymous. Similarly the Koran: "God leadeth astray whom He will"; the commentators specify that "God leadeth astray" in turning away from those who wish to go astray and in thus leaving them to the resources

*From *CI*, Chapter 11 (trans G. Polit)

of their own darkness. The expression "God leadeth astray"— or Yahweh hardened — is explainable by the concern to recall that the cause of our lights is God, and that in consequence the cause of our darknesses can only be the absence of God;[1] absence provoked by the luciferian desire to be absent from Him, or more profoundly: to be, like Pharaoh, wisdom and power outside the wisdom and the power of God.

"God leadeth astray," says the Koran, in conformity with a very Semitic ellipsism; now in being led astray — and we have seen that God is here the cause in an altogether indirect and non-acting manner — the initiative comes from man, that is, it manifests the fundamental and global possibility which the man concerned impersonates; unless being led astray is only temporary, in which case the possibility is only a secondary modality. The fundamental and characteristic possibility of the individual, that which determines his ultimate destiny, derives in the final analysis from universal Possibility and not from a decree of the creating Principle; the latter — the personal and legislating God — limits Himself, with regard to the individual possibilities, to clothe them with concrete and cosmic existence, as Ibn 'Arabi has very well specified; they are what they "want to be," as is suggested by the Koranic passage wherein the souls, before their projection into the cosmos, attest that God is their Lord. In other words, the diverse possibilities, negative as well as positive, result indirectly from the Infinitude and Radiation of the divine Self: they are positive by their participation and negative by their distance.

*   *   *

Grosso modo, it is inconceivable that God create an animal or a plant without at the same time creating its subsistence, and this relationship between the creature and its vital surroundings marks an obligation on the part of the Creator, if one keeps to moral terms in expressing oneself. God did not create an intelligent being so that the latter might grovel before the unintelligible; He created him in order to be known starting from contingency, and that is precisely why He created him intelligent. If God wished to owe nothing to man, He would not have created him.

In a general fashion, the error of the partisans of an integral obedientialism consists in transferring — by excess of zeal — the ontological "servitude" (*ubūdiyah*) of man onto the moral plane, by abusively applying the ontological absoluteness of this subordination of the creature as such to man insofar as he is intelligent and free. Now one thing is the existential determination of man, which he shares with every pebble, and another thing is his liberty, which he owes to his deiform personality and which causes him to participate in the Divine Nature.[2]

Firstly and fundamentally, the Divinity "wills" Itself; there is no difference between its "Willing" and its Being; the word "Willing" has no extrinsic meaning here, it coincides simply with the Infinitude of the Absolute, which amounts to saying that it expresses the essence of what will be, within *Māyā*, the dynamic and cosmogonic dimension or function of the Principle: namely the Radiation of the Sovereign Good (the Socratic or Platonic *Agathón*).

Secondly and more relatively: at the degree of this Radiation, the Divine Will has but one single object: to existentiate, that is, to project the All-Possibility of the Infinite — thereby differentiating it — into contingency, relativity — Existence, precisely; this is the second aspect of the Divine Will.

Thirdly and lastly, and on this basis or within this framework, the Divinity — now involved in the play of *Māyā* — wills to manifest its own nature, which is the Good; in consequence, the personal, legislating and saving God regulates human conduct: He orders virtue and forbids vice; He rewards good and punishes evil. But His Will cannot extend, retrospectively as it were, to His own Root or Essence; He "must" and "wishes" to accept the fundamental and general cosmic consequences of the existentiating Radiation, since to be able to manifest the Good in a world it is necessary first of all that there be a world. The Will of Radiation, which precedes and conditions this manifestation, produces fatally a distancing with respect to the divine Source, and this distance, together with the diversifying, graduated and contrasting unfolding of the possibilities, gives rise to that limited and transitory phenomenon which we call "evil."

If we wish to explain the apparent contradictions of the Divine Will, we are obliged to have recourse to the perspective which we have just outlined and which reveals three degrees of the Divine Will, thus of the "Subjectivity" of the Principle. It is absurd to acknowledge that one and the same subjectivity or will, on the one hand does not will sin and on the other hand wills a given sin; that one and the same subject orders obedience while creating a given disobedience, or that He desires that which He nevertheless hates. In this order of ideas, the Christian *distinguo* between what God "wills" and what He "permits" is full of interest: God permits evil because He knows that evil is the ontologically inevitable shadow of a global good and that all evil concurs in the final analysis towards the good; in permitting evil, God indirectly envisages the good of which this evil is like an infinitesimal, transitory and necessary fragment, contingency requiring and provoking by its very nature contrasts, fissures, or dissonances. And it is only in this sense that one can affirm that all is good because God wills it, and that no possibility can be situated outside of the Divine Will.

If the Asharites limited themselves to affirming that the Will of God is one, as God is one, we would have nothing to say against them, for the simple reason that the hypostatic modes of the Divine Will do not preclude its essential unity. The Divine Will which wills the good in the world is in effect only an application of the Divine Will which wills existentiating Radiation, or which wills the good as Radiation; and this initial Will in its turn is only a projection of the intrinsic Will of the Essence — Beyond-Being — which has in view its own Being. The most "exterior" Divine Will always comprises in its nature the hypostatic modes which precede it ontologically, if it be permitted here to term "mode" what, at the summit at least, is on the contrary pure Essence; in other words, that the Divine Will is necessarily one cannot preclude that it be diversified extrinsically in function of its applications at diverse universal degrees.

On Predestination and Free Will*

. . . Another example of the helplessness of the human mind when left to its own resources is the problem of predestination. This idea of predestination is simply an expression, in the language of human ignorance, of the Divine Knowledge that in its perfect simultaneity embraces all possibilities without any restriction. In other words, if God is omniscient He knows future events, or rather events

*From *TUR*, pp. 50-51.

that appear thus to beings limited by time; if God did not know these events He would not be omniscient; from the moment that He knows them they appear as predestined relative to the individual. The individual will is free insofar as it is real; if it were not in any degree or in any way free it would be deprived of all reality; and in fact, compared with absolute Liberty, it has no reality, or more precisely, it is totally nonexistent. From the individual standpoint, however, which is the standpoint of human beings, the will is real in the measure in which they participate in the Divine Liberty, from which individual liberty derives all its reality by virtue of the causal relationship between the two; whence it follows that liberty, like all positive qualities, is Divine in itself and human insofar as it is not perfectly itself, in the same way that a reflection of the sun is identical with the sun, not as reflection but as light, light being one and indivisible in its essence.

The metaphysical link between predestination and liberty might be illustrated by comparing the latter to a liquid that settles into all the convolutions of a mold, the latter representing predestination: in that case the movement of the liquid is equivalent to the free exercise of our will. If we cannot will anything other than what is predestined for us, this does not prevent our will being what it is, namely, a relatively real participation in its universal prototype; it is precisely by means of this participation that we feel and live our will as being free.

The life of a man, and by extension the whole individual cycle of which that life and the human state itself are only modalities, is in fact contained in the Divine Intellect as a complete whole, that is to say, as a determined possibility that, being what it is, is not in any of its aspects other than itself, since a possibility is nothing else than an expression of the absolute necessity of Being; hence the unity or homogeneity of every possibility, which is accordingly something that cannot not be. To say that an individual cycle is included as a definitive formula in the Divine Intellect comes to the same thing as saying that a possibility is included in the Total Possibility, and it is this truth that furnishes the most decisive answer to the question of predestination. The individual will appears in this light as a process that realizes in successive mode the necessary interconnection of the modalities of its initial possibility, which is thus symbolically described or recapitulated. It can also be said that since the possibility of a being is necessarily a possibility of manifestation, the cyclic process of that being is the sum of the aspects of his manifestation and therefore of his possibility, and that the being, through the exercise of his will, merely manifests in deferred mode his simultaneous cosmic manifestation; in other words, the individual retraces in an analytic way his synthetic and primordial possibility, which, for its part, occupies a necessary place in the hierarchy of possibilities, the necessity of each possibility, as we have seen, being based metaphysically on the absolute necessity of the Divine All-Possibility.

Tracing the Notion of Philosophy*

Were Ibn 'Arabī, Jīlī and other theoreticians of Sufism philosophers? Yes and no, depending on the meaning given to this word.

According to Pythagoras, wisdom is *a priori* the knowledge of the stellar world and of everything that is situated above us; *sophia* being the wisdom of the gods, and *philosophia* that of men. For Heraclitus, the philosopher is one who applies himself to the knowledge of the profound nature of things; for Plato, philosophy is the knowledge of the Changeless and of the Ideas; and for Aristotle, it is the knowledge of first causes and principles, together with the sciences that are derived from them. In addition, philosophy implies for all of the Ancients a moral conformity to wisdom: only he is wise, *sophos*, who lives wisely. In this particular and precise sense, the wisdom of Solomon is philosophy; it is to live according to the nature of things, on the basis of piety— of the "fear of God"— with a view to whatever is essential and liberating.

All this shows that, to say the least, the word "philosopher" in itself has nothing restrictive about it, and that one cannot legitimately impute to this word any of the negative associations of ideas that it may elicit; usage applies this word to all thinkers, including eminent metaphysicians — some Sufis consider Plato and other Greeks to be prophets — so that one would willingly reserve it for sages and simply use the term "rationalists" for profane thinkers. It is nevertheless legitimate to take account of a misuse of language that has become conventional, for unquestionably the terms "philosophy" and

*From *SVQ*, Chapter 5.

"philosopher" have been seriously compromised by ancient and modern practitioners of reason; in fact, the serious inconvenience of these terms is that they conventionally imply that the norm for the mind is reasoning pure and simple[1], in the absence, not only of intellection, but also of the indispensable objective data. Admittedly one is neither ignorant nor rationalistic just because one is a logician, but one is both if one is a logician and nothing more.[2]

In the opinion of all profane thinkers, philosophy means to think "freely", as far as possible without presuppositions, which precisely is impossible; on the other hand, gnosis, or philosophy in the proper and primitive sense of the word, is to think in accordance with the immanent Intellect and not by means of reason alone. What gives rise to confusion is that in both cases the intelligence operates independently of outward prescriptions, although for diametrically opposed reasons: that the rationalist if need be draws his inspiration from a pre-existing system does not prevent him from thinking in a way that he deems to be "free"— falsely, since true freedom coincides with truth — and likewise, *mutatis mutandis*: that the gnostic — in the orthodox sense of the term — bases himself extrinsically on a given Scripture or on some other gnostic, cannot prevent him from thinking in an intrinsically free manner by virtue of the freedom proper to the immanent Truth, or proper to the Essence which by definition escapes formal constraints. Or again: whether the gnostic "thinks" what he has "seen" with the "eye of the heart", or whether on the contrary he obtains his "vision" thanks to the intervention — preliminary and provisional and in no wise efficient — of a thought which then takes on the role of occasional cause, is immaterial with regard to the truth, or with regard to its almost supernatural gushing forth in the spirit.

The reduction of the notion of intellectuality to that of simple rationality often has its cause in the prejudice of a school: St. Thomas is a sensationalist — in other words he reduces the cause of all non-theological knowledge to sensible perceptions — in order to be able to underestimate the human mind to the advantage of Scripture; in other words, because this allows him to attribute to Revelation alone the glory of "supernatural" knowledge. And Ghazali inveighs against the "philosophers" because he wishes to reserve for the Sufis the monopoly of spiritual knowledge, as if faith and piety, in combination with intellectual gifts and with grace — all the Arab philosophers were believers — did not provide a sufficient basis for pure intellection.

According to Ibn 'Arabī, the "philosopher"—which for him means practically the skeptic—is incapable of knowing universal causality except by observing causations in the outward world and by drawing from his observations the conclusions that impose themselves on his sense of logic. According to another Sufi, Ibn al-'Arīf, intellectual knowledge is only an "indication" pointing to God: the philosopher only knows God by way of a "conclusion", his knowledge only has a content "with a view to God", and not "by God" as does that of the mystic. But this *distinguo* is only valid, as we have said, if we assimilate all philosophy to unmitigated rationalism, and forget in addition that in the doctrinaire mystics there is an obvious element of rationality. In short, the term "philosopher" in current speech signifies nothing else than the fact of expounding a doctrine while respecting the laws of logic, which are those of language, and those of common sense, without which we would not be human; to practise philosophy is first and foremost to think, whatever may be the reasons which rightly or wrongly incite us to do so. But it is also, more especially and according to the best of the Greeks, to express by means of the reason certainties "seen" or "lived" by the immanent Intellect, as observed earlier; now the explanation necessarily takes on the manner imposed on it by the laws of thought and language.

Some will object that the simple believer who understands nothing of philosophy can derive much more from scriptural symbols than does the philosopher, with his definitions, abstractions, classifications and categories; an unjust reproach, for theoretical thought, firstly does not exclude supra-rational intuition—this is completely obvious—and secondly does not pretend to provide by itself anything that it cannot offer by virtue of its nature. This something may be of immense value, otherwise it would be necessary to suppress all doctrines; Platonic *anamnesis* can have as occasional cause doctrinal concepts as well as symbols provided by art or virgin nature. If in intellectual speculation there is a human danger of rationalism, and thus of skepticism and materialism—at least in principle—mystical speculation for its part comprises, with the same reservation a danger of exaggeration, or even of rambling and incoherence, whatever may be said by the esoterizing zealots who take pleasure in question-begging and sublimizing euphemisms.

•   •   •

We must here say a few words in defence of the Arab philosophers who have been accused, amongst other things, of confusing Plato, Aristotle and Plotinus; we consider that on the contrary they had the merit of integrating these great Greeks in one and the same synthesis, for what interested them was not systems, but truth itself. We shall no doubt run counter to certain esoterist prejudices if we say that metaphysically orthodox philosophy—that of the Middle Ages as well as that of antiquity—pertains to sapiential esoterism, either intrinsically by its truth, or extrinsically with regard to the simplifications of theology; it is "thinking", if one will, but not ratiocination in the void. If it be objected that the errors that one may find in some philosophers who overall are orthodox prove the nonesoteric and consequently profane nature of all philosophy, this argument can be turned against theology and the mystical or gnostic doctrines, for in these sectors too erroneous speculations can be found on the margin of real inspirations.

To give a concrete example, we shall mention the following case, which in any event is interesting in itself and apart from any question of terminology: the Arab philosophers rightly accept the eternity of the world for, as they say, God cannot create at a given moment without putting Himself in contradiction with His very nature, and thus without absurdity;[3] most ingeniously Ghazali replies—and others have repeated the same argument—that there is no "before" with regard to creation, that time "was" created with, for and in the world. Now this argument is invalid since it is unilateral: for if it safeguards the transcendence, the absolute freedom and the timelessness of the Creator with regard to creation, it does not explain the temporality of the latter; in other words it does not take account of the temporal limitations of a unique world projected into the void of non-time, a limitation which engages God since He is its cause and since it exists in relation to His eternity;[4] the very nature of duration demands a beginning. The solution of the problem is that the co-eternity of the world is not that of our "actual" world—which of necessity had an origin and will have an end—but consists in the necessity for successive worlds: God being what He is—with his absolute Necessity and His absolute Freedom—He cannot not create necessarily, but He is free in the modes of creation, which never repeat themselves since God is infinite. The whole difficulty comes from the fact that the Semites envisage only one world, namely ours, whereas the non-Semiticized Aryans, either accept an indefinite series of creations — this is the Hindu doctrine of cosmic cycles — or else envisage the world as the necessary manifestation of the Divine Nature and not as a contingent and particular phenomenon. In this confrontation between two theses, the theological and the philosophical, it is the philosophers, and not the theologians — even if they be Sufis like Ghazali — who were right; and if doctrinal esoterism provides the explanation of problems posed but not clarified by faith, we do not see why those philosophers who provide this explanation thanks to intellection — for reasoning pure and simple would not succeed in doing so, and it is moreover metaphysical truth that proves the worth of the intuition corresponding to it — do not have the same merit as the recognized esoterists; especially since, to paraphrase St. Paul, one cannot testify to great truths except by the Holy Spirit.

For the theologians, to say that the world is "without beginning" amounts to saying that it is eternal *a se* — this is why they reject the idea — whereas for the philosophers it means that it is eternal *ab alio*, for it is God who lends it eternity; now an eternity that is lent is a completely different thing from eternity in itself, and it is precisely for this reason that the world is both eternal and temporal: eternal as a series of creations or a creative rhythm, and temporal from the fact that each line in this flux has a beginning and an end. It is Universal Manifestation in itself that is co-eternal with God by reason of the fact that it is a necessary expression of His eternal Nature — the sun being unable to abstain from shining — but eternity cannot be reduced to a given contingent phase of this divine Manifestation. Manifestation is "co-eternal", not eternal, as only the Essence is: and this is why it is periodically interrupted and totally re-absorbed into the Principle, so that it is both existent and non-existent, and does not enjoy a plenary and so to speak "continuous" reality like the Eternal itself. To say that the world is "co-eternal" nevertheless means that it is necessary as an aspect of the Principle, and that it is therefore "something of God", which is already indicated by the term "Manifestation"; and it is precisely this truth that the theologians refuse to accept; for obvious reasons since in their eyes it abolishes the difference between creature and Creator.[5]

The "co-eternity" of the world with God evokes the universal *Materia* of Empedocles and Ibn Masarrah, which is none other than the Logos as Substance *amā* "cloud" or *habā* "dust"):[6] it is not creation as such that is co-eternal with the Creator, it is the creative virtuality, which comprises — according to these doctrines — four fundamental formative principles. These are, symbolically speaking, "Fire", "Air", "Water", "Earth",[7] which recall the three principial determinations (*gunas*) included in *Prakriti: Sattva, Rajas, Tamas*; the difference in number indicating a secondary difference in perspective.[8]

•   •   •

As regards the confrontation between Sufis and philosophers, the following remark must be made: if Ghazali had limited himself to asserting that there is no possible esoteric realization without an initiation and a corresponding message, and that the philosophers in general demand neither the one nor the other,[9] we would have no reason to reproach him; but his criticism is levelled at philosophy as such, that is to say, it is situated above all on the doctrinal and epistemological plane. In fact, the Hellenizing philosophy that is in question here is neutral from the initiatic point of view, given that its intention is to provide an exposition of the truth, and nothing else; particular opinions — such as rationalism properly so-called — do not enter into the definition of philosophy.[10] Be that as it may, Ghazali's ostracism makes us think of those ancient theologians who sought to oppose the "vain wisdom of the world" with the "tears of repentance", but who at the end of the day did not refrain from constructing systems of their own, and in doing so could not do without the help of the Greeks, to whom nevertheless they denied the co-operation of the "Holy Spirit" and therefore any supernatural quality.

The Sufis do not wish to be philosophers, that is understood; and they are right if they mean by this that their starting point is not doubt and that their certainties are not rational conclusions. But we completely fail to see how, when they reason, they can do so in any different way than do the philosophers; nor how a philosopher, when he conceives a truth whose transcendent and axiomatic nature he recognizes, can do so in any different way than do the Sufis.

It was not as a gnostic, but as a "thinker" that Ibn 'Arabī treated the question of evil, explaining it by subjectivity and relativity, with an entirely Pyrrhonic logic. What is serious is that by practically abolishing evil — since it is reduced to a subjective angle of vision — by the same stroke one abolishes good, whether this was the intention or not; and in particular one abolishes beauty, by depriving love of its content, whereas it is precisely on their reality and their necessary connection that Ibn 'Arabī's doctrine insists. It is beauty that determines love, not vice versa: the beautiful is not what we love and because we love it, but that which by its objective value obliges us to love it; we love the beautiful because it is beautiful, even if in fact it may happen that we lack judgement, which does not invalidate the principle of the normal relationship between object and subject. Likewise, the fact that one may love because of an inward beauty and in spite of an outward ugliness, or that love may be mixed with compassion or other indirect motives, cannot invalidate the nature either of beauty or of love.

On the contrary, it is as a gnostic that Ibn 'Arabī responded to the question of freedom; every creature does what it wills because every creature is basically what it wills to be: in other words, because a possibility is what it is and not something else. Freedom in the last analysis coincides with possibility, and this moreover is attested by the Koranic story of the initial pact between human souls and God; destiny, consequently, is what the creature wills by his nature, and thus by his possibility. One may wonder which we should here admire more: the gnostic who penetrated the mystery or the philosopher who knew how to express it.

But if man does what he is or if he is what he does, why strive to become better and why pray to this end? Because there is the distinction between substance and accident: both demerits and merits come from either one or the other, without man being able to know from which they come, unless he is a "pneumatic" who is aware of his substantial reality, an ascending reality because of its conformity with the Spirit (*Pneuma*), "Whoso knoweth his own soul, knoweth his Lord"; but even then, the effort belongs to man and the knowledge to God, in other words, it suffices that we strive while being aware that God knows us. It suffices us to know that we are free in and through our movement towards God; our movement towards our "Self".

•   •   •

In a certain respect, the difference between philosophy, theology and gnosis is total; in another respect, it is relative. It is total when one understands by "philosophy" rationalism alone; by "theology", the explanation of religious teachings alone; and by "gnosis", intuitive and intellective, and thus supra-rational, knowledge; but the difference is only relative when one understands by "philosophy" the fact of thinking, by "theology" the fact of speaking from a dogmatic point of view about God and religious things, and by "gnosis" the fact of presenting pure metaphysics, for then the genres are interpenetrating. It is impossible to deny that the most illustrious Sufis, while being "gnostics" by definition, were at the same time to some extent theologians and to some extent philosophers, or that the great theologians were both to some extent philosophers and to some extent gnostics, the last word having to be understood in its proper and not sectarian sense.

If we wish to retain the limitative, or indeed pejorative sense of the word philosopher, we could say that gnosis or pure metaphysics takes certainty as its starting-point, whereas philosophy on the contrary has doubt as its starting-point, and strives to overcome this only with the means that are at its disposition and which do not pretend to be more than purely rational. But since neither the term "philosophy" in itself, nor the usage that has been made of it since the earliest times, oblige us to accept only the restrictive sense of the word, we shall not consider criminal those who employ it in a wider sense than what may seem to be opportune.[11]

Theory, by definition, is not an end in itself, it is only — and seeks only — to be a key with a view to a cognition on the part of the "heart". If there is attached to the notion of "philosophy" a suspicion of superficiality, insufficiency and pretension, it is precisely because only too often — and indeed always in the case of the moderns — it is presented as being sufficient unto itself. "This is only philosophy": we readily accept the use of this turn of phrase, but only on condition that one does not say that "Plato is only a philosopher", Plato who said that "beauty is the splendor of the truth"; beauty that includes or demands all that we are or can be.

If Plato maintains that the *philosophos* should think independently of received opinions, he is referring to intellection and not to logic alone; whereas Descartes, who did everything to restrict and compromise the notion of philosophy, reaches such a conclusion from the starting-point of systematic doubt, so that for him philosophy is synonymous not only with rationalism, but also with skepticism. This is a first suicide of the intelligence, inaugurated moreover by Pyrrho and others, in the guise of a reaction against what one looked on as metaphysical "dogmatism". The "Greek miracle" is in fact the substitution of the reason for the Intellect, of the fact for the Principle, of the phenomenon for the Idea, of the accident for the Substance, of the form for the Essence, of man for God; and this applies to art as well as to thought. The true Greek miracle, if miracle there be — and in this case it would be related to the "Hindu miracle"— is doctrinal metaphysics and methodic logic, providentially utilized by the monotheistic Semites. . .

NOTES

Evidence and Mystery

1. Wrongly, if one understands emanation in the physical sense; rightly, if one acknowledges that it is purely causal while at the same time implying a certain consubstantiality due to the fact that reality is one.

2. According to Genesis "God created man in his own image" and "male and female created He them." Now according to one Father of the Church, the sexes are not made in the image of God; only the features that are identical in the two sexes resemble God, for the simple reason that God is neither man nor woman. This reasoning is fallacious because, although it is evident that God is not in Himself a duality, He necessarily comprises the principial Duality in His Unity, exactly as He comprises the Trinity or the Quaternity; and how can one refuse to admit that the Holy Virgin has a prototype in God not only as regards her humanity but also as regards her femininity?

3. The fact that we have drawn attention on a number of occasions to this Vedantine notion must not prevent our insisting on it once more; we shall return to it again later. Here the reader may be reminded that the term *Māyā* combines the meanings of "productive power" and "universal illusion"; it is the inexhaustible play of manifestations, deployments, combinations and reverberations, a play with which *Ātmā* clothes itself even as the ocean clothes itself with a mantle of foam ever renewed and never the same.

4. The Orthodox Church speaks more prudently of a "transmutation".

5. If one had to interpret literally every word of the Gospels, one would have to believe that Christ is a vine or a door, or one would have to hate father and mother, or to pluck out one's eye, and so on.

6. Rejected because of an inability to combine it with the complementary thesis. The truth is here antinomic, not unilateral: the hypostases are at the same time three modes of the one Divine Person and three relatively distinctive Persons.

On the Divine Will

1. "Let no man say when he is tempted, I am tempted of God: for God cannot be tempted with evil, neither tempteth He any man." (Epistle of Saint James I 13.)

2 The fact that in the Moslem prayer the vertical positions alternate with the prostrations expresses in its way the two aspects of man, that of "slave" (*'abd*) and that of "viceregent" (*khalīfah*); these are two aspects and also two relationships which must not be confused, when there is a need to distinguish them. Quite clearly, Islam knows this since it has the notions of intelligence, responsibility and merit, but piety nonetheless seeks to reduce the vicar to the slave, which is possible only in respect of ontological causality, in which precisely the notion of "viceregency" does not intervene.

Concerning the Notion of Philosophy

1. Naturally the most "advanced" of the modernists seek to demolish the very principles of reasoning, but this is simply fantasy *pro domo*, for man is condemned to reason as soon as he uses language; unless he wishes to convey nothing at all. In any case, one cannot assert the impossibility of asserting anything, if words are still to have any meaning.

2. A German author (H. Türck) has proposed the term "misosopher"–"enemy of wisdom"– for those thinkers who undermine the very foundation of truth and intelligence. We will add that misosophy – without mentioning some ancient precedents – begins *grosso modo* with "criticism" and ends with subjectivisms, relativisms, existentialisms, dynamisms, psychologisms and biologisms of every kind. As for the ancient expression "misology", it designates above all the hatred of the fideist for the use of reason.

3. Indeed the uniqueness of God excludes that of the world, in succession as well as in extent; the infinity of God demands the repetition of the world, in two respects: creation cannot be a unique event, any more than it can be reduced to the human world alone.

4. All the same, there is in favour of this argument – which moreover is repeated by Ibn 'Arabī – the attenuating circumstance that it is the only way of reconciling the emanationist truth with the creationist dogma without giving the latter an interpretation too far removed from the "letter"; we say "emanationist truth" in order to emphasize that it is a question of the authentic metaphysical idea and not of some pantheistic or deistic emanationism. Be that as it may, Ibn 'Arabī, when speaking of creation – at the beginning of his *Fuūs alHikam* – cannot prevent himself from speaking in temporal mode: "When the Divine Real willed to see . . . its Essence" *(lammā shā'a 'l-Haqqu subhānahu an yara . . . 'aynahu.*); it is true that in Arabic the past tense has in principle the sense of the eternal present when it is a case of God, but this applies above all to the verb to be (*kāna*) and does not prevent creation from being envisaged as an "act" and not as a "quality".

5. The total Universe can be compared either to a circle or to a cross, the centre in both cases representing the Principle; but whereas in the first image the relationship between the periphery and the centre is discontinuous, this being the dogmatist perspective of theology, analogically speaking, in the second image the same relationship is continuous, this being the perspective of gnosis. The first perspective is valid when phenomena as such are envisaged — something that gnosis would not contest — whereas the second perspective adequately takes account of things and of the Universe.

6. This idea like the terms used to express it belongs to Islam, apart from the Greek anologies noted later; there is nothing surprising in this, since truth is one.

7. This Empedoclean quaternity is found in another form in the cosmology of the Indians of North America, and perhaps also of Mexico and other more southern regions: here it is Space that symbolizes Substance, the universal "Ether", while the cardinal points represent the four principial and existentiating determinations.

8. *Sattva* — analogically speaking — is the "Fire" which rises and illumines; *Tamas* is then the "Earth" which is heavy and obscure. *Rajas* — by reason of its intermediary position — comprises an aspect of lightness and another of heaviness, namely "Air" and "Water", but both envisaged in violent mode: on the one hand it is the unleashing of the winds and on the other that of the waves.

9 Silence in this matter in any case proves nothing against the rightness of a given philosophy; Plato said moreover in one of his letters that his writings did not include all of his teachings. It may be noted that according to Synesius the goal of monks and philosophers is the same, namely the contemplation of God.

10. In our first book, *The Transcendent Unity of Religions*, we adopted the point of view of Ghazali as regards "philosophy": that is to say, bearing in mind the impoverishment of modern philosophers, we simplified the problem, as others have done before us, by making "philosophy" synonymous with "rationalism". According to Ghazali, to practise philosophy is to operate by syllogisms — but he cannot do without them himself — and thus to use logic; the question remains whether one does so *a priori* or *a posteriori*.

11. Even Ananda Coomaraswamy does not hesitate to speak of "Hindu philosophy", which at least has the advantage of making clear the "literary genre", more especially as the reader is deemed to know what the Hindu spirit is in particular and what the traditional spirit is in general. In an analogous manner, when one speaks of the "Hindu religion", one knows perfectly well that it is not a case — and cannot be a case — of a Semitic and Western religion, a religion refractory to every differentiation of perspective; also one speaks traditionally of the Roman, Greek and Egyptian "religions", and the Koran does not hesitate to say to the pagan Arabs: "To you your religion and to me mine", although the religion of the pagans had none of the characteristic features of Judeo-Christian monotheism.

PART II

THE STUDY OF RELIGIONS

Comparative Religion—Methodology

Diversity of Revelation*

SEEING THAT THERE IS BUT ONE TRUTH, must we not conclude that there is but one Revelation, one sole Tradition possible? To this our answer is, first of all, that Truth and Revelation are not absolutely equivalent terms, since Truth is situated beyond forms, whereas Revelation, or the Tradition which derives from it, belongs to the formal order, and that indeed by definition; but to speak of form is to speak of diversity, and so of plurality; the grounds for the existence and nature of form are: expression, limitation, differentiation. What enters into form, thereby enters also into number, hence into repetition and diversity; the formal principle—inspired by the infinity of the Divine Possibility—confers diversity on this repetition. One could conceive, it is true, that there might be only one Revelation or Tradition for this our human world and that diversity should be realised through other worlds, unknown by man or even unknowable by him; but that would imply a failure to understand that what determines the difference among forms of Truth is the difference among human receptacles. For thousands of years already, humanity has been divided into several fundamentally different branches, which constitute so many complete humanities, more or less closed in on themselves; the existence of spiritual receptacles so different and so original

*From *GDW*, Chapter 2.

149

demands differentiated refractions of the one Truth. Let us note that this is not always a question of race, but more often of human groups, very diverse perhaps, but none the less subject to mental conditions which, taken as a whole, make of them sufficiently homogeneous spiritual recipients; though this fact does not prevent some individuals from being able to leave their framework, for the human collectivity never has anything absolute about it. This being so, it can be said that the diverse Revelations do not really contradict one another, since they do not apply to the same receptacle, and since God never addresses the same message to two or more receptacles of divergent character, corresponding analogically, that is, to dimensions which are formally incompatible; contradictions arise only on one and the same level. The apparent antinomies between Traditions are like differences of language or of symbol; contradictions are in human receptacles, not in God; the diversity in the world is a function of its remoteness from the divine Principle, which amounts to saying that the Creator cannot will both that the world should be, and that it should not be the world.

If Revelations more or less exclude one another, this is so of necessity because God, when He speaks, expresses Himself in absolute mode; but this absoluteness relates to the universal content rather than to the form; it applies to the latter only in a relative and symbolical sense, because the form is a symbol of the content and so too of humanity as a whole, to which this content is, precisely, addressed. It cannot be that God should compare the diverse Revelations from outside as might a scholar; He keeps Himself so to speak at the center of each Revelation, as if it were the only one. Revelation speaks an absolute language, because God is absolute, not because the form is; in other words, the absoluteness of the Revelation is absolute in itself, but relative *qua* form.

The language of the sacred Scriptures is divine, but at the same time it is necessarily the language of men; it is made for men and could be divine only in an indirect manner. This incommensurability between God and our means of expression is clear in the Scriptures, where neither our words, nor our logic are adequate to the celestial intention; the language of mortals does not *a priori* envisage things *sub specie aeternitatis*. The uncreated Word shatters created speech while directing it towards the Truth; it manifests thus its transcendence in relation to the limitations of human powers of logic; man must be able to overstep these limits if he wishes to attain the divine meaning of the words, and he oversteps them in metaphysical knowledge, the fruit of pure intellection, and in a certain fashion also in love, when he touches the essences. To wish to reduce divine Truth to the conditionings of earthly truth is to forget that there is no common measure between the finite and the Infinite.

The absoluteness of a Revelation demands its unicity; but on the level of facts such unicity cannot occur to the extent of a fact being produced that is unique of its kind, that is to say constituting on its own what amounts to a whole genus. Reality alone is unique, on whatever level it is envisaged: God, universal Substance, divine Spirit immanent in this Substance; however, there are 'relatively unique' facts, Revelation for example, for since all is relative and since even principles must suffer impairment, at any rate in appearance, and in so far as they enter into contingencies, uniqueness must be able to occur on the plane of facts; if unique facts did not exist in any fashion, diversity would be absolute, which is contradiction pure and simple. The two must both be capable of manifesting themselves, unicity as well as diversity; but the two manifestations are of necessity relative, the one must limit the other. It results from this, on the one hand that diversity could not abolish the unity which is its substance, and on the other that unity or unicity must be contradicted by diversity on its own plane of existence; in other words, in every manifestation of unicity, compensatory diversity must be maintained, and indeed a unique fact occurs only in a part and not in the whole of a cosmos. It could be said that such and such a fact is unique in so far as it represents God for such and such an environment, but not in so far as it exists; this existing however does not abolish the symbolism of the fact, it repeats it outside the framework, within which the unique fact occurred, but on the same plane. Existence, which conveys the divine Word, does not abolish the unicity of such and such a Revelation in its providentially appointed field, but it repeats the manifestation of the Word outside this field; it is thus that diversity, without abolishing the metaphysically necessary manifestation of unicity, none the less contradicts it outside a particular framework, but on the same level, in order thus to show that the uncreated and non-manifested Word alone possesses absolute unicity.

If the objection is raised that at the moment when a Revelation occurs, it is nonetheless unique for the world, and not for a part of the world only, the answer is that diversity does not necessarily occur in simultaneity, it extends also to the temporal succession, and this is clearly the case when it is a question of Revelations. Moreover, a uniqueness of fact must not be confused with a uniqueness of principle; we do not deny the possibility of a fact unique to the world in a certain period, but that of a fact unique in an absolute sense. A fact which appears unique in space, is not so in time, and inversely; but even within each of these conditions of existence, it could never be affirmed that a fact is unique of its kind — for it is the genus or the quality, not the particularity, which is in question — because we can measure neither time nor space, and still less other modes which elude us.

This whole doctrine is clearly illustrated by the following example: the sun is unique in our solar system, but it is not so in space; we can see other suns, since they are situated in space like ours, but we do not see them as suns. The uniqueness of our sun is belied by the multiplicity of the fixed stars, without thereby ceasing to be valid within the system which is ours under Providence; the unicity is then manifested in the part, not in the totality, although this part is an image of the totality and represents it for us; it then 'is', by the divine Will, the totality, but only for us, and only insofar as our mind, whose scope is likewise willed by God, does not go beyond forms; but even in this case, the part 'is' totality so far as its spiritual efficacy is concerned.

•   •   •

We observe the existence, on earth, of diverse races, whose differences are 'valid' since there are no 'false' as opposed to 'true' races; we observe also the existence of multiple languages, and no one thinks of contesting their legitimacy; the same holds good for the sciences and the arts. Now it would be astonishing if this diversity did not occur also on the religious plane, that is to say if the diversity of human receptacles did not involve diversity of the divine contents, from the point of view of form, not of essence. But just as man appears, in the framework of each race, simply as 'man' and not as a 'White' or a 'Yellow', and as each language appears in its own sphere as 'language' and not as such and such a language among others, so each religion is of necessity on its own plane 'religion', without any comparison or relative connotation which, in view of the end to be attained, would be meaningless; to say 'religion' is to say 'unique religion'; explicitly to practise one religion, is implicitly to practise them all.

An idea or an enterprise which comes up against insurmountable obstacles is contrary to the nature of things; the ethnic diversity of humanity and the geographical extent of the earth suffice to make highly unlikely the axiom of one unique religion for all men, and on the contrary highly likely — to say the least — the need for a plurality of religions; in other words, the idea of a single religion does not escape contradiction if one takes account of its claim to absoluteness and universality on the one hand, and the psychological and physical impossibility of their realisation on the other, not to mention the antinomy between such claims and the necessarily relative character of all religious mythology; only pure metaphysic and pure prayer are absolute and therefore universal. As for 'mythology', it is — apart from its intrinsic content of truth and efficacy — indispensable for enabling metaphysical and essential truth to 'gain a footing' in such and such a human collectivity.

The Limitations of Exoterism*

The exoteric point of view is fundamentally the point of view of individual interest considered in its highest sense, that is to say, extended to cover the whole cycle of existence of the individual and not limited solely to terrestrial life. Exoteric truth is limited by definition, by reason of the very limitation of the end it sets itself, without this restriction, however, affecting the esoteric interpretation of which that same truth is susceptible thanks to the universality of its symbolism, or rather, first and foremost, thanks to the twofold nature, inward and outward, of Revelation itself; whence it follows that a dogma is both a limited idea and an unlimited symbol at one and the same time. To give an example, we may say that the dogma of the unicity of the Church of God must exclude a truth such as that of the validity of other orthodox religious forms, because the idea of religious universality is of no particular usefulness for the purpose of salvation and may even exert a prejudicial effect on it, since, in the case of persons not possessing the capacity to rise above an individual standpoint, this idea would almost inevitably result in

*From *TUR*, Chapter 2.

religious indifference and hence in the neglect of those religious duties the accomplishment of which is precisely the principle condition of salvation. On the other hand, this same idea of religious universality — an idea that is more or less indispensable to the way of total and disinterested Truth — is nonetheless included symbolically and meta-physically in the dogmatic or theological definition of the Church or of the Mystical Body of Christ; or again, to use the language of the other two monotheistic religions, Judaism and Islam, we may find in the respective conceptions of the "Chosen People," *Yisraèl*, and "submission," *Al-Islam*, a dogmatic symbol of the idea of universal orthodoxy, the *Sanatana Dharma* of the Hindus.

It goes without saying that the outward limitation of dogma, which is precisely what confers upon it its dogmatic character, is perfectly legitimate, since the individual viewpoint to which this limitation corresponds is a reality at its own level of existence. It is because of this relative reality that the individual viewpoint, except to the extent to which it implies the negation of a higher perspec-tive, that is to say, insofar as it is limited by the mere fact of its nature, can and even must be integrated in one fashion or another in every path possessing a transcendent goal. Regarded from this standpoint, exoterism, or rather form as such, will no longer imply an intellec-tually restricted perspective but will play the part of an accessory spiritual means, without the transcendence of the esoteric doctrine being in any way affected thereby, no limitation being imposed on the latter for reasons of individual expediency. One must not there-fore confuse the function of the exoteric viewpoint as such with the function of exoterism as a spiritual means: the viewpoint in ques-tion is incompatible, in one and the same consciousness, with esoteric knowledge, for the latter dissolves this viewpoint as a preliminary to reabsorbing it into the center from which it came; but the exoteric means do not for that reason cease to be utilizable, and will, in fact, be used in two ways: on the one hand, by intellectual transposition into the esoteric order — in which case they will act as supports of intellectual actualization; and on the other hand, by their regulating action on the individual portion of the being.

The exoteric aspect of a religion is thus a providential disposi-tion that, far from being blameworthy, is necessary in view of the fact that the esoteric way can only concern a minority, especially under the present conditions of terrestrial humanity. What is blame-worthy is not the existence of exoterism, but rather its all-invading autocracy — due primarily perhaps, in the Christian world, to the narrow precision of the Latin mind — which causes many of those who would be qualified for the way of pure Knowledge not only to stop short at the outward aspect of the religion, but even to reject entirely an esoterism that they know only through a veil of prejudice and deformation, unless indeed, not finding anything in exoterism to satisfy their intelligence causes them to stray into false and artificial doctrines in an attempt to find something that exoterism does not offer them, and even takes it upon itself to prohibit.

The exoteric viewpoint is, in fact, doomed to end by negating itself once it is no longer vivified by the presence within it of the esoterism of which it is both the outward radiation and the veil. So it is that religion, according to the measure in which it denies metaphysical and initiatory realities and becomes crystallized in a literalistic dogmatism, inevitably engenders unbelief; the atrophy that overtakes dogmas when they are deprived of their internal dimension recoils upon them from the outside, in the form of heretical and atheistic negations.

•   •   •

The presence of an esoteric nucleus in a civilization that is specifically exoteric in character guarantees to it a normal development and a maximum of stability; this nucleus, however, is not in any sense a part, even an inner part, of the exoterism, but represents, on the contrary, a quasi-independent "dimension" in relation to the latter. Once this dimension or nucleus ceases to exist, which can only happen in quite abnormal, though cosmologically necessary, circumstances, the religious edifice is shaken, or even suffers a partial collapse, and finally becomes reduced to its most external elements, namely, literalism and sentimentality. Moreover, the most tangible criteria of such a decadence are, on the one hand, the failure to recognize, even to the point of denial, metaphysical and initiatory exegesis, that is to say, the mystical sense of the Scriptures — an exegesis that has moreover a close connection with all aspects of the intellectuality of the religious form under consideration; and on the other hand, the rejection of sacred art, that is to say, of the inspired and symbolic forms by means of which that intellectuality is radiated and so communicated in an immediate and unrestricted language to all intelligences. This may not perhaps be quite sufficient to explain why it is that exoterism has indirectly need of esoterism, we do not say in order to enable it to exist, since the mere fact of its existence is not a question any more than the incorruptibility of its means of grace, but simply to enable it to exist in normal conditions. The fact is that the presence of this transcendent dimension at the center of the religious form provides its exoteric side with a life-giving sap, universal and Paracletic in its essence, without which it will be compelled to fall back entirely upon itself and, thus left to its own resources, which are limited by definition, will end by becoming a sort of massive and opaque body the very density of which will inevitably produce fissures, as is shown by the modern history of Christianity. In other words, when exoterism is deprived of the complex and subtle interferences of its transcendent dimension, it finds itself ultimately overwhelmed by the exteriorized consequences of its own limitations, the latter having become, as it were, total.

Now, if one proceeds from the idea that exoterists do not understand esoterism and that they have in fact a right not to understand it or even to consider it nonexistent, one must also recognize their right to condemn certain manifestations of esoterism that seem to encroach on their own territory and cause "offence," to use the Gospel's expression; but how is one to explain the fact that in most, if not all, cases of this nature, the accusers divest themselves of this right by the iniquitous manner in which they proceed? It is certainly not their more or less natural incomprehension, nor the defense of their genuine right, but solely the perfidiousness of the means that they employ that constitutes what amounts to a "sin against the Holy Ghost"; this perfidiousness proves, moreover, that the accusations that they find it necessary to formulate, generally serve only as a pretext for gratifying an instinctive hatred of everything that seems to threaten their superficial equilibrium, which is really only a form of individualism, therefore of ignorance . . .

•   •   •

Exoteric doctrine as such, considered, that is to say, apart from the "spiritual influence" that is capable of acting on souls independently of it, by no means possesses absolute certitude. Theological knowledge cannot by itself shut out the temptations of doubt, even in the case of great mystics; as for the influences of Grace that may intervene in such cases, they are not consubstantial with the intelligence, so that their permanence does not depend on the being who benefits from them. Exoteric ideology being limited to a relative point of view, that of individual salvation — an interested point of view that even influences the conception of Divinity in a restrictive sense — possesses no means of proof or doctrinal credentials proportionate to its own exigencies. Every exoteric doctrine is in fact characterized by a disproportion between its dogmatic demands and its dialectical guarantees: for its demands are absolute as deriving from the Divine Will and therefore also from Divine Knowledge, whereas its guarantees are relative, because they are independent of this Will and based, not on Divine Knowledge, but on a human point of view, that of reason and sentiment. For instance, Brahmins are invited to abandon completely a religion that has lasted for several thousands of years, one that has provided the spiritual support of innumerable generations and has produced flowers of wisdom and holiness down to our times. The arguments that are produced to justify this extraordinary demand are in no wise logically conclusive, nor do they bear any proportion to the magnitude of the demand; the reasons that the Brahmins have for remaining faithful to their spiritual patrimony are therefore infinitely stronger than the reasons by which it is sought to persuade them to cease being what they are. The disproportion, from the Hindu point of view, between the immense reality of the Brahmanic tradition and the insufficiency of the religious counter-arguments is such as to prove quite sufficiently that had God wished to submit the world to one religion only, the arguments put forward on behalf of this religion would not be so feeble, nor those of certain so-called "infidels" so powerful; in other words, if God were on the side of one religious form only, the persuasive power of this form would be such that no man of good faith would be able to resist it. Moreover, the application of the term "infidel" to civilizations that are, with one exception, very much older than Christianity and that have every spiritual and historic right to ignore the latter, provides a further demonstration, by the very illogicality of its naive pretensions, of the perverted nature of the religious claims with regard to other orthodox traditional forms.

An absolute requirement to believe in one particular religion and not in another cannot in fact be justified save by eminently relative means, as, for example, by attempted philosophico-theological, historical, or sentimental proofs; in reality, however, no proofs exist in support of such claims to the unique and exclusive truth, and any attempt so made can only concern the individual dispositions of men, which, being ultimately reducible to a question of credulity, are as relative as can be. Every exoteric perspective claims, by definition, to be the only true and legitimate one. This is because the exoteric point of view, being concerned only with an individual interest, name-ly salvation, has no advantage to gain from knowledge of the truth of other religious forms. Being uninterested as to its own deepest truth, it is even less interested in the truth of other religions, or rather it denies this truth, since the idea of a plurality of religious forms might be prejudicial to the exclusive pursuit of individual salvation, This clearly shows up the relativity of form as such, though the lat-ter is nonetheless an absolute necessity for the salvation of the in-dividual. It might be asked, however, why the guarantees, that is to say, the proofs of veracity or credibility, which religious polemicists do their utmost to produce, do not derive spontaneously from the Divine Will, as is the case with religious demands. Obviously such a question has no meaning unless it relates to truths, for one cannot prove errors; the arguments of religious controversy are, however, in no way related to the intrinsic and positive domain of faith; an idea that has only an extrinsic and negative significance and that, fundamentally, is merely the result of an induction — such, for ex-ample, as the idea of the exclusive truth and legitimacy of a particular religion or, which comes to the same thing, of the falsity and il-legitimacy of all other possible religions — an idea such as this evident-ly cannot be the object of proof, whether this proof be divine or, for still stronger reasons, human. So far as genuine dogmas are con-cerned — that is to say, dogmas that are not derived by induction but are of a strictly intrinsic character — if God has not given theoretical proofs of their truth it is, in the first place, because such proofs are inconceivable and nonexistent on the exoteric plane, and to demand them as unbelievers do would be a pure and simple contradiction; secondly, as we shall see later, if such proofs do in fact exist, it is on quite a different plane, and the Divine Revelation most certainly implies them, without any omission. Moreover, to return to the ex-oteric plane where alone this question is relevant, the Revelation in its essential aspect is sufficiently intelligible to enable it to serve as a vehicle for the action of Grace, and Grace is the only sufficient and fully valid reason for adhering to a religion. However, since this action of Grace only concerns those who do not in fact possess its equivalent under some other revealed form, the dogmas remain without persuasive power — we may say without proofs — for those who do possess this equivalent. Such people are therefore "unconvertible" — leaving aside certain cases of conversion due to the suggestive force of a collective psychism, in which case Grace intervenes only *a posteriori* — for the spiritual influence can have no hold over them, just as one light cannot illuminate another. This is in conformity with the Divine Will, which has distributed the one Truth under different forms or, to express it in another way, between different humanities, each one of which is symbolically the only one. It may be added that if the extrinsic relativity of exoterism is in conformity with the Divine Will, which affirms itself in this way according to the very nature of things, it goes without saying that this relativity cannot be done away with by any human will.

Thus, having shown that no rigorous proof exists to support an exoteric claim to the exclusive possession of the truth, must we not now go further and admit that even the orthodoxy of a religious form cannot be proved? Such a conclusion would be highly artificial and, in any case, completely erroneous, since there is implicit in every religious form an absolute proof of its truth and so of its orthodoxy; what cannot be proved, for want of absolute proof, is not the intrinsic truth, hence the traditional legitimacy, of a form of the universal Revelation, but solely the hypothetical fact that any particular form is the only true and legitimate one, and if this cannot be proved it is for the simple reason that it is untrue.

There are, therefore, irrefutable proofs of the truth of a religion; but these proofs, which are of a purely spiritual order, while being the only possible proofs in support of a revealed truth, entail at the same time a denial of the pretensions to exclusiveness of the form. In other words, he who sets out to prove the truth of one religion either has no proofs, since such proofs do not exist, or else he has the proofs that affirm all religious truth without exception, whatever the form in which it may have clothed itself.

. . .

The exoteric claim to the exclusive possession of a unique truth, or of Truth without epithet, is therefore an error purely and simply; in reality, every expressed truth necessarily assumes a form, that of its expression, and it is metaphysically impossible that any form should possess a unique value to the exclusion of other forms; for a form, by definition, cannot be unique and exclusive, that is to say, it cannot be the only possible expression of what it expresses. Form implies specifications or distinction, and the specific is only conceivable as a modality of a "species," that is to say, of a category that includes a combination of analogous modalities. Again, that which is limited excludes by definition whatever is not comprised within its own limits and must compensate for this exclusion by reaffirmation or repetition of itself outside its own boundaries, which amounts to saying that the existence of other limited things is rigorously implied in the very definition of the limited. To claim that a limitation, for example, a form considered as such, is unique and incomparable of its kind, and that it excludes the existence of other analogous modalities, is to attribute to it the unicity of Existence itself; now, no one can contest the fact that a form is always a limitation or that a religion is of necessity always a form — not, that goes without saying, by virtue of its internal Truth, which is of a universal and supraformal order, but because of its mode of expression, which, as such, cannot but be formal and therefore specific and limited. It can never be said too often that a form is always a modality of a category of formal, and therefore distinctive or multiple, manifestation, and is consequently but one modality among others that are equally possible, their supraformal cause alone being unique. We will also repeat — for this is metaphysically of great importance — that a form, by the very fact that it is limited, necessarily leaves something outside itself, namely, that which its limits exclude; and this something, if it belongs to the same order, is necessarily analogous to the form under consideration, since the distinction between forms must needs be compensated by an indistinction or relative identity that prevents them from being absolutely distinct from each other, for that would entail the absurd idea of a plurality of unicities or Existences, each form representing a sort of divinity without any relationship to other forms.

As we have just seen, the exoteric claim to the exclusive possession of the truth comes up against the axiomatic objection that there is no such thing in existence as a unique fact, for the simple reason that it is strictly impossible that such a fact should exist, unicity alone being unique and no fact being unicity; it is this that is ignored by the ideology of the "believers," which is fundamentally nothing but an intentional and interested confusion between the formal and the universal. The ideas that are affirmed in one religious form (as, for example, the idea of the Word or of the Divine Unity) cannot fail to be affirmed, in one way or another, in all other religious forms; similarly the means of grace or of spiritual realization at the disposal of one priestly order cannot but possess their equivalent elsewhere; and indeed, the more important and indispensable any particular means of grace may be, the more certain it is that it will be found in all orthodox forms in a mode appropriate to the environment in question.

The foregoing can be summed up in the following formula: pure and absolute Truth can only be found beyond all its possible expressions; these expressions, as such, cannot claim the attributes of this Truth; their relative remoteness from it is expressed by their differentiation and multiplicity, by which they are strictly limited...

It was pointed out earlier that in its normal state humanity is composed of several distinct "worlds." Certain people will doubtless object that Christ, when speaking of the "world," never suggested any such delimitation, and furthermore that He made no reference to the existence of an esoterism. To this it may be an answer that neither did He explain to the Jews how they should interpret those of His words that scandalized them. Moreover, an esoterism is addressed precisely to those "that have ears to hear" and who for that reason have no need of the explanations and "proofs" that may be desired by those for whom esoterism is not intended. As for the teaching that Christ may have reserved for His disciples, or some of them, it did not have to be set forth explicitly in the Gospels, since it is contained therein in a synthetic and symbolic form, the only form admitted in sacred Scriptures...

In the final analysis the relationship between exoterism and esoterism is equivalent to the relationship between "form" and "spirit" that is discoverable in all expressions and symbols; this relationship must clearly also exist within esoterism itself, and it may be said that only the spiritual authority places itself at the level of naked and integral Truth. The "spirit," that is to say, the supraformal content of the form, which, for its part, corresponds to the "letter," always displays a tendency to breach its formal limitations, thereby putting itself in apparent contradiction with them. It is for this reason that one may consider every religious readaptation, and therefore every Revelation, as fulfilling the function of an esoterism in relation to the preceding religious form; Christianity, for example, is esoteric relatively to the Judaic form, and Islam relatively to the Judaic and Christian forms, though this is, of course, only valid when regarded from the special point of view that we are here considering and would be quite false if understood literally. Moreover, insofar as Islam is distinguished by its form from the other two monotheistic religions, that is to say, insofar as it is formally limited, these religions also possess an esoteric aspect as between Christianity and Judaism. However, the relationship to which we referred first is a more direct one than the second, since it was Islam that, in the name of the spirit, shattered the forms that preceded it, and Christianity that shattered the Judaic form, and not the other way around. . .

Contours of the Spirit*

Anthropomorphism is inevitable in religions, but it is a two-edged sword. Inevitably it brings with it contradictions which can be only imperfectly neutralized, and that by calling them 'mysteries'.

What people fail to understand is that the divine nature implies manifestation, creation, objectivation, and what is 'other-than-the-Self', and that this projection implies imperfection and therefore evil, since what is 'other-than-God' cannot be perfect, God alone being good.

This goodness God projects into His manifestation in which, by reason of the separative remoteness, imperfection is implicit. God never directly wills evil, but He accepts it inasmuch as it manifests by metaphysical necessity the world, the 'projection' of Himself willed by His infinity. The mystery lies, not in evil, but in infinity. The divine Person never directly wills evil, except through justice for the re-establishing of equilibrium, and the possibility of evil comes, not from the will, from the Person of God, but from the infinity of His nature. The Vedantists express this mystery of infinity by saying that *Maya* is without origin.

The Infinite is what it is; one may understand it or not understand it.[1]

*From *SPHF*, Part Three, Chapter 1.

Metaphysic cannot be taught to everyone but, if it could be, there would be no atheism.

Anthropomorphism cannot avoid attributing, indirectly, absurdities to God; now it is impossible to speak of God to most men without using an anthropomorphic symbolism and this is especially so since God really includes a personal aspect of which the human person is precisely a reflection.

When we say that God wills only what is good, that is only fully true if God is envisaged from a definite, and so a restricted, aspect, and if we specify that evil must be seen as such, that is to say as it appears to creatures. It must be added that, even in the world, good has the upper hand over evil in spite of the sometimes contrary appearances which a particular section of the cosmos may, in a particular existential situation, present.

Mercy is the first word of God; thus it must also be His last word. Mercy is more real than the whole world . . .

According to Christian doctrine Adam sinned and the fall was the first sin.

For Islam Adam could not sin. He was the first of the prophets, and they are beyond sin. On the other hand Adam was a man, and human nature implies limitations and so the possibility of faults; otherwise nothing would distinguish it from God. It is a fault (*dhanb*), that is, a sort of inadvertence or confusion and not an intentional transgression (*ithm, zhulm*), which caused the loss of Eden. The first pair were pardoned for this fault after suffering the consequent sanction on this earth. It is particular to the faults of prophets to carry with them sanctions in this life and not in the other life. David and Solomon had to suffer here below and not in the beyond. According to this way of seeing things it is only through Cain that sin came into the world.

Christianity does not admit the absence of sin in prophets in general and in Adam in particular. Since however it cannot admit that prophets suffered the pains of fire even till the coming of Christ, it placed the prophets in limbo. Now this conception of limbo, 'not-heaven' which is also not hell, has a theological function analogous to the Islamic conception of a fault, a 'demerit' which is not sin.

Christianity, with its 'historical' mode of thinking, attributes to original sin what Islam attributes to earthly nature as such. In a sense the Christian perspective is in 'time' and that of Islam in 'space'.

The Christian perspective is founded on the fall of Adam, which requires as its complement the messianic redemption. The Islamic perspective for its part envisages humanity as it is and, so to speak, in the collective state and, further, it rests on the idea of the 'message', or *risâlah*, of the 'envoys', or *rusul*, that is, on the necessarily multiple manifestation, of the eternal Word. This lineage of messengers, since it has a beginning, requires a final synthesis — the Prophet, who is the 'seal', or *khâtam*, of the prophetic cycle. The 'mythologies' cross one another without inner contradiction and the mutual misinterpretations arise from ignorance of their respective points of departure and from the mistake of attributing to others one's own postulates.

The Hindu perspective starts from Reality, not from man, whose fall becomes one cosmic accident among thousands of others.

The Buddhist, like the Christian, perspective starts from man: it is founded on the distinction between suffering and Deliverance, but it speaks of man only to reduce him to nothingness. This apparent nothingness is the sole Reality, the infinite Plenitude.

Between the Buddhist reaction and that of Shankara there is a certain complementary relationship: Buddhism reacted against a Brahmanism which had become somewhat sophistical and pharisaical; Shankara reacted against the doctrinal simplifications of Buddhism — simplifications not, it is true, erroneous in themselves, but contrary to the traditional metaphysic of India. If Brahmanic spirituality had not become darkened, the peaceful expansion of Buddhism would not have been possible; in the same way, if the Buddhist point of view had not been centered on man and his last ends, Shankara would not have had to reject it in the name of a doctrine centered on the Self.

Herein lies the great difference: the Buddha delivers by eliminating what is human after first defining it as suffering; Shankara delivers by the sole knowledge of what is real, what is pure Subject, pure Self. But the eliminating of everything that is human does not work without metaphysic, and to know the Self does not work without the eliminating of what is human: Buddhism is a spiritual therapy which as such requires a metaphysic, whereas Hinduism is a metaphysic which implies, under the same necessity, a spiritual therapy.

In Shankara's terminology ignorance appears as the superimposition of an 'I' on the 'Self' and then, secondly, and by way of consequence, as desire.

Hinduism sees in the first place ignorance, Buddhism sees first desire.

Buddhism starts, not from the notion of the ego as do the religions of Semitic origin, but from the wholly empirical reality of suffering; its spiritual starting point is, not the container which we are, but the content which we live. The 'I' is an ephemeral collection of sensations: hence the apparent denial of the 'soul' which results from the same outlook as does the apparent negation of 'God'. Buddhism is only logically consistent with itself in denying the continuity of the sensory soul.

Only when the abstract container, which is the ego, becomes in its turn an empirical content does the metaphysical outlook intervene, which excludes *a fortiori* all egocentricity. Buddhism becomes metaphysical when the 'I' is, in the process of extinction, concretely perceived as 'desire' and so also as 'suffering'.

If Buddhism sees the world only as a chaos of irreducible substances (*dharmas*) of which the numberless combinations produce subjective and objective appearances, this is for the same reason which results in Christianity having, strictly speaking, no cosmology: it is because both these two great perspectives regard the world, not in view of its reality or unreality, but solely in connection with the way of coming out of it. For the Buddhist even more than for the Christian to seek to know the nature of the world is a distraction; for the Hindu on the contrary knowledge of the cosmos is an aspect of knowledge of the Absolute, it being nothing other than *Atma* as *Maya*, or the 'Universal Soul' as 'Creative Illusion'. This perspective, which starts from the Absolute, is truly metaphysical, whereas the Buddhist and Christian perspectives, which start from man, are initiatic, that is, centered first of all on spiritual realization, though, since they are intrinsically true, they contain the Hindu metaphysical perspective just as it in turn contains the initiatic.

Shankara's refutation, taken as a whole, shows, not why Buddhism is false, but why Hinduism cannot admit it without nullifying itself.

Christianity starts with the fall of Adam and presupposes that man means the fall; Islam starts with the illumination of Adam after the fall ('And Adam received from his Lord words, and the Lord turned Himself towards him.' Quran, *surat el-baqarah*, 35), that is, with the first revelation; or again, and more directly, it starts with the illumination of Abraham, which is nothing other than the revelation of monotheism.

In other words Christianity is founded on the primordial fall of one single man, Islam on the nature of mankind, or rather of man as such, Buddhism on the suffering of man and Hinduism on the illusion of existence, whether human existence or other. Judaism — the Mosaic Law — sees in man permanent revolt against the Law and so the moral consequence of the fall of Adam rather than the fact of the fall; it might be said that it neutralizes this consequence, whereas Christianity eliminates its cause.

A traditional perspective or 'mythology' is to total and divine Truth as a geometrical form is to space. Each fundamental geometrical form — such as the point, the circle, the cross or the square — is a complete picture of the whole of space, but each of them excludes the others.

In empty space every point is the center and thus the starting point of a symbolically valid measure; but no 'measure' of space is absolutely adequate, else it would be space itself. The various starting points of the traditional mythologies — the creation of the world, the fall of Adam, the revelation to Abraham, the suffering of ignorance — are, so to speak, so many points of reference in metaphysical space.

The Human Margin*

Christ, in rejecting certain rabbinical prescriptions as "human" and not "Divine", shows that according to God's scale of measurement there is a sector which, while being orthodox and traditional, is none the less human in a certain sense; this means that the Divine influence is total only for the Scriptures and for the essential consequences of the Revelation, and that it always leaves a "human margin" where it exerts no more than an indirect action, letting ethnic or cultural factors have the first word. It is to this sector or margin that many of the speculations of exoterism belong. Orthodoxy is on the one hand homogeneous and invisible; on the other hand it admits

*From *IPP*, Chapter 3.

of degrees of absoluteness and relativity. We should not therefore be too scandalized at the anathemas which Dyophysites, Monophysites, Aphthartodocetae, Phartolatrae, Agnoetae, Aktistetae, and Ktistolatrae hurl at one another over the question of knowing whether Christ is of an incorruptible substance or whether there was any human ignorance in the soul of Christ, or whether the body of Christ is uncreated while being at the same time visible, or whether it was created, and so on.

What is surprising in most cases, though not always equally so, is the vehement desire to pin oneself and others down on questions which are not of crucial importance, and the incapacity to allow a certain latitude as regards things which the Revelation did not deem it indispensable to be altogether precise about; yet all that was necessary, both from the mystical and from the dogmatic point of view, was to admit that Christ as living God could not help showing in his humanity supernatural prerogatives which it would be vain to seek to enumerate, but that inasmuch as he was incontestably man, he was bound to have certain limits; this is proved by the incident of the fig tree whose sterility he did not discern from afar. The question of the *filioque* is a clear example of this tendency to pointless preciseness, and to a dogmatization which yields a luxuriant crop of variances and anathemas.

One fact which forces itself upon us in this connection is that fallen or post-edenic man is a kind of fragmentary being; we are therefore bound to open our eyes to the obvious truth that a man's sanctity does not preclude the possibility of his being a poor logician or more sentimental than intellectual and yet feeling, nonetheless, a call to fulfil some teaching function, not of course through pretension, but through "zeal for the house of the Lord". Inspiration by the Holy Ghost cannot mean that the Spirit replaces human intelligence, liberating it from all its natural limitations, for that would be Revelation; inspiration means simply and solely that the Spirit guides man in accordance with the Divine intention and according to the capacities of the human receptacle. If this were not so, there would be no theological elaboration, nor would there be any divergences in orthodoxy, and the first Father of the Church would have written one single theological treatise which would have been exhaustive and definitive; there would never have been a Thomas Aquinas or a Gregory Palamas. There are, moreover, men who are inspired by the Holy Ghost because they are Saints and in proportion to their sanctity, whereas there are others who are Saints because they are inspired by the Holy Ghost and whose sainthood is in proportion to their inspiration.

The most ordinary examples of the human margin which Heaven concedes to traditions are to be found in the scissions within the intrinsically orthodox religions; and this has nothing to do with the question of heterodoxy, for intrinsic heresies lie beyond the margin in question. There is no denying that collective human thought is not good at conceiving the fluctuations between different points of view on the one hand and aspects to which they correspond on the other, or between the different modes of the subjective and the objective; this leads to polarizations and scissions which, however inevitable and providential they may be, are nontheless dangerous imperfections. Heaven allows man to be what he is, but this condescension or patience does not mean complete approval on the part of God . . .

A religion is not limited by what it includes but by what it excludes; this exclusion cannot impair the religion's deepest contents — every religion is intrinsically a totality — but it takes its revenge all the more surely on the intermediary plane which we call the "human margin" and which is the arena of theological speculations and fervours both moral and mystical. It is certainly not pure metaphysics nor is it esoterism which would put us under the obligation of pretending that a flagrant contradiction is not a contradiction; all that wisdom allows us to do — or rather it obliges us — is to recognize that extrinsic contradictions can hide an intrinsic compatibility or identity, which amounts to saying that each of the contradictory theses contains a truth and thereby an aspect of the whole truth and a way of access to this totality.

When one religion places the human Logos of another religion in hell, or when one confession does the same with the Saints of another confession, it cannot really be maintained, on the pretext that the essential truth is one, that there is no flagrant contradiction or that this contradiction is not by definition a serious infirmity on its own plane; the only extenuating circumstance that can be adduced is to say that this plane is not essential for the tradition which is being understood, and this means that its essential spirituality is not necessarily impaired by the error in question, inasmuch as contemplatives are not necessarily preoccupied by the extrinsic anathemas of their religion; and it could be argued also that in these anathemas the persons aimed at become negative symbols, so that there is merely an error of attribution and not of idea, an error of fact, not of principle.

As regards the ordinary theological ostracisms—whether of the West or of the East—there is a profound lesson to be learned from the fables of Aesop and of Bidpai; the story of the fox and the grapes which were too high for him to reach and which he therefore declared to be sour repeats itself in all the sectors of human existence. In the name of wisdom, one vilifies one's neighbour's wisdom to console oneself—or to take one's revenge—for not having found it oneself; eminent theologians have not hesitated to say that the inner voice of Socrates was the devil and to declare diabolic all the wisdom of the Greeks—a pointless extravagance to say the least, seeing that Christianity, even in its Oriental branches, has not been able to renounce the help of that wisdom altogether.

In the closed space of theology there are two openings: gnosis and the liturgy. It is immediately clear that gnosis constitutes such an opening towards the Unlimited; but it is necessary to know that the formal language of the sacred, whether it be the language of sanctuaries or of nature, is, as it were, complementary to, or the prolongation of, metaphysical wisdom. For beauty, like pure truth, is calm and generous; it is disinterested and escapes from passional suffocations and from disputes about words; and one of the reasons for the existence of sacred art—however much of a paradox this might seem—is that it may speak to the intelligence of the sage as also to the imagination of the simple man, satisfying both sensibilities at one and the same time and nourishing them according to their needs. . .

• • •

The human margin is clearly not confined to the plane of doctrine or dialectic, and we have already alluded to this when speaking of rabbinical exaggerations which are stigmatized by Christ. Analogous to these are certain excessive practices, consecrated by tradition or tolerated by it, particularly in Hinduism, where certain opinions or attitudes, without being in general altogether unintelligible, are in any case disproportionate to the point of being actually superstitious. These things are to be explained partly by the con-

stant care that is taken to preserve the tradition in its original purity
— against one set of wrongs other wrongs are then brought to bear —
and partly by a certain totalitarianism which is engrained in human
nature; the care for purity goes clearly together with the awareness
that collectivities need formulations which are precise and therefore
incisive and, practically speaking, inordinate; otherwise the teachings
would be toned down to the point of vanishing altogether.

But in some of these excesses there may be a realism which has
the purpose of exhausting negative possibilities within the framework
of the tradition itself, in much the same way that Holy Scriptures
contain wisely providential imperfections, or that sacred art shows
us monsters side by side with divinities, and devils side by side with
angels, in order to reduce to a minimum, by a kind of preventive
and disciplined anticipation, the inevitable reactions of the powers
of darkness.

• • •

If there are some variations, or even divergences, which are
spiritually and traditionally legitimate or admissible, this is ultimately
because there are three basic human types together with their diverse
combinations: the passional, the sentimental, the intellectual.

Every man is an "I" placed in the "world"; that world has "forms",
and the "I" has "desires". Now the great question is to know how a
man first reacts to or interprets, by his very nature, these four facts
of human existence; for it is this spontaneous conception which is
the mark of his spiritual type.

For the passional man the contingent facts of existence, the world
and the "I" with their contents, men and things, good deeds and sins,
partake, practically speaking, of the absolute; God appears to him
as a sort of abstraction, a background which does not *a priori* impose itself upon him. Passion dominates him and plunges him deeply
into the world of appearances; his path is thus first and foremost a
penitential one, whether he redeems himself by a violent asceticism
or whether he sacrifices himself in some holy war, or in a servitude
dedicated to God. The passional man is incapable of being intellectual in the full sense of the word; the doctrine, as far as he is concerned, is made up of threats and promises, and of the metaphysical
and eschatological minimum required by an intelligence that is over-
run with passion.

For the man of the intellectual type, on the contrary, the contingent facts of existence are immediately apparent as such, they are as it were transparent; before asking "what do I want?", he will ask "what is the world?" and "what am I?", which determines in advance a certain detachment with regard to forms and desires. It is true that he may have attachments in virtue of heavenly realities which shine through their earthly reflections; the most contemplative child can be strongly attached to things which, in the human desert with which destiny may have surrounded him, seem like reminders of a Paradise both lost and immanent. However that may be, it is the Invisible which is the reality for the deeply contemplative man, whereas "life is a dream" (*la vida es sueño*); in him the Platonic sense of beauty takes the place of brute passion.

The third type is the emotional man, who might be called the musical type; he is intermediate, for he may tend towards the passional as well as towards the intellectual type, and he is moreover reflected in each. It is love and hope which constitute in him the dominant and operative element; and he will be inclined to put special stress on devotional manifestation, with a predilection for musical liturgy; his is the spirituality of happiness, but it is also the spirituality of homesickness.

•   •   •

It is a great temptation to attribute the apparent naïvety of the Holy Scriptures to the "human margin", stretched out as it is in the shadow of Divine inspiration; it goes without saying that there is no connection between the two, unless we take this margin in a transposed and altogether different way, as we will do later, but it is clearly no such transposition that modern critics have in view when they bring up as arguments against the sacred books the apparent scientific errors which they contain. The data — said to be naïve — of Genesis for example prove, not that the Bible is wrong, but that man ought not to be told any more; needless to say, no knowledge is harmful in itself, and there are necessarily always men who are capable of spiritually integrating all possible knowledge; but the only kinds of knowledge that the average man can cope with are those which come to him through elementary, universal, age-old and therefore normal experience, as the history of the last centuries clearly proves.

It is a fact not only that scientific man — rough-cast by classical Greece and developed by the modern West — loses religion in proportion to his involvement with physical science but also that the more he is thus involved, the more he closes himself to the infinite dimension of suprasensory knowledge — the very knowledge that gives life a meaning.

It is true that Paradise is described in the Scriptures as being "up above", "in Heaven", because the celestial vault is the only height that can be empirically or sensorially grasped; and for an analogous reason, hell is "down below", "under the earth", in darkness, heaviness, imprisonment. Similarly, for the Asiatics, *samsaric* rebirths — when they are neither celestial nor infernal — take place "on earth", that is, on the only plane that can be empirically grasped; what counts, for Revelation, is the efficacy of the symbolism and not the indefinite knowledge of meaningless facts. It is true that no fact is totally meaningless in itself, otherwise it would be nonexistent, but the innumerable facts which escape man's normal experience and which the scientific viewpoint accumulates in our consciousness and also in our life are only spiritually intelligible for those who have no need of them.

Ancient man was extremely sensitive to the intentions inherent in symbolic expressions, as is proved on the one hand by the efficacy of these expressions throughout the centuries and on the other hand by the fact that ancient man was a perfectly intelligent being, as everything goes to show; when he was told the story of Adam and Eve, he grasped so well what it was all about — the truth of it is in fact dazzlingly clear — that he did not dream of wondering "why" or "how"; for we carry the story of Paradise and the Fall in our soul and even in our flesh. The same applies to all eschatological symbolism: the "eternity" of the hereafter denotes first of all a contrast in relation to what is here below, a dimension of absoluteness as opposed to our world of fleeting and therefore "vain" contingencies, and it is this and nothing else that matters here, and this is the divine intention that lies behind the image. In transmigrationist symbolisms, on the contrary, this "vanity" is extended also to the hereafter, at least in a certain measure and by reason of a profound difference of perspective; and here likewise there is no preoccupation with either "why" or "how", once the penetrating intention of the symbol has been grasped as it were in one's own flesh.

In the man who is marked by the viewpoint of modern science, intuition of the underlying intentions has vanished, and that is not all; modern science, axiomatically closed to the suprasensory dimensions of the Real, has endowed man with a crass ignorance and thereby warped his imagination. The modernist mentality is bent on reducing angels, devils, miracles — in a word all non-material phenomena which are inexplicable in material terms — to the domain of the "subjective" and the "psychological", when there is not the slightest connection between the two, except that the psychic itself is also made — but objectively — of substance which lies beyond matter; a contemporary theologian, speaking of the Ascension, has gone so far as to ask slyly, "where does this cosmic journey end?", which serves to measure out the self-satisfied imbecility of a certain mentality that wants to be "of our time". It would be easy to explain why Christ was "carried up" into the air and what is the meaning of the "cloud" which hid him from sight, and also why it was said that Christ "will come after the same fashion"; every detail corresponds to a precise reality which can easily be understood in the light of the traditional cosmologies; the key lies in the fact that the passage from one cosmic degree to another is heralded in the lower degree by "technically" necessary and symbolically meaningful circumstances which reflect after their fashion the higher state and which follow one another in the order required by the nature of things.

In any case, the deficiency of modern science lies essentially in its neglect of universal causality; it will no doubt be objected that science is not concerned with philosophical causality but with phenomena, which is untrue, for evolutionism in its entirety is nothing other than a hypertrophy, thought out as a means of denying real causes, and this materialistic negation, together with its evolutionist compensation, belongs to philosophy and not to science.

From an altogether different point of view, it must be admitted that the progressives are not entirely wrong in thinking that there is something in religion which no longer works; in fact the individualistic and sentimental argumentation with which traditional piety operates has lost almost all its power to pierce consciences, and the reason for this is not merely that modern man is irreligious but also that the usual religious arguments, through not probing sufficiently to the depths of things and not having had previously any need to do so, are psychologically somewhat outworn and fail to satisfy certain needs of causality. If human societies degenerate on the one hand with the passage of time, they accumulate on the other hand experience by virtue of old age, however intermingled with errors their experience may be; this paradox is something that any pastoral teaching bent on efficacy should take into account, not by drawing new directives from the general error but on the contrary by using arguments of a higher order, intellectual rather than sentimental; as a result, some at least would be saved — a greater number than one might be tempted to suppose — whereas the demagogic scientistic pastoralist saves no one.

* * *

The notion of the "human margin" can be understood in a higher sense which entirely transcends both the psychological and the terrestrial, and in this case we enter into an altogether new dimension which must on no account be confused with the vicissitudes of thought. What we have in mind here is the fact that this notion can also be applied to the Divine order and to the level of the Logos, inasmuch as certain human divergences are providentially prefigured in the Divine Intelligence; from this point of view there is no question of an excess of divergences such as spring in the main from human weakness, but of adaptations willed by the Divine Mercy. Without there being any total difference of principle here, there is an eminent difference of dimension, analogous to the differences between the square and the cube, or between whiteness and light.

When it is said that religious divergences are mere differences of formulation, this may be enough, provisionally, for those who are convinced in advance and in the abstract; but it is not enough when there is any question of entering concretely into details, for then it also needs to be known why these formulations are manifested as so many mutually incompatible affirmations, and not as simple differences of style. It is not enough simply to tell ourselves that the diverse traditional doctrines express "points of view" and therefore different "aspects" of the one Truth; we need to know that it is necessarily so, that it could not possibly be otherwise, because a means of expression cannot possibly be exhaustive, though it provides a key which is perfectly sufficient for the total Truth. The same can be said of physical experience: it is impossible to describe a landscape so validly as to exclude all other descriptions, for no one can see the landscape in all its aspects at the same time, and no single view can prevent the existence and the validity of other equally possible views.

For man, the historical facts on which his religion is based prove its exclusive truth precisely because they are facts and therefore realities; for God, these same facts have merely the value of symbols used as arguments for the purpose of demonstration, and they can therefore be replaced by other facts just as one demonstration or one symbol can be replaced — always provided there is good reason for the change — by another demonstration or another symbol; the essential content is always the same Truth, on the one hand celestial and on the other hand salvational, but approached in diverse ways, since no angle of vision is the only possible one. This is what is indicated by the contradictions contained in the Holy Scriptures and also, no doubt to a lesser degree, by the divergences in the visions of the Saints.

Religious belief is always based on a point of view from which it, and it alone, appears sublime and irrefutable; not to share this opinion seems not only the worst of perversities, for it means standing in opposition to God, but also the worst of absurdities, for it means failing to see that two and two make four. Everyone in the West knows what grounds there are for feeling that Christianity is obviously true, but it is much less known why other religions decline to accept this feeling. It cannot be contested that Christianity, in its immediate and literal expression — not in its necessarily universal and therefore polyvalent essence — addresses itself to sinners, to those who "have need of the physician"; its starting-point is sin, just as that of Buddhism is suffering. In Islam as in Hinduism — the oldest religion and the most recent religion paradoxically come together in certain features — the starting point is man himself; by comparison, the Christian perspective — still according to its literality which, outwardly speaking, is its "crowning proof"— will appear as limited to a single aspect of man and the human state, an aspect which, for all its undoubted reality, is not the only one and not exhaustive. It is not within the scope of prodigies, whatever they may be, to be able to shake this conviction, seeing that it relates to the nature of things and that nothing phenomenal can take precedence over the Truth.

But it is unanimity that matters, not separative diversity, and there would be small profit in talking about the second without thinking of the first. If by "science" we mean a knowledge that is related to real things — whether or not they can be directly ascertained — and not exclusively a knowledge determined by some narrowly limited and philosophically defective programme with a method to match, religion will be the science of the total hierarchy, of equilibrium, and of the rhythms of the cosmic scale; it takes account, at one and the same time, of God's outwardly revealing Manifestation and of His inwardly absorbing Attraction, and it is only religion that does this and that can do it *a priori* and spontaneously.

• • •

There can be no doubt that the Epistles of the New Testament are divinely inspired, but it is inspiration in the second degree; in other words they are not direct Revelation like the words of Jesus and Mary or like the Psalms; it is this difference that accounts for a further difference of degree within this secondary inspiration, according to whether the Spirit is speaking or whether it is allowing man to be almost entirely himself the speaker. Man, in this context, is a saint, but he is not the Holy Ghost. The apostle recognizes this himself when, in giving certain counsels, he specifies that he does so of himself and not under the inspiration of the Paraclete. "And unto the married I command, yet not I, but the Lord . ." Here it is clearly the Spirit that is speaking. "Now concerning virgins I have no commandment of the Lord: yet I give my judgement as one that hath obtained mercy of the Lord to be faithful . ." Here it is man who speaks. And likewise: "To the rest speak I, not the Lord . ." And again: "She is happier if she so abide, after my judgement: and I think also that I have the Spirit of God." (I Cor. VII, 10, 12, 25, 40.)

We are here in the presence of the "human margin", but it comprises yet another degree. Following the apostle who gives his opinion, there come at a later date the Roman theologians who — not without unrealistic idealism and an ultimate confusion of asceticism with morals — deduce from it celibacy for all priests, a measure that is bound up with putting too extrinsic a motive on the sacrament of marriage and with forgetting, in consequence, the spiritual aspects of sexuality. The result of this was, positively, the flowering of a sanctity of a determined type and, negatively, an accumulation of tensions responsible for all sorts of disequilibrium and culminating in the Renaissance and what followed it; not that the morally unrealistic and spiritually narrow pietism of a certain type of Christianity was the only cause of the subsequent naturalistic explosions, but it contributed strongly to this end and is suffering the consequences in its own flesh to this day. . .

NOTES

Contours of Spirit
1. The word 'understanding' has here a quite relative and provisional meaning.

Archaic Religions

The Ancient Worlds in Perspective*

THE WHOLE EXISTENCE of the peoples of antiquity, and of traditional peoples in general, is dominated by two presiding ideas, the idea of Center and the idea of Origin. In the spatial world we live in, every value is related back in one way or another to a sacred Center, to the place where Heaven has touched the earth; in every human world there is a place where God has manifested Himself to spread His grace therein. Similarly for the Origin, the quasi-timeless moment when Heaven was near and when terrestrial things were still half-celestial; but the Origin is also, in the case of civilizations having a historical founder, the time when God spoke, thereby renewing the primordial alliance for the branch of humanity concerned. To conform to tradition is to keep faith with the Origin, and for that very reason it is also to be situated at the Center; it is to dwell in the primordial Purity and in the universal Norm. Everything in the behaviour of ancient and traditional peoples can be explained, direct-ly or indirectly, by reference to these two ideas, which are like land-marks in the measureless and perilous world of forms and of change.

It is a "mythological subjectivity" of this kind that makes under-standable, for example, the imperialism of ancient civilizations, for one cannot simply put everything down to the "law of the jungle",

*From *LAW*, Chapter 1.

178

even though that law may in fact be biologically inevitable and to
that extent legitimate; one must also take into account, and even,
since human beings are concerned, give precedence to, the fact that
each ancient civilization can be said to live on a remembrance of
the lost Paradise, and that it believes itself—in so far as it is the vehicle
of an immemorial tradition or of a Revelation that restores the "lost
word"—to be the most direct branch of the "age of the Gods". It is
therefore in every case "our own people" and no other who perpetuate
primordial humanity from the point of view of both wisdom and
of the virtues; and this outlook, it must be recognized, is neither more
nor less false than the exclusivism of the religions nor, on the purely
natural plane, than each ego's experience that he alone is "I". There
are many peoples who do not call themselves by the name by which
they are known to others; they call themselves simply "the people"
or "men"; other tribes are unbelievers, they have separated themselves
from the main stem. Such a point of view is, broadly speaking, that
of the Roman Empire as well as of the confederation of the Iroquois.

The purpose of the ancient imperialism was to spread an "order",
a condition of equilibrium and stability that conforms to a divine
model, and is in any case reflected in nature, notably in the planetary
world. The Roman emperor, like the monarch of the celestial Middle Kingdom, wields his power thanks to a "mandate from Heaven".
Julius Caesar, holder of this mandate and "divine man" (*divus*), was
conscious of the range of his mission; as far as he was concerned,
nothing had the right to oppose it; Vercingetorix was in his eyes a
sort of heretic. If the non-Roman peoples were regarded as "bar-
barians", it is precisely because they were outside the "order"; they
manifested, from the point of view of the *pax romana*, disequilibrium,
instability, chaos, perpetual menace. In Christianity (*corpus mysticum*)
and Islam (*dar-al-islam*) the theocratic essence of the imperial idea
is clearly apparent; without theocracy there could be no civilization
worthy of the name. So true is this that the Roman emperors, in the
midst of the pagan break-up and from the time of Diocletian, felt
the need to divinize themselves or to allow themselves to be divinized,
while improperly attributing to themselves the title of conquerors
of the Gauls descended from Venus. The modern idea of "civilization" is not without relation, historically speaking, to the traditional
idea of "empire"; but the "order" has become purely human and wholly
profane, as the notion of "progress" proves, since it is the very negation of any celestial origin; "civilization" is in fact but urban refine-

ment in the framework of a worldly and mercantile outlook, and this explains its hostility to virgin nature as well as to religion. According to the criteria of "civilization", the contemplative hermit — who represents human spirituality and at the same time the sanctity of virgin nature — can be no better than a sort of "savage", whereas in reality he is the earthly witness of Heaven.

These considerations lead naturally to a few observations on the complexity of Authority in Western Christianity. The emperor, as opposed to the Pope, incarnates temporal power; but more than that he also presents, by virtue of his pre-Christian but nevertheless celestial origin, an aspect of universality, whereas the Pope is identified by his function with the Christian religion alone. The Muslims in Spain were not persecuted until the clergy had become too powerful in comparison with the temporal power; the temporal power, which appertains to the emperor, represents in this case universality or "realism" and therefore "tolerance", and therefore also in the nature of things a certain element of wisdom. This ambiguity in the imperial function — of which the emperors were conscious to a greater or less extent — partly explains what may be called the traditional disequilibrium of Christianity; and one might well think that the Pope had recognized this ambiguity — or this aspect of superiority paradoxically accompanying an inferiority — by prostrating himself before Charlemagne after his coronation . . .

•   •   •

When one is speaking of ancient traditional peoples it is important not to confuse healthy and integral civilizations with the great paganisms — for the term is justified here — of the Mediterranean and the Near East, of whom Pharaoh and Nebuchadnezzar have become the classic incarnations and conventional images. What strikes one first in these "petrified" traditions of the world of the Bible is a cult of the massive and the gigantic, as well as a cosmolatry often accompanied by sanguinary rites, not forgetting a development to excess of magic and the arts of divination. In civilizations of this kind the supernatural is replaced by magic, and the here and now is divinized while nothing is offered for the hereafter, at least in the exoteric field which in fact overwhelms everything else; a sort of marmorean divinization of the human is combined with a passionate humanization of the Divine; potentates are demigods and the gods preside over all the passions.

A question that might arise here is the following: how was it that these old religions could deviate into paganism and then become extinct, where as a similar destiny seems to be excluded in the case of the great traditions that are alive today in the West and in the East? The answer is that traditions having a prehistoric origin are, symbolically speaking, made for "space" and not for "time"; that is to say, they saw the light in a primordial epoch when time was still but a rhythm in a spatial and static beatitude, and when space or simultaneity still predominated over the experience of duration and change. The historical traditions on the other hand must take the experience of "time" into account and must foresee instability and decadence, since they were born in periods when time had become like a fast-flowing river and ever more devouring, and when the spiritual out look had to be centered on the end of the world. The position of Hinduism is intermediate in the sense that it has the faculty, exceptional in a tradition of the primordial type, of rejuvenation and adaptation; it is thus both prehistoric and historic and realizes in its own way the miracle of a synthesis between the gods of Egypt and the God of Israel.

To return to the Babylonians: the lithoidal character of this type of civilization cannot be explained in terms of a tendency to excess alone; it may also be explained in terms of a sense of the changeless; it is as if they had seen the primordial beatitude evaporating and had therefore wanted to build a fortress, with the result that the spirit was stifled instead of being protected; seen from this angle the marmorean and inhuman side of these paganisms looks like a titanic reaction of space against time. From this point of view the implacability of the stars is paradoxically combined with the passions of bodies; the stellar vault is always present, divine and crushing, while an overflowing life takes the place of a terrestrial divinity. From another point of view, many of the characteristics of the civilizations of antiquity are explained by the fact that in the beginning the celestial Law was of an adamantine severity while at the same time life still retained something of the celestial. Babylon lived falsely on this sort of recollection; but there existed nontheless, at the very heart of the most cruel paganisms, mitigations that can be accounted for by changes in the cyclical atmosphere. The celestial Law becomes less demanding as the end of our cycle approaches; Clemency grows as man becomes weaker. The acquittal by Christ of the adulterous woman carries this meaning—apart from other meanings no less admissible—and so does the intervention of the angel in the sacrifice of Abraham.

Nobody would think of complaining of the mitigation of moral laws; it is, however, proper to consider it, not in isolation, but in its context, because it is the context that reveals its intention, its range and its value. In reality the mitigation of moral laws—to the extent that it is not illusory—can represent an intrinsic superiority only on two conditions, namely, firstly that it confers a concrete advantage on society, and secondly that it be not obtained at the cost of that which gives meaning to life. Respect for the human person must not open the door to a dictatorship of error and baseness, to the crushing of quality by quantity, to general corruption and the loss of cultural values, for if it does so it is, in relation to the ancient tyrannies, but an opposite extreme and not the norm. When humanitarianism is no more than the expression of an over-valuation of the human at the expense of the Divine, or of the crude fact at the expense of the truth, it cannot possibly be counted as a positive acquisition. It is easy to criticize the "fanaticism" of our ancestors when one has lost the very notion of a truth that brings salvation, or to be "tolerant" when one despises religion.

The Religions of the American Indians

The Sacred Pipe of the Red Indians*

...THE TRADITION OF THE INDIANS of North America[1] has, in the Sacred Pipe, an all-important symbol and "means of grace" which represents not only a doctrinal synthesis, both concise and complex, but an instrument of ritual around which centers their whole spiritual and social life. To describe the symbolism of the Sacred Pipe and of its rites is thus, in a certain sense, to expound the sum of Redskin wisdom. It will not be necessary to treat this subject here in all its fullness; to do so would be difficult inasmuch as the Red Indian tradition varies considerably in its forms of expression (as may be seen for example in the myth of the origin of the Calumet and the symbolism of colours), such variations being due to the scattering of the tribes in the course of the centuries; we will therefore dwell rather upon the fundamental aspects of this wisdom which, as such, remain always the same beneath the variety of the ways in which they are expressed. We will use, however, in preference to others, the doctrinal symbols found among the Sioux, well known to our friend J. Epes Brown who recorded, from the lips of the late Black Elk (Hehaka Sapa), the account of the rites of the Sioux nation (*The Sacred Pipe*, University of Oklahoma Press: Norman).

The Indians of North America are one of the races which have

*From *LS*, Chapter 11.

been most studied by ethnographers; yet it cannot be said that everything about them is fully known, for the simple reason that ethnog-
raphy does not embrace all possible forms of knowledge and therefore
cannot possibly be regarded as a general key. There is in fact a sphere
which by definition is beyond the reach of ordinary science ("outward" or "profane" science, that is to say), but which is the very basis
of civilization: this is spirituality—the knowledge of Divine Reality
and of the means of realizing It, in some degree or other, in oneself.
Clearly no one can understand any one form of spirituality without
knowing spirituality in itself;[2] to be able to know the wisdom of a
people we must first of all possess the keys to such wisdom, and these
indispensable keys are to be found, not in any subsidiary branch of
learning, but in intellectuality at its purest and most universal level.
To disallow that which is the very essence of all true wisdom is to
bar ourselves in advance from understanding any wisdom at all;
in other words, the forms of a known wisdom are the necessary keys
to the understanding of any other wisdom as yet unknown.

Some writers feel the need to question whether the idea of God
is really present in the Red Indian religion, because they think they
see in it a sort of "pantheism" or "immanentism"; but this misunder-
standing is simply due to the fact that most of the Indian terms for
the Divinity refer to all its possible aspects, and not merely, as is the
case with the word "God" (at least in practice), to its personal aspect
alone; *Wakan-Tanka* (the "Great Spirit") is God not only as Creator
and Lord but also as Impersonal Essence.

Objections are sometimes raised to this name "Great Spirit" as
a translation of the Sioux word *Wakan-Tanka*, and of similar terms
in other Indian languages; but though *Wakan-Tanka* (and the terms
which cor respond to it) can also be translated by "Great Mystery"
or "Great Mysterious Power" (or even "Great Medicine"), and though
"Great Spirit" is no doubt not absolutely adequate, it none the less
serves quite well enough and in any case conveys the meaning in
question better than any other term; it is true that the word "spirit"
is rather indefinite, but it has for that reason the advantage of implying no restriction, and this is exactly what the "polysynthetic"
term *Wakan* requires. The expression "Great Mystery" which has been
suggested as a translation of *Wakan-Tanka* (or of the analogous terms,
such as *Wakonda* or *Manitu*, in other Indian languages) is no better
than "Great Spirit" at expressing the idea in question: besides, what
matters is not whether the term corresponds exactly to what we mean

by "Spirit", but whether the ideas expressed by the Red Indian term may be translated by "Spirit" or not. . .

It is through the animal species and the phenomena of nature that the Indian contemplates the angelic Essences and the divine Qualities; in this connection we will quote from one of Joseph Epes Brown's letters: "It is often difficult for those who look on the tradition of the Red Man from the outside or through the educated mind, to understand their preoccupation with the animals, and with all things in the Universe. But for these people, as of course for all traditional peoples, every created object is important simply because they know the metaphysical correspondence between this world and the Real World. No object is for them what it appears to be, but it is simply the pale shadow of a Reality. It is for this reason that every created object is *wakan*, holy, and has a power according to the loftiness of the spiritual reality that it reflects; thus many objects possess negative powers as well as those which are positive and good, and every object is treated with respect, for the particular power that it possesses can be transferred into man — of course they know that everything in the Universe has its counterpart in the soul of man. The Indian humbles himself before the whole of creation, especially when lamenting (that is, when he ritually invokes the Great Spirit in solitude), because all visible things were created before him and, being older than he, deserve respect (this priority of created things may also be taken as a symbol of the priority of the Principle); but although the last of created things, man is also the first, since he alone may know the Great Spirit (*Wakan-Tanka*)". . .

The Calumet was "revealed", or "sent down from Heaven"; its coming into this world is supernatural, as the sacred accounts bear witness.

When the Indian performs the rite of the Calumet, he greets the sky, the earth and the four cardinal points, either by offering them the pipe stem forward (in accordance with the ritual of the Sioux, for example) or by blowing the smoke towards the "central fire" which burns in front of him; the order of these gestures may vary, but their static plan remains always the same, since it is the doctrinal figure of which the rite is to be the enactment.

In keeping with certain ritual practices, we will begin our enumeration with the West: this "West Wind" brings with it thunder and rain, that is, Revelation and also Grace; the "North Wind" purifies and gives strength; from the East comes Light, that is, Knowl-

edge, and these, according to the Indian perspective, go together with
Peace; the South is the source of Life and Growth; it is there that
the "Good Red Road" begins, the way of welfare and felicity. The
Universe thus depends on four primordial determinations —"Water",
"Cold", "Light", "Warmth"; the first of these, "Water", is none other
than the positive aspect of darkness which should normally stand
in opposition to light, just as cold is the opposite of warmth; the
positive aspect of darkness is in fact its quality of "shade" which gives
protection against the parching strength of the sun and which produces or favours moisture; the sky must grow dark before it can give
rain, and God manifests Anger (thunder) before granting Grace of
which rain is the natural symbol. As to "Cold" ("the sanctifying and
purifying wind which gives strength"), its positive aspect is purity
so that the "Purity" of the North may be placed in opposition to the
"Warmth" of the South, just as the "Rain" of the West is opposable
to the "Light" from the East; the connection between "Cold" and
"Purity" is evident: inanimate, "cold" things, that is, minerals —
unlike animate, "warm" beings — are not subject to corruption. The
"Light" of the East is, as we have already said, "Knowledge" ; and
"Warmth" is "Life" and therefore "Love", and also "Goodness", "Beauty", "Happiness".

   Before going further, we may reply to an objection which might
arise from the fact that in the Sioux mythology, the "Four Winds"
seem to correspond to a rather secondary function of the Divinity,
which is here divided into four Aspects, each of which contains four
subdivisions. The Sioux doctrine, by a remarkable derogation of the
ordinary mythological hierarchy, gives a pre-eminence to these four
Principles over the other Divinities, showing thereby very clearly
that, in the rite of the Calumet or rather in the perspective which
is attached to it, the cardinal points represent the four essential Divine
Manifestations.

   It would also be possible to speak of the four "cosmic Places"
in the following terms, here again, as always, starting from the "West"
and moving towards the "North": "Moisture", "Cold", "Drought",
"Warmth"; the "West's" negative aspect, the correlative of moisture,
is darkness, and the "East's" positive aspect, the correlative of drought,
is light. The "Thunder-Bird" (*Wakinyan-Tanka*) whose abode is in the
West, and who protects the earth and its vegetation against drought
and death, is said to flash lightning from its eyes and to thunder
with its wings; the analogy with the Revelation on Mount Sinai,

which was accompanied by "thunders and lightnings, and a thick cloud" (*Exodus, XIX 16*), is all the more striking in that this Revelation took place on a rock, while in the Indian mythology it is precisely the "Rock" which is connected with the "Thunder-Bird", as we shall see from what follows. As to the symbolic connection between Revelation and the West, it may seem unusual and even paradoxical, but it should always be remembered that in Indian symbolism the cardinal points are necessarily positive in their meaning: thus, as we have already said, the West is not the opposite of the East, not "Darkness" and "ignorance ", but the positive complement of the East, that is "rain" and "Grace". It might also seem surprising that the Indian tradition should establish a symbolical link between the "West Wind", bearer of thunder and rain, and the "Rock" which is an "angelic" or "semi-divine" personification of a cosmic Aspect of *Wakan-Tanka*; but this connection is admissible, for in the rock are united the same complementary aspects as in the storms: the terrible aspect by reason of its destructive hardness (the rock is, for the Indians, a symbol of destruction — hence his stone weapons of which the connection with thunder-bolts is obvious), and the aspect of Grace through its giving birth to springs which, like the rain, quench the thirst of the land.

We now come to another aspect of the rite of the Calumet, and here may be seen the analogy between the smoke of the sacred tobacco (*kinni kinnik*) and incense: in most religions incense is as it were a "human response" to the Divine Presence and the smoke marks the "spiritual presence" of man in the Face of the supernatural Presence of God, as is affirmed by this Iroquois incantation: "Hail! Hail! Hail! Thou Who hast created all things, hear our voice. We are obeying Thy Commandments. That which Thou hast created returneth back unto Thee. The smoke of the holy plant riseth up unto Thee, whereby it may be seen that our speech is true."

In the rite of the Calumet man represents the state of "individuation" ; space (with its six directions) represents the Universal into which what is individual has — after being transmuted — to be reabsorbed; the smoke disappearing into space, with which it finally identifies itself, marks well this transmutation from the "hard", "opaque" or "formal" into the "dissolved", "transparent" or "formless"; it marks at the same time the unreality of the "ego" and so of the world which, spiritually, is identical with the human microcosm. But this resorption of the smoke into space (which stands for God) transcribes at the same time the Mystery of "Identity" in virtue of which, to use a Sufic expression, "the Sage is not created"; it is only in illusion that man is a "weight" cut out of space and isolated in it: in reality he "is" that space and he must "become what he is", as the Hindu Scriptures say. By absorbing, together with the sacred smoke, the "Perfume of Grace", and by breathing himself out with it towards the unlimited, man spreads himself supernaturally throughout the "Divine Space", so to speak: but at the same time God is represented by the fire which consumes the tobacco. The tobacco itself represents man or, from the macrocosmic point of view, the Universe; space is here "incarnate" in the fire of the Calumet, just as the cardinal points are united, according to another symbolism, in the Central Fire...

We have seen that Nature (landscape, sky, stars, elements, wild ani mals) is a necessary support for the Indian tradition, just as are temples for other religions; all the limitations imposed on Nature by artificial, heavy-weighing, unmoveable works (limitations that are likewise imposed on man through his becoming a slave to these works) are thus sacrileges, even "idolatries", and they carry within them the seeds of death. The result of this outlook is that the destiny of the Red man is tragic in the proper sense of the term: tragedy is a desperate situation caused not by chance but by the fatal clash of two principles. The crushing of the Indian race is tragic because the Red man could only conquer or die; it is the spiritual basis of this alternative which confers on the destiny of the Red race an aspect of grandeur and martyrdom. It was not simply because they were the weaker side that the Red men succumbed; they did so because they represented a spirit which was incompatible with the white man's commercialism. This great drama might be defined as the struggle, not only between a materialistic civilization and another that was chivalrous and spiritual, but also between urban civilization (in the strictly human and evil sense of this term, with all its implications of "artifice" and "servility") and the kingdom of Nature considered as the majestic, pure, unlimited apparel of the Divine Spirit. And it is from this idea of the final victory of Nature (final because it is primordial) that those Indians who have remained faithful to their ancestors draw their inexhaustible patience in the face of the misfortunes of their race; Nature, of which they feel themselves to be embodiments, and which is at the same time their sanctuary, will end by conquering this artificial and sacriligious world, for it is the Garment, the Breath, the very Hand of the Great Spirit.

NOTES

The Sacred Pipe of the Red Indians

1. Or rather, to be more precise: the Indians of the plains and forests which stretch from the Rocky Mountains (and even from farther West) to the Atlantic Ocean.

2. It is quite evident that a knowledge of skull shapes, idioms and folklore customs in no wise qualifies a person for an intellectual penetration of ideas and symbols Certain ethnologists believe themselves justified in calling "vague" every conception they themselves fail to understand.

Hinduism

The Vedanta*

THE VEDANTA APPEARS among explicit doctrines as one of the most direct formulations possible of that which makes the very essence of our spiritual reality. This direct character is compensated by its requirement of renunciation, or, more precisely, of total detachment (*vairagya*).

The Vedantic perspective finds its equivalents in the great religions which regulate humanity, for truth is one. The formulations may, however, be dependent on dogmatic perspectives which restrict their immediate intelligibility or make direct expressions of them difficult of access. In fact, whereas Hinduism is, as it were, made up of autonomous fractions, the monotheistic religions are organisms in which the various parts are formally and solidly linked with the whole.

If Hinduism is organically linked with the Upanishads, it is not, however, reducible to the Shivaite Vedantism of Shankara, although this latter must be considered as the essence of the Vedanta and so of the Hindu tradition.

The Vedanta of Shankara, which is here more particularly being considered, is divine and immemorial in its origin and by no means the creation of Shankara, who was only its great and provi-

*From *SPHF*, Part Four, and *LS*, Chapter 2.

dential enunciator. This Vedanta has in view above all the virtues of the mind, those which converge towards perfect and permanent concentration, whereas moralities — whether Hindu or Monotheist — extend these same principles to the domain of action, which is almost suppressed in the case of the wandering monk (or *sannyâsi*). Thus calm of the spirit (*shama*) becomes, in the case of the Moslem for example, contentment (*ridhâ*) or confidence in God (*tawakkul*), which in fact produces calm of the spirit. The Vedanta retains the alchemical essence of the virtues.

According to the Vedanta the contemplative must become absolutely 'Himself'; according to other perspectives, such as that of the Semitic religions, man must become absolutely 'Other' than himself — or than the 'I'— and from the point of view of pure truth this is exactly the same thing...

The demiurgic tendency is conceived in the Vedanta as an objectivation, and in Sufism it is conceived as an individuation, and so in fact as a subjectivation, God being then, not pure 'Subject' as in the Hindu perspective, but pure 'Object', 'He' (*Hua*), That which no subjective vision limits. This divergence lies only in the form, for it goes without saying that the 'Subject' of the Vedanta is anything but an individual determination and that the Sufic 'Object' is anything but the effect of an 'ignorance'. The 'Self' (*Atma*) is 'He', for it is 'purely objective' in as much as it excludes all individuation and the 'He' (*Hua*) is 'Self' and so 'purely subjective' in the sense that it excludes all objectivation.

The Sufic formula *Lâ ana wa lâ Anta: Hua* (Neither I nor Thou but He) is thus equivalent to the formula of the Upanishads *Tat tvam asi* (That art thou).

When the Vedantist speaks of the 'unicity of the Subject' (or, more precisely, 'non-duality', *advaita*), a Sufi would speak of the 'unicity of Existence' (that is, of 'Reality', *wahdat el-Wujûd*). In Hindu terms the difference is that the Vedantist insists on the aspect of *Chit* ('Consciousness') and the Sufi on the aspect of *Sat* ('Being').

That which in man goes beyond individuality and all separateness is not only pure 'Consciousness' but also pure 'Existence'. Ascesis purifies the existential side of man and thus indirectly purifies the intellectual side.

If man could be limited to 'being' he would be holy; this is what Quietism thought it had understood.

Atma is pure Light and Bliss, pure 'Consciousness', pure 'Subject'. There is nothing unrelated to this Reality; even the 'object' which is least in conformity with It still is It, but It 'objectivized' by *Maya*, the power of illusion consequent on the infinity of the Self.

This is the very definition of universal objectivation. But within it one must distinguish between two fundamental modes, one 'Subjective' and the other 'Objective'. The first mode is this: between the object as such and the pure and infinite Subject there stands in some sort the objectivized Subject, that is to say the cognitive act through which, by analysis and synthesis, the bare object is brought back to the Subject. This function of objectivizing (in relation to the Subject, which then, as it were, projects Itself upon the objective plane), or of subjectivizing (in relation to the object which is integrated in the subjective and so brought back to the divine Subject), is the spirit which knows and discerns, the manifested intelligence, the consciousness, which is relative and so can be an object of knowledge.

The other fundamental mode of objectivation may be described thus: in order to realize the Subject, which is *Sat* (Being), *Chit* (Knowledge or Consciousness) and *Ananda* (Bliss), it is needful to know that objects are superimposed upon the Subject and to concentrate one's spirit on the Subject alone. Between the objective world, which then becomes identified with 'ignorance' (*avidyâ*) and the Subject, the Self (*Atma*), there is interposed an objectivation of the Subject. This objectivation is direct and central; it is revelation, truth, grace and therefore it is also the *avatâra*, the *guru*, the doctrine, the method, the *mantra*.

Thus the sacred formula, the *mantra*, symbolizes and incarnates the Subject by objectivizing It and, by 'covering' the objective world, this dark cavern of ignorance, or rather by 'substituting' itself for it, the *mantra* leads the spirit lost in the labyrinth of objectivation back to the pure Subject.

That is why in the most diverse traditions the *mantra* and its practice, *japa*, are referred to as 'recollection' (the *dhikr* of Sufism): with the aid of the symbol, of the divine name, the spirit which has gone astray and become separated 'recollects' that it is pure 'Consciousness', pure 'Subject ', pure 'Self'.

The 'non-difference' of Real and unreal does not in any way imply either the unreality of the Self or the reality of the world. To start with, the Real is not 'non-different' in function of the unreal; it is the unreal which is 'non-different' in function of the Real, not, that is, inasmuch as it is unreality, but inasmuch as it is a 'lesser Reality', the latter being none the less 'extrinsically unreal' in relation to Absolute Reality . . .

The conceptions of Ramanuja are contained in those of Shankara and are transcended by them. When Shankara sees in the localization and duration of sensory objects a direct and tangible manifestation of their unreality, he does not say, as Ramanuja seems to have believed, that they do not exist *qua* objects, but he says that *qua* existing objects they are unreal. Ramanuja affirms against Shankaracharya truths which the latter never denied on their own level. Ramanuja shows a tendency to make everything 'concrete' in function of the created world, and this indeed agrees both with the Vishnuite point of view and with the spirit of the West which is related to the same perspective.

The antagonism between Shankara and Nagarjuna is of the same order as that which opposes Ramanuja to Shankara, with this difference, however, that, if Shankara rejects the doctrine of Nagarjuna, it is because the form of the latter corresponds — independently of its real content and of the spiritual virtuality it represents — to a more restricted perspective than that of the Vedanta; when, on the other hand, Ramanuja rejects the doctrine of Shankara it is for the opposite reason. The perspective of Shankara goes beyond that of Ramanuja, not merely in respect of its form, but in respect of its very basis.

In order really to understand Nagarjuna, or the Mahayana in general, one must before everything else take account of two facts, first that Buddhism presents itself essentially as a spiritual method and so subordinates everything to the point of view of method and, secondly, that this method is essentially a negative one. From this it follows that, on the one hand, metaphysical reality is considered in function of method, that is as 'state' and not as 'principle', and, on the other hand, it is conceived in negative terms: *Nirvana*, 'Extinction', or *Shunya*, the 'Void'. In Buddhist wisdom affirmation has the same sense and function as 'subjectivism', and hence ignorance, in Hindu wisdom. To describe *Nirvana* or *Shunya* in positive terms would amount — speaking as a Vedantist — to wishing to know the pure Subject, the 'divine Consciousness', *Atma*, on the plane of objectivation itself, hence on the plane of ignorance. . .

It is useless to seek to realize that 'I am *Brahma*' before understanding that 'I am not *Brahma*'; it is useless to seek to realize that '*Brahma* is my true Self' before understanding that '*Brahma* is outside me'; it is useless to seek to realize that 'Brahma is pure Consciousness' before understanding that 'Brahma is the Almighty Creator'.[1]

It is not possible to understand that the enunciation 'I am not Brahma'is false before having understood that it is true. Similarly it is not possible to understand that the enunciation 'Brahma is outside me' is not exact before having understood that it is; and, similarly again, it is not possible to understand that the enunciation 'Brahma is the Almighty Creator' enfolds an error before having understood that it expresses a truth.

If in order to be able to speak of the Self, one must have realized the Self, how can one who has not realized it know that one must have realized it in order to be able to speak of it? If some sage can alone know that it is the Self, because he has himself realized it, how can his disciples know he has realized it and that he alone knows what the Self is?

Under these conditions there would remain only absolute ignorance face to face with absolute knowledge, and there would be no possible contact with the Self, no spiritual realization and no difference between the intelligent man and the fool, or between truth and error. To attribute to knowledge a purely subjective and empirical background which is at the same time absolute amounts to the very negation of intellect, and consequently of intellection. At one stroke this is a denial, first, of intelligence, then, of its illumination by the Self and, finally, of the Prophetic and Lawgiving manifestation of the Self in a given world. And so it means the destruction of tradition, for in these conditions the unicity and permanence of the Veda would remain inexplicable. Every 'being who had attained to realization' would write a new Veda and found a new religion. The *Sanatana Dharma* would be a concept devoid of meaning.

Intellection, inspiration, revelation. These three realities are essential for man and for the human collectivity. They are distinct one from another, but none can be reduced simply to a question of 'realization'. The 'realized' man can have inspirations that are — as to their production — distinct from his state of knowledge, and on the other hand he could not add one syllable to the Veda. Moreover inspirations may depend on a spiritual function, for instance on that of a Pontiff, just as they may also result from a mystical degree. As for revelation, it is quite clear that the most perfect spiritual realization could not bring it about, although such realization is its *sine qua non*.

As for intellection, it is an essential condition of the realization in question, for it alone can give to human initiative its sufficient reason and its efficacy. This fundamental role of pure intelligence is an aspect of 'becoming what one is'.

Revelation is, in a certain sense, the intellection of the collectivity, or rather it takes the place of that. For the collectivity as such it is the only way of knowing, and it is for this reason that the *avatara* through whom the revelation is brought about must, in his normalizing perfection, incarnate the humanity which he both represents and illuminates.

This is why the prayer of a saint is always a prayer of all and for all.

To believe, with certain 'neo-yogists', that 'evolution' will produce a superman 'who will differ from man as much as man differs from the animal or the animal from the vegetable' is a case of not knowing what man is. Here is one more example of a pseudo-wisdom which deems itself vastly superior to 'those separatist religions', but which in point of fact shows itself more ignorant than the most elementary of catechisms. For the most elementary catechism does know what man is: it knows that by his qualities and as an autonomous world he can be opposed to the other kingdoms of nature taken together; it knows that in one particular respect — that of spiritual possibilities, not that of animal nature — the difference between a monkey and a man is infinitely greater than that between a fly and a monkey. For man alone[2] is able to come forth from the world; man alone is able to return to God; and that is the reason why he cannot in any way be surpassed by a new earthly being. Among the beings of this earth man is the central being; this is an absolute position; there cannot be a center more central than the center, if definitions have any meaning.

This neo-yogism, like other similar movements, pretends that it can add an essential value to the wisdom of our ancestors; it believes that the religions are partial truths which it is called upon to stick together, after hundreds or thousands of years of waiting, and to crown with its own naive little system.

It is far better to believe that the earth is a disk supported by a tortoise and flanked by four elephants than to believe, in the name of 'evolution', in the coming of some 'superhuman' monster.

A literal interpretation of cosmological symbols is, if not positively useful, at any rate harmless, whereas the scientific error — such as evolutionism — is neither literally nor symbolically true; the repercussions of its falsity are beyond calculation.

The intellectual poverty of the neo-yogist movements provides an incontestable proof that there is no spirituality without orthodoxy. It is assuredly not by chance that all these movements are as if in league against the intelligence; intelligence is replaced by a thinking that is feeble and vague instead of being logical, and 'dynamic' instead of being contemplative. All these movements are characterized by the detachment they pretend to feel in regard to pure doctrine. They hate its incorruptibility, for in their eyes this purity is 'dogmatism'; they fail to understand that Truth does not deny forms from the outside, but transcends them from within.

Orthodoxy includes and guarantees incalculable values which man could not possibly draw out of himself. . . .

Principle of Distinction in the Social Order*

The first prerequisite, when setting out to evaluate any institution, especially a sacred one, that has for contingent reasons become a subject of controversy, is to disengage the question at issue, by a clear-cut act of discernment, from all the accretions that human passion, whether individual or collective, may have imposed upon it; otherwise it is useless to speak of forming a judgement and still less of a possible reform.

The subject of caste — for it is of this we are about to treat — is one which nowadays is apt to arouse so much feeling that it is not easy to bring people back into a mood of calm consideration, yet this is what we — and they themselves — must try and bring about, for neither a "conservatism" that is merely defensive nor a bias in favour of precipitate innovation is adequate to meet the challenge of a situation as confused as the present one; there must be clear perception, informed understanding of the question before us, which amounts to this: what is "caste" essentially, not only in relation to the Hindu social system but also, in a more general sense, as an ever present factor in any human collectivity? However, before attempting to discuss the operative principle behind the phenonema of social distinction, it would seem prudent to clear the ground somewhat

*From *LS*, *Chapter 7*.

by disposing of certain accessory matters that have, over this question of caste, played a part in fogging the issue for many people both in India itself and elsewhere.

In the first place it should be noted that contemporary criticism of caste (or rather of some of its workings) have been of two distinct kinds, with no less differing motives behind them: on the one hand there have been persons of religious bent whose wish was to eliminate from the social system — whether rightly or wrongly is here beside the point — what they deemed to be abuses that had grown with time; while, on the other, there were the out and out modernists whose outlook had been refashioned, as a result of a Westernised education, on entirely profane lines and who attacked caste in the most vicious tones on grounds of its incompatibility with the latest socio-political theories prevailing in the West, theories they wished to propagate at all costs among their fellow countrymen.

The first-named attitude, even if it has been mistaken in its actual assessment of relevant facts and still oftener in the remedies it proposed, is one with which it is possible to come to terms, on the basis of a more accurate appraisal of those same facts in the light of traditional wisdom; to be desirous of removing such defects as its mishandling by fallible men (unavoidable in this world) may have introduced even into a sacred institution is in no wise incompatible with the traditional spirit, provided it be accompanied by a sense of proportion as well as by a reverent attitude generally; whereas with the second-named attitude no accommodation is possible inasmuch as it represents an expression of insubordination in the face of the sacred such as can properly be described as *"asuric"*.

To pass to another aspect of the question, mention must be made of certain current misinterpretations that originated with the Western ethnologists and which have gained credence with regrettable ease in some Indian circles. We are referring to the attempted explanation of caste simply in terms of an expedient used by ancient fair-skinned conquerors for the purpose of keeping a "coloured" population permanently in subjection. This is a case both of overlooking the fact that a hierarchical arrangement of society analagous to caste has been common to many civilisations besides the Hindu, if in less perfected form, and also of reading into a Vedic setting something akin to that "racist" theory that provided the modern colonialists with a convenient "doctrine" by which to justify their claims.

A similar error consists in turning caste into a synonym for social "classes" in the sense given to this word after the Industrial Revolution in Europe, a sense that subsequently has undergone a still further extension in the Marxist doctrine of the "class war". In point of fact this notion of class, resting as it does, not on qualitative but entirely on economic distinctions, went with the bourgeois mentality of the 19th century and has no place in any traditional conception, whether Indian or European. The peasantry of Europe, for example, wherever they still exist, do not form a "class", being in fact much nearer to a caste in the Indian sense, as is proved by their innate dignity when one compares them with the rootless masses of the big towns, and this also explains the extreme pressure exerted, under the Communist dictatorship, in order to "collectivise" the peasantries; for as long as something like a caste spirit survives among a people, they can never be turned into the physical and mental "proletarians" that the Marxist party overlords have in mind. Incidentally, those who so readily spend their indignation over the shortcomings, sometimes real enough but also often exaggerated, of a hierarchically ordered social system, would do well to turn their attention occasionally to some of the oppressions and cruelties carried out in our time, often on an unheard of scale, in the name of a supposed equality, for this might help to bring them to that more balanced view of things which alone can save the would-be reformer from becoming a tyrant in his turn.

The periodic onset of corruption is in the nature of human frailty, the price of preventing it being an unsleeping vigilance such as belongs only to the Saints. Failing this protection, if abuses develop beyond certain proportions some need for readaptation — a *re-form* in the strict sense of the word — may well arise; the history of all the great religions is full of such examples. It is neither the mere fact of abuses nor even the occasional need for the reform we wish to deny, but the reformist competence of those who, without regard for tradition or any sacred values, are prepared to abandon principles and their applications, good use and misuse both together, untaught by the manifold disasters that elsewhere have flowed from similar attempts.

One last point needs mentioning before we take up the main thread of our subject: it is a point that has generally passed unnoticed during discussion of the causes that have led up to the present crisis; we are thinking of the psychological effects that have accompanied the widespread adoption, among large sections belonging to superior castes, of profane Western tastes and ways of thinking such as might very justly have been treated as "untouchable" because of their obviously anti-spiritual character.

When a man, of set preference, fills his house with the shoddiest products of European manufacture while contemptuously banishing all objects of traditional craftsmanship (thus incidentally helping to starve out of existence one of society's most precious elements) or when that man is heard on all occasions quoting the catchwords of modern sociology, psychology and the like as if they were *śruti* or, if that man be a scholar, when he labels the sacred doctrines of Hinduism (even Vedānta!) as a "philosophy" thus classing them with the purely ratiocinative constructions which in the West go under that name, it becomes difficult for the people around him to take his caste status or his abstentions from contact with this or that any longer at their face value; unconsciously his surviving scruples are bound to convey an impression of mere conventionality, of hypocrisy even. Such an argument is, of course, not strictly valid, for it harbours a certain confusion between things of different orders. It does, however, contain a kind of rough and ready logic that cannot be ignored in times of upheaval like the present, when only the taking up of a firmly intelligent standpoint can save a man from being sucked under by the tide of profaneness flowing on every side.

It should be added, moreover, in respect of the example given above, that here at least is one sphere in which any man is able, within the limits of his own home and family life, to effect something like a traditional restoration by deliberately reversing the process of alienation, at least to a considerable degree. Such initiative, applied without waiting for everybody else to follow suit, has a real spiritual value for the person concerned and it also can have great influence on the views of others, for bad example is not alone in being contagious. This is an aspect of the crisis which should not be overooked by those who would fain strengthen the traditional loyalties which caste, among other things, engenders. . .

• • •

In common with all other sacred institutions the system of castes is founded on the very nature of things or, to be more exact, on one aspect of that nature, and thus on a reality which in certain circumstances cannot but manifest itself; this statement is equally valid as regards the opposite aspect, that of the equality of men before God. In short, in order to justify the system of castes it is enough to put the following question: does diversity of qualifications and of heredity exist? If it does, then the system of castes is both possible and legitimate. In the case of an absence of castes, where this is traditionally imposed, the sole question is: are men equal, not just from the point of view of their animality which is not here in question, but from the point of view of their final end? Since every man has an immortal soul this is certain; therefore in a given traditional society this consideration can take precedence over that of diversity of qualifications. The immortality of the soul is the postulate of religious "egalitarianism", just as the quasi-divine character of the intellect — and hence of the intellectual elite — is the postulate of the caste system.

One could not imagine any greater divergence than that between the hierarchical system of Hinduism and the levelling outlook of Islam, yet there is here only a difference of emphasis, for truth is one: indeed, if Hinduism considers first of all in human nature those fundamental tendencies which divide men into so many hierarchical categories, it nevertheless realises equality in the super-caste of wandering monks, the *sannyāsis*, in which social origin no longer plays any part. The case of the Christian clergy is similar in the sense that among them titles of nobility disappear: a peasant could not become a prince, but he could become Pope and crown an Emperor. Inversely, some form of hierarchy appears even in the most "egalitarian" religions: in Islam, where every man is his own priest, the Sherifs, descendants of the Prophet, form a religious nobility and are thus superimposed on the rest of society, though without assuming in it any exclusive function. In the Christian world a citizen of note might be enobled, whereas in the Hindu system such a thing is altogether excluded, because there the essential object of the higher castes is the "maintenance" of a primordial perfection; it is the "descending" sense given to the origin of castes that explains why caste can be lost but not acquired. [1] Indeed this perspective of "hereditary maintenance" is the very key to the caste system: it also explains the exclusiveness of admission to Hindu temples — the temples are not pulpits for preaching — and in a more general way the preponderant part played by rules of purity. The "obsession" of Hinduism is not the conversion of "unbelievers" but on the contrary the maintaining of a primordial purity which is as much intellectual as moral and ritual.

What are the fundamental tendencies of human nature to which castes are more or less directly related? They could be defined as so many different ways of envisaging an empirical "reality": in other words the fundamental tendency in a man is connected with his "feeling" or "consciousness" of what is "real". For the *brāhmaṇa* — the purely intellectual, contemplative and "sacerdotal" type — it is the changeless, the transcendent which is "real"; in his innermost heart he does not "believe" either in "life" or in "earth"; something in him remains foreign to change and to matter; broadly speaking such is his inner disposition — what might be called his "imaginative life"— whatever may be the personal weaknesses by which it is obscured. The *kṣattriya* — the "knightly" type — has a keen intelligence, but it is turned towards action and analysis rather than towards contemplation and synthesis; his strength lies especially in his character; he makes up for the aggressiveness of his energy by his generosity and for his passionate nature by his nobility, self-control and greatness of soul. For this human type it is action that is "real", for it is by action that things are determined, modified and ordered; without action there is neither virtue nor honour nor glory. In other words the *kṣattriya* believes in the efficacy of action rather than in the fatedness of a given situation: he despises the slavery of facts and thinks only of determining their order, of clarifying a chaos, of cutting Gordion knots. Thus, just as for the *brāhmaṇa* all is changeful and unreal except the Eternal and whatever is attached to It — truth, knowledge, contemplation, ritual, the Way — so for the *kṣattriya* all is uncertain and peripheral except the constants of his *dharma* — action, honour, virtue, glory, nobility — on which for him all other values depend. This perspective can be transposed on to the religious plane without any essential change in its psychological quality.

For the *vaiśya* — the merchant, the peasant, the artisan, the man whose activities are directly bound up with material values not merely *de facto* and accidently but by virtue of his inner nature — it is riches, security, property and "well-being" that are "real"; in his instinctive life other values are secondary and in his innermost heart he does not "believe" in them; his imagination expands on the plane of economic stability, of the material perfection of work and the return it yields, and when this is transposed on to the religious plane it becomes exclusively a perspective of accumulating merit with a view to posthumous security. Externally this mentality is analogous to that of the *brāhmana* by reason of its static and pacific character; but it is remote from the mentality both of the *brāhmaṇa* and the *kṣattriya* because of a certain pettiness of the intelligence and will;[2] the *vaiśya* is clever and possesses common sense, but he lacks specifically intellectual qualities and also chivalrous virtues, "idealism" in the higher sense of the term. Here it must be repeated that we are speaking, not of "classes", but of "castes", or, to be more precise, of "natural castes", since institutions as such, though they may reproduce nature, are never wholly free from the imperfections and vicissitudes of all manifestations. One does not belong to some particular caste because one follows a certain profession and is the issue of certain parents, but, at any rate under normal conditions, one follows a particular profession because one belongs to a certain caste and the latter is largely — though not absolutely — guaranteed by heredity; at least this guarantee is sufficient to render the Hindu system possible. The system has never been able to exclude exceptions, which as such confirm the rule; the fact that the exceptions have attained the largest possible number in our days of over-population and of the "realisation of impossibilities" could not in any case vitiate the principle of hereditary hierarchy. . .

The principle of caste is reflected, not only in the ages of man, but also in a different way in the sexes: woman is opposable to man, in a sense, as the chivalrous type is opposable to the sacerdotal, or again, in another relationship, as the "practical" type is opposable to the "idealist", one might say. But, just as the individual is not absolutely bound by caste, neither can he be bound in an absolute way by sex: the metaphysical, cosmological, psychological and physiological subordination of woman is apparent enough, but woman is none the less the equal of man from the point of view of human condition and so also of immortality; she is his equal in respect of sanctity, but not in respect of spiritual functions: no man can be more holy than the Blessed Virgin, and yet, whereas any priest can celebrate the Mass and preach in public, she could not do so.[3] From another angle woman assumes, face to face with man, an aspect of Divinity: her nobility, compounded of beauty and of virtue, is for man like a revelation of his own infinite essence and so of what he "would wish to be" because that is what he "is".

Finally we want to touch on a certain connection between the actualisation of castes and sedentary conditions of existence: it is an undeniable fact that the lower types are less frequently found among warrior nomads than among sedentary peoples; an adventurous and heroic nomadism results in the qualitative differences becoming as it were submerged in a generalised nobility; the materialist and servile type is kept in abeyance and in compensation the priestly type does not become completely distinct from the chivalric type. According to the conceptions of these peoples human quality— "nobility"— is maintained by a fighting mode of life: no virtue, they say, without virile and therefore perilous activity; man becomes vile when he ceases to look suffering and death in the face; it is impassiveness which makes a man; it is events, or, if you will, adventure which makes life. This perspective explains the attachment of these peoples — Bedouins, Tuaregs, Red Indians and ancient Mongols — to their ancestral nomadic or semi-nomadic condition and the contempt they feel for sedentary folk and especially for town-dwellers; the deepest evils from which humanity is suffering do in fact come out of the great urban agglomerations and not out of virgin nature. . . [4]

Caste in its spiritual sense is the "law" or *dharma* governing a particular category of men in accord with their qualifications. It is in this sense, and only in this sense, that the *Bhagavad-Gītā* says: "Better for each one is his own law of action, even if it be imperfect, than the law of another, even well applied. It is better to perish in one's own law; it is perilous to follow the law of another" (III, 35).[5] And similarly the *Mānava-Dharma Śāstra* says: "It is better to carry out one's own proper functions in a defective manner than to fulfil perfectly those of another; for he who lives accomplishing the duties of another caste forthwith loses his own" (X, 97).

NOTES

The Vedanta

1. 'No man cometh unto the Father but by me.' The following *hadith* bears the same meaning: 'He who desires to meet Allah must first meet His Prophet.'

2. Animals and other peripheral beings have, as such, no possibility of coming forth from the world. They must first enter a 'central' state.

Principle of Distinction in the Social Order

1   The late Pandit Hari Prasad Śastri did, however, assure us that there could be exceptions to this rule quite apart from the possible reintegration of a family through successive marriages. He quoted the case of King Viśvamitra In that case one should no doubt take into account the quality of the cyclic period and the special conditions created by the proximity of an *avatāra* of Viṣṇu

2. In the nineteenth century the bourgeois laity in Europe had for reasons of equilibrium to realise in their turn the qualities of the classes that had been eliminated; we are not referring here to the fact of belonging to the bourgeois class, which is in itself unimportant, but to the bourgeois spirit, which is quite a different thing. The preoccupation with science in the nineteenth and twentieth centuries, proves, not indeed that "humanity" has "progressed", but that the "intellectuality" of men of mercantile type is hardly able to rise above the level of mere facts. The current illusion that man can rejoin metaphysical realities by dint of scientific discoveries is quite characteristic of this heaviness of spirit and only goes to prove that, as Guénon wrote, "the rise of the *vaiśyas* spells intellectual night". Moreover "civilisation", without any qualifying epithet and taken as *the* civilisation, is a typically *vaiśya* concept, and this explains on the one hand the hatred now often felt for anything supposed to partake of "fanaticism" and on the other hand an element of pretentious kindliness which is a deadly feature of the systematic oppression dealt out by the civilisation in question.

3. In the framework of a traditional Christian world.

4. A certain easing of the Hindu system among the Balinese can be explained by facts qualitatively analogous to nomadism, namely their insular isolation and the necessarily restricted number of the inhabitants; also the Balinese show a proud and independent character which makes them akin to the nomads.

5. The *Bhagavad-Gītā* cannot mean that every individual must, when he meets a traditional teaching, follow his personal opinions and tastes, otherwise Hinduism, which is a tradition, would long ago have ceased to exist.

The Chinese Religions*

CONFUCIANISM DIVIDES MEN into rulers and ruled. From the former it requires a sense of duty and from the latter filial piety. Here we see that the social Law is in no wise detached from the spiritual meaning of the whole tradition; inevitably it has concomitant spiritual elements which concern man as such, that is, man envisaged independently from society. Indeed every man rules or determines something which is placed in some way in dependence on him, even if it is only his own soul, made up of images and desires; and, again, every man is governed or determined by something which in some way surpasses him, even if it is only his own intellect. Thus each man bears in himself the double obligation of duty in relation to the inferior and of piety in relation to the superior, and this double principle is capable of incalculable applications: it includes even inanimate nature in the sense that each thing can have in relation to us, according to the circumstances, the function of being either a celestial principle or a terrestrial substance.

Chinese wisdom foresees an application that is first social and secondly personal of the universal pair 'Heaven-Earth' (*Tien-Ti*) and thus a conformity with the 'Ineffable' (*Wu-Ming*) from which this pair proceeds, the *Tao*. The point of junction between Confucianism and Taoism is in the virtues. The former envisages their social and human value and the second their intrinsic and spiritual quality. Man is the place where Earth and Heaven meet.

Egoism must be extinguished between devotion and duty.

*From *SPHF*, Part Three, Chapter 1.

205

Buddhism

Originality of Buddhism*

WHOEVER SETS OUT to define a spiritual phenomenon situated in the almost heavenly era of the great Revelations has to beware of assessing it according to the impoverished categories of later ages or, still worse, those belonging to the inbuilt profanity of the 'free-thinking' world. Buddhism, which many have tried to reduce to the level of a commonplace philosophical empiricism, is anything but a purely human ideology; were it such, its quality as a way of enlightenment or salvation would be unintelligible. To deny the celestial character of Sākyamuni and his Message is after all tantamount to saying that there can be effects without a cause, and this remark moreover holds good for all inspired Messengers and all sacred institutions. The Buddha, despite certain appearances, was not a 'reformer' in the current sense of the word — which implies heterodoxy — and could not be such; all that weighs with a reformer in that sense is to bring back the religion to which he adheres, or thinks he adheres, to its 'primitive purity'; this task he tries to accomplish by rejecting essential elements rather like a man who, wishing to refer a tree back to its root, would saw off all its branches and even its trunk. The would be reformer, whose idea of 'purity' is entirely external and in no wise transcendent, fails to perceive that the branches normally and legitimately

*From *ITB*, Chapter 1.

206

contain the root and even the seed and that the sap is the same throughout the tree down to its smallest shoot and that every organism has its laws of growth, determined not only by its own particular nature but also by its medium of expansion; such a person forgets that time as such is irreversible and that the qualitative differences of temporal cycles necessitate readaptions, for any given tradition, in a more explicit or more differentiated sense just as happens with the tree, analogically speaking, the branches of which are more complex than the trunk. The Buddha, direct manifestation of the Spirit, had both the power and the right to place himself outside the tradition in which he was born; he had no call to concern himself with the purity of Hinduism nor did he think of reforming the latter; the pre-existing frameworks, which were moreover and humanly speaking decadent in his time, represented for him no more than formalism as such; they stood for a pharisaism whereof 'the letter' kills.

Be it noted, however, that here the reference is to formalism and pharisaism, not to form and orthodoxy; it is a question of abuses and not of the things themselves that have been abused; this must be remembered even while saying that the Buddhist perspective, as such, had no need to make this particular distinction in regard to Hinduism. In any case, orthodox reformers have also existed, such as Tsongkhapa in Tibetan Buddhism and, in the West, SS. John of the Cross and Teresa of Avila, not forgetting Savonarola; but in their case there never had been a question of invalidating any principle of the tradition, indeed quite the contrary.

The first question to be put concerning any doctrine or tradition is that of its intrinsic orthodoxy; that is to say one must know whether that tradition is consonant, not necessarily with such another traditionally orthodox perspective, but simply with Truth. As far as Buddhism is concerned, we will not ask ourselves therefore whether it agrees with the letter of the *Veda* or if its 'non-theism' (not 'atheism') is reconcilable, in its expression, with the Semitic theism or any other, but only whether Buddhism is true in itself; which means, if the answer be affirmative, that it will agree with the Vedic spirit and that its non-theism will express the truth, or a sufficient aspect of the truth, whereof theism provides another possible expression, opportune in the world governed by it. In point of fact, a particular spiritual perspective is commonly discoverable somewhere within the framework of a tradition that seems to exclude it; thus, theism reappears in a certain sense in the framework of Buddhism despite its characteristic non-theism, both in a diffused form as the countless Buddhas and Bodhisattvas manifested in, or revealed to, the worlds and to whom worship is due, and also, to cite one particularly striking example, in the cult of the Buddha Amitābha, infinite Light, associated with the Pure Land schools of China and Japan. Conversely, the Buddhist 'non-theism' reappears in its turn with the conception of the 'impersonal Essence' of the Divinity pertaining to all the monotheistic esotericisms: from the above examples it will be seen that religious frameworks have nothing exclusive about them; rather always it is a question of emphasis or spiritual economy.

The not infrequent employment, by the Buddha, of terms proper to the Brahmanical theism clearly shows that the Buddhist perspective has nothing in common with atheism properly so called; it is a perversity of some Western propagandists on behalf of Buddhism as also of some Orientals wishful of appearing in line with modern 'humanism' to have confused the issue in this respect. 'Extinction' (*Nirvāna*) or 'the Void' is but 'God' subjectivised, as a state of realization; 'God' is but the Void objectively regarded, as Principle. If Buddhists, except when taking up the standpoint of Mercy, abstain from objectivising the Void or the Self, this is because they have nothing to ask of it, given their own anti-individualist point of view; if nevertheless there are certain 'dimensions' where things appear otherwise, this is because the 'objective aspect' of Reality is too much in the nature of things to pass unperceived and without being turned to account on occasion.

All that has just been said means implicitly that Buddhism, inasmuch as it is a characteristic perspective and independently of its various modes, answers to a necessity: it could not but come to be, given that a nonanthropomorphic, impersonal and 'static' consideration of the Infinite is in itself a possibility; such a perspective had therefore to be manifested at a cyclic moment and in human surroundings that rendered it opportune, for whatever the receptacle is, there the content imposes itself. People have sometimes remarked on the fact that the Buddhist perspective is not distinguishable in any very essential way from such and such doctrines found in Hinduism; this is true up to a point, being all the more likely inasmuch as Hinduism is characterized by an uncommon wealth of doctrines and methods; but it would be wrong to infer from this that Buddhism does not represent as spontaneous and autonomous a reality as do the other great Revelations; what may be said is that Buddhism is some thing like a Hinduism universalized, just as Christianity and Islam, each in its own way, are a Judaism rendered universal and therefore detached from its particular ethnic environment and thus made accessible to men of all manner of racial origins. Buddhism in a way extracted from Hinduism its yogic sap, not through a borrowing, be it understood, but through a divinely inspired remanifestation, and it imparted to this substance an expression that was simplified in certain respects, but at the same time fresh and powerfully original.

This is proved, among other things, by Buddhist art, of which the prototypes may doubtless be discerned in the yogic postures common to Indian sacred iconography or again in the dance which, for its part, is like an intermediary between *yoga* and the temple statuary: Buddhist art — and here one is thinking chiefly of images of the Buddha — seems to have extracted from Hindu art, not such and such a particular symbolism, but its contemplative essence. The plastic arts of India evolve in a last analysis round the human body in its postures of recollection; in Buddhism the image of this body and this visage has become a symbol of extraordinary fecundity and a means of grace of unsurpassable power and nobility, to which the genius of the yellow race has added, on the basis of the Indian prototypes, something not far short of a fresh dimension; fresh, not from the point of view of the symbolism as such, but from that of expression. It is through this artistic crystallization that what Buddhism comprises of absoluteness and therefore also of universality is most vividly displayed to an outside observer. The sacred image transmits a message of serenity: the Buddhist Dharma is not a passionate struggle against passion, it dissolves passion from within, through contemplation. The lotus, supporting the Buddha, is the nature of things, the calm and pure fatality of existence, of its illusion and finally of its disappearance; but it is also the luminous centre of *Māyā* whence arises Nirvāna become man.

From the doctrinal point of view the great originality of Buddhism is to consider the Divine, not in relation to its cosmic manifestations as ontological cause and anthropomorphic personification, but rather in relation to its acosmic and anonymous character, as supraexistential 'state' which then will appear as Voidness (*shūnyatā*) from the point of view of the false plenitude of existence (*samsāra*); the latter is the realm of 'thirst' (*trishnā*). By this view of things stress is laid on the unconditional character of the divine Goodness, or rather of the 'nirvānic Grace' projected, as this is, through a myriad of Buddhas and Bodhisattvas into the round of trans migration and even down to the hells; faith in the infinite mercy of the Buddha, himself an illusory appearance of the beatific Void, already constitutes a grace or a gift. Salvation consists in coming out of the infernal circle of 'concordant actions and reactions'; seen from this standpoint, morality appears like a provisional and fragmentary thing and even as inoperative in the sight of the Absolute, if only because it is itself involved in the indefinite chain of acts and the existential fruit of acts. Forms such as Zen and the Pure Land doctrine of Amitābha's 'original vow' are particularly effective in allowing one to sense the subtle relationships, made up of imponderables and paradoxes, at once separating and connecting the world of Transmigration and Extinction, Samsāra and Nirvāna.

Mystery of the Bodhisattva*

There is a side of Buddhism which makes it akin to the Semitic religions — paradoxically so, considering its non-theistic character — in the sense that its starting point is related to a human point of view rather than to the metaphysical nature of things. When, for instance, it is said that Existence is but suffering and that the Absolute is the cessation of suffering, and further that human perfection lies in 'compassion for all living beings', this does indeed open up a perspective conformable to our human situation and to our ultimate interests, but it does not straightway give the most direct possible definition of 'that which is', if one can thus describe a thought which seeks to embrace at the same time both the manifested Universe and that which surpasses it.

Such an observation is not, however, of a kind that logically need embarrass Buddhists, and this for two reasons; firstly, because they are in no danger of overlooking the fact that the doctrines of the Buddhas are only 'celestial mirages' intended to catch, as in a golden net, the greatest possible number of creatures plunged in ignorance, suf-

*From *ITB*, Chapter 15.

fering and transmigration, and that it is therefore the benefit of creatures and not the suchness of the Universe which determines the contingent form which the Buddhist Message must take; and secondly, because Buddhism, within the framework of its own wisdom, reaches beyond 'the letter' of a formal 'mythology' and ultimately transcends all possible human powers of expression, thus realizing a degree of contemplative disinterestedness not surpassed by the Vedānta, Taoism or any other purely metaphysical doctrine.

Hence the question that Sākyamuni might have asked himself— if he had had to ask one—was, 'Which is the most effective way of conveying the saving Truth to men in these latter times?' and not 'Which is the most adequate (or least inadequate) formulation of the metaphysical nature of things?'

Neither the Vedānta nor Neo-Platonism include the possibility of addressing their teaching effectively to all men and thus of serving as the vehicle of an entire tradition, nor indeed is this their purpose. But Buddhism of necessity has to envisage this possibility, and it cannot therefore fail to offer itself first of all as an *upāya*, a 'provisional means', for pursuing an objective which is above all charitable, in the widest and most complete sense of that word. Buddhists, it must be stressed, are all the better equipped for the recognition of this need since they are very far from claiming that the truth of Nirvāna can be closed in a definitive sense within the mould of any dialectic whatsoever. Nevertheless there results from this general situation, and apart from any fluctuations of terminology, a certain difficulty in speaking of Knowledge in such a way as to satisfy at one and the same time the demands of metaphysical truth and of that side of Buddhism which is concerned with the human will and human emotions.

• • •

Primitive Buddhism distinguishes extrinsically between a *Samyaksam-Buddha* and a *Pratyeka-Buddha*; the former corresponds to what Hindus would call a major Avatara, having by definition the function of 'founder of a religion', and the latter to a *Jīvan-Mukta*—a man 'delivered in his lifetime'—who neither has the quality of a major or plenary Avatara nor consequently the function attaching to such a one; and not having had a Buddha as master, neither does he have disciples. After this comes the *Srāvaka* or 'hearer' who is a disciple, or the disciple of a disciple of the Buddha; like the Pratyeka-Buddha, he is an Arahant or perfected saint, but is such thanks to the direct influence of the Master, if one may so put it. Finally there is the *Bodhisattva* who, in principle, is a saint destined for Buddhahood.

Now, when it is stated, as in the Mahāyāna writings, that the condition of a Pratyeka-Buddha is inferior to that of a Bodhisattva because the realization of the former is 'self-centered' and lacks compassion for creatures, it seems to be forgotten — or at least this logical objection obtrudes itself *a priori* — that Nirvāna implies by definition the abolition of all egoity and the realization of total charity. This is an objection which the Mahāyāna itself raises in its own way and in its sapiential dimension; but this does not imply any contradiction if it be remembered that two truths here are recognized, the one being relative and provisional and the other absolute and final and that the doctrinal form of the Mahāyāna is essentially apophatic and antinomic. In other words, when it is said that the Mahāyāna is 'great' (*mahā*) for the sole reason that its aim is the salvation of 'all living beings' thanks to the sacrificial ideal of the Bodhisattva — and not the salvation of a single individual as is the case with the Hīna yāna or 'lesser vehicle'— then it is proper to object, in accordance with the higher teaching of the Mahāyāna itself, that the alleged reason carries no weight with respect to Nirvana or, what amounts to the same thing, with respect to Knowledge; not to mention the fact that this world of ignorance and suffering, Samsāra, the Round of Existence, is metaphysically necessary and has not to be considered solely from a volitional and emotional angle.

However that may be, the Mahāyāna under its sapiential aspect aims at maintaining its solidarity with the heroic ideal of the Bodhisattva, while nonetheless referring back that ideal to a strictly metaphysical perspective. It first declares that Compassion is a dimension of Knowledge, then it adds that one's 'neighbour' is non-real and that charity must therefore be exercised 'quietly when the occasion arises' and without slipping into the dualist and objectivist illusion, for, as it says, there is no one whom our charity could concern, nor is there a charity which could be 'ours'. In this way, though taking the compassionate interpretation of the Bodhisattva's function for its starting point, the gnosis of the Mahāyāna follows a roundabout route to rejoin the most rigorous, and therefore the most objective and disinterested metaphysical positions.

To speak as precisely as possible, Buddhism can be said to present itself under the following fundamental aspects: first of all, primitive Buddhism; then Theravāda Buddhism which is its continuation as to form if not as to content; finally, Mahāyāna (the 'Great Vehicle') which qualifies whatever preceded it as Hīnayāna ('Lesser Vehicle') and which in its general form exalts the heroic ideal of the Bodhisattva; then, within the actual framework of the Mahāyāna, a sapiential perspective which corrects and counterbalances the elements of 'love' as specifically embodied in the mahāyānic ideal; while parallel with this perspective there is another which is devotional and centered particularly on the cult of the Buddha Amitābha as found in China and Japan. If then the 'greatness' of the Great Vehicle be admitted, this is not for the sake of the altruistic ideal which appears as its mythological mantle and its elementary thesis, but because of the two quintessences just mentioned — the one sapiential and the other devotional — the ultimate crystallizations of which are, in Japan, Zen and Jōdo.

While maintaining solidarity with the sacrificial ideal of its basic thesis, but without following it into its literal and too human interpretations, the sapiential Mahāyāna adopts the terminology of this thesis and projects into it its own certainties. Consequently it will say, not that Nirvāna requires charity to complete it but that the condition of the Pratyeka-Buddha is not Nirvāna in the fullest sense, or that it is a Nirvana on a transitory level; in which case, the use here of the title 'Buddha' seems to indicate a change of terminology, since it is *a priori* abnormal to call a man Buddha when he is placed lower than a Bodhisattva. It is however possible to justify such a use of this title seeing that it refers to a state which is already nirvānic in the sense that there is 'extinction' at least in relation to the formal world, this by itself being enough to dispense the one concerned from any further obligation to return to the round of births and deaths.

The Mahāyānist polemic against the Pratyeka-Buddhas should therefore not astonish us unduly, springing as it does from a perspective of sacrificial idealism. To mention a parallel case in Hinduism, the Vishnuite *bhakti*, which is also a way of Love, often represents the Shivaite *jnāni*, (gnostic) as being a rationalist, sterile, sad and lacking what is essential until one day, touched by Grace, he discovers devotional love — as if the latter were not already, and eminently, comprised in Gnosis itself.

In considering the Bodhisattvic ideal, account must be taken of the following fundamental situation: Buddhism unfolds itself in a sense between the empirical notions of suffering and cessation of suffering; the notion of Compassion springs from this very fact and is an inevitable or necessary link in what might be called the spiritual mythology of the Buddhist tradition. The fact of suffering and the possibility of putting an end to it must needs imply compassion, unless a man were living alone upon the earth. This is where the Bodhisattva enters on the scene: he incarnates the element of compassion — the ontological link as it were between Pain and Felicity — just as the Buddha incarnates Felicity and just as ordinary beings incarnate suffering; he must be present in the cosmos as long as there is both a Samsāra and a Nirvāna, this presence of his being expressed by the statement that the Bodhisattva wishes to deliver 'all beings'.

From a more contingent point of view, it could also be admitted that concern for personal salvation, while irreproachable in itself, does in practice involve a certain danger of egotism when acknowledged by a numerous collectivity in which exoteric tendencies are bound to manifest themselves; from this angle the intervention of the Mahāyāna ideal is seen to be providential. At the time when it first appeared on the scene in specific form the Buddhist tradition had doubtless begun to be affected by all kinds of narrow and pharisaical currents; the same had applied to Brahmanism in the Buddha's time as also to Judaism at the time of Christ; which does not mean, however, that either of these traditions had succumbed entirely or in regard to their innermost life. For this reason also there can be no question nowadays of applying the polemic of the ancient Mahāyānists to the Theravādins of Ceylon, Burma and Indo-China.

Furthermore, concerning the tradition itself when regarded in a more fundamental sense, the very necessity of its developing an emotional element, in the absence of a theism properly so called and given the conditions of the 'latter times', explains the opportuneness of the cult of the Bodhisattva in correlation with the way of works and the way of love; in this respect, the difference between the Buddhism of the North and that of the South is no more than one of style and 'mythology'; it in no wise affects their common supra-formal essence. To give one particular illustration, it can be admitted that, if, for instance, in the climate of the Mahāyāna the Buddhist Amitābha has become the object of a quasi-personal cult, this is because, as Bodhisattva, he has been able to accumulate the merits capable of creating a 'Buddha-field' and a 'Pure Land'; but this retrospective motive evidently need not affect contemplation, whether in its devotional or its gnostic dimension, and especially since the same causal connection may also be conceived as working in the opposite direction: this is the same as saying that here the 'prime mover' is not a contingency like the merit accumulated by an individual (or by a 'karmic nexus' if one so prefers). but a principle of Mercy that creates at the same time both the merit itself and the saint who accumulates the merit. The principle of Mercy results from the very nature of the Ādi-Buddha, the Absolute who is at the same time both Knowledge and Love...

• • •

A distinction must be made between the personal transmigratory Bodhisattva and the celestial or universal Bodhisattva endowed with ubiquity; the former, if he be not simply a manifestation of the latter, accumulates merits by his virtues and his actions; the latter is the cosmic emanation of a Buddha, or, in western terms, he is the Archangel who manifests a given Divine Quality; his reintegration into Nirvāna coincides with the *Mahāpralaya*, the Apocatastasis which effects the return of all manifestation to the Principle or of all contingency to the Absolute. The human Bodhisattva can be (to use Hindu terminology) either a *bhakta* or a *jnāni*: in the former case the way is shared between devotion and compassion — devotion in the respect of the Buddhas and celestial Bodhi sattvas and compassion towards the creatures wandering in Samsara — whilst in the latter case it is the way of gnosis that takes precedence over everything else. Here compassion is not something added in sentimental fashion to a supposedly imperfect mode of knowledge; on the contrary compassion is regarded as the secondary dimension or internal complement of a knowledge which is virtually or effectively perfect, because it is situated on the axis of Buddhahood or is identified with Buddhahood itself.[1]

Some will doubtless object that the gnosis of the Bodhisattva is not that of the Buddha: whereas the compassion of the latter is intrinsic in the sense that he carries all things in himself, the universal pity of the Bodhisattva is extrinsic and therefore still situated under the sign of duality. This view, however, does not do full justice to the nature of the great Bodhisattvas, whose sacrificial sojourn in the world is an occasion for realizing Nirvāna in a certain sense within the samsāric condition itself. This must needs be so, for the simple reason that a being cannot deprive himself, from life to life, of that very Enlightenment which constitutes the meaning and the end of all his efforts, all his virtues and all his merits. It is neither possible on the one hand to persist in an exclusively negative situation nor, on the other, to regard the ultimate Wisdom merely as a means of coming to another's aid, which would amount in effect to making a means of the end or a contingency of the Absolute; Knowledge as such cannot be an instrument designed for charity any more than the Real can be subordinate to the illusory: as the Tibetan Arahant Milarepa put it 'one should not show oneself rash and hasty in the intention to serve others as long as one has not realized the Truth oneself; otherwise one risks becoming a blind man leading the blind'. The condition of the gnostic Bodhisattva would be neither conceivable nor tolerable if it were not a matter of contemplating the Absolute in the heart and in the world at one and the same time. Above all it must be stressed that Knowledge, by definition, has no connection with the quantity of merits or the number of incarnations. This is what Zen teaches in the most uncompromising manner: texts like the *Diamond Sūtra* or the Chinese *Sūtra of Huang-Po* formulate the decisive truth in the most explicit possible fashion and thereby express, in terms of doctrine, the very quintessence of Buddhism. Only a bhaktism with an exoteric bias could imagine perfect Knowledge as being the fruit of a process of accumulating elements of one kind or another; one must not let oneself be deceived on that score even if these elements appear sublime from the human point of view; in short there is nothing quantitative or moral about the Spirit. According to the *Lankavatāra-sūtra*, the Bodhisattvas, while holding back from entry into Nirvana, are there already in fact, 'for in their love and compassion there is no cause of illusory distinction and consequently no intervention of such distinction'. The *Diamond Sūtra* mentions this saying of the Buddha: 'A Bodhisattva who says: "I will deliver all beings" must not be called a Bodhisattva'.

Something should be said about the distinction between Nirvana and Parinirvāna: only death allows of a total reintegration (for those who in their lifetime have realized 'Extinction') in that 'Supreme Extinction' which is none other than the Vedantine Selfhood. Living beings, whatever may be their degree of spirituality, remain of necessity linked with Being, which belongs to the realm of Nirvāna since it represents a perfect transcendence in relation to all manifestation and to the whole cosmic enmeshment, but which, being still of the realm of *Māyā* whereof it is the summit or quintessence, is not yet the Self. If in a certain respect death brings no change for one who has realized Nirvāna it nonetheless in another respect effects a considerable change, so that it can be said that death for the 'living liberated one' is neither a modification nor a non-modification, or that it is both at once. However, if we say that the Buddha, in dying, entered Parinirvāna, this is again only an earthly mode of speech: in reality, he was always there in his capacity of *Dharmakāya*, 'body of the Dharma'; similarly he did not cease to dwell in Heaven in his capacity of *Sambhogakaya*, 'body of Bliss', even while he was manifest among mortals by virtue of *Nirmanakāya*, the 'body of supernatural metamorphosis'. In monotheistic terms it can be said that to every Prophet there corresponds an Archangel and, beyond creation, a divine Name, and that every divine Name reflects in its own way the Divinity one and undivided.

An important point touching the mystery of the Bodhisattva in his capacity of a 'virtual Buddha' is the comprehension of the nirvanic essence of Samsāra: just as it has been said elsewhere that the finite is a sort of internal dimension of the Infinite — an indispensably necessary dimension, by reason of the intrinsic character of infinity — with equal justice Samsāra could be defined as a sort of dimension of Nirvāna, or an 'ignorant' manner (in the sense of the Indian term *avidyā*, nescience) of envisaging the latter, the factor of 'ignorance' being called forth by the very infinity of the divine 'Voidness'. The actual substance of this 'reality in reverse' is constituted by those countless 'grains of sand' which are the *dharmas*, the elementary qualities, these being like the segmented, innumerable and inverted crystallizations of the Void or of the pure nirvānic Substance. The 'impermanence' of things is none other than their own relativity. . .

Glimpses into Zen*

The interest in Zen manifested of late years in the Western countries has resulted from an understandable reaction against the coarseness and ugliness prevalent in the world today, and also from a certain weariness in regard to concepts rightly or wrongly judged to

*From *ITB*, Chapter 10.

be inoperative; while on the other hand people have tended to feel increasingly bored by the habitual philosophical battles of words. Unfortunately, these justifiable motives get only too easily mingled with anti-intellectual and falsely 'concretist' tendencies — this was only to be expected — in which case the reaction becomes deprived of all effective value. For it is one thing to take up a stand beyond the scope of the thinking faculty and another to remain far short of that faculty's highest possibilities even while imagining one has transcended things of which one does not comprehend the first word. He who truly rises above verbal formulations will ever be ready to respect those which have given direction to his thinking in the first place; he will not fail to venerate 'every word that proceedeth out of the mouth of God'. There is a rustic proverb which says that only the pig overturns its trough after emptying it and the same moral is to be found in the well-known fable of the fox and the grapes. If Zen is less given to doctrinal formulation than other schools, this is because its own structure allows it to be so; it owes its consistency to factors that are perfectly rigorous, but not easily grasped from the outside; its silence, charged with mystery, is quite other than a vague and facile mutism. Zen, precisely by reason of its direct and implicit character, which is admirably suited to certain possibilities of the Far Eastern mind, presupposes so many conditions of mentality and environment that the slightest lack in this respect jeopardizes the result of any effort however sincere; at the same time we must not forget that a typical man of the Japanese *élite* is in many respects a product of Zen.

But there is also an inverse danger, this time affecting Far Eastern people themselves: followers of Zen (as also Theravādins in a different way) in the course of their scholastic and academic contacts with the West find it hard to resist making capital of what is, in a sense, the adogmatic character of their own tradition, as if the absence of dogmas bore the same meaning and colour for a contemplative Asiatic as for a Western agnostic. Similar misunderstandings have also been apparent in the realm of art, where contemporary 'abstract' productions have been confused, in Japan, with works inspired by Tao-Zen, at least as regards their intention. With this can be compared the confusion persistently fostered by European psychologists as between drawings by insane patients and Tantrik Buddhist *māndalas*; in the latter case, just as in the case of the Zen 'adogmatism', appearances are equated which in reality are at the antipodes of one an other and this, moreover, is precisely the reason why they are thus confused.

In a quite general way, that which calls for suspicion and for implacable vigilance is the reducing of the spiritual to the psychic, a practice which by now has become a commonplace to the point of characterizing Western interpretations of the traditional doctrines. This so-called 'psychology of spirituality' or this 'psychoanalysis of the sacred' is the breach through which the mortal poison of modern relativism infiltrates into the still living Oriental traditions. According to Jung the figurative emergence of certain contents of the 'collective unconscious' is accompanied empirically, as its psychic complement, by a noumenal sensation of eternity and infinitude. This is the way to ruin insidiously all transcendence and all intellection for, according to this theory, it is the collective unconscious, or subconscious, which is at the origin of 'individuated' consciousness, human intelligence having two components, namely the reflexions of the subconscious on the one hand and the experience of the external world on the other; but since experience is not in itself intelligence, on this showing intelligence will have the subconscious for its substance, so that one has to try and define the subconscious on the basis of its own ramification. This is the classical contradiction of all subjectivist and relativist philosophy.

Assuredly, there is no question here of denying that whatever is truly spiritual, though essentially determined by supra-individual factors, will also include secondary modalities of a psychic, and even of a corporeal order from the very fact that it necessarily sets in motion 'all that we are'. Granted that this is so, a 'psychology of the spiritual' nevertheless is a contradictory notion that can only end up in falsifying and negating the spirit; one might just as well speak of 'a biology of truth' and indeed one can be pretty sure that someone has already done so. In an analogous way, many people are apt to confuse what is supra-logical with the illogical and viceversa: as soon as a, to them, uncomfortable demonstration is found to be logically faultless, these people hasten to write it off as 'Aristotelian' or 'Cartesian' in order to stress the artificial and outmoded character they fain would attribute to it.

When referring to the much canvassed 'non-dogmatism' of the Buddhist teachings one has to be extremely cautious how one expresses this thought, since it is useless to lay down, out of contempt for dogmatic forms, conditions that could never in fact be fulfilled or to let oneself be involved in conclusions which may be quite logical in form perhaps, but which are erected on false bases, contrary to reality. One can never cease wondering at the levity with which some people, in their scorn of all dogmas for reasons allegedly spiritual, forget to consult tradition concerning such and such an order of possibilities while blithely claiming that their little personal recipe is at long last going to inaugurate a new world where all will be happy even if they be plunged in illusion — when the Buddha himself did not succeed in accomplishing this, even supposing he had wished to do so. Apart from the sheer inanity of such a pretension, one finds here a fundamental ignorance regarding the qualitative differences of historical phases; these people wish to lay down the law about things situated in the Universe without having the least notion of the laws whereby it is governed and with a complete contempt of the traditions that reveal those laws. The nondogmatism of Zen and kindred spiritualities in reality is chiefly aimed at the mental crystallizations of partial truths; it in no wise confers a general mandate against Truth as such; if it closes the door, as it does, against any fixation in a half-truth, this does not mean that it leaves the door open for every error. For the modernistically minded neo-Zen exponent, on the other hand, this same non-dogmatism becomes a licence to do anything one pleases and this, in the name of a tradition to which, if he be Japanese, he himself remains attached atavistically and sentimentally; the sheer want of imagination sometimes displayed by persons who seem in other respects intelligent is one of the more baffling and all too common symptoms of the semi-Europeanized East.

According to the *Lankāvatara-Sūtra* the being who has entered into the state of a Buddha accomplishes mysterious actions that are 'impossible to conceive' (*achintya*) and 'carried out without purpose and outside any feeling of usefulness' (*anābhoga-charyā*); this statement is poles apart from a utilitarian, not to say materialistic and demagogic Neo-Buddhism. Like other men, a Buddhist assuredly may busy himself with such and such a useful activity in response to circumstances good or bad, but only on condition he does not forget that external activities in themselves are without relation to Buddhahood and Reality; they are neither situated outside Samsāra nor opposed to illusion. More especially should it be remembered that any useful activity a man undertakes will imply the condition that he never claims to be adding anything whatsoever to tradition or to sanctity, as if these had hitherto been lacking in some essential quality which at last has been discovered thanks to Kant or Rousseau after countless centuries of insufficiency. Relativities are not things to be grafted on the Absolute. . .

The above considerations on Zen may lead people to put the question whether that school, or else some other, most faithfully reflects the original teachings of Sākyamuni. On the level of intrinsic orthodoxy this is a meaningless question, however; it is as if one were to ask which of the branches of a tree best conforms to the root. Concerning the manifold forms of historical Buddhism the only question worth asking is that of their orthodoxy or heterodoxy; all that is orthodox today, whatever form may have developed around it, was contained in Buddhism from the beginning. All orthodox Buddhism is 'the real Buddhism'; the deployment of a more or less subtle aspect of the Dharma is never an 'evolution' in the progressivist sense of the word; inspiration is not an invention any more than a metaphysical perspective is a rationalist system. With many Asian authors, the Western terms they introduce into their writings are often employed carelessly though without an erroneous intention; but in that case it is the Western reader who must be forewarned, since otherwise he will infallibly be misled by the association of ideas normally implied in the terms that have thus been carelessly borrowed from his vocabulary.

As for the Western world itself, one may recall, for instance, the case of a Christian 'avant-garde' theologian who, out of a wish to prove that 'tradition' is the equivalent of 'progress' and not an immobilism, went so far as to maintain that St Paul, in wishing to formulate such and such truths in his Epistles, 'was compelled to invent'. His general aim doubtless was to claim 'modern progress' as an outcome of Christianity and to align in one and the same glory the Apostles and the inventors of machines, serums and explosives. In the same line of thought, when a man is not intelligent enough to understand what St Thomas and the Scholastics were trying to say, this is called 'being in tune with one's own time'; while to deceive oneself thus regarding one's own intellectual obtuseness by making of it a norm will doubtless be described as 'humility'.

To declare that the primitive Dharma was merely 'practical' and not 'speculative'— the *sūtras* are there to prove the contrary — amounts to reducing the Dharma to an individual experience devoid of any possibility of further radiation. Knowledge of a doctrine cannot be rendered fully adequate except on the basis of the notions of orthodoxy and tradition.

One has heard it said that Buddhism, just as it needed at a certain moment in its history to find a 'new form', namely the Mahāyāna, should in our day likewise 'be rejuvenated' consonantly with 'the spirit of the age', a statement — need one say it? — which is false twice over: firstly, because the Mahayana was not concocted by men nor did it seek to make itself acceptable to any 'age' whatsoever, and secondly because it constitutes, for that humanity to which its message was addressed, a definitive expression of Buddhism, valid therefore till the end of the world and the coming of Maitreya.

If our age, not because of its hypothetical superiority, but on the contrary because of its misery, requires a certain readaptation of the Eternal message, this has been effected long since: Jōdo, Pure Land, is the last utterance, providential and infinitely merciful, of this message and as it addresses itself to those who are most miserable nothing could exceed it in timeliness. The man of our time can lay claim to no spiritual originality unless it be a superabundance of distress, to which the answer will be, by way of compensation, a secret outpouring of Graces, always provided that man does not close himself from beforehand to the celestial offer to save him. The greatest of all human miseries is a refusal to lay oneself open to Mercy.

NOTES

Mystery of the Bodhisatva

1. A Buddhist friend has rightly pointed out to the author that the merits, compassion and knowledge of the Bodhisattva correspond respectively to *karma, bhakti* and *jnāna* and consequently are addressed to those who follow those ways; for each of them the Bodhisattva reveals himself under a particular aspect. To use Buddhist terms, these are the three aspects called *upekshā* ('passionlessness'), *maitrī* ('love of one's neighbour') and *prajnā* ('knowledge'). In the framework of gnosis, compassion nevertheless changes its mode.

*Shintoism**

...POSSIBLY SHINTŌ IS THE MOST INTACT and hence the most complete form belonging to a traditional current that might be described as 'Hyperborean Shamanism', one that extends across Siberia and the adjoining Mongolian lands as far as North America; many mythological and cultural concordances and even vestimentary similarities go to support such a supposition; such a parallelism contains no cause for surprise, since Mongols, Japanese and Red Indians all embody—or have embodied—the heroic side of the Yellow Race, in the broadest sense of the word. For these peoples it is above all Nature that is the sanctuary—a truth which in Japan finds concrete utterance in the *torii* placed in front of sacred landscapes—and this holiness of virgin nature and this 'transcendent immanence' is not without connexion, among the peoples concerned, with their thirst for freedom, their contempt for luxury, their taciturnness and other similar characteristics.

The likeness of the ancient Shintoist songs and those of the Red Indians is striking: 'Ho, now is the time! — Ho, now is the time! — Ho! Ha! Psha! Come on my children! — Come on my children!' (The most ancient Japanese *uta*, that has come down from the warriors of Jimmu Tennō) —'They shall appear! — May you see them! — A horse-people appeareth. — A thunder people appeareth. —They shall appear, look!' (Sioux) —'Now the rising sun — has sent his rays towards

*From *ITB*, Chapter 11.

223

earth — coming from afar — coming from afar — coming from afar — a great number (of warriors) coming from afar, he yo!' (Pawnee) — 'Make us see, is it real? — Make us see, is it real, this life I am leading? —You, divine Beings, who abide everywhere — make us see, is it real — this life I am leading?' (Pawnee). It would not be altogether easy to guess from the mode of expression to which of the two traditions, so remote from one another geographically and historically, a given phrase belongs.

There is nevertheless in the Shintō civilization, apart from any thought of later Chinese or Buddhist influences, one element that partly separates it from the Northern Shamanist world and this is a certain degree of Malayan or Malayo-Polynesian admixture; additional causes of its originality are its insular situation, with all the psychological consequences that this entails, and also the extreme plasticity of the Yamato race, which has made of Japan a reservoir of the principal spiritual and artistic currents of Asia. All the above factors, and more besides, joined in the creating of that kind of bewitching polyphony that might well be called the 'Japanese miracle'.

To return to the analogies pointed out above, it can be said that Shintō, like the North American tradition, knows the cult of the grand phenomena of Nature: sun, moon, rain-bearing hurricane, wind, thunder and lightning, fire, wild animals, rocks, trees, not forgetting sky and earth that are their containers; above it all there is to be found, as 'Great Spririt', *Ameno-Minakanushi-no-kami*, the 'Lord of the true Centre of Heaven'.

Judaism

The Torah and the Mischna*

... According to the Jewish tradition it is not the literal form of the holy Scriptures which has the force of law, but solely their orthodox commentaries. The Torah is a 'closed' book and does not open itself to a direct approach; it is the sages who 'open' it, for it is in the very nature of the Torah to require from the beginning the commentary of the Mischna. It is said that the Mischna was given out in the Tabernacle, when Joshua transmitted it to the Sanhedrin; by this the Sanhedrin was consecrated and thus instituted by God like the Torah and at the same time. And this is highly important: the oral commentary, which Moses had received on Sinai and transmitted to Joshua, was in part lost and had to be reconstituted by the sages on the basis of the Torah: this shows very clearly that gnosis includes both a 'horizontal' and a 'vertical' continuity, or rather that it accompanies the written Law in a manner that is both 'horizontal' and continuous and also 'vertical' and discontinuous; the secrets are passed hand to hand, but the spark may at any time leap forth on mere contact with the revealed Text in function of a particular human receptacle and the imponderables of the Holy Spirit. It is also said that God gave the Torah during the daytime and the Mischna by night; and again, that the Torah is infinite in itself whereas the Mischna

*From *UI*, p. 47.

225

is inexhaustable by its movement in time. We would add that the Torah is like the ocean, and the Mischna like a river. *Mutatis mutandis* all this applies to every Revelation and particularly to Islam . . .

The Supreme Commandment*

"Hear, O Israel: the Lord our God is one Lord. And thou shalt love the Lord thy God with all thine heart, and with all thy soul and with all thy might." (*Deuteronomy*, VI,5). This fundamental expression of Sinaitic monotheism contains the two pillars of all human spirituality, namely metaphysical discernment on the one hand and contemplative concentration on the other; or in other words: doctrine and method, or truth and way. The second element is presented under three aspects: according to a certain rabbinical interpretation, man must firstly "unite himself with God" in his heart, secondly "contemplate God" in his soul, and thirdly "work in God" with his hands and through his body.

The Gospel gives a slightly modified version of the Sinaitic words, in the sense that it makes explicit an element which in the Torah was implicit, namely "mind"; this word is found in each of the synoptic Gospels, whereas the element strength is only found in the versions of Mark and Luke, which may indicate a certain change of accent or perspective with regard to the "Old Law": the element mind is detached from the element "soul" and gains in importance over the element "strength", which refers to works; and one may see in this the sign of a tendency towards interiorization of activity. In other words, whereas for the Torah the "soul" is both active or operative and passive or contemplative, the Gospel seems to denote by the term "soul" the passive contemplative element and by the term "mind" the active operative element; it may be supposed that this is to mark the superiority of inward activity over outward works.

Thus the element "strength" or "works" seems to have a different emphasis in Christianity than in Judaism: in the latter, "mind" is in a certain fashion the inward concomitance of outward observance,

*From *EPW*, pp. 151-157.

whereas in Christianity works appear rather as the exteriorization, or the external confirmation, of the activity of the soul. The Jews contest the legitimacy and efficacy of this relative interiorization; inversely, Christians readily believe that the complication of outward prescriptions (*mitsvoth*) does harm to the inward virtues;[1] in reality, if it it true that the "letter" can kill the "spirit", it is not less true that sentimentalism can kill the "letter", quite apart from the fact that no spiritual fault is the exclusive prerogative of any religion. At all events, the sufficient reason of a religion is precisely to put the emphasis on a determinate spiritual possibility; the latter is the framework for those possibilities that are apparently excluded, in so far as they are destined to be realized, and so of necessity we find in each religion elements which seem to be reflections from the other religions. What can be said is that Judaism, in its basic form, is a *karma-marga* rather than a *bhakti*, whereas the relationship is inverse in Christianity; but *karma*, "action", necessarily comprises an element of *bhakti*, "love", and vice versa.

What has just been said as well as what immediately follows, can serve as an illustration of the fact that of necessity the profoundest truths are already to be found in the fundamental and initial formulations of the religions. Esoterism, in fact, is not an unpredictable doctrine that can only be discovered, should the occasion arise, by means of detailed researches; what is mysterious in esoterism is its dimension of depth, its particular developments and its practical consequences, but not its starting-points, which coincide with the fundamental symbols of the religion in question;[2] moreover its continuity is not exclusively "horizontal" as is that of exoterism; it is also "vertical", in other words esoteric mastery is related to prophecy, without for all that departing from the framework of the mother-religion.

*   *   *

In the Gospels the law of the love of God is immediately followed by the law of the love of one's neighbour, which is enunciated in the Torah in the form: "Thou shalt not hate thy brother in thine heart: thou shalt in any wise rebuke thy neighbour, and not suffer sin upon him. Thou shalt not avenge, nor bear any grudge against the children of thy people, but thou shalt love thy neighbour as thyself. I am the Lord." (*Leviticus*, XIX, 17 and 18).[3]

From the Biblical passages quoted there results a triple law; firstly, recognition by the intelligence of the oneness of God; secondly,
union, both volitive and contemplative, with the One God, and thirdly, transcending the misleading and deforming distinction between
"I" and "the other".[4]

Love of one's neighbour receives all its meaning through the
love of God: it is impossible to abolish the separation between man
and God — to the extent that it can and must be abolished — without
also abolishing in a certain fashion, and bearing in mind all the
aspects comprised in the nature of things, the separation between
the *ego* and the *alter*; in other words, it is impossible to realize consciousness of the Absolute without realizing consciousness of our
relativity. To understand this fully, it is sufficient to consider the illusory, and illusion-producing, nature of egohood: there is indeed
something thoroughly absurd in believing that "only I" am "I"; God
alone can say this without contradiction. It is true that we are condemned to this absurdity, but we are so only existentially, and not
morally; what determines that we are men and not animals is precisely the concrete awareness that we have of the "I" of other people, and
so of the relative falseness of our own ego; we must draw the consequences from this and spiritually correct what is unbalanced and
mendacious in our existential egohood. It is with this imbalance in
view that it is said: "Judge not that ye be not judged", and also: "Thou
considerest not the beam that is in thine own eye", or again: "All things
whatsoever ye would that men should do to you, do ye even so to
them". (*Matthew*, VII, 3 and 12).

After proclaiming the Supreme Commandment, Christ added that
the second Commandment was "like unto" the first, which implies
that the love of one's neighbour is essentially contained in the love
of God and that the former is real and acceptable only in so far as
it derives from the latter, for "whoever gathereth not with Me, disperseth"; the love of God may thus sometimes contradict our love
for men, as in the case of those who must "hate father and mother
in order to follow Me", although men can never be frustrated by such
an option. It is not enough to love one's neighbour, we must love
him in God, and not against God, as atheistic moralists do; and in
order to love him in God, we must love God.

What enables divine injunctions to be both simple and absolute
is that any adaptations necessitated by the nature of things are always
implied, and cannot but be implied; thus, charity does not abolish

natural hierarchies: the superior treats the inferior — when the relationship of hierarchy applies — as he himself would like to be treated if he were the inferior, and not as if the inferior were superior; or again, charity does not imply that we should share in the errors of others, or that others should escape a punishment that we would have deserved ourselves, if we had participated in their errors or their vices, and so on.

In this connection, the following should also be said: one is only too familiar with the prejudice which would have contemplative love justify itself and excuse itself before a world that despises it, and which would have the contemplative engage himself unnecessarily in activities that turn him away from the end he has in view; those who think in this manner are obviously unaware that contemplation represents for human society a sort of sacrifice which is salutary for it and of which it is strictly in need. The prejudice in question is analogous to the one that condemns the ostentation of sacred art, of sanctuaries, of priestly vestments, and of liturgy: here again there is a refusal to understand, firstly, that not all riches redound to men,[5] but that some redound to God, and do so in the interests of all; secondly, that sacred treasures are offerings or sacrifices that are due to His greatness, His beauty and His glory; and thirdly, that in a society, the sacred must of necessity make itself visible, so as to create a presence or an atmosphere without which it fades from men's minds. The fact that a spiritual individual may be able to do without forms is beside the question, for society is not this individual; and the individual needs society in order to blossom, just as a plant needs earth in order to live. Nothing is more vile than envy with regard to God; poverty dishonours itself when it covets the gold decoration of sanctuaries;[6] it is true that there have always been exceptions to the rule, but they have no connection with the cold and strident demands of iconoclastic utilitarians.

* * *

In the Torah there is a passage which has been much misused in order to support an argument in favour of a so-called "vocation of the earth" and a consecration of the devouring materialism of our age: "Be fruitful and multiply, and replenish the earth, and subdue it: and have dominion over the fish of the sea, and over the fowl of

the air, and over every living thing that moveth upon the earth".
(*Genesis*, I, 28)[7] This order in fact only defines human nature in its
relationships with the earthly environment or, in other words, it
defines the rights resulting from our nature; God says to man: "thou
shalt do such and such a thing", as He would say to fire to burn and
to water to flow; every natural function necessarily depends on a
Divine Order. By this imperative form of the Divine Words, man
knows that if he dominates on earth, it is not by an abuse, but according to the Will of the most High and therefore according to the
logic of things; but these Words in no wise mean that man must abuse
his capacities by giving himself over exclusively to the inordinate,
enslaving, and finally destructive exploitation of earthly resources.
For here as in other cases, it is necessary to understand the words
in the context of other words which necessarily complete them, which
is to say that the passage quoted is intelligible only in the light of
the Supreme Commandments: "Thou shalt love the Lord thy God
with all thy heart, with all thy soul, and with all thy might." Without
this key, the passage on fruitfulness could be interpreted as forbidding celibacy and excluding all contemplative preoccupation; but
the Supreme Commandment shows precisely what are the limits of
this passage, what is its necessary basis and its total meaning: it shows
that the right or the duty to dominate the world derives from what
man is in himself.

• • •

The equilibrium of the world and of creatures depends on the
equilibrium between man and God, and so on our knowledge, and
on our will, with regard to the Absolute. Before asking what man
must do, it is neces sary to know what he is.

We have seen that the Supreme Commandment comprises, so
to speak, three dimensions: firstly, the affirmation of Divine Oneness,
and this is the intellectual dimension; secondly, the obligation of loving God, and this is the volitive or affective dimension; and thirdly,
the obligation of loving one's neighbour, and this is the active and
social dimension; this third mode is indirect, and takes effect outwardly, while necessarily having its roots in the soul, in the virtues
and in contemplation.

As for the first dimension, which constitutes the fundamental
enunciation of Judaism[8] — prefigured in the ontological witness of

the burning bush[9] — it comprises two aspects, one concerning intellection and the other faith; as for the second dimension, we will recall that it comprises the three aspects "union", "contemplation" and "operation", the first relating to the heart, the second to the soul or the mental element, or to virtues and to thought, and the third to the body. And finally the third dimension, love of one's neighbour, derives from the generosity that is necessarily engendered by the knowledge and the love of God; it is thus both condition and consequence.

Having enunciated the two Commandments — unconditional and "vertical" love of God and conditional and "horizontal" love of one's neighbour[10] — Christ adds: "On these two commandments hang all the law and the prophets." (*Matthew*, XXII,40). In other words the two Commandments on the one hand constitute the *Religio perennis* — the primordial, eternal and *de facto* underlying[11] Religion[12] — and on the other hand are to be found, by way of consequence, in all manifestations of this *Religio* or of this *Lex*, namely in the religions that govern humanity; herein therefore is contained a doctrine proclaiming both the unity of the Truth and the diversity of its forms, and at the same time defining the nature of this Truth by means of the two Commandments of Love.

NOTES

The Supreme Commandment

1. Hassidism would suffice to prove the contrary, if proof were needed for something so obvious.

2. This is why it is unreal to ask "where Christian esoterism has gone" and to suppose, for example, that it is founded on the Cabbala and the Hebrew language; Christian esoterism can be founded only on the Gospel and on the symbolism of the dogmas and the sacraments — and by extension on the "Old Testament" in translation, especially on the Psalms and the Song of Solomon — although it can certainly annex "on the margin" elements from Jewish and Hellenic esoterism; it even does so of necessity, since these elements are within its reach and correspond to certain vocations.

3. Or again: "But the stranger that dwelleth with you shall be unto you as one born among you, and thou shalt love him as thyself: for ye are strangers in the land of Egypt: I am the Lord your God." (*ibid 34*)

4. For "all things are *Atma*." Consequently: "Inasmuch as ye have done it unto one of the least of these my brethren, ye have done it unto Me." (*Matthew*, XXV,40) — "He that hath pity upon the poor lendeth unto the Lord; and that which he hath given will He pay him again." (*Proverbs*, XIX,17)

5. The notion of poverty, moreover is capable of many fluctuations, given the artificial and inexhaustable nature of the needs of "civilized" man. There are no "underdeveloped" peoples, there are only overdeveloped peoples.

6. It will be recalled that gold decoration is prescribed by God Himself. And it is significant that neither St Vincent de Paul nor the holy Curé d'Ars — both so ardently concerned with the welfare of the poor without for all that forgetting the spiritual welfare without which material welfare has no meaning — ever dreamt of begrudging God His riches; for the Curé d'Ars, no expense was great enough for the beauty of the house of God.

7. Rabbinical exegesis no doubt explains the meaning of this enumeration, but it is not this aspect that concerns us here.

8. "Hear, O Israel, the Lord our God is one Lord."

9. "And God said unto Moses, I am that I am." (*Exodus*, III,l4)

10. The Decalogue contains, and develops, these two crucial Commandments.

11. "The Lord possessed me (Wisdom) in the beginning of his way, before his words of old. I was set up from everlasting, from the beginning, or ever the earth was" (*Proverbs*, VIII, 22 and 23)

12. We say "primordial Religion", and not "Tradition", because the first of these terms has the advantage of expressing an intrinsic reality (*religere* = "to bind" the earthly with the heavenly), and not simply an extrinsic reality like the second (*tradere* = "to hand down" scriptural, ritual and legal elements). Moreover, one may with reason ask if there could be any question of "tradition" in an age in which spiritual knowledge was innate or spontaneous, or again, if the necessity of a "tradition", and thus of an outward handing down, does not *ipso facto* involve the necessity of a plurality of formulations.

Christianity

The Christian Tradition
Some Thoughts on its Nature*

IN THE PERSPECTIVE of gnosis, Christ, 'Light of the world,' is the universal Intellect, as the Word is the 'Wisdom of the Father.' Christ is the Intellect of microcosms as well as that of the macrocosm. He is then the Intellect in us[1] as well as the Intellect in the Universe and *a fortiori* in God; in this sense, it can be said that there is no truth nor wisdom that does not come from Christ, and this is evidently independent of all consideration of time and place. Just as 'the Light shineth in darkness; and the darkness comprehended it not,' so too the Intellect shines in the darkness of passions and illusions. The relationship of the 'Son' to the 'Father' is analogous to the relationship of pure Love to Being or of the Intellect to the 'Self,' and that is why we are, in the Intellect or in sanctifying Grace, 'brothers' of Christ.

Likewise Christ is prefigured in the whole of creation; this too has one aspect of incarnation and another of crucifixion. On a lesser scale, humanity, and with it the individual human, is an image of Christ, and comprises both aspects: man is 'incarnation' by his Intellect and his freedom, and 'crucifixion' by his miseries . . .

*From *GDW*, Chapter 10

233

. . .

The Church of Peter is visible, and continuous like water; that of John — instituted on Calvary and confirmed at the sea of Tiberias — is invisible, and discontinuous like fire. John became 'brother' of Christ and 'Son' of the Virgin, and, further, he is the prophet of the Apocalypse; Peter is charged to 'feed my sheep,' but his Church seems to have inherited also his denials, whence the Renaissance and its direct and indirect consequences; however, 'the gates of hell shall not prevail against it.' John 'tarries till I come,' and this mystery remains closed to Peter.[2]

. . .

The Holy Spirit is given by Confirmation, through the medium of fire, for oil is none other than a form of liquid fire, as too is wine; the difference between Baptism and Confirmation could be defined by saying that the first has a negative — or 'negatively positive'— function, since it 'takes away' the state of the fall, while the second sacrament has a purely positive function in the sense that it 'gives' a light and a power that are divine.[3]

This transmission acquires a new 'dimension' and receives its full efficacy through the vows which correspond to the 'Gospel counsels'; these vows — true initiatic leaven — denote at the same time a death and a second birth, and they are in fact accompanied by symbolic funeral rites; the consecration of a monk is a sort of burial.[4] By poverty, man severs himself from the world; by chastity he severs himself from society; and by obedience, he severs himself from himself.[5]

. . .

The whole of Christianity hangs on these words: Christ is God. Likewise on the sacramental plane: the bread 'is' His body and the wine 'is' His blood.[6] There is, further, a connection between the eucharistic and the onomatologic mysteries: the Named one is 'really present' in His Name, that is to say He 'is' His Name.

The Eucharist is in a sense the 'central' means of grace of Christianity; it must then express integrally what characterises that tradition, and it does so in recapitulating not only the mystery of Christ as such, but also its double application to the 'greater' and the 'lesser mysteries'; the wine corresponds to the first and the bread to the second, and this is clearly shown not only by the respective natures of the sacred elements, but also by the following symbolic facts: the bread is 'quantitative,' in the sense that Christ multiplied what already existed, while the miracle of the wine is 'qualitative,' for Christ conferred on the water a quality which it did not have, namely that of wine. Or again, the body of the crucified Redeemer had to be pierced in order that blood might flow out; blood thus represents the inner aspect of the sacrifice, which is moreover underlined by the fact that blood is liquid, hence 'non-formal,' while the body is solid, hence 'formal' ; the body of Christ had to be pierced because, to use the language of Meister Eckhart, 'if you want the kernel, you must break the shell.' The water which flowed from Christ's side and proved His death is like the negative aspect of the transmuted soul: it is the 'extinction' which, according to the point of view, either accompanies or precedes the beatific plenitude of the divine blood; it is the 'death' which precedes 'Life,' and which is as it were its external proof.

．．．

Christianity hangs also on the two supreme commandments, which contain 'all the law and the prophets.' In gnosis, the first commandment — total love of God — implies awakened consciousness of the Self, while the second — love of the neighbour — refers to seeing the Self in what is 'not-I.' Likewise for the injunctions of *oratio et jejunium*: all Christianity hangs on these two disciplines, 'prayer' and 'fasting.'

Oratio et jejunium: 'Fasting' is, first, abstention from evil and next the 'void for God' (*vacare Deo*) where 'prayer'— the 'remembrance of God' — establishes itself, thus fulfilling the victory already won by the Redeemer.

'Prayer' culminates in a constant recalling of divine Names, in so far as it is a question of an articulated 'remembrance.' The Golden Legend, so rich in precious teachings, contains stories which bear witness to this: a knight wished to renounce the world and entered

the Cistercian order; he was illiterate and, further, incapable of re-
taining, from all the teachings he received, anything but the words
Ave Maria; these words 'he kept with such great collectedness that
he pronounced them ceaselessly for himself wherever he went and
whatever he was doing.' After his death, a beautiful lily grew on his
grave, and on each petal was written in golden letters *Ave Maria*; the
monks opened the grave and saw that the root of the lily was grow-
ing from the knight's mouth.—To this story we have only one word
to add concerning the 'divine quality' of the Name of the Virgin:
he who says Jesus, says God; and equally, he who says Mary, says
Jesus, so that the *Ave Maria*—or the Name of Mary—is, of the divine
Names, the one which is closest to man.

The Golden Legend recounts also that the executioners of St.
Ignatius of Antioch were astonished by the fact that the saint pronounced the Name of Christ without ceasing: 'I cannot keep from
doing so,' he told them, 'for it is written in my heart.' After the saint's
death, the pagans opened his heart and there saw, written in golden
letters, the Name of Jesus.[7]

·   ·   ·

God is Love, and He is Light: but He is also, in Christ, sacrifice
and suffering, and that again is an aspect or an extension of Love.
Christ has two natures, divine and human, and He offers also two
ways, gnosis and charity: the way of charity, in so far as it is distinguished from gnosis, implies grief, for perfect love is willing to suffer; it is in suffering that man best proves his love; but there is also
in this as it were a price to be paid for the 'intellectual easiness' of
such a perspective. In the way of gnosis where the whole emphasis
is on pure contemplation and the chief concern is with the glorious
aspect of Christ rather than with his grievous humanity—and there
is in certain respects a participation in the divine nature, which is
ever blissful and immutable—suffering is not imposed in the same
way; that is, it does not, in principle, have to exceed the exigencies
of a general ascesis, such as the Gospel designates by the term *jejunium*; a quasiimpersonal detachment here takes precedence over
individual desire for sacrifice. All Christian spirituality oscillates between these two poles, although the aspect of charity-suffering greatly
preponderates, in practice —and for obvious reasons—over the
aspect gnosis-contemplation.

The question: 'What is God?' or: 'What am I?' outweighs, in the soul of the gnostic, the question: 'What does God want of me?' or: 'What must I do?' although these questions are far from being irrelevant, since man is always man. The gnostic, who sees God 'everywhere and nowhere,' does not first of all base himself on alternatives outside himself, although he cannot escape them; what matters to him above all is that the world is everywhere woven of the same existential qualities and poses in all circumstances the same problems of remoteness and proximity. . .

• • •

'And the light shineth in darkness; and the darkness comprehended it not.' The message of Christ, by its form, is addressed *a priori* to the passional element in man, to the point of fall in his nature, but it remains gnostic or sapiential in Christ Himself and therefore in trinitarian metaphysics, not to speak of the sapiential symbolism of Christ's teachings and parables. But it is in relation to the general form — the volitional perspective — of the message that Christ could say: 'They that are whole have no need of the physician, but they that are sick: I came not to call the righteous, but sinners to repentance' (Mark ii, 17). Again, when Christ says 'Judge not, that ye be not judged,' He is referring to our passional nature and not to pure intelligence, which is neutral and is identified with those 'that are whole.' If Christ shall come to 'judge the quick and the dead,' that is again a matter of the Intellect — which alone has the right to judge — and of the equating of Christ and Intellect.

The volitional perspective, to which we have just alluded, is affirmed in the clearest possible way in biblical history: we see there a people at once passionate and mystical struggling in the grip of a Law which crushes and fascinates it, and this prefigures, in a providential way, the struggles of the passional soul — of every soul in so far as it is subject to passions — with the truth which is the final end of the human state. The Bible always speaks of 'that which happens' and almost never of 'that which is,' though it does so implicitly as the Kabbalists point out; we are the first to recognise this, but it alters nothing in the visible nature of these Scriptures, nor in the human causes behind this nature. From another angle, Judaism had hidden what Christianity was called on to make openly manifest;[8]

in turn, the Jews had openly manifested, from the moral point of view, what Christians, later, learnt to hide; the ancient crudity was replaced by an esotericism of love, no doubt, but also by a new hypocrisy.

It is necessary to take account equally of this: the volitional perspective has a tendency to retain the *ego* because of the idea of moral responsibility, while gnosis, on the contrary, tends to reduce it to the cosmic powers of which it is a combination and an outcome. And again: from the point of view of will and passion, men are equal; but they are not so from the point of view of pure intellection, for the latter introduces into man an element of the absolute which, as such, exceeds him infinitely. To the moralising question: 'Who art thou that judgest another?'—a question by which some would like to obliterate all 'wisdom of serpents' or all 'discerning of spirits' in a vague and would-be charitable psychologism — to this question one would have the right to reply 'God' in every case of infallible judgement; for intelligence, in so far as it is 'relatively absolute,' escapes the jurisdiction of virtue, and consequently its rights surpass those of man regarded as passional and fallible *ego*; God is in the truth of every truth. The saying that 'no one can be judge and party in his own cause' could be applied to the *ego* only in so far as the latter limits or darkens the mind, for it is arbitrary to attribute in principle to the intelligence as such a limit with respect to an order of contingencies; to assert, as certain moralists would, that man has no right to judge, amounts to saying that he has no intelligence, that he is only will or passion and that he has no kind of likeness to God.

The sacred rights of the Intellect appear besides in the fact that Christians have not been able to dispense with the wisdom of Plato, and that, later, the Latins found the need for recourse to Aristotelianism, as if there by recognising that *religio* could not do without the element of wisdom, which a too exclusive perspective of love had allowed to fall into discredit. But if knowledge is a profound need of the human spirit, it is by that very fact also a way.

To return to our earlier thought, we could also express ourselves thus: contrary to what is the case in gnosis, love scarcely has the right to judge another; it takes all upon itself and excuses everything, at least on the level where it is active, a level the limits of which vary according to individual natures; 'pious fraud'[9] — out of charity — is the price of volitional individualism. If gnosis, for its part, discerns essentially — and on all levels — both spirits and values, this is because

its point of view is never personal, so that in gnosis the distinction
between 'me' and 'other', and the subtle and paradoxical obstinacies
attaching to this, scarcely have meaning; but here too, the application of the principle depends on the limitations imposed on us by
the nature of things and of ourselves.

Charity with regard to our neighbour, when it is the act of a
direct consciousness and not just of a moral sentiment, implies seeing ourselves in the other and the other in ourselves; the scission between *ego* and *alter* must be overcome, that the cleavage between
Heaven and earth may be healed.

• • •

According to St. Thomas, it is not in the nature of free will to
choose evil, although this possibility derives from having freedom
of agency associated with a fallible creature. Will and liberty are thus
connected; the Doctor, that is, introduces into the will an intellectual element and makes the will, quite properly, participate in intelligence. Will does not cease to be will by choosing evil — we have
already said this on other occasions — but it ceases fundamentally
to be free, and so intellective; in the first case, it is the dynamic faculty, power of the passions — animals also have a will — and in the
second, the dynamisation of discernment. It could be added that
neither does intelligence cease to be itself when in error, but in this
case the relationship is less direct than for the will; the Holy Spirit
(Will, Love) 'is delegated' by the Son (Intellect, Knowledge) and
not inversely.

Christian doctrine does not claim that moral effort produces
metaphysical knowledge, but it does teach that the restoring of the
fallen will — the extirpation of the passions — releases the contemplative power latent in the depths of our theomorphic nature; this
contemplative power is like a window on which the divine Light cannot but fall, whether as Justice or still more as Mercy; in gnosis, this
process of mystical alchemy is accompanied by appropriate concepts
and states of consciousness. Seen from this angle, the primacy of
love is not opposed to the perspective of wisdom, but illumines its
operative aspect.

• • •

The morality which offers the other cheek—so far as morality can here be spoken of—means not an unwonted solicitude towards one's adversary, but complete indifference towards the fetters of this world, or more precisely a refusal to let oneself be caught up in the vicious circle of terrestrial causations. The man who wants to be right at any price on the personal plane, loses serenity and moves away from the 'one thing needful'; the affairs of this world bring with them only disturbances, and disturbances take one farther from God. But peace, like every spiritual attitude, can be independent from external activity; holy anger is internally calm, and when to execute judgement is an unavoidable task—unavoidable because motivated by higher and nonpersonal interests—it is quite compatible with a mind free from attachment and hatred. Christ fights against passions and interest, but not against the performance of duty or the collective interest; in other words, He is opposed to personal interest when the latter is passionate or harmful to the interests of others, and He condemns hatred, even when it serves a higher interest.

The 'non-violence' advocated by the Gospels symbolises—and makes effective—the virtue of the mind preoccupied with 'what is' rather than with 'what happens.' As a rule, man loses much time and energy in questioning himself about the injustice of his fellows as well as about supposed hardships of destiny; whether there be human injustice or divine punishment, the world—the 'current of forms' or the 'cosmic wheel'—is what it is, it simply follows its course; it is conformable to its own nature. Men cannot not be unjust, seeing that they form part of this current; to be detached from the current and to act contrary to the logic of facts and of the slaveries which it engenders is bound to appear as madness in the eyes of the world, but it is, in reality, to adopt here below the point of view of eternity. And to adopt this point of view is to see oneself from very far away: it is to see that we ourselves form part of this world of injustice, and that is one reason the more for remaining indifferent amid the uproar of human quarrelling. The saint is the man who acts as if he had died and returned to life; having already ceased to be 'himself,' in the earthly sense, he has absolutely no intention of returning to that dream, but maintains himself in a kind of wakefulness that the world, with its narrowness and impurities, cannot understand.

Pure love is not of this world of oppositions; it is by origin celestial and its end is God; it lives, as it were in itself, by its own light and in the ray of God-Love, and that is why charity 'seeketh not her own, is not easily provoked, thinketh no evil; rejoiceth not in iniquity, but rejoiceth in the truth; beareth all things, believeth all things, hopeth all things, endureth all things' (I Cor. XIII, 5-7).

Mysteries of Christ and of the Virgin*

God became man, that man might become God. The first mystery is the Incarnation, the second is the Redemption.

However, just as the Word, in assuming flesh, was already in a sense crucified, so too man, in returning to God, must share in both mysteries: the *ego* is crucified to the world, but the grace of salvation is made incarnate in the heart; sanctity is the birth and life of Christ in us.

This mystery of the Incarnation has two aspects: the Word on the one hand and His human receptacle on the other; Christ and the Virgin Mother. To be able to realise this mystery in itself, the soul must be like the Virgin; for just as the sun can be reflected in water only when it is calm, so the soul can receive Christ only in virginal purity, in original simplicity, and not in sin, which is turmoil and unbalance.

By 'mystery' we do not mean something incomprehensible in principle — unless it be on the purely rational level — but something which flows out into the Infinite, or which is envisaged in this respect, so that intelligibility becomes limitless and humanly inexhaustible. A mystery is always 'something of God.'

•   •   •

Ave Maria gratia plena, dominus tecum: benedicta tu in mulieribus, et benedictus fructus ventris tui, Jesus.

Maria is the purity, the beauty, the goodness and the humility of the cosmic Substance; the microcosmic reflection of this Substance is the soul in a state of grace. The soul in the state of baptismal grace corresponds to the Virgin Mary; the blessing of the Virgin is on him

---

*From *GDW*, Chapter 11.

who purifies his soul for God. This purity — the Marial state — is the
essential condition, not only for the reception of the sacraments, but
also for the spiritual actualisation of the real Presence of the Word.
By the word *ave*, the soul expresses the idea that, in conforming to
the perfection of Substance, it puts itself at the same time in connection with it, whilst imploring the help of the Virgin Mary, who
personifies this perfection.

Gratia plena: primordial Substance, by reason of its purity, its
goodness and its beauty, is filled with the divine Presence. It is pure,
because it contains nothing other than God; it is good, because it
compensates and absorbs all forms of cosmic disequilibrium, for it
is totality and therefore equilibrium; it is beautiful, because it is totally
submissive to God. It is thus that the soul, the microcosmic reflection of Substance — corrupted by the fall — must again become pure,
good and beautiful.

Dominus tecum: this Substance is not only filled with the divine
Presence in an ontological or existential manner, in the sense that
it is penetrated with it by definition, that is to say by its very nature,
but it is also constantly communicating with the Word as such. So,
if *gratia plena* means that the divine Mystery is immanent in the Substance as such, *Dominus tecum* signifies that God, in His metacosmic
transcendence, is revealed to the Substance, just as the eye, which
is filled with light, sees in addition the sun itself. The soul filled with
grace will see God.

Benedicta tu in mulieribus: compared with all secondary substances,
the total Substance alone is perfect, and totally under the divine
Grace. All substances derive from it by a rupture of equilibrium;
equally, all fallen souls derive from the primordial soul through the
fall. The soul in a state of grace, the soul pure, good and beautiful,
regains primordial perfection; it is, thereby, 'blessed among all'
microcosmic substances.

Et benedictus fructus ventris tui, Jesus: that which, in principle, is
Dominus tecum, becomes, in manifestation, *fructus ventris tui, Jesus*: that
is to say that the Word which communicates with the ever-virgin
substance of the total Creation, is reflected in an inverse sense within
this Creation: it will there appear as the fruit, the result, not as the
root, the cause. And again: the soul submissive to God by its purity,
its goodness and its beauty, seems to give birth to God, according
to appearances; but this God being born in it will transmute and
absorb it, as Christ transmutes and absorbs His mystical body, the

Church, which from being militant and suffering becomes triumphant. But in reality, the Word is not born in the Substance, for the Word is immutable; it is the Substance which dies in the Word. Again, when God seems to germinate in the soul, it is in reality the soul which dies in God. *Benedictus*: the Word which becomes incarnate is itself Benediction; nevertheless, since according to appearances it is manifest as Substance, as soul it is called blessed; for it is then envisaged, not in respect of its transcendence — which would render Substance unreal — but in respect of its appearance, its Incarnation: *fructus*.

Jesus: the Word, which determines Substance, reveals itself to the latter. Macrocosmically, it is the Word which manifests itself in the Universe as the divine Spirit; microcosmically, it is the Real Presence affirming itself at the centre of the soul, radiating outwards and finally transmuting and absorbing it.[1]

• • •

The virginal perfections are purity, beauty, goodness and humility; it is these qualities which the soul in quest of God must realise.

Purity: the soul is empty of all desire. Every natural movement which asserts itself in the soul is then considered in respect of its passional quality, its aspect of concupiscence, of seduction. This perfection is cold, hard and transparent like a diamond. It is immortality excluding all corruption.

Beauty: the beauty of the Virgin expresses divine Peace. It is in the perfect equilibrium of its possibilities that the universal Substance realises its beauty. In this perfection, the soul quits all dissipation to repose in its own substantial, primordial, ontological perfection. We said above that the soul must be like a perfectly calm expanse of water; every natural movement of the soul will then appear as agitation, dissipation, shrivelling up, and so as ugliness.

Goodness: the mercy of the cosmic Substance consists in this, that, virgin in relation to its products, it comprises an inexhaustible power of equilibrium, of setting aright, of healing, of absorbing evil and of manifesting good; being maternal towards beings who address themselves to it, it in no way refuses them its assistance. Likewise, the soul must divert its love from the hardened *ego* and direct it towards the neighbour and the whole of creation; the distinction between 'I' and 'other' is as if abolished, the 'I' has become 'other' and the 'other' become 'I.' The passional distinction between 'I' and 'thou' is a state of death, comparable to the separation between the soul and God.

Humility: the Virgin, despite her supreme sanctity, remains woman and aspires to no other role; the humble soul is conscious of its own rank and effaces itself before what surpasses it. It is thus that the *Materia Prima* of the Universe remains on its own level and never seeks to appropriate to itself the transcendence of the Principle.

The mysteries, joyful, sorrowful and glorious of Mary are so many aspects of cosmic reality on the one hand, and of mystical life on the other.

Like Mary — and like universal Substance — the sanctified soul is 'virgin,' 'spouse,' and 'mother.'

. . .

The Lord's Prayer is the most excellent prayer of all, since it has Christ for its author; it is, therefore, more excellent, as a prayer, than the *Ave*, and that is why it is the first prayer of the Rosary. But the *Ave* is more excellent than the Lord's Prayer in that it contains the Name of Christ, mysteriously identified with Christ Himself, since 'God and His Name are one.' Christ is more than the Prayer He taught, and the *Ave*, which contains Christ through His Name, is thus more than this Prayer; this is why the recitations of the *Ave* are much more numerous than those of the *Pater*, and why the *Ave* constitutes, with the Name of the Lord that it contains, the very substance of the Rosary. What we have just stated amounts to saying that the prayer of the 'servant' addressed to the 'Lord' corresponds to the 'Lesser Mysteries'— and we recall that these concern the realisation of the primordial or edenic state, and hence the fullness of the human state — while the Name of God itself corresponds to the 'Great Mysteries,' the finality of which is beyond all individual states.

From the microcosmic point of view, as we have seen, 'Mary' is the soul in the state of 'sanctifying grace,' qualified to receive the 'Real Presence'; 'Jesus' is the divine Seed, the 'Real Presence' which brings about the transmutation of the soul, namely its universalisation, or its reintegration in the Eternal. 'Mary'— like the 'Lotus'— is 'surface' or 'horizontal'; Jesus — like the 'Jewel'[2] — is 'centre' and, in the dynamic relationship, 'vertical.' 'Jesus' is God in us, God who penetrates us and transfigures us.

Among the meditations of the Rosary, the 'joyful Mysteries' concern, from the point of view adopted here, and in connection with jaculatory prayers, the 'Real Presence' of the Divine in the human; as for the 'sorrowful Mysteries', they describe the redemptive 'imprisonment' of the Divine in the human, the inevitable profanation of the 'Real Presence' by human limitations; finally, the 'glorious Mysteries' relate to the victory of the Divine over the human, the freeing of the soul by the Spirit.

The Problem of Evangelism*

Christianity is divided into three great denominations: Catholicism, Orthodoxy, Evangelism, not to mention the Copts and other ancient groups close to Orthodoxy. This classification may astonish some of our regular readers since it seems to place Protestantism on the same level as the ancient Churches; now we have in view here, not liberal Protestantism or no matter what sect, but Lutheran Evangelism, and the latter incontestably manifests a Christian possibility, a limited one, no doubt, and excessive through certain of its features, but not intrinsically illegitimate, and consequently representative of certain theological, moral and even mystical values. If Evangelism — to use the term favored by Luther — were situated in a world such as that of Hinduism, it would appear therein as a possible way, that is to say it would be, no doubt, a secondary *darshana* amongst others; in Buddhism it would not be more heterodox than is Amidism or the school of Nichiren, both of which, however, are independent with regard to the global tradition surrounding them.

To understand our point of view, one has to know that the religions are determined by archetypes which are so many spiritual possibilities: on the one hand, every religion *a priori* manifests an archetype, but on the other hand, every archetype can manifest itself *a posteriori* within every religion. It is thus that Shi'ism for example is due, not to a Christian influence of course, but to a manifestation, within Islam, of the religious possibility — or the spiritual arche-

*From *CI*, Chapter 3 (trans. G. Polit)

type—which affirmed itself in a direct and plenary fashion in Christianity; and this same possibility gave rise, within Buddhism, to Amidist mysticism, but accentuating another dimension of the archetype, namely that of a cosmic prodigy of Mercy, which requires, and at the same time confers, the quasi-charisma of saving Faith; whereas in the case of Shi'ism the accent is upon the divine man opening Heaven to earth.

It could be said analogously that the Germanic soul—treated by Rome in too Latin a manner, but this is another question—that this soul, which is neither Greek nor Roman, felt the need of a more simple and more inward religious archetype, one less formalistic therefore, and more "popular" in the best sense of the word; this in certain respects is the religious archetype of Islam, a religion based on a Book and conferring priesthood upon every believer. At the same time and from another point of view, the Germanic soul had a nostalgia for a perspective that integrates the natural into the supernatural, that is, tending towards God without being against nature; a piety that was non-monastic, yet accessible to every man of good will in the midst of earthly preoccupations; a way founded upon Grace and confidence and not upon Justice and works; and this way incontestably has its premises in the Gospel itself.

•   •   •

Here it is once again—for we have done so upon other occasions —appropriate to define the difference between a heresy which is extrinsic hence relative to a given orthodoxy, and another that is intrinsic, hence false in itself and with respect to all orthodoxy or to the truth as such. To simplify the matter, we may limit ourselves to noting that the former manifests a spiritual archetype—in a limited manner, no doubt, but nonetheless efficacious—whereas the latter is merely human workings and in consequence based solely on its own productions[1] which decides the entire question. To claim that a "pious" spirit is assured of salvation is meaningless, for in total heresies there is no element that can guarantee posthumous beatitude, even though—apart from all question of belief—a man can always be saved for reasons which escape us; but he is certainly not saved by his heresy...

On the subject of Arianism, which was a particularly invasive heresy, the following remark ought to be made: it is unquestionably heterodox by the fact that it sees in Jesus merely a creature; this idea can have a meaning in the perspective of Islam, but it is incompatible with that of Christianity. However, the lightning-like expansion of Arianism shows that it answered to a spiritual need—conformable to the archetype of which Islam is the most characteristic manifestation—and it is precisely to this need or to this expectation that Evangelism finally responded,[2] not in humanizing Christ, of course, but in simplifying the religion and Germanizing it in a certain manner. Another well-known heresy was Nestorianism, which rigorously separated the two natures of Christ, the divine and the human, and by way of consequence saw in Mary the mother of Christ but not of God; this perspective corresponds to a possible theological point of view, and thus it is a question of an extrinsic, and not a total, heresy. . .

• • •

It is not difficult to argue, against the Reformation, that it is impossible that the traditional authorities and the councils, by definition inspired by the Holy Spirit, were mistaken; this is true, but does not exclude paradoxes that attenuate this quasi-evidentness. First of all, and it is this that gave wings to the reformers, starting with Wycliff and Huss, Christ himself challenged many "traditional" elements supported by the "authorities" in calling them "prescriptions of men"; then, the excesses of "papism" at the time of Luther and well before then, prove if not that the papacy in itself is illegitimate, at least that it comprises excesses which the Byzantine Church is the first to note and to stigmatize. We mean to say that the pope, instead of being *primus inter pares* as Saint Peter had been, has the exorbitant privilege of being at once prophet and emperor: as prophet, he places himself above the councils, and as emperor, he possesses a temporal power that surpasses that of all the princes including the emperor himself; and it is precisely these unheard-of prerogatives which permitted, in our time, the entry of modernism into the Church, like a Trojan horse and despite the warnings of the preceding popes; that popes may personally have been saints does not at all weaken the valid arguments of the Eastern Church. In a word, if the Church of the West had been such that it could have avoided casting the Church of the East into the "outer darknesses"— and with what manifestation of barbarism — it would not have had to undergo the counterblow of the Reformation.

Moreover, to say that the Roman Church is intrinsically orthodox and integrally traditional does not mean that it conveys in a direct, compelling and exhaustive manner all aspects of the world of the Gospel, even though it necessarily contains them and manifests them occasionally or sporadically; for the world of the Gospel was Oriental and Semitic and plunged in a climate of holy poverty, whereas the world of Catholicism is European, Roman, imperial; this is to say that the religion was Romanized in the sense that the characteristic traits of the Roman mentality have determined its formal elaboration. Suffice it to mention in this respect its juridicism and its administrative and even military spirit; traits which are manifested by, among others, the disproportionate complication of rubrics, the prolixity of the missal, the dispersing complexity of the sacramental economy, the pedantic manipulation of indulgences; then by a certain administrative centralization — indeed militarization — of monastic spirituality; without forgetting, on the level of forms — which is far from being negligible — the pagan titanism of the Renaissance and the nightmare of Baroque art. Still from the point of view of formal outwardness, the following remark could be made: in the Catholic world, and already by the end of the Middle Ages, the difference between religious and laical dress is often abrupt to the point of incompatibility; when the essentially worldly and vain, indeed erotic trappings of the princes is compared with the majestic garments of the priests, it is hard to believe that the former are Christians like the latter, whereas in the Oriental civilizations the style of dress is in general homogeneous. In Islam, there does not even exist a dividing line between religious figures and the rest of society; there is no laical society opposed at the level of appearances to a priestly one. This being said, let us close this parenthesis, the point of which was simply to show that the Catholic world presents traits — on its surface as well as in its depths — which certainly do not express the climate of the Gospels.[3]

It has been argued to satiety that it is sacred institutions that count and not the human accidents that disfigure them; this is obvious, yet the very degree of this disfiguration indicates that in the institutions themselves part of the imperfection was due to some human zeal. Dante and Savonarola saw this clearly in their way. and the very phenomenon of the Renaissance proves it. If it be said to us that the papacy, such as it was throughout the centuries, represents the only possible solution for the West, we agree, but then one should have foreseen the risks that this inevitable adaptation fatally comprised, and have done everything to diminish, not to increase them; if a strongly marked hierarchy was indispensable, one should have insisted all the more on the sacerdotal aspect of every Christian.

However that may be, what permitted Luther to separate himself from Rome,[4] was his awareness of the principle of the "decadence of orthodoxy," that is of the possibility of a fall within the immutable framework of a traditional orthodoxy, an awareness inspired by the example of the scribes and the pharisees in the Gospel, with their "prescriptions of men"; objectively, what is meant by this are the specifications, developments, elaborations, clarifications and stylizations required by one given temperament, but not by another.[5] Another association of ideas which was useful to Luther and to Protestantism in general is the Augustinian opposition between a *civitas dei* and a *civitas terrena* or *diaboli*: the witnessing of the disorders of the Roman Church easily led him to the identity of Rome with the "earthly city" of Saint Augustine. There is also, and fundamentally, a tendency in the Gospel which answers with particular force to the needs of the Germanic soul: namely the tendency towards simplicity and inwardness, hence contrary to theological and liturgical complication, to formalism, to dispersion of worship, to the all too often off-handed tyranny of the clergy. From another viewpoint, the Germans were sensitive to the nobly and robustly popular character of the Bible, which has no relationship with democracy, for Luther was a supporter of a theocratic regime upheld by the emperor and the princes.

Without question, the perspective of Evangelism is typically Pauline; it is founded on the so to speak gnostic dualism of the following elements: the flesh and the spirit, death and life, servitude and Freedom, the Law and Grace, justice through works and justice through faith, Adam and Christ. From another point of view, Evangelism is founded, like Christianity as such, on the Pauline idea of the universality of salvation responding to the universality of sin or to the state of the sinner; only the redemptive death of Christ could deliver man from this curse; by the Redemption, Christ became the luminous head of all humanity. But the typically Pauline accentuation of the Message is the doctrine of justification through faith, which Luther made the pivot of the religion, or more precisely of his mysticism.

•   •   •

After the defeat of Wycliff and Huss — from whom it would have been proper to retain, if not the entire doctrine, then at least certain of its tendencies — the popes contributed by their obduracy to the Lutheran explosion;[6] after the defeat — within the very framework of Catholic orthodoxy — of Dante, and other warners, Luther by his violence caused the Catholic renovation; Providence willed both outcomes, the Evangelical Church as well as the Tridentine Church. Ideally speaking: after the Council of Trent, Catholicism should have assimilated — without denying itself — the essence of the message of Evangelism, as the latter should have rediscovered the essence of the Catholic reality; instead of that, both parties hardened in their respective positions, and in fact, they could not have done otherwise, if only for the same reason that there are diverse religions: that is, it is necessary for spiritual perspectives, before they start to shade their meanings, to be entirely themselves, all the more so in that their overaccentuation answers to racial or ethnic needs.[7]

Each denomination manifests the Gospel in a certain manner; now this manifestation seems to us to be the most direct, the most ample and the most realistic possible in the Orthodox Church, which can already be seen in the outer forms of the latter, whereas the Catholic Church offers an image that is more Roman, less Oriental, in a certain sense even more worldly since the Renaissance and the Baroque epoch, as we have pointed out above. Latin civilization has nothing to do with the world and the spirit of the Gospel; but after all, the Roman West is Christian and in consequence Christianity has the right to be Roman. There remains the Evangelical Church; the question of its cultural forms does not arise, since in this respect it participates in the Catholic culture, with the difference however that it introduces into the latter a principle of rather iconoclastic sobriety, while having the advantage of not accepting the Renaissance and its prolongations; this is to say that Evangelism stopped, artistically speaking and in the intention of Luther, at the forms of the Middle Ages, while simplifying them, and that it thus escaped that unqualifiable aberration which was Baroque art. From the spiritual point of view, Protestantism retains from the Gospel the spirit of simplicity and inwardness while accentuating the mystery of faith, and it presents these aspects with a vigor the moral and mystical value of which cannot be denied; this accentuation was necessary in the West, and since Rome did not wish to take it upon itself, it is Wittenberg that did so.

In connection with Protestant quasi-iconoclasm, we would point out that Saint Bernard also wished to have chapels empty, bare and sober, in short that "sensible consolations" be reduced to a minimum; but he desired it for the monasteries and not for the Cathedrals; the sense of the sacred in this case, is concentrated on the essential of the rites. We meet with this point of view in Zen as well as in Islam, and above all we meet with it repeatedly in Christ, so much so that it would be unjust to deny any precedent in the Scripture to the Lutheran attitude; Christ wanted one to adore God "in spirit and in truth" and that one not do so with "vain repetitions as the heathen" in praying; it is the accentuation of faith, with the primacy of sincerity and intensity.

• • •

The celibacy of priests, imposed by Gregory VII after one thousand years of practice to the contrary — the latter being always maintained by the Church of the East — presents several serious drawbacks: it needlessly repeats the celibacy of the monks and cuts off the priests more radically from lay society, which becomes all the more laic thereby; that is, this measure reinforces in the laity the feeling of dependence and of lesser moral value, marriage being in practice belittled by still another edict. Next, the celibacy imposed upon an enormous number of priests — for society has all the more need of priests as it is numerous and Christianity is all of the West — that is, upon too great a number, necessarily created moral disorders and contributed to the loosening of morals, whereas it would have been better to have good married priests than bad celibate priests; unless the number of priests be reduced, which is impossible since society is large and has need of them. Finally, the celibacy of the clergy prevents the procreation of men of religious vocation, it thus impoverishes society; if only men without religious vocation can have children, the society will become more and more worldly and "horizontal," and less and less spiritual and "vertical."

However that may be, Luther lacked realism in his turn: he was astonished that during his absence from Wittenberg—this was the year of Wartburg—the promoters of the Reformation gave themselves up to all kinds of excesses; at the end of his life, he even went so far as to regret that the mass of the mediocre had not remained under the rod of the pope. Scarcely occupying himself with collective psychology, he believed that the simple principle of piety could replace the material supports which contribute so powerfully to regulate the behavior of the crowds; not only to put this behavior in equilibrium within space, but also to stabilize it in time. He was unaware, in his mystical subjectivism, that a religion has need of symbolism in order to be able to subsist; that the inward cannot live in a collective consciousness without outward signs;[8] but, prophet of inwardness, he scarcely had a choice.

The Latin West had too often lacked realism and measure, whereas the Greek Church, like the East generally, knew better how to reconcile the exigencies of spiritual idealism with those of the everyday human world. From a particular viewpoint, we would like to make the following remark: it is very unlikely that Christ, who washed the feet of his disciples and who taught them that "the first shall be the last," would have appreciated the imperial pomp of the Vatican court: such as the kissing of the foot, the triple crown, the *flabelli*, the *sedia gestatoria*; to the contrary, there is no reason to think that he would have disapproved of the ceremonies—of sacerdotal and not imperial style—which surround the Orthodox patriarch; he would no doubt have disapproved of the cardinalate, which on the one hand raises so to speak the princely throne of the pope, and on the other hand constitutes a dignity that is non-sacerdotal and more worldly than religious.[9]

We have spoken above of the celibacy of priests imposed by Gregory VII, and we must add a word concerning the Evangelical councils and the monastic vows. When one reads in the Gospel that "there is no man that hath left house, or brethren, or sisters, or father, or mother, or wife, or children, or lands, for my sake, and the gospel's," one immediately thinks of monks and nuns; now Luther thought that it was solely a question of persecutions, in the sense of this saying from the Sermon on the Mount: "Blessed are they who are persecuted for righteousness' sake: for theirs is the kingdom of Heaven";[10] and he is all the more sure of his interpretation in that there were neither anchorites nor monks before the IVth century.

•   •   •

Viewed in its totality, Protestantism has something ambiguous about it due to the fact that, on the one hand it is inspired sincerely and concretely by the Bible, yet on the other hand it is bound up with humanism and the Renaissance. It is Luther who incarnates the first kind: his perspective is medieval and so to speak retrospective, and it gives rise to conservative and at times esoterically tending pietism. In Calvin, it is on the contrary tendencies of humanism, hence of the Renaissance which, if they do not determine the movement, at least mingle with it rather strongly; no doubt, he is greatly inspired in his doctrine by Luther and the Swiss reformers, but in his republican fashion — on a theocratic basis of course — and not in monarchist fashion like the German reformer; and it can be said on the whole that in a certain manner he was more opposed to Catholicism than was the latter.[11]

For some time already, the fundamental ideas of the Reformation had been "in the air," but it is Luther who lived them and who made of them a personal drama. His Evangelism — like that of other particular perspectives enclosed within a general perspective — is an overaccentuated "decoupage," but sufficient and efficacious, hence "non-illegitimate." [12]

One cannot study the problem of Evangelism without taking into consideration the powerful personality of its real, or at least its most notable, founder. First of all, and this follows from what we have just said, nothing allows one to affirm that Luther was a modernist ahead of his time, for he was in no wise worldly and sought to please no one; his innovations were assuredly of the most audacious kind, to say the least, but they were Christian and nothing else; they owed nothing to any philosopher or to any scientism.[13] He rejected Rome, not because it was too spiritual, but on the contrary because it seemed to him too worldly; too "according to the flesh" and not "according to the spirit," from his particular point of view.

The mystic of Wittenberg[14] was a German Semiticized by Christianity, and he was representative in both respects: fundamentally German, he loved what is sincere and inward, not facile and formalistic; Semitic in spirit, he admitted only Revelation and faith and did not wish to hear talk of Aristotle or the Scholastics.[15] On the one hand, there was in his nature something robust and powerful (*gewaltig*), with a complement of poetry and gentleness (*Innigkeit*); on the other hand, he was a voluntarist and an individualist who expected nothing from either intellectuality or metaphysics. To be sure, his impetuous genius was capable of uncouthness —which is the least that can be said— but he lacked neither patience nor generosity; he could be vehement, but not more so than a Saint Jerome or other saints who reviled their adversaries, "devoured" as they were by "zeal for the house of the Lord"; and no one can contest that they found precedents for this in both Testaments.[16]

The message of Luther is essentially expressed in two legacies, which testify to the personality of the author and to which it is impossible to deny grandeur and efficaciousness: the German Bible and the hymns. His translation of the Scripture, while conditioned in certain places by his doctrinal perspective, is a jewel both of language and piety; as for his hymns—most of which are not from his hand, although he composed their models and thus gave the impulse to their flowering— these hymns we say, became a fundamental element of worship, and for Evangelism they were a powerful factor of expansion.[17] The Catholic Church itself could not resist this magic; it ended by adopting several Lutheran hymns, which had become popular to the point of imposing themselves like the air one breathes. In summary, the whole personality of Luther is in his translation of the Psalms and in his famous hymn "A Mighty Fortress Is Our God" (*Ein feste Burg ist unser Gott*), which became the "war song" (*Trutzlied*) of Evangelism, and whose qualities of power and grandeur cannot be denied. But more gently, this personality is also in his commentary on the *Magnificat*, which testifies to an inner worship of the Holy Virgin whom Luther never rejected; Pope Leo X, having read this commentary without knowing its author made this remark: "Blessed be the hands that wrote this!" No doubt the German reformer was not able to maintain the public worship of the Virgin, but this was because of the general reaction against the dispersion of religious sentiment, hence in favor of worship concentrated on Christ alone, which became absolute and consequently exclusive, as is the worship of *Allah* for the Moslems. Besides, Scripture treats the Virgin with a somewhat surprising parsimony—which played a certain role here—but there are also the crucial, and doctrinally inexhaustible, declarations that Mary is "full of grace" and that "all generations shall call me blessed."[18]

The German reformer was a mystic in the sense that his way was purely experimental and not conceptual; the pertinent demonstrations of a Staupitz were of no help to him. To discover the efficacy of Mercy, he needed first the "event of the tower"; having meditated in vain on the "Justice of God," he had the grace of under-standing in a flash that this Justice is merciful and that it liberates us in and by faith.

• • •

The great themes of Luther are the Scripture, Christ, the Inward, Faith; the first two elements on the divine side, and the latter two on the human side. By accentuating Scripture — at the expense of Tradition — Evangelism is close to Islam, wherein the Koran is everything; by accentuating Christ — at the expense of the pope, of hierarchy, of the clergy — Evangelism recalls devotional Buddhism which places everything in the hands of *Amitabha*; the worshipful and ritual expression of this primacy of Christ being Communion, which for Luther is as real and as important as for the Catholics. The Lutheran tendency towards the "inward," the "heart," if one will, is incontestably founded on the perspective of Christ, and likewise the accenting of faith, which moreover evokes — we repeat — Amidist mysticism as well as Moslem piety. We would not dream of making these comparisons, at first glance needless, if they did not serve to illustrate the principle of the archetypes which we have spoken of above and which is of crucial importance.

As regards Christ concretized in Communion, it is not true that Luther reduced the Eucharistic rite to a simple ceremony of remembrance, as did his adversary Zwingli;[19] quite to the contrary, he admitted the real Presence, but neither transubstantiation — which the Greeks did not accept either as such, although they ended by accepting the word — nor the bloodless renewal of the historical sacrifice; however, the sacramental realities perceived by the Catholics are implicitly comprised in the Lutheran definition of the Eucharist — objectively but not subjectively — so much so that it could even be said, even from the Catholic point of view, that this definition is acceptable on condition of being conscious of this implication. For the Catholics, this latter condition constitutes the very definition of the mystery, which is perhaps disproportionate if one takes account of the somewhat dispersing and "free" usage that Catholicism makes of its Mass;[20] certain psychological facts — human nature being what it is — no doubt would have required that the mystery be presented in a more veiled fashion and be handled with more discretion. To be sure, the Lutheran Communion is not the equivalent of the Catholic Communion, but we have reasons for believing—given its context as a whole—that it nonetheless communicates to a sufficient degree the graces Luther expected of it,[21] which presupposes that the intention of the ritual change was fundamentally Christian—and free from all rationalist, let alone political, hindsight—as was the case in fact.

If the Lutheran Communion is not the equivalent of the Catholic Communion, it is because it does not comprise spiritual virtualities as extensive as those of the latter; but precisely, these initiatic virtualities are too lofty for most mortals, and to impose them upon the latter is to expose them to sacrilege. From another point of view, if the Mass were still equal to the historical Sacrifice of Christ, it would become sacrilege due to its profanation by the more or less trivial manner of its usage: hasty low Masses, Masses attributed to this or that, including the most contingent and profane occasions. To be sure, the Mass coincides potentially with the event of Golgotha, and this potentiality, or this virtuality, can always give rise to an effective coincidence;[22] but if the Mass had in itself the character of its blood prototype, at each Mass the earth would tremble and would be covered with darkness.

• • •

In summary: according to Luther, the grace obtained by and in faith regenerates the soul and permits it to unite itself to the Divine Life; it permits man to resist evil, to combat it and to exercise charity towards the neighbor. It is faith which saves, and not works; because we have no need to add our insignificant merits to the infinite merits of Christ. Works are useful when we do not consider them meritorious; in that case they become integrated into faith.

• • •

What fundamentally constitutes the Lutheran message is the accentuation of faith within the awareness of our misery; by this very awareness, but also in spite of it. All the limitations of this point of departure have indirectly the function of a key or a symbol; they are compensated, beyond the words, by the ineffable response of

Mercy; the initial torment is resolved in the final analysis in the quasi-mystical experience of the faith that appeases, vivifies and liberates.

•   •   •

One recognizes in Luther tendencies quite analogous to those of the "friends of God" (*die Gottesfreunde*), a mystical society which flowered in the XIVth century in the Rhineland, Swabia and Switzerland, and whose most eminent representatives were Tauler and the blessed Suso. The former—known to Luther— made himself the spokesman of the Eckhartian doctrine of "quietude" (*Gelassenheit*) and fought against "justice through works" (*Werkgerechtigkeit*) and against outward religiosity.

According to Tersteegen[23]—one of the saintly men of the Evangelical Church—"the true theosophers, about whom we know very little after the time of the Apostles, were all mystics, but it is very far from the case that all mystics are theosophers; not one amongst thousands. The theosophers are those whose spirit (not reason) has explored the depths of the Divinity under Divine guidance, and whose spirit has known such marvels thanks to an infallible vision."[24]

What exoterism—Catholic, Orthodox or Evangelical—does not say, and cannot say is that the Pauline or Biblical mystery of faith is none other at its root than that of gnosis: that is, the latter is the prototype and the underlying essence of the former. If faith can save, it is because intellective knowledge delivers; this knowledge which, being transcendent, is immanent, and conversely. The Lutheran theosophers were gnostics within the framework of faith, and the most metaphysical Sufis accentuate faith on the basis of knowledge; no doubt there is a faith without gnosis, but there is not gnosis without faith. The soul can go to God without the direct concurrence of pure intellect, but the latter cannot manifest itself without giving the soul peace and life, and without demanding from it all the faith of which it is capable.

NOTES

The Christian Tradition Some Thoughts on its Nature

1. "The Word was the true Light, which lighteth every man. . ." (John i, 9).

2. It is significant that the Celtic Church, that mysterious springtime world which appeared as a sort of last prolongation of the golden age, held itself to be attached to St. John.

3. According to Tertullian, 'the flesh is anointed that the soul may be sanctified; the flesh is signed that the soul may be fortified; the flesh is placed in shadow by the laying on of hands that the soul may be illumined by the Holy Spirit.' As for Baptism, the same author says that 'the flesh is washed that the soul may be purified.'—According to St. Dionysius, Baptism, Eucharist and Confirmation refer respectively to the ways of 'purification,' 'illumination' and 'perfection'; according to others, it is Baptism which is called an 'illumination'; this clearly does not contradict the foregoing perspective, since all initiation 'illumines' by definition: the taking away of 'original sin' opens the way to a 'light' pre-existing in edenic man.

4. These funeral rites remind one of the symbolic cremation which, in India, inaugurates the state of *sannyâsa*.

5. The married man can be chaste 'in spirit and in truth,' and the same necessarily holds good for poverty and obedience, as is proved by the example of St. Louis and other canonised monarchs. The reservation expressed by the words 'in spirit and in truth,' or by the Pauline formulation 'the letter killeth, but the spirit giveth life,' has a capital importance in the Christian perspective, but it also contains — and moreover providentially — a 'two-edged sword.'

6. For Clement of Alexandria, the body of Christ, or the eucharistic bread, concerns active life or faith, and the blood or the wine, contemplation and gnosis.

7. The same fact is recounted of a Dominican saint, Catherine of Racconigi. Apart from the *Ave Maria* and the Name of Jesus, mention should be made of the double invocation *Jesu Maria*, which contains as it were two mystical dimensions, as also of *Christe eleison* which is in effect an abridgement of the 'Jesus Prayer' of the Eastern Church; it is known that the mystical science of jaculatory prayer was transmitted to the West by Cassian, who appears retrospectively as the providential intermediary between the two great branches of Christian spirituality, whilst in his own time he was, for the West, the representative of the mystical tradition as such. And let us recall here equally those liturgical words: ' *Panem celestem accipiam et nomen Domini invocabo,*' and: '*Calicem salutaris accipiam et nomen Domini invocabo.*'— in Greek and Slav monasteries a knotted chaplet forms part of the investiture of the Small Schema and the Great Schema: it is conferred ritually on the monk or the nun The Superior takes the chaplet in his left hand and says: "Take, brother N., the sword of the Spirit which is the word of God, to pray to Jesus without ceasing, for you must constantly have the Name of the Lord Jesus in the mind, in the heart and on the lips, saying: 'Lord Jesus Christ, Son of God, have mercy on me, a sinner.'" In the same order of ideas, we would draw attention to the 'act of love'— the perpetual prayer of the heart — revealed, in our times, to Sister Consolata of Testona.

8. The commentators of the Torah state that the impediment of speech from which Moses suffered was imposed on him by God so that he should not be able to divulge the Mysteries which, precisely, the Law of Sinai had to veil and not to unveil; but these Mysteries were, basically, none other than the 'Christ-given Mysteries.'

9. Veracity, which in the end has more importance than moral conjectures, implies in short the consequent use of logic, that is to say: to put nothing higher than truth, nor to fall into the contrary fault of believing that to be impartial means not to consider anyone right or wrong. One must not stifle discernment for the sake of impartiality, for objectivity consists, not in absolving the wrong or accusing the right, but in seeing things as they are, whether that pleases us or not: it is, consequently, to have a sense of proportion as much as a sense of subtlety of degrees. It would be useless to say such elementary things if one did not meet at every turn this false virtue which distorts the exact vision of facts but could dispense with its scruples if only it realised sufficiently the value and efficacy of humility before God.

Mysteries of Christ and of the Virgin
1. This expression should not be taken quite literally any more than other expressions of union which will follow; here, what is essential is to be aware of 'deification, ' whatever significance one may give to this term.

2. We are here alluding to the well-known Buddhist formula: *Om mani padmê hum*. There is an analogy worth noticing between this formula and the name 'Jesus of Nazareth': the literal meaning of *Nazareth* is 'flower,' and *mani padmê* means 'jewel in the lotus.'

The Problem of Evangelism
1. Such as Mormonism, Bahaism, the Ahmadism of Kadyan, and all the "new religions" and other pseudo-spiritualities which proliferate in today's world.

2. Arius of Alexandria was not a German, but his doctrine went out to meet an aspiration of the Germanic mentality, whence its success with the Visigoths, the Ostrogoths, the Vandals, the Burgundians and the Langobards.

3. For a Joseph de Maistre, whose intelligence moreover had great merits, the reformers could not be other than "nobodies" who dared to set their personal opinions against the traditional and unanimous certitudes of the Catholic Church; he was far from suspecting that these "nobodies" spoke under the pressure of an archetypal perspective which, being such, could not not become manifested in appropriate circumstances. The same author accused Protestantism with having done an immense evil in breaking up Christianity, but he readily loses sight of the fact that Catholicism did as much in rashly excommunicating all of the Patriarchs of the East; without forgetting the Renaissance, whose evil was, to say the least, as "immense" as those of the political and other effects of the Reformation

4. He separated himself from the Roman Church only after his condemnation, by burning the bull of excommunication; and it is appropriate moreover not to lose sight of the fact that at the time of the Reformation there was no unanimity on the question of the pope and the councils, and even the question of the divine origin of the papal authority was not secure from all controversy.

5. Hinduism also — without mentioning the Mediterranean paganisms — furnishes an example of this kind, with the heavy and endless pedantry of the Brahmans which, however, was not too difficult to escape, given the plasticity of the Hindu spirit and the suppleness of the corresponding institutions.

6. This is something which, within the Catholic camp, Cardinal Newman and others have acknowledged.

7. In so saying, we do not lose sight of the fact that the Germans of the South — the Allamanis (the Germans of Baden, the Alsatians, the German Swiss, the Swabians) and the Bavarians (including the Austrians) — have a rather different temperament than that of the Germans of the North, and that everywhere there are mixtures; racial and ethnic frontiers in Europe are, in any case, rather fluctuating. We do not say that every German is made for Evangelism, for Germanic tendencies can obviously manifest within Catholicism just as, conversely, Protestant Calvinism manifests above all a Latin possibility.

8. This is, moreover, be it said in passing, what is forgotten by most of the even impeccable *gurus* of contemporary India, starting with Rāmakrishna.

9. "But be not ye called Rabbi: for one is your Master, even Christ; and all ye are brethren." "Neither be ye called masters: for one is your Master, even Christ." (Matth. xxiii, 8 and 10)

10. He says so in a marginal note of his translation: "Whosoever believes, must suffer persecution, and risk all" (*alles dran setzen*). And he repeats it in his song *Ein feste Burg ist unser Gott*: "Even if they (the persecutors) take body, goods, honor, child and wife, let them go (*lass fahren dahin*); they shall receive no benefit; the Kingdom (of God) shall be ours" (*das Reich muss uns doch bleiben*).

11. As for Protestant liberalism, Luther, after a while, foresaw its abuses and he would in any case be horrified to see this liberalism such as it presents itself in our time; he who could bear neither self-sufficient mediocrity nor iconoclastic fanaticism.

12. Evangelism properly so-called, which is at the antipodes from liberal Protestant-ism, was perpetuated in pietism, whose father was De Labadie, a mystic converted to the Reformation in the XVth century, and whose most notable representatives were no doubt Spener and Tersteegen; this pietism or this piety exists always in various places, either in a diminished or quite honorable form.

13. As is, on the contrary, the case in Catholic modernism. That this modernism is open not only towards Evangelism, but also towards Islam and other religions, gets us nowhere, since this same modernism is also altogether open to no matter what, except to Tradition.

14. For he was a mystic rather than a theologian, which explains many things.

15. It could be objected that the Semites adopted the Greek philosophers, but that is not the question, for this adoption was diverse and graded, not to mention many reservations. Besides, Luther — a cultivated man — was also a logician and could not not be one; in certain respects, he was Latinized of necessity — as was an Albert the Great or an Eckhart — but that was on the surface only.

16. When the reformer terms the "papist mass" an abomination, we are made to think of the bonze Nichiren who claimed that it sufficed to invoke Amida once to fall into Hell; not to mention the Buddha who rejected the Veda, the castes and the gods.

17. Among the composers of hymns, there were notably the pastor Johan Valentin Andrea, author of the "Chemical Marriages of Christian Rosenkreutz," and later Paul Gerhardt, Tersteegen and Novalis, whose hymns are among the jewels of German poetry; and let us add that the religious music of Bach testifies to the same spirit of powerful piety

18. As Dante said: "Lady, thou art so great and possesseth such power, that whosoever desireth grace and has recourse to thee, it is as if his desire wished to fly without wings." (*Paradiso*, XXXIII, 13-15)

19. Whose thesis has been retained by liberal Protestantism; Calvin attempted to bring it back more or less to that of Luther The idea of a commemorative rite pure and simple is intrinsically heretical since "to do in memory of" makes no sense from the point of view of sacramental efficaciousness.

20. For one must not "cast pearls before swine" nor "give what is holy unto the dogs." With the Orthodox, the Mass is the center disposed of by the priests, whereas it could be said that with the Catholics it is the priest who is, in practice, the center who disposes of the Masses.

21. The same could be admitted, with perhaps certain reservations which are difficult to make precise, for the Calvinist and Anglican Communions, but not for those of the Zwinglians or the liberal Protestants or, further — which at first will seem paradoxical — for the "conciliary" or post-conciliary masses, which are not covered by a valid archetype and which are, along with their ambiguous intentions, merely the result of human arbitrariness.

22. And this is independent of the intrinsic efficaciousness of the sacrament, notwithstanding that this efficaciousness is realized in function of the holiness, hence receptivity, of the communicant.

23. In a chapter entitled *Kurzer Bericht von der Mystik.*

24. The theosopher Angelus Silesius would not perhaps have left the Lutheran Church had he not been expelled for his esoterism; in any case, Bernardine mysticism seemed to correspond best to his spiritual vocation. This makes us think somewhat of Shri Chaitanya who, a great Advaitin, threw out his books to think only of Krishna; and let us note at this point that this bhakta, while accepted as being orthodox, rejected the ritual of the brahmans and the castes in order to put the entire accent on faith and love, not on works.

Islam

Islam*

ISLAM IS THE MEETING between God as such and man as such.

God as such: that is to say God envisaged, not as He manifested Himself in a particular way at a particular time, but independently of history and inasmuch as He is what He is and also as by His nature He creates and reveals.

Man as such: that is to say man envisaged, not as a fallen being needing a miracle to save him, but as man, a theomorphic being endowed with an intelligence capable of conceiving of the Absolute and with a will capable of choosing what leads to the Absolute.

To say 'God' is to say also 'being,' 'creating,' 'revealing'; in other words it is to say 'Reality,' 'Manifestation,' 'Reintegration': to say 'man' is to say 'theomorphism,' 'transcendent intelligence' and 'free will.' These are, in the author's meaning, the premises of the Islamic perspective, those which explain its every application and must never be lost sight of by anyone wanting to understand any particular aspect of Islam.

Man thus appears *a prior* as a dual receptacle made for the Absolute, and Islam comes to fill that receptacle, first with the truth of the Absolute and secondly with the law of the Absolute. Islam then is in essence a truth and a law—or the Truth and the Law—the former

*From *UI*, Chapter 1.

answering to the intelligence and the latter to the will. It is thus that Islam sets out to abolish both uncertainty and hesitation and, *a fortiori*, both error and sin; error in holding that the Absolute is not, or that it is relative, or that there are two Absolutes, or that the relative is absolute; sin places these errors on the level of the will or of action. These two doctrines of the Absolute and of man are respectively to be found in the two 'testimonies' of the Islamic faith, the first (*Lā ilāha illa'*Llāh) concerning God and the second (*Muhammadun rasūlu' Llāh*) concerning the Prophet.

The idea of predestination, so strongly marked in Islam, does not do away with the idea of freedom. Man is subject to predestination because he is not God, but he is free because he is 'made in the image of God.' God alone is absolute freedom, but human freedom, despite its relativity — in the sense that it is 'relatively absolute'— is not something other than freedom any more than a feeble light is something other than light. To deny predestination would amount to pretending that God does not know events 'in advance' and so is not omniscient: *quod absit*.

To sum up: Islam confronts what is immutable in God with what is permanent in man. For 'exoteric' Christianity man is *a priori* will, or, more exactly, he is will corrupted; clearly the intelligence is not denied, but it is taken into consideration only as an aspect of will; man is will and in man will is intelligent; when the will is corrupted, so also is the intelligence corrupted in the sense that in no way could it set the will to rights. Therefore a divine intervention is needed: the sacrament. In the case of Islam, where man is considered as the intelligence and intelligence comes 'before' will, it is the content or direction of the intelligence which has sacramental efficacy: whoever accepts that the Transcendent Absolute alone is absolute and transcendent, and draws from this its consequences for the will, is saved. The Testimony of Faith — the *Shahādah* — determines the intelligence; and the Islamic Law — the *Sharī'ah* — determines the will; in Islamic esotericism — the *Tarīqah* — there are initiatic graces which serve as keys and underline our 'supernatural nature.' Once again, our salvation, its texture and its development, are prefigured by our theomorphism: since we are transcendent intelligence and free will it is this intelligence and this will, or it is transcendence and freedom, which will save us; God does no more than fill the receptacles man had emptied but not destroyed; to destroy them is not in man's power.

Again in the same way: only man has the gift of speech, because

he alone among earthly creatures is 'made in the image of God' in
a direct and integral manner; now, if it is this theomorphism which,
thanks to a divine impulsion, brings about salvation or deliverance,
speech has its part to play as well as intelligence and will. These last
are indeed actualized by prayer, which is speech both divine and
human, the act relating to the will and its content to intelligence;
speech is as it were the immaterial, though sensory, body of our will
and of our understanding; but speech is not necessarily exteriorized,
for articulated thought also involves language. In Islam nothing is
of greater importance than the canonical prayers (*salāt*) directed
towards the Kaaba and the 'mentioning of God' (*dhikru 'Llāh*) directed
towards the heart; the speech of the Sufi is repeated in the universal
prayer of humanity and even in the prayer, often inarticulate, of all
beings.

What constitutes the originality of Islam is not the discovery
of the saving function of intelligence, will and speech — that function is clear enough and is known to every religion — but that it has
made of this, within the framework of Semitic monotheism, the point
of departure in a perspective of salvation and deliverance. Intelligence
is identified with its content which brings salvation; it is nothing other
than knowledge of Unity, or of the Absolute, and of the dependence
of all things on it; in the same way the will is *el-islām*, in other words
conformity to what is willed by God, or by the Absolute, on the one
hand in respect of our earthly existence and our spiritual possibility,
and on the other in respect both of man as such and of man in a
collective sense; speech is communication with God and is essentially prayer and invocation. When seen from this angle Islam recalls
to man not so much what he should know, do and say, as what intelligence, will and speech are, by very definition. The Revelation
does not superadd new elements but unveils the fundamental nature
of the receptacle...

The doctrine of Islam hangs on two statements: first 'There is
no divinity (or reality, or absolute) outside the only Divinity (or Reality, or Absolute)' (*Lā ilāha illa 'Llāh*), and 'Muhammad (the "Glorified,"
the Perfect) is the Envoy (the mouthpiece, the intermediary, the
manifestation, the symbol) of the Divinity' (*Muhammadun rasūlu 'Llāh*);
these are the first and the second 'Testimonies' (*Shahādāt*) of the faith.

Here we are in the presence of two assertions, two certitudes,
two levels of reality: the Absolute and the relative, Cause and effect, God and the world. Islam is the religion of certitude and equilib-

rium, as Christianity is the religion of love and sacrifice. By this we mean, not that religions have monopolies but that each lays stress on one or other aspect of truth. Islam seeks to implant certitude — its unitary faith stands forth as something manifestly clear without in any way renouncing mystery — and is based on two axiomatic certainties, one concerning the Principle, which is both Being and Beyond-Being, and the other concerning manifestation, both formal and supraformal: thus it is a matter on the one hand of 'God'— or of 'The Godhead' in the sense in which Eckhart used that term — and on the other of 'Earth' and 'Heaven.' The first of these certainties is that 'God alone is' and the second that 'all things are attached to God.' In other words: 'nothing is absolutely evident save the Absolute'; then, following on this truth: 'All manifestation, and so all that is relative, is attached to the Absolute.' The world is linked to God — or the relative to the Absolute —both in respect of its cause and of its end: the word 'Envoy,' in the second *Shahādah*, therefore enunciates, first a causality and then a finality, the former particularly concerning the world and the second concerning man.

All metaphysical truths are comprised in the first of these 'testimonies' and all eschatological truths in the second. But it could also be said that the first *Shahādah* is the formula of discernment or 'abstraction' (*tanzīh*) while the second is the formula of integration or 'analogy' (*tashbīh*): in the first *Shahādah* the word 'divinity' (*ilāh*) — taken here in its ordinary current sense — designates the world inasmuch as it is unreal because God alone is real, while the name of the Prophet (*Muhammad*) in the second *Shahādah* designates the world inasmuch as it is real because nothing can be outside God; in certain respects all is He. Realizing the first *Shahādah* means first of all — 'first of all' because this *Shahādah* includes the second in an eminent degree — becoming fully conscious that the Principle alone is real and that the world, though on its own level it 'exists,' 'is not'; in one sense it therefore means realizing the universal void. Realizing the second *Shahādah* means first of all becoming fully conscious that the world — or manifestation — is 'not other' than God or the Principle, since to the degree that it has reality it can only be that which alone 'is,' or in other words it can only be divine; realizing this *Shahādah* thus means seeing God everywhere and everything in Him. 'He who has seen me,' said the Prophet, 'has seen God'; now everything is the 'Prophet,' on the one hand in respect of the perfection of existence and on the other in respect of the perfections of mode or expression.

If Islam merely sought to teach that there is only one God and not two or more, it would have no persuasive force. In fact it is characterized by persuasive ardour and this comes from the fact that at root it teaches the reality of the Absolute and the dependence of all things on the Absolute. Islam is the religion of the Absolute as Christianity is the religion of love and of miracle; but love and miracle also pertain to the Absolute and express nothing other than an attitude It assumes in relation to us. . .

Here there is a point to be touched on, the question of Moslem morality. If we want to understand certain seeming contradictions in that morality we must take into account the fact that Islam distinguishes between man as such and collective man, the latter appearing as a new creature subject in a certain degree, but no further, to the law of natural selection. This is to say that Islam puts everything in its proper place and treats it according to its own nature; collective man it envisages, not through the distorting perspective of a mystical idealism which is in fact inapplicable, but taking account of the natural laws which regulate each order and are, within the limits of each order, willed by God. Islam is the perspective of certainty and of the nature of things rather than of miracles and idealist improvisation. This is said, not with any underlying intention of indirectly criticizing Christianity, which is what it should be, but in order better to bring out the intention and justification of the Islamic perspective. . .

If there is a clear separation in Islam between man as such and collective man, these two realities are none the less profoundly linked together, given that the collectivity is an aspect of man — no man can be born without a family — and that conversely society is a multiplication of individuals. It follows from this interdependence or reciprocity that anything that is done with a view to the collectivity, such as the tithe for the poor or the holy war, has a spiritual value for the individual and conversely; this converse relationship is the more true because the individual comes before the collectivity, all men being descended from Adam and not Adam from men.

What has just been said explains why the Moslem does not, like the Buddhist and the Hindu, abandon external rites in following some particular spiritual method which can compensate for them, or because he has attained a spiritual level of a nature to authorize such abandonment. A particular saint may no longer have need of the canonical prayers since he finds himself in a state of being steeped in prayer, in a state of 'intoxication'[1] — none the less he continues to accomplish the prayers in order to pray with and for all and in order that all may pray in him. He is the incarnation of that 'mystical Body' which every believing community constitutes, or, from another point of view, he incarnates the Law, the tradition and prayer as such. Inasmuch as he is a social being he should preach by his example and, inasmuch as he is individual man, permit what is human to be realized and in some sense renewed through him.

The metaphysical transparency of things and the contemplativity answering to it mean that sexuality (within the framework of its traditional legitimacy, which is one of psychological and social equilibrium) can take on a meritorious character, as the existence of this framework indeed already shows. In other words it is not only the enjoyment which counts — leaving aside the care to preserve the species — for sexuality also has its qualitative content, its symbolism which is both objective and something lived. The basis of Moslem morality is always in biological reality and not in an idealism contrary to collective possibilities and to the undeniable rights of natural laws; but this reality, while forming the basis of our animal and collective life, has no absolute quality since we are semi-celestial beings; it can always be neutralized on the level of our personal liberty, though never abolished on that of our social existence. What has just been said of sexuality applies by analogy, but only in respect of merit, to food: as in the case of all religions, overeating is a sin, but to eat in due measure and with gratitude to God is, in Islam, not only not a sin but a positively meritorious action. The analogy is not, however, total, for in a well-known *hadith*, the Prophet said he 'loved women,' not that he loved 'food.' Here the love of woman is connected with nobility and generosity, not to mention its purely contemplative symbolism which goes far beyond this.

Islam is often reproached with having propagated its faith by the sword; what is overlooked is, first, that persuasion played a much greater part than war in the expansion of Islam as a whole, and, secondly, that only polytheists and idolators could be compelled to embrace the new religion,[2] thirdly, that the God of the Old Testament is no less a warrior than the God of the Quran, quite the opposite, and, fourthly, that Christianity also made use of the sword from the time of Constantine's appearance on the scene. The question to be put here is simply the following: is it possible for force to be used with the aim of affirming and diffusing a vital truth?

Beyond doubt the answer must be in the affirmative, for experience proves that we must at times do violence to irresponsible people in their own interest. Now, since this possibility exists it cannot fail to be manifested in appropriate conditions,[3] exactly as in the case of the opposite possibility of victory through the force inherent in truth itself; it is the inner or outer nature of things which determines the choice between two possibilities. On the one hand the end sanctifies the means, and on the other hand the means may profane the end, which signifies that the means must be found prefigured in the divine nature; thus the right of the stronger is prefigured in the 'jungle' to which beyond question we belong to a certain degree and when regarded as collectivities; but in that 'jungle' no example can be found of any right to perfidy and baseness and, even if such characteristics were to be found there, our human dignity would forbid us to participate in them. The harshness of certain biological laws must never be confused with that infamy of which man alone is capable through his perverted theomorphism . . .

On the Quran[*]

. . . A sacred text with its seeming contradictions and obscurities is in some ways like a mosaic, or even an anagram; but it is only necessary to consult the orthodox, and so divinely guided, commentaries in order to find out with what intention a particular affirmation was made and in what respects it is valid, or what are the underlying implications that enable one to connect elements which at first sight appear incongruous. These commentaries sprang from the oral tradition which from the beginning accompanied the Revelation, or else they sprang by inspiration from the same supernatural source; thus their role is not only to intercalate missing, though implicit, parts of the text and to specify in what relationship or in what sense a given thing should be understood, but also to explain the diverse symbolisms, often simultaneous and superimposed one on another:

[*]From *UI*, Chapter 2.

in short the commentaries providentially form part of the tradition; they are as it were the sap of its continuity, even if their committal to writing or in certain cases their remanifestation after some interruption occurred only at a relatively late date in order to meet the requirements of a particular historical period. 'The ink of the learned (in the Law or in the Spirit) is like the blood of the martyrs, said the Prophet, and this indicates the capital part played in every traditional cosmos by orthodox commentaries.[1]

In order to understand the full scope of the Quran we must take three things into consideration: its doctrinal content, which we find made explicit in the great canonical treatises of Islam such as those of Abū Hanīfah and Et-Tahāwī; its narrative content, which depicts all the vicissitudes of the soul; and its divine magic or its mysterious and in a sense miraculous power;[2] these sources of metaphysical and eschatological wisdom, of mystical psychology and theurgic power lie hidden under a veil of breathless utterances, often clashing in shock, of crystalline and fiery images, but also of passages majestic in rhythm, woven of every fibre of the human condition.

But the supernatural character of this Book does not lie only in its doctrinal content, its psychological and mystical truth and its transmuting magic, it appears equally in its most exterior efficacy, in the miracle of the expansion of Islam; the effects of the Quran in space and time bear no relation to the mere literary impression which the written words themselves can give to a profane reader. Like every sacred Scripture the Quran is also *a priori* a 'closed' book, though 'open' in another respect, that of the elementary truths of salvation.

It is necessary to distinguish in the Quran between the general excellence of the Divine Word and the particular excellence of a content which may be superimposed, as, for instance, when it is a question of God or of His qualities; it is like the distinction between the excellence of gold and that of some masterpiece made from gold. The masterpiece directly manifests the nobility of gold; similarly the nobility of the content of one or another verse of the sacred book expresses the nobility of the Quranic substance, of the Divine Word, which is in itself undifferentiated; it cannot, however, add to the infinite value of that Word. This is also connected with the 'divine magic,' the transforming and sometimes theurgic virtue of the divine speech to which allusion has already been made.

This magic is closely linked with the actual language of the Revelation, which is Arabic, and so translations are canonically illegitimate and ritually ineffectual. When God has spoken in it a language is sacred;[3] and in order that God should speak in it it must have certain characteristics such as are not found in any modern language; finally, it is essential to grasp that after a certain period in the cycle accompanied by a certain hardening in the situation on earth God has spoken no more, or at any rate not as Revealer; in other words, after a certain period whatever is put forward as new religion is inevitably false; the Middle Ages mark *grosso modo* the final limit.[4]

The Quran is, like the world, at the same time one and multiple. The world is a multiplicity which disperses and divides; the Quran is a multiplicity which draws together and leads to Unity. The multiplicity of the holy Book—the diversity of its words, sentences, pictures and stories—fills the soul and then absorbs it and imperceptibly transposes it into the climate of serenity and immutability by a sort of divine 'cunning.' The soul, which is accustomed to the flux of phenomena, yields to this flux without resistance; it lives in phenomena and is by them divided and dispersed—even more than that, it actually becomes what it thinks and does. The revealed Discourse has the virtue that it accepts this tendency while at the same time reversing the movement thanks to the celestial nature of the content and the language, so that the fishes of the soul swim without distrust and with their habitual rhythm into the divine net.[5] To the degree that it can bear it the mind must have infused into it a consciousness of the metaphysical contrast between 'substance' and 'accidents'; a mind thus regenerated is a mind which keeps its thoughts first of all on God and thinks all things in Him. In other words, through the mosaic of texts, phrases and words, God extinguishes the appearance of mental agitation. The Quran is like a picture of everything the human brain can think and feel, and it is by this means that God exhausts human disquiet, infusing into the believer silence, serenity and peace.

In Islam, as also in Judaism, Revelation relates essentially to the symbolism of the book: the whole universe is a book whose letters are the cosmic elements—the *dharmas* as Buddhists would say—which, by their innumerable combinations and under the influence of the divine Ideas, produce worlds, beings and things. The words and phrases of the book are the manifestations of the creative possibilities, the words in respect of the content, the phrases in respect of the container; the phrase is, in effect, like a space or a duration conveying a predestined series of compossibles and constituting what may be called a 'divine plan.' This symbolism of the book is distinguished from that of speech by its static character; speech is situated in duration and implies repetition whereas books contain affirmations in a mode of simultaneity; in a book there is a certain levelling out, all the letters being alike, and this is moreover highly characteristic of the Islamic perspective. Only, this perspective, like that of the Torah, also includes the symbolism of speech; speech is however then identified with the origin; God speaks and His Speech is crystallized in the form of a Book. Clearly this crystallization has its prototype in God, and indeed it can be affirmed that the 'Speech' and the 'Book' are two sides of pure Being, which is the Principal that both creates and reveals; however, it is said that the Quran is the Word of God, not that the Word proceeds from the Quran or from the Book.

First of all the 'Word' is Being as the eternal Act of Beyond-Being, of the Divine Essence; but, taken as the sum of the possibilities of manifestation, Being is the 'Book.' Then, on the level of Being itself, the Word, or according to another image the Pen, is the creative Act while the Book is the creative Substance; here there is a connection with *Natura naturans* and *Natura naturata* in the highest sense attributable to these concepts. Finally, on the level of Existence (or, it could be said, of Manifestation) the Word is the 'Divine Spirit,' the central and universal Intellect which gives effect to and perpetuates the miracle of creation, as it were by 'delegation'; in this case the Book is the sum of the 'crystallized' possibilities, the world of innumerable creatures. The 'Word' is then the aspect of 'dynamic' simplicity or of simple' action,' while the 'Book' is the aspect of 'static' complexity or differentiated 'being.'

Or it can be said that God created the world like a Book and His Revelation came down into the world in the form of a Book; but man has to hear the Divine Word in Creation and by that Word ascend towards God; God became Book for man and man has to become Word for God; man is a 'book' through his microcosmic multiplicity and his state of existential coagulation whereas God, when envisaged in this context, is pure Word through His metacosmic Unity and His pure principial 'activity.'

In Christianity the place of the 'Book' is taken by the 'Body' with its two complements of 'flesh' and 'blood' or 'bread' and 'wine'; *in divinis* the Body is, first, the primary autodetermination of Divinity, and thus the first 'crystallization' of the Infinite; next it is Universal Substance, the true 'mystical Body of Christ'; and finally it is the world of creatures, the 'crystallized' manifestation of this Body.

We have seen that God-as-Being is The Book *par excellence*, and that, on the level of Being, the pole of Substance is the first reflection of this Book; the Word, which is its dynamic complement, then becomes the Pen, the vertical axis of creation. In contra-distinction man too has an aspect of Word represented by his name; God created man in naming him; the soul is a Word of the Creator when envisaged from the aspect of its simplicity or its unity.

The most obvious content of the Quran is made up, not of doctrinal expositions, but of historical and symbolical narratives and eschatological imagery; the pure doctrine emerges from these two sorts of pictures in which it is enshrined. Setting aside the majesty of the Arabic text and its almost magical resonances a reader could well become wearied of the content did he not know that it concerns ourselves in a quite concrete and direct way, since the 'misbelievers' (the *kāfirūn*), the 'associaters ' of false divinities with God (the *mushrikūn*) and the hypocrites (the *munāfiqūn*) are within ourselves; likewise that the Prophets represent our intellect and our conscience, that all the tales in the Quran are enacted almost daily in our souls, that Mecca is our heart and that the tithe, the fast, the pilgrimage and the holy war are so many virtues, whether secret or open, or so many contemplative attitudes.

Running parallel with this microcosmic and alchemical interpretation there is the external interpretation which concerns the phenomena of the world around us. The Quran is the world, both outside and within us, always connected to God in the two respects of origin and end; but this world, or these two worlds, show fissures announcing death or destruction or, to be more precise, transformation, and this is what the apocalyptic and eschatological surats teach us; everything that concerns the world also concerns us, and conversely. These surats transmit to us a multiple and striking picture of the fragility both of our earthly condition and of matter, a picture too of the destined reabsorption of space and of the elements in the invisible substance of the causal 'protocosm'; this is the collapse of the visible world into the immaterial — a collapse, to para-

phrase Saint Augustine, 'inwards' or 'upwards'; it is also the confronting of creatures, snatched from the earth, with the flashing reality
of the Infinite.

By its 'surfaces' the Quran presents a cosmology which treats
of phenomena and their final end, and, by its 'pinnacles,' a metaphysic of the real and the unreal . . . If the Quran contains elements
of polemic concerning Christianity and, for stronger reasons, concerning Judaism, it is because Islam came after these religions, and
this means that it was obliged — and there is a point of view which
allows of its doing so — to put itself forward as an improvement on
what came before it. In other words the Quran enunciates a perspective which makes it possible to 'go beyond' certain formal aspects of
the two more ancient monotheisms. Something analogous can be
seen, not only in the position of Christianity in relation to Judaism —
where the point is self-evident by reason of the messianic idea and
the fact that the former is like a 'bhaktic' esotericism of the latter —
but also in the attitude of Buddhism towards Brahmanism; here too
the later appearance in time coincides with a perspective that is symbolically, though not intrinsically, superior. Of this fact the tradition that is apparently being superseded clearly has no need to take
account since each perspective is a universe for itself — and thus a
centre and a standard — and since in its own way it contains all valid
points of view. By the very logic of things the later tradition is 'condemned' to the symbolical attitude of superiority, on pain of non-
existence one might almost say; but there is also a positive symbolism
of anteriority and in this respect the new tradition, which is from
its own point of view the final one, must incarnate 'what came before,'
or 'what has always existed'; its novelty — or glory — is consequently
its absolute 'anteriority.'

Pure intellect is the 'immanent Quran'; the uncreated Quran —
the Logos — is the Divine Intellect; and this is crystallized in the form
of the earthly Quran and answers 'objectively' to that other immanent and 'subjective' revelation which is the human intellect. In Christian terms it could be said that Christ is like the 'objectivation' of
the intellect and the intellect is like the 'subjective' and permanent
revelation of Christ. Thus there are two poles for the manifestation
of Divine Wisdom and they are: first, the Revelation 'above us' and,
secondly, the intellect 'within us'; the Revelation provides the symbols while the intellect deciphers them and 'recollects' their content,

thereby again becoming conscious of its own substance. Revelation is a deployment and intellect a concentration; the descent is in accord with the ascent.

But there is another *haqīqah* (truth) on which we should wish to touch at this point, and it is this: in the sensory order the Divine Presence has two symbols or vehicles — or two 'natural manifestations' — of primary importance: the heart within us, which is our centre, and the air around us, which we breathe. The air is a manifestation of ether, the weaver of forms, and it is at the same time the vehicle of light, which also makes manifest the element ether. When we breathe, the air penetrates us and, symbolically, it is as though it introduced into us the creative ether and the light too; we inhale the Universal Presence of God. Equally there is a connection between light and coolness, for the sensation of both is liberating; what is light externally is coolness inwardly. We inhale luminous, cool air and our respiration is a prayer, as is the beating of our heart; the luminosity relates to the Intellect and the freshness to pure Being. In Islam it is taught that at the end of time light will become separated from heat and heat will be hell whereas light will be Paradise; the light of heaven is cool and the heat of hell dark.

The world is a fabric woven of threads of ether, and into it we and all other creatures are woven. All sensory things come forth from ether, which contains all; everything is ether crystallized. The world is an immense carpet; we possess the whole world in each breath because we breathe the ether from which all things are made, and we 'are' ether. Just as the world is an immeasurable carpet in which everything is repeated in a rhythm of continual change, or where everything remains similar within the framework of the law of differentiation, so too the Quran — and with it the whole of Islam — is a carpet or fabric, in which the centre is everywhere repeated in an infinitely varied way and in which the diversity is no more than a development of the unity. The universal 'ether,' of which the physical element is only a distant and grosser reflection, is none other than the divine Word which is everywhere 'being' and 'consciousness' and everywhere 'creative' and 'liberating' or 'revealing' and 'illuminating.'

The nature which surrounds us — sun, moon, stars, day and night, the seasons, the waters, mountains, forests and flowers — is a kind of primordial Revelation; now these three things — nature, light and breath — are profoundly linked with one another. Breathing should be linked with the remembrance of God; we should breathe with reverence, with the heart so to speak. It is said that the Spirit of God—the Divine Breath—was 'over the waters' and that it was by breathing into it that God created the soul, as it is also said that man, who is 'born of the Spirit,' is like the wind; 'thou hearest the sound thereof, but canst not tell whence it cometh, and whither it goeth.'

It is significant that Islam is defined in the Quran as an 'enlarging (*inshirāh*) of the breast,' that it is said, for example, that God 'hath enlarged our breast for Islam'; the connection between the Islamic perspective and the initiatic meaning of breathing and also of the heart is a key of the first importance for understanding the arcana of Sufism. It is true that by the very force of things the same path also opens out on to universal gnosis.

The 'remembrance of God' is like breathing deeply in the solitude of high mountains: here the morning air, filled with the purity of the eternal snows, dilates the breast; it becomes space and heaven enters our heart.

This picture includes yet another symbolism, that of the 'universal breath': here expiration relates to cosmic manifestation or the creative phase and inspiration to reintegration, to the phase of salvation or the return to God.

One reason why Western people have difficulty in appreciating the Quran and have even many times questioned whether this book does contain the premises of a spiritual life lies in the fact that they look in a text for a meaning that is fully expressed and immediately intelligible, where as Semites, and Eastern peoples in general, are lovers of verbal symbolism and read 'in depth.' The revealed phrase is for them an array of symbols from which more and more flashes of light shoot forth the further the reader penetrates into the spiritual geometry of the words: the words are reference points for a doctrine that is inexhaustible; the implicit meaning is everything, and the obscurities of the literal meaning are so many veils marking the majesty of the content.[6]

On the Prophet*

. . .The Prophet is the human norm in respect both of his individual and of his collective functions, or again in respect of his spiritual and earthly functions.

Essentially he is equilibrium and extinction: equilibrium from the human point of view and extinction in relation to God.

The Prophet is Islam; if Islam offers itself as a manifestation of truth, of beauty and of power — and it is indeed these three elements which inspire it and which, on various planes, it tends by its very nature to actualize — the Prophet for his part incarnates serenity, generosity and strength. These virtues could also be enumerated in the inverse order according to the ascending hierarchy of their values and by reference to the levels of spiritual realization. Strength is the affirmation — which may at need be combative — of Divine Truth both in the soul and in the world, and here lies the distinction drawn in Islam between the two kinds of holy warfare, the greater (*akbar*) and the lesser (*asghar*), or the inner and the outer. Generosity compensates for the aggressive aspect of strength; it is charity and pardon. These two complementary virtues of strength and generosity culminate, or are in a sense extinguished, in a third virtue, serenity, which is detachment from the world and from the ego, extinction in face of God, knowledge of the divine and union with it.

There is a certain, no doubt paradoxical, relationship between virile strength and virginal purity in the sense that both are concerned with the inviolability of the sacred, strength in a dynamic and combative manner and purity in a static and defensive manner; it could also be said that strength, a 'warrior' quality, includes a mode or complement that is static or passive, and this is sobriety, love of poverty and of fasting and incorruptibility, all of which are 'pacific' or 'non-aggressive' qualities. In the same way generosity, which 'gives', has its static complement in nobility, which 'is'; or rather nobility is the intrinsic reality of generosity. Nobility is a sort of contemplative generosity; it is love of beauty in its widest sense: for the Prophet and for Islam it is here that aestheticism and love of clean-

*From *UI*, Chapter 3.

liness enter, for the latter removes from things, and especially from the body, the mark of being earthly and fallen and so brings them back, both symbolically and in a certain manner even in virtuality, to their immutable and incorruptible prototypes, or to their essences. As for serenity, that also has a necessary complement in truthfulness which is as it were its active or discriminative aspect; it is the love of truth and of intelligence, so characteristic of Islam, and therefore it is also impartiality and justice. Now nobility compensates the aspect of narrowness in sobriety and these two complementary virtues find their culmination in truthfulness in the sense that they subordinate themselves to it and, if need be, efface themselves or seem to do so, in its presence.

The virtues of the Prophet form, so to speak, a triangle: serenity with truthfulness is the apex of the triangle and the two other pairs of virtues — generosity with nobility and strength with sobriety — form the base; the two angles of the base are in equilibrium and at the apex are reduced to unity. As was said above the soul of the Prophet is in its essence equilibrium and extinction.

Imitation of the Prophet implies, first, strength as regards oneself, next, generosity as regards others and, thirdly, serenity in God and through God. It could also be said: serenity through piety, in the most profound sense of that term.

Such imitation moreover implies: first, sobriety in relation to the world; secondly, nobility within ourselves in our being; thirdly, truthfulness through God and in Him. But we must not lose sight of the fact that the world is also within us, and that, conversely, we are not other than the creation which surrounds us and, finally, that God created 'by the Truth' (*bil-Haqq*); the world is, both in its perfections and in its equilibrium, an expression of the Divine Truth.

The aspect of 'force' is at the same time and indeed above all the active and affirmative character of the spiritual means or method; the aspect of 'generosity' is also the love of our immortal soul; while the aspect of 'serenity,' which is, first, seeing all things in God, is also seeing God in all things. One may be serene because one knows that 'God alone is,' that the world and all its troubles are 'non-real,' but equally one may be serene because — admitting the relative reality of the world — one realizes that 'all things are willed by God,' that the Divine Will acts in all things, that all things symbolize God in one or another respect and that symbolism is for God what might be called a 'manner of being.' Nothing is outside God; God is not absent from anything.

Imitation of the Prophet means actualizing a balance between our normal tendencies, or more exactly between our complementary virtues and, following from this and above all, it is extinction in the Divine Unity on the basis of this harmony. It is thus that the base of the triangle is in a certain sense absorbed into its apex, which appears as its synthesis and its origin or as its end and the reason for its existence.

If we now return to the description given above but formulate it somewhat differently, we can say that Muhammad is the human form orientated towards the Divine Essence; this 'form' has two chief aspects, corresponding respectively to the base and to the apex of the triangle, and these are nobility and piety. Now nobility is compounded of strength and generosity, while piety — at the level here in question — is compounded of wisdom and sanctity; it should be added that by 'piety' we must understand the state of 'spiritual servitude' (*'ubūdiyah*) in the highest sense of the term, comprising perfect 'poverty' (*faqr*, whence the word *faqīr*) and 'extinction' (*fanā'*) before God, and this is not unrelated to the epithet 'unlettered' (*ummī*) which is applied to the Prophet. Piety is what links us to God; in Islam this something is, first of all an understanding, as deep as is possible, of the evident Divine Unity — for one who is 'responsible' must grasp this evidentness and there is here no sharp demarcation between 'believing' and 'knowing'— and next it is a realization of the Unity that goes beyond our provisional and 'unilateral' understanding which is itself ignorance when regarded in the light of plenary knowledge: there is no saint (*wali*, 'representative,' and so 'participant') who is not a 'knower through God' (*'ārif bil-Llāh*). This explains why in Islam piety, and *a fortiori* the sanctity which is its flowering, has an air of serenity;[1] it is a piety of which the essence is that it opens out into contemplation and gnosis.

Or again, the phenomenon of Muhammad could be described by saying that the soul of the Prophet is made up of nobility and serenity, the latter comprising sobriety and truthfulness and the former strength and generosity. The Prophet's attitude to food and sleep is determined by sobriety and his attitude to woman by generosity; here the real object of generosity is the pole of 'substance' in humankind, this pole — woman — being envisaged in its aspect of being a mirror of the beatific infinitude of God.

Love of the Prophet constitutes a fundamental element in Islamic spirituality, although this love must not be understood in

the sense of a personalistic *bhakti* which would presuppose diviniz-
ing the Prophet in an exclusive way. It arises because Moslems see
in the Prophet the prototype and model of the virtues which make
the theomorphism of man and the beauty and equilibrium of the
universe and are so many keys or ways towards the Unity which
delivers, so that they love him and imitate him even in the very
smallest details of daily life. The Prophet, like Islam as a whole, is
as it were a heavenly mould ready to receive the influx of the intelligence and will of the believer and one wherein even effort becomes
a kind of supernatural repose. . .

Seeds of a Divergence*

Islam gushed forth as an epic. Now a heroic history is written
with the sword, and in this religious context the sword assumes a
sacred function. The taking of life does not have the same meaning
as in profane history; combat is an ordeal, as it was in the climate
of the Bible. The genesis of a religion amounts to the creation of
a moral and spiritual type that is apparently new, and even *de facto*
new in certain contingent respects. In the case of Islam, this type
consists of an equilibrium — paradoxical from the Christian point
of view — between the qualities of the contemplative and the combative, and then between holy poverty and sanctified sexuality. The
Arab — and the man Arabized by Islam — has, so to speak, four poles:
the desert, the sword, woman and religion. For the contemplative
these become inward, the desert, the sword and woman becoming
so many states or function of the soul. God is not only the All-Powerful
Lord; the more profoundly His Power is understood, the more He
reveals Himself as immanent Love.

On the most general and *a priori* outward level, the sword represents death — death dealt out and death courted — so that its perfume is always present. Woman represents an analogous reciprocity;
she is love received and love given, and thus she incarnates all the
generous virtues; she compensates for the perfume of death with that

*From *IPP*, Chapter 5.

of life. The profoundest meaning of the sword is that there is no nobility without renunciation of life, and this is why the Sufi's initiatic
vow—in so far as it relates historically to the "Pact of the Divine Good
Pleasure" (*Bay'at ar-Riḍwān*)—includes the promise to fight to the
point of death, bodily in the case of warrior and martyr (*shahīd*), and
spiritually in the case of the dervishes or the "poor" (*faqīr*). The symbiosis of love and death within the framework of poverty and before
the face of the Absolute constitutes all that is essential in Arab nobility,
so much so that we do not hesitate to say that here lies the very
substance of the primitive Muslim soul.

From the point of view of the objective aspects of the Arab-
Islamic phenomenon, it is important to bear in mind that Islam has
an essentially political dimension which was foreign to primitive
Christianity and which Christianity as a state religion knows only
as a profane appendage. Now political activity is divisive by its very
nature, because of the diversity of possible solutions to any problem
and because of the diversity of individual qualificiations. The Companions of the Prophet were therefore politically divided by the force
of circumstances, and what was at stake was nothing less than the
final and lasting victory of Islam. They lived side-by-side like closed
systems, somewhat as different religious perspectives exist side-by-
side without understanding each other. Each identified himself, in
his very being, with his own intuitions of what was right and efficacious. The remarkable stability of Islamic institutions through
all the vicissitudes of history proves that the Companions were not
thinking in terms of worldly ambitions and that they had, at the very
heart of their dissensions, a concern for immutability and incorruptibility. In a word, each enclosed himself in his own viewpoint with
holy obstinacy, if one may so describe it, rigidity of attitude being
the result of sincerity.

In the intertwining of destinies which concern us here, there
is the strange case of Fāṭimah. Embodying, according to unanimous
tradition, the purest sanctity, she was put aside, frustrated and forgotten. On occasion she was treated in a hard way even by the Prophet,
her father. Herein is the whole drama of a celestial soul predestined
to be the martyr of terrestrial life. Her abasement is, as it were, the
shadow cast by her spiritual elevation, human individuals appearing in her destiny as the cosmic instruments of her painful alchemy.
There is something of this likewise in the case of the Blessed Virgin
treated not without a certain coldness by the Gospels and passed over

largely in silence by most of the New Testament, to reappear afterwards in all the greater splendour. A comparable example, in a totally different world, is Sītā, the wife of Rāma, never happy on earth but made divine in Heaven; or again Māyā, mother of the Buddha, halfforgotten yet ultimately glorified in the form of Tara, "Mother of all the Buddhas." We mention these things to show that the destinies of saints of the highest order manifest symbolic elements which it would be vain to analyse from the point of view of individual responsibilities alone. So far as Fāṭimah is concerned, the attachment of this saint to her father clashed, after his death, with the inflexibility of the first Caliph who refused her certain elementary favours in strict adherence to Islamic principles which, in reality, could have been interpreted more broadly in her case; but it was the destiny of Fāṭimah to be deprived of the consolations of this lower world. This example is typical of the oppositions between the Companions; it is not their passions that clash, but their good intentions, inspired by a totalitarian mentality always ready to deal in terms of irreducible alternatives.

The drama of the Companions is, in sum, the drama of human subjectivity; there would be no problem if there were only the good and the bad, but the great paradox is the existence of the good who differ to the point of not being able to understand each other, and who differ not so much by nature as in terms of situation and vocation. The great epic poems, such as the Iliad or the Song of the Nibelungs, show in all their tragic grandeur this intertwining of temperaments, positions, responsibilities and destinies; combat outwardly, in the current of forms, but unity within, in the unchanging quest for the Light which liberates.

• • •

In every religion there are three spheres or levels: the Apostolic, the theological and the political. The first has a certain quality of absoluteness; the other two are more or less contingent, although, clearly, at very different levels. In Christianity, the theological element is directly joined with the Apostolic, the political era beginning only with Constantine. In Islam, on the other hand, the political element is found in conjunction with the Apostolic; theological elaboration, properly speaking, comes later. Moreover, the Apostolic sphere — the intimate circle of the Prophet — inevitably comprises opposite points of view when the political element comes into play, offering as it does different solutions to the problems of efficacy; but it cannot comprise, in its very substance, elements of hypocrisy or other forms of baseness — differences of perspective, certainly, but not conflicts of petty and sordid self-interest. The Apostolic sphere is pure or it is nothing, and it is in this sense that Sunnism judges the Apostolic epoch of Islam. But to be adequate, the traditional Sunnī version of events must implicitly express the all but Avataric nature of Fāṭimah's posterity, which it does through its doctrine of the *sharīfs*. These cannot suffer damnation, any sins they may commit being forgiven them in advance; they are entitled to respect and love; they easily become saints; in short, they are "pneumatics," in gnostic terms, even if in most cases they are so only in virtuality. None of this should be taken to mean that a "psychic" can never become a saint or that there are no "pneumatics" outside the Fatimid line — for Sunnīs, Abū Bakr is the first and even the providential example of the "pneumatic" type in question.

From a certain point of view, the significance of the battles between Umayyads and 'Alids is in practice the conflict between political effectiveness and sanctity, the impossibility, that is, of always combining the two. Abū Bakr and 'Umar succeeded in doing so, apart from certain blunders which need not concern us here. As far as the Caliphate of 'Uthmān is concerned, and still more that of 'Alī, it is important not to underestimate the terrible difficulty of holding the balance among a mass of men as passionate, ambitious and turbulent as the ancient Arabs were, always at odds among themselves and thus unaccustomed to unity and discipline. This state of affairs is, moreover, one of the gauges of the incomparable genius of the founder of Islam.

The early Caliphs were fully aware of the danger that the austere Bedouins, become conquerors, might adopt the decadent customs of the Sasanids and the Byzantines; this is what the later Caliphs did all too readily, to the extent of betraying the dignity and virtue of their race, and this is what the Shī'ites were concerned to prevent in claiming the Caliphate for the 'Alids alone. Moses, upon seeing the Golden Calf, broke the Tablets of the Law and then, it is said, received others of a less rigorous nature. This expresses a principle of fluctuation or adaptation, the effects of which may be observed in diverse traditional climates and, not least, in primitive Islam, where the political régime which was finally viable did not correspond to the original ideal. The Sunnīs resign themselves to this fatality, whereas the Shī'ites enwrap themselves in the bitter memory of lost purity which combines with the recollection of the drama of Kerbala and, on the level of mystical life, with the noble sadness aroused by the awareness of our earthly exile — an exile which is then seen above all in its aspect of injustice, oppression and frustration as regards primitive virtue and divine rights.

.   .   .

Whatever secondary explanations may be forthcoming, Shi'ism cannot be explained in depth or given its *raison d'être* on the political plane alone. What needs to be said is that in Islam and, above all, in the person of the Prophet, there are two tendencies or two mysteries — this last word being used to indicate what is rooted in the celestial order — namely "Fear" and "Love," or "Cold" and "Heat," or "Dryness" and "Humidity," or "Water" and "Wine." Now there are grounds for saying that 'Alī, Fāṭimah, Ḥasan and Ḥusain represented the second of these two dimensions, whereas 'A'ishah, Abū Bakr, 'Umar and 'Uthmān personified the first at least from the point of view of outward accentuation. 'Alī and his family — politically ineffectual — came up against the world of "Fear" and effectiveness; and what is remarkable is that Fāṭimah came up against this not only in the person of the first Caliph but even in relation to her father the Prophet, who combined, as we have said, the two tendencies. It goes without saying that the element of "Love" could not be lacking in Abū Bakr's group — the intense love of the Prophet among all the Companions proves this — and, inversely, it is unthinkable that the element of "Fear" should have been lacking in 'Alī and his people, for in their case too it can only be a question of emphasis, not of deprivation. In short what was more or less implicit in the case of the Sunnīs became no doubt more explicit in that of the Shī'ites. There is no end to what might be said about this interlacing of religious attitudes, and we would have preferred not to have to speak of it, if only because it is a difficult and thankless task to do justice in a few words — we will not say to all those concerned — but to all the angles of vision. There is one consideration which in any case imposes itself in this context and this is that upon contact with the

Sunnī world — in which the general atmosphere is one of resignation to God and serenity through faith — one does not in any way
have the impression of being concerned with a perspective of Love,
whereas one does have this impression in the climate of Shīʿism,
whatever may be the reasons. It is true that resignation and serenity
characterize Islam as a whole; it is equally true that in Shīʿism there
is added to it — to the extent of superimposition — an emotional element, a kind of equivalent to which is found, among Sunnīs, only
in the Sufi brotherhoods.

However this may be, there is a most important point which
has still to be made: when we speak of the element of "Love" in the
case of the Prophet, there can clearly be no question of anything other
than the love of God; when we attribute this element to the Companions, it becomes somewhat fluid as regards its object, which may
be either God or the Prophet, or both at the same time, or it may
include ʿAlī and his family, whereas the object of "Fear" is always God.
What is to be understood above all is that in Islam the love of God
is not the point of departure; it is a grace which God may bestow
upon him who fears Him. The point of departure is obedience to
the Law and the entirely logical fear of punishment. "What matters
is not that you should love God, but that God should love you,"
declares a work on the Prophet based on canonical sources, and it
continues to this effect: if you wish God to love you, you must love
His Messenger by following his Sunnah. The love of God thus passes
by way of the love of the Messenger; among the Shīʿites, the love
of the Messenger passes *de facto* by way of love of ʿAlī and his family,
which introduces into this mysticism — for pla··sible reasons — an element of hatred and mourning, on the level where such motivations
may be reconciled with movement towards God...

• • •

For the Shīʿites, and according to a perspective tending both
to the symbolic and the schematic, and therefore to simplification
and abstraction, the protagonists of the "dry" dimension or the dimension of earthly effectiveness become the personifications of the "world";
only ʿAlī's family represents the "spirit." This makes it possible to
recognize the intrinsic orthodoxy of Shīʿite mysticism, but does not
lend conviction on the exoteric level to the polemics against the pillars

of Sunnism, inasmuch as Sunnī doctrine embraces, in a positive sense, not only 'Alī and Fāṭimah, but also the great "Imams" upon whom the Shī'ites themselves rely. In short, it is paradoxical and tragic that a branch of tradition, whose whole point is to be a dimension of esoterism or of "wine," should at the same time be associated in the exoteric realm with a particularly obtrusive and questionable ostracism. However, from the metaphysical-mystical point of view — we must insist yet again upon this — names and events are symbols of realities inscribed in the Empyrean before the creation of the human world; the adequacy of the spiritual sense compensates for any inadequacy in the earthly symbols. Shī'ism is a mysticism based upon the necessary defeat — changed ultimately into victory — of the earthly manifestation of the Logos, and it is thereby linked to the mystery enunciated by the Gospel according to St John: "And the light shineth in darkness and the darkness comprehended it not." We are thus far from the idea — at first sight the only plausible one — of outright and inevitable victory simply as a result of the Divine origin of the Message. The criteria are now inverted in that the minority situation of Shī'ism is, from the Shī'ite viewpoint, a sign of superiority; for Sunnism, which is the necessarily victorious perspective of the Divine Message and the one adhered to by the majority, it is a sign of heresy to be in the minority, whereas it is a criterion of orthodoxy for the Shī'ites since *lux in tenebris lucet et tenebrae eam non comprehenderunt.* This criteriology applies unquestionably to esoterism and, in this respect, Islam's two confessional viewpoints coincide, Sunnī Sufism being by definition in a minority in the context of the general religion; it is so to the precise extent that it represents a perspective of "light" or pure "gnosis." To summarize: whereas Sunnism is a message that is victorious by definition, since it comes from God and contains esoterically a message of "light" which is by definition precarious and hidden, Shī'ism for its part is an eso-exoterism deriving directly from the element "light" and thus condemned to be both tragic and in a minority. Shī'ites seem to be asserting, "Islam *is* esoterism"; to which the rejoinder of Sunnīs appears to be, "First of all let Islam exist on earth." It is worth mentioning that most of the descendents of 'Alī and Fāṭimah are Sunnis, and that there have been 'Alid dynasties which, even so, were not Shī'ite.

This leads to the following conclusion: if the political failure of 'Alī and his successors on the general level of Islam proves that the Prophet's son-in-law could not be the personification, alone and in every respect, of both spiritual and temporal authority for Islam as such, the very existence of Shī'ism is an equally irrefutable proof of an element of victory and, thereby, of a spiritual reality of the highest eminence and of a very particular kind in 'Alī himself and, by extension, in his family. Sunnīs do not dispute this eminence since they pray for blessings upon the Prophet, "his Family (*Āl*) and his Companions (*Ṣaḥb*)" and honour the "*sharīfs*"; but they do not give them the same place as do the Shī'ites...

The exclusion from Shī'ism of the element of "dryness" may basically explain — but not justify — the Shī'ites' misinterpretation of the first three Caliphs and the Prophet's favourite wife, and this is the price paid for the exoteric coagulation of Shī'ism; it is indeed the way of all exoterism to become hypnotized by a single aspect of reality and to interpret everything in terms of that segment. Let us recall in this connection the total condemnation of all forms of "paganism" by each of the three monotheistic religions, or, in particular, Christian underestimation of the Torah and of the inward dimension of Judaism, or again, the reduction of Christ's role in Islam to that of a forerunner. For Shī'ite spirituality, the question of knowing who an Abū Bakr or an 'Ā'ishah really were does not arise; only principles — positive or negative — count , in whatever images they find expression. Moreover, the theses which are most hostile to Sunnism and — it must be admitted — most passionate and most unconvincing, seem to be of somewhat indeterminate range; they are found above all from the Safavid period onwards in theological works which do not possess any absolute authority, given that the application of the canonical principle of "personal judgement" (*ijtihād*) is freer among the Shī'ites than among the Sunnis and thus opens the door to far more pronounced divergencies, whence, by way of compensation, the less compelling nature of the opinions expressed...

•   •   •

One can understand all aspects of Shī'ism on the sole condition of being fully aware of a certain typological difference between Muhammad and 'Alī, in virtue of which there is a fascinating element peculiar to 'Alī, which determines a cult which is almost independent of that of the Prophet. 'Alī appears above all as the "Solar

Hero," he is the "Lion" (*Asad* or *Ḥaydar*) of God; he personifies the combination of physical heroism on the field of battle with a sanctity wholly detached from the things of the world; he is the personification of the wisdom, both impassive and combative, which the Bhagavad-gītā teaches. He is not a statesman; he uses the sword, but not strategy or diplomacy; he is incautious out of a spirit of purity, and indecisive because of his detachment from earthly things; this explains why at the time of his election he did not rally all his supporters. In the personality of Muhammad, by contrast, it is not the physical hero who stands out, but rather the leader of men, the farsighted and invincible statesman, who not merely wins a day's battle by the strength of his sword, but who creates by his genius, humanly speaking, a millennial world-empire. Now Abū Bakr, 'Umar and others were more responsive to this kind of power than to the heroic radiance of an 'Alī; for men such as the first three Caliphs there could not, for that matter, be any question of cult or hostility in relation to the Messenger's son-in-law.

If we may express ourselves without ambiguity, at the risk of appearing to simplify or to go too far in humanizing matters, we would say that there was between the Prophet and his son-in-law a different kind of splendour which made possible a different kind of love, depending upon affinities; one could be dazzled by the personality of 'Alī in another way — and subjectively to a greater degree — than by the personality of Muhammad; and the inverse was even truer. It is the imperative and almost exclusive element in the love for 'Alī which explains the need to add his name to that of the Prophet in the Shī'ite testification of faith; this is because the powerful originality of the "Lion of Allāh" is, from a certain point of view, irreplaceable; it is such that it provides precisely the basis for a cult which is perpetuated through the Imāms, necessary mediators between man and God in terms of this particular perspective. These considerations, imposed upon us by the search for causes proportionate to the immensity of the effects, are corroborated by an historical factor of the first importance, although of a rather outward character, which will perhaps cause surprise by its simplicity; the fact emerges on the one hand from the *aḥādīth* as a whole and, on the other, from certain particular traditions, that the Prophet liked to insist upon the practical side of things and that his spiritual teachings tended to conciseness, whereas his son-in-law 'Alī readily gave theological instruction and complex spiritual directives, even on the battlefield. Now it is not difficult to see how this altogether extrinsic difference of manifestation could give rise to preferences and misunderstandings, not, doubtless, to the disadvantage of the Prophet, but to the detriment of those of his Companions who, by nature or by vocation, were integrated into his reticent and legalist style of manifestation.

While insisting upon these primary factors, one must not, however, lose sight of the role played in the genesis of Shī'ism by political contingencies after the death of 'Uthmān and in particular, after the death of 'Alī. After the latter event, the town of Kūfah expected to remain the capital of the Empire and had no intention of deferring to Damascus, Mu'wiyyāh's capital. If it is true that ideas create vested interests, it is no less undeniable that vested interests can, in their turn, create ideas or ideologies, in the sense that they make for particular points of emphasis — and corresponding doctrinal elaborations — with all the prejudices and ostracization that can follow. These two factors, idea and interest, are sometimes difficult to disentangle in a climate of passions that are at once mystical and political. From an entirely different point of view, it is possible that Shī'ism, which was at first a purely Arab movement, was subjected later to the influence of concepts of Babylonian and Mazdean origin; we are thinking here particularly of the metaphysic of Light and of the related idea of an esoteric and quasi-superhuman Priesthood.

Islamic Poverty*

One of the fundamental characteristics of Islam is its cult of poverty, which extends from the Sunnah to art. The splendour of the mosques is a richness upon which the mark of poverty has been stamped, their brilliance neutralized by an unvaried calm, even in Persian and Turkish art, in which the richness is more pronounced than in that of the Arabs. The Quran is the model for this equilib-

*From *IPP*, Chapter 2.

rium; to chant the Quran is to imbibe holy poverty; the element of intoxication is not lacking, but it is a sober intoxication, comparable to the poetry of the desert. The dryness of Quranic style — with the exception of certain Sūrahs and certain passages — has often been remarked upon, without allowance being made for the virile power of this style; to speak of God in Arabic is to speak forcefully. In fact the level and dry style of the Quran prevents the development of any individualism of a titanic and dangerously Promethean kind; it has created a human type rooted in pious poverty and holy childishness.

The Arab soul is composed of poverty and it is out of this depth that the qualities of ardour, courage, tenacity and generosity emerge. All is derived from poverty, unfolds within its framework and is reabsorbed into it; the originality of Arab eloquence, whether chivalrous or moralizing, lies in its poverty; its prolixity is that of the desert.

There is a universal message in the Islamic cult of poverty, found equally in the Gospels, but with less obsessive invariability; it is concerned to remind man that the norm of well-being is not a maximum, but a minimum, of comfort, and that the cardinal virtues in this context are contentment and gratitude. But this message would amount to little were it not the expression of a truth which encompasses our whole being, and which the Gospels express in these terms: "Blessed are the poor in spirit, for theirs is the kingdom of Heaven." The Quranic basis for spiritual poverty in Islamic terms is the following verse: "Oh men, ye are the poor in relation to God, and God is the Rich to whom all praises are due." The "poor" are those who know that they possess nothing in their own right and need to receive everything from another; the "Rich" is He who is self-sufficient and lives from His own substance. Islam, in so far as it is "resignation" to the Divine Will, is poverty. But poverty is not an end in itself; the whole reason for its existence is its positive complement, by which perfect poverty opens out onto the richness we carry within ourselves, since the Transcendent is also the Immanent. To die for this Transcendence is to be born into this Immanence.

The Quintessential Esoterism of Islam*

The first Testimony of Faith (*Shahādah*) comprises two parts, each of which is composed of two words: *lā ilāha* and *illā 'Llāh*, "no divinity — except the (sole) Divinity." The first part, the "negation" (*nafy*), corresponds to Universal Manifestation, which in regard to the Principle is illusory, whereas the second part, the "confirmation" (*ithbāt*), corresponds to the Principle, which is Reality and which in relation to Manifestation is alone real.

And yet, Manifestation possesses a relative reality, lacking which this order could not be the cause of Manifestation, and therefore of what is relative by definition; this is what is expressed graphically by the Taoist symbol of the *Yin-Yang*, which is an image of compensatory reciprocity. That is to say, the Principle comprises at a lower degree than its Essence a prefiguration of Manifestation, which makes the latter possible; and Manifestation for its part comprises in its center a reflection of the Principle, lacking which it would be independent of the latter, which is inconceivable, relativity having no consistency of its own.

The prefiguration of Manifestation in the Principle — the principial Logos — is represented in the *Shahādah* by the word *illā* ("except" or "if not"), whereas the name *Allāh* expresses the Principle in itself; and the reflection of the Principle — the manifested Logos — is represented in its turn by the word *ilāha* ("divinity"), while the word *lā* ("there is no" or "no"), refers to Manifestation as such, which is illusory in relation to the Principle and consequently cannot be envisaged outside or separately from it.

This is the metaphysical and cosmological doctrine of the first Testimony, that of God (*lā ilāha illā 'Llāh*). The doctrine of the second Testimony, that of the Prophet (*Muhammadun Rasūlu 'Llāh*), refers to Unity, not exclusive this time, but inclusive; it enunciates, not distinction, but identity; not discernment, but union; not transcendence, but immanence; not the objective and macrocosmic discontinuity of the degrees of Reality, but the subjective and microcosmic continuity of the one Consciousness. The second Testimony is not static and separative like the first, but dynamic and unitive.

*From *SVQ,* Chapter 6.

Strictly speaking, the second Testimony— according to the quintessential interpretation— envisages the Principle only in terms of three hypostatic aspects, namely: the manifested Principle (*Muhammad*), the manifesting Principle (*Rasūl*) and the Principle in itself (*Allāh*). The entire accent is put on the intermediate element, *Rasūl*, "Messenger"; it is this element, the Logos, that links the manifested Principle to the Principle in itself. The Logos is the "Spirit" (*Rūh*) of which it has been said that it is neither created nor uncreated or again, that it is manifested in relation to the Principle and non-manifested or principial in relation to Manifestation.

The word *Rasūl*, "Messenger," indicates a "descent" of God towards the world; it equally implies an "ascent" of man toward God. In the case of the Mohammedan phenomenon, the descent is that of the Koranic Revelation (*laylat al-qadr*), and the ascent is that of the Prophet during the "Night Journey" (*laylat al-miʿrāj*); in the human microcosm, the descent is inspiration, and the ascent is aspiration; the descent is divine grace, while the ascent is human effort, the content of which is the "remembrance of God" (*dhikru 'Llāh*); whence the name *Dhikru 'Llāh* given to the Prophet.[1]

The three words *dhākir, dhikr, madhkūr*— a classical ternary in Sufism— correspond exactly to the ternary *Muhammad, Rasūl, Allāh*: *Muhammad* is the invoker, *Rasūl* the invocation, *Allāh* the invoked. In the invocation, the invoker and the invoked meet, just as *Muhammad* and *Allāh* meet in the *Rasūl*, or in the *Risālah*, the Message.[2]

The microcosmic aspect of the *Rasul* explains the esoteric meaning of the "Blessing upon the Prophet" (*salāt ʿala 'n-Nabī*), which contains on the one hand the "Blessing" properly so called (*Salāt*) and on the other hand "Peace" (*Salām*), the latter referring to the stabilizing, appeasing and "horizontal" graces, and the former to the transforming, vivifying and "vertical" graces. The "Prophet" is the immanent universal Intellect, and the purpose of the formula is to awaken within us the Heart-Intellect both in respect of receptivity and illumination; of the Peace that extinguishes and of Life that regenerates, by God and in God.

•   •   •

The first Testimony of Faith, which refers *a priori* to transcendence, comprises secondarily and necessarily a meaning according to immanence: in this case, the word *illā*, "except" or "if not", means that every positive quality, every perfection, every beauty, belongs to God or even, in a certain sense, "is" God, whence the Divine Name "the Outward" (*az-Zāhir*) which is complementarily opposed to "the Inward" (*al-Bātin*).[3]

In an analogous but inverse manner, the second Testimony, which refers *a priori* to immanence, comprises secondarily and necessarily a meaning according to transcendence: in this case, the word *Rasūl*, "Messenger", means that Manifestation — *Muhammad* — is but the trace of the Principle, *Allāh*; that Manifestation is thus not the Principle.

These underlying meanings must accompany the main meanings by virtue of the principle of compensatory reciprocity to which we referred when speaking of the first Testimony, and in regard to which we made mention of the well-known symbol of *Yin-Yang*. For Manifestation is not the Principle, yet it is the Principle by participation, in virtue of its "nonexistence"; and Manifestation — the word indicates this — is the Principle manifested, but without being able to be the Principle in itself. The unitive truth of the second Testimony cannot be absent from the first Testimony, any more than the separative truth of the first can be absent from the second.

And just as the first Testimony, which has above all a macrocosmic and objective meaning, also necessarily comprises a microcosmic and subjective meaning,[4] likewise the second Testimony, which has above all a microcosmic and subjective meaning also comprises, necessarily, a macrocosmic and objective meaning.

The two Testimonies culminate in the word *Allāh*, which being their essence contains them and thereby transcends them. In the name *Allāh*, the first syllable is short, contracted, absolute, while the second is long, expanded, infinite; it is thus that the Supreme Name contains these two mysteries, Absoluteness and Infinity, and thereby also the extrinsic effect of their complementarity, namely Manifestation, as is indicated by this *hadīth qudsī*: "I was a hidden treasure and I willed to be known, thus I created the world." Since absolute Reality intrinsically comprises Goodness, Beauty, Beatitude (*Rahmah*), and since it is the Sovereign Good, it comprises *ipso facto* the tendency to communicate itself, thus to radiate; herein lies the aspect of Infinity of the Absolute; and it is this aspect that projects Possibility, Being, from which springs forth the world, things, creatures.

The Name *Muhammad* is that of the Logos, which is situated between the Principle and Manifestation, or between God and the world. Now the Logos, on the one hand is prefigured in the Principle, which is expressed by the word *illā* in the first *Shahādah*, and on the other hand projects itself into Manifestation, which is expressed by the word *ilāha* in the same formula. In the Name *Muhammad*, the whole accent and all the fulgurating power are situated at the center, between two short syllables, one initial and one final, without which this accentuation would not be possible; it is the sonorous image of the victorious Manifestation of the One.

• • •

According to the school of *Wujūdiyah*,[5] to say that "there is no divinity (*ilāha*) if not the (sole) Divinity (*Allāh*)" means that there is only God, that consequently everything is God, and that it is we creatures that see a multiple world where there is but one Reality; it remains to be seen why creatures see the One in multiple mode, and why God Himself, in so far as He creates, gives laws, and judges, sees the multiple and not the One. The correct answer is that multiplicity is objective as well as subjective — the cause of diversifying contingency being in each of the two poles of perception — and that multiplicity or diversity is in reality a subdivision, not of the Divine Principle of course, but of its manifesting projection, namely existential and universal Substance; diversity or plurality is therefore not opposed to Unity, it is within the latter and not alongside it. Multiplicity as such is the outward aspect of the world; however it is necessary to look at phenomena according to their inward reality, and thus as a diversified and diversifying projection of the One. The metacosmic cause of the phenomenon of multiplicity is All-Possibility, which coincides by definition with the Infinite, the latter being an intrinsic characteristic of the Absolute. The Divine Principle, being the Sovereign Good, tends by this very fact to radiate and thus to communicate itself; to project and to make explicit all the "possibilities of the Possible."

To say radiation is to say increasing distance, and thus progressive weakening or darkening, which explains the privative — and in the last analysis subversive — phenomenon of what we call evil; we call it such rightly, and in conformity with its nature, and not because of a particular, or even arbitrary, point of view. But evil, on pain of not being possible, must have a positive function in the

economy of the universe, and this function is two-fold: there is firstly contrasting manifestation, in other words, the throwing into relief
of the good by means of its opposite, for to distinguish a good from
an evil is a way of understanding better the nature of the good;[6]
then there is transitory collaboration which means that the role of
evil is also to contribute to the realization of the good.[7] It is however
absurd to assert that evil is a good because it is "willed by God" and
because God can only will the good; evil always remains evil in respect
of the privative or subversive character that defines it, but it is indirectly a good through the following factors: through existence,
which detaches it so to speak from nothingness and makes it participate, together with everything that exists, in Divine Reality, the
only one there is; through superimposed qualities or faculties, which
as such always retain their positive character; and finally, as we have
said, through its contrasting function with regard to the good and
its indirect collaboration in the realization of the good.

To envisage evil in relation to cosmogonic Causality is at the
same stroke and *a priori* to envisage it in relation to Universal Possibility: if manifesting radiation is necessarily prefigured in the Divine
Being, the privative consequences of this Radiation must likewise
be so, in a certain manner; not as such, of course, but as "punitive"
functions — morally speaking — pertaining essentially to Power and
Rigour, and consequently making manifest the "negation" (*nafy*) of
the *Shahādah*, namely the exclusiveness of the Absolute. It is these
functions that are expressed by the Divine Names of Wrath such as
"He who contracts, tightens, tears (*Al-Qābid*)," "He who takes revenge
(*Al-Muntaqim*)," "He who gives evil (*Ad-Darr*)," and several others; [8]
completely extrinsic functions, for: "Verily, my Mercy precedeth my
Wrath (*Ghadab*)," as the inscription on the throne of *Allah* declares;
"precedes", and thus "takes precedence over", and in the last analysis
"annuls". Moreover, the terrible divine functions, like the generous
ones, are reflected in creatures, either positively by analogy, or negatively by opposition; for holy anger is something other than hatred,
just as noble love is something other than blind passion.

We would add that the function of evil is to permit or to introduce the manifestation of Divine Anger, which means that the latter in a certain way creates evil with a view to its own ontologically
necessary manifestation: if there is Universal Radiation, there is by
virtue of the same necessity, both the phenomenon of evil and the
manifestation of Rigor, then victory of the Good, thus the eminent-

ly compensatory manifestation of Clemency. We could also say, very elliptically, that evil is the "existence of the inexistant" or the "possibility of the impossible"; this paradoxical possibility being required, as it were by the unlimitedness of All-Possibility, which cannot exclude even nothingness, however null in itself, yet "conceivable" both existentially as well as intellectually.

Whoever discerns and contemplates God, firstly in conceptual mode and then in the Heart, will finally see Him also in creatures, in the manner permitted by their nature, and not otherwise. From this comes, on the one hand charity towards one's neighbor and on the other hand respect towards even inanimate objects, always to the extent required or permitted by their qualities and their defects, for it is not a question of deluding oneself but of understanding the real nature of creatures and things;[9] this means that one has to be just and, depending on the case, to be more charitable than just, and also that one must treat things in conformity with their nature and not with a profanating inadvertence. This is the most elementary manner of seeing God everywhere, and it is also to feel that we are everywhere seen by God; and since in charity there are no strict lines of demarcation, we would say that it is better to be a little too charitable than not charitable enough.[10]

• • •

Each verse of the Koran, if it is not metaphysical or mystical in itself, comprises besides its immediate sense, a meaning that pertains to one or the other of these two domains; this certainly does not authorize one to put in the place of an underlying meaning an arbitrary and forced interpretation, for neither zeal nor ingenuity can replace the real intentions of the Text, whether these be direct or indirect, essential or secondary. "Lead us on the straight path": this verse refers first of all to dogmatic, ritual and moral rectitude; however, it cannot but refer also, and more especially, to the way of gnosis; on the contrary, when the Koran institutes some rule or other or when it relates some incident, no superior meaning imposes itself in a necessary way, which is not to say that this is excluded *a priori*, provided that the symbolism be plausible. It goes without saying that the exegetic science (*'ilm al-uṣūl*) of the theologians, with its classification of explanatory categories, does not take account — and this is its right — of the liberties of esoterist readings.

A point that we must bring up here, even if only to mention it, is the discontinuous, allusive and elliptical character of the Koran: it is discontinuous like its mode of revelation or "descent" (*tanzīl*), and allusive and therefore elliptical through its parabolism, which insinuates itself in secondary details, details that are all the more paradoxical in that their intention remains independent of the context. Moreover, it is a fact that the Arabs, and with them the Arabized, are fond of isolating and accentuating discontinuity, allusion, ellipsis, tautology and hyperbolism; all this seems to have its roots in certain characteristics of nomadic life, with its alternations, mysteries and nostalgias.

Let us now consider the Koranic "signs" in themselves. The following verses, and many others in addition, have an esoteric significance which if not always direct, is at least certain and therefore legitimate; or more precisely, each verse has several meanings of this kind, be it only because of the difference between the perspectives of love and gnosis, or between doctrine and method.

"God is the light of the heavens and of the earth (the Intellect that is both 'celestial' and 'terrestrial', principial or manifested, macrocosmic or microcosmic, the transcendent or immanent Self)" (*Sura of Light*, 35); "And to God belong the East and the West. Wheresoe'er ye turn, there is the Face of God" (*Sura of the Cow*, 115); "He is the First and the Last and the Outward (the Apparent) and the Inward (the Hidden), and He knows infinitely all things" (*Sura of Iron*, 3); "He it is who hath sent down the profound Peace (*Sakīnah* = Tranquility through the Divine Presence) into the hearts of the believers (the heart being either the profound soul or the intellect), in order to add a faith unto their faith (an allusion to the illumination that superposes itself upon ordinary faith): (*Sura of Victory*, 4); "Verily we belong to God and unto Him we shall return" (*Sura of the Cow*, 152); "And God calleth to the Abode of Peace and leadeth whom He will (whoever is qualified) on the straight (ascending) Path" (*Sura Yūnus*, 26); "Those who believe and those whose hearts find peace through the remembrance (mention = invocation) of God; is it not through the remembrance of God that hearts find peace?" (*Sura of the Cattle*, 91); "O men! Ye are the poor (*fuqarā*', from *faqīr*) in relation to God and God is the Rich (*al-Ghanī* = the Independent), the universally Praised (every cosmic quality referring to Him and bearing witness to Him)" (*Sura of the Creator*, 15); "And the beyond (the principial night) is better for thee than the herebelow (the phenomenal world)" (*Sura of the Dawn*, 4); "And worship God until certainty (metaphysical certainty, gnosis) comes to thee" (*Sura of the Rock*, 99).

We have quoted these verses as examples, without undertaking to clarify the properly esoteric underlying meanings contained in their respective symbolisms. But is is not only the verses of the Koran that are important in Islam, there are also the sayings (*ahādīth*) of the Prophet, which obey the same laws and in which God sometimes speaks in the first person; a saying in this category to which we referred above, because of its doctrinal importance, is the following: "I was a hidden treasure and I willed to be known, and so I created the world." And a saying in which the Prophet speaks for himself, and which we also quoted, is the following: "Spiritual virtue (*ihsān* = right doing) is that thou shouldst worship God as if thou sawest Him, for, if thou seest Him not, He nevertheless seeth thee."

A key formula for Sufism is the famous *hadīth*, in which God speaks through the mouth of the Messenger: "My slave ceaseth not to draw nigh unto Me by devotions freely accomplished, until I love him; and when I love him, I am the hearing whereby he heareth and the sight whereby he seeth and the hand wherewith he smiteth and the foot whereon he walketh." It is thus that the Absolute Subject, the Self, penetrates into the contingent subject, the ego, and that the latter is reintegrated into the former; this is the principal theme of esoterism. The "devotions freely accomplished" culminate in the "remembrance of God" or are directly identified with it, all the more so since the profound reason for the existence of every religious act is this remembrance, which in the last analysis is the reason for the existence of man.

But let us return to the Koran: the quasi "eucharistic" element in Islam — in other words, the element of "heavenly nourishment"— is the psalmody of the Book; the Canonical Prayer is the obligatory minimum of this, but it contains, as if by compensation, a text that is considered to be the equivalent of the whole Koran, namely the *Fātihah*, the "Sura that opens". What is important in the rite of reading or reciting the Revealed Book is not only the literal understanding of the text, but also, and almost independently of this understanding, the assimilation of the "magic" of the Book, either by elocution, or by audition, with the intention of being penetrated by the Divine Word (*Kalāmu 'Llāh*) as such, and consequently forgetting the world and the ego...

•   •   •

The two-fold Testimony is the first and the most important of the five "Pillars of the Religion" (*arkān ad-Dīn*). The others only have meaning in reference to it, and they are the following: Canonical Prayer (*Salāt*); the Fast of Ramadan (*Siyām*); Almsgiving (*Zakāt*); Pilgrimage (*Hajj*). The esoterism of these practices resides not only in their obvious initiatic symbolism, it resides also in the fact that our practices are esoteric to the extent that we ourselves are, firstly by our understanding of the Doctrine and then by our assimilation of the Method; these two elements being contained, precisely, in the two-fold Testimony. Prayer marks the submission of Manifestation to the Principle; the Fast is detachment with regard to desires, thus with regard to the ego; the Almsgiving is detachment with regard to things, thus with regard to the world; the Pilgrimage, finally, is the return to the Center, to the Heart: to the Self. A sixth pillar is sometimes added, the Holy War: this is the fight against the profane soul by means of the spiritual weapon; it is therefore not the Holy War that is outward and "lesser" (*asghar*), but the Holy War that is inward and "greater" (*akbar*), according to a *hadīth*. The Islamic initiation is in fact a pact with God with a view to this "greater" Holy War; the battle is fought by means of the *Dhikr* and on the basis of *Faqr*, inward Poverty; whence the name of *faqīr* given to the initiate.

Amongst the "Pillars of the Religion", that which the Prayer has in particular is that it has a precise form and comprises bodily positions which, being symbols, necessarily have meanings belonging to esoterism; but these meanings are simply explanatory, they do not enter consciously and operatively into the accomplishment of the rite, which only requries a sincere awareness of the formulas and a pious intention regarding the movements. The reason for the existence of the Canonical Prayer lies in the fact that man always remains an individual interlocutor before God and that he does not have to be anything else. When God wills that we speak to Him, He does not accept from us a metaphysical meditation. As regards the meaning of the movements of the Prayer, all that need be said here is that the vertical positions express our dignity as free and theomorphic vicar (*khalīfah*), and that the prostrations on the contrary manifest our smallness as "servant" (*ʿabd*) and as dependent and limited creature; man must be aware of the two sides of his being, made as he is of clay and spirit.

•   •   •

For obvious reasons, the Name *Allāh* is the quintessence of Prayer, as it is the quintessence of the Koran; containing in a certain manner the whole Koran, it thereby also contains the Canonical Prayer, which is the first sura of the Koran, "the opening" (*Al-Fātihah*). In principle, the Supreme Name (*al-Ism al-A'zam*) even contains the whole religion, with all the practices that it demands, and it could consequently replace them; but in fact, these practices contribute to the equilibrium of the soul and of society, or rather they conditon them.

In several passages, the Koran enjoins the faithful to remember God, and thus to invoke Him, and frequently repeat His Name. Likewise, the Prophet said: "It behoves you to remember your Lord (to invoke Him)." He also said: "There is a means of polishing every thing, and of removing rust; what polishes the heart is the invocation of *Allāh*; and there is no act which removes God's punishment as much as does this invocation." The Companions (of the Prophet) said: "Is the fight against infidels equal to that?" He replied: "No, not even if one fights until one's sword is broken." And he said further, on another occasion: "Should I not teach you an action that is better for you than fighting against infidels?" His Companions said: "Yes, teach us." The Prophet said: "This action is the invocation of *Allāh*."

The *Dhikr*, which implies spiritual combat since the soul tends naturally towards the world and the passions, coincides with the *Jihād*, the Holy War; the Islamic initiation — as we said above — is a pact with a view to this War; a pact with the Prophet and with God. The Prophet, on returning from a battle declared: "We have returned from the lesser Holy War (performed with the sword) to the greater Holy War (performed with invocation)."

The *Dhikr* contains the whole Law (*Sharīah*) and it is the reason for the existence of the whole Law;[11] this is declared by the Koranic verse: "Verily prayer (the exoteric practice) prevents man from committing what is shameful (sullying) and blameworthy; and verily the remembrance (invocation) of God (the esoteric practice) is greater." (*Sura of the Spider*, 45).[12] The formula "the remembrance of God is greater" or "the greatest thing" (*wa la-dhikru 'Llāhi akbar*) evokes and paraphrases the following words from the Canonical Prayer: "God is greater" or "the greatest" (*Allāhu akbar*) and this indicates a mysterious connection between God and His Name; it also indicates a certain relativity—from the point of view of gnosis—of the outward rites, which are nevertheless indispensable in principle and in the majority of cases. In this connection we could also quote the following *hadīth*: one of the Companions said to the Prophet: "O Messenger of God, the prescriptions of Islam are too numerous for me; tell me something that I can hold fast to." The Prophet replied: "Let thy tongue always be supple (in movement) with the mention (the remembrance) of God." This *hadīth*, like the verse we have just quoted, expresses by allusion (*ishārah*) the principle of the inherence of the whole *Sharī'ah* in the *Dhikr* alone.

"Verily ye have in the Messenger of God a fair example for whosoever hopeth in God and in the Last Day and remembereth God much." (*Sura of the Confederates*, 21). "Whosoever hopeth in God": this is he who accepts the Testimony, the *Shahādah*, not merely with his mind, but also with his heart; this is expressed by the word "hopeth". Now faith in God implies by way of consequence faith in our final ends; and to act in consequence is quintessentially to "remember God"; it is to fix the spirit on the Real instead of dissipating it in the illusory; and it is to find peace in this fixation, according to the verse quoted above: "Is it not in the remembrance of God that hearts find peace?"

"God makes firm those who believe by the firm Word, in the life of this world and in the beyond." (*Sura Ibrāhīm* 27). The "firm Word" (*al-qawl ath-thābit*) is either the *Shahādah*, the Testimony, or the *Ism*, the Name, the nature of the *Shahādah* being *a priori* intellectual or doctrinal, and that of the *Ism* being existential or alchemical; but not in an exclusive manner, for each of the two Divine Words participates in the other, the Testimony being in its way a Divine Name and the Name being implicitly a doctrinal Testimony. By these two Words, man becomes rooted in the Immutable, in this world as in the next. The "firmness" of the Divine Word refers quintessentially to the Absolute, which in Islamic language is the One; also, the affirmative part of the *Shahādah*—the words *illā 'Llāh*—is called a "firming" (*ithbāt*), which indicates reintegration into immutable Unity.

The whole doctrine of the *Dhikr* emerges from these words: "And remember Me (*Allāh*), I shall remember you (*Fadhkurūnī adhkurkum*)" (*Sura of the Cow*, 152). This is the doctrine of mystical reciprocity, as it appears in the following saying of the early Church: "God became man so that man become God"; the Essence became form so that form become Essence. This presupposes within the Essence a formal potentiality, and within form a mysterious immanence of the essential Reality; the Essence unites because it is one.

• • •

The whole of Sufism, it seems to us, is summed up in these four words: *Haqq, Qalb, Dhikr, Faqr*: "Truth ", "Heart", "Remembrance", "Poverty". *Haqq* coincides with the *Shahādah*, the two-fold Testimony: the metaphysical, cosmological, mystical and eschatological Truth. *Qalb* means that this Truth must be accepted, not by the mind alone, but with the Heart, thus with all that we are. *Dhikr*, as we know, is the permanent actualization, by means of the sacramental word, of this Faith or this Gnosis; while *Faqr* is simplicity and purity of soul, which makes possible this actualization by conferring on it the sincerity without which no act is valid.

The four most important formulas in Islam, which correspond in a certain sense to the four rivers of Paradise gushing forth from beneath the Throne of *Allāh* — the earthly reflection of this throne being the Kaaba — are the first and second *Shahādahs*, then the Consecration and the Praise: the *Basmalah* and the *Hamdalah*. The first *Shahādah*: "There is no divinity except the (sole) Divinity"; the second *Shahādah*: "Mohammed is the Messenger of God (of the sole Divinity)"; the *Basmalah*: "In the Name of God, the Clement, the Merciful";[13] the *Hamdalah*: "Praise be to God, the Lord of the worlds."

On the Life Cycle of Sufism*

Certain clarifications with regard to Sufism may be opportune at this point. It has been claimed, with a somewhat surprising assurance, that original Sufism was acquainted only with fear, that the Sufism of love comes later, and that of gnosis later still; and this succession has been presented, without hesitation, as an evolution, the

*From *IPP*, Chapter 2.

different phases of which have been attributed to alien influences. In reality, this unfolding in three phases is a normal cyclical projection of the spiritual potentialities of Islam. What in principle is of the highest order must be manifested — from the point of view of general emphasis — last of all, and this can obviously give the illusion of a kind of progress so long as one is unaware of the profound reasons for the phenomenon and unaware also that the three elements — fear, love, knowledge — necessarily existed from the beginning, and above all in the very person of the Prophet, as the Quran and the Sunnah bear witness; without which they could not have flowered at a later stage in specific forms of doctrine and method.

There are two parallel movements which balance each other: on the one hand, the collectivity degenerates as it moves further away from the origin; but, on the other, without there being — needless to say — any general increase in spirituality, there are successive stages of blossoming in the order of progression we have described, in the sense that values which were implicit from the beginning are unfolded as doctrine and become explicit, to the extent that one could point to a progressive and compensatory illumination in the very framework of general decadence. This is a phenomenon which may be observed in all religious cycles — that of Buddhism gives us another striking example — and this is why, within each religion, there arise "renewers" (*mujaddidūn*) who are "prophets" in a derivative and secondary sense. In Islam, Rābiʿah al-ʿAdawiyyah, Dhu 'l-Nun al-Miṣrī, an-Niffarī, al-Ghazālī, ʿAbd al-Qādir al-Jīlānī, Ibn ʿArabī, Abu 'l-Hasan ash-Shādhilī and Rūmī are of their number.

A paradoxical reason for the phenomenon is that the full flowering of the perspective of love presupposes a human environment forged in the perspective of fear, and that the blossoming of the perspective of gnosis presupposes an environment informed by that of love. In other words, a religion must have time to mould its segment of mankind before it can project upon it a particular spiritual emphasis once the ground has been prepared; the same is true of sacred art and the liturgy in general.

The Sufi ternary, "fear" (*makhāfah*), "love" (*maḥabbah*) and "knowledge" (*maʿrifah*) is manifested, in the framework of integral Monotheism, in the forms of the three Semitic religions respectively, each comprising in its turn and after its own fashion, with greater or lesser accentuation, the three modes in question. Christianity begins with the primitive desert fathers; it flowers again more gently, under the sign of the Virgin Mother, in the Middle Ages, to give place — although somewhat precariously, since the entire emphasis is on charity — to manifestations of gnosis which are particularly discernible, at various levels, among the Rhineland mystics and in Scholasticism, not forgetting the German theosophists — in a sort of traditional exile — and other more or less isolated groups.

In Judaism too, the period of the Psalms and the Song of Songs could not be that of the Pentateuch, and the Qabbalists could not emerge or unfold their doctrine before the Middle Ages. And let us remember in this context that Judaism, which stresses the Pact between God and Israel, is in its entirety a perspective of faith and fear; the fear of God frames the perspectives of love and knowledge, which could not be absent from it, love being in this case closely linked with hope.

Christianity, for its part, does not *a priori* put the accent on the Divine Nature, but on the redemptive Divine Manifestation; this is a perspective of love which frames after its fashion those of fear and knowledge, with fear and love being in this case derived from faith. These points have been raised here, not for the sake of defining the three perspectives yet again, but in order to underline the fact that each contains implicitly the other two. . .

NOTES

Islam

1. The Quran says: 'Do not go to the prayer in a state of drunkenness,' and this can be understood in a higher and positive sense; the Sufi who enjoys a 'station' (*maqām*) of bliss, or even merely the *dhākır* (the man given up to *dhikr*, the Islamic equivalent of the Hindu *japa*) could, considering his secret prayer to be like a 'wine' (*khamr*), in principle abstain from the general prayers, 'in principle' for in fact the care for equilibrium and solidarity, so marked in Islam, make the balance tend in the other direction.

2. This attitude ceased in relation to Hindus, at any rate in large measure, once the Moslems had grasped that Hinduism was not equivalent to the paganism of the Arabs; Hindus were in that case assimilated to the 'people of the Book' (*ahl al-Kıtāb*), that is to the Monotheists of the Western Semitic traditions.

3. Christ, in using violence against the money-changers in the temple, showed that this attitude could not be excluded.

On the Quran

1. Jalāl ed-Dīn Rumi, in his *Discourses* or *Fīhi mā fīhi*, wrote: 'God the Most High does not speak to just any man; like the kings of this world He does not speak with any casual fool; He has chosen ministers and deputies. Man accedes to God by going through the intermediaries He has appointed. God the Most High has made an election among his creatures in order that a man may come to Him by going through him whom He has chosen.' This passage, which refers to the Prophets, is also applicable to the authorized interpreters of the tradition.

2. Only this power can explain the importance of the recitation of the Quran. In his *Risālat el-Quds* Ibn 'Arabī quotes the case of Sufis who spent their whole life in reading or in ceaselessly reciting the Quran, and this would be inconceivable and even impossible of realization were there not, behind the husk of the literal text, a concrete and active spiritual presence which goes beyond the words and the mind. Moreover it is by virtue of this power of the Quran that certain verses can chase away demons and heal the sick, given the concurrence of the requisite conditions.

3. From this the reader might conclude that Aramaic is a sacred language since Christ spoke it, but here three reservations must be made; first, in Christianity, as in Buddhism, it is the Avatara himself who is the Revelation so that, apart from their doctrine, the Scriptures have not the central and plenary function which they have in other traditions; secondly, the precise Aramaic words used by Christ have not been preserved, which corroborates what has just been said; thirdly, for Christ himself Hebrew was the sacred language. Though the Talmud affirms that 'the Angels do not understand Aramaic,' this language has none the less a particularly high liturgical value; long before Christ it was 'made sacred' by Daniel and Esdras.

4. In fact Islam is the last world religion. As for the Sikh brotherhood, this is an esotericism analogous to that of Kabīr, the special position of which is explained by the quite exceptional conditions arising from the contiguity of Hinduism and Sufism; but here too it is a case of the very latest possibility.

5. This is true of every sacred Scripture and is notably true of the Bible story: the vicissitudes of Israel are those of the soul seeking its Lord. In Christianity this function of 'transforming magic' appertains especially to the Psalms.

6. Thus, moreover, was the Bible read — following in the footsteps of antiquity — in the Middle Ages. The denial of the hermeneutical interpretation, which was the bulwark of traditional and integral intellectuality, inevitably led in the end to 'criticism'— and destruction — of the sacred Texts; for instance there is nothing left of the Song of Songs once only the literal meaning is accepted.

On the Prophet

1. It is on this account that some have reproached this piety with being 'fatalistic' or 'quietist.' The real tendencies in question in fact already show in the term *'islām'*, which means 'abandonment' (to God).

The Quintessential Esoterism of Islam

1. Jacob's ladder is an image of the Logos, with the angels descending and ascending, God appearing at the top of the ladder, and Jacob remaining below.

2. Another ascending ternary is that of *makhāfah, mahabbah, maʿrifah*: fear, love, knowledge, modes which are both simultaneous and successive.

3 This interpretation has given rise to the accusation of pantheism, wrongly of course, because God cannot be reduced to outwardness; in other words, because outwardness does not exclude inwardness, any more than immanence excludes transcendence.

4. An initiatic or, one might say, "advaitic" sense: "There is no subject (no 'ego'), except the sole Subject (the 'Self')." It should be noted that Ramana Maharshi, as well as Ramakrishna, seem to have failed to recognize, in their teachings, the vital importance of the ritual and liturgical framework of the way, whereas neither the great Vedantists nor the Sufis ever lost sight of this.

5. The ontological monism of Ibn ʿArabī. It should be noted that even in Islam this school does not have a monopoly on unitive metaphysics, in spite of the prestige of its founder.

6. At first sight one might think that this throwing into relief is merely a secondary factor because it is circumstantial, but such is not the case since it is a question here of the quasiprincipial opposition of phenomena — or of categories of phenomena — and not of accidental confrontations. Qualitative "contrasting" is indeed a cosmic principle and not a question of encounters or comparisons.

7. Evil in its aspect of suffering contributes to the unfolding of Mercy which, in order to be plenary, must be able to save in the fullest meaning of this word; that is to say that Divine Love in its dimension of unlimited compassion implies evil in its dimension of abysmal misery; to this the Psalms and the Book of Job bear witness, and to this the final and quasi-absolute solution is the Apocatastasis which integrates everything in the Sovereign Good.

8. Vedantic doctrine discerns in the substantial or feminine pole (*Prakriti*) of Being three tendencies, one ascending and luminous (*Sattva*), one expansive and fiery (*Rajas*) and one descending and obscure (*Tamas*); this last does not in itself constitute evil, but it prefigures it indirectly and gives rise to it on certain levels or under certain conditions.

9. It is in this context as well that the love of beauty and the sense of the sacred are situated.

10. According to the Koran, God rewards merit much more than he punishes faults and He forgives the latter more readily on account of a little merit, than he lessens a reward on account of a little fault; always according to the measures of God, not according to ours.

11. This is the point of view of all invocatory disciplines, such as the Hindu *japa-yoga* or the Amidist *nembutsu (buddhanusmriti)*. This *yoga* is found in *jñana* as well as in *bhakti*. "Repeat the Sacred Name of the Divinity," said Shankaracharya in one of his hymns.

12. "God and His Name are identical," as Ramakrishna said; and he certainly was not the first to say so

13 God is clement or benevolent in Himself, in the sense that Goodness, Beauty and Love are comprised in His very Essence (*Dhāt*) and that He therefore manifests them necessarily in and through the world; this is expressed by the Name *Rahmān*, which is almost synonymous with the Name *Allāh*. And God is in addition good towards the world in the sense that He manifests His goodness towards creatures by according them subsistence and all possible gifts, including eminently salvation; it is this that is expressed by the Name *Rahīm*.

PART III

THE NATURE OF REALITY

Metaphysics

Dimensions, Modes and Degrees of the Divine Order*

THE IDEA THAT the Supreme Principle is both Absolute Reality and, for that very reason, Infinite Possibility, can suffice unto itself, for it contains everything, notably the necessity for a universal Manifestation. From a less synthetic point of view, however, and one closer to *Maya*, we may envisage a third hypostatic element, namely the Perfect Quality; being the Absolute, the Principle is thereby the Infinite and the Perfect. Absoluteness of the Real, infinitude of the Possible, perfection of the Good; these are the "initial dimensions" of the Divine Order.

This order also comprises "modes": Wisdom, Power, Goodness, that is, the content or the substance of the Supreme Principle consists in these three modes and each of them is at once Absolute, Infinite and Perfect; for each divine mode participates by definition in the nature of the divine Substance and thus comprises absolute Reality, infinite Possibility and perfect Quality. In Wisdom, as in Power and as in Goodness, there is in fact no contingency, no limitation, or any imperfection; being Absolute, these modes cannot not be, and being Infinite, they are inexhaustible; being Perfect, they lack nothing.

The Principle not only possesses "dimensions" and "modes," it

*From *STRP*, Chapter 2 (trans. G Polit).

309

also has degrees, and this in virtue of its very Infinitude, which projects the Principle into Relativity and thus produces, so to speak, this metacosmic "space" which we term the Divine Order. These degrees are the divine Essence, the divine Potentiality and the divine Manifestations; or Beyond-Being, Being, the Creator, and the Spirit, the existentiating Logos, which constitutes the divine Center of the total cosmos.

• • •

Necessity and Liberty; Unicity and Totality.[1] On the one hand, the Absolute is "necessary" Being, that which must be, which cannot not be, and which for that very reason is unique; on the other hand, the Infinite is "free" Being, which is unlimited and which contains all that can be, and which for that very reason is total.

This absolute and infinite, necessary and free, unique and total Reality is *ipso facto* perfect: for it lacks nothing, and it possesses in consequence all that is positive; it suffices unto itself. That is, the Absolute, like the Infinite which is as its intrinsic complement, its *shakti*, coincides with Perfection; the Sovereign Good is the very substance of the Absolute.

In the world, the existence of things, hence their relative reality, is derived from the Absolute; their containers, their diversity and their multiplicity, thus space, time, form, number, are derived from the Infinite; and finally, their qualities, whether substantial or accidental, are derived from Perfection. For Perfection, the Sovereign Good, contains the three Modes or hypostatic Functions which we have just mentioned, namely: Intelligence or Consciousness, or Wisdom, or Ipseity; Power or Strength; Goodness, which coincides with Beauty and Beatitude. It is Infinitude which so to speak projects the Sovereign Good into relativity, or in other words, which creates relativity, *Māyā*; it is in relativity that the supreme Qualities become differentiated and give rise to the Qualities of the creating, inspiring and acting Divinity, thus to the personal God; it is from Him that are derived all the cosmic qualities with their indefinite gradations and differentiations.

To say Absolute is to say Reality and Sovereign Good; to say Infinite is to say in addition communication, radiation, and in consequence, rela tivity; hence also differentiation, contrast, privation; the Infinite is All-Possibility. *Atmā* wills to clothe even nothingness, and it does so by and in *Māyā*.[2]

. . .

It is necessary to distinguish between the Good in itself and the manifestations of the Good: The Good in itself has no opposite, but from the moment that it is reflected in the manifested order, which is the cosmic order, it appears in the form of a given good, and this particularism implies, necessarily, the possibility of a given evil; relative good can be produced only in a world of contrasts.

To say, out of a concern for transcendence, that the Absolute is "be yond good and evil, beauty and ugliness," can only mean one thing, namely that it is the Good in itself, Beauty in itself; it cannot mean that it is de prived of goodness or beauty. Moreover, if on the one hand the possibility of the manifestation of a good necessarily renders possible that of an evil, on the other hand all manifested good, being limited by definition, implies the possibility of another mani- fested good; God alone is unique, because He alone remains out- side of manifestation.

The quasi-fragmentariness of manifested goods appears in an eloquent manner in sexual love or more precisely in the natural selec- tion which it implies: a given limited good — a given individual viewed in respect of his qualities — wishes to complete himself by another given limited but complementary good, and thus to create a new being in whom the fragments are united. This new being is limited in his turn, of course, since he is still comprised within manifesta- tion, but he is less limited in terms of a given intention of natural selection, and less limited in terms of the love which tends to tran- scend individuals — intrinsically by its spiritual magic and extrin- sically by the unitive creation of a new being. It is thus that man is in search of himself, his totality and his deiformity; and in seek- ing himself, he seeks God, unconsciously or consciously: either binding or liberating himself.

. . .

In the Absolute, there is no differentiation, for the latter by definition pertains to relativity, to *Māyā*; if it be objected that the Infinite and the Good — or Infinitude and Perfection — pertain to the Absolute, our reply is that the separation of these aspects or dimensions is subjective, that it is in our spirit, whereas in the Absolute these same aspects are undifferentiated while remaining real in respect of their intrinsic nature.

In the Essence — in the "pure Absolute"— Intelligence, Power and Goodness are also situated,[3] not alongside one another, but within one another, so much so that we can say, either that the Absolute — or the Absolute-Infinite-Good — is Intelligence, or that it is Power, or that it is Goodness, always in their intrinsic and purely principial reality. In relation to the first term, it will be said that the Absolute is the Self, which is, moreover, what is expressed by the term *Atmā*; thus viewed, the Absolute is the Subject as such, the real and unique Subject; extrinsically and combined with *Māyā*, this Subject will be the root of all possible subjectivities, it will be the immanent "divine I." In relation to the second term, Power, it will be said that the Absolute is the "absolutely Other", the Transcendent as well as the principial Omnipotent; extrinsically and combined with *Māyā*, it will be the underlying Agent of all acts as such, not inasmuch as they are intentions and forms.[4] In relation to the third term, finally, Goodness or Beauty, it will be said that the Absolute coincides with supreme Beatitude, and that extrinsically and combined with *Māyā*, it will be the generous "Father," but also the merciful "Mother": infinitely blissful in itself, it gives existence and the goods of existence; it offers all that it is in its Essence.

The Infinite, by its radiation brought about so to speak by the pressure — or the overflowing — of the innumerable possibilities, transposes the substance of the Absolute, namely the Sovereign Good, into relativity; this transposition gives rise *a priori* to the reflected image of the Good, namely the creating Being. The Good, which coincides with the Absolute, is thus prolonged in the direction of relativity and gives rise first of all to Being, which contains the archetypes, and then to Existence, which manifests them in indefinitely varied modes and according to the rhythms of the diverse cosmic cycles.

The Absolute is that which "cannot not be"; and the necessity of Being excludes all "that which is not It." In an analogous but as it were inverse manner, the Infinite is that which "can be all"; and the liberty of Being includes all "that which is It", hence all that is possible, this "all" being limitless, precisely. In other words: God alone is necessary Being: in Him there is nothing contingent or, for all the more reason, arbitrary, and on the contrary, outside of Him, there are only contingent existences; and God alone is free Being: in Him there is no determination *ab extra* or any constraint, and on the contrary, outside of Him, there are only the existences that He determines. On the one hand, an existence may or may not be, and that is its contingency; on the other hand, the existence of a thing contains but one possibility, that of that thing and nothing else — and that is its limitation — whereas the being of God contains all that is possible.

Or again: God, by His nature, hence by necessity, "must" create, but He "is free" to create what He wills in virtue of His liberty; He is "necessary" in the In-Itselfness, yet He is free in the modalities. In other words: God "is free" to create what He wills — and He can will only in conformity with His nature — but He "must" follow the logic of things; His activity is necessary in laws and structures, while being free in their contents.

• • •

Existence is subject to Being, but Being in its turn is subject or subordinate to Beyond-Being; in other words, the world is subject to God, but God in His turn is subject to His own Essence: to the "pure Absolute," to *Ātmā* without trace of *Māyā*. God can do all in the world; but He can do nothing outside of what His Essence or His Nature "dictates," and He can will nothing else. God cannot be what He "wills," except in the sense that He wills only what He is; now He is the Sovereign Good. Certainly, God the Creator is the absolute Master of the created world; but *Ātmā* is the absolute Master of *Māyā*, and the Creator pertains to *Māyā* since He is, within it, the direct and central reflection of *Ātmā*.

That Beyond-Being can have "on its level"— if one may express oneself thus provisionally — a will other than that which Being has on its level, is not more contradictory than the fact that a given aspect of Being or a given "Divine Name" can have a will different from that of another given aspect of Being. The "Generous" for example, can or must will something other than what is willed by the "Avenger";

now the "vertical" diversity in the Divine Order is not more contrary to Unity than is the "horizontal" diversity. That God as Legislator does not will sin whereas God as All-Possibility wills it — but from an altogether different point of view of course — is as plausible as the fact that the Divine Justice has aims other than those of the Divine Mercy.[5]

"God doeth what He will": quite paradoxically, it is just this Koranic expression, and analogous expressions,[6] which indicate absolute transcendence and which refer — in the very language of creating and revealing Being — to the fathomless Beyond-Being, hence to the transpersonal Essence of the Divinity. The very paradox of the expression, which eludes all explanation, all logical and moral satisfaction, insinuates a reality that transcends the domain of the personal Divine Subject; the apparently arbitrary here opens the way to metaphysical clarification. The word by word evasions are in reality keys towards profundity; the function of the words here is the reverse of the interpretations of the Hanbalite, Asharite and other theologians. "God doeth what He will" means, in the final analysis, "God is not what you think," or rather: "what you can understand"; namely an anthropomorphic being having a unique subjectivity and thereby a unique will.

God can will what He is, He cannot be what He wills, assuming — with regard to the second proposition — that He could will no matter what, which precisely His Being excludes. A remark which imposes itself here is the following: in a certain respect, God is the absolute Good; but in another respect, He is "beyond good and evil," according to the interpretation of the words, as we have noted above. On the one hand, He is the Good in the sense that all good derives from His nature, whereas He cannot cause evil as such; on the other hand, He is "beyond good and evil" in the sense that He is necessarily the cause of all that exists, since there is no other cause in the universe; now existence in itself is neither good nor bad, even though it can be viewed in terms of both aspects. Compared to the "Sovereign Good," the whole world can appear as a kind of "evil" since it is not God —"why callest thou me good?"— whereas in another respect, "God saw that it was good," that is, the world is good as divine Manifestation, which shows clearly that, if on the one hand God is "the Good," on the other hand He is "beyond good and evil";[7] in this latter relationship — and in this latter only — it can be said that the distinction in question means nothing to God, and that consequently human morality does not concern Him.

The Divine Order — if one may express oneself thus — is made of Wisdom, Power and Goodness, each of these Hypostases being Absolute, Infinite and Perfect. In addition, this Order comprises three degrees of Reality, namely Beyond-Being, Being and Existence: the latter is here, not cosmic Existence as a whole, but the divine Manifestation, that is, the direct and central reflection of Being in the cosmic order;[8] it is thus that the Divine Order enters into the cosmos without ceasing to be what it is and without the cosmos ceasing to be what it is. And that is at the same time the mystery of the Logos, of the *Avatāra*: of the human theophany that is "true man and true God."

The polarization into distinct Qualities is produced starting from the degree of "Being" and is accentuated starting from the degree of "Existence." Among the Divine Qualities, those which manifest Rigor, Justice, Anger, pertain in the final analysis and in a particular manner to the pole "Absolute," which in itself cannot be a pole, yet appears thus as soon as its *shakti* of Infinitude is viewed separately; correlatively and complementarily, the Qualities that manifest Gentleness, Compassion, Love, pertain in an analogous manner to the pole "Infinite"; this is the Islamic distinction between "Majesty" (*Jalāl*) and "Beauty" (*Jamāl*). But the "Just" is the "Holy" just as the "Merciful" is the "Holy"; for God is One and He is holy by virtue of His Essence, not by virtue of a given Quality. Justice or Rigor, which derives in a certain manner from the pole "absolute," cannot not be; thus there must be supports in the cosmos which permit its manifestation. Likewise for Clemency or Gentleness, which derives from the pole "Infinite": it can manifest itself only through created elements which serve as receptacles of its action. This evokes the Pauline doctrine of the vessels of Wrath and the vessels of Mercy, thus the idea of predestination; the latter being none other than the substance of a given existential possibility.

•   •   •

All-Possibility, whatever be its hypostatic level,[9] prefigures, with its limitlessness both static and dynamic, the complementarity "space-time," or more concretely that of the ether and its vibratory power; the ether being, in our material world, the basic substance which prefigures in its turn the complementarity "mass-energy." And let us recall at this point that the spatial void is in reality the ether, that it is consequently a relative and symbolic void; likewise, the temporal void, so to speak — the absence of change or movement — is in reality the latent energy of the etheric element, for there is no absolute inertia. And this concrete space is a substance, or the substance, the first of all substances; concrete space is a vibration, or the vibration, the one which vehicles all the others. If the empirical void were absolute as only a principle can be, it would be a pure nothingness, and there would be no extension possible — temporal or spatial — for a nothingness cannot be added onto another nothingness; the point then could not concretely engender the line, or the moment, time. Only a substance — by definition energetic or vibratory — can vehicle contents, either static or dynamic.

Certainly, space as container pure and simple is empty and without life — it nonetheless realizes this aspect only in a relative and fragmentary fashion — but as the field of the manifestation of formal possibilities, thus in its integral nature, it is plenitude and movement; hence it is not without reason that in fact there is no total space without celestial bodies, and there are no celestial bodies without change and displacement. If space were merely an emptiness devoid of substantiality and energy, and containing forms by miracle, it would be merely a museum of crystals; we say "by miracle," for an absolute void, being nothing, can contain nothing.

It is necessarily thus because divine Possibility, while being a void with respect to manifestation, is in itself Plenitude and Life.[10]

The Interplay of the Hypostases*

To say Absolute, is to say Infinite; Infinitude is an intrinsic aspect of the Absolute. It is from this "dimension" of Infinitude that the world necessarily springs forth; the world exists because the Absolute, being such, implies Infinitude.

This Absolute-Infinite is the Sovereign Good; the *Agathón* of Plato. Now the Good — according to the Augustinian formula — tends essentially to communicate itself; being the Sovereign Good, the Absolute-Infinite cannot but project the world; which is to say that

*From *DH*, Chapter 3 (trans. G.Polit).

the Absolute, being the Sovereign Good, comprises thereby Infinitude and Radiation.

If we were to be asked what the Absolute is, we would reply first of all that it is necessary and not merely possible Reality; absolute Reality, hence infinite and perfect, precisely; and we would add — in conformity with the level of the question asked — that the Absolute is that which, in the world, is reflected as the existence of things. Without the Absolute, there is no existence; the aspect of absoluteness of a thing is what distinguishes it from inexistence, if one may so put it. Compared to empty space, each grain of sand is a miracle.

If we were to be asked further what the Infinite is, we would reply, with the quasi-empiricist logic demanded by the question itself, that the Infinite is that which, in the world, appears as modes of expanse or of extension, such as space, time, form or diversity, number or multiplicity, matter or substance. In other words, and to be more precise: there is a conserving mode, and this is space; a transforming mode, and this is time; a qualititative mode, and this is form, not inasmuch as it limits, but inasmuch as it implies indefinite diversity; a quantitative mode, and this is number, not inasmuch as it fixes a given quantity, but inasmuch as it too is indefinite; a substantial mode, and this is matter, it too being without limit as is shown by the star-filled sky. Each of these modes has its prolongation — or more exactly its basis — in the animic state and beyond, for these modes are the very pillars of universal existence.

Finally, if we were to be asked what Perfection or the Sovereign Good is — for to say God is to say Goodness, as is indicated by the very expression of a "good God" — we would say that it is that which, in the world, is manifested as qualities and, more concretely, as qualitative phenomena; perfections and perfect things. We say "that which manifests" and not "that which is": the Absolute, the Infinite, the Good are not respectively existence, the existential categories, the qualities of things, but all of these factors manifest, precisely, what the Divine Hypostases — if one may say so — are in themselves and beyond the world.

• • •

Infinitude and Perfection are intrinsic dimensions of the Absolute; but they also affirm themselves in a "descending sense" and in view of cosmogonic manifestation, in which case it could be said that Perfection or the Good is the "image" of the Absolute produced by Radiation, hence in function of the Infinite. It is here that intervenes the Divine *Māyā*, Relativity *in divinis*: whereas on the one hand the Absolute by definition possesses Infinitude and Perfection, on the other hand — in virtue of the Relativity necessarily implied by the Infinite — the Absolute gives rise to an operative Infinitude and to a manifested Good; thus to a hypostatic hierarchy in a "descending direction," and in the final analysis "creative."

The Absolute is infinite; therefore it radiates, and in radiating, it projects itself; the content of this projection being the Good. The Absolute could neither radiate nor produce thereby the image of the Good if it were not itself in its Immutability both the Good and the Radiation, or in other words, if it did not possess these intrinsic dimensions — and indistinctly since Relativity is transcended. This is the very foundation of what Christian doctrine terms the Hypostases.

To say projection is to say polarization: the Infinite — at the degree of *Maya* or, more precisely, at the summit of Relativity — projects the Absolute and thus produces the image, and from the moment there is image — this is the Logos — there is polarization, that is to say refraction of the Light which in itself is undivided. The good refracted, or the Logos, contains all Perfections possible, it translates the potentiality of the Essence into an inexhaustible unfolding of possibilities, and it is thus the divine "place" of the archetypes.

Geometrically speaking, we could say that the point by its very nature contains both the circle and the rays; that being the case, it projects them. The point here stands for the Absolute; the cluster of rays, for operative Infinity; the circle, for the Projected Good, hence for the totality of perfections. That is to say that the divine Order comprises on the one hand "degrees," and on the other hand "modes": degrees in projecting itself, and modes in polarizing itself.

* * *

God is also Perfection, we have said; however, evil cannot not exist, but its existence is always limited in respect of spatial as well as of temporal extension, whereas the Sovereign Good has no limit. And yet, man as such is not able to understand totally the existence

of evil; there always remains a point at which man, instead of understanding concretely, has to resign himself and accept what his sensibility and his imagination, and even his logic, do not seem able
to grasp. And this is not without relation to the fact that man as such
cannot exhaustively comprehend the divine nature, even though the
Intellect in principle comprehends all, for it is God who comprehends
Himself in it; but this ultimate comprehension, to which man has
access in principle, coincides with the Inexpressible; whereas language
is man, and infinite knowledge cannot pertain to that which in human
nature is bound up with language, thought and desire. In other words:
there is always in evil an element of unintelligibility or of absurdity,
which is reducible intellectually, but not imaginatively or sentimentally, therefore humanly; which is not a reproach, but the taking note
of a natural fact. The logic of the metaphysician can be satisfied
without difficulty; but human sentiment, let us repeat, has no choice
other than to submit, which amounts to saying, precisely, that human
nature has its limits. Humanly, no one escapes the obligation to
"believe in order to be able to understand" (*credo ut intelligam*).

But if concrete evil is partially incomprehensible to man, that
good which is abstract in practice — namely, spiritual good — is quite
as much so; man, though he well knows that prayer places him before
God and in contact with Mercy, if he were capable of understanding this totally and in a concrete manner, would spare himself many
disturbances and anxieties; and he would better grasp, eschatological-
ly speaking, that evil cannot but brush, though not overcome, the
free, responsible and immortal man who gives himself to God.

But let us return to the question of privative possibility in itself:
all things considered, one need not seek too far for the causes of
human perplexity in the face of concrete evil; if a particular phenomenon of evil seems incomprehensible to us, it is not so much
because of our understanding has limits as it is for the simple reason
that there is nothing to understand, except in an abstract manner.
Which is to say that we understand perfectly that evil is either a privation or an excess and that it is necessary for such and such metaphysical reasons; we understand evil as such, but we do not understand such and such an evil. The concrete understanding of the
absurd is a contradiction in terms, the absurd being precisely that
which offers nothing to our understanding, except for its simple
possibility and its evident falseness. If our ultimate refuge is God,
intellectually as well as morally, it is because He alone is absolutely

intelligible, whether we understand this *a priori* or not; He alone being that which is, total intelligibility coinciding with pure Being.

• • •

In Trinitarian theology, the Absolute in itself corresponds to Being and Power;[1] the Infinite, to Will or Love, therefore to the function of projection or radiation; and the Good, to Intelligence or Knowledge, therefore to the polarization of the potentialities of the Essence.

The Absolute, the Good, the Infinite: *Sat, Chit, Ananda.* In considering this analogy between the Trinity just mentioned and the Vedantic Ternary—"Being, Consciousness, Beatitude"— it could be asked what relationship there is between the Good and Consciousness (*Chit*); now the Good, from the moment that It springs as such from the Absolute — which contains it in an undifferentiated or undeterminate manner — coincides with the distinctive consciousness which the Absolute has of itself; the Divine Word, which is the "Knowledge" which God has of Himself, cannot but be the Good, God being able to know Himself only as Good.

The principle of radiation or projection — inherent in the Absolute, in the "Father"— corresponds to the "Holy Spirit"; and the principle of polarization or refraction, to the "Son."[2] The "Son" is to the "Father" what the circle is to the center; and the "Holy Spirit" is to the "Father" what the radius is to the center. And as the radius, which "emanates" from the center, does not stop at the circle, but traverses it, it could be said that starting from the circle, the radius is "delegated" by the circle, as the "Spirit" emanates from the "Father" and is delegated by the "Son"; the character of the *filioque*, at once justifiable and problematical, becomes clear with the aid of this image.

To say that the "Father" is nothing without the "Son"— we have somewhere encountered this ill-sounding expression — can mean only this, if one wishes to find a plausible meaning in it: that the Absolute would not be the Absolute wihout its potentiality, both hypostatic and cosmogonic, of "exteriorization"— therefore also of repetition. Between the Absolute and its both intrinsic and extrinsic projection[3] — depending on the ontological degree — there is at once inequality and equality, which Catholic theology expresses by the elliptical notion of "subsistent relations"; "relation" refers logically to inequality, and "subsistent," to equality, which latter, for the theologians, in practice abolishes its contrary.[4] It can be seen from this that dogmatist thought is so to speak static and exclusive, that it is unaware of the play of *Māyā*; in other words, it admits of no movement, no diversity of points of view and of aspects, no degrees in Reality. It offers keys, but also veils; appeasing and protective veils assuredly, but veils which it itself will not lift.

. . .

The "Father" is always "greater" than the "Son" and the "Holy Spirit": greater than the Son, because precisely He is the Father — otherwise the words would mean nothing — and greater than the Holy Spirit since the latter emanates from the former and not conversely.

The Son, is therefore, always "less great" than the Father — apart from the relationship of equality which is that of the Essence and which does not intervene here — whereas in regard to the Holy Spirit He is either greater or less great: He is greater inasmuch as He "delegates" or sends the Spirit, and less great inasmuch as He is manifested by it, at the time of the Incarnation and also as "Child" of the Virgin; the latter is the impersonation of the Holy Spirit, as the expressions *gratia plena* and *Mater Dei* clearly indicate.

The Holy Spirit is always less great than the Father, in the sense that It is His Radiation, whereas It is either greater or less great than the Son: It is greater inasmuch as It vehicles or projects the Son, but less great inasmuch as It is delegated or sent by Him. It is thus that the radii which emanate from a point are "greater" than the circle which they project so to speak, but this circle is "greater" than they once it is situated at the interior of the radiation and thereby in practice assumes the central situation of the point.

The Hypostases are not "relative," that is to say "non-absolute" or "less absolute," inasmuch as they are "contained" in the Essence — which latter, according to a certain early perspective, coincides with the "Father" — they are relative inasmuch as they "emanate" from It; if they were not "contained, " they could not "emanate." The Hypostases are relative with respect to the Essence, and absolute with respect to the world, which amounts to saying — paradoxically, but necessarily — that they are "relatively absolute"; that they are so at the ontological levels of "emanation," and not in essentiality wherein they coincide with the Absolute pure and simple.

We are here at the limit of the expressible; it is the fault of no one if within every enunciation of this kind there remain unanswerable questions, at least in respect of a given need for causality and on the plane of dialectic; for the science of the heart needs no discussion. In any case, it is all too evident that wisdom cannot start from the intention of expressing the ineffable; but it intends to furnish points of reference which permit us to open ourselves to the ineffable to the extent possible, and according to what is foreseen by the Will of God.

The Mystery of the Veil*

The veil is a notion which evokes the idea of mystery, because it hides from view something that is either too sacred or too intimate; but it also enfolds a mystery within its own nature when it becomes the symbol of universal veiling. The cosmic and metacosmic veil is a mystery because it has its root in the depths of the Divine Nature. According to the Vedantists, it is impossible to explain *Maya*, even though one cannot help admitting its presence; *Maya*, like *Atma*, is without origin and without end.

The Hindu notion of "Illusion," *Maya*, coincides in fact with the Islamic symbolism of the "Veil," *Hijāb*: the universal Illusion is a power which on the one hand hides and on the other hand reveals; it is the Veil before the Face of *Allāh*[1] or, according to a multiplying extension of the symbolism, the series of sixty-six thousand veils of light and darkness which either through clemency or rigour screen the fulgurating radiance of the Divinity.[2]

The Veil is a mystery because Relativity is. The Absolute, or the Unconditioned, is mysterious by sheer evidentness; but the Relative or the Conditioned is so by dint of unintelligibility. If it is impossible to understand the Absolute, it is because its luminosity is blinding; on the contrary, if it is impossible to understand the Relative, it is because its obscurity offers no reference to mark. At least this is so when we consider Relativity in its seeming arbitrariness,

*From *EPW*, pp. 47-64.

for it becomes intelligible to the extent that it is the vehicle of the Absolute, or to the extent that it appears as an emanation of the Absolute. To be the vehicle of the Absolute, while veiling it, is the purpose of the Relative.

One must therefore seek to penetrate the mystery of Relativity from the starting point of the Absolute or in terms of it, and this compels us — or allows us — to find the root of Relativity in the Absolute itself: and this root is none other than Infinity, which is inseparable from the Real which, being absolute, is necessarily infinite. This Infinity implies Radiation, for the good tends to communicate itself, as St. Augustine observed; the Infinity of the Real is none other than its power of Love. And the mystery of Radiation explains everything: by radiating, the Real as it were projects Itself "outside Itself," and in separating Itself from Itself, It becomes Relativity to the very extent of this separation. It is true that this "outside " is necessarily situated in the Real Itself, but it none the less exists *qua* outwardness and in a symbolic fashion, which is to say that it is "thought" by the Infinite by virtue of Its tendency to Radiation and hence to expansion in a void that in reality does not exist. This void has no reality except through the Rays that are projected into it; Relativity is only real through its contents which, for their part, pertain essentially to the Absolute. Thus it is that space has no existence except through what it contains; an empty space would no longer be a space, it would be nothingness.

The principial prototype of the Veil, therefore, is the divine dimension of Infinity, which radiates so to speak from the Unconditioned while remaining a rigorously intrinsic quality; in the Absolute, *Shiva* and *Shakti* are identical. Separative and playful *Maya* which creates illusion, does not emerge inexplicably from nothingness, it proceeds from the very nature of *Atma*; for since the good has by definition a tendency to communicate itself, the "Sovereign Good" cannot but radiate for itself and in its Essence, and then — and as a consequence — from itself and outside itself; being Truth, "God is Love."

This amounts to saying that there is in God a first Veil, namely the purely principial and essential tendency towards communication and thus towards contingency, a tendency which remains strictly within the Divine Essence. The second Veil is as it were the extrinsic effect of the first: this is the ontological Principle, creative Being, which conceives the Ideas or the Possibilities of things. Being gives rise to a third Veil, the creative Logos that produces the Universe, and this too, and to some extent *a fortiori*, is a Veil which both dissimulates and transmits the treasures of the Sovereign Good.

•   •   •

Beyond-Being is the Absolute or Unconditioned, which by definition is infinite and thus unlimited; but one can also say that Beyond-Being is the Infinite, which by definition is absolute; in the first case, the accent is put on the symbolism of virility; in the second case, it is put on femininity; the Supreme Divinity is either Father or Mother.[3] The notions of the Absolute and the Infinite thus do not in themselves indicate a polarity, except when they are juxtaposed, which already corresponds to a relative point of view. On the one hand, as we have said, the Absolute is the Infinite, and inversely; on the other hand, the first suggests a mystery of oneness, exclusion and contraction, whereas the second suggests a mystery of totality, inclusion and expansion.

As mentioned above, Relativity arises from the aspect of Illimitation of the Unconditioned, and proceeds by successive veilings up to the limitpoint of separation — a point which is never reached since it is illusory, or which is only reached symbolically; for our world this limit-point is matter, but one can conceive of limit-points indefinitely more solidified, and *a fortiori* much more subtle. There is no cosmogenesis without theogenesis; this term is metaphysically plausible, but it offends the ear owing to the fact that it seems to attribute becoming to the Hypostases, whereas it can only be a case of principial succession in the direction of the relative. The end-point of theogenesis is the most relative or the most outward Hypostasis, namely the "Spirit of God" which, while already being created, since it occupies the luminous centre of creation, is nevertheless still Divine; this is the Logos which prefigures, on the one hand, the human species as natural representative of God on earth, and on the other hand the *Avatara* as supernatural representative of God amongst men.

The polarity "Unconditioned-Unlimited"— in so far as there is here a polarity resulting, not from the meaning of these words but solely from their comparative juxtaposition, which precisely restricts their meanings — is repeated in the very structure of the Veil, or of *Maya*, or of Relativity, which brings us to the symbolism of weaving. The first term of the polarity becomes the warp, or the vertical or masculine dimension, while the second term becomes the woof, or the horizontal or feminine dimension; and each of these dimensions, at all levels, comprises elements of Existentiality, Consciousness and Bliss, in conformity with the Vedantic ternary, and in either an active or a passive manner, depending on whether the elements refer to the warp or the woof. The complementarity "Unconditioned-Unlimited," which comprises these three elements, thus produces, in an indefinite and iridescent display the measureless river of phenomena; the universe is thus a veil which on the one hand exteriorizes the Essence and on the other hand is situated within the Essence itself, inasmuch as it is Infinitude.

In Islamic terms, the divine polarity, which we have just compared to the warp and the woof, is expressed by the letter *alif*, which is vertical, and the letter *ba*, which is horizontal; these are the first two letters of the Arabic alphabet, one symbolizing determinativity and activity, and the other receptivity or passivity.[4] The same functions are expressed by the Calamus (*Qalam*) and the Tablet (*Lawh*): in every phenomenon and at every level, there is an "Idea" which is incarnated in an existential receptacle; the Calamus is the creative Logos, whereas the Ideas that it contains and projects refer to the ink (*Midād*). We find the same polarity in the human microcosm, man being both "vicar" (*khalīfah*), and "servant" (*'abd*),[5] or intellect and soul.

According to a famous *hadīth*, God was a hidden treasure who wished to be known and who for this reason created the world. He was hidden from men as yet inexistent; it is consequently the inexistence of men that was the first veil; God thus created the world for men in order to be known by them and in order to project His own Felicity into innumerable relative consciousnesses. This is why it has been said that God created the world out of love.

Wherever *Atma* is, there also is *Maya*, intrinsic Life and extrinsic Power of deployment. In Islamic terms, and apart from the notion of the *Hijāb*, it is said that wherever *Allāh* is, there also is *Rahmah*, the infinite Clemency and Mercy, and it is this that is expressed by the fundamental formula that introduces the Suras of the Koran and, in human life, everything written and everything undertaken "In the Name of God, the most Clement, the most Merciful." The fact that these Names of infinite Goodness are added to the Name *Allāh* indicates that Goodness is in the very Essence of God and that, unlike most of the divine qualities, it is not an element that appears only by refraction on the already relative plane of the attributes; this means that *Rahmah* belongs to *Dhāt*, the Essence, and not to the attributes, *Sifāt*.[6] *Rahmah* is *Maya*, not with respect to Relativity and Illusion, but with respect to Infinitude, Beauty, Generosity. [7]

• • •

In the Vedanta, *Atma* is clothed in three great veils (or "envelopes," *koshas*), which correspond analogically, by prefiguring them causatively, to the states of wakefulness, dreaming, and deep sleep: these veils or states are *Vaishvarana, Taijasa,* and *Prajna*; what they veil is unconditioned and ineffable Reality, *Turiya*, which in the human microcosm is the Divine Presence in the depth of the heart. This reality, or this fourth "state" in the ascending sense, is Beyond-Being or *Atma* in itself; it is said of it that it is "neither manifested (*vyakta*) nor unmanifested (*avyakta*)," and this calls for an explanation.

The idea of the unmanifested has two different meanings: there is the absolutely unmanifested, *Parabrahma* or *Brahma nirguna* ("unqualified"), and the relatively unmanifested, *Ishvara* or *Brahma saguna* ("qualified"); this relatively unmanifested, Being as existentiating principle or matrix of the archetypes, may be called the "potentially manifested" in relation to the "effectively manifested," namely the world; for in the divine order itself, Being is the "manifestation" of Beyond-Being, otherwise manifestation properly so called, or Existence, would be neither possible nor conceivable. To say that the absolutely unmanifested is the principle both of the manifested — the world — and of the relatively unmanifested — Being — would be a tautology: as the principle of Being, Beyond-Being is implicitly the principle of Existence. In the sight of the absolutely unmanifested, the distinction between the potentially manifested — which is relatively unmanifested and creative — and the effectively manifested or the created, the distinction, that is, between Being and Existence, has no reality; in the sight of Beyond-Being it is neither a complementarity nor an alternative.

It is important to take account, in the principial or divine order, firstly of the Absolute in itself, and secondly of the Absolute in so far as it is deployed in *Maya*, or in the mode of *Maya*; in this second respect, "all things are *Atma*." In an analogous manner, but within the context of *Maya* itself, one can look on things firstly in themselves, and thus from the standpoint of the separate existence which determines them as phenomena, and secondly in Being, and thus as archetypes. Every aspect of relativity — even principial — or of manifestation is *vyakta*, and every aspect of absoluity — even relative — or of non-manifestation is *avyakta*.

In order to realize Beyond-Being, which is the absolute Self, it is necessary, according to the *Katha Upanishad*, to "pass beyond obscurity"; this "beyond obscurity" is obviously the intrinsic luminosity of the Self, which is revealed after the obscurity presented by the unmanifested in relation to the illusory luminosity of the manifested. Since "extremes meet," the maximum of "inward" knowledge will have as its complement the maximum of "outward" knowledge, not of course in the sense of scientific knowledge, but in the sense that the man who sees God perfectly within and beyond phenomena will see Him perfectly in the outward or in phenomena;[8] thus the "ascent" of the spirit towards God entails subjectively a "descent" of God into things.[9] This "divine vision" of the world may well carry with it a "mandate from Heaven" or a spiritual mission whatever be its degree of importance, which will vary according to the profundity or totality of the inward knowledge. Inversely, one could say that a particular predestined mandate providentially coincides with supreme knowledge; but one cannot in any event affirm that a degree of knowledge or realization *ipso facto* entails a law-giving prophetic mission; otherwise every perfect sage would be the founder of a religion. Be that as it may, what we were concerned to point out here is that the lifting of the veil in the inward and intellective dimension is accompanied by an illumination or a transparency of the veils in which and through which we live; and of which we are made, from the very fact of our existence.

· · ·

The veil can be thick or transparent, unique or multiple; it veils or it unveils, violently or gently, suddenly or progressively; it includes or it excludes, and it separates thus two regions, one inward and one outward. All these modes are manifested in the microcosm as well as in the macrocosm, or in the spiritual life as well as in the cosmic cycles.

The impenetrable veil covers from sight something that is too sacred or too intimate; the veil of Isis suggests the two relationships, since the body of the Goddess coincides with the Holy-of-Holies. The "sacred" refers to the divine aspect of *Jalāl*, "Majesty"; the "intimate" for its part refers to *Jamāl*, "Beauty"; blinding Majesty and intoxicating Beauty. The transparent veil, on the contrary, communicates both the sacred and the intimate, like a sanctuary that opens its door, or a bride who gives herself, or a bridegroom who welcomes and takes possession.

When the Veil is thick, it hides the Divinity: it is made of the forms that constitute the world, but these are also the passions within the soul; the thick Veil is woven out of sensorial phenomena around us and passional phenomena within us; and be it noted that an error is a passional element to the extent that it is serious and that man is attached to it. The thickness of the Veil is both objective and subjective, in the world and in the soul: it is subjective in the world in so far as our minds fail to penetrate to the essence of forms, and it is objective in the soul in the sense that passions and thoughts are phenomena.

When the Veil is transparent, it reveals the Divinity: it is made of forms in so far as these communicate their spiritual contents, whether we understand them or not; in an analogous fashion, the virtues allow the Divine Qualities to shine through, while the vices indicate their absence, or their opposites, which comes to the same thing. The transparency of the Veil is both objective and subjective, which can be understood without difficulty after what has just been said; for if on the one hand forms are transparent, not in respect of their existence but in respect of their messages, on the other hand it is our mind which makes them transparent by its penetration. Transcendence thickens the Veil; immanence renders it transparent, either in the objective world or in ourselves, through our awareness of the underlying Spirit. From quite a different standpoint, however, the understanding of transcendence is a phenomenon of transparency, while on the contrary the brutish enjoyment of what is offered to us by virtue of immanence, is obviously a phenomenon of thickening.[10]

The ambiguity of the Veil is expressed in Islam by means of the two notions of "abstraction" (*tanzīh*) and "resemblance" (*tashbīh*). From the first standpoint sensible light is nothing in regard to Divine

Light which alone "is"; "nothing resembleth Him," says the Koran, thus proclaiming transcendence. From the second point of view, sensible light "is" Divine Light — or "is not other" than it — but manifested on a particular plane of existence, or through a particular existential veil; "God is the Light of the Heavens and the earth," the Koran also says; thus sensible light resembles Him, it "is He" in a certain respect, that of immanence. To metaphysical "abstraction" corresponds mystical "solitude," *khalwah*, the ritual expression of which is the spiritual retreat; "resemblance," for its part, gives rise to the grace of "radiance," *jalwah*,[11] of which the ritual expression is the invocation of God performed in common. Mystery of transcendence or "contraction" (*qabd*) on the one hand, and mystery of immanence or "dilation" (*bast*) on the other; *khalwah* withdraws us from the world, *jalwah* transforms it into a sanctuary.

According to a theory of Ibn 'Arabī, there is a correspondence between Adam and Mohammed, in the sense that each of them manifests a synthesis — initial in the first case and terminal in the second — whereas Seth and Jesus correspond in the sense that the first manifests the exteriorization of the divine gifts, and the second, their interiorization towards the end of the cycle; we give here the meaning, not the literal words, of the doctrine concerned. One might also say that Seth manifests *tashbīh*, "resemblance" or "analogy," thus symbolism, the participation of the human in the divine, and that, inversely, Jesus manifests "abstraction," thus the tendency towards a pure "beyond," the kingdom of Christ not being of this world; Adam and Mohammed in this case manifest the equilibrium between *tashbīh* and *tanzīh*, Adam *a priori* and Mohammed *a posteriori*. Seth, the revealer of crafts and arts, illumines the veil of earthly existence; Christ rends the dark veil;[12] Islam, like the primordial religion, combines the two attitudes.

Besides the word *hijāb*, "veil," there is also the word *sitr*, which means "curtain," "veil," "cover" and "modesty"; likewise *satīr*, "chaste," and *mastūr*, "modest."[13] From the sexual point of view, one veils that which, in different respects, is earthly and heavenly, fallen and incorruptible, animal and divine, so as to be protected against the eventuality either of a humiliation or a profanation, according to the perspectives or circumstances.

There are iridescent silks in which two opposed colours appear alternately on the same surface, depending on the position of the material; this play of colours evokes cosmic ambiguity, namely the mixture of "nearness" (*qurb*) and "distance" (*buʻd*) — we might also say of greatness and smallness — that characterizes the fabric of which the world is made and of which we ourselves are made. This brings us to the question of the subjective attitude of man before the objective ambiguity of the world. The noble man, and consequently the spiritual man, sees in positive phenomena the substantial greatness and not the accidental smallness, but he is indeed obliged to discern smallness when it is substantial and when, in consequence, it determines the nature of the phenomenon. The base man, on the contrary, and sometimes the simply worldly man, sees the accidental before the essential and gives himself over to the consideration of the aspects of smallness which enter into the constitution of greatness, but which cannot detract from its greatness in the least degree, except in the eyes of the man who is himself made of smallness.

The two iridescent colours, it goes without saying, can have an exclusively positive meaning: activity and passivity, rigour and gentleness, strength and beauty, and other complementarities. The universal Veil comprises a play of contrasts and shocks, and also and even more profoundly and more really, a play of harmony and love.

• • •

The symbolism of the Veil widens when one envisages a new element superimposed upon it, namely embroidery, ornamental weaving, decorative printing: the veil thus enriched[14] suggests the play of *Maya* in all its diversity and all its iridescence, as does also, with the accent on the unfolding, the mysterious plumage of the peacock, or as does a painted fan which on being opened displays its message and its splendour.[15] The peacock and the fan are emblems or attributes of *Vishnu*; and it is especially worthy of note that the fan, in the Far East and elsewhere, is a ritual instrument which, like universal *Maya*, can both open and shut, manifest and reabsorb, revive and extinguish. The opening or unfolding, whatever be its image, is the projection of Existence, which manifests all virtualities; the shutting signifies reintegration in the Essence and return to potential plenitude; the play of *Maya* is a dance between Essence and Existence, Existence being the Veil, and Essence, Nudity. And Essence is inaccessible to the existent as such, as was said by the inscription on the statue of Isis at Sais: "I am all that has been, all that is, and all that will be; and no mortal has ever lifted my veil."

. . .

Veils are divine or human, without speaking of the veilings that other creatures represent or constitute. The divine veils are, in our cosmos, the existential categories: space, time, form, number, matter; then the creatures with their faculties, and also, on a completely different level, the revelations with their truths and their limits. The human veils are, firstly, man himself, the ego in itself, then the passional and darksome ego, and finally passions, vices, sins, without forgetting, on a normal and neutral plane, concepts and thoughts in so far as they clothe the truth.

One of the functions of the Veil is to separate; the Koran alludes to this in several connections, either when the the curtain separates man from the truth that he rejects, or when it separates him from God who speaks to him, or when it separates men from women to whom they have no right, or finally when it separates the damned from the elect; but the most fundamental separation, the one that comes first and foremost, is the one between the Creator and creation, or between the Principle and its manifestation. In total or strict metaphysics, one would include the separation between Beyond-Being and Being, the latter pertaining to *Maya*, and so to Relativity; thus the line of demarcation between the two orders of reality — the Veil in other words — is situated within the divine order itself.

If we understand by *Maya* its global cosmic manifestation, we may say that *Atma* is reflected in *Maya* and assumes there a central and prophetic function, *Buddhi*, and that *Maya* in its turn is prefigured in *Atma* and anticipates or prepares therein the creative projection. Similarly, it is *Maya* contained in *Atma* — and thus the Creator *Ishvara* — that produces *Samsara*, or the macrocosm, the hierarchy of worlds and concatenation of cycles; and it is *Atma* contained in *Maya* — in the sacramental *Mantra* — that unmakes *Samsara* as microcosm. Mystery of prefiguration and mystery of reintegration: the first is that of Creation and also that of Revelation; the second is that of the Apocatastasis and also that of Salvation.

All of this evokes the Taoist symbolism of *Yin-Yang*: a white field and a black field, the first containing a black spot and the second a white spot; in the present context this means that the relationship between the Face and the Veil is repeated on both sides of the Veil, firstly on the inside, *in divinis*, and then on the outside, at the heart of the universe. In Sanskrit terms: there are *Atma* and *Maya*, but there are also — since Reality is one and since the nature of things could not imply a fundamental dualism — *Maya* in *Atma* and *Atma* in *Maya*.[16]

* * *

In earthly usage, that is to say as a material object and human symbol, the Veil on the one hand hides the sacred pure and simple, and on the other hand hides the ambiguous or the perilous. From this latter point of view, we may say that *Maya* possesses a character of ambiguity by virtue of the fact that it veils and unveils and also, from the point of view of its dynamism, by virtue of the fact that it separates from God because it creates, while bringing close to God because it reabsorbs or liberates. Beauty in general and music in particular provide an eloquent image of the power of illusion, in the sense that they possess both an exteriorizing and interiorizing quality and act in one direction or the other depending on the nature and intention of each man: a passional nature and an intention of pleasure, or a contemplative nature and an intention of "remembrance" in the Platonic sense of the word. Woman is veiled as in Islam wine is forbidden, and she is unveiled — in certain rites or certain ritual dances[17] — with the aim of operating a kind of magic by analogy, the unveiling of beauty with an erotic vibration evoking, in the manner of a catalyst, the revelation of the liberating and beatific Essence; of the *Haqīqah*, the "Truth-Reality," as the Sufis would say. It is by virtue of this analogy that the Sufis personify beatific and intoxicating Knowledge in the form of *Laila*, or sometimes *Salma*, a personification which moreover is concretized, from the point of view of human reality and in the Semitic world, in the Blessed Virgin, who combines in her person the substance of sanctity and concrete humanity; dazzling and inviolable sanctity and the merciful beauty that communicates it with purity and sweetness. Like every heavenly being, Mary manifests the universal Veil in its function by transmission: she is Veil because she is a form, but she is essence by her content and consequently by her message. She is both closed and open, inviolable and generous;[18] she is "clothed in the sun" because she is clothed in Beauty, "the splendour of the True," and she is "black but beautiful" because the Veil is both closed and transparent, or because, after having been closed by virtue of inviolability, it opens by virtue of mercy. The Virgin is "clothed in the sun" because, as Veil, she is transparent: the Light, which is at the same time Beauty, is communicated with such a power that it seems to consume the Veil and abolish veiling, so that the Inward, which is the purpose of the form, seems so to speak to envelop the form by transubstantiating it. "Whoever has seen me, has seen God":'these words, or their equivalent, are found in the most diverse traditional worlds, and they apply especially also to the "divine Mary," "clothed in the sun" because reabsorbed in it and as it were contained therein. [19] To see God by seeing the Divine in human form, is in some fashion to see the Essence before form: it is to undergo the imprint of the divine Content together with that of the human container, and "before" the latter by reason of the pre-eminence of the Divine. The Veil has become Light, there is no longer any Veil.

· · ·

There is nothing but Light; the veils of necessity originate in the Light itself, they are prefigured in it. They do not come from its luminosity, but from its radiation; not from its clarity but from its expansion. The Light shines for itself, then it radiates to communicate itself, and by radiating, it produces the Veil and the veils; by radiating and spreading out it creates separation, veils, gradations. The intrinsic tendency to radiation is the first Veil, that which later defines itself as creative Being, and then manifests itself as cosmos. Esoterism or gnosis, being the science of Light, is thereby the science of veilings and unveilings, and necessarily so since on the one hand discursive thought and the language that expresses it constitute a veil, while on the other hand the purpose of this veil is the Light.

God and the world do not mix; there is but one sole Light, seen through innumerable veils; the saint who speaks in the name of God does not speak by virtue of a divine inherence, for Substance cannot be inherent in accidence; it is God who speaks, the saint being only a veil whose function is to manifest God, "as a light cloud makes the sun visible," according to a comparison used by the Moslems.

Every accident is a veil which makes visible, more or less indirectly, Substance-Light.

In the *Avatara* there is quite obviously a separation between the human and the divine — or between accident and Substance — then there is a mixing, not of human accident and divine Substance, but of the human and the direct reflection of Substance in the cosmic accident; relatively to the human this reflection may be called divine, on condition that the Cause is not in any way reduced to the effect. For some, the *Avatara* is God "descended"; for others, he is an "opening" which allows God immutably "on high" to be seen. [20]

Universal radiation is the unfolding of accidence, starting from initial Relativity; necessary Being, radiating by virtue of its infinitude, gives rise to Contingency. And the Heart that has become transparent communicates the one Light and thus reintegrates Contingency in the Absolute; this means that we are only truly ourselves through our awareness of Substance and through our conformity to this awareness, but not that we must depart from all relativity — supposing that we were able — for God, in creating us, wishes us to exist.

• • •

To summarize: the possibilities are the veils which on the one hand restrict the absolute Real and on the other hand manifest it; Possibility as such, in the singular and in the absolute sense, is the supreme Veil, that which envelops the mystery of One-and-Onliness and at the same time deploys it, while remaining immutable and without depriving itself of anything; Possibility is none other than the Infinitude of the Real. To say Infinitude is to say Potentiality: and to affirm that Possibility as such, or Potentiality, both veils and unveils the Absolute, is only a way of expressing the two-dimensional nature — in itself undifferentiated — which we may discern analytically in the absolutely Real. Likewise, we can discern in it a three-dimensional nature, also intrinsically undifferentiated but heralding a possible deployment: these dimensions are "Being," "Consciousness," "Felicity." It is by virtue of the third element — immutable in itself — that Divine Possibility, "out of love," opens onto and gives rise to that mystery of exteriorization that is the universal Veil, whose warp is made of the worlds, and whose woof is made of beings.

Symbolism and Grace*

. . . It remains to speak of the Symbol and of Grace: the latter is interior and non-formal, the former is exterior and formal. Every form which expresses God — whether naturally or traditionally, but not artificially — is a symbol having power to save, in other words it can be a vehicle of, and a key to, Grace; in grace, God is manifest not as form, but as presence or essence. Grace, Revelation, Intellect, and the universal Spirit can be called 'uncreated,' having regard to the essential identity which unites them to their divine Source; and by extension the same could be said of their respective receptacles, the symbol, the *Avatara*, man, Creation — to specify their function — if this did not involve a contradiction in terms or if one could risk the expression 'uncreated created'; in fact, it is by this contradictory expression that the total Creation could legitimately be distinguished from any individual creature, or man from the animals, or the *Avatara* from fallen humanity, or the symbol from arbitrary or artificial forms; but this would imply an ellipsis which would do too much violence to reason and language. Moreover a distinction must be made between two kinds of symbol; those of nature and those of Revelation. The first have spiritual efficacy only by virtue of their 'consecration' or 'revalorisation' by the *Avatara* or the revealed Word, or by virtue of a very exalted degree of knowledge which restores to them their fundamental reality. Before the Fall, every river was the Ganges, and every mountain was Dailasa, for the Creation was still 'interior,' the 'knowledge of good and evil' not having yet 'exteriorised' or 'materialised' it; likewise for the sage every river is still a river of Paradise. Nature symbolism, which assimilates, for example, the sun to the divine Principle, derives from a 'horizontal' correspondence; revealed symbolism, which makes this assimilation spiritually effective — in ancient solar cults and before their 'petrifaction'— derives from a 'vertical' correspondence; the same holds good for gnosis, which reduces phenomena to 'ideas' or archetypes. Much might be said here on the natural symbolism of bread and wine — or of body and blood — and their 'sacramentalisation' by Christ;

*From *SW*, pp. 96-98.

likewise the sign of the Cross, which expresses with its two dimensions the respective mysteries of the Body and Bread and the Blood and Wine, has, of course, always had its metaphysical sense but received its quasi-sacramental virtue — at least in its specifically Christian form — through the incarnate Word; in other terms, it is necesary for the *Avatara* to 'live' a form in order to make it 'effective,' and that is why sacred formulae or divine Names must come from Revelation in order to be capable of being 'realised.'[1]

Just as there are two kinds of symbol there are two kinds of grace: natural graces, which are accessible to us on the basis of our existence itself — through the virtues, for example, or even in an apparently quite gratuitous manner, or through 'sensible consolations'— and supernatural graces, which occur in direct or indirect connection with the various media of a Revelation, or which come from intellection; these graces are 'supernatural' because they do not come from 'cosmic reserves' but from the divine Source, 'vertically' therefore and not 'horizontally.'[2]

It could be asked whether graces and symbols deriving from nature still deserve to be classed as manifestations of the divine; they deserve it in principle and in a very broad sense, too broad doubtless to be safe from all accusations of abuse of language. It is obvious that every good, whether it be of an objective or subjective kind, can come only from God, but account must be taken of the fact that man is no longer capable of seeing spontaneously the celestial Cause in the terrestrial effect; God must then be 'incarnated' anew in forms that have become 'emptied' or 'dead', at least in cases where this 'revalorisation' is essential. This reservation signifies that the Intellect certainly possesses, in principle, the same powers as Revelation, but since Revelation exists, these powers cannot be actualised in opposition to it within the framework of a given Tradition; in fact, there is little likelihood of the Intellect being actualised without the help of this framework, or of such frameworks if several traditional sources are available.[3]

The Science of the Study of Myth*

. . .The question of the spiritual sense underlying the myths is one of those which people gladly relegate to the realm of feeling and imagination and which 'exact science' refuses to treat otherwise than through the medium of psychological and historical conjectures.[1] For those of us, however, who disbelieve in the efficacy of a knowledge isolated from the truth as a whole (unless it be a mere matter of knowing physical things, actually palpable) a science run on these lines suffers precisely from this, namely that it is prone to substitute 'exactness' for intelligence, let this be said plainly; it is in effect this very exactness, practically confined as it is to the quantitative order, which stands in the way of the decisive operations of pure intelligence, just because a meticulous and often arbitrary cataloguing of facts, possibly of small significance or rendered such thanks to the point of view adopted, replaces the intellectual and qualitative perception of the nature of things. Science claims to be characterized by its refusal of all purely speculative premisses (the *voraussetzungsloses Denken* of the German philosophers) and at the same time by a complete liberty of investigation; but this is an illusion since modern science, like every other science before it moreover, cannot avoid starting out in its turn from an idea: this initial idea is the dogma concerning the exclusively rational nature of the intelligence and its more or less universal diffusion. In other words, it is assumed that there exists a unique and polyvalent intelligence (which in principle is true) and that this intelligence is possessed by everybody and furthermore that this is what allows investigation to be entirely 'free' (which is radically false). There are truths which intuitive intellection alone allows one to attain, but it is not a fact that such intellection lies within the capacity of every man of ordinarily sound mind. Moreover the Intellect, for its part, requires Revelation, both as its occasional cause and as vehicle of the 'Perennial Philosophy,' if it is to actualize its own light in more than a fragmentary manner.

In any case, when people speak of 'objective analysis' they nearly always forget the principal interested party, namely the intelligence (or unintelligence) of the man who analyses; they forget that, in many

*From *ITB*, pp. 82-84.

cases, the analysis of facts intended to prove such and such a thing whereof the existence or nonexistence is nevertheless evident *a priori* only serves to cover the absence, whether basic or accidental, of intellection and therefore of an intelligence proportioned to the magitude of the problem as set.

When true myths are done away with, they inevitably come to be replaced by artificial myths. In practice, a mode of thought which is content to rely on its own logic alone while operating in a realm where ordinary logic opens up no vistas, thereby becomes defenseless against the various scientific mythologies of the time, rather in the same way as when religion is done away with, this leads in fact, not to a rational view of the Universe, but to a counter-religion, with its own 'faith,' its dogmas, its taboos, in the name of which it will not be long before rationalism itself is eaten up. To treat man as absolutely free — man who plainly is not absolute — is to set free all manner of evils in him, without there remaining any principle whereby their propagation might be kept within bounds. All this goes to show that basically it is a kind of abuse of language to give the bare name of 'Science' to a knowledge that only leads to practical results while revealing nothing concerning the profound nature of phenomena; a science which by its own showing eschews transcendent principles can offer no sort of guarantee as to the ultimate results of its own investigations.

Pure and simple logic amounts only to a very indirect manner of knowing things; it is, before all else, the art of coordinating data (whether true or false) according to a given need of causal satisfaction and within the limits of a given imagination, so much so that an apparently faultless argument can yet be quite erroneous in function of the falseness of its premisses; the more elevated the order of the thing to be made known, the more vulnerable will be the mind in that case. What one is criticizing here is not the exactitude of science, far from that, but the exclusive level imposed on that exactitude, whereby this quality is rendered inadequate and inoperative: man can measure a distance by his strides, but this does not make him able to see with his feet, if one may so express oneself. Metaphysics and symbolism, which alone provide efficient keys to the knowledge of supra-sensible realities, are highly exact sciences — with an exactitude greatly exceeding that of physical facts — but these sciences lie beyond the scope of unaided *ratio* and of the methods it inspires in a quasiexclusive manner. . .

NOTES

Dimensions, Modes and Degrees of the Divine Order

1. Even in the natural order, a thing that is positively or qualitatively unique is always total; perfect beauty cannot be poor, it is by definition a synthesis, whence its aspect of unlimitedness and appeasement.

2. Principially and analogically speaking, *Māyā* is not only "spatial," it is also "temporal": there are not only extension and hierarchy, there are also change and rhythm; there are worlds and cycles.

3. If one refers to the Vedantine ternary Sat ("pure Being"), Chit ("Consciousness"), Ananda ("Beatitude"), it is necessary to bear in mind that the aspect "Power" pertains to the aspect "pure Being." In physics, it will be said that "energy" is bound up with "mass"; the proof of this is that the force of attraction in celestial bodies is proportional to their size or density.

4. It is here that is situated the Asharite theory of the human "acquisition" (*kasb*) of the divine Acts: it is God alone who acts, since He alone is capable of it; it is He who " creates" our acts, but it is we who "acquire" them (*naksibūn*).

5. This is what the "polytheists" understand very well.

6. There are notably the allusions to the "hidden" (*ghayb*) and sayings like this one: "God knoweth and ye know not."

7. It should be noted that, if the Koran did not specify that it is God who "created evil" (*mın sharri mā khalaq*), the door would remain open for a Mazdean or Manichean dualism: one would risk admitting two divinities, one good and one evil. The Koranic solution is situated so to speak between two pitfalls: the idea of two antagonistic Gods, and the negation pure and simple of evil; the Arab or Near-Eastern collective mentality does not seem to have left any other choice.

8. This "Dıvine Manifestation" is none other than the *Buddhı* of the Vedantins, or the archangelic domain of the monotheists.

9. Beyond-Being, Being or Existence; either the pure Infinite (*Ananda*), or its prolongation in Being (= *Prakriti*), or again the limitlessness of the existentiating cosmic Substance (= *Saraswati-Lakshmi-Parvati*) According to Paracelsus, God "the Son" presupposes, not only "the Father," but also "the Mother"; the latter is more or less hidden in the "Father," and it is Mary who impersonates her on the human plane. This opinion is plausible in the sense that the Infinite can be considered metaphorically — if we accept this kind of symbolism and assuming a framework that makes it possible — as the "Spouse" (*Shakti*) of the Absolute and the "Mother" of the Divine Perfection or of the Supreme Good; the Infinite is then necessarily reflected, in a mode of "major import" in the Woman-*Avatāra*.

10. In rationalism, it will be said that All-Possibility is an abstraction, whereas in reality it is a potentiality, or Potentiality pure and simple. We would add that All-Possibility is not only a divine "dimension," it is also total *Māyā*, from Being down to our world.

The Interplay of the Hypostases
1. Which is reflected, in the physical world, as the relationship "mass-energy." As for the notion of "Being," it should not be interpreted here in its narrowly ontological and determinative sense, but simply as a synonym for Reality.

2. This complementarity is equally represented by "Mary" and "Jesus," whence the feminization — as regards Mary — of the *Pneuma* on the part of certain gnostics.

3. The expression "intrinsic projection" seems contradictory, but it comprises — like the expression "relatively absolute"— a metaphysical nuance which it is impossible to express otherwise and which, in spite of the paradox, is perfectly graspable.

4. "The Father is greater than I" (John XIV, 28), but "I and the Father are one" (John X, 30). Theology does not draw all of the consequences implied by the former; and it draws too many from the latter.

The Mystery of the Veil
1. In the Sufi terminology derived from the Koran, the Divine Essence (*Dhāt*) is called "Face" (*Wajh*), which at first sight seems paradoxical, but becomes comprehensible through the symbolism of veiling.

2. Omar Khayyam: "Neither thou nor I shall solve the mystery of this world; neither thou nor I read this secret writing. We both would like to know what this veil hides; but when the veil falls there is neither thou nor I."

3. A well known example of Divine Femininity can be seen in Isis of the Egyptians, whom we mention here because of her connection with the Veil. Isis is *Maya*, not as the opposite, but as an aspect or function of *Atma*, and thus as his *Shakti*, and she represents not so much the power of cosmic illusion as that of initiatic disillusion. By drawing back the veils, which are accidents and darkness, she reveals her Nudity, which is Substance and Light; being inviolable, she can blind or kill, but being generous, she regenerates and delivers.

4. Nevertheless the woof, represented by the shuttle, is active, which does not contradict feminine passivity, because woman is active in child-bearing, whereas man in this connection remains passive; this is why, in Hindu doctrine, creative activity is attributed to Universal Substance, *Prakriti*, which in fact "produces" beings, whereas *Purusha* "conceives" them as ideas. This appearance of inversion provides an illustration of the Taoist doctrine of *Yin Yang* which in short is the theory of reciprocal compensation; without this compensation, the dualities would be absolute and irreducible, which is an impossibility since Reality is one.

5. This is why the Prophet is called both *Rasūl*, "Messenger," and *'Abd*, "Servant"; the latter is extinguished before God, while the former prolongs Him.

6. *Allāh* "was" good and loving "before" creation, and this is expressed by the Name *Rahmān*, "most Clement"; and He is good and loving "since" creation and towards creation, and this is expressed by the Name *Rahīm* "most Merciful." According to the Koran, *Ar-Rahmān* is synonymous with *Allāh*, — which shows that it pertains to *Dhāt* and not to the *Sifāt*, — and it is *Ar-Rahmān* who created man, taught him speech (*bayān*, the capacity to express himself with intelligence, and thus to think) and revealed the Koran. It should be noted that the Name *Rahīm* pertains to the At-

tributes and not to the Essence, though it nevertheless prolongs the Name *Rahmān* in the created order.

7. In other words, it is *Shaktı* rather than *Maya*; this amounts to saying that *Maya* insofar as it is inherent in *Atma* has no ambiguity, and that it is thus properly the *Shaktı*, the Power of Divine Life and of cosmic Manifestation.

8. God, insofar as he manifests himself in the cosmos, being called "the Outward" (*Az-Zāhır*) in the Koran.

9. "It is not I who have left the world, it is the world that has left me," an Arab *faqīr* once said to us; we would add that, by way of compensation, God makes himself present in the world to the very extent that the world becomes absent for us.

10. Mention should be made in this context, from the point of view of sacred art, of the use of the cloud in Taoist painting. This cloud sometimes expresses more than the landscape, which on the one hand it obscures and on the other hand enhances, thus creating an atmosphere both of secrecy and translucence

11. A word derived from *jılwah*, "unveiling," when speaking of a bride; the sense of "radiance" is contained in the root of the word itself *Jalwah* is the concrete awareness of the Divine Omnipresence, an awareness which makes it possible to understand the "language of the birds," metaphorically speaking, and to hear the universal praise that rises to God

12 It goes without saying that Christianity, in its general and characteristic form, sees in this sacrificial rending the only possible solution; it nevertheless comprises the inverse or complementary attitude to the extent that it is esoteric.

13. One should also note the invocation *yā* Sattār, "Thou who coverest," to express a desire for protection.

14. The most famous example of which is the Kashmir shawl, without forgetting the decorated sari which adds to the play of envelopment a communicative magic, as if by hiding the body, it sought to reveal the soul; the same applies, in particular, to all princely and priestly vestments.

15 The Japanese screen, which is often decorated with paintings inspired by Zen or Taoism, is not unconnected with the general symbolism under discussion; the same is true of the Islamic screen of perforated wood and of windows of the same kind. In these examples it is a question of a partition that is either mobile, which distinguishes it from a fixed wall, or else made transparent, so that it may be open even when it has been shut, and this ambiguity corresponds well to the mobility or the transparency of the veil. The perforated screen allows one to see without being seen, and is thus a kind of veil that is transparent from one side and opaque from the other, which brings to mind the *hadıth* of spiritual virtue (*ihsān*): God must be worshipped "as if thou sawest Him, for, if thou seest Him not, He nevertheless seeth thee."

16. A revealed Book, a Prophet, a rite, a sacred formula, a Divine Name belong to the formal order, and are thus *Maya*, but it is a *Maya* that delivers since it essentially is the vehicle of *Atma*. It is *"Atma* in *Maya,"* whereas the creative Word, or the Logos, is *"Maya* in *Atma."*

17. One speaks of a "dance of the seven veils," in a malefic sense in the case of Salomé dancing before Herod, and in a benefic sense in the case of the Queen of Sheba dancing before Solomon, which evokes precisely the dual function of beauty, of woman and of wine.—In the case of the Blessed Virgin and according to the Koranic commentators, the seven veils become seven doors, which Zacharias had to open with a key each time he visited Mary in the Temple; Zacharias represents the privileged soul that penetrates the mystery thanks to a "key," which is another image of "unveiling."—It is thus that the seventh day of creation marks the return to the Origin, or the "peace in the Void," as the Taoists would say, or the meeting with principial Reality, "naked" because unmanifested. There is an analogous meaning in the notion of the "seventh Heaven," which coincides with the "Garden of the Essence."

18. The Russian Church celebrates a "feast of the Veil" in remembrance of an apparition of Mary at Constantinople, in the course of which the Virgin lifted her luminous veil and held it, in a miraculous fashion, above those present. The Russian word *pokrov* means both "veil" and "intercession": the *Maya* which dissimulates Essence is at the same time the *Maya* which communicates graces.

19. The *avataras* are "contained" in the heavenly Logos, which they represent on earth or of which they manifest a function, as they are likewise contained pre-existentially in the Divine Names, which diversify the undifferentiated mysteries of the Essence and whose aspects are innumerable. In Sufism, the Blessed Virgin personifies the pre-existential and existing *Sophia*: the Logos inasmuch as it "conceives" creatures, then "engenders" them and finally "forms" or "embellishes" them; if Mary thus represents the unmanifested and silent Logos — *nigra sum sed formosa* —, Jesus is the manifested and law-giving Logos.

20. What "incarnates" in the *Avatara* is an aspect of *Buddhi* such as *Vishnu* or *Shiva*; it is not *Atma* in itself. It should be recalled in this connection that the purpose of Christianity is to emphasize the "Divine Phenomenon," whereas that of Islam, on the contrary, is to reduce the phenomenon to the Principle or the effect to the Cause.

Symbolism and Grace

1. For example, rites of ablution whether Brahminical, Jewish, Christian or Islamic, obtain their efficacy not from water as such — for this is 'dead,' 'exteriorised' or 'materialised' since the fall from the edenic state — but from its consecration by the respective Revelation, which restores to water, within the framework of certain conditions, its primordial virtue.

2. In Moslem terms, this is the difference between the 'blessing' (*salat*) and the 'peace' (*salam*) which accompanies the name of the Prophet.

3. Such is the case, for example, with those Christians who were Platonists or Neo-Platonists, and so nourished to one degree or another on Orphic and Pythagorean wisdom.

The Science of the Study of Myth

1. Some honourable exceptions are to be found among the anthropologists of recent years, whose approach to the peoples and the folklore they study in various parts of the world is neither patronizing nor hampered by an ingrained rationalist or materialist prejudice. in short they take into account the spiritual dimension of man, at least in some degree. However, the question remains open as to how far their studies are officially admitted into the category of 'exact science.'

Epistemology

Consequences Flowing from the Mystery of Subjectivity*

THE FIRST ASCERTAINMENT which should impose itself upon man when he reflects on the nature of the Universe is the primacy of that miracle, intelligence — or consciousness or subjectivity — and consequently the incommesurability between these and material objects, be it a question of a grain of sand or of the sun, or of any creature whatever as an object of the senses. The truth of the Cartesian *cogito ergo sum* is not that it presents thought as the proof of being but simply that it enunciates the primacy of thought — hence of consciousness or of intelligence — in relation to the material world which surrounds us; certainly it is not our personal thought which preceded the world, but it was — or is — absolute Consciousness, of which our thought is precisely a distant reflection; our thought which reminds us — and proves to us — that in the beginning was the Spirit. Nothing is more absurd than to have intelligence derive from matter, hence the greater from the lesser; the evolutionary leap from matter to intelligence is from every point of view the most inconceivable thing that could be.

We shall no doubt be told that the reality of a creator God has not been demonstrated; but aside from the fact that it is not difficult to demonstrate this reality with arguments proportionate to its nature — but which for that very reason are inaccessible to certain

*From *DH*, Chapter 1 (trans. G.Polit).

344

spirits — the least that can be said is that evolution has never been proved by anybody whatsoever, and with good reason; transformist evolution is accepted as a useful and provisional postulate, as one accepts no matter what, provided no obligation is felt to accept the primacy of the Immaterial, since the latter escapes the control of our senses. And yet, starting from the recognition of the immediately tangible mystery that is subjectivity or intelligence, it is easy to understand that the origin of the Universe is, not inert and unconscious matter, but a spiritual Substance which, from coagulation to coagulation and from segmentation to segmentation — and other projections both manifesting and limiting — finally produces matter by causing it to emerge from a more subtle substance, but one which is already remote from principial Substance. It will be objected that there is no proof of this, to which we reply — apart from the phenomenon of subjectivity which precisely comprises this proof, leaving aside other possible intellectual proofs, not needed by Intellection — that there are infinitely fewer proofs for this inconceivable absurdity, evolutionism, which has the miracle of consciousness springing from a heap of earth or pebbles, metaphorically speaking.

Within the same order of ideas, we shall assert that the ideas of "Great Spirit" and of the primacy of the Invisible are natural to man, which does not even need to be demonstrated; now what is natural to human consciousness, which is distinguished from animal consciousness by its objectivity and its totality — its capacity for the absolute and the infinite, we might say — what is natural to human consciousness proves *ipso facto* its essential truth, the reason for the existence of intelligence being adequation to the real.[1] From another point of view, if Intellection and Revelation are "supernaturally natural" to man, their refusal is also a possibility of human nature, of course, otherwise it would not occur; but since man is integrally intelligent, and thereby integrally free, this means by way of consequence that he alone, among terrestrial creatures is free to go against his own nature. Now he possesses this liberty only in the wake of a fall which, precisely, separates him first of all from this immanent Revelation that is Intellection, and then sets him against prophetic Revelation which, for its part, compensates for the absence of immanent Science; and which by this compensation, awakens It, at least in principle.

Extrinsic arguments contribute to proving — as points of reference or as keys — the intellectual and existential primacy of the Spirit, but, let it be said again, we have no need of these proofs; if there are people for whom the shadow of a cat does not prove the presence of the real cat, or for whom the sound of a waterfall does not prove the proximity of water, this could not mean that our knowledge of this animal or of this waterfall necessarily or exclusively depends upon the shadow or the sound. Our axiom is that on the one hand all that exists is inscribed *a priori* in the theomorphic substance of our intelligence — there is no integral consciousness that does not prolong absolute Consciousness — and on the other hand that the intellectual actualisation of the real or of the possible depends either on the perfection of our nature or else on an external factor which brings out the value of this perfection, or which fulfils it if it is partial; a factor such as Revelation or, in a more particular way, such as an experience which provokes the archetypal remembrance of which Plato spoke.

● ● ●

Man's liberty is total, but it could not be absolute, since the quality of absoluteness pertains solely to the supreme Principle and not to its manifestation, even if it be direct or central. To say that our liberty is total, means that it is "relatively absolute," that is to say that it is such on a particular level and within certain limits; nonetheless, our liberty is real — that of an animal is also real in a certain way, otherwise a bird in a cage would not feel deprived of freedom — and it is so because liberty as such is liberty and nothing else, whatever may be its ontological limits. As for absolute Liberty, that of the divine Principle, man participates in it to the extent that he conforms to it, and this possibility of communion with Liberty in Itself or with the Absolute originates precisely from the total — although relative — character of our liberty; which amounts to saying that in God and through Him, man can be reunited with pure Liberty; only in God are we absolutely free.

To acknowledge that man is by definition situated between an intellection which connects him to God and a world which has the power to detach him from Him, and that consequently man, being free correlatively to his intelligence, possesses the paradoxical freedom to wish in his turn to make himself God, is to acknowledge at the same stroke that the possibility of a rupture between Intellection and reason as such is present from the start, on account of the very ambiguity of the human condition; for the *pontifex* suspended between the Infinite and the finite cannot not be ambiguous, so much so that it is inevitable that "offenses must needs come": that man — starting from the original fall and passing from fall to fall — should end in rationalist luciferism,[2] which turns against God and thereby opposes itself to our nature; or which turns against our nature and thereby opposes itself to God. The rational faculty detached from its supernatural context is necessarily opposed to man and is bound to give rise in the end to a way of thought and a form of life both of which are opposed to man; in other words: Intellection is not altogether safe except in souls providentially exempted from certain risks inherent in human nature; but it is not — and cannot be — safe in man as such, for the simple reason that man comprises by definition passional individuality, and it is the presence of the latter precisely that creates the risk of a rupture with pure Intellect, and consequently the risk of the fall.

That is human which is natural to man, and that is most essentially or most specifically natural to man which refers to the Absolute and consequently points to the transcending of terrestrial humanity.[3] And even prior to symbols, doctrines and rites, our very subjectivity — as we have said — points as clearly as possible to our relationship with the Spirit and the Absolute; but for the absolute primacy of the Spirit, relative subjectivity would be neither possible nor conceivable, it would be like an effect without a cause.

Intelligence separated from its supra-individual source is accompanied *ipso facto* by that lack of sense of proportions which one calls pride; conversely, pride prevents intelligence, when it has become rationalism, from rising to its source; it can only deny Spirit and replace it with matter; it is from matter that it makes consciousness spring forth, to the extent that it does not succeed in denying consciousness by reducing it to a particularly refined or "evolved" kind of matter — and efforts to do so are not lacking.[4] Rather than bow to the evidence of the Spirit, proud reason will deny its own nature which, nonetheless, enables it to think; in its concrete conclusions, it lacks as much imagination and sense of proportions as intellectual perspicacity, and this precisely is a consequence of its pride. *Corruptio optimi pessima*: it is this that proves, once again, the monstrous disproportion between the cleverness of reason, become luciferian, and the falseness of its results; torrents of intelligence are wasted for the sake of conjuring away the essential and proving the absurd brilliantly, namely that spirit has sprung from a piece of earth — or, let us say, from an inert substance — in the course of billions of years, the quantity of which, in relation to the supposed result is ridiculous, and which proves nothing. In all this there is a loss of common sense and a perversion of the imagination which strictly speaking no longer have anything human about them, and which can only be explained in terms of the well-known scientistic prejudice which explains everything from below; to erect no matter what hypothesis provided it excludes real causes, which are transcendent and not material, and whose concrete and tangible proof is precisely our subjectivity.

•   •   •

Spirit is Substance, matter is accident: that is to say that matter is but a contingent and transitory modality of the radiation of the Spirit which projects the worlds and the cycles while remaining transcendent and immutable. This radiation produces the polarisation into subject and object: matter is the final point of the descent of the objective pole, sensorial consciousness being the corresponding subjective phenomenon. For the senses, the object is matter, or let us say the perceptible physical domain; for the Intellect, objective reality is the Spirit in all its forms. It is by it that we exist, and that we know; were it not immanent in physical substances these could not exist for one instant. And in this Spirit precisely the subject-object opposition is resolved; it is resolved in the Unity which is at once exclusive and inclusive, transcendent and immanent. The alpha as well as the omega, while transcending us infinitely, reside in the depths of our heart.[5]

That which we can and must know, that we are; and this is why we can know it, infallibly, on condition that we are liberated from the veils which separate us from our true nature. Man imposes these veils upon himself because his luciferian will identifies itself with them; he believes therefore that he recognises himself in them; and because, in consequence, to remove them is to die. That at least is what man feels so long as he has not understood that "I am black, but beautiful".

There are, moreover, in favor of the primacy of the Spirit, extrinsic proofs which are not negligible; we have often alluded to them, and they result from the very nature of man. If everything has begun with matter, and if there is no Spirit, thus no God, how can we explain that men were able to firmly believe the contrary for thousands of years, and that they even brought out a maximum of intelligence in affirming it and a maximum of heroism in living up to it. One cannot put forth progress, since the unbelievers of every kind are far from being superior to believers and sages, and nowhere does one see an evolutive passage from the latter to the former; materialistic ideas have manifested and spread, so to speak, under our eyes — since the "Age of Enlightenment"—without it being possible to note therein an evolution in the direction of a qualitative ascent, both intellectual and moral — quite to the contrary.

Those who uphold the evolutionist argument of an intellectual progress like to explain religious and metaphysical ideas by inferior psychological factors, such as fear of the unknown, childish hope of a perpetual happiness, attachment to an imagery that has become dear, escape into dreams, the desire to oppress others at small expense, *et caetera*; how can one fail to see that such suspicions, presented shamelessly as demonstrated facts, comprise psychological inconsequentialities and impossibilities, which cannot escape any impartial observer? If humanity has been stupid for thousands of years, one cannot explain how it could have ceased being so, all the more so as it occurred in a very short period of time; and one can explain it still less when one observes with what intelligence and heroism it has been stupid for so long and with what philosophic myopia and moral decadence it finally became "lucid" and "adult."[6]

The essence of the real is the banal or the trivial, the scientists and other pseudo-realists seem to say. To which we could answer: the essence of the real is the miraculous; the miracle of consciousness, intelligence, knowledge. In the beginning was, not matter, but Spirit, which is the Alpha and the Omega.

NOTES

Consequences Flowing from the Mystery of Subjectivity
1. We have heard it said by someone that the wings of birds prove the existence of air, and that in the same way the religious phenomenon, common *a priori* to all peoples, proves the existence of its content, that is to say God and the after-life; which is to the point if one takes the trouble to examine the argument in depth.

2. Or existentialist luciferism, which on the whole amounts to the same thing, since there is no greater reasoner than a negater of intellectual efficacy.

3. The word "humanism" constitutes a curious abuse of language in view of the fact that it expresses a notion which is contrary to the integrally human, hence to the human properly so called: indeed, nothing is more fundamentally inhuman than the "purely human," the illusion of constructing a perfect man starting from the individual and terrestrial, whereas the "ideally human" draws its reason for existence and its entire content from that which transcends the individual and the earthly.

4. The fact that "energy" should be spoken of, rather than "matter "—and other subtleties of the kind—changes nothing in relation to the basis of the problem and merely pushes back the limits of the difficulty. Let us mention that a so-called "socio-biologist"—this word implies a whole program—has carried ingenuity to the point of replacing matter with "genes," whose blind egoism combined with the instinct of ants or bees, would have ended by forming not only bodies but also consciousness and finally, human intelligence, miraculously capable of delivering a dissertation on the very genes which had amused themselves by producing this same intelligence.

5. The key to the Delphic mysteries is, "Know thyself" (*Gnóthi seautón*); to know the nature of subjectivity is to know the structure of the world.

6. A characteristic trait of "our times," is that one everywhere "puts the cart before the horse": that which normally should be the means, becomes the end, and inversely. Machines are supposed to be there for men, but in fact men are there for the machines; whereas formerly roads were there for the towns, now the towns are there for the roads; instead of *mass-media* being those for "culture" the latter is there for the *mass-media* and so forth. The modern world is an inextricable tangle of revolvings that no one can stop.

Cosmology & The Traditional Sciences

Hypostatic and Cosmic Numbers*

THE SYMBOLISM OF NUMBERS and geometrical figures provides a relatively simple way of describing the modes and degrees of veiling and unveiling; not that the understanding of these things can in itself be made easy, but the symbols at least provide keys and clarifying elements.

One can represent Absolute Reality, or the Essence, or Beyond-Being, by the point; it would doubtless be less inadequate to represent it by the void, but the void is not properly speaking a figure, and if we give the Essence a name, we can with the same justification, and the same risk, represent it by a sign; the simplest and thus the most essential sign is the point.

To say Reality is to say Power or Potentiality, or *Shakti* if one prefers; there is thus in the Real a principle of polarization, perfectly undifferentiated in the Absolute, but capable of being discerned and the cause of every subsequent deployment. We can represent this Principial polarity by an axis, either horizontal or vertical: if it is horizontal, it signifies that Potentiality, or Supreme *Maya*, remains within the Supreme Principle, *Paramatma*, as an intrinsic dimension of latent potency; if the axis is vertical, it signifies that Potentiality becomes Virtuality, that it radiates and communicates itself, and that

*From *EPW*, pp. 65-77.

351

consequently it gives rise to the first hypostasis, Being, the creative principle.[1] It is in this first bipolarity, or in this principial duality, that are prefigured or pre-realized all possible complementarities and oppositions: subject and object, activity and passivity, static and dynamic, oneness and totality, exclusive and inclusive, rigour and gentleness. These couples are horizontal when the second term is the qualitative and thus harmonious complement of the first, in other words, if it is its *Shakti*; they are vertical when the second term tends in an efficient manner towards a more relative level or when it is already at such a level. We do not have to mention here pure and simple oppositions, in which the second term has only a privative character and which cannot have any divine archetype, except in a purely logical and symbolic manner.

In the human microcosm, duality is manifested, for example, by the double function of the heart, which is both Intellect and Love, the latter referring to the Infinite and the former to the Absolute; also, from another standpoint, which reflects the descending hypostatic projection, the Intellect corresponds to Beyond-Being, and the mental element to Being.

*   *   *

The divine archetype of all positive ternaries is the Vedantic trinity *Sat, Chit, Ananda*: God, from the starting point of His supra-ontological Essence, is pure "Being," pure "Spirit," pure "Felicity." [2]

Like the binary, the ternary presents two different aspects depending on the position of the triangle, geometrically speaking. In the upright triangle, the duality of the base is contemplative in the sense that it indicates, through the summit, a turning back towards unity; the ternary here represents relativity intent on conforming to absolutity and refusing to move away from it; it brings to an end the movement towards the multiple. In the inverted triangle, the duality is operative in the sense that it tends, through the inverted summit, towards extrinsic radiation or production.

This amounts to saying that the element *Ananda*, on the one hand, constitutes the internal and intrinsic radiation of *Atma*, which desires nothing other—if one may so put it—than the enjoyment of its own infinite Possibility, and on the other hand tends towards the manifestation of this Possibility—now overflowing—through numberless refractions. Thus it is that in sexual love the end or the result can be outward and quasisocial, namely the child; but it can also be inward and contemplative, namely realization — by means, precisely, of this lived symbolism — of the one Essence in which the two partners melt, which is a birth in an upward direction and a reabsorption into Substance.[3] In this case the result is essentiality, whereas in the preceding case it is perfection; this amounts to saying that the dimensions of absoluity and infinity, on the one hand pertain to the Essence, which unites them, and on the other hand produce perfection, which manifests them.

But there is still another type of ternary, the most immediate example of which is the hierarchy of the constituent elements of the microcosm, *corpus, anima, spiritus*, or *soma, psyché, pneuma*; the Vedantic ternary of the cosmic qualities, *tamas, rajas, sattwa*, is of the same order. This ternary is founded, not on the union of two complementary poles with a view to a third element, either higher or lower, or inward or outward, but on the qualitative aspects of space measured from the starting point of a consciousness which is situated within it: ascending dimension or lightness, descending dimension or heaviness, horizontal dimension open to both influences.

The ternary previously considered — that of *Sat-Chit-Ananda* — also has a spatial foundation, but in this case purely objective, namely the three dimensions of space: height, breadth and depth; the first corresponds to the masculine principle, the second to the feminine principle, and the third to the fruit, which is either intrinsic or extrinsic; this last distinction is expressed precisely by the position of the triangle. The new ternary just mentioned — body, soul, spirit, or darkness, warmth, light — is also to be found in the triangle, and in two ways that are highly instructive. In the first instance the spirit is regarded as being situated at the summit, and in this case the image expresses the transcendence of the intellect with regard to the sentient soul and the body, which are then placed on the same level, with the difference however that the soul is situated on the right, the positive or active side. Alternatively the body is situated at the inverted summit, and in this case the image expresses the superiority of the soul and the spirit with regard to the body.

And this indicates two aspects of the corresponding divine ternary: in one sense, the world is the "Body" of God, while Being, as the matrix of the archetypes, is His "Soul" and the Essence His "Spirit"; in another sense — and here we rejoin the Vedantic rigour —

the Essence, or Beyond Being, is the "Spirit" of God, while the subordination of *Maya* or Relativity is expressed by the juxtaposition, on the base of the triangle, of Being and Existence, and so of "Soul" and "Body."

But let us return to the ternary *Sat-Chit-Ananda* represented by the triangle, the summit indicating *Sat*, and the two lower angles indicating respectively *Chit* and *Ananda*. By inverting the triangle, the summit, which is Being and radiating Power in the upright triangle, becomes separating and coagulating power, and thus in fact subversive, in the inverted triangle; this is the image of the fall of Lucifer, in which the highest point becomes the lowest, an image which explains the mysterious and paradoxical relationship between powerful, but immutable, Being and the manifesting power which separates from Being until it finally rises up against it.[4] The positive and innocent cosmogonic power terminates at the point of fall that is matter, whereas the subversive centrifugal power terminates in evil; these are two aspects that must not be confused.

There is a particularly concrete image of the Vedantic ternary and this is the sun: the solar star, like all fixed stars, is matter, form and radiation. Matter, or mass-energy, manifests *Sat*, which is Being-Power; form is equated with *Chit*, Consciousness or Intelligence;[5] radiation corresponds to *Ananda*, which is Beatitude or Goodness. Radiation comprises both warmth and light, just as *Ananda* participates in both *Sat* and *Chit*, warmth referring to Goodness and light to Beauty; light spreads far and wide the image of the sun, just as Beauty transmits Truth; "Beauty is the splendour of the True." According to a somewhat different and no less plausible symbolism, the sun presents itself to human experience as form, light and warmth: *Sat, Chit, Ananda*; in this case, substance is one with form, which indicates fundamental Power, while light manifests Intelligence, and warmth manifests Goodness.[6]

· · ·

As far as the reflection of the hypostatic ternary in the human being is concerned, we would say that the Intellect, which is the "eye of the heart" or the organ of direct knowledge, is projected into the individual soul by limiting and polarizing itself; it is then manifested under a triple aspect, or in other words, it divides into three modes, namely intelligence, will and sentiment. This means that the Intellect itself is at once cognitive, volitive and affective in the sense that it comprises three dimensions which refer respectively to the "Consciousness" (*Chit*), the "Being" (*Sat*) and the "Beatitude" (*Ananda*) of the Principle (*Atma*).

The intelligence operates the understanding of God, of the world, of man; the knowing subject is entirely determined by the object known or to be known; God appears *a priori* in the relationship of transcendence. The will for its part operates, spiritually speaking, the movement towards God, and thus above all contemplative concentration, on the basis of the required conditions, of course; here, it is the subject that predominates, and this results moreover from the fact that, of necessity, God is in practice envisaged from the standpoint of immanence. In the third domain, the soul, man is reduced neither to the known object nor the realizing subject; because this is the plane of confrontation between man and God; it is consequently the plane of devotion and faith, and of the humanly divine — or divinely human — dialogue between the person and his Creator.

A point that needs to be made here is that, in knowledge, the subject is extinguished in the face of the object: if the latter is positive, it so to speak absorbs the subject while extinguishing it, but if it is negative the extinction of the subject simply signifies the exactness of the perception. In contemplative and realizatory concentration on the other hand, which is dependent on the will from the point of view of the immediate operation, the human subject is unitively absorbed by the Divine Subject, and this obviously at the time implies an extinction with regard to the latter.

The natural symbol of the trinity is provided by the three dimensions of space: interpreted in connection with the human microcosm, height evokes intelligence, breadth sentiment, and depth will. For intelligence tends upwards, towards the essential and the transcendent; when it is perverted by error, it falls by contradicting its own nature. Sentiment, for its part, is ourselves in our existential totality, *hic et nunc*, and this is expressed by breadth, with a qualitative difference between the right and the left; in other words, sentiment, in the complete and profound meaning of the word that we have in view here, represents the human person and the choice that he can make of his destiny. As for the will, it moves forward as do our steps in walking; it plunges into the future as our steps plunge into the space in front of us, unless it draws back by opposing its own spiritual and eschatological vocation; in both cases, there is a reference to the dimension of depth.

. . .

When one sets out to give an account of metacosmic Reality by means of the numerical hypostases, one might without being in the least arbitrary stop at the number three, which constitutes a limit that is all the more plausible in that to some extent it marks a falling back on Unity; it may be said to express unity in the language of plurality and seems to set up a barrier to the further unfolding of the latter. But with no less reason one can proceed further, as indeed various traditional perspectives do.

Envisaged with respect to the principle of quaternity, the Essence comprises four qualities or functions which are reflected on earth by North, South, East and West. With the help of this analogical correspondence, we shall the more easily be able to discern, in the Essence itself and consequently in a latent and undifferentiated state — where "all is in all" — but obviously as a potentiality of *Maya*, the four following principles: firstly Purity or Vacuity, Exclusivity; secondly as the complementary opposite — symbolically the North-South axis — Goodness, Beauty, Life or Intensity, Attraction; thirdly Strength or Activity, Manifestation; and fourthly — this is the East-West axis--Peace, Equilibrium or Passivity, Inclusivity, Receptivity. To these principles may be referred the Koranic Names *Dhu'l-Jalal, Dhu'l-Ikram*,[7] *Al-Hayy, Al-Qayyum*: the Possessor of Majesty, the Possessor of Generosity, the Living, the Changeless,[8] Names whose meaning could also be expressed by the following notions: inviolable Purity, overflowing Love, invincible Power, unalterable Serenity; or Truth, which is Rigour and Purity, Life, which is Gentleness and Love, Strength, which is active Perfection, and Peace, which is passive Perfection.

The image of quaternity is the square, and also the cross; the latter is dynamic, the former static.[9] Quaternity signifies stability or stabilization; represented by the square, it is a solidly established world, and a space which encloses; represented by the cross, it is the stabilizing Law that proclaims itself to the four directions, indicating thereby its character of totality. The static quaternity is the radiation of ordaining Grace, which is both Law and Benediction.[10] All of this is prefigured in God, in the Essence, in an undifferentiated manner, and in Being, in a differentiated manner.

When static, the Quaternity is intrinsic and in a certain fashion turned in on itself, and this is *Maya* radiating as Infinitude within the heart of *Atma*; when dynamic, Quaternity radiates, and this is *Maya* in its function of communicating *Atma* and deploying its potentialities; in this case, it establishes the cosmos according to the principles of totality and stability — this is the meaning of quaternity as such — and infuses into it the four qualities which it needs to subsist and to live,[11] and this is the meaning of the four Archangels who, emanating from the Divine Spirit (*Ruh*) whose functions they represent, sustain and govern the world.

The Quaternity is but a development of the Duality *Atma-Maya*, *Deva* and *Shakti*: the Divinity and its Power both of internal Life and theophanic Radiation.

But the Quaternity does not refer only to equilibrium, it also determines unfolding, and so time, or the cycles: hence the four seasons, the four parts of the day, the four ages of creatures and worlds. This unfolding cannot apply to the Principle, which is immutable; what it entails is a successive projection, in the cosmos, of the principial and consequently extratemporal quaternity. The temporal quaternity has above all a cosmogonic meaning, and it is contained moreover in a so to say crystallized state in the four great degrees of universal unfolding: the material world corresponding to winter, the vital world to autumn, the animic world to summer, and the spiritual world — angelic or paradisal — to spring; and this applies in the microcosm as well as in the macrocosm.[12]

The passage from trinity to quaternity is effectuated, if one may so put it, by the bipolarization of the summit of the triangle, which comprises virtually a duality by reason of its double origin; it is the passage from the triangle to the square. The trinity, let us say, is the father, the mother and the child; but the child cannot be neuter, it is of necessity either male or female; if it is either one, this logically calls for the presence of the other. In an analogous manner, the complementary opposition between North and South calls for an intermediate region which, by polarizing into two in its turn, gives rise to East and West, the latter in a certain manner participating in the North, the former in the South.

This principial process of progression is repeated in the case of the quaternity, as it is repeated for the other numbers, *mutatis mutandis*: every quaternity is a virtual quinary and owes its character only to the fact that the centre is so to speak projected into the four extremities: the quaternity is the centre envisaged in its quaternary aspect. But it is sufficient to accentuate the centre independently of its prolongations in order to obtain the quinary: thus, when one speaks of the four ages, the individual that goes through them, is comprised in each age; and in the four seasons, the earth that goes through them is also implied; otherwise the seasons, like the ages, would be abstractions.

•   •   •

The Divine Quaternity is reflected in each of the three modes of the human microcosm: intelligence, will, sentiment; or intellective, volitive and affective consciousness; or again understanding, concentration and conformity or virtue. In the place of sentiment, one could say simply "soul," for the reference here is to the human person as such, who by definition is loving, or more precisely, who is capable of including or excluding from his fundamental love the things that present themselves to his experience.

We have discerned in the divine nature the four following "cardinal points": Purity, Strength, Life, Peace; or Vacuity, which excludes, Activity, which manifests, Attraction, which reintegrates, and Equilibrium, which includes. Intelligence illumined by truth — in conformity with its *raison d'être* — comprises these poles inasmuch as it is capable of abstraction, discrimination, assimilation or certainty, contemplation or serenity.

Still in connection with the intelligence, we must take account of yet another quaternity, whose constituent elements are to the four qualities just described what the intermediary regions are to the cardinal points. These elements are reason and intuition on the one hand, and imagination and memory on the other, corresponding respectively to the North-South and East-West axes. The reason operates, not intellection, but cohesion, interpretation, ordering, concluding; intuition, which is its complementary opposite, operates immediate perception — immediate, but nonetheless veiled and mostly approximate, and confined to the plane of external and internal phenomena, because what is in question here is the mind and not the pure Intellect. As for imagination and memory, the first is prospective and operates invention, creation, and production in one degree or another; the second on the other hand is retrospective and operates conservation, association with origins, empirical continuity. It might be added here that the quality associated with imagination is vigilance, which is prospective; that associated with intuition is generosity which is subjective; and that associated with memory is gratitude, which is retrospective.

Analogous things could be said concerning the two other planes of the microcosm, namely the will and sentiment, or the volitive soul and the affective soul if one prefers, but it is not our intention to push this analysis further, having presented it only by way of application and illustration.

What Is Matter and Who Is Mara?*

Matter, as was pointed out before, is nothing else but the extreme limit or precipitation-point in the process of manifestation, at least for our world; consequently, it is the 'lowest' thing to be found within that reality that concerns us. It might nevertheless be asked whether this lowest thing is not on the contrary a 'consciousness' of sorts, namely the principle of evil, that Mara who tempted the Buddha or Satan who tempted Christ? This difficulty is resolved, however, if one distinguishes in the Cosmos two poles, the one existential, blind and passive and the other intellectual, therefore conscious and active: matter is the point of precipitation in relation to the existential pole only, while the intellectual pole gives rise, at the extreme limit of the process of flight from God, to that 'personifiable force,' or that perverted consciousness, who is Satan or Mara. In other words, Matter is the existence most remote from pure Being, and the Devil is the consciousess most remote from pure Intelligence, the divine Intellect; and since on the intellectual plane this remoteness can only spell subversion or opposition, that intelligence which is most remote from the Absolute will be the one that denies the Absolute as 'intelligibly,' or rather as consciously, as possible. Existence

*From *ITB*, Chapter 8

— the *materia secunda* or *natura naturata* of the medieval Schoolmen, opposed by them to *Natura naturans* or divine Prototype — in course of drawing away from pure Being becomes 'hardened' and at the same time segmented: Matter is the most 'weighted' and the most 'broken' existence of all — regarded from the human point of view, be it understood, since assuredly there can be worlds other than ours, implying other limits of manifestation; while Mara is the most subversive possible intelligence, the most perverse; as compared with Mara, however, matter though hardened and corrupted remains innocent.

Howbeit, we must not make the mistake of confusing stupidity with satanism or vulgarity with mere materiality. There is a consciousness that is diminished through contact with the pole of matter and this is unintelligence, human or other; and there is an existence enhanced through contact with the pole of intelligence (if indirectly) and this is the nobility of material substances, whether of noble metals and precious stones or, passing through the vegetable order, the bodily beauty of living things. Intelligence, in the process of drawing away from the Self, is not necessarily diabolical, it can sink passively, becoming diminished without subversion. Likewise existence, in drawing away from Being, is not exclusively hardness and undifferentiated inertia; it can be accompanied by qualities that bring it near to the pole of 'Spirit' and in this sense it is not farfetched to say of the diamond or of a flower that it displays more intelligence than such and such a stupid man. The power to teach inherent in the things of Nature, especially when in her virgin state, is bound up with this qualitative possibility attaching to natural things: for the North American Indians wild Nature is their Book of Scriptures rendering all written texts needless in their tradition and even writing as such; all that is wanted is the science enabling them to read the signs;[1] by comparison, urbanized and sophisticated man has become largely blind and his opportunities to learn from his surroundings have been catastrophically reduced in practice.

Before proceeding further and even at some risk of repetition, let us once again go into the question of the limitation of matter and of such science as would confine itself to matter; or (what comes to the same) the question of the reality that lies 'behind' the material plane. Modern science, by its own showing, remains strictly horizontal and linear; at no point does it reach above and beyond the plane of sensible manifestation. When speaking of 'science,' the author has in mind the general scientific outlook, which is based principally on the physical sciences; psychology belongs on this same level, more-over, inasmuch as it does not include the recognition of one or more supra-sensorial dimensions, in the sense of concrete and objective realities and not merely in the sense of psychological dreams. It must be added that for those who do accept these dimensions — some an-thropologists or ethnologists for instance — an unequivocal rejection of psycho-analytical speculations is of the utmost importance.

Magic for example, be it 'white' or 'black,' enters into a supra-sensorial (but in no case transcendent) dimension, a dimension of 'depth' as one might say: the point about magic is that it does not, like official science, confine itself to reducing material phenomena to 'energies' or 'movements' of a more or less physical character in-cludable, that is to say, in the post-paradisial solidification of the ter-restrial or spacial substance;[2] but it bypasses the material shell 'in the direction of the interior' by entering into the underlying subtle or *animic* substance: hence the power to 'dematerialize' and transform displayed by *Shamans* and other practioners of magic, be it of a benign or of an evil kind. This power, despite so much evidence, is denied by official science, which fails to perceive the subtle intermediary linking the seemingly contradictory phenomena of magical trans-locations and metamorphoses. The same science fails to perceive, *a fortiori*, the dimension of 'height' any more than that of 'depth,' that is to say the Spiritual World, concerning which magic can also re-main in ignorance; now it is this spiritual dimension that explains theurgic action and miracles. From the standpoint of this latter dimension, the subtle or animic order, that which both magical sci-ence and spiritualistic empiricism[3] deal with, is 'a shell' in its turn, just as matter is a shell from the standpoint of the subtle world. By way of illustration the subtle substance might perhaps best be com-pared to a heavy liquid like blood, and the spiritual or supra-formal substance to air or a gas.

Metaphysically, it is necessary to add yet another dimension: the divine or nirvanic dimension whereof the spiritual dimension is but the cosmic reflexion or 'angelic' emanation. In the most diverse traditional symbolisms the three dimensions described above are respectively represented by 'earth,' 'fire' and 'light.'

When speaking of Matter, one is not oblivious of the fact that from the Buddhist point of view it tends to be regarded in a subjec-tive and empirical sense chiefly; but this fact does not essentially af-fect the question we have been discussing; the fact that Matter may

only interest some people in its capacity of a phenomenon of consciousness is itself independent of the relatively objective content of
that phenomenon as such. . .

The grand reabsorption of the sensible world — not implying
the least fusion — will be heralded by cataclysms on a cosmic scale
which will be like the cracking of the shell of our existence; matter,
by passing through the fire, will be vapourized, not in the physical
sense of the word (which would in no wise take us out of the material
world), but in the sense that it will be 'discomposed towards the interior,' as it were, that is to say in the direction of the subtle and principial order and will rejoin, in due course, the protomatter of the
terrestrial Paradise, that of the non-evolutive creation of species.
Moreover death, for the human microcosm, is none other than this
same regression, for the macrocosm; herein is to be seen the distinction between a 'particular judgment' and the 'general judgment.' In
both cases, man has every interest in keeping himself watchful and
ready; as an old German proverb has it 'he who dies before dying,
dies not when he dies.' Man in dying needs to be at the level of his
new condition, failing which he will be clothed in the very form of
his own insufficiency or of his own internal contradiction or, shall
we say, of his 'sin': his separation from his own norm or prototype
will then make itself felt as an inextinguishable fire.

The following quotation from the *Bhagavadgita* (XVI.4) puts the
position with particular clearness: 'hypocrisy, arrogance, vanity, fury,
insolence and ignorance belong to him who is born, oh Partha, for
a demoniac destiny.' According to Shankara's commentary, we are
to understand by 'hypocrisy' (or ostentation) the claim to be just and
without defects; by 'arrogance' is meant pride in erudition, wealth
or social status; by 'insolence' is meant any statement implying that
the blind see clearly or that the ugly is beautiful or, in other words,
a contempt for truth, falsification of facts, inversion of normal relationships; lastly 'ignorance' means a false conception of our own
duties.

In Judeo-Christian parlance, it is because Adam after the fall
was no longer at the level of the paradisial ambiency that the state
of semi-death that is post-edenic matter came to be produced: we
die because this matter is itself a substance of death, an accursed
substance; our state is something like that of fishes unknowingly
enclosed in a block of ice. According to one text of the Pali Canon,
the *Agganna-sutta*, the progressive materialization of man and his sur-

roundings is due to the fact that the primordial and 'prematerial' men, who formerly had shone like stars and had glided through the air and fed on Beatitude, began to eat soil at the same time when the terrestrial surface emerged from the waters. This earliest earth was colourful, scented and sweet, but men, through feeding on it, lost their own radiance; then it was that the sun and moon appeared, days and nights, therefore also the external light with its alternations and its measurable duration. Later the soil itself ceased to be edible and became limited to producing edible plants; later again, only a small number of plants could be eaten and man had to nourish himself at the price of hard labouring. Passions and vices, and with them adversities, increasingly found a place in the world. Myths like this one, describing the hardening of the primordial substance, are to be found almost everywhere and constitute, like all the most basic traditional data, a testimony whereof the traces are lost in the night of centuries; this is tantamount to saying that they form part of man himself. . .

The manifested Universe comprises two rhythms, the one horizontal and the other vertical: the cosmic cycles follow each other in an incommensurable coming and going, but all this manifestation will disappear in its turn; it will ultimately be breathed in by its immutable Cause.

NOTES

Hypostatic and Cosmic Numbers

1. The combination of point, horizontal stroke and vertical stroke is transcribed by the circle, which expresses the union between the Divinity and its radiating Power, or between the *Deva* and his *Shakti*; it is, so to speak, Divine "Totality," whereas the point represents "Oneness."

2. "Being" is to be understood here not merely as the ontological and creative Principle, but as Reality as such. As regards the distinction between Creative Being and Beyond-Being, we may observe that the terms *esse* and *posse*, in their juxtaposition and correlation, provide a clear indication of the relationship between the two aspects in question.

3. The two points of view can be combined, and must even necessarily be so, when there is coincidence between a social vocation and a contemplative vocation, a coincidence which is encouraged by the Islamic perspective and in particular by the example of the Prophet.

4. The devil being the humanized personification — humanized on contact with man — of the subversive aspect of the centrifugal existential power; not the personification of this power in so far as its mission is positively to manifest Divine Possibility.

5. In every kind of creature, human, animal, vegetable or mineral, form expresses *Chit*; matter, *Sat*; and extension or growth, *Ananda*. It is nevertheless impossible to isolate one of these dimensions from the other, for they always "operate" together: if the form which distinguishes one flower from another manifests the element "Knowledge," *Chit*, it nonetheless expresses, within the very framework of this element, the element "Joy," *Ananda*, whence the beauty of the flower. It should be added that in the case of conscious beings, a psychological application of the ternary is obviously superimposed on the physico-vegetative application which we have just outlined.

6. It is curious to note that in liturgical images of the sun, such as the monstrance or the framing of the monogram of Jesus, straight rays alternate with flames; this expresses the distinction between the "light" and the "warmth" of the Divine Being.

7. Re-united in a single name: *Dhu 'l-Jalāli wa 'l-ikrām*, "Possessor of Majesty and Generosity" (Sura of the All-Merciful, 78). The Sunna records the two equivalent Names of *Jalīl*, "Majestic," and *Jamīl*, "Beautiful," whence these two fundamental Divine aspects: *Jalāl*, "Majesty," and *Jamāl*, "Beauty," that is to say: Rigour and Gentleness.

8. Or more precisely: He who subsists by Himself. "Passivity" signifies here pure "Substantiality" and implies the ideas of Harmony and Peace; God is "passive" in the sense that He is infinitely in conformity with Himself, or with the Essence when it is Being that is in question.

9. Logically, there would perhaps be a certain advantage in representing the dynamic quaternity by a square standing on one of its corners rather than by a cross, since the central intersection of the latter already constitutes a fifth element; this would replace the sides of the square with corners, which would effectively indicate radiation as opposed to a contemplative turning inwards.

10. One will recall here, on the one hand, the Kaaba, whose interior is a sanctuary protected by its walls, and thus enclosed and not open, and on the other hand, the call to prayer on the minarets, which is made towards the four directions of space. Moreover, whoever prays inside the Kaaba, no longer being able to turn towards the centre since he is there himself, must prostrate himself towards the four directions, and this combines the static symbolism of the square with the dynamic symbolism of the cross.

11. The Heavenly Jerusalem corresponds to the square, being a city and a sanctuary; the earthly Paradise, with its four rivers, corresponds to the cross. The Islamic Paradise — the "Garden" (*Jannah*) — combines the two images: on the one hand it is a world and a sanctuary, and on the other hand four rivers spring from its centre. Beatitude of security in the first case, and of radiation in the second.

12. This hierarchy is that of the earthly kingdoms: mineral, vegetable, animal and human, the human species detaching itself from the animal kingdom by the Intellect.

What is Matter and Who is Mara?

1 Islam attributes a similar illuminative function to the various signs (*ayat*) of Nature: the nomad of the Arabian desert and his fellow of the North American prairie have shared this truth, each in his own way.

2. In *The Reign of Quantity and the Signs of the Times* by René Guénon (Luzac, 1953) is to be found a clear explanation of the *qualitative* inequality of temporal phases or periods of history. This doctrine is of the highest importance and this is doubtless why it is side-tracked, with a sort of infallible instinct, by all the modernistically minded representatives of religion of both West and East, who evidently have a strong motive for preferring equivocal explanations concerning the possibilities of the age they live in, given the fact that they already believe dogmatically in an integral and indefinite progress.

3. This latter empiricism is one that operates blindly, being linked with a false doctrine into the bargain; but this fact does not in itself prevent this type of phenomenon from being real at its own level. Here one has to distinguish between certain given phenomena and the quite false explanations wished onto them.

PART IV

ART AND THE SPIRITUAL
SIGNIFICANCE OF BEAUTY

Aesthetics

Aesthetics and Symbolism in Art and Nature*

IN THE ECONOMY of spiritual means beauty, which is positive and compassionate, stands in a sense at the very antipodes from asceticism, which is negative and implacable; none the less the one always contains something of the other, for both are derived from truth and express truth, though from different points of view.

Search for the disagreeable is justified in so far as it is a form of asceticism. It must not, however, be carried to the point of becoming a cult of what is ugly, for that would amount to a denial of one aspect of truth. This question could hardly arise in a civilization still wholly traditional, for in it ugliness would have occurred more or less accidentally. Only in the modern world has ugliness become something like a norm or a principle; only here does beauty appear as a specialty, not to say a luxury. Hence the frequent confusion, at all levels, of ugliness with simplicity.

In our times the discerning of forms assumes a quite special importance. Error appears in all the forms around us among which we live. There is a danger of its poisoning our sensibility—even our intellectual sensibility —by introducing into it a kind of false indifference, a hardening and a kind of triviality.

*From *SPHF*, Part Two, Chapter 1.

A true aesthetic,[1] is nothing but the science of forms and so its aim must be what is objective and real, not subjectivity as such: Forms, intellections; the whole of traditional art in its very widest sense is founded on this correspondence. Moreover a feeling for form may also play an important part in intellectual speculation. The rightness — or the logic — of proportions is a criterion of truth or error in every domain into which formal elements enter.

The reflection of the supra-formal in the formal is not the formless; on the contrary it is strict form. The supra-formal is incarnated in forms that are both 'logical' and 'generous' and thus in beauty.

At any rate in practice, ignorant and profane aestheticism puts the beautiful — or what its sentimental idealism takes to be beautiful — above the true and thus exposes itself to errors on its own level. But if aestheticism is the unintelligent cult of the beautiful, or more exactly of aesthetic feeling, this in no way implies that a feeling for beauty is mere aestheticism.

This is not to say that man has no choice save between aestheticism and aesthetics, or, in other words, between idolizing of the beautiful and the science of beauty. Love of beauty is a quality which exists apart from its sentimental deviations and its intellectual bases.

Beauty is a reflection of divine bliss and, since God is Truth, the reflection of His bliss will be that mixture of happiness and truth which is to be found in all beauty.

Forms allow of a direct, 'plastic' assimilation of the truths — or of the realities — of the spirit. The geometry of the symbol is steeped in beauty, which in its turn and in its own way is also a symbol. The perfect form is that in which truth is incarnate in the rigour of the symbolical formulation and in the purity and intelligence of the style.

A man with feeling for form may prefer a cottage to a magnificent temple and will always prefer a cottage to a palace in bad taste.

An ignorant and impassioned aesthete always prefers the magnificent temple, and sometimes even the palace in bad taste, to the cottage.

Herein lies the difference between them.

Beauty mirrors happiness and truth. Without the element of 'happiness' there remains only bare form — geometrical, rhythmical or other — and without the element of 'truth' there remains only a wholly subjective enjoyment or, it might be said, luxury. Beauty stands between abstract form and blind pleasure, or rather so combines them as to imbue veridical form with pleasure and veridical pleasure with form.

Beauty is a crystallization of some aspect of universal joy; it is something limitless expressed by means of a limit.

Beauty is in one sense always more than it gives, but in another sense it always gives more than it is. In the first sense the essence shows as appearance; in the second the appearance communicates the essence.

Beauty is always beyond compare; no perfect beauty is more beautiful than another perfect beauty. One may prefer this beauty to that, but this is a matter of personal affinity or of complementary relationship and not of pure aesthetics. Human beauty, for instance, can be found in each of the major races, yet normally a man prefers some type of beauty in his own race rather than in another; inversely, sometimes affinities between qualitative and universal human types show themselves to be stronger than racial affinities.

Like every other kind of beauty artistic beauty is objective, and so can be discovered by intelligence, not by 'taste.' Taste is indeed legitimate, but only to the same extent as individual peculiarities are legitimate, that is, just in so far as these peculiarities translate positive aspects of some human norm. Different tastes should be derived from pure aesthetic and should be of equal validity, just as are the different ways in which the eye sees things. Myopia and blindness are certainly not different ways of seeing—they are merely defects of vision.

In beauty man 'realizes,' passively in his perception and externally in his production of it, that which he should himself 'be' after an active or inward fashion.

When man surrounds himself with the ineptitudes of an art that has gone astray how can he still 'see' what he should 'be'? He runs the risk of 'being' what he 'sees' and assimilating the errors suggested by the erroneous forms among which he lives.

Modern satanism is manifested, no doubt in a very external way but in the most directly tangible way and in the way which makes the greatest inroads, in the unintelligible ugliness of forms. 'Abstracted' people, who never 'see' things, none the less allow themselves to be influenced in their general mental outlook by the forms around them to which they sometimes, with astonishing superficiality, deny all importance, just as though traditional civilizations did not unanimously proclaim the contrary. In this connection the spiritual aesthetics of some of the great contemplatives will be recalled as evidence that, even in a world of normal forms, the sense of the beautiful may acquire a special spiritual importance. . .

Poetry should express with sincerity a beauty of the soul; it could also be said that with beauty goes sincerity. It would be useless to bring up so obvious a point but for the fact that in these days definitions of art have become more and more falsified, either through the abuse of attributing to one art the characteristics of another or by introducing into a definition of one art, or of all art, perfectly arbitrary elements such as the desire to be up-to-date; just as though the value or lack of value of a work of art could depend on the fact of knowing it to be modern or ancient, or on one's believing it to be ancient if it is modern or vice versa.

Contemporary poetry is mostly lacking in beauty and sincerity; in beauty for the simple reason that the souls of poets — or rather of those who fabricate what takes the place of poetry — are lacking in beauty, and also in sincerity on account of the artificial and paltry searching for unusual expressions which excludes all spontaneity. It is no longer a question of poetry but of a sort of jeweller's work, frigid and encrusted with false gems, or of a meticulous elaboration which is at the very antipodes of what is beautiful and true. Since the muse no longer gives anything, because it is already killed — for the last thing to which a man 'of to-day' would consent is to appear naïve — men provoke morbid vibrations in the soul and cut the soul to fragments.[2]

Whatever the vagaries of 'up-to-dateness,' it is illogical to cultivate a non-poetical poetry and to define poetry in terms of its own absence.

Metaphysical or mystical poets such as Dante and some of the troubadours or the Sufi poets, expressed spiritual realities through the beauty of their souls. Here is a matter of breadth of intelligence far more than of procedure, for it is not given to every man sincerely to formulate truths which are beyond the range of ordinary humanity; even if there were no question of introducing a symbolical terminology into a poem, it would still be necessary to be a true poet in order to succeed in it without betrayal. Whatever one may think of the symbolical intention of the *Vita Nuova* or the *Khamriyah* (the 'Song of Wine' by Omar ibn al-Faridh) or the quatrains of Omar Khayyam, it is not possible with full knowledge to deny the poetical quality of such works, and this is the quality which, from the artistic point of view, justifies the intention in question.

And, further, the same symbiosis of poetry and symbolism is to be found in such prototypes of divine inspiration as the 'Song of Songs.'

Sometimes it is said that the Eastern civilizations are dead, and are producing no more poetry. To the extent that this is true they are in the right; it is better to confess to being dead than to pretend to have life.

Architecture, painting and sculpture are objective and static. These arts chiefly express forms, and their universality lies in the objective symbolism of these forms.

Poetry, music and dance are subjective and dynamic. These arts, first of all, express essences, and their universality lies in the subjective reality of these essences.

Music distinguishes essences as such and does not, like poetry, distinguish their degrees of manifestation. Music can express the quality of 'fire' without being able to specify (since it is not objective), whether it is a question of visible fire, of passion, of fervour, of mystical glow or of universal fire (that is to say the angelic essence from which all these expressions are derived). All this music expresses at one and the same time when it sings of the igneous spirit, and it is for this reason that some men hear the voice of passion and others the corresponding spiritual function, either angelic or divine. Music has a way of presenting numberless combinations and modes of these essences by means of secondary differentiations and characters of melody and rhythm, rhythm being more essential than melody because it is the principial or masculine determination of musical language, whereas melody is its expansive and feminine substance.

The angelic essences have been compared to streams of pure water, of wine, milk, honey and fire, and correspond to so many melodies, so many musical categories.

A true building, whether it is a temple, a palace or a house, represents the universe, or some world or microcosm, seen in conformity with a particular traditional perspective. Thus it also represents the 'mystical body', the caste or the family according to the particular case.

Dress exteriorizes, either the spiritual or the social function, or the soul. Indeed these two aspects may be combined. Clothing is opposed to nakedness as the soul is opposed to the body or as the spiritual function — the priestly function for example — is opposed to animal nature. When clothing is combined with nakedness — as, for example, among the Hindus — then the latter appears in its qualitative and sacred aspect.

Byzantine, Roman and primitive Gothic arts are arts which

postulate God, or rather 'realize' Him on a certain level.

The pseudo-Christian art which the neo-paganism of the Renaissance inaugurated only seeks and only realizes man. It suffocates the mysteries it should suggest in the superficial and powerless hubbub which inevitably characterizes individualism, and in any case inflicts, chiefly by its ignorant hypocrisy, very great harm on society. How could it be otherwise seeing that this art is only disguised paganism and takes no account in its formal language of the contemplative chastity and the immaterial beauty of the spirit of the Gospels? How could one unreservedly call 'sacred' an art which, forgetful of the almost sacramental character of holy pictures and forgetful, too, of the traditional rules of the craft, offers to the veneration of the faithful carnal and flashy copies of nature and even portraits of concubines painted by libertines? In the ancient Church, and in the Eastern Churches even down to our own times, icon painters prepared themselves for their work by fasting, by prayer and by sacraments; to the inspiration which had fixed the immutable type of the picture they added their own humble and pious inspirations; scrupulously they respected the symbolism — always susceptible of an endless series of precious nuances — of the forms and colours. They drew their creative joy, not from inventing pretentious novelties, but from a loving recreation of the revealed prototypes, and hence came a spiritual and artistic perfection such as no individual genius could ever attain.

The Renaissance retained certain qualities of intelligence and grandeur, but the Baroque style could hardly express anything but the spiritual poverty and the hollow and miserable turgidity of its period.

Late Gothic statuary shows all the marks of bourgeois art, dense and lacking in intelligence. The Renaissance had an easy game to play in setting against it the noble and intelligent art of a Donatello or a Cellini. But none the less, taken as a whole, the misdeeds of Gothic art are a small matter beside those of the Renaissance with its profane, passionate and pompous art.

No doubt bad taste and lack of capacity are to be met with everywhere, but tradition neutralizes them and reduces them to a minimum that is always tolerable.

The first thing which strikes one in a traditional masterpiece is its intelligence: an intelligence which surprises either by its complexity or by its power of synthesis; an intelligence which envelops, penetrates and uplifts.

Humanly speaking some artists of the Renaissance are great, but with a greatness which becomes small in face of the greatness of the sacred. In sacred art genius is as it were hidden; what is dominant is an impersonal, vast and mysterious intelligence. The sacred masterpiece has a touch of the infinite, an imprint of the absolute. In it individual talent is disciplined; it is intermingled in the creative function of the tradition as a whole; this could not be replaced, far less could it be surpassed, by human resources...

There are two aspects in every symbol: the one adequately reflects the divine Function and so constitutes the sufficient reason for the symbolism; the other is merely the reflection as such and so is contingent. The former of these aspects is the content; the latter is the mode of its manifestation. When we say 'femininity', we have no need to consider what are the possible modes of expression of the feminine principle; the species, race or individual does not matter at all, only the feminine quality. It is the same for every symbolism: on the one hand the sun shows a content, which is its luminosity, its emanation of heat, its central position and its immutability in relation to its planets; on the other hand it has a mode of manifestation, which is its matter, its density and its spatial limitation. Now it is clearly the qualities of the sun and not its limitations which show forth something of God.

And the manifestation is adequate, for in reality the symbol is nothing other than the Reality it symbolizes, in so far as that Reality is limited by the particular existential level in which it 'incarnates.' And thus it must of necessity be, for, in an absolute sense, nothing is outside God; were it otherwise there would be things that were absolutely limited, absolutely imperfect, absolutely 'other than God' — a supposition that is metaphysically absurd. To say that the sun is God is false in so far as it implies that 'God is the sun'; but it is equally false to pretend that the sun is only an incandescent mass and absolutely nothing else. That would be to cut it off from its divine Cause; and at the same time it would be to deny that the effect is always something of the Cause. It is superfluous to introduce into the definition of symbolism reservations which, though they pay tribute to the absolute transcendence of the divine Principle, are none the less foreign to a purely intellectual contemplation of things.

Apart from this there exist mere metaphors: these are pseudo-symbols, i.e. pictures which are in short ill-chosen. A picture which does not touch the essence of what it seeks to express is not a symbol but an allegory.

Foundations of an Integral Aesthetics*

Esoterism comprises four principal dimensions: an intellectual dimension, to which doctrine bears witness; a volitive or technical dimension, which includes the direct and indirect means of the way; a moral dimension, which concerns the intrinsic and extrinsic virtues; and an aesthetic dimension, to which pertain symbolism and art from both the subjective and objective point of view.

Exoterically, beauty represents either an excusable or an inexcusable pleasure, or an expression of piety and thereby the expression of a theological symbolism; esoterically, it has the role of a spiritual means in connection with contemplation and interiorizing "remembrance." By "integral aesthetics" we mean in fact a science that takes account not only of sensible beauty but also of the spiritual foundations of this beauty,[1] these foundations explaining the frequent connection between the arts and initiatic methods.

• • •

The Divine Principle is the Absolute and, being absolute, it is the Infinite; it is from Infinity that manifesting or creating *Maya* arises; and this Manifestation realizes a third hypostatic quality, namely Perfection. Absoluteness, Infinity, Perfection; and consequently beauty, in so far as it is a manifestation, demands perfection, and perfection is realized on the one hand in terms of absoluteness and on the other hand in terms of infinity: in reflecting the Absolute, beauty realizes a mode of regularity, and in reflecting the Infinite, it realizes a mode of mystery. Beauty, being perfection, is regularity and mystery; it is through these two qualities that it stimulates and at the same time appeases the intelligence and also a sensibility which is in conformity with the intelligence.

In sacred art, one finds everywhere and of necessity, regularity and mystery. According to a profane conception, that of classicism,

*From *EPW*, pp. 177-182.

it is regularity that produces beauty; but the beauty concerned is devoid of space and depth, because it is without mystery and consequently without any vibration of infinity. It can certainly happen in sacred art that mystery outweighs regularity, or vice versa, but the two elements are always present; it is their equilibrium which creates perfection.

Cosmic Manifestation necessarily reflects or projects the Principle both according to absoluteness and according to infinity; inversely, the Principle contains or prefigures the root of Manifestation, and so of Perfection, and this is the Logos. The Logos combines *in divinis* regularity and mystery, it is so to speak the manifested Beauty of God; but this manifestation remains principial, it is not cosmic. It has been said that God is a geometer, but it is important to add that He is just as much a musician.

Absolute, Infinite, Perfection: the first could be represented by a point, the second by the radii extending from it, and the third by the circle. Perfection is the Absolute projected, by virtue of Infinitude, into relativity; it is by definition adequate, but it is not the Absolute, or in other words, it is a kind of Absolute — namely, the manifested Absolute — but not the Absolute as such; and by "manifested Absolute" one must always understand: manifested in such and such a way. The Infinite is Divine Femininity, and it is from it that Manifestation proceeds; in the Infinite, Beauty is essential, and so formless, undifferentiated and unarticulated, whereas in and through Manifestation it coagulates and becomes tangible, not only because of the very fact of exteriorization, but also, and positively, by virtue of its content, image of the Absolute and factor of necessity, and so of regularity.

The cosmic, or more particularly the earthly function of beauty is to actualize in the intelligent creature the Platonic recollection of the archetypes, right up to the luminous Night of the Infinite.[2] This leads us to the conclusion that the full understanding of beauty demands virtue and is identifiable with it: that is to say, just as it is necessary to distinguish, in objective beauty, between the outward structure and the message in depth, so there is a *distinguo* to make, in the sensing of the beautiful, between the aesthetic sensation and the corresponding beauty of soul, namely such and such a virtue. Beyond every question of "sensible consolation" the message of beauty is both intellectual and moral: intellectual because it communicates to us, in the world of accidentality, aspects of Substance, without for all that having to address itself to abstract thought; and moral, because it reminds us of what we must love, and consequently be.

•   •   •

In conformity with the Platonic principle that like attracts like, Plotinus states that "it is always easy to attract the Universal Soul . . . by constructing an object capable of undergoing its influence and receiving its participation. The faithful representation of a thing is always capable of undergoing the influence of its model; it is like a mirror which is capable of grasping the thing's appearance."[3]

The passage states the crucial principle of the almost magical relationship between the conforming recipient and the predestined content or between the adequate symbol and the sacramental presence of the prototype. The ideas of Plotinus must be understood in the light of those of the "divine Plato": the latter approved the fixed types of the sacred sculptures of Egypt, but he rejected the works of the Greek artists who imitated nature in its outward and insignificant accidentality, while following their individual imagination. This verdict immediately excludes from sacred art the productions of an exteriorizing, accidentalizing, sentimentalist and virtuoso naturalism, which sins through abuse of intelligence as much as by neglect of the inward and the essential.

Likewise, and for even stronger reasons: the inadequate soul, that is to say, the soul not in conformity with its primordial dignity as "image of God," cannot attract the graces which favour or even constitute sanctity. According to Plato, the eye is "the most solar of instruments," which Plotinus comments on as follows: "The eye would never have been able to see the sun if it were not itself of solar nature, any more than the soul could see the beautiful if it were not itself beautiful." Platonic Beauty is an aspect of Divinity, and this is why it is the "splendour of the True": this amounts to saying that Infinity is in some fashion the aura of the Absolute, or that *Maya* is the *shakti* of *Atma*, and that consequently every hypostasis of the absolute Real — whatever be its degree — is accompanied by a radiance which we might seek to define with the help of such notions as "harmony," "beauty," "goodness," "mercy" and "beatitude."

"God is beautiful and He loves beauty," says a *hadith* which we have quoted more than once:[4] *Atma* is not only *Sat* and *Chit*, "Being" and "Consciousness"— or more relatively: "Power" and "Omniscience"— but also *Ananda*, "Beatitude," and thus Beauty and Goodness; [5] and what we want to know and realize, we must *a priori* mirror in our own being, because in the domain of positive realities[6] we can only know perfectly what we are.

The elements of beauty, be they visual or auditive, static or dynamic, are not only pleasant, they are above all true and their pleasantness comes from their truth: this is the most obvious, and yet the least understood truth of aesthetics. Furthermore, as Plotinus remarked, every element of beauty or harmony is a mirror or receptacle which attracts the spiritual presence to its form or colour, if one may so express it; if this applies as directly as possible to sacred symbols, it is also true, in a less direct and more diffuse way, in the case of all things that are harmonious and therefore true. Thus, an artisanal ambience made of sober beauty— for there is no question of sumptuousness except in very special cases — attracts or favours *barakah*, "blessing"; not that it creates spirituality any more than pure air creates health, but it is at all events in conformity with it, which is much, and which, humanly, is the normal thing.

In spite of these facts, which would seem to be quite obvious and which are corroborated by all the beauties that Heaven has bestowed on the traditional worlds, some will doubtless ask what connection there can be between the aesthetic value of a house, of an interior decoration, or of a tool and spiritual realization: did Shankara ever concern himself with aesthetics or morality? The answer to this is that the soul of a sage of this calibre is naturally beautiful and exempt from every pettiness, and that furthermore, an integrally traditional environment — especially in a milieu like that of the brahmins — largely if not absolutely excludes artistic or artisanal ugliness; so much so that Shankara had nothing to teach — nor *a fortiori* to learn — on the subject of aesthetic values, unless he had been an artist by vocation and profession, which he was not, and which his mission was far from demanding.

To be sure, the sensation of the beautiful may in fact be only a pleasant experience, depending on the degree of receptiveness; but according to its nature and of course by virtue of its object, it offers to the intellect, in parallel with its musicality, an intellectual satisfaction, and thus an element of knowledge.

It is necessary to dissipate here an error which would have it that everything in nature is beautiful and everything of traditional production is likewise beautiful because it belongs to tradition; according to this view, ugliness does not exist either in the animal or the vegetable kingdoms, since, it seems, every creature "is perfectly what it should be," which has really no connection with the aesthetic question; likewise it is said that the most magnificent of sanctuaries possesses no more beauty than some tool or other, always because the tool "is everything that it should be." This is tantamount to maintaining not only that an ugly animal species is aesthetically the equivalent of a beautiful species, but also that beauty is such merely through the absence of ugliness and not through its own content, as if the beauty of a man were the equivalent of that of a butterfly, or of a flower or a precious stone. Beauty, however, is a cosmic quality which cannot be reduced to abstractions foreign to its nature; likewise, the ugly is not only that which is not completely what it is supposed to be, nor is it only an accidental infirmity or a lack of taste; it is in everything which manifests, accidentally or substantially, artificially or naturally, a privation of ontological truth, of existential goodness, or, what amounts to the same, of reality. Ugliness is, very paradoxically, the manifestation of a relative nothingness: of a nothingness which can affirm itself only by denying or eroding an element of Being, and thus of beauty. This amounts to saying that, in a certain fashion and speaking elliptically, the ugly is less real than the beautiful, and in short that it exists only thanks to an underlying beauty which it disfigures; in a word, it is the reality of an unreality, or the possibility of an impossibility, like all privative manifestations . . .

NOTES

Aesthetics and Symbolism in Art and Nature

1. This word is used in its present-day, current meaning; it is not used to designate theories of sensory knowledge.

2. The same remarks are valid in relation to contemporary music; it is no longer music but something else. At the opposite end of the scale from the vibratory or 'sonorous' arts one may meet with inverse tendencies, which are in fact the complement of these, that is, attempts at 'dynamic,' or even 'vegetative,' architecture.

Foundations of an Integral Aesthetics

1. One must not confuse aesthetics with aestheticism: the second term, used to describe a literary and artistic movement in England in the 19th century, means in general an excessive preoccupation with aesthetic values real or imaginary, or at any rate very relative. However, one must not too readily cast aspersions upon romantic aesthetes, who had the merit of a nostalgia that was very understandable in a world that was sinking into a hopeless mediocrity and a cold and inhuman ugliness.

2. According to Pythagoras and Plato, the soul has heard the heavenly harmonies before being exiled on earth, and music awakens in the soul the remembrance of these melodies.

3. This principle does not prevent a heavenly influence manifesting itself incidentally or accidentally even in an image which is extremely imperfect—words of perversion and subversion being excluded—through pure mercy and by virtue of the "exception that proves the rule."

4 Another *hadith* reminds us that "the heart of the believer is sweet, and it loves sweetness (*halawah*)." The "sweet," according to the Arabic word, is at the same time the pleasing, coupled with a nuance of spring-like beauty; which amounts to saying that the heart of the believer is fundamentally benevolent because having conquered the hardness that goes with egoism and worldliness, he is made of sweetness or generous beauty.

5. When the Koran says that God "has prescribed for Himself Mercy (*Rahmah*)," it affirms that Mercy pertains to the very Essence of God; moreover, the notion of Mercy does not do justice, except in a partial and extrinsic way, to the beatific nature of the Infinite.

6. This reservation means that we do not know privative realities—which, precisely, manifest unreality—except by contrast; for example, the soul understands moral ugliness to the extent that it itself is morally beautiful, and it cannot be beautiful except by participation in Divine Beauty, Beauty in itself.

PART V

MAN

The Nature of Man

On the Creation of Man*

...ACCORDING TO A RED INDIAN MYTH, the Great Spirit created man three times over, each time destroying what He had made before; the first two attempts were abortive; only the third was to survive.[1] The various forms of animal fossils (gigantic saurians and so forth) prove, not a generic continuity between species, but first efforts towards incarnating certain 'ideas' out of the primordial chaos. At the epoch of the great waves of creation, 'matter' was not yet definitely separated from the subtle world, to which, for example, the psychic elements belong, whether they are conceived in subjective or objective mode;[2] creation could thus take place, not by 'evolution' starting from a single cell — an impossible hypothesis, anyway, and one which only pushes the limits of the difficulty further back — but by successive 'manifestations' or 'materialisations' starting from the subtle state, the cosmic matrix of 'ideas' to be incarnated.[3] This way of seeing things does not exclude very partial evolutions, or adaptations to environment, but reduces them to proportions compatible with metaphysical and cosmological principles.[4]

Ancient and medieval narratives furnish many illustrations —

*From SW, pp. 94-96.

convincing for those who conceive this order of possibilities — of this 'transparency' of matter, or of this interpenetration of material and subtle states: Angels and spirits manifested themselves readily in those days given certain conditions; the marvelous was 'the order of the day' it might be said; matter was not yet the impenetrable shell which it has become in the course of the last thousand years, and above all in the course of these last centuries, correlatively with the mental hardening of men. In primordial ages, cosmic analogies were still much more direct than later: the sun was much more directly 'divine' than in more 'solidified' ages and the same remark holds good for all the salient phenomena of nature: stars, elements, mountains, rivers, lakes, forests, stones, plants, animals; 'sacred geography' still kept all its spiritual efficacy.

Creation — or 'creations'— should then be represented not as a process of transformism taking place in 'matter' in the naïvely empirical sense of the word, but rather as an elaboration by the life-principle, that is to say, something rather like the more or less discontinuous productions of the imagination: images arise in the soul from a non-formal substance with no apparent link between them; it is not the images which transform themselves, it is the life substance which causes their arising and creates them. That man should appear to be the logical issue not indeed of an evolution but of a series of 'sketches,' more and more centred on the human form — sketches of which the apes seem to represent disparate vestiges — this fact, or this hypothesis, we say, in no way signifies that there is any common measure, and so a kind of psychological continuity, between man and the anthropomorphic and more or less 'embryonic' bodies which may have preceded him. The coming of man is a sudden 'descent' of the Spirit into a receptacle that is perfect and definitive because it conforms to the manifestation of the Absolute; the absoluteness of man is like that of the geometrical point, which, strictly speaking, is quantitatively unattainable starting from the circumference. . . [5]

Man as Divine Manifestation*

Man is a divine manifestation, not in his accidentality and his fallen state, but in his theomorphism and his primordial and principial perfection. He is the 'field of manifestation' of the intellect, which reflects the universal Spirit and thereby the divine Intellect; man as such reflects the cosmic totality, the Creation, and thereby the Being of God. The divine Intelligence confers on man intellect, reason and free will; it is by these features — and by speech which manifests them — that the human being is distinguished from animals in a 'relatively absolute' fashion; it is true that every intelligence, even that of plants, is 'intellect,' but the human intellect alone is direct and transcendent; it alone has access to the Divine. The quasi-divine character of man — which is still affirmed in sacred and primordial collectivities — implies that it is impossible to 'realise God' without first realising the human norm; consequently, this latter is 'Prophet' in relation to the fallen individual . . .

Man being 'made of clay' is corruptible, whence the necessity of his ransom. Non-formal manifestation is beyond corruptibility, or rather it is corruptible only at a single point, or 'just once'— the fall of Lucifer — for the corruptibility inherent in the formal world presupposes a corrupted essence which makes it possible, an essence which in relation to man is 'personified' by Satan. Lucifer being an essence — that is to say something which is 'totally itself'— cannot be converted,[1] but man, who is a form, and so something which 'is not altogether itself'—'itself' here being divine — can be converted 'to himself' or to his divine nature, in the likeness of Adam, just as he can become identified with the satanic essence, if he detaches his form from its divine Essence.[2] Damnation is the fall of the form which denies its essence; with the devil the case is the reverse, for he is an essence who denied the 'form of God' in refusing to worship Adam.[3] The ambiguity of the human state is that we are as it were suspended between God — our Essence — and the human form, which is 'made of clay'; we are so to speak a mixture of divinity and dust. To say

*From *SW*, pp. 81-88.

that Man is a form is to say that he falls, to some extent, under the control of the 'demiurgic' essence which hardens and separates, and which is the principle of individuation in so far as it is dark and subversive; Satan is its passional aspect, and in fact those men are lost who direct their passion into egocentric hardness — whence by compensation their intellectual softness — and who find their satisfaction in fury against the universal 'Otherness,' the necessarily 'objective' Truth, and so against everything opposed to their own subjectivity which is itself both hardened and passional;[4] that is why Dante's hell contains both fire and ice. In the beyond, where the reality of human positions is laid bare, this fury is like a joy which lacerates, the joy being in the subjective passion, and the laceration in the objective reality; hell is as it were the revolt of the cipher, of the nothingness which seeks to be the All.[5] When man turns away from his divine Essence, his *ego* becomes like a stone dragging him downwards, and his Essence turns away from him; what then fills this *vacuum* is the dark essence, that of formal compression and the fall.

But what we would like to consider now is the actual appearance of man, his physical quality of 'image of God,' which distinguishes him *a priori* from all other creatures on earth, so that to speak of the human body is almost to speak of man as such; our bodily form would in fact be unintelligible if it were not for our faculties of intelligence and liberty; it is on the contrary explicable only in terms of these qualities. Let us say at once that the profanation of human beauty by the passions in no way authorises contempt for this work of the Creator: despite the good intentions of those who seek to defend virtue at the expense of truth and intelligence, to disparage this beauty is a kind of blasphemy and all the more so since the *Avatara* of necessity synthesises the total Creation in his body and so in its beauty. Some will doubtless insist that all earthly beauty is imperfect and carries blemishes, but this is false in so far as they go on to deduce from this that there is no true beauty on earth. On the other hand, if earthly beauty can be perfect in its kind, it is none the less exclusive of other kinds, and so in a certain sense limited: the beauty of a rose cannot realise that of a water-lily, and in the same way human beauties, whether individual or racial, exclude one another; God alone possesses simultaneously all possible beauty, the Essence being beyond the segmentation of form.

What constitutes the theomorphism of the human body is its

quality of totality and its nobility; its totality is shown above all in the richness — or the universality — of its faculties in so far as this determines bodily structure; and its nobility, by its vertical — and so celestial — position and its gait which is free and sovereign because detached from the ground. Certain animal species do indeed have nobility — the same can be said of certain vegetable and mineral species — but they are fragmentary in comparison to man and so lack totality; the case of monkeys is the opposite, in the sense that they certainly possess physical totality, or nearly so, but they lack nobility, that is to say they are not fashioned either for the human gait, nor for the human carriage of the head, defects which suffice to rivet them to animality. The monkey is man prefigured as regards animality alone, whilst in the human beast the animality devours the man; in such a beast, humanity is like an accident.

In man alone is the head 'freed' from the body so as to dominate it, as if it were a new and autonomous being, like the Spirit dominating chaos.[6] In the opposition between the head and the body — and each appears as a world for itself — the head represents man, Consciousness, and the body woman, Existence; but the whole body assumes a feminine aspect when it is opposed to the heart, which then indicates the divine Intellect, in relation to which the creature — mental as well as corporeal — appears in its dependent and lunar character.[7]

The question of theomorphism raises that of the bodily and mental difference between the sexes, since each of these is theomorphic while being distinct from the opposite sex. The male body appears like a revelation of the Spirit, it evinces intelligence, force triumphant, impassibility, active perfection; the female body is like a revelation of Existence, it reveals Substance — or Totality not, as does the male body, Centrality — and it evinces beauty, moving innocence, fecundity, passive perfection.

Man expresses — always within the same framework of human theomorphism which confers on both sexes the same character of centre and of totality, setting aside any question of predominance — man, then, expresses knowledge and woman love; again, the masculine body is more 'geometrical'— it is, after all, the 'abstract' image of the divine Person — while the feminine body is 'musical' and appears like a 'concrete' expression of our existential Substance and, *in divinis*, of the infinite Beatitude. The feminine body is compounded of nobility and innocence, that is, it is noble by its theomorphism — in this respect it is not distinct from the masculine body, except in its mode — and innocent because it reflects the innocence of existence; its nobility it manifests by its vertical lines, and its innocent fecundity by its curves, and thus it bears in its flesh the fundamental aspects of the *Materia Prima*: the loftiness, purity and mercy of the *Virgo Genitrix*, 'full of grace.' The beauty of woman appears to man as the revelation of the bliss of the Essence of which he is himself as it were a crystallisation — and in this respect femininity transcends man — and this explains the alchemical role and the 'dissolving' power of woman's beauty: the vibratory shock of the aesthetic event — in the deepest sense of this word — should be the means of 'liquefaction of the hardened heart,' whereas passional emotion, when its 'idolatrous' side is not neutralised by a traditional consecration, cannot be exempt from a chaotic and, in principle, promethean and mortal animality. And here it may be pointed out that, from a spiritual point of view, the body has something of the quality of a 'two-edged sword': it may be the vehicle of a 'consciousness of being,' a contemplative 'non-thought' or a kind of ontological and blessed calm, but also of a merely physical and sensual assurance; the body is then 'lived' with a view to 'existence' and not to pure Being. The opportunity of a contemplative junction between the bodily and the spiritual — and we are not here thinking primarily of sexuality — will then depend on individual as well as collective mental structures.[8]

The human being is compounded of geometry and music, of spirit and soul, of virility and femininity: by geometry, he brings back order to the chaos of existence, that is he gives back to blind substance an ontological significance and thus sets up a reference point between Earth and Heaven, a 'sign-post' pointing towards God; by music he brings the segmentation of form back to unitive life, reducing form, which is a death, to Essence, at least symbolically and virtually, so that it vibrates with a joy which is at the same time a nostalgia for the Infinite.[9] As symbols, the masculine body indicates a victory of the Spirit over chaos, and the feminine body, a deliverance of form by Essence; the first is like a magic sign which would subjugate the blind forces of the Universe, and the second like celestial music which would give back to fallen matter its paradisiac transparency, or which, to use the language of Taoism, would make trees flower beneath the snow.

Matter can indeed assume a divine form but this form must be 'wilted' by hardships recalling its exile. The human body has something of the divine by reason of its theomorphism, so that there is a risk of its feeling itself God — or of being deified — if it is not humbled in its very existence; we meet everywhere in nature this humiliation of the theomorphic, for example in the fact that the sun, the physical reflection of the divine Intellect, has to set 'in order to prostrate itself,' as Moslems put it, 'before the throne of Allah.' In all cases of this kind — direct theomorphism on the one hand and existential humiliation on the other — spiritual significance coincides with physical necessity; the latter could never furnish a sufficient explanation of the imperfections in question, precisely because it presupposes metaphysical conditions without which it would itself have no existence. We will add that the devil has every interest in making us believe that physical animality is what we are, that here there is a kind of squalid accident in creation, as if natural blemishes did not, on the contrary, remind us that we are other than this and that our homeland is elsewhere. There is no reason for asking whether it is nature which by its impurities mocks man, or whether it is man who by his prejudices mocks nature; man is not 'of this world,' and it is in the name of God that this world makes him aware of this; for nothing is chance, all is a divine message. Nothing so purifies us from the psychic traces of our materiality as consciousness of the profound necessity of things, as also of their nothingness.

The Fall of Man*

. . . In a certain sense, Adam's sin was a sin arising from inquisitiveness, if such an expression be admissible. Originally, Adam saw contingencies in the aspect of their relationship to God and not as independent entities. Anything that is considered in that relationship is beyond the reach of evil; but the desire to see contingency as it is in itself is a desire to see evil; it is also a desire to see good

*From *LAW*, pp. 43-49.

as something contrary to evil. As a result of this sin of inquisitiveness —Adam wanted to see the "other side" of contingency—Adam himself and the whole world fell into contingency as such; the link with the divine Source was broken and became invisible; the world became suddenly external to Adam, things became opaque and heavy, they became like unintelligible and hostile fragments. This drama is always repeating itself anew, in collective history as well as in the life of individuals.

A meaningless knowledge, a knowledge to which we have no right either by virtue of its nature, or of our capacities, and therefore by virtue of our vocation, is not a knowledge that enriches, but one that impoverishes. Adam had become poor after having acquired knowledge of contingency as such, or of contingency in so far as it limits. We must distrust the fascination which an abyss can exert over us; it is in the nature of cosmic blind-alleys to seduce and to play the vampire; the current of forms does not want us to escape from its hold. Forms can be snares just as they can be symbols and keys; beauty can chain us to forms, just as it can also be a door opening towards the formless.

Or again, from a slightly different point of view: the sin of Adam consists in effect of having wished to superimpose something on existence, and existence was beatitude; Adam thereby lost this beatitude and was engulfed in the anxious and deceptive turmoil of superfluous things. Instead of reposing in the immutable purity of Existence, fallen man is drawn into the dance of things that exist, and they, being accidents, are delusive and perishable. In the Christian cosmos, the Blessed Virgin is the incarnation of this snow-like purity; She is inviolable and merciful like Existence or Substance; God in assuming flesh brought with Him Existence, which is as it were His Throne; He caused it to precede Him and He came into the world by its means. God can enter the world only through virgin Existence.

• • •

The problem of the fall evokes the problem of the universal theophany, the problem that the world presents. The fall is only one particular link in this process; moreover it is not everywhere presented as a "shortcoming'' but in certain myths it takes the form of an event unconnected with human or angelic responsibility. If there is a cosmos, a universal manifestation, there must also be a fall or falls, for to say "manifestation" is to say "other than God" and "separation."

On earth, the divine Sun is veiled; as a result the measures of things become relative, and man can take himself for what he is not, and things can appear to be what they are not; but once the veil is torn, at the time of that birth which we call death, the divine Sun appears; measures become absolute; beings and things become what they are and follow the ways of their true nature.

This does not mean that the divine measures do not reach this world, but they are as it were "filtered" by its existential shell; previously they were absolute but they become relative, hence the floating and indeterminate character of things on earth. The star which is our sun is none other than Being seen through this carapace; in our microcosm the Sun is represented by the heart. It is because we live in all respects in such a carapace that we have need — that we may know who we are and whither we are going — of that cosmic cleavage which constitutes Revelation; and it could be pointed out in this connection that the Absolute never consents to become relative in a total and uninterrupted manner.

In the fall, and in its repercussions through duration, we see the element of "absoluteness" finally devoured by the element of "contingence"; it is in the nature of the sun to be devoured by the night, just as it is in the nature of light to "shine in the darkness" and not to be "comprehended." Numerous myths express this cosmic fatality, inscribed in the very nature of what could be called the "reign of the demiurge."

The prototype of the fall is in fact the process of universal manifestation. The ideas of manifestation, projection, "alienation," egress, imply those of regression, reintegration, return, apocatastasis; the error of the materialists — whatever subtleties they may employ in seeking to dissolve the conventional and now "obsolete" idea of matter — is to take matter as their starting point as if it were a primordial and stable fact, whereas it is only a movement, a sort of transitory contraction of a substance that is in itself inaccessible to our senses. The matter we know, with all that it comprises, is derived from a supra-sensory and eminently plastic protomatter; it is in this protomatter that the primordial terrestrial being is reflected and "incarnated"; in Hinduism this truth is affirmed in the myth of the sacrifice of *Purusha*. Because of the tendency to segmentation inherent in this protomatter, the divine image was broken and diversified; but creatures were still, not individuals who tear one another to pieces, but contemplative states derived from angelic models and, through those models, from divine Names. It is in this sense that it could be said that in Paradise sheep lived side by side with lions; but in such a case only "hermaphrodite" prototypes — of supra-sensory spherical form — are in question, divine possibilities issuing from the qualities of "clemency" and of "rigour, " of "beauty" and of "strength," of "wisdom" and of "joy." In this protomaterial *hyle* occurred the creation of species and of man, a creation resembling the "sudden crystallization of a super-saturated chemical solution." After the "creation of Eve"— the bipolarization of the primordial "androgyne" — there occurred the "fall", namely the "exteriorization" of the human couple, which brought in its train — since in the subtle and luminous protomatter everything was bound together and as one — the exteriorization or the "materialization" of all other earthly creatures, and thus also their "crystallization" in sensible, heavy, opaque and mortal matter.

Plato in his *Symposium* recalls the tradition that the human body, or even simply any living body, is like half a sphere; all our faculties and movements look and tend towards a lost centre — which we feel as if "in front" of us — lost, but found again symbolically and indirectly, in sexual union. But the outcome is only a grievous renewal of the drama: a fresh entry of the spirit into matter. The opposite sex is only a symbol: the true centre is hidden in ourselves, in the heart-intellect. The creature recognizes something of the lost centre in his partner; the love which results from it is like a remote shadow of the love of God, and of the intrinsic beatitude of God; it is also a shadow of the knowledge which consumes forms as by fire and which unites and delivers.

The whole cosmogonic process is found again, in static mode, in man: we are made of matter, that is to say of sensible density and of "solidification," but at the centre of our being is the suprasensible and transcendent reality, which is at once infinitely fulminating and infinitely peaceful. To believe that matter is the "alpha" which gave to everything its beginning amounts to asserting that our body is the starting point of our soul, and that therefore the origin of our *ego*, our intelligence and our thoughts is in our bones, our muscles, our organs. In reality, if God is the "omega", He is of necessity also the "alpha", on pain of absurdity. The cosmos is a "message from God to Himself by Himself" as the Sufis would say, and God is "the First and the Last", and not the Last only. There is a sort of "emanation", but it is strictly discontinuous because of the transcendence of the Principle and the essential incommensurability of the degrees of reality; emanationism, on the contrary, is based on the idea of a continuity such as would not allow the Principle to remain unaffected by manifestation. It has been said that the visible universe is an explosion and consequently a dispersion starting from a mysterious centre; what is certain is that the total Universe, the greater part of which is invisible to us in principle and not solely *de facto*, describes some such movement — in an abstract or symbolical sense — and arrives finally at the deadpoint of its expansion; this point is determined, first by relativity in general and secondly by the initial possibilities of the cycle in question. The living being itself resembles a crystallized explosion, if one can put it in that way; it is as if the being had been turned to crystal by fear in the face of God.

* * *

Man, having shut himself off from access to Heaven and having several times repeated, within ever narrower limits, his initial fall, has ended by losing his intuition of everything that surpasses himself. He has thus sunk below his own true nature, for one cannot be fully man except by way of God, and the earth is beautiful only by virtue of its link with Heaven. Even when man retains belief, he forgets more and more what the ultimate demands of religion are; he is astonished at the calamities of this world, without its occurring to him that they may be acts of grace, since they rend, like death, the veil of earthly illusion, and thus allow man "to die before death," and so to conquer death...

Even believers themselves are for the most part too indifferent to feel concretely that God is not only "above" us, in "Heaven", but also "ahead" of us, at the end of the world, or even simply at the end of our own lives; that we are drawn through life by an inexorable force and that at the end of the course God awaits us; that the world will be submerged and swallowed up one day by an unimaginable irruption of the purely miraculous — unimaginable because surpassing all human experience and standards of measurement. Man cannot possibly draw on his past to bear witness to anything of the kind, any more than a may-fly can expatiate on the alternation of the seasons; the rising of the sun can in no way enter into the habitual sensations of a creature born at midnight whose life will last but a day; the sudden appearance of the orb of the sun, unforeseeable by reference to any analogous phenomenon that had occurred during the long hours of darkness, would seem like an unheard of apocalyptic prodigy. And it is thus that God will come. There will be nothing but this one advent, this one presence, and by it the world of experiences will be shattered . . .

Man in the Universe*

Modern science, which is rationalist as to its subject and materialist as to its object, can describe our situation physically and approximately, but it can tell us nothing about our extra-spatial situation in the total and real Universe. Astronomers know more or less where we are in space, in what relative "place", in which of the peripheral arms of the Milky Way, and they may perhaps know where the Milky Way is situated among the other assemblages of star-dust; but they do not know where we are in existential "space", namely, in a state of hardness and at the centre or summit thereof, and that we are simultaneously on the edge of an immense "rotation", which is not other than the current of forms, the "samsaric" flow of phenomena, the *panta rhei* of Heraclitus. Profane science, in seeking to pierce to its depths the mystery of the things that contain — space, time, matter, energy — forgets the mystery of the things that are contained: it tries to explain the quintessential properties of our bodies and the intimate functioning of our souls, but it does not know what intelligence and existence are; consequently, seeing what its "principles" are, it cannot be otherwise than ignorant of what man is.

When we look around us, what do we see? Firstly existence; secondly, differences; thirdly, movements, modifications, transformations; fourthly, disappearances. All these things together manifest a state of universal Substance: that state is at once a crystallization and a rotation, a heaviness and a dispersion, a solidification and

*From *LAW*, Chapter 7.

a segmentation. Just as water is in ice, and the movement of the hub in the rim, so is God in phenomena; He is accessible in them and through them; this is the whole mystery of symbolism and of immanence. God is "the Outward" and "the Inward," "the First" and "the Last."

God is the most dazzlingly evident of all evidences. Everything has a centre; therefore the totality of things — the world — also has a centre. We are at the periphery of "something absolute," and that "something" cannot be less powerful, less conscious, less intelligent than ourselves. Men think they have "solid earth" under their feet and that they possess a real power; they feel perfectly "at home" on earth and attach much importance to themselves, whereas they know neither whence they came nor whither they are going and are drawn through life as by an invisible cord.

All things are limited. Now the idea of limitation is inseparable from that of effect, and similarly the idea of effect from that of cause; thus it is that all things, by their limitation no less than by their content, prove God, prime Cause and correspondingly limitless.

Or again: what proves the Absolute extrinsically? In the first place the relative, because it is meaningless save through the absoluteness it restricts, and in the second place the "relatively absolute", that is to say, the reflection of the Absolute in the relative. The question of intrinsic or direct proofs of the Absolute does not arise, the evidence being in the Intellect itself and consequently in all our being, so that indirect proofs can do no more than serve as supports or occasional causes; in the Intellect subject and object are not distinct, they could be said to interpenetrate. Certitude exists in fact, otherwise the word would not exist; there is therefore no reason to deny it on the plane of pure intellection and of the universal.

* * *

The *ego* is at the same time a system of images and a cycle; it is something like a museum, and a unique and irreversible journey through that museum. The *ego* is a moving fabric made of images and tendencies; the tendencies come from our own substance, and the images are provided by the environment. We put ourselves into things, and we place things in ourselves, whereas our true being is independent of them.

Alongside this system of images and tendencies that constitutes our *ego* there are myriads of other systems of images and tendencies. Some of them are worse or less beautiful than our own, and others are better or more beautiful.

We are like foam ceaselessly renewed on the ocean of existence. But since God has put Himself into this foam, it is destined to become a sea of stars at the time of the final crystallization of spirits. The tiny system of images must become, when its terrestrial contingency is left behind, a star immortalized in the halo of Divinity. This star can be conceived on various levels; the divine Names are its archetypes; beyond the stars burns the Sun of the Self in its blazing transcendence and in its infinite peace.

Man does not choose; he follows his nature and his vocation, and it is God who chooses.

•   •   •

A man who has fallen into the mire and who knows that he can get out in this way or in that and with a certain amount of effort does not think of rebelling against natural laws nor of cursing existence; it is obvious to him that mud can exist and that there is such a thing as weight, and he only thinks of getting out of the mire. Now, we are in the mire of earthly existence and we know that we can escape from it, whatever trials we may undergo; Revelation gives us the assurance and the Intellect can become aware of the fact *a posteriori*. It is therefore absurd to deny God and to abuse the world for the sole reason that existence presents fissures which it cannot do otherwise than present, on pain of not existing and of being unable to "existentiate."

We are situated as it were under a sheet of ice which neither our five senses nor our reason enable us to pierce, but the Intellect — at once mirror of the supra-sensible and itself a supernatural ray of light — passes through it without trouble, once Revelation has allowed it to become conscious of its own nature. Religious belief also passes through this cosmic shell, in a less direct and more affective manner no doubt, but none the less intuitively in many cases; the divine Mercy, which is comprised in universal Reality and proves the fundamentally "beneficent" character of that Reality, desires moreover that Revelation should intervene wherever that sheet of ice or that shell exists, so much so that we are never completely shut in, except it be in our refusal of Mercy. Mistaking the ice that imprisons us for Reality, we do not acknowledge what it shuts out and experience no desire for deliverance; we try to compel the ice to be happiness. Within the order of physical laws nobody thinks of refusing the Mercy that dwells indirectly in the nature of things: no man on the point of drowning refuses the pole held out to him; but too many men refuse Mercy in the total order, because it surpasses the narrow bounds of their daily experience and the no less narrow limits of their understanding. Man does not in general want to be saved except on condition that he need not surpass himself.

The fact that we are imprisoned in our five senses contains within itself an aspect of Mercy, paradoxical though this may appear after what has just been said. If the number of our senses were multiplied — and there is theoretically no limit in principle to their multiplication — objective reality would tear through us like a hurricane; it would break us in pieces and crush us at the same time. Our "vital space" would be transparent, we would be as if suspended over an abyss or as if rushed through an incommensurable macrocosm, with its entrails exposed so to speak, and filled with terror. Instead of living in a maternal, charitably opaque and watertight compartment of the universe — for the world is a matrix and death a cruel birth — we would find ourselves forever faced with a totality of spaces or abysses, as well as with myriads of creatures and phenomena, such that no individual could possibly endure the experience. Man is made for the Absolute or the Infinite, not for limitless contingency.

Man, then, is as if buried under a sheet of ice. His experience of it takes various forms; at one time it is the cosmic ice that matter has become in its present and post-Edenic state of solidity, and at another time it is the ice of ignorance.

Goodness is in the very substance of the Universe, and for that reason it penetrates right into the matter we know, "accursed" though that matter be. The fruits of the earth and the rain from the sky, which make life possible, are nothing if not manifestations of the Goodness that penetrates everywhere and warms the world; and we carry that Goodness within ourselves, at the bottom of our chilled hearts.

•   •   •

The symbolism of a fountain reminds us that all things are by definition an exteriorization projected into a void in itself non-existent, but nevertheless perceptible in phenomena; water, in this imagery, is the "stuff that dreams are made of" (Shakespeare) which produces worlds and beings. The distance of the drops of water from their source corresponds on the macrocosmic scale to a principle of coagulation and of hardening, also of individuation on a certain plane; the weight that makes the drops fall back is then the supernatural attraction of the divine Centre. The image of the fountain does not however take into account the degrees of reality, nor especially the absolute transcendence of the Centre or of the Principle; what it does take into account is the unity of "substance" or of "nonunreality", but not the existential separation that cuts the relative off from the Absolute; the first relationship goes from the Principle to manifestation, and the second from manifestation to the Principle; that is to say, there is unicity "from the point of view" of the Principle, and diversity or separativity from the point of view of creatures in so far as they are themselves and nothing more.

In a certain sense worlds are like living bodies and beings are like the blood or like the air that courses through them; the contents as well as the containers are "illusory" projections out of the Principle, —illusory because in reality nothing can be separated from it,— but the contents are dynamic and the containers static; this distinction is not apparent in the symbolism of the fountain, but it is apparent in the symbolism of respiration or of the circulation of the blood.

The sage looks at things in connection with their necessarily imperfect and ephemeral exteriorization, but he also looks at them in connection with their perfect and eternal content. In a moral and therefore strictly human and volitional context, this exteriorization coincides indirectly with the idea of "sin", and that is an aspect of the matter that man, in so far as he is an active and passionate creature, must never lose sight of . . .

● ● ●

One must know that which contains and not become dispersed among that which is contained. That which contains is in the first place the miracle of existence, and in the second place the miracle of consciousness or of intelligence, and in the third place the miracle of the joy that, like an expansive and creative power, fills as it were the existential and intellectual "spaces." All that is not capable of immortality must burn; accidents perish, Reality alone remains.

There is in every man an incorruptible star, a substance called upon to become crystallized in Immortality; it is eternally prefigured in the luminous proximity of the Self. Man disengages this star from its temporal entanglements in truth, in prayer and in virtue, and in them alone.

NOTES

On the Creation of Man

1. This myth coincides in a remarkable way with the teaching of the *Saura-Purana*: while *Shiva*, as *Kala*, was meditating on the new Creation — after the destruction of the old one, or rather its reabsorption into *Prakriti* — there appeared first of all the elements deriving from *tamas*, namely darkness, blindness, ignorance, inertia. This Creation being insufficient, a new one was conceived, and so on until man.

2. The world was not yet 'solidified' as Guénon would say. See on this subject, as also on questions of 'sacred geography,' his *The Reign of Quantity* (Luzac, 1953) and our *Spiritual Perspectives and Human Facts* (Faber, 1954).

3. Such things can still take place today, *mutatis mutandis*, under exceptional conditions and on a very restricted scale, in magical — or 'spiritualistic'— operations, in which objects may 'dematerialise' and 'rematerialise,' and psychic influences can assume human forms. The 'ectoplasm' of séances is like a magic and non-formal imitation of primordial matter.

4. It is quite wrong to assume, as does a widely current view, that it is only religious opinion which is opposed to evolutionism

5. The same thing is repeated in the womb; as soon as the body is formed the immortal soul is suddenly fixed in it like a flash of lightning, so that there is complete discontinuity between this new being and the embryonic phases which have prepared its coming. It has rightly been maintained, against transformism, not only that 'the greater cannot come from the less' (Guénon), but also that even though something extant may gain more precision or become atrophied, there cannot on the other hand be a motive, in a species, for the adjunction of a new element, not to mention that nothing could guarantee the hereditary character of such an element (according to Schubert-Soldern).

Man as Divine Manifestation

1. Satan not being a person, Origen speaks of the 'destruction' of 'Death' and not of the conversion of the devil; all the same, this final destruction is not total annihilation, for what is destroyed is not the actual substance of the powers of evil, but their state of perversion. Apocatastasis is a transmutation which implies no 'personal' reintegration. Among the angels — good or bad — personifications are indeed only 'accidental,' and related to their contacts with the human world.

2. The essence of Angels — except in the case of the supreme or 'central' Angels — is not directly God, but the divine Attributes; the Angels are, however, superior to men by their character of being pure essences, or in other words, by the absence of formal crystallisation: man is their superior by his central position, and that is why Brahmins can 'command' the *devas*. As for the supreme Angels, we spoke of them in the chapter ' *En-Nur*' in our book, *Dimensions of Islam*.

3. This is the doctrine of the fall of *Iblis*. It is to be noted that according to the Koran *Iblis* was 'created of fire' and that he is therefore a *jinn*, that is to say a being not 'of light' but 'of flame.' In Hindu terms, we would say that *tamas* (the principle of darkness, 'earth,' existential 'hardening,' ignorance) derives indirectly, by 'detaching' itself, from *rajas* (the principle of 'fire,' existential 'expansion,' 'passion'), which in its turn proceeds, in an equally 'oblique' manner, from *sattwa* (the principle of luminosity, spiritual 'transparency,' knowledge). The name *Lucifer* indicates that the spirit of evil proceeds — evidently by falling, and so indirectly — from the 'support of light,' that is to say from *sattwa*; in this perspective, the intermediary *rajas* is assimilated to *tamas*, exactly as, from the point of view of knowledge, passion is assimilable to ignorance, although the difference between these two terms remains real on their own level.

4. This passional tendency to condensation, separation and fall can rest on very diverse attitudes; it can be located in thought or in the flesh; idolatry of the latter can be as mortal, or nearly so, as rejection of the Truth, not to mention malice, in which the combination of hardening and passion is particularly obvious.

5. Boehme, and in Islam El-Jīlī, have very rightly insisted on this aspect of enjoyment attaching to infernal states. Let us remark here that if hell were 'eternal' in the true sense of the word, instead of being simply 'perpetual' and so perishing with duration, the devil would be partly right in his pretension to divinity; but this is impossible, since 'nothingness' cannot 'be.'

6. Infra-human creatures all the same should not be underestimated. The classical example of a 'anthropocentrism' that is metaphysically inadmissible, though doubtless opportune in certain perspectives, is the opinion according to which animals and plants were created with the sole object of preserving man's animal life, as though all plants and all animals were useful to man, and as though this usefulness explained the forms, colours and other infinitely varied features of these beings, not to speak of the psychological individuality and the contemplative side of the higher animals. Moreover all these aspects are largely useless to the subsistence of the animals and plants themselves. The fact that the lion firstly is not useful to man, and secondly possesses a mane which is not useful for his own subsistence shows

in its way that the animal has an end independent of his material life on the one hand and of utility to man on the other; no doubt he does not possess reason, but he has consciousness, which also transcends crude matter; now the purpose of a consciousness cannot be in the unconscious; everything in nature is made 'to praise God.'

7. See on this subject F. Schuon, *Gnosis*, the chapter 'Ternary Aspect of the Human Microcosm' (Murray, 1959).

8. *Hatha-yoga* is a kind of 'corporeal-existential thought' which would be not only impracticable, but even inconceivable in a people suffering from a moralism about clothing.

9. This function of reducing formal crystallisations to Essence shows well the symbolical correspondence between woman and wine, or between love and drunkenness. Dissolution downwards, towards infra-formal, obscure and chaotic essences, gives rise to many illusions, which explains why exotericism cannot make use of certain symbols Geometrical coordination moreover can equally give rise to sinister counterfeits, namely to limitative crystallisations of the mind, to a spirit of systematisation and partition, to the 'logical error' which denies and compromises the non-formal clarities of the Essence; it is these latter that are then falsely identified with chaos, while form becomes a synonym of the Absolute; the idea of the Infinite is replaced by that of Perfection or of Being, as is shown by certain aspects of 'classical' thought.

Woman

Woman and Interiorization*

'WOMEN, PERFUMES AND PRAYER' these three things, according to a famous *hadith* 'were made worthy of love' to the Prophet; and this symbolism provides us with a concise doctrine of the outward reverberations of the love of the Inward. Woman, synthesizing in her substance virgin nature, the sanctuary and spiritual company, is for man what is most lovable; in her highest aspect, she is the formal projection of merciful and infinite Inwardness in the outward; and in this regard she assumes a quasi-sacramental and liberating function. As for 'perfumes,' they represent qualities or beauties that are formless, exactly in the same way as music; that is to say that side by side with the formal projection of Inwardness, there exists also a complementary formless projection, symbolized, not by visual or tangible qualities, but by auditory and olfactory ones; perfumes are silent music.

As for 'prayer,' the third element mentioned in the *hadith*, its function is precisely to lead from outward to Inward, and it both consecrates and transmutes the qualitative elements of the outward realm; from this it may be seen that the ternary comprised in the saying of Muhammad, far from being of an astonishing arbitrariness and a shocking worldliness — as is believed by those who have no idea

*From *DI*, Chapter 9.

either of Oriental symbolism in general or of the Islamic perspective in particular — provides on the contrary a doctrine which is entirely homogeneous, and which is founded, not on the moral or ascetical alternative[1] — that goes without saying — but on the metaphysical transparency of things. The nature of the three elements of the ternary can be further delineated with the help of the notions — enumerated in the corresponding order — of 'beauty,' 'love' and 'sanctity': it is beauty and love that reflect the Inward in the outward world, and it is sanctity, or the sacred, which establishes the bridge — in both directions — between the outward and inward planes.

'All that is beautiful comes from the Beauty of God,' says a *hadith*. Moslems readily affirm the link between beauty and love and show little inclination to dissociate these two elements which for them are but the two faces of one and the same reality; whoever says beauty, says love, and conversely, whereas for Christians mystical love is almost exclusively associated with sacrifice, except in chivalric esoterism and its prolongations.[2] The *hadith* just quoted really contains the whole doctrine of the earthly concomitances of the love of God, in conjunction with the following *hadith*: 'God is beautiful, and He loves beauty'; this is the doctrine of the metaphysical transparency of phenomena. This notion of beauty or harmony, with all the subtle rhythms and symmetries which it implies, has in Islam the widest possible significance: 'to God belong the most beautiful Names,' says the Qoran more than once, and the virtues are called 'beautiful things' (*husnā*). 'Women and perfumes': spiritually speaking these are forms and qualities, that is to say, they are truths that are both dilating and fruitful, and they are also the virtues which these truths exhale and which correspond to them within us.

'Everything on earth is accursed except the remembrance of God,' said the Prophet, a saying which must be interpreted not only from the standpoint of abstraction (*tanzīh*) but also from that of analogy (*tashbīh*); that is to say, the remembrance of God is not only an inwardness free from images and flavours, but also a perception of the Divine in the symbols (*āyāt*) of the world. To put it another way: things are accursed — or perishable — in so far as they are purely outward and externalizing, but not in so far as they actualize the remembrance of God and manifest the archetypes contained in the inward and Divine Reality. And everything in the world that surrounds us which gives rise to a concomitance of our love of God or of our choice of the 'inward dimension,' is at the same time a concomitance of the love which God shows towards us, or a message of hope from the 'Kingdom of Heaven which is within you.'

These considerations — or even simply the notion of the 'love of God'— lead us to a related question, that of the Divine Person in relation to our capacity for love: what, it may be asked, is the meaning of the masculine character attributed to God by the Scriptures, and how can man — the male — accord all his love, naturally centered on woman, on a Divine Person who seems to exclude femininity? The answer to this is that the masculine character of God in Semitic monotheism signifies, not that the Divine Perfection could possibly exclude the feminine perfections (which is unthinkable), but simply that God is totality and not part, and this totality has its image, precisely, in the human male, whence his priority with regard to woman — a priority which in other respects is either relative or nonexistent; it is indeed important to understand that the male is not totality in the same way that God is, and likewise that woman is not 'part' in an absolute manner, for each sex, being equally human, shares in the nature of the other.

If each of the sexes constituted a pole, God could neither be masculine nor feminine, for it would be an error of language to reduce God to one of two reciprocally complementary poles; but if, on the contrary, each sex represents a perfection, God cannot but possess the characteristics of both — active perfection, however, always having priority over passive perfection. Whether one likes it or not, in Christianity the Blessed Virgin assumes the function of the feminine aspect of the Divinity, at least in practice, and in spite of every theological precaution; however, this observation, far from being a cause of reproach in the eyes of the writer, has on the contrary for him the most positive meanings. In Islam it is sometimes said that man has a feminine character in relation to God; but from another point of view, the doctrine of the Divine Names implies that the Divinity possesses all conceivable qualities, and if we see in the perfect woman certain qualities which are proper to her, she cannot have them except in so far as they are a reverberation of the corresponding Divine Qualities . . .

NOTES

Woman and Interiorization

1. Principle: to realize God one must reject the world, since the latter moves us away from God in a variety of ways. This perspective is incarnated by Buddha and Christ.

2 Some may think that the relationship 'beauty-love' is purely 'natural' and therefore foreign to spirituality; this is to overlook that a positive natural relationship is rooted in the supernatural and comprises the virtues of the latter in function of the spiritual value and ritual attitude of man. At the exoteric level, this is the fruitless dialogue between two different orders of truth, one ascetical and one alchemical; this is stressed once again because, at least on the moral plane, it is the main stumbling block between West and East. In this connection it may be added that all exoterism — be it *de facto* or *de jure* — tends to put humility in the place of intelligence, and merit in the place of beauty, as if these were unavoidable alternatives.

Sexuality

The Problem of Sexuality*

IT WOULD IN PRINCIPLE be impossible for the spiritual life to exclude a domain as fundamental, humanly speaking, as sexuality; sex is an aspect of man. Traditionally the West is marked by a theology of Augustinian inspiration, which explains marriage from a more or less utilitarianist angle, while neglecting the intrinsic reality of the thing. According to this perspective — leaving aside every apologetic euphemism — sexual union in itself is sin; consequently the child is born in sin, but the Church compensates, or rather more than compensates, for this evil with a greater good, namely baptism, faith, sacramental life. According to the primordial perspective, on the other hand, which is founded on the intrinsic nature of the realities concerned, the sexual act is a "naturally supernatural" sacrament. In primordial man sexual ecstasy coincides with spiritual ecstasy, it communicates to man an experience of mystical union, a "remembrance" of the Divine Love of which human love is a distant reflection; an ambiguous reflection, certainly, since the image is at one and the same time both adequate and inverted. It is in this ambiguity that the whole problem resides: the primitive, "pagan," Greco-Hindu perspective — a *de facto* esoteric perspective in the Christian context — is based on the adequateness of the image, for a tree reflected in water

*From *EPW*, pp. 129-145.

408

is still a tree and not something else; the Christian, penitential, ascetical and in fact exoteric perspective is on the contrary based on the inversion of the image, for a tree has its branches above and not below, and the reflection is thus no longer the tree. But there is a great disparity between the two points of view: while esoterism accepts the relative and conditional justice of the penitential perspective, this perspective is unable in its turn to accept the legitimacy of the "natural ," primordial and participative perspective; and this is exactly the reason why the latter cannot but be "esoteric" in an Augustinian context, although in itself it may nevertheless be integrated into an exoterism, as is proved, for example, by Islam.[1]

In a Christian atmosphere, sexuality in itself, isolated from every distorting context, readily acquires the opprobrium of "bestiality," whereas in reality nothing that is human is bestial by its nature; that is why we are men and not beasts. Nevertheless, in order to escape from the animality in which we participate, it is necessary that our attitudes should be integrally human, in accordance with the norm imposed upon us by our deiformity; they must embrace both our soul and our spirit, or in other words, devotion and truth. Moreover, it is only the blind passion of fallen man that is bestial, and not the innocent sexuality of the animals; when man is reduced to his animality, he becomes worse than the animals, who betray no vocation and violate no norm; we must not implicate the animal, which may be a noble creature, in the taboos and anathemas of human moralism.

If the sexual act were by its nature a sin — as basically the Christian and penitential perspective would have it[2] — this nature would be transmitted to the child that is conceived in it; if on the contrary the sexual act represents, through its profound and spiritually integral nature, an act that is meritorious because in principle sanctifying[3] — or a primordial sacrament evoking and actualizing in the required conditions union with God — the child that is conceived according to this nature will be hereditarily predisposed to spiritual union, no more and no less than he would be predisposed to sin in the contrary case; the fact that the act by itself is *de jure* if not *de facto* a sort of sacrament implies, moreover, that the child is a gift, and not the exclusive culmination of the act.[4]

The Church blesses marriage with a view to the procreation of men, of whom it will make believers; it blesses it while taking upon itself the inevitable but provisional drawback of the "sin of the flesh." We are tempted to say that it is here nearer to St. Paul than to Christ;

in other words, St. Paul, without inventing anything—which is out of the question—nevertheless accentuated things with a view to a particular application which was not necessary in itself. Unquestionably, Christ indicated the way of abstinence; but abstinence does not necessarily signify that the sexual act is sinful in nature; it may signify on the contrary that sinners profane it; for in sexual union sinners rob God of enjoyment which belongs to Him. Seen from this angle, the sin of Adam consisted in monopolizing enjoyment —in attributing to himself enjoyment as such, so that the fault lay both in the theft and in the manner of envisaging the object of the theft, namely a pleasure that is substantially divine. Thus his sin was to usurp the place of God while withdrawing from the divine subjectivity in which man participated at the origin; it was to cease to participate in this divine subjectivity and to make himself absolute subject. The human subject, by practically making himself God, at the same stroke limited and degraded the object of his happiness and even the whole cosmic ambience.

Obviously, in the intention of Christ, there could not simply have been a desire not to see a natural and primordial sacrament profaned; there was also, and even above all, the offering of a spiritual means congenial to an ascetical perspective, for chastity is necessarily the ferment of a way, given precisely the ambiguity of sexual things. At Cana, Christ consecrated or blessed marriage, without one being able to say that he did so from the Pauline or Augustinian angle: he changed the water into wine, which is an eloquent symbolism, and which refers with much more probability to the possibility of a union that is both carnal and spiritual than to the moral and social opportunism of the theologians; if it was a question of an exclusively carnal union, it would indeed no longer be human.[5]

Moreover, if procreation is such an important thing it is impossible that the act which is its *conditio sine qua non* should be a regrettable accident, and that this act should not, on the contrary, possess a sacred character proportionate to the importance and holiness of procreation itself. And if it is possible to isolate—as do the theologians—procreation from the sexual act by stressing only the former, it must be equally possible to isolate the sexual act from procreation by accentuating the act alone in conformity with its own nature and its immediate context; this amounts to saying that love possesses a quality that makes it independent of its purely biological and social aspect, as moreover its theological and mystical symbolism proves.

One can procreate without loving, and one can love without procreating; the love of Jacob for Rachel does not lose its meaning because Rachel was for a long time sterile, and the Song of Solomon does not seek to justify itself by any demographic considerations.

Without any doubt, Christ was not opposed to marriage, nor was he, perhaps, opposed to polygamy either; the parable of the ten virgins seems to bear witness to this.[6] In the Christian world, polygamy should have been permitted to princes, if not to all believers; many wars and many tyrannical pressures on the Church would have been avoided — amongst others, the Anglican schism. Man must not put asunder what God has joined together, Christ said when condemning divorce; the marriages of princes, however, were for the most part the result of political bargaining, and this has nothing to do with God, any more than it has to do with love. Polygamy, like monogamy rests on natural factors: if monogamy is normal because the first marriage was of necessity monogamous and because femininity, like virility, resides entirely in a single person, then polygamy for its part is explained, on the one hand, by the biological facts and by social or political opportuneness — at least in certain societies — and on the other hand by the fact that the infinitude which woman represents permits a diversity of aspects; man is prolonged towards the periphery, which liberates, just as woman is rooted in the centre, which protects.[7] To this it should be added, leaving aside all considerations of opportuneness, that the more or less Nordic peoples tend to favour monogamy, and this for obvious reasons of climate and temperament, whereas the majority of southern peoples seem to have a natural tendency towards polygamy, whatever be its form or degree. Be that as it may, it was an error, in the West, to impose on a whole continent a morality for monks: a morality that is perfectly legitimate in its methodic context, but which is nevertheless based on the error — as regards its extension to the whole of society — that sexuality is a kind of evil; an evil that should be reduced to a minimum and tolerated only by virtue of an approach that treats as incidental all that is essential.

No doubt a distinction should be made between a polygamy in which several women keep their personality, and a princely "pantogamy" in which a multitude of women represent femininity in a quasi-impersonal manner; the latter would be an affront to the dignity of human persons if it were not founded on the idea that a given bridegroom is situated at the summit of human kind. Pantogamy is possible because Krishna is Vishnu, because David and Solomon are prophets, because the sultan is the "shadow of *Allah* on earth"; it could also be said that the innumerable and anonymous harem has a function analogous to that of the imperial throne adorned with precious stones; a function that is analogous but not identical, for the throne made of human substance — the harem, that is — indicates in an eminently more direct and more concrete manner the real or borrowed divinity of the monarch. At a profane level, this pantogamy would not be possible; as to whether it is legitimate or excusable in any particular case, this is a question that can be settled only on the basis of the distinction between the individual, who may be commonplace, and the function, which is sublime and may on that account attenuate human disproportions and illusions.

We have written the foregoing in order to explain existing phenomena and not to express preferences or their opposite; our personal sensibility is not at issue and may even be opposed to a particular moral or social solution, of which nevertheless we have sought to demonstrate the justification from a given point of view or in a given context.

•   •   •

A very important possibility that must be taken into account here is abstinence within the framework of marriage; this moreover goes hand in hand with the virtues of detachment and generosity, which are the essential conditions for the sacramentalization of sexuality. Nothing is more opposed to the sacred than tyranny or triviality on the plane of conjugal relations; abstinence, the breaking of habits and freshness of soul are indispensable elements of any sacred sexuality. In a permanent confrontation of two beings, there must be two equilibrium-producing openings, one towards Heaven and the other on earth itself: there must be an opening towards God, who is the third element above the two spouses, without which the duality would become opposition; and there must be an opening or a void — a ventilation, so to speak — on the immediate human plane, and this is abstinence, which is both a sacrifice before God and a homage of respect and gratitude towards the spouse. For the human and spiritual dignity of the spouse demands that he or she should not become a habit, should not be treated in a way that lacks imagination and freshness and should thus keep his or her mystery; this

condition demands not only abstinence, but also, and above all, loftiness of character, which in the last analysis results from our sense
of the sacred or from our state of devotion.

Devotion, in fact, demands on the one hand separative respect
and on the other hand participative intimacy; on the one hand one
must extinguish oneself and remain poor, and on the other hand one
must radiate or give; whence the complementarity of detachment
and generosity. And in this context it is necessary to stress that the
patient and charitable comprehension of the spouse's physical temperament is a condition not only of human dignity but also of the
spiritual value of the marriage; periodical abstinence being, precisely,
an expression of this comprehension or of this tolerance.[8]

In order not to omit any possibility, we must even consider the
case, no doubt rare but in no wise illegitimate in itself, where this
abstinence is definitive and where the ideal of a brother-and-sister
relationship is combined with that of chastity;[9] in such a case, the
tone will not be that of a pedantic or tormented moralism, but that
of holy childhood. Obviously Platonic marriage presupposes rather
special vocational qualifications, at the same time as a spiritual point
of view which supports this solution, in conformity with the words
from Genesis "It is not good that man should be alone; I shall make
for him a helpmeet like unto him."[10]

. . .

Certainly the flesh was cursed by the fall, but only in a certain
respect, that of existential and formal discontinuity, not in respect
of spiritual and essential continuity: the human body, male or female,
is a theophany, and remains so in spite of the fall;[11] by loving one
another, the spouses legitimately love a divine manifestation, each
one according to a different aspect and in a different respect; the
divine content of nobility, goodness and beauty remaining the same.
It is by basing itself on this relationship that Islam, on the one hand
implicitly recognizes the sacred character of sexuality in itself, and
on the other hand — by way of consequence — considers that every
child is born *muslim* and that it is its parents who make of it an infidel, if so be the case.

Christian theology, by concerning itself with sin and seeing a
seductress in Eve in particular and in woman in general, has been

led to evaluate the feminine sex with a maximum of pessimism. According to some, it is man alone and not woman who was made in
the image of God, whereas the Bible affirms, not only that God
created man in His image, but also that "male and female created
He them," which has been misinterpreted with much ingenuity. In
principle, one might be surprised at this lack of more or less visual
intelligence on the part of the theologians; in fact, such a limitation
has nothing surprising about it, given the will-bound and sentimental
character of the exoterist perspective in general, which disposes it
to prejudices and bias.[12] A first proof — if proof is needed — that
woman is divine image like man, is that in fact she is a human being like him; she is not *vir* or *andros*, but like him she is *homo* or *anthropos*; her form is human and consequently divine. Another proof —
but a glance ought to suffice — resides in the fact that, in relation
to man and on the erotic plane, woman assumes an almost divine
function — similar to the one which man assumes in relation to
woman — which would be impossible if she did not incarnate, not
the quality of absoluteness, to be sure, but the complementary quality
of infinitude; the Infinite being in a certain fashion the *shakti* of the
Absolute.

    And this leads us, in order to rectify the excessively unilateral
opinions to which the question of the sexes has given rise, to define
three relationships which govern the equilibrium between man and
woman: firstly the sexual, biological, psychological and social relationship; then the simply human and fraternal relationship, and finally the properly spiritual or sacred relationship. In the first relationship, there is obviously inequality, and from this results the social
subordination of woman, a subordination already prefigured in her
physical constitution and her psychology; but this relationship is not
everything, and it may even be more than compensated for — depending on the individuals and the confrontations — by other dimensions.
In the second relationship, that of the human quality, woman is equal
to man since like him she belongs to the human species; this is the
plane, not of subordination, but of friendship; and it goes without
saying that on this level the wife may be superior to her husband
since one human individual may be superior to another, whatever
be the sex. Finally, in the third relationship there is, highly paradoxically, reciprocal superiority: in love, as we have said earlier, the
woman assumes in regard to her husband a divine function, as does
the man in regard to the woman . . .

Krishna, the great *avatara* of Vishnu, had numerous wives, as did, moreover, at a period closer to ourselves, the prophet-kings David and Solomon; the Buddha, likewise a major *avatara*, had none;[13] the same is true of Shankara, Ramanuja and other minor incarnations, who nevertheless were Hindu by tradition like Krishna. This proves that if the choice of sexual experience or chastity may be a question of superiority or inferiority on the spiritual level, it can also be an affair of perspective and vocation, and with the same justification; the whole problem is then reduced to the distinction between "abstraction" and "analogy", or to the opportuneness, be it intellectual, methodic, psychological or quasi-existential, or perhaps even simply social, of one or other of these options which in principle are equivalent. The question that arises here is to know not simply what man chooses, or what his particular nature requires or desires, but also and even above all how God wants to be approached: whether through the void, the absence of everything that is not He, or through the plenitude of His manifestations, or again through the void and through plenitude alternately, of which the hagiographies provide many examples. In the last analysis it is God Himself who seeks Himself through the play of His veilings and unveilings, His silences and His words, His nights and His days.

Fundamentally, every love is a search for the Essence or the lost Paradise; the melancholy, gentle or violent, which often appears in poetic or musical eroticism bears witness to this nostalgia for a far-off Paradise and doubtless also the evanescence of earthly dreams, of which the sweetness is, precisely, that of a Paradise which we no longer perceive, or which we do not yet perceive. Gipsy violins evoke not only the heights and the depths of a love that is too human, they also celebrate, in their profoundest and most poignant accents, a thirst for the heavenly wine that is the essence of Beauty; all erotic music, to the extent of its authenticity and nobility, rejoins the sounds, both captivating and liberating, of Krishna's flute.[14]

Like that of woman, the role of music is equivocal, and so are the related arts of dancing and poetry: there is either a narcissistic inflation of the ego, or an interiorization and a beatific extinction in the essence. Woman, incarnating *Maya*, is dynamic in a double sense: either in the sense of an exteriorizing and alienating radiation, or in that of an interiorizing and reintegrating attraction; whereas man, in the fundamental respect in question, is static and unequivocal.

Man stabilizes woman, woman vivifies man; furthermore, and quite obviously, man contains woman within himself, and vice versa, given that both are *homo sapiens*, man as such; and if we define the human being as *pontifex*, it goes without saying that this function includes woman, although she adds to it the mercurial character proper to her sex.[15]

Man, in his lunar and receptive aspect, "withers away" without the woman-sun that infuses into the virile genius what it needs in order to blossom; inversely, man-sun confers on woman the light that permits her to realize her identity by prolonging the function of the sun.

Chastity can have as its aim, not only resistance to the dictates of the flesh, but also, and more profoundly, an escaping from the polarity of the sexes and a reintegration of the unity of the primordial *pontifex*, of man as such; it is certainly not an indispensable condition for this result, but it is a clear and precise support for it, adapted to given temperaments and imaginations.

· · ·

If for Christianity, as for Buddhism in general, the sexual act is identified with sin — every euphemistic subtlety apart — this is easily explained by the fact that inasmuch as the "spirit" is above and the "flesh" below, the most intense pleasure of the flesh will be the lowest pleasure in relation to the spirit. This perspective is plausible to the extent that it takes account of a real aspect of things, that of the existential discontinuity between the phenomenon and the archetype, but it is false to the extent that it excludes the aspect of essential continuity, which precisely compensates, and on its level annuls, that of discontinuity. For if, on the one hand, the flesh as such is separated from the spirit, on the other hand it is united to it in so far as it manifests it and prolongs it, that is to say, in so far as it is recognized as being situated in the unitive vertical axis or the radius, and not on the separative horizontal axis or the circle; in the first case the centre is prolonged, and in the second it is concealed.

The spiritual exploitation of the mystery of continuity depends either on the real and not imaginary contemplativity of the individual or on a religious system allowing an indirect and passive participation in this mystery; the risks of a centrifugal effect are in this case neutralized and compensated by the general perspective and the particular dispositions of the religion, on condition, of course, that the individual submits to this in a sufficient manner. For the true contemplative, each pleasure that we can qualify as noble is a meeting with the eternal, not a fall into the temporal and the impermanent.

According to Meister Eckhart even the simple fact of eating and drinking would be a sacrament if man understood in depth what he was doing. Without entering into the details of this assertion, which in fact can be applied at various levels — especially that of craftsmanship and art — we would say that in these cases the sacramental character has a significance which relates it to the "lesser mysteries"; sexuality on the other hand, and this is what proves its dangerous ambiguity, refers to the "greater mysteries", as is indicated by the wine at Cana. Let us note in this connection that the passive complement of sexual union is deep sleep: here too there is a prefiguration of supreme union, with the difference nevertheless that in sleep the sacramental initiative is entirely from the side of God, who confers His grace on whoever may receive it; in other words, deep sleep is a sacrament of union to the extent that man is already sanctified.

In Islam there is a notion which effectively acts as a bridge between the sacred and the profane or between the spirit and the flesh, and this is the notion of *barakah*, of "immanent blessing": it is said of every licit pleasure experienced in the name of God and within the permitted limits, that it vehicles a *barakah*, which amounts to saying that it has a spiritual value and a contemplative perfume, instead of being limited to a purely natural satisfaction, tolerated because it is inevitable or to the extent that it is so. . .

•   •   •

In this context, as we were saying, woman appears as the exteriorizing and fettering element: feminine psychology, indeed, on the purely natural plane and failing a spiritual adjustment of values, is characterized by a tendency towards the world, the concrete, the existential if one will, and in any case towards subjectivity and sentiment, and also by a more or less unconscious guile in the service of this in-born tendency.[16] It is with regard to this tendency that Christians as well as Muslims have felt justified in saying that a holy woman is no longer a woman, but a man — a formulation that is absurd in itself, but defensible in the light of the axiom we are speaking of. But this axiom concerning the innate tendency of woman happens to be relative and not absolute, given that woman is a human being like a man and that sexual psychology is necessarily a relative thing; one can make use as much as one likes of the fact that Eve's sin was to call Adam to the adventure of outwardness, but one cannot forget that the function of Mary was the opposite and that this function also enters into the possibility of the feminine spirit. Nevertheless the spiritual mission of woman will never be linked with a revolt against man, in as much as feminine virtue comprises submission in a quasi-existential manner: for woman, submission to man — not to no matter what man — is a secondary form of human submission to God. It is so because the sexes, as such, manifest an ontological relationship, and thus an existential logic which the spirit may transcend inwardly but cannot abolish outwardly.

To allege that the woman who is holy has become a man by the fact of her sanctity, amounts to presenting her as a denatured being: in reality, a holy woman can only be such on the basis of her perfect femininity, failing which God would have been mistaken in creating woman — *quod absit* — whereas according to Genesis she was, in the intention of God, "a helpmeet for man"; and so firstly a "help" and not an obstacle, and secondly "like unto him", and not sub-human; to be accepted by God, she does not have to stop being what she is.[17]

The key to the mystery of salvation through woman, or through femininity, if one prefers, lies in the very nature of *Maya*: If *Maya* can attract towards the outward, she can also attract towards the inward.[18] Eve is life, and this is manifesting *Maya*; Mary is Grace, and this is reintegrating *Maya*. Eve personifies the demiurge under its aspect of femininity; Mary is the personification of the *Shekhinah*, of the Presence that is both virginal and maternal. Life, being amoral, can be immoral; Grace, being pure substance, is capable of absorbing all accidents.

Sita, the wife of Rama, seems to combine Eve with Mary: her drama, at first sight disconcerting, describes in a certain fashion the ambiguous character of femininity. In the midst of the vicissitudes of the human condition, the divinity of Sita is significantly maintained: the demon Ravana, who had succeeded in abducting Sita — following a fault on her part — believes that he has ravished her, but he has ravished only a magical appearance, without having been able to touch Sita herself. The fault of Sita was an unjust suspicion, and her punishment was likewise such a suspicion: this is the form taken here by the sin of Eve; but at the end of her earthly career, the Ramayanic Eve reintegrates the Marial quality: Sita, the incarnation of Lakshmi,[19] disappears into the earth which opens for her and this signifies her return to Divine Substance which the earth visibly manifests. The name of Sita, in fact, means "furrow": Sita, instead of being born a woman, emerged from the Earth-Mother, that is from *Prakriti*, the metacosmic Substance that is pure and at the same time creating.

The Hindus excuse Sita by emphasizing the fact that her fault[20] was due to an excess of love for her spouse Rama; by universalizing this interpretation, one can conclude that the origin of evil is not curiosity or ambition as in the case of Eve, but an immoderate love, and thus the excess of a good.[21] This seems to rejoin the Biblical perspective in the sense that the sin of the first couple was to misappropriate love: to love the creature more than the Creator, to love the creature outside the Creator and not in Him. But in this case the "love" is more of a craving on the part of the soul than a form of worship; a desire for novelty or fullness of experience rather than an adoration; and therefore a lack of love rather than a deviated love.

• • •

An indispensable condition for the innocent and natural experience of earthly happiness is the spiritual capacity of finding happiness in God, and the incapacity to enjoy things outside of Him. We cannot validly and persistently love a creature without carrying him within ourselves by virtue of our attachment to the Creator; not that this inward possession must be perfect, but it must at all events be present as an intention which allows us to perfect it.

The state — or the very substance — of the normal human soul is devotion or faith, and this comprises an element of fear as well as an element of love; perfection is the equilibrium between the two poles, and this once again brings us back to the Taoist symbolism of *Yin-Yang*, which is the image of balanced reciprocity: we mean that the love of God, and by reflection the love of the husband or the wife, implies an element of fear or respect.

To be at peace with God is to seek and find our happiness in Him; the creature that He has joined to us may and must help us to reach this with greater facility or with less difficulty, in accordance with our gifts and with grace, whether merited or unmerited.[22] In saying this we evoke the paradox — or rather the mystery — of attachment with a view to detachment, or of outwardness with a view to inwardness, or again, of form with a view to essence. True love attaches us to a sacramental form while separating us from the world, and it thus rejoins the mystery of exteriorized Revelation with a view to interiorizing Salvation.

NOTES

The Problem of Sexuality

1. Islam being in this respect even more explicit than Judaism.

2. No doubt this perspective is not exclusively Christian, but we want to deal with it here in its best known form.

3 This is related to the fact that in several traditional worlds the sexual act of the prince is reputed to fertilize, through the woman, the soil of the country, or to increase the prosperity of the people.

4. If the sexual act is a double-edged sword that can give rise to totally opposite eschatological consequences, depending on the objective and subjective conditions that accompany it, it may call to mind, *mutatis mutandis*, the sacrament of the Eucharist which, in the absence of the required conditions, results not in grace but in condemnation, as the Apostle has emphasized.

5. When the Church teaches that Mary was "conceived without sin," this refers to the fact that her soul was created without the stain of original sin; but many uninstructed believers think this attribute refers to the extraordinary manner of her conception, realized without carnal union on the part of her parents — according to a tradition — or at least without desire or enjoyment in their union, and so without "concupiscence." If this interpretation is not theological, its existence is nevertheless significant, for such a sentiment is typical of the Christian perspective.

6. At least in a symbolical way, if one disregards the words "and of the bride" added by the Vulgate, and justified, so it appears, by a certain Jewish custom.

7. Polyandry, on the other hand, finds no support in the facts of nature; extremely rare, it is doubtless to be explained by very special economic reasons and perhaps also by concepts proper to shamanism. There is also the case of sacred prostitution — hetaerae, hierodules, *devadasis*, geishas — in which woman becomes the centre because she gives herself to a number of men; we are compelled to admit that this phenomenon is a possibility within the framework of archaic traditions, but it is at all events excluded from the later religions, apart from a few exceptions, which however are too marginal to merit explicit mention.

8. It may be noted that the Redskins saw in sexual abstinence, to which they were sometimes constrained for practical reasons, a sign of strength and consequently of fulfilled virility.

9. The marriage of Ramakrishna offers us an example of this. The Paramahamsa adored his wife without touching her; which is of infinitely greater worth than touching her without adoring her.

10. This is also translated as "who will be a match for him" or "who will be worthy of him"; this passage, if one takes the trouble to understand it, rules out the pious misogyny and the holy unthinkingness of some exegetes.

11. "Whoever has seen me, has seen God": this *hadith* applies first and foremost to the avataric person, but it applies equally to the human form as such; in this case it is not a question of "such and such a man", but of "man as such."

12. It may be objected that the doctors were inspired by the Holy Spirit; without doubt, but this inspiration is conditioned in advance, if one may express it thus, for water takes on the colour of its recipient. The Holy Spirit excludes intrinsic error and error that is harmful to the soul, but not necessarily every error that is extrinsic and opportune, and thus in practice neutral as regards essential truth and salvation.

13. That is, he was married in his youth, while he was still *Boddhisatva* and not *Buddha*.

14. Visible forms manifest the heavenly essences by crystallizing them; music in a certain fashion interiorizes forms by recalling their essences by means of a language made of unitive sweetness and unlimitedness. Earthly beauty evokes in the soul the transforming "remembrance" of heavenly music, although with regard to this it may appear hard and dissonant: *"Qualunque melodia più dolce sona—qua giù, e più a sè l'anima tira,—parebbe nube che squarciata tona,—comparata al sonar di quella lira—onde si coronava il bel zaffiro—del quale il ciel più chiaro s'inzaffira."* (Dante, *Paradiso* XXIII, 97-102).

15. If woman is "of one flesh" with man—if she is "flesh of his flesh and bone of his bones"—this shows, in relation to the Spirit, which man represents, an aspect of continuity or prolongation, not of separation.

16. We are here in the realm of imponderables, but what is decisive is that the psychological differences between the sexes really exist, in a vertical or qualitative sense as well as in a horizontal or neutral sense. Perhaps one should add, in order to forestall easily foreseeable objections, that woman finds a means of manifesting her particular worldliness within the very framework of a *de facto* masculine worldliness; in other words, generally human weaknesses do not abolish the specific— but certainly not obligatory—weaknesses of the feminine sex. Finally, it is necessary to recall in this context that modern life ends in devirilizing men and defeminizing women, which is to the advantage of no one, since the process is contrary to nature and transfers or even accentuates faults instead of correcting them.

17. *Ave gratia plena*, said the angel to Mary. "Full of grace": this settles the question, given that Mary is a woman. The angel did not say *Ave Maria*, because for him *gratia plena* is the name that he gives to the Virgin; this amounts to saying that *Maria* is synonymous with *gratia plena*.

18. When it is said that *Samsara* is *Nirvana* and vice versa, this means that there is only *Nirvana* and that *Samsara* is its radiance, which is both centrifugal and centripetal, projecting and reabsorbing, creating and saving.

19. Lakshmi is a divine but already cosmic personification of *Prakriti*, the feminine pole of Being, of which she manifests the aspect of goodness, beauty and happiness.

20. Namely a damaging suspicion cast on the virtuous Lakshmana, who refused to go in search of Rama since his mission was to protect Sita; he finally obeyed, and this allowed Ravana to abduct the heroine.

21. The Ramayana, in relating the incident, states that the mind of a woman is "covered with clouds" when the interest of the beloved is at stake; her trust is "inconstant" and her tongue "venomous"; the compensatory quality being the love of her *alter ego*, and consequently the perfect gift of self. In another place, the Ramayana points out the gentle wisdom of the wife in contradistinction from the unreflecting anger of the warrior.

22. According to a well-known *hadith*, "marriage is half of the religion."

PART VI

THE SPIRITUAL LIFE

Elements and Goal of the Spiritual Path

Nature and Function of the Spiritual Master*

THERE IS A VEDANTIC NOTION which, being fundamental, can serve as a key in the most diverse realms, and this is the ternary *Sat, Chit, Ananda*: Being, Consciousness and Bliss. Here it will be applied to the spiritual master, not for any lack of other ways of approaching this subject, but because the Vedantic ternary provides in this connection a particularly appropriate means of access.

The master, in fact, represents and transmits, firstly a reality of being (*Sat*), secondly a reality of intelligence or truth (*Chit*), and thirdly a reality of love, union, or happiness (*Ananda*).

The element "being" which the master represents and transmits, and without which he would be as if deprived of reality and existence, is the religion to which he belongs and by which he is mandated, or the spiritual organization within the framework of this religion. The religion, or the esoteric cell which sums it up and offers us its essence, confers on man the "being" without which there is no concrete and efficacious way. The function of the founders of religion is *a priori* to give back to fallen man his primordial "being"; the first condition, then, of spirituality is to be virtually "reborn" and thus to realize the as it were ontological basis of the two constituent elements of the way, namely, discernment or doctrine on the one hand, and concentration or method on the other.

*From *SCR*, Spring, 1967, and *LT, Chapter 15.*

425

Representing *a priori* a "substance" or a "being," *Sat*, the spiritual master is *a posteriori*, and on this very basis, the vehicle of an " intellection" or of a "consciousness," *Chit*: by this is to be understood a providential doctrine which determines the flavour or style of every subsequent formulation. It is necessary to understand that this doctrine depends on a Revelation in the direct and plenary sense and that consequently its regular ramifications have a quality of absoluteness and infinitude which makes unnecessary any recourse to extraneous sources, although it is perfectly possible that formulations originating in such a source, to the extent that they are mentally compatible with the dogmatic or mythological system in question, may be extrinsically adopted by a given master and integrated into the perspective which he incarnates. Such was the case, notably, of the Neoplatonic concepts adopted by certain Sufis, or of Christianized Aristotelianism. It would be wrong to see syncretism in this, for the extraneous concepts are accepted only because they are assimilable, and they are only assimilable by reason of their inward concordance with the tradition in question, and because Truth is one. Another aspect of this question of intellectuality is infallibility: the master is in principle infallible with regard to the revealed doctrine which he represents, and which he even personifies by virtue of his "being" or "substance," of his *Sat*, so to say; but this infallibility, which is not unconnected with Grace, is conditioned by the equilibrium between knowledge and virtue, or between intellectuality and spirituality — one might even say, between intelligence and humility.

Thus, the spiritual master must realize the ternary "being," "discernment," "concentration." By "being" must be understood the "new substance" or "consecration," or "initiation"; by "discernment" is meant truth which distinguishes between the Real and the illusory, or between *Ātmā* and *Māyā*; and by "concentration" must be understood the method which allows the "initiated" and "consecrated" contemplative to fix himself, at first mentally and later with the centre of his being, on the Real, whose evidence we carry in ourselves. It is this fixation which, being a reality of union, and thus of "love" and of "bliss," corresponds analogically and operatively to the element *Ananda* in the Vedantic ternary.

The importance in spirituality of what we have called the existential element results from the principle that it is impossible to approach the Absolute, or the Self, without the blessing and the aid of Heaven: "No man cometh to the Father but by Me" (Christianity), and "no one will meet *Allāh* who has not met his Envoy" (Islam); "whosoever gathereth not with Me, disperseth," and "without Me you can do nothing" (Christianity); "and you cannot wish unless *Allāh* wishes" (Islam). This *conditio sine qua non*, the pivots of which are first and foremost the elements of "consecration" and "orthodoxy"— related respectively to *Sat* and *Chit* — explains why a spirituality deprived of its bases can only end up as a psychological exploit without any relation to the development of our higher states.

The profane man being "non-existent" from the point of view at issue here, the master gives him "spiritual existence" by affiliation or consecration; next he gives him the doctrine — or "intelligence"—, and finally he gives him "life," that is to say, the spiritual means referring to the element "concentration." Now this means, which is an engagement "to the death"— for in order to "live" inwardly, one must "die" outwardly — is essentially a gift from the master and from Heaven, for otherwise it would be lacking in the indispensable Grace. Doubtless there have been very exceptional cases in which other modalities have come into play, but this was always on behalf of persons whose sanctity guaranteed their purity of intention, and protected the spiritual means from any profanation.

In a word: we can only make use of a spiritual means on condition of a concrete and solemn engagement, recognizing thereby that Heaven disposes of us according to its good pleasure; and this engagement is irreversible — the way is one of no return.

•   •   •

Inasmuch as he is the guide of the personal way of the disciple — always within the general way laid down by divine authority through tradition — the spiritual master is as it were the continuation of the *ego* of the disciple. Every spiritual alchemy involves an anticipated death and consequently also certain losses of equilibrium, or periods of obscuration, in which the disciple is not fully master of himself; he is no longer completely of this world, nor yet completely of the other, and his experience seems to call in question all the existential categories of which, so to say, we are woven. In these "trials," and in the "temptations" which accompany them — for lower *maya*, or the downward quality (*tamas*), takes advantage of the slightest fissure — the spiritual master plays the role of "motionless centre": to the temptation of giving rational form to irrational troubles he opposes objective, immutable and incorruptible truth. The same is true in the case of temptations of inverse character, when the disciple, submerged by some contemplative state which surpasses his usual capacity — and such a state may only be accidental and does not prove any realization — may think that to some degree he has become superhuman. In this case, lower *maya* — or the devil, which here amounts to the same thing — will not fail to suggest to the disciple that he should declare himself master, or give way to some other pretension of this kind. The case is rather like that of a drunken man who no longer perceives the true proportions of things. The master, for his part, has realized "sober drunkenness," his human substance is adapted to his spiritual state, for mastership is precisely "keeping a cool head" — without any pretension, however — in the beatific experience. All that has been said shows clearly that faith is indispensable on the part of the disciple. Without faith there is no spiritual continuity, and thus no bridging of "hells," nor any possible victory over the *ego.* . . .

What has gone before clearly shows that spiritual mastership is a very special function and that it is consequently false to describe every teaching authority as a "spiritual master." The functions of "doctor" and "master" often coincide — but they may also not do so — in the same personage. The master does not necessarily write treatises, but he always possesses a sufficient doctrinal authority. . .

The Servant and Union*

Imām Abū-l-Hasan Ash-Shādhilī has said: 'Nothing removes man further from God than the desire for union with Him.' At first sight this statement may seem surprising coming from one who was one of the great promoters of esoterism in Islam; but everything becomes clear once it is understood that it refers to the ego and not to the pure Intellect. Indeed, the 'servant' (*'abd*) as such can never cease to be the servant; consequently he can never become the 'Lord' (*Rabb*). The 'servant-Lord' polarity is irreducible by its very nature,

*From *DI*, Chapter 3.

the nature of the servant or the creature being in a certain sense the sufficient reason for the Divine intervention under the aspect of Lord. Man cannot become 'God';[1] the servant cannot change into the Lord; but there is something in the servant that can — not without the Lord's grace — surpass the axis 'servant-Lord' or 'subject-object' and realize the absolute 'Self.' This Self is God in so far as He is independent of the 'servant-Lord' axis and of every other polarity: while the Lord is in a certain manner the object of the servant's intelligence and will — and inversely — the Self has no complementary opposite; It is pure Subject, that is to say It is Its own Object at once unique and infinite, and innumerable on the plane of a certain diversifying relativity. *Māyā*, which breaks up and diversifies both Subject and Object, is not opposed to the Self, of which it is simply the emanation or prolongation in illusory mode; and this mode proceeds from the very nature of the Self, which implies the possibility — through Its infinitude — of an 'unreal reality,' or conversely, of an 'existing nothingness.' The Self radiates even into nothingness and lends it, if one may provisionally expresss oneself in a more or less paradoxical manner, Its own Reality made of Being, Consciousness, and Life or Beatitude.[2]

The way of Union, then, by no means signifies that the servant as such unites himself to the Lord as such, or that man ends by identifying himself with God; it signifies that that something which in man — and beyond his individual outwardness — is already potentially and even virtually Divine, namely the pure Intellect, withdraws from the 'subject-object' complementarism and resides in its own transpersonal being, which, never entering into this complementarism, is no other than the Self. To the objection that the Self is the object of human intelligence, and that in consequence It fits perfectly into the 'subject-object' polarity, it must be answered that it is only the notion of the Self which is such an object, and that the existence of this notion proves precisely that there is in the human mind something which already is 'not other' than the Self; it is in virtue of this mysterious inward connection with the Self that we are able to conceive the latter objectively. If this something *increatum et increabile* were not within us, it would never be possible for us to escape, at the centre of our being, from the 'servant-Lord' polarity.

Monotheistic theology, like the doctrine of the *bhaktas*, is in fact strictly bound up with this polarity; it cannot therefore surpass it, and for this reason the Intellect will always be reduced for it to an aspect of the servant. Its general and as it were 'collective' language cannot be that of sapiential esoterism, any more in the East than in the West. In the Christian climate, the Self is conceivable only within the framework of a 'theosophy'; that is to say, it is the element of *sophia* which indicates emergence from the domain of polarities and the surpassing of the latter. As for Moslems, they will say, not that the Intellect (*'Aql*) is 'uncreated' in its essence, but that the Divine Intellect (*'Ilm*, 'Science') takes possession of — or replaces — the human Intellect, which amounts to the same thing metaphysically; and this mode of expression is in conformity with the Divine *hadīth* according to which 'I (Allāh) will be the ear by which he shall hear, the sight by which he shall see. . .'

It follows from what has been said above that it would be completely wrong to speak of the Lord 'and' the Self, for God is One. If we speak of the Self, there is neither servant nor Lord, there is but the Self alone, possible modes of which are the Lord and the servant — or what are so called from a certain standpoint; and if we speak of the Lord, there is no Self in particular or different from the Lord; the Self is the essence of the Lord of the worlds. The Attributes of the Lord (*Sifāt*, in Arabic) concern the servant as such, but the Essence (*Dhāt*) does not.

From this it follows that man can speak to the Lord, but not realize Him, and that he can realize the Essence or Self, but not speak to It. With regard to the Self, there is no opposite nor interlocutor, for the Self or Essence, let it be repeated, is entirely outside the axis 'Creator-creature' or 'Principle-manifestation,' although in this relationship It is present within the Creator; but It does not then concern us as creatures or servants, and we are unable to attain It on the plane of this polarity, if we except the possibility of conceiving It, a possibility accorded by the Lord by virtue of the universal nature of our intelligence, and also by virtue of the universality of the Self. In other words, if we are able to attain the Self outside the said polarity, it is solely by the Will of the Lord and with His help; the Self cannot be realized in defiance of the Lord or in defiance of the 'Lord-servant' relationship. To put it in another way: although the object of unitive realization is the superontological Essence, and not the Lord, it cannot be effected without the Lord's blessing; and though the true subject of that union is the supra-personal Intellect, and not the servant, it cannot be brought about without the servant's participation.

The ego, which is 'accident,' is extinguished—or becomes absolute 'itself'—in the Self, which is 'substance.' The Way is the withdrawal of the intelligence into its pure 'Substance,' which is pure Being, pure Consciousness, and pure Beatitude.

The subject of the realization of the Self is strictly speaking the Self Itself: that is to say, the Essence of the servant 'rejoins' the Essence of the Lord by a cosmic detour, through the operation of a sort of 'Divine respiration'; it is in this sense that it has been said that 'the Sufi is not created,' and again that the process of union (*tawhīd*) is 'a message from Him by Him.'[3] Realization of the Essence or Self is not so much effected from the starting point of the servant as through the latter; it is effected from God to God through man, and this is possible because, in the perspective of the Self—which has no opposite and of which *Māyā* is an emanation or a 'descent'—man himself is a manifestation of the Self and not a sort of contrary situated on a separative axis. 'There are paths going from God to men'—states Abū Bakr As-Ṣaydalānī—'but there is no path from man reaching to God': this means, not only that the servant is unable to attain the Lord, but also that the path of Union is not of the making of the servant as such.[4] On the other hand, when Abū Bakr Ash-Shiblī affirms that 'in the realization of God (of the Essence) there is a beginning to be savoured but not an end,' he is referring, on the one hand, to the irruption of Grace such as it is experienced by the servant, and on the other to the Essence, which is Itself infinite and consequently has no common measure with the initial and fragmentary experience of man.[5]

It has been stated that from the standpoint of the Self there is no confrontation between a Principle and a manifestation, there is nothing but the Self alone, the pure and absolute Subject which is its own Object. But, it will be asked, what then becomes of the world that we still cannot help perceiving? This question has to some extent already been answered, but it may perhaps be useful to enlarge upon this crucial point: the world is *Ātmā*—the Self—in the guise of *Māyā*; more especially it is *Māyā* in so far as the latter is distinct from *Ātmā*, that goes without saying, for otherwise the verbal distinction would not exist; but whilst being *Maya*, it is implicitly—and necessarily—*Ātmā*, in rather the same way that ice is water or is 'not other' than water. In the Self, in the direct or absolute sense, there is no trace of *Māyā*—save the dimension of infinitude that has been referred to and from which *Māyā* indirectly proceeds—but at the

degree of *Māyā*, the latter is 'not other' than the Self; [6] it is not the
servant, since the polarities are surpassed. *Maya* is the reverberation of the Self in the direction of nothingness,[7] or the totality of the
reverberations of the Self; the innumerable relative subjects 'are' the
Self under the aspect of 'Consciousness' (*Chit*), and the innumerable
relative objects are once again the Self, but this time under the aspect
of 'Being' (*Sat*). Their reciprocal relationships — or their 'common
life'— constitute 'Beatitude' (*Ānanda*), in manifested mode, of course;
this is made up of everything in the world which is expansion, enjoyment or movement.

     According to the 'servant-Lord' perspective, as has been stated
above, the Essence is implicitly 'contained' in the ontological Principle
— whence the infinite Majesty of the latter[8] — but this is the mystery
of all mysteries and in no way concerns us. In order to illustrate more
clearly the diverse angles of vision comprised in the science of the
supernatural, this perspective of discontinuity or separativity may
be represented by a system of concentric circles — or of polygons, if
preferred[9] — which are so many isolated images of the centre. We
have seen that according to the perspective of the Self, everything
'is' the Essence, and that if none the less we establish a distinction
on this plane — as our existence obliges us to do — it is between the
Essence as such and the Essence as 'me' or 'world.'[10] This is the perspective of continuity, of universal homogeneity or immanence,
represented by such figures as the cross, the star, the spiral; in these
figures the periphery is attached to the centre, or rather, the whole
figure is simply an extension or a development of the latter; the whole
figure is the centre, if one may so put it, whereas in the figures with
discontinuous elements the centre is to all intents nowhere, since
it is without extent.

     What, then, is the practical consequence of these affirmations
so far as our spiritual finality is concerned? Just this: if we consider
the total Universe under the relationship of separativity, according
to the 'Creator creature' axis, no union is possible, unless it be a union
of 'grace' which safeguards or maintains the duality; but if we consider the Universe under the relationship of the unity of the Essence
or Reality, that is to say from the standpoint of the homogeneity and
indivisibility of the Self, union is possible, since it 'exists' *a priori* and
the separation is only an illusory 'fissure'; it is this 'fissure' that is
the mystery, not the union;[11] but it is a negative and transitory
mystery, an enigma which is only an enigma from its own stand-

point and within the limits of its subjectivity; it can be resolved intellectually and, for still stronger reasons, ontologically.[12]

Since Paradise affords perfect beatitude, it may be asked how and why anyone could desire something else and something more, namely a realization that transcends the created and reintegrates the individual accident in the Universal Substance. To this objection, which is justifiable in certain psychological cases, the reply is that it is not a question of choosing this and scorning that, but of following our spiritual nature such as God has willed it, or in other words, of following Grace in the manner in which it concerns us. The true metaphysician cannot but accept the consequences implied by the scope of his intelligence; which is to say that man follows what is imprescriptible in his 'supernatural nature' with the help of God, but man as servant will take what the Lord grants him. True, the Sufis have not hesitated to qualify Paradise as a 'prison' and to make use of other metaphors of the kind in order to underline the absolute transcen dence of the supreme Union, but they have also called that Union 'Paradise of the Essence,' an expression which has the advantage of conforming to scriptural symbolism; the word 'Paradise' or 'Garden' then becomes synonymous with 'supernatural beatitude,' and if on the one hand it specifies no degree of reality, it also implies no limitation.

The objection mentioned above might equally well be countered by the assertion that it is impossible to assign limits to the love of God; it is therefore unreasonable to ask why a given soul, possessing the intuition of the Essence, tends towards the Reality which it senses through the existential darkness. Such a question is devoid of meaning, not only in relation to the 'naturally supernatural' aspirations of the gnostic, but also on the plane of the affective mystic, where the soul aspires to everything it can conceive above itself, and not to anything less. It is obviously absurd to want to impose limits upon knowledge; the retina of the eye catches the rays of infinitely distant stars, it does so without passion or pretension, and no one has the right or the power to hinder it.

NOTES

The Servant and Union

1. If formulations of this sort are nevertheless encountered here and there, they are elliptical and are not intended to be taken literally. When St Irenaeus speaks of 'becoming God' he understands thereby the Essence, or in other words he places himself intellectually outside the polarity in question; no doubt he understands also, and perhaps even *a priori*, a union that is indirect or virtual, but which is already a kind of participation in the supreme Union, at least according to the perspective that concerns us here.

2. This is the Vedantine ternary *Sat, Chit, Ananda*. By 'Being' we mean here, not the sole ontological Principle — which is *Ishvara* and not *Sat* — but the preontological Reality which is the complementary opposite of the pole 'Knowing' (*Chit*). For *Chit* the Sufis would say '*Ilm* ('Science') or *Shuhud* ('Perception'), the second term being the equivalent of the Vedantine *Sākshin* ('Witness'); for *Sat* they would say *Wujūd* ('Reality'), and for *Ananda, Hayāt* ('Life') or *Irādah* ('Will,' or 'Desire').

3. Dhū 'n-Nūn Al-Miṣrī: 'True knowledge is knowledge of the Truth through the Truth, as the sun is known through the sun itself.'—'The true knower (*'ārif*) exists not in himself, but by God and for God.'—'The end of knowledge is that man comes to the point where he was at the origin.' Bāyazīd: 'He who knows God by God becomes immortal.'

4. Al-Junayd: 'The Sufi is someone who becomes without (personal) attributes and meets God.'

5. Bāyazīd: 'The knower receives from God, as reward, God himself.'—'Whosoever enters into God, attains the truth of all things and becomes himself the Truth (*Al-Haqq* = God); it is not cause for surprise that he then sees in himself, and as if it were him, everything that exists outside God.'— Similarly Shankaracharya: 'The Yogi, whose intelligence is perfect, contemplates all things as dwelling in himself, and thus he perceives by the eye of Knowledge, that everything is *Atmā*.'

6. It is in this sense that it is said in the *Mahāyāna* that *Samsāra* 'is' *Nirvāna*.

7. Nothingness cannot exist, but the 'direction towards' nothingness exists, and indeed this observation is fundamental in metaphysics.

8. The 'Personal God' is in fact none other than the personification of the Essence.

9. In this case, the dimensions or constitutive structures of the worlds and microcosms will be taken into account, not just their existence.

10. Pantheism is the error of introducing the nature of *Atmā-Māyā* into the 'Lord-servant' polarity, or of denying that polarity on the very plane where it is real.

11. For the Vedantists, *Māyā* is in a sense more mysterious — or less obvious — than *Atma*.

12. The intellectual solution being the notion of contradictory or privative possibility, such possibility being necessarily included in the All-Possibility, or in the very nature of Infinitude. It would be absurd to object that this notion is insufficient, since anything more adequate is of the order of 'being,' not of 'thinking.'

Prayer

Modes of Prayer*

THE MOST ELEMENTARY mode of prayer—of contact between man and God —is no doubt prayer in the most ordinary sense of the word, for this is the direct expression of the individual, of his desires and fears, his hopes and gratitude. This prayer is however less perfect than canonical prayer which, for its part, has a universal character due to the fact that God is its author and that the subject, in reciting it, does so not as a particular individual, but in his capacity as man, the human species; also this prayer contains nothing which does not concern man—every man—and this is as much as to say it includes, 'eminently' or in addition, all possible individual prayers; it can even render them superfluous, and, in fact, the Revelations permit or recommend individual prayer, but do not impose it. Canonical prayer shows its universality and its timeless value by being very often expressed in the first person plural, and also by its preference for using a sacred or liturgical, and therefore symbolically universal, language, so that it is impossible for whoever recites it not to pray for all and in all.

As to individual prayer, grounds for its existence are incontestably to be found in our nature, since individuals do in fact differ from one another and have different destinies and desires.[1] The

---

*From *SW*, Chapter 5.

aim of this prayer is not only to obtain particular favours, but also the purification of the soul: it loosens psychological knots or, in other words, dissolves subconscious coagulations and drains away many secret poisons; it externalises before God the difficulties, failures and distortions of the soul, always supposing the prayer to be humble and genuine, and this externalisation — carried out in relation to the Absolute — has the virtue of re-establishing equilibrium and restoring peace, in a word, of opening us to grace. All this is offered us equally and *a fortiori* by canonical prayer, but the human spirit is in general too weak to extract from it all the remedies to be found there.

The personal character of non-canonical prayer does not imply that it is free from rules, for human souls — as the Psalms admirably show — are always alike in their miseries and joys, and therefore in their duties towards God; it is not enough for a man to formulate his petition, he must express also his gratitude, resignation, regret, resolution and praise. In his petition, man is concerned to look for some favour, provided it be of a nature agreeable to God, and so to the universal Norm; thankfulness is the consciousness that every favour of destiny is a grace which might not have been given; and if it be true that man has always something to ask, it is just as true, to say the least, that he has always grounds for gratitude; without this, no prayer is possible. Resignation is the acceptance in advance of the non-fulfilment of some request; regret or contrition — the asking of pardon — implies consciousness of what puts us in opposition to the divine Will; resolution is the desire to remedy some transgression, for our weakness must not make us forget that we are free;[2] finally, praise signifies not only that we relate every value to its ultimate Source, but also that we see every trial in terms of its necessity or its usefulness, or in its aspect of fatality and of grace. If petition is a capital element of prayer, it is because we can do nothing without the help of God; man's resolves offer no guarantee — the example of St. Peter shows this — if he does not ask this help.

•   •   •

Another mode of prayer is meditation; the contact between man and God here becomes one between the intelligence and Truth, or relative truths contemplated as approaches to the Absolute. There is a certain exterior analogy between meditation and individual prayer in that man formulates his thought spontaneously in both cases; the difference, which is infinitely more important, is that meditation is objective and intellectual — unless it is a question of imaginative, even sentimental, reflections, which are not what we have in mind here — while prayer is subjective and volitive. In meditation, the aim is knowledge, hence a reality which in principle goes beyond the *ego* as such; the thinking subject is then, strictly speaking, the impersonal intelligence, hence man and God at the same time, pure intelligence being the point of intersection between the human reason and the divine Intellect.

Meditation acts on the one hand on the intelligence, in which it 'awakens' certain consubstantial 'memories,' and on the other on the subconscious imagination which ends by incorporating in itself the truths meditated, resulting in a fundamental and as it were organic process of persuasion. Experience proves that one man can do great things even in unfavourable circumstances, provided that he believes himself capable of accomplishing them, while another, more gifted perhaps, but doubting himself, will do nothing even in favourable conditions; man walks fearlessly on flat ground, but imagination may prevent him taking a single step when he has to pass between two chasms. From this one sees the importance of meditation even simply from the point of view of auto-suggestion; in the spiritual life, as in other fields, it is a precious help to be deeply persauded both as to the things towards which we are tending, and also of our capacity to attain them, with the help of God.

Meditation — as defined in the language of the Vedanta — is essentially 'investigation' (*vichara*) leading to the assimilation of theoretical truth, and then discrimination (*viveka*) between the Real and the unreal; there are two levels in it, one ontological and dualist, and the other centred on Beyond-Being or the Self, and consequently non-dualist; here lies the whole difference between *bhakti* and *jnana*.

Pure concentration also is a prayer, on condition that it has a traditional basis and is centred on the Divine; this concentration is none other than silence which, indeed, has been called a 'Name of Buddha' thanks to its connection with the idea of the Void.[3]

• • •

We have distinguished canonical prayer from individual prayer by saying that in the latter it is some individual who is the subject, while in the former the subject is man as such; but there is a prayer where God himself is in a sense the Subject, and that is the pronouncing of a revealed divine Name. The foundation of this mystery is, on the one hand, that 'God and his Name are one' (Ramakrishna), and on the other, that God Himself pronounces His Name in Himself, hence in eternity and outside of all creation, so that His unique and uncreated Word is the prototype of jaculatory prayer and even, in a less direct sense, of all prayer. The first distinction that the intellect conceives in the Divine Nature is that of Beyond-Being and Being; but since Being is so to speak the 'crystallisation' of Beyond-Being, it is like the 'Word' of the Absolute, in which the latter expresses Itself, determines Itself, or names Itself. Another distinction which is essential here and which derives from the preceding by principial succession, is that between God and the world, the Creator and the creation: just as Being is the Word or Name of Beyond-Being, so too the world — or Existence — is the Utterance of Being, of the 'personal God'; the effect is always the 'name' of the cause.

But while God, in naming Himself, firstly determines Himself as Being and secondly, starting from Being, manifests Himself as Creation — that is to say that He manifests Himself 'within the framework of nothingness' or 'outside of Himself,' and so 'in illusory mode'[4] — man, for his part, describes the inverse movement when he pronounces the same Name, for this Name is not only Being and Creation, but also Mercy and Redemption; in man, It does not create, but on the contrary 'undoes,' and that in a divine manner since It brings man back to the Principle. The divine Name is a metaphysical isthmus (in the sense of the Arabic word *barzakh*): as 'seen by God,' it is determination, limitation, 'sacrifice'; as seen by man, it is liberation, limitlessness, plenitude. We have said that this Name, invoked by man, is none the less always pronounced by God; human invocation is only the 'external' effect of eternal and 'internal' invocation by the Divinity. The same holds good for every other Revelation: it is sacrificial for the divine Spirit and liberating for man; Revelation, whatever may be its form or mode, is 'descent' or 'incarnation' for the Creator, and 'ascent' or 'ex-carnation' for the creature.[5]

The sufficient reason for the invocation of the Name lies in its being the 'remembering of God'; and this, in the last analysis, is consciousness of the Absolute. The Name actualises this consciousness and, in the end, perpetuates it in the soul and fixes it in the heart, so that it penetrates the whole being and at the same time transmutes and absorbs it. Consciousness of the Absolute is the prerogative of the human intelligence, and also its aim.

Again: we are united to the One by our being, by our pure consciousness and by the symbol. It is by the symbol — the Word — that man, in central and quintessential prayer, realises both Being and Consciousness, the latter in the former and conversely. The perfection of Being, which is Extinction, is prefigured by deep sleep, and also, in other ways, by beauty and virtue; the perfection of Consciousness, which is Identity — or Union, if this term be preferred — is prefigured by concentration, and also, *a priori*, by intelligence and contemplation. Beauty does not, of course, produce virtue but it favours in a certain way a pre-existing virtue; equally, intelligence does not produce contemplation, but it broadens or deepens a contemplation that is natural. Being is passive perfection and Consciousness active perfection. 'I sleep, but my heart waketh.'

Why is it that Being is 'Word' or 'Name'[6] rather than 'Thought,' 'Act' or 'Sacrifice,' and why is it that jaculatory prayer also is not thought, act, sacrifice, and so on? First it is quite true that Being has all these aspects, and many others as well; these aspects are to be found in every Revelation. None the less, speech on the one hand realises all possible aspects of affirmation, and on the other has a kind of pre-eminence from the fact that it is the feature which most notably distinguishes man from animals. Speech implies thought, since it is its exteriorisation, but thought does not imply speech; similarly, speech, while itself an act, adds to action a new dimension of intelligibility. Likewise again, speech has an aspect of sacrifice in the sense that it limits what it expresses; and as for jaculatory prayer — which being speech, is at the same time thought, act and sacrifice — it includes yet another aspect of sacrifice or asceticism from the fact that it excludes all other preoccupation of the heart and thereby is a 'poverty' or a *vacare Deo*. Or again, man, at the moment of birth, manifests his voice before any other faculty, and this cry is already, though doubtless unconsciously, a prayer, as being a prefiguration or a symbol; likewise for the last gasp of the dying man, or his last breath, since voice and breath refer to the same symbolism.

Every normal activity, needless to say, reflects in its way the eternal Act of God: thus a weaver could say that Being is the first divine 'fabric,' in the sense that Beyond-Being weaves in it the principial possibilities — the 'divine Names'— and that Being in its turn weaves manifestations in Existence, hence angels, worlds, beings;[7] not every man is a weaver, however, but every man speaks, which shows clearly that speech has priority over secondary and more or less 'accidental' activities; these are too external to be assimilable to 'prayers,' but they can be the vehicle of prayer by virtue of their symbolical quality.[8] In other words, any kind of occupation, whether a craft or otherwise, provided that it is 'natural,' can be a spiritual support not only thanks to the symbolism inherent in it, which would not suffice by itself, but above all by virtue of the contemplative prayer superimposed on it, which actualises the value of the symbol.

• • •

The principle according to which 'prayer of the heart' can replace all other rites — on condition of sufficient spiritual maturity — is to be found in Hesychasm, but is much more emphasised in the Hindu and Buddhist ways, where the abandonment of general ritual prayers and practices is considered normal and sometimes even a *sine qua non* of such prayer. The profound reason for this is that it is necessary to distinguish between the realm of the 'divine Will' and that of the 'divine Nature'; the latter 'is what it is' and is expressed by the Name alone, while the former projects into the human world differentiated — and necessarily relative — wills and is expressed by complex prayers, corresponding to the complexity of human nature.[9] Rites, however — especially those of a purifying or sacramental character — can be considered as necessary aids to support prayer of the heart; this belongs to a point of view deriving from a perspective differing from the one just envisaged, and better suited to certain temperaments.

We should doubtless hesitate to speak of these things if others — Europeans as well as Asiatics — did not speak of them, and if we were not living at a time when all sorts of testimonies are demanded and when the compensating Mercy simplifies many things, though this cannot mean that everything will become easily accessible. It is obvious that a spiritual means has significance only within the rules assigned to it by the tradition which offers it, whether it is a question of external or of internal rules; nothing is more dangerous than to give oneself up to 'improvisations' in this field. This reservation will not fail to surprise those who hold that man is free in all respects before God, and who will ask by what right we seek to subject prayer to conditions and to enclose it within frameworks; the reply is simple, and it is the Bible itself which gives it: 'Thou shalt not take the name of the Lord thy God in vain; for the Lord thy God will not acquit him that takes his name in vain' (Exod. xx, 7; Deut. v, II). Man is *a priori* 'vain' according to certain spiritual criteria, those precisely which apply when it is a question of direct 'mystagogic' methods; man then is not absolutely free, apart from the fact that absolute Liberty belongs to God alone. That alone has value for salvation which is given by Him, not that which is taken by man; it is God who has revealed His Names, and it is He who determines their usage; and if, according to the Apostle 'whosoever shall eat this (divine) bread...unworthily...eateth...damnation to himself' (I Cor. xi, 27-29), the same holds good for the presumptuous use of jaculatory prayers.

If this be admitted, we can return to the positive side of the question: in whatever degree it may be opportune, according to circumstances and surroundings, jaculatory prayer meets these two requirements of prayer: perfection and continuity. 'Pray without ceasing' says the Apostle (I Thess. v, 17),[10] and 'Likewise the Spirit also helpeth our infirmities: for we know not what we should pray for as we ought: but the Spirit itself maketh intercession for us with groanings which cannot be uttered' (Rom. viii, 26).[11]

• • •

The Divine Names have significations which are particular because belonging to a revealed language and also universal because referring to the supreme Principle. To invoke a Divinity is to enunciate a doctrine: he who says 'Jesus', says implicitly that 'Christ is God',[12] which signifies that God 'came down' in order that man should be able to 'ascend'; [13] moreover, to say that 'God was made man' signifies at the same time that man is fallen, since the justification for the Divine descent is the fact that man exists 'below'; God 'takes on flesh' because man is 'flesh', and this is fall, passion, misery. The starting-point of Christianity is the volitional aspect of man; it is grafted, so to speak, not on the fundamentally theomorphic properties of our nature, but on the 'accident'— an accident practically decisive for the majority—of our fall; but starting from this point of view—and this is of capital importance—the Christian tradition can give access to gnosis and thus rejoin the perspectives founded on the intellectual theomorphism of the human being, and this it owes to the evident—and dazzling—analogy between Christ and the Intellect, as equally to the idea of 'deification' deriving from it.

To say that 'God became man in order that man might become God'[14] means in the final analysis—if we want to pursue this reciprocity to its ultimate foundations—that Reality has entered into nothingness, so that nothingness might become real. If it be objected here that nothingness, being nothing, can play no part, the answer lies in two questions: how is the existence of the very idea of nothingness to be explained? How is it that there is a 'nothing' on the level of relativities and in everyday experience? Nothingness certainly has neither being nor existence, but it is none the less a kind of metaphysical 'direction', something we can conceive and pursue, but never attain; 'evil' is none other than 'nothingness manifested' or 'the impossible made possible.' Evil never lives from its own substance, which is non-existent, but it corrodes or perverts the good, just as disease could not exist without the body which it tends to destroy; evil, says St Thomas, is there to allow the coming of a greater good, and in fact qualities have need of corresponding privations to enable them to be affirmed distinctively and separately.

But in Christianity reciprocity has first of all a meaning of love, witness its solicitude in regard to efficacy for salvation: the Name of Christ signifies that God loved the world, that the world might love God; and since God loves the world, man must love his neighbour, thus repeating on the human plane God's love for the world. Likewise, man must 'lose his life' because God sacrificed Himself for him;[15] the cross is the instrument and the symbol of this sacrificial meeting, it is as it were the point of intersection between the human and the Divine. Christianity presents itself above all as a volitive reciprocity between Heaven and earth, not as an intellective discrimination between Absolute and relative; but this discrimination is none the less implicit in the reciprocity as such, so that the Christian perspective could not exclude it: the Subject makes itself object in order that the object should become Subject, which is the very definition of the mystery of knowledge. Gnosis is based—'organically' and not artificially—on the polyvalent symbolism of the Incarnation and the Redemption, which implies that such a 'symbiosis' is in the nature of things and consequently within 'the divine intention'.

The Name of Christ is 'Truth' and 'Mercy'; all the same, this second quality is crystallised in a particular fashion in the Name of the Virgin, so that the two Names appear like a polarisation of the divine Light, Christ is 'Truth and Power' and the Virgin, 'Mercy and Purity'[16] . . .

• • •

Prayer implies an inner alternative, a choice between an imperfection arising from our nature, and the 'memory of God', which is perfection by reason of its prime mover as well as of its object. If this alternative is above all an inner one — otherwise we should have no right to any external action — it is because prayer can be superimposed on any legitimate action; likewise, if the alternative is relative and not absolute — otherwise we should have no right to any thought outside of prayer — it is because prayer if it cannot be superimposed on every beautiful or useful thought, can at least continue to vibrate during the passage of such a thought; and then mental articulation, although in practice excluding prayer (to the extent that the mind cannot do two things at once), nevertheless does not interrupt the 'remembrance' in the eyes of God. In other words, just as prayer cannot be superimposed on a base or illicit action, so the fragrance of prayer cannot survive a thought opposed to the virtues; further, it is obvious that the vibration of prayer in the absence of its articulation — when the mind is engaged elsewhere — presupposes a habit of prayer in the subject, for there is no scent without a flower; it presupposes also the intention to persevere in prayer and to intensify it; it is thus that the 'past' and the 'future', the acquired and the intended, participate in the inarticulate continuity of prayer.

Life is not, as children and worldly people believe, a kind of space filled with possibilities offering themselves to our good pleasure; it is a road which runs, getting ever shorter, from the present moment to death. At the end of this road there is death and the encounter with God, then eternity; but all these realities are already present in prayer, in the timeless actuality of the divine Presence.

What matters, for man, is not the diversity of the events he may experience as they stretch out along the magic thread we call duration, but perseverance in this 'remembrance' which takes us outside time and raises us above our hopes and our fears. This remembrance already dwells in eternity; here the succession of actions is only illusory, prayer being one; it is, thereby, already a death, a meeting with God, an eternity of blessedness.

What is the world if not the outflowing of forms, and what is life if not a bowl which seemingly is emptied between one night and another? And what is prayer, if not the sole stable point — a point of peace and of light — in this dream universe, and the strait gate leading to all that the world and life have sought in vain? In the life of a man, these four certitudes are all; the present moment, death, the encounter with God, eternity. Death is an exit, a world which closes down; the meeting with God is like an opening towards a flashing and immutable infinitude; eternity is a fullness of being in pure light; and the present moment is, in our duration, an almost unseizable 'place' where we are already eternal — a drop of eternity amid the ceaseless shiftings of forms and melodies. Prayer gives to the terrestrial instant its full weight of the eternal and its divine value; it is the sacred ship bearing its load, through life and death, towards the further shore, towards the silence of light — but at bottom it is not prayer which traverses time as it repeats itself, it is time which, so to speak, halts before this oneness of prayer which belongs already to heaven.

Prayer Fashions Man*

To think of God. In the mind the divine presence is like snow; in the heart — inasmuch as it is the existential essence — it is like fire. Freshness, purity, peace; warmth, love, bliss. The lily and the rose.

The divine presence penetrates the soul — the existential ego, not thought in itself — like a gentle heat, it pierces the heart — inasmuch as it is the centre of intellect — like an arrow of light.

Prayer — in the widest sense — triumphs over the four accidents of our existence: the world, life, the body and the soul; or we might also say: space, time, matter and desire. It is situated in existence

*From *SPHF*, pp. 212-213.

like a shelter, like an islet. In it alone are we perfectly ourselves, because it puts us into the presence of God. It is like a miraculous diamond which nothing can tarnish and nothing can resist.

Man prays and prayer fashions man. The saint has himself become prayer, the meeting-place of earth and Heaven; and thus he contains the universe and the universe prays with him. He is everywhere where nature prays and he prays with and in her: in the peaks which touch the void and eternity, in a flower which scatters itself or in the abandoned song of a bird.

He who lives in prayer has not lived in vain.

NOTES

Modes of Prayer

1. With the *Avataras* every personal prayer becomes polyvalent and canonical, as is shown by the Psalms for example; but these great Messengers give us at the same time the pattern of spontaneous prayer, since they but rarely repeat the prayers of others, and in any case show us that canonical prayer must be said with spontaneity, as if it were the first or the last prayer of our life.

2. Logically, regret and resolution are inseparable, but a regret can be conceived without resolution, and this is tepidness or despair, as also a resolution without regret, and this is pride, unless it is based on wisdom. It is not a question here primarily of sentimentality, but of attitudes of the will, whether or not these are accompanied by feelings.

3. *Shunyamurti*, 'Manifestation of the Void,' is one of the Names of Buddha. The silent prayer of the North American Indians, which presupposes a symbolist outlook and the framework of virgin nature, offers striking analogies with Zen.

4. In the Torah, God says to Moses: 'I am that I am' (*Eheieh asher Eheieh*); this refers to God as Being, for it is only as Being that God creates, speaks and legislates, since the world exists only in relation to Being. In the Koran, this same utterance is rendered as follows: 'I am God' (*Ana 'Llah*); this means that Being (*Ana*, 'I') derives from Beyond-Being (*Allah*, this Name designating the Divinity in all Its aspects without any restriction); it is thus that the Koranic formula refers to the divine Prototype of the pronouncing of the Name of God. *Ana 'Llah* signifies implicitly that 'God and his Name are one'—since Being 'is' Beyond-Being inasmuch as it is its 'Name'—and for the same reason the 'Son' is God, while not being the 'Father.' What gives its metaphysical force to the Hebraic formula is the return of 'being' on itself; and what gives its force to the Arabic formula is the juxtaposition, without copula, of 'subject' and 'object.'

5. In Japanese Amidic Buddhism, there have been controversies over the question whether invocations of the Buddha must be innumerable or whether on the contrary one single invocation suffices for salvation, the sole condition being, in both cases, a perfect faith and, as a corollary, abstention from evil, or the sincere intention so to abstain. In the first case, invocation is envisaged from the human side, that is from the angle of duration, whilst in the second case, it is conceived in its principial, hence its divine and therefore timeless reality; the *Jodo-Shinshu*, as also the Hindu *Japa-Yoga*, combines both perspectives.

6. Meister Eckhart says in his commentary on the Gospel of St John that 'the Father neither sees, nor hears,nor speaks, nor wishes anything but His own Name. It is by means of His Name that the Father sees, hears and manifests Himself. The Name contains all things. Essence of the Divinity, it is the Father Himself. The Father gives thee His eternal Name, and it is His own life, His being and His divinity that He gives thee in one single instant by His Name.'

7. It is this second proposition which the artisan will adopt in fact, the first belonging to the province of pure metaphysics, and not necessarily entering into the outlook of craft initiations, which have a cosmological basis.

8. It is thus that it is necessary to understand every fundamental and naturally 'ritual' activity, the gesture of the sower for example, or the work of the mason; is not God He who sows the cosmic possibilities in the *Materia prima* and, in the soul, the truths and graces, and is He not the 'Great Architect of the Universe'?

9. Here lies the whole difference between form and essence, which penetrates every domain. If 'in the resurrection they neither marry, nor are given in marriage', this relates to mode or form, not to essence; if on the other hand Paradise shelters *houris*, this relates to essence and not to mode; and it is in relation to essence that St Bernard could speak of 'torrents of voluptuous delight'.

10. Basing himself on the Gospel: 'And he spake a parable unto them to this end, that men ought always to pray, and not to faint' (Luke xviii, 1); 'Watch ye therefore, and pray always, that ye may be accounted worthy to escape all these things...' (Luke xxi, 36). St Bernardino of Sienna says in a sermon that 'the name (of Jesus) is origin without origin' and that it is 'as worthy of praise as God himself'; and again: 'Everything which God has created for the salvation of the world is hidden in this Name of Jesus' (San Bernardino da Sienna: *Le Prediche Volgari*). It is not by chance that Bernardino gave to his cypher of the Name of Jesus the appearance of a monstrance: the divine Name, carried in thought and in the heart, through the world and through life, is like the Holy Sacrament carried in procession. This cypher of the Greek letters I H S, signifying *Iesouss*, but interpreted in Latin as *In Hoc Signo* or as *Jesus Hominum Salvator* and often written in Gothic letters, can be analysed in its primitive form into three elements — a vertical straight line, two vertical lines linked together, and a curved line — and thus contains a symbolism at once metaphysical, cosmological and mystical; there is in it a remarkable anology, not only with the name *Allah* written in Arabic, which equally comprises the three lines of which we have just spoken (in the form of the *alif*, the two *lam* and the *ha*), but also with the Sanskrit monosyllable *Aum*, which is composed of three *matras* (A U M) indicating a 'rolling up' and thereby a return to the Centre. All these symbols mark, in a certain sense, the passage from 'coagulation' to 'solution'.

11. 'At all times let us invoke Him, the object of our meditations, in order that our mind may always be absorbed in Him, and our attention concentrated on Him daily' (Nicholas Cabasilas: *Life in Jesus Christ*). What the invocation of the divine Name is in relation to other prayers, the Eucharist is for the other sacraments: 'One receives the Eucharist last, precisely because one can go no further, add nothing to it: for clearly the first term implies the second, and this the last. Now, after the Eucharist there is nothing further towards which one could tend: a stop must be made there, and thought given to the means of keeping, to the end, the good acquired' (ibid.).

12. That is to say 'Christ alone is God'— not: 'God is Christ'— just as the sun alone is 'our sun', that of our planetary system. We need not here return to the question — practically non-existent as it is for the vast majority of ancient and even modern Christians — of knowing where the bounds of the 'planetary system' which is Christianity are drawn; this involves the whole problem of the refraction of the celestial in the terrestrial, or more precisely of the concordance between the divine light and different human receptacles.

13. And because the Absolute has entered into man, into space, into time, the world and history have become as if absolute, whence the danger of an anti-metaphysical conception of the 'real', or the temptation of involving God — the Absolute that has become in a sense human or historical — in the 'current of forms'. This is not unconnected with a theological 'personalism' which would seek to substitute the humanised Divine for the Divine-in-itself, as It reveals itself to pure Intellect. When we say 'absolute' in speaking of the Word or of Being, it is not through failing to recognise that these aspects belong metaphysically to the relative realm, of which they mark the summit *in divinis*, but because, in relation to the cosmos, every aspect of God is absolute.

14. For example St Irenaeus: 'Thanks to His boundless love, God made Himself what we are, in order to make us what He is.'

15. In the Eucharistic rite, man eats or drinks God in order to be eaten or drunk by Him; the 'elect of the elect' are those who drink and are consumed in a divine wine where there is no more 'Thee' or 'Me'

16. In many icons the Holy Virgin expresses mercy by the inclined and spiral-like movement of her attitude, while the severity of her facial expression indicates purity in its aspect of inviolability; other icons express solely this purity, emphasising the severity of the features by a very upright position; others again express mercy alone, combining the inclination of the body with softness of expression.

The Spiritual Virtues*

...TRUTH HAS, IN ITS MANIFESTATION, something of humility and charity; humility is false if it has neither truth nor charity, and charity is false if it has neither truth nor humility. The virtues mutually control one another.

Truth, when it appears on the level of our will, becomes virtue, and it is then veracity and sincerity.

* * *

The three fundamental virtues of veracity, charity and humility must penetrate even into our thinking, which is also an action. There is no level of activity into which the virtues should not enter. When pure truth manifests itself it cannot do so without the virtues, for manifestation is an action.

Humility means to look on oneself in the limiting state of individuation; it means to gaze on the ego, on limitation and on nothingness. Charity means looking around one; it means seeing God in one's neighbour, and also seeing oneself there, but this time not as pure limitation, but as a creature of God made in His image. Veracity means to look towards Truth and to submit and attach oneself to it and to become penetrated by its implacable light. And each one of the three virtues must be found again in each of the other virtues, for they are criteria one of another.

* * *

Charitable humility will avoid causing scandal and thus injuring one's neighbour; it should not be contrary to the self-effacement which is its sufficient reason.

*From *SPHF*, Part six.

448

Veridical humility will avoid overestimation: virtue must not run counter to truth. But it may be more 'true' than some sterile and external truth, and in this case it is virtue which is truth and the contradiction is only an apparent one.

Humble charity will avoid showing itself when it is not useful. Man must not grow proud of his generosity: 'Let not your left hand know what your right doeth.' The gift of oneself should above all be inward; otherwise external well-doing is devoid of spiritual value or of blessing.

Veridical charity is conscious of the nature of things. I am not less than my neighbour, since I exist and have an immortal soul like him. But it may be that some higher interest comes before temporal interest, whether it is a question of my 'neighbour' or of 'myself'.

Humble veracity will not hide our ignorance. To pretend to a knowledge we do not possess is hurtful to the knowledge we do possess.

Charitable veracity will neglect nothing in order to make the truth understood. If truth is a good, it should also be a gift.

Effacing the ego, the giving of oneself, the realization of truth. It might be said that these attitudes respectively correspond to the stages — or states — of purification, expansion and union. These are the three 'dimensions' of perfect gnosis.

* * *

A spiritual virtue is nothing other than consciousness of a reality. It is natural — but it is indifferent — if some feeling or other is added to it. When virtue is only sentimental, in the sense of being ignorant of the reality to which it relates, it may have relative utility, but it is none the less a spiritual obstacle and a source of errors.

* * *

If metaphysic is a sacred thing, that means that it could not be presented as though it were only a profane philosophy sufficient unto itself, or in other words limited to the framework of a play of the mind. It is illogical and dangerous to talk of metaphysic without being preoccupied with the moral concomitances it requires, the criteria of which are, for man, his behaviour in relation to God and to his neighbour.

* * *

The key to understanding the spiritual necessity of the virtues lies in this, that metaphysical truths are also reflected in the will and not only in intellect and reason. To a principial truth there corresponds an attitude of the will. This is a necessary aspect — or a consequence—of the principle that 'to know is to be'.

* * *

To meditate on the divine qualities is at the same time to meditate on the virtues—and consequently on the vices—of human beings. Spirituality has both concentric circles and radii, both modes of analogy and modes of identity: virtues and intellections. When these latter are replaced by rational operations, then the virtues in their turn will appear as modes of identity, as 'relatively direct' participations in the divine Being...

* * *

Certain Hindus of old blessed our epoch, not because it is good, but because, being bad, it includes by compensation spiritual graces which make easy what is in itself difficult, provided always that man is sincere, pure, humble and persevering. In former ages the spirit was more or less everywhere, but was more difficult to reach and to realize just because it was everywhere present. Its very superfluity excluded easiness. It was there, but had a tendency to disappear; to-day it is hidden, but has a tendency to give itself.

There is an economy of mercy although in its essence mercy goes beyond any economy, for principially it comes before justice. Mercy is not measured except in its external aspect; and justice, which is neither the first nor the last work of God, limits it only accidentally and in terms of a particular level of existence.

Apart from compensatory graces, which are in themselves independent of the evil of our times, there are advantages in this evil itself. The world has become so emptied of substance that it is hard for a spiritual man to be too much attached to it. The man of today, if he is a contemplative, is already half broken through this very fact. Formerly, worldliness offered the more seduction from having aspects that were intelligent, noble and full. It was far from being contemptible as it is in our day. It made possible, no doubt, in the souls of the *élite*—who alone interest us here—a sort of simple-minded and total attachment which required a corresponding renunciation. The evil of the world had not yet become affirmed in the very appearance of the world.

* * *

Why cannot man enter into contemplation so long as his heart is full of anger against his neighbour? It is because man cannot get beyond his 'I'—individuality—except on condition that he sees it as individuality as such without any distinction of person.

Before sacrificing, say the Gospels, man must be reconciled with his brother. Some saint — we forget which — said it is just as absurd to want to contemplate God with one's heart full of bitterness against one's neighbour as it is to pluck out one's eye in order to see better.

Moral imperfection is here only the human expression of incompatibility of perspectives. Hatred of a particular person, or of a collectivity, which amounts to the same thing, is opposed to love of the totality. And it is the totality that one must love in order to be able to love God. Perfection requires loving man, not loving some particular man.

* * *

Spiritual realization is theoretically the easiest thing and practically the most difficult thing there is. It is the easiest because it is enough to think of God. It is the most difficult because human nature is forgetfulness of God.

Sanctity is a tree which grows between impossibility and miracle...

* * *

It is necessary to dig deep into the soil of the soul through layers of aridity and bitterness in order to find love and to live from it.

The depths of love are inaccessible to man in his state of hardness but reveal themselves externally through the language of art and also through that of nature. In sacred art and in virgin nature the soul can taste by analogical anticipation something of the love which sleeps in itself and for which it has a nostalgia though it has not experience of it.

* * *

In this nether world there is the immense problem of separation. How to make men understand that in God they are separated, from nothing?

To the angels our formal — or separative — world presents itself as a pile of debris. What is in reality united is separated in form and by form. The formal world is made up of coagulated essences.

* * *

The soul is a tree whose roots go deep down into the 'world'— into the things which, in ourselves as well as around us, are capable of being felt, tasted and lived. The 'world' is diversity and the passional movements which answer to it, whether in the flesh, or in feelings or in thought.

'The one thing necessary' is the transferring of our roots into what appears as nothing, as void, as unity. And, as the soul cannot plant its roots in the void, the void is 'incarnated' in the symbol; it is in everything that brings us nearer to God.

* * *

There is a great certainty in life, and this is death. He who really understands this certainty is already dead in this life. Man is hardly at all preoccupied with his past sufferings if his present state is happy; what is past in life, whatever its weight, is no longer. Now everything will one day be past; that is what a man understands at the moment of death. To know that is to be dead; it is to rest in peace.

But there is yet another certainty in life — whether we can have this certainty depends only on ourselves — and it is the certainty of living in the divine will. This certainty compensates for that of death and conquers it. In other words, when we have the certainty of being conformed to the divine will, the certainty of death is full of sweetness. Thus the meaning of our life on earth can be reduced to two certainties: that of the inevitability of our destiny and that of the meaning or value of our will. We cannot avoid the meaning of life any more than we can avoid death. That great departure, which cannot have a shadow of doubt for us, proves to us that we are not free to act 'just anyhow', that from this present moment we ought to conform to a will stronger than our own.

* * *

In his empirical existence man finds himself in contact with God, with the world, with the soul and with his neighbour. On each of these levels it might be said that God speaks a different language. In the world he touches us through destiny, which is in time, and by the symbols that surround us, and which are in space. In the soul he is truth, which is objective, and the voice of conscience, which is subjective. In our neighbour he appears as the need we must supply and also as the teaching we must accept, so that the divine function of the neighbour is at once passive and active.

One cannot serve God without also seeing him in destiny, in the truth and in the neighbour.

* * *

What are the great troubles of the soul? A false life, a false death, a false activity, a false rest. A false life: passion which engenders suffering; a false death: egoism which hardens the heart and separates from God and his mercy; a false activity: dispersal, which drives the soul into an insatiable whirlwind and makes it forget God who is peace; a false rest or a false passivity: the feebleness and laziness which deliver up the soul without resistance to the countless solicitations of the world.

* * *

To this false life is opposed a true death: the death of passion. This is spiritual death, the cold and crystalline purity of the soul conscious of its immortality. To false death is opposed a true life: the life of the heart turned towards God and open to the warmth of his love. To false activity is opposed a true rest, a real peace: the rest of the soul which is simple and generous and is content with God, the soul which turns aside from agitation and curiosity and ambition, to rest, if one can so put it, in the divine beauty. To false rest is opposed a true activity: the battle of the spirit against the multiple feebleness which squanders the soul — and this precious life — as in a game or in a dream.

To false knowledge, to empty thought, is opposed a way of being: that of the spirit united to its divine Source, beyond the mind which is split up and indefinitely scattered, in a movement with no upshot. To false existence, to the crude and blind fact, is opposed a true knowledge, a true discernment: to know that God alone is absolute Reality, that the world is only through him and in him and that, outside him, I am not...

PART VII

ESCHATOLOGY AND THE AFTERLIFE

Reflections on Eschatological Problems

Some Observations on a Problem of the Afterlife*

THE GREAT REVELATIONS are at one and the same time, in varying degrees, both total and fragmentary: total by reason of their absolute content or their esoterism and fragmentary by reason of their particular symbolism or their exoterism; but even this exoterism always contains elements which make it possible to reconstitute the total truth. In Islam, for example, one of these elements is the idea, expressed in various ways, of the relativity — or non-eternity — of Paradise and Hell. The Qoran mentions the blessed and the damned as abiding respectively in Paradise and Hell 'so long as the heavens and the earth endure, except as thy Lord wisheth'.[1] The everlastingness in question is thus doubly relative. As regards Paradise we may quote also the saying of the Prophet: 'God will say (to the people of Paradise): are ye content? They will answer: wherefore should we not be content, seeing that Thou hast given us what Thou hast not given to any of Thy creation? Then He will say: I will give you better than that. They will say: What thing, O Lord, is better? Then will He say: I will let down upon you My Beatitude and never afterwards shall I be wroth with you.'[2] This recalls the verse of the Qoran: 'Beatitude from God is greater (than Paradise).'[3] Mention must also be made of the saying of the Sufis that Paradise is 'the prison of the

*From *DI*, Chapter 10.

457

gnostic' or that it is 'inhabited by fools'; and the Qoran itself affirms that 'everything is perishable but the Face (Essence) of Allah.'[4]

The profound meaning of all these allusions is as follows: towards the completion of a major cosmic cycle, in the words of a *ḥadīth*: 'the flames of Hell will grow cold';[5] correlatively, but without there being any true symmetry—for 'My Mercy takes precedence over my Wrath'—the Paradises, at the approach of the Apocatastasis, will of metaphysical necessity reveal their limitative aspect, as if they had become less vast or as if God were less close than before; they will experience a sort of nostalgia for the One without a second or for the Essence, for proximity is not Unity and comprises an element of otherness and separativity. Without involving suffering of any kind, which would be contrary to the very definition of Heaven, the aspect 'other than God' will manifest itself to the detriment of the aspect 'near to God'. This will be no more than a passing shadow, for then will come the Apocatastasis whose glory will surpass all promises and all expectation, in conformity with the principle that God never fulfils less than He promises, but on the contrary always more.[6] At the very moment when, perhaps, one of the blessed will ask himself whether he is still in Paradise, the great veil will be torn asunder and the uncreated Light will flood all and absorb all: the 'garden' will return to the 'Gardener'; Universal Manifestation will be transmuted and everything will be reintegrated within the ineffable Plenitude of the Principle; Being itself, together with its possibilities of creation, will no longer be detached from the indivisible Self; its possibilities will expand into what might be called, notwithstanding a certain inherent absurdity in the expression, the 'absolute Substance'. This aspect of Paradisal 'twilight' reveals itself to the Sufis as a direct consequence of the contingency of the celestial states themselves; it is also implicit in the *Shahādah*—the testimony of Unity —which is the key to discernment between the Absolute and the contingent;[7] it is this discernment which allows them to compare Paradise—or the Paradises—to a 'prison'; in other words, they see the effects in the causes and perceive *a priori* the limits of all that is not God, while at the same time, and from another standpoint, they see God through phenomena. On the other hand, the Sufis analogically rejoin the Buddhist perspective when describing the Divine Beatitude as the 'Paradise of the Essence', which corresponds directly to Nirvana; the latter is in fact 'God' considered from the standpoint of Beatitude and Permanence. All this reveals an important point of contact between the Semitic and Brahmano-Buddhic eschatologies, and illustrates the crucial idea of the 'impermanence of all things'.

We have just seen that as the final absorption of the Paradises into the Essence approaches, the aspect of separativity will be accentuated at the expense of the aspect of nearness, at least in a certain measure. The case of Hell — or the Hells — is however analogically inverse, in the sense that they comprise, on the one hand an aspect of remoteness (from God) which is their *raison d'être*, and on the other hand, an aspect of necessity or existence which perforce attaches them to the Will of God, and thus to Reality itself; at the beginning the first aspect will predominate, but the second aspect is bound to be affirmed towards the end of the cycle, and this is precisely the reason for the 'cooling'— as the *hadīth* expresses it — of the flames of Hell. God being Love or Mercy — more essentially than Justice or Rigour — his Goodness is included in Existence and in all existential substances, and it will finally take possession of everything that exists. In each thing and in each creature, that which is good is firstly its pure and simple existence, then its deiformity, even the most indirect, and lastly its particular qualities; these positive aspects, without which nothing can exist, will in the end triumph over the negative accidents, and they will do so by virtue of the universal law of equilibrium with its two-fold aspect of wearing out and compensation.[8] Considerations of this kind, whether relating to Heaven or Hell, can only be schematic, and cannot take account of all possible modalities, which in the nature of things are unknown to us; Revelation teaches us directly or indirectly that Paradise and Hell comprise regions and degrees — in both the 'horizontal' and 'vertical' dimensions[9] —, but the 'life' or 'movements' in these abodes cannot be penetrated by earthly understanding, unless it be through rare and fragmentary images. In any case, the metaphysical basis of the whole of this doctrine rests on the most solid of foundations, for it coincides with the very notion of contingency.

Existence necessarily implies particularity and change; this is demonstrated by space and time on the plane of corporeal existence, and by the cosmic cycles on the plane of universal Existence. Existence is, analogically speaking, both a 'form' and a 'movement'; it is at once both static and dynamic, but at the same time comprises the alternation of unfolding and crystallization; the transmigration of souls has no other meaning.[10] At the summit of universal Existence this 'migratory vibration' comes to a stop, because it turns inwards in the direction of the Immutable; there remains only a single movement, a single cycle, that of Paradise, which opens onto the Essence. In God Himself, who is beyond Existence, there is an element which pre-figures Existence, and this is the Divine Life, which the Christian doctrine attributes to the Holy Spirit and which it calls Love; towards this Life converge those existences that are plunged in the light of Glory and sustained by it; and it is this Light, this 'Divine Halo', which keeps the Paradises outside the 'migratory vibrations' of existences that are still corruptible. The sage does not strictly speaking emerge from his existential movement — although from the standpoint of the cosmic wheel he does so — but turns it inwards: the movement becomes lost in the Infinite or expands in the 'changeless movement' of the 'Void'.

To identify oneself with movement is to engender movement and therefore change, the series of movements; to identify oneself with pure being engenders being and therefore the interiorization and transmutation of movement, or the cessation of movement in the Immutable and the Unlimited. Desire is movement, and contemplation is being.

Revelation offers truths that are not only explicit but also implicit; it presents both postulates and conclusions, causal ideas and consequential ideas; it cannot escape from reckoning with these consequences concretely once it has provided the keys to them. These keys necessarily imply the corresponding consequences, of which they are as it were the living anticipations. The 'totality' of love in Christianity, and the 'sincerity' of faith and knowledge in Islam, imply the most decisive metaphysical truths, even though these truths must needs reveal the illusory nature, not of the literal interpretations which are always valid on their own levels, but of these levels themselves. It is for this reason that the criterion of traditional orthodoxy does not necessarily consist in agreement with a particular exoteric thesis, but in agreement with the principle of knowledge or realization by which this thesis is accompanied: he who says 'ice' says 'water', even if from the point of view of immediate vision — which only counts at a certain level — there is opposition between solidity and liquidity. It is also for this reason that it is absurd to expect from Revelation explicit teachings about every truth; it needs to be explicit in regard to those truths which necessarily concern all men, but it has no cause to be explicit in regard to truths which are neither comprehensible nor necessary to the majority of men, and which should remain in a state of potentiality that only esoterism is called upon to actualize. For example, when the Scriptures proclaim that 'God is Love', that implies metaphysically the relativity and even the end of Hell; he who says 'relativity', says 'limit', and so 'end'; but this end derives from a 'dimension' that is higher than the reality of Hell; it is not therefore Hell which comes to an end, but the end which does away with Hell. It is as though the dimension of depth were to absorb one of the other two dimensions, or rather both of them at the same time, by dissolving or transmuting the plane surface; neither of the two dimensions would cease to exist in relation to their common plane, it is this plane itself which would cease to exist.

Universal Eschatology*

Eschatology is part of cosmology, and the latter is a prolongation of metaphysics, which is essentially identical to the *sophia perennis*. It may be asked by what right is eschatology part of this *sophia*, given that, epistemologically speaking, pure intellection does not seem to reveal our destinies beyond the grave, whereas it reveals to us the universal principles; but in reality, the knowledge of these destinies is accessible thanks to the knowledge of principles, or thanks to their correct application. It is in fact by comprehending the profound nature of subjectivity, and not exclusively by that outward way that is Revelation,[1] that we can know the immortality of the soul, for to say total or central subjectivity — and not partial and peripheral as is that of animals — is to say thereby capacity of objectivity, intuition of the Absolute and immortality.[2] And to say that we are immortal, means that we have existed before our human birth — for what has no end cannot have a beginning — and in addition, that we are subject to cycles; life is a cycle, and our former existence must also have been a cycle in a chain of cycles. Our existence to come may also proceed by cycles, that is, it is condemned to them if we

*From *STRP*, Chapter 7 (trans. G. Polit).

have not been able to realize the reason for the existence of the human state which, being central, permits precisely of escaping the "round of existences."

The human condition is in fact the door towards Paradise: towards the cosmic Center which, while forming a part of the manifested Universe, is nonetheless situated — thanks to the magnetic proximity of the divine Sun — beyond the rotation of the worlds and destinies, and thereby beyond "transmigration". And it is for that reason that "human birth is hard to attain", according to a Hindu Text; in order to be convinced of this, it suffices to consider the incommensurability between the central point and the innumerable points of the periphery.

•   •   •

There are souls who, fully or sufficiently conformed to the human vocation, enter directly into Paradise: they are either the saints or the sanctified. In the former case, they are great souls illuminated by the divine Sun and dispensers of beneficent rays; in the latter case, they are souls who, having neither faults of character nor worldly tendencies, are free — or freed — from mortal sins, and sanctified by the supernatural action of means of grace of which they have made their viaticum. Between the saints and the sanctified there are doubtless intermediary possiblities, but God alone is the judge of their position and their rank.

Nevertheless, among the sanctified — those saved by sanctification both natural and supernatural[3] — there are those who are not perfect enough to enter directly into Paradise; thus they will wait their maturity in a place which the theologians have termed an "honorable prison," but which in the opinion of the Amidists is more than that since, they say, this place is situated in Paradise itself; they compare it to a golden lotus bud, which opens when the soul is ripe. This state corresponds to the "limbo of the fathers" (*limbus* = "edge") of the Catholic doctrine: the just of the "Ancient Alliance", according to this very particular perspective, found themselves therein before the "descent into the hells" of the Christ-Savior;[4] a conception above all symbolic, and very simplifying; but perfectly adequate as to principle, and even literally true in cases which we need not define here, given the complexity of the problem.

After the "lotus" we have to envisage "purgatory" properly so-called: the soul faithful to its human vocation, that is, sincere and persevering in its moral and spiritual duties, cannot fall into hell, but it can pass, before entering Paradise, by that intermediary and painful state which the Catholic doctrine terms "purgatory": it must pass through it if it has faults of character, or if it has worldly tendencies, or if it is charged with a sin for which it has not been able to compensate by its moral and spiritual attitude or by the grace of a sacramental means. According to Islamic doctrine "purgatory" is a transient abode in hell: God saves from the fire "whomsoever He will," that is to say that He alone is the judge of the imponderables of our nature; or in other words, He alone knows what is our fundamental possibility or our substance. If there are Christian denominations which deny Purgatory, it is at root for the same reason: because the souls of those who are not damned, and who *ipso facto* are destined for salvation, are in the hands of God and concern only Him.

Regarding Paradise, it is necessary here to take into account its "horizontal" regions as well as its "vertical" degrees: the former correspond to circular sectors, and the latter to concentric circles. The former separate the diverse religious or denominational worlds, and the latter, the diverse degrees within each of these worlds: on the one hand, the *Brahma-Loka* of the Hindus for example, which is a place of salvation like the Heaven of the Christians, does not however coincide with this latter;[5] and on the other hand, within the same Paradise, the place of Beatitude of modest saints or of the "sanctified" is not the same as that of the great saints. "There are many rooms in my Father's mansion,"[6] without there being for all that impenetrable barriers between the diverse degrees, for the "communion of saints" forms part of Beatitude;[7] neither is there any need to maintain that there is no communication possible between the diverse religious sectors, on the esoteric plane where it can have a meaning. [8]

• • •

It is necessary for us on the one hand to comment on the infernal possibility, which maintains the soul in the human state, and on the other hand the possibilities of "transmigration," which on the con-

trary cause it to leave the human state. Strictly speaking, hell also
is in the final analysis a phase of transmigration, but before releas-
ing the soul to other phases or other states, it imprisons it "perpetual-
ly", but not "eternally"; eternity pertains to God alone, and in a certain manner to Paradise in virtue of a mystery of participation in
the divine Immutability. Hell crystallizes a vertical fall; it is "invincible" because it lasts until the exhaustion of a certain cycle of which
God alone knows the extent. Those who enter hell are not those who
have sinned accidentally, with their "shell" so to speak, but those who
have sinned substantially or with their "kernel", and this is a distinction that may not be perceptible from without; they are in any case
the proud, the wicked, the hypocrites, hence all those who are the
contrary of the saints and the sanctified.

Exoterically speaking, man is damned because he does not accept a given Revelation, a given Truth, and does not obey a given
Law; esoterically, he damns himself because he does not accept his
own fundamental and primordial Nature, which dictates a given
knowledge and a given comportment.[9] Revelation is only the objective and symbolic manifestation of the Light which man carries
in himself, in the depths of his being; it only reminds of what he
is and what he should be since he has forgotten what he is. If all
human souls, before their creation, must attest that God is their
Lord — according to the Koran[10] — it is because they know "pre-
existentially" what Being, the Truth and the Law are; fundamental
sin is a suicide of the soul.

On the Notion of Hell*

. . .The notion of an 'eternal' hell, after having for many centuries stimulated fear of God and efforts towards virtue, has today
rather the opposite effect and contributes to making the doctrine of
the world beyond seem improbable; and, by a strange paradox, in
a period which is one of contrasts and compensations, and at the

*From *UI*, pp. 74-79.

same time generally speaking as refractory as it could be to pure metaphysic, only the esotericism of gnosis is in a position to render intelligible the very precariously held positions of exotericism and to satisfy certain needs of causality. Now the problem of divine punishment, which our contemporaries have such difficulty in admitting, can be summed up in two questions: first, is it possible for man who is responsible and free to oppose the Absolute either directly or indirectly, even if only in an illusory sense? Certainly he can, since the individual essence can be impregnated with any cosmic quality and there are consequently states that are 'possibilities of impossibility'.[1] And the second question is this: can exoteric truth, for instance in regard to Hell, be total truth? Certainly not, since it is determined — in a certain sense 'by definition'— by a particular moral interest, or by particular reasons of psychological opportuneness. The absence of various compensating shades of expression in certain religious teachings can be explained in this way; the eschatologies relating to these religious perspectives are of course not antimetaphysical, but they are 'non-metaphysical' and anthropocentric,[2] and so much is this the case that in the context of these teachings certain truths appear 'immoral' or at least rather 'unseemly': it is therefore not possible for them to discern in infernal states aspects that are more or less positive, or the converse in paradisal states. By this we do not mean to say that there is symmetry as between Mercy and Rigour — the former has priority over the latter[3] — but rather that the relationship 'Heaven-hell' corresponds by metaphysical necessity to what is expressed in the Far Eastern symbolism of the *yin-yang*, in which the black portion includes a white point and the white portion a black point; if then there are compensations in gehenna because nothing in existence can be absolute and the divine Mercy penetrates everywhere,[4] there must also be in Paradise, not indeed sufferings, but shadows bearing an inverse testimony to the same principle of compensation and signifying that Paradise is not God, as also that all existences are conjoined. Now this principle of compensation is esoteric — to make a dogma of it would be wholly contrary to the spirit of 'either. . .or' so characteristic of Western exotericism — and indeed we find Sufic writings giving expression to views remarkable for their shades of meaning: Jili, Ibn Arabi and others admit an aspect of enjoyment in the infernal state for, if on the one hand the man who has been reproved suffers from being cut off from the Sovereign Good and, as Avicenna emphasises, from deprivation of his earthly body although the passions subsist, on the other hand he remembers God, according to Jalal ed-Din Rumi, and 'nothing is sweeter than the remembrance of Allah'. Indeed in hell the wicked and the proud know that God is real, whereas on earth they either took no account of this or were always able to bring themselves to doubt it; thus something is changed in them by the mere fact of their death and this something is indescribable from the point of view of earthly life. 'The dead alone know the worth of life', say the Moslems. Here it is perhaps as well to recall also that those in hell would be *ipso facto* delivered if they had the supreme knowledge — of which they certainly possess the potentiality — so that even in hell they hold the key to their liberation; but what must above all be pointed out is that the second death referred to in the Apocalypse, as also the reservation expressed in the Quran where certain sayings about hell are followed by the phrase 'unless thy Lord wills otherwise' (*illā mā shā'a Llāh*,[5] indicate the point of intersection between the Semitic conception of perpetual hell and the Hindu and Buddhist conception of transmigration. In other words the hells are in the final count passages to individual non-human cycles and thus to other worlds. The human state, or any other analogous 'central' state, is, as it were, surrounded by a ring of fire: in it there is only one choice, either to escape from 'the current of forms' upwards, towards God, or else to leave humanity downwards through the fire, the fire which is like the sanction of the betrayal on the part of those who have not realized the divine meaning of the human condition. If 'the human state is hard to obtain', as is held by Asiatic believers in transmigration, it is for the same reason of its centrality and theomorphic majesty equally hard to leave. Men go to the fire as being gods and they come out of the fire as being but creatures: God alone could go to hell eternally — if He could sin. Again: the human state is very near to the divine Sun, if we can at all speak of proximity in such a connection; the fire is the ultimate price — in reverse — of that privileged situation, how privileged can be gauged by the intensity and inextinguishability of the fire. From the gravity of hell we must infer the grandeur of man; we must not inversely infer from the seeming innocence of man the supposed injustice of hell. . . .

The Two Paradises*

The Vedantine notion of "Deliverance" (*moksha, mukti*) evokes, rightly or wrongly, the paradoxical image of a refusal of Paradise and a choice of Supreme Union, the latter seeming to imply — according to some formulations — a dissolution of the individual and the identification of the intellect nucleus with the Self. If such an outcome is presented as the object of a strictly human option, it is right to object that no individual could have a motive for choosing anything except his own survival and happiness; all the rest is pretentiousness and bookish speculation, and so has nothing to do with the Vedantine notion in question.

To begin with, the following two points must be borne in mind: first, that the idea of "Deliverance" or "Union" corresponds to a metaphysical truth, however much its true meaning may have come to be altered by pedantic or extravagant interpretations; secondly, that there are in man two subjects — or two subjectivities — with no common measure and with opposite tendencies, even though there is also coincidence between them in a certain sense. On the one hand there is the *anima* or empirical ego, which is woven of contingencies, both objective and subjective, such as memories and desires; on the other hand, there is the *spiritus* or pure Intelligence, the subjectivity of which is rooted in the Absolute and which therefore sees in the empirical ego only a shell, something outward and alien to the true "oneself", that is, to the transcendent and immanent "Self".

Now if it is incontestable that the human ego normally desires happiness and survival in happiness, to the point of having no possible motive for desiring more than this, it is equally true that pure Intelligence exists and that its nature is to tend towards its own source. The whole question is one of knowing, spiritually speaking, which of these two subjectivities predominates in a human being. One has a perfect right to deny that the choice of a supra-individual state has any sense for the individual as such, but one cannot deny that there is something in man which goes beyond individuality and which may take precedence over its aspirations.

*From *IPP*, Chapter 12.

We speak of taking precedence over its aspirations, not of abolishing them, and here we touch on another aspect of the problem, and by no means the least important. When tradition speaks of a "dissolution" or an "extinction" of individuality, it is the private limitations of the ego that are meant, not its existence as such. If there is no common measure between the ego of the being "delivered in life" (*jīvan-mukta*) and his spiritual reality, and if there is therefore no need to deny, when saying that he "is Brahma", that he is a particular man, the same incommensurability — and, together with it, the same compatibility or the same parallelism — is to be found in the next world. Were it not so, we should have to conclude that the Avatars had totally disappeared from the cosmos, and this has never been admitted in traditional doctrine. Christ "is God", but this in no way prevents him from saying: "Today shalt thou be with me in Paradise", or from predicting his own return at the end of the cycle.

The "world" is the sphere of phenomena or contingencies; the ordinary ego, the *anima*, is thus an integral part of the world and is situated "on the outside" for one who is able to see it from the point of view of the *spiritus* which, by definition, belongs to the *Spiritus Sanctus*; and this could never be a matter of ambition or of affection, for it is a question of real understanding and of an inborn perspective. In other words, subjectivity may be conceived, or realized, according to three degrees, which correspond precisely to the ternary "*corpus*", "*anima*", "*spiritus*". The first degree is that of animality, albeit human; the second is that of the microcosm of dreaming, in which the subject no longer identifies itself with the mere body, but with the ever-growing mirage that is woven out of the experiences of imagination and feeling; the third degree is that of pure Intelligence which is the trace, in man, of the one "transcendentally immanent" Subject. The soul is the inner witness of the body, as the spirit is the inner witness of the soul.

It is the nature of Intelligence not to identify itself passively, and as it were blindly, with the phenomena which it registers but, on the contrary, by reducing these to their essences, to come in the end to know That which knows. At the same time, the sage — precisely because his subjectivity is determined by Intelligence — will tend to "be That which is" and to "enjoy that which enjoys", which brings us back to the Vedantine ternary: Being, Consciousness, Beatitude (*Sat, Chit, Ananda*). There is in reality but a single Beatitude, just as there is but a single Subject and a single Object. The three poles are united in the Absolute, and separated in so far as the Absolute engages itself in Relativity, in accordance with the mystery of *Māyā*; the final issue of this descent is, precisely, the diversification of subjects, objects and experiences. Object, Subject, Happiness: all our existence is woven out of these three elements, but in illusory mode; the sage does what the ignorant man does, that is, he lives on these three elements, but he does so in the direction of the Real, which alone is Object, Subject, Happiness.

• • •

When the Sufis say that "Paradise is inhabited by fools", one must take it as referring to subjects attached to phenomena rather than to the one and only Subject, which is its own Object and its own Beatitude. All paradoxical expressions tending to make a distinction between the "saved" and the "elect" are to be understood, above all, as metaphors which affirm a particular principle or a specific tendency. The paradox is occasioned by the fact that the image is naïvely human, and therefore psychological, whilst the principle itself has no common measure with psychology. Two subjectivities, two languages: herein lies the whole enigma of esoterism. A doctrine is esoteric in so far as it appeals to "inward subjectivity" and thereby puts aside "outward subjectivity"; on the other hand, it is exoteric in so far as it accepts the empirical ego as a closed system and an absolute reality and confines itself to subjecting this system to prescriptions that are equally absolute. For the Sufis, the attestation that there is no god but God is esoteric because it ultimately excludes outward egoity; "ultimately", that is, when it is understood "sincerely", and therefore totally. The traditional expression "knowing through God" (*'ārif bi'Llāh*) — and not "knowing God"— is characteristic in this connection, the proposition "through" serving to indicate the practically divine subjectivity within pure Intellection.

The outward ego is by definition nourished on phenomena, and is in consequence thoroughly dualistic; it is matched by the revealed and objective religion whose Prophet is a particular historic personage. The inward ego looks towards its own transcendent and immanent Source; to it corresponds the innate and subjective religion whose Avatar is the heart; but this wisdom is in fact inaccessible without the concurrence of objective and revealed religion, just as the inward ego is inaccessible without the concurrence of the sanctified outward ego.

The crystallization of metaphysical truth in a religious — and therefore dogmatic — phenomenon is a result of the principle of individuation. Falling into the human atmosphere, Divine Truth is coagulated and individualized; it becomes a point of view and it is personified, so that it is impossible to reconcile one particular religious form with another on the actual level of this personification, just as it is impossible to change one's own human ego for another human ego, even though we know perfectly well that our neighbour's ego is no more illogical nor any less legitimate than our own. On the other hand, this passage from one form to another, and so from one metaphysical-mystical subjectivity to another, is always possible if one reascends to the source of religious coagulations, which belongs to universal Subjectivity or, we might way, to Intelligence itself; man has access to it, in principle and in fact, in pure Intellection; and that is the subjectivity which is concerned with "Deliverance" in the Vedantine sense of the term.

When Sufis disdain Paradise and want only God, it goes without saying that they mean Paradise as being created and therefore "other than God", and not as being Divine by virtue of its substance and its content, quite apart from its existential degree. Otherwise, they could not speak with perfect logic as they do of the "Paradise of the Essence", which is situated beyond creation. Analogously, if the Sufis sometimes appear to reject good works or even the virtues, they are rejecting these values in so far as they appear to be "their own" and not in so far as they belong to God. Or again, when some Sufi says that he is equally indifferent to good and to evil, this means that he is envisaging them in relation to the contingency which they have in common and which in its turn appears "evil" in comparison with that "good" which is the quality of the Absolute alone. If we compare good to light and evil to an opaque stone, whitening the stone does not transform it into light. The stone may be striped white and black in terms of "good" and "evil", but it will not be any less, by reason of its opaqueness and its heaviness, a kind of "evil" in relation to the luminous ray.

The two human subjects, the outward or empirical and the inward or intellective, correspond analogically to the two aspects of the Divine Subject, the ontological or personal and the supraontological or impersonal; in man, as *in divinis*, duality is perceptible or actualized only in relation to the element *Māyā*. Or again, to return to the ternary *corpus, anima, spiritus*, these three subjectivities reflect respectively the three hypostases — if indeed this term is applicable here — Existence, Being and Beyond-Being, so that man is totally himself only in the Intellect; while the empirical ego is nourished on phenomena, the intellective ego burns them up and tends towards the Essence. This difference in principle does not, in any case, imply an alternative in fact, because there is simply no common measure between them; the norm is equilibrium between the two levels, and not a "dehumanization" inconceivable in concrete terms.

•   •   •

The paradoxical expression "absolutely Absolute" calls for certain explanations. Orthodox theologians, according to Palamas, make a distinction in God between the Essence and the Energies; error, say the Catholics, for the Divine nature is simple; no error, reply the Orthodox, for the laws of logic do not concern God, who is beyond them; a dialogue between the deaf, we say, for logic in no way prevents one from admitting that the Divine Nature comprises Energies, even while being simple. To understand this, it is enough to possess the notion of Divine Relativity, which is precisely what the theologians' totalitarian cult of sublimity precludes by refusing to allow any combination of the antinomic relationships which in pure metaphysics are part of the nature of things. There can be no symmetry between the relative and the Absolute; in consequence, if there is clearly no such thing as the "absolutely relative", there is none the less something that is "relatively absolute", and this is Being in its creative, revealing and saving aspect, absolute for the world, but not for the Essence which is Beyond-Being or "Non-Being". If God were the Absolute in every context and without any hypostatic limitation, there could be no contact between Him and the world, and the world would not even exist. In order to be able to create, speak and act, it is necessary for God Himself to make Himself "world", after a certain fashion, and He does so by the ontological self-limitation which gives rise to the "personal God", the world itself being the most extreme and also the most relative of self-limitations. Pantheism would be right, in its way, if it confined itself to this aspect of things without denying transcendence.

Monotheistic exoterism readily loses sight of these aspects of inclusiveness; but it has the advantage — and this is the reason for its existence — of placing man as such face-to-face with this "human Absolute", God the Creator; it must none the less pay the price for this simplification, in terms of theological "dead ends", which the Christians explain in terms of "mystery" and the Muslims in terms of God's "good pleasure", testifying to the need to account in one and the same breath for both the unity of God and the antinomic complexity of Divine intervention in the world. Now this complexity can never be explained in terms of unity; it is explained, on the contrary, by relativity *in divinis*, that is, by hypostatic gradation with a view to the unfolding of creation; this relativity in no way affects unity, any more than the dimensions of space affect either the oneness of the central point or the homogeneity of total space which derives from that point and deploys it.

The situation of the theologies, faced with the paradoxical complexity of metaphysical Reality, can be summarized as follows: first, there is the axiom that God is the Absolute, since nothing can be above Him; there follows the logical observation that there is something relative in God; finally, the conclusion is drawn that, since God is the Absolute, this apparent element of relativity can only be absolute. The fact that this is contrary to logic proves that logic does not attain to God, who is "mystery" (Christianity) and who "doeth as He will" (Islam). Now we have seen that the solution of the problem rests upon two points: objectively, the Absolute is subject to gradation, at least unless one prefers not to speak of it; subjectively, it is not logic that is at fault, but the opaqueness of our axioms and the rigidity of our reasoning. Certainly, "God does as He wills", but this illusion of arbitrariness springs from our inability to discern, on the phenomenal level, all His motives; certainly He is "mystery", but this is because His Subjectivity — ultimately the one and only Subjectivity — is inexhaustible and yields up its secrets only to the extent that it embraces us in its light.

It stands to reason that the ego is not wholly itself in so far as it is determined by objects, which are "other than oneself"; the true ego, the pure Subject, bears its object within itself, like the Divine Essence, which "tends towards its own infinite Centre" — if this inadequate image is admissible — whereas Being tends towards creation, but obviously "without emerging from itself" and without being affected by the world and its contents. The subject-intellect, like

Beyond-Being, bears its object within itself; but the empirical or psychic ego has its object both outside itself and within itself, in the manner of Being; and just as Existence has its object outside itself, in the things that exist, so the sensory ego has its object outside and tends towards the outward. Now God can be simultaneously Beyond-Being, Being and even Existence, that is, from the point of view of *Māyā*, for ultimately Beyond-Being can never be unfolded but contains everything within itself in a state that is undifferentiated but infinitely real. Yet for man, who is made in the image of God, it is possible to be unfaithful to this image, since he is not God and since he is free. Having committed this act of infidelity, and bearing it in his inborn nature he must — if he is to become theomorphic once again — tend towards Divine Inwardness. The subject as *anima* must make itself independent of the corporeal subject, and the intellectual subject must make itself independent of the subject *anima*, in conformity with this teaching: "Whosoever shall seek to save his life shall lose it; and whosoever shall lose his life shall preserve it" (*Luke*, 17, 33); and again, "Except a corn of wheat fall into the ground and die, it abideth alone; but if it die it bringeth forth much fruit. He that loveth his life, shall lose it; and he that hateth his life in this world shall keep it unto life eternal" (*John* 12, 14-15).

The "life" or the "soul" to be sacrificed is, we repeat, the ego as passional nucleus and not as a particular subjectivity; nor is the criterion of a spiritual degree the absence of consciousness of self, which could not be a habitual condition — otherwise Christ could never have moved in the world — but it is being rid of passional entanglement rooted in desire, ostentation and optical illusion. The first spiritual phase is isolation, for the world is the ego; the summit is to "see God everywhere", for the world is God. In other words, there is one spiritual perfection in which the contemplative sees God only inwardly, in the silence of the heart; and there is another that is superior to this and derives from it — for the second of these can only be conceived as an extension of the first — in which the contemplative perceives God equally in the outward, in phenomena; in their existence, and then in their general and particular qualities, and indirectly even in their privative manifestations. In this realization, not only does the ego appear extrinsic — which happens also in the case of the first perfection — but the world appears as inward inasmuch as it reveals its Divine substance, things becoming as it were translucent. It is to this realization, at once radiating and all-embracing, that the Sufis allude when they say, with Shibli: "I have never seen. anything but God."

But to "see God everywhere" may also have a more particular meaning, which in a sense coincides with the understanding of the "language of the birds" and at the same time brings us back to the principle that "extremes meet": the intelligence that is penetrated by what is most inward may thereby possess, as if by a divine gift, the faculty of understanding the secret intentions of outward things and so of forms in an altogether general sense.

• • •

Above, we quoted the words of Christ on "life", to the effect that those who would save it lose it, and that those who are willing to lose it save it for eternity. No doubt this teaching makes a first distinction — an entirely general one — between worldly and spiritual men; but it refers equally, since it is sacred and therefore polyvalent, to the two subjectivities which particularly concern us, the phenomenal and the intellectual, or the empirical "self" and transcendent "self-hood". In the latter case, the notion of "perdition" has to be transposed; it refers simply to the ambiguous situation of the predominantly "psychic" man. Whereas the "pneumatic" is saved by his ascendent nature, his subjectivity being intellective, the "psychic" risks being lost by reason of the contingent and passive character of his egoity.

But it is in the nature of things for the spiritual subjectivity to occasion an intermediate solution more sacrificial than intellectual, according to which the subject, without being the microcosmic prolongation of the Self in Shankara's sense of the term, is not limited either to being the empirical "self". This is the heroic subjectivity of the way of Love, which tears itself away from phenomena without, however, being able to integrate itself into the transcendent and immanent Witness. A ray of Mercy then enters into the subjectivity withdrawn from the world; deprived of the worldly "self", the immortal soul ends by living on the Grace which upholds and adopts it.

• • •

Since the distinction between the two subjectivities is essential, no spiritually complete civilization can be without it. Even if we did not know of a Meister Eckhardt, we would none the less have to admit that this point of view is not absent from Christianity. Meister Eckhardt, with characteristic audacity, prayed God to free him from God, but made it clear that this referred to God as the origin of creatures and that our essential being is above God envisaged in this fashion; "the essence of God and the essence of the soul are one and the same," he said, thus providing the key to the enigma. This way of putting things expresses a compensatory reciprocity between the Absolute and the Relative, or between *Ātmā* and *Māyā*: for joined to the mystery of incommensurability (in Islam: *Lā ilāha illā 'Llāh*) is the compensatory mystery of reciprocity (in Islam: *Muhammadun Rasūlu'Llāh*). In other words, there is in *Ātmā* a point which is *Māyā*, and that is Being or the Personal God, while there is in *Māyā* a point which is *Ātmā*, and that is Beyond-Being or the Divine Essence present in the Intellect; it is the immanent "absoluteness" in human "relativity". This brings us back once again to the Taoist symbolism of *Yin-Yang* where the white part has a black centre, and the black part has a white centre. The fact that man can conceive of the limitation of Being in relation to the pure Absolute proves that he can in principle realize this pure Absolute and thus transcend what emanates from Being in the way of legislation, namely religion; we say "in principle", because it is in fact very rare; otherwise the religions would not exist.

"If I were not, God would not be either," says Meister Eckhardt, and his meaning becomes clear in the light of the doctrine that has just been expounded; and he is careful to add, for those who do not understand this "stark naked truth which has issued forth from the very heart of God", that they should not "beat their heads against a wall", for this truth is understood only by one who is "like unto it". In other words, the doctrine of the Supreme Subjectivity demands a providential predisposition to receive it; we say a "predisposition" rather than a "capacity", for the principal cause of metaphysical incomprehension is not so much a fundamental incapacity of the intellect as a passional attachment to concepts which conform to man's natural individualism. By transcending this individualism man becomes on the one hand predisposed to this kind of comprehension; metaphysics itself, on the other hand, contributes to this transcending; every spiritual realization has two poles or points of departure, one situated in our thinking and the other in our being.

The *Sūrat ar-Rahmān, LV* (The All-Merciful) attributes "to him who fears the Station of his Lord" two gardens of Paradise, and then goes on to mention two further gardens. According to the commentators, the first two gardens are destined respectively for men and the jinn, or again, according to others, for each believer, but without the difference in the gardens being explained; as far as the two further gardens are concerned, Bayḍāwī—and there are many who follow him—takes the view that they are for believers of lesser merit or lesser quality. According to others, headed by Kāshānī, the second two are, on the contrary, higher than the first two, but this question, which depends on the symbolic descriptions of the Paradises, is of no importance here. It seems to us in any case admissible to make a distinction in each of the two pairs mentioned, between a "horizontal" garden and a "vertical" one, this second Paradise being none other than God Himself as He communicates Himself or manifests Himself in relation to the degree envisaged; this is the exact equivalent of the distinction between the "celestial body" of the Buddhas and their "divine body".

In the case of the "chosen" or those "brought near" (*muqarrabūn*), the "vertical" garden is the state of Union; we have already seen that this state could not prevent the personal presence of the "bodies of glory" in a created Paradise, for without this possibility many passages of the Scriptures and many sacred phenomena would be inexplicable. As for the two lower gardens, the higher of the two will not be a Paradise of "Union" but of "beatific vision", this vision being, like Union, "vertical" in relation to a "horizontal" and therefore phenomenal and, strictly speaking, human beatitude. One of the symbolisms which denotes celestial "verticality" in relation to celestial "horizontality" is that of the "crowns of uncreated light" which, according to a Christian tradition, the elect will wear; and this meaning applies first and foremost, at an unsurpassable level of reality, to the "Coronation of the Virgin".

In the celebrated Prayer of Ibn Mashīsh, which is concerned with the Logos or the *Ḥaqīqah al-muḥammadiyyah*, there is mention of "the loveliness of Beauty" and "the overflowing of Glory"; apart from other meanings, this may be taken to refer to the two "axial" degrees of Heaven. In erotic symbolism, it is the difference between "vision" of the beloved and "union"; in the latter event form is extinguished in the same way as accidents are re-absorbed into the Substance and the Divine Qualities become undifferentiated in the Essence. This extinction, or re-absorption or, again, indifferentiation, relates to what has been called on other occasions the "perspective of centripetal rays" as opposed to that of "concentric circles". In terms of the first mystery, which is that of continuity or inclusivity—and here it is a question of something infinitely more than a "way of seeing things"—"all is *Ātmā*", and direct union is consequently possible; in terms of the second mystery, "*Brahma* is not in the world", and separation between the created and the uncreated orders is consequently absolute, and therefore irreducible (this is the mystery of discontinuity or exclusivity). It is only on the basis of this irreducibility that the inclusive homogeneity of the Real can be adequately conceived together with its spiritual consequence, the mystery of Identity or of the "Paradise of the Essence".

NOTES

Some Observations on a Problem of Afterlife
1. xi, 107-8.

2. Bukhār/mī, *Rıqaqq* 1.

3. ix, 72.

4. xxviii, 88. So also the Gospel: 'Heaven and earth shall pass away, but my Words shall not pass away' (St Luke, xxi, 33).

5. Abdul-Qādir Al-Jīlānī states in the place of Hell, when it is extinguished, there will spring up a green tree called *Jarjir*, 'and the best of the colours of Paradise is green', opposed to the red of fire.

6. This explains an apparent contradiction in the Qoran which, having limited Paradise to 'so long as the heavens and the earth endure' immediately adds that Paradise is 'a gift which shall not be cut off'.

7. Christianity possesses the same key in this saying of Jesus 'There is none good but one, that is, God' (*Nemo bonus nisi unus Deus*) (St Mark x, 18). This sentence contains the whole doctrine of the relationship of the contingent to the Absolute and consequently expresses the non-eternity of created states: Heaven, not being God, could not be 'good', it is thus of necessity ephemeral when considered on the scale of the 'Lives of *Brahmā*' and in relation to 'existence'.

8. A Hindu text describing the Apocatastasis says that *tamas* will be converted into *rajas*, and *rajas* into *sattva*. In the Apocalypse of St Peter, the risen Christ speaks of the Apocatastasis while at the same time forbidding the disclosure of this doctrine, in order that men may not sin the more; it is indeed only logical that it has not been retained in the general teaching of the church. But in our days the situation is quite different, at least as regards the opportuneness of certain truths, though not as regards the dogmas.

9. 'There are many mansions in my Father's house,' said Christ. St Irenaeus refers to this saying when echoing a doctrine according to which some will enter Heaven, others the earthly Paradise, and others again the celestial Jerusalem; all will see the Saviour, but in different manners according to their degree of dignity.

10. The meeting point between the monotheistic eschatology and Indian 'transmigrationism' lies hidden — in Monotheism — in the concepts of Limbo and Hell, and also in the 'resurrection of the flesh', in which the being is not however invested with a new individuality.

Universal Eschatology

1. Although the latter always constitutes the occasional cause, or the initial cause, of the corresponding intellection.

2. As we have demonstrated on other occasions, above all in our book *From the Divine to the Human*, in the chapter "Consequences Flowing from the Mystery of Subjectivity."

3. This is not a contradiction, for the specific nature of man comprises by definition elements disposed towards supernaturalness.

4. It is in this place that Dante places *de facto* — all things considered — the sages and heroes of antiquity, even though he associates them with the Inferno, for reasons of theology since they were "heathens".

5. Those Hindu Paradises from which one is expelled after the exhaustion of "good karma" are places, not of salvation but of transient reward; "peripheral" and not "central" places, and situated outside the human state since they pertain to transmigration.

6. This saying also, and implicitly, comprises an esoteric reference to the celestial sectors of the diverse religions.

7. And let us specify that, if there are degrees in Paradise, there are also rhythms, which the Koran expresses in saying that the blessed will have their nourishment "morning and evening". There is, moreover, no world without hierarchic levels or cycles, that is without "space" or "time".

8. This possibility of interreligious communication clearly has a meaning as well when one and the same personage, at once historical and celestial, appears in different religions, as is the case of the Biblical Prophets, even though their functions differ according to the religion in which they manifest themselves.

9. "God wrongeth not mankind in aught; but mankind wrong themselves." (*Koran*, Sura *Yūnus*, 44)

10. "And (remember) when thy Lord brought forth from the Children of Adam, from their reins, their seed, and made them testify of themselves, (saying): Am I not your Lord? They said: Yes, verily. We testify. (That was) lest ye should say at the Day of Resurrection: Lo! of this we were unaware; Or lest ye should say: (It is) only (that) our fathers ascribed partners to God of old and we were (their) seed after them..." (Sura The Heights, 172 and 173) —These preexistential creatures are the individual possibilities necessarily contained within All-Possibility, and called forth to Existence — not produced by a moral Will — by the existentiating Radiation.

On the Notion of Hell

1. 'And they say: The Fire will not touch us save for a certain number of days. Say: Have ye received a covenant from Allah — truly Allah will not break His covenant — or tell ye concerning Allah that which ye know not? Nay, but whosoever hath done evil and his sin surroundeth him; such are the rightful owners of the Fire; they will abide therein' (*khālidūn*). (Quran, II, 80-81). Here the whole emphasis is on the proposition: '. .and his sin surroundeth him' (*wa aḥātat bihi khatī 'atuhu*), which indicates the essential, and so 'mortal' character of the transgression. This passage is a reply to men who believed, not that Hell as such is metaphysically limited, but that the duration of the punishment is equal to that of the sin.

2. Theologians are not in principle unaware that the 'eternity' of hell — the case of paradise is somewhat different — is not on the same level as that of God and could not be identical with it; but this subtlety remains for them without consequences. If, in the Semitic Scriptures, exotericism is predicated by such ideas as creation *ex nihilo* and a survival both individual and eternal, the exoteric tendency likewise appears in Hindu and Buddhist Scriptures — though in a different fashion — in the sense that these texts appear to place on this earth those phases of transmigration which are neither celestial nor infernal; in the climate of Hinduism exotericism, always averse to subtle explanations, is reduced to simplicity of the symbols. Certainly one eschatology may be more complete than another, but none could be absolutely adequate by reason of the very limitation of human and earthly imagination.

3. There is assymmetry as between celestial and infernal states because the former are eminently nearer to pure Being than the latter; their 'eternity' is thus on any reckoning different from that of the hells.

4. El-Ghazzālī relates in his *Durrat el-fākhirah* that one man, when plunged into the fire, cried out more loudly than all the others: 'And he was taken out all burned. And God said to him: Why did you cry out more loudly than all the other people in the fire? He replied: Lord, Thou hast judged me, but I have not lost faith in Thy mercy. . . .And God said: Who despairs of the mercy of his Lord if not those who have gone astray? (Quran, XV, 56) Go in peace, I have pardoned you.' From a Catholic point of view this would refer to 'purgatory'. Buddhism knows of Bodhisattvas, such as Kshitigarbha, who give relief to the damned with celestial dew or bring them other alleviations, and this is an indication that there are angelic functions of mercy which reach even to hell.

5. (Surats VI, 129 and XI, 107). The same reservation concerns Paradise: '. . .they will abide there. . .so long as the heavens and the earth endure unless thy Lord willeth otherwise; a gift never failing' (XI, 108). This last proposition relates most

directly to the participation by 'those brought nigh' (*muqarrabūn*) in the Divine Eternity by virtue of the supreme union; in their case (that of the *karma-mukti* of Vedantic doctrine) Paradise opens out into Divinity at the end of the cycle ('so long as the heavens and the earth endure'), as is also the case of the Paradises of Vishnu and of Amida. As for the reservation mentioned above, it indicates the possibility of later, though always beneficial changes for those who, to use a Sufi expression, 'prefer the garden to the Gardener'—those, that is, whose state is the fruit of action and not of knowledge or pure love. Here may also be mentioned the possibility of the Bodhisattvas who, while remaining inwardly in Paradise, enter a particular world which is by analogy 'earthly', and also, at a much lower level, those non-human benedictions which, thanks to a particular *karma*, a being may use up passively like a plant absorbing food. But none of this enters into the perspective of what are called the monotheisms, a perspective which, moreover, does not include either the rhythm of the cosmic cycles or, *a fortiori*, the rhythm of the universal cycles (the 'lives of *Brahma*'), although certain *ahādīth* and passages in the Bible (including, no doubt, the 'reign of a thousand years') refer to these ideas more or less overtly.

PART VIII

CRITICISM OF THE MODERN WORLD

Criticism of Modern Philosophy

Modern Philosophy, Logic and Intuition*

THE FOLLOWING POINT cannot be sufficiently stressed: philosophy, in the sense in which we understand the term (which is also its current meaning) primarily consists of logic; this definition of Guénon's puts philosophic thought in its right place and clearly distinguishes it from "intellectual intuition", which is the direct apprehension of truth. It is important, however, to establish yet another distinction on the rational plane itself. Logic can either operate as part of an intellection, or else, on the contrary, put itself at the service of an error; moreover unintelligence can diminish or even nullify logic, so that philosophy can in fact become the vehicle of almost anything: it can be an Aristotelianism carrying ontological insights, just as it can degenerate into an "existentialism" in which logic has become a mere shadow of itself, a blind and unreal operation; indeed, what can be said of a "metaphysic" which idiotically posits man at the centre of the Real, like a sack of coal, and which operates with such blatantly subjective and conjectural concepts as "worry" and "anguish"? When unintelligence — and the variety we mean here is in no wise incompatible with what passes for intelligence in "worldly" circles — and passion prostitute logic, it is impossible to escape from that mental satanism which is so frequently to be found in contemporary thought.

*From *LS*, pp. 7-9.

The validity of a logical demonstration thus depends on the knowledge which we, as demonstrators, have of the subject in view, and it is evidently wrong to take as our starting-point not this direct knowledge but pure and simple logic. When man has no "visionary" knowledge of Being, and merely "thinks" with his "brain" instead of "seeing" with his "heart", all his logic is useless to him, because it starts out from an initial fallacy. Moreover, the validity of a demonstration must be distinguished from its dialectical efficacy; the latter evidently depends on the intuitive disposition available for the recognition of truth when demonstrated, and therefore on an intellectual capacity. Logic is nothing but the science of mental co-ordination and of arriving at rational conclusions; it cannot, therefore, attain the transcendent through its own resources; a supralogical — not an illogical — dialectic, based on symbolism and analogy, and therefore descriptive rather than ratiocinative, may be harder for some people to assimilate, but it conforms more closely to transcendent Reality. Contemporary philosophy, on the other hand, really amounts to a decapitated logic: what is intellectually evident it calls "prejudice"; wishing to free itself from servitude to the *mental*, it sinks into infra-logic; shutting itself off from the intellectual light above, it exposes itself to the obscurity of the lowest "subconscious" beneath.[1] Philosophic scepticism takes itself for a healthy attitude and for an absence of "prejudices", whereas it is in fact something completely artificial; it proceeds, not from real knowledge, but from sheer ignorance, and for this reason it is as alien to intelligence as it is to reality.

The fact that the philosophic type of thought is centred on logic and not directly on intuition implies that the latter is left at the mercy of the needs of the former: in the Scholastic disputations of medieval Europe, it was sometimes less a question of truth than of a certain opportunism in the field of logic, the point being to steer clear of certain dangerous conclusions. Christian Scholasticism, it must not be forgotten, was above all a rampart against error; it aimed at being an apologetic, and not an auxiliary to meditation or contemplation as is the case with the doctrines of "operative" metaphysic — of gnosis or *jñāna*. Prior to Scholasticism, Greek philosophy, for its part, aimed at satisfying a certain logical need to determine causes rather than at furnishing intelligence with a means to realization: moreover, the fact that truth possesses the quality of disinterestedness leads easily, on the plane of speculative logic, to a tendency to pursue "art for art's sake" and hence to fall into that "windy loquacity of the philosophers" stigmatized by St. Bernard . . .

Conceptual Dimensions*

The true and complete understanding of an idea goes far beyond the first apprehension of the idea by the intelligence, although more often than not this apprehension is taken for understanding itself. While it is true that the immediate evidence conveyed to us by any particular idea is, on its own level, a real understanding, there can be no question of its embracing the whole extent of the idea, since it is primarily the sign of an aptitude to understand that idea in its completeness. Any truth can in fact be understood at different levels and according to different conceptual dimensions, that is to say, according to an indefinite number of modalities that correspond to all the possible aspects, likewise indefinite in number, of the truth in question. This way of regarding ideas accordingly leads to the question of spiritual realization, the doctrinal expressions of which clearly illustrate the dimensional indefinitude of theoretical conceptions.

Philosophy, considered from the standpoint of its limitations — and it is the limitations of philosophy that confer upon it its specific character — is based on the systematic ignoring of what has been stated above. In other words, philosophy ignores what would be its own negation; moreover, it concerns itself solely with mental schemes that, with its claim to universality, it likes to regard as absolute, although from the point of view of spiritual realization these schemes are merely so many virtual or potential and unused objects, insofar at least as they refer to true ideas; when, however, this is not the case, as practically always occurs in modern philosophy, these schemes are reduced to the condition of mere devices that are unusable from a speculative point of view and are therefore without any real value. As for true ideas, those, that is to say, that more or less implicitly suggest aspects of the total Truth, and hence this Truth itself, they become by that very fact intellectual keys and indeed have no other function; this is something that metaphysical thought alone is capable of grasping. So far as philosophical or ordinary theological thought is concerned, there is, on the contrary, an ignorance affecting not only the nature of the ideas that are believed to be completely under-

*From *TUR*, Chapter 1.

stood, but also and above all the scope of theory as such; theoretical understanding is in fact transitory and limited by definition, though its limits can only be more or less approximately defined...

In order to forestall possible misunderstandings we feel we should warn the reader that we do not necessarily subscribe to every assessment, conclusion, or theory formulated in the name of metaphysical, esoteric, or broadly traditional principles; in other words, we do not espouse any theory simply because it belongs to some particular school, and we wish to be held responsible solely for what we write ourselves. This question of "school" reminds us of a further classificatory term, that of "traditionalism"; like "esoterism", it has nothing pejorative about it in itself and one might even say that it is less open to argument and a far broader term, in any case, than the latter; in fact, however, with a particularly reprehensible arbitrariness it has been associated with an idea which inevitably devalues its meaning, namely the idea of "nostalgia for the past"; it is hardly credible that such an idiotic and dishonest circumlocution should be freely resorted to as an argument against strictly doctrinal positions or even purely logical ones. Those who look back longingly at some past age because it embodied certain vital values are reproached for adhering to these values because they are found in the past, or because one would like to situate them there "irreversibly"; one might as well say that the acceptance of an arithmetical proof is the sign, not of the unimpaired functioning of the intelligence, but of a morbid obsession with numbers. If to recognize what is true and just is "nostalgia for the past", it is quite clearly a crime or a disgrace not to feel this nostalgia.

The same goes for other accusations prompted by the idea of tradition, such as those of "romanticism", "aestheticism", or "folklore"; far from disclaiming any affinity with these things, we adopt them in the precise measure that they have a relationship either with tradition or with virgin nature, restoring to them in consequence their legitimate and, at the very least, innocent meanings. For "beauty is the splendor of the true"; and since it is possible to be capable of perceiving this without lacking "seriousness", to say the least, we do not feel obliged to offer excuses for being particularly sensitive to this aspect of the Real.

Rationalism, Real and Apparent*

The effectiveness of a metaphysical reasoning depends essentially upon two conditions, the one internal and the other external: namely the acuity and profundity of the intelligence, on the one hand, and the worth or amplitude of the available information, on the other. These two conditions do not lie wholly within the sphere of rationalism, the first because it may call into play pure Intellection over and above the indirect processes of the reason, and the second because it does not apply only to simple sensorial and psychological acts, but may involve the supernatural (though in no wise irrational) phenomenon of Revelation.[1] The rationalist is not a person who reasons adequately in terms of total and supralogical intelligence and on the basis of the necessary data — data that are traditional in origin when it comes to things that escape the limitations of common experience — but, on the contrary, a person who thinks he can resolve every problem, be it even by denying its existence, by means of logic alone and on the basis of some arbitrarily exploited fact.

Such being the case, all integral rationalism is false by definition; and since nothing is ever rejected without its being replaced by something else, it will be individual tendencies that will supplant the missing Intellection. A reasoning that is square in shape — if such an image be permitted — will reject a spherical reality and will replace it with a square error based on a personal tendency that is opposed to the global reality of existence and the spirit; in other words, a profane system of thought is always the portrait of an individual, even when it is mingled with some glimmerings of knowledge, as must always be the case since the reason is not a closed vessel.

Reason, then, to the extent that it is artificially divorced from the Intellect, engenders individualism and arbitrariness. This is exactly what happens in the case of someone like Kant, who is a rationalist even while rejecting "dogmatic rationalism"; while the latter is doubtless rationalism, the Kantian critical philosophy is even more deserving of the name, indeed it is the very acme of rationalism.

*From *LT,* Chapter 3

As is well known this critical philosophy looks upon metaphysics, not as the science of the Absolute and of the true nature of things, but as the "science of the limits of human reason", this reason (*Vernunft*) being identified with intelligence pure and simple, an utterly contradictory axiom, for in terms of what can the intelligence limit itself, seeing that by its very nature it is in principle unlimited or it is nothing? And if the intelligence as such is limited, what guarantee do we have that its operations, including those of critical philosophy, are valid? For an intellectual limit is a wall of which one has no awareness. One cannot therefore have it both ways: either the intelligence by definition comprises a principle of illimitability or liberty,[2] whatever be the degree of its actualization, in which case there is no call to attribute limits to it with an arbitrariness that is all the more inexcusable in that the power of a particular individual intelligence (or mode of intelligence) is not necessarily a criterion for the appraisal of intelligence as such; or else, on the contrary, the intelligence comprises, likewise by definition, a principle of limitation or constraint, in which case it no longer admits of any certitude and cannot function any differently from the intelligence of animals, with the result that all pretension to a "critical philosophy" is vain.

If the normal functioning of the intelligence has to be subjected to a critique, then the criticizing consciousness has to be subjected to a critique in its turn by asking, "what is it that thinks?" and so forth — a play of mirrors whose very inconclusiveness demonstrates its absurdity, proved more over in advance by the very nature of cognition. A thought is "dogmatist", or else it is nothing; a thought that is "criticist" is in contradiction with its own existence. A subject who casts doubt on man's normal subjectivity thereby casts doubt upon his own doubting; and this is just what has happened to critical philosophy, swept away in its turn, and through its own fault, by existentialism in all its forms.

•   •   •

According to the sensationalists, all knowledge originates in sensorial experience; theologians hasten to add that this applies only to man's "natural" capacity for knowledge — a comment that does not render the above opinion any the less debatable — whereas the extreme sensationalists go so far as to maintain that human knowledge can have no other source than the experience in question: which merely proves that they themselves have no access to any suprasensory knowledge and are unaware of the fact that the suprasensible can be the object of a genuine perception and hence of a concrete experience. Thus, it is upon an intellectual infirmity that these thinkers build their systems, without their appearing to be in the least impressed by the fact that countless men as intelligent as themselves (to put it mildly) have thought otherwise than they do. How, for example, did a man like Kant explain to himself the fact that his thesis, so immensely important for humankind, if it were true, was unknown to all the peoples of the world and had not been discovered by a single sage, and how did he account for the fact that men of the highest abilities labored under lifelong illusions (in his eyes) which were totally incompatible with those abilities — even founding religions, producing sanctity, and creating civilizations? Surely the least one might ask of a "great thinker" is a little imagination.

• • •

Apart from the forms of sensory knowledge, Kant admits the categories, regarded by him as innate principles of cognition; these he divides into four groups inspired by Aristotle,[3] while at the same time subjectivizing the Aristotelian notion of category. He develops in his own way the Peripatetic categories that he accepts while discarding others, without realizing that, regardless of Aristotelianism, the highest and most important of the categories have eluded his grasp.[4]

The categories are *a priori* independent of all experience since they are innate; Kant recognized this, yet he considered that they were capable of being "explored" by a process he called "transcendental investigation". But how will one ever grasp the pure subject who explores and who investigates?

Another feature of this suicidal rationalism is the following: we are asked to believe that knowledge, thus reduced to a combination of sensory experiences and the innate categories, shows us things such as they appear to be and not such as they are; as if the inherent nature of things did not pierce through their appearances, given that the whole point of knowledge is the perception of a thing-in-itself — an aseity — failing which the very notion of perception would not exist.

To speak of a knowledge that is incapable of adequation is a contradiction in terms, disproved moreover by experience at every level of the knowable; in short, it is absurd to deduce from the obvious fact that our knowledge cannot become totally identified with its objects — at least when these objects are relative[5] — that all speculations on the aseity of things are "empty and vain" (*leer und nichtig*). To turn this dictatorial conclusion into an argument against metaphysical "dogmatism", so far from unmasking the latter, serves only to demonstrate the emptiness and vanity of critical philosophy, thus causing the argument to rebound upon itself.

All the hopeless pedantism of this philosophy becomes glaringly apparent in the notion of "sophistications": this is the name it gives to reasonings which are devoid of "empirical premises", and which enable us to infer something of which (so it appears) we have no idea — as, for example, when we infer the reality of God from the existence of the world or the qualities it manifests. The philosopher, who in other respects displays so little of the poet, does nevertheless have enough poetic imagination to describe conclusions of this kind as "sophistical mirages" (*sophistische Blendwerke*); that a reasoning might simply be the logical and provisional description of an intellectual evidence, and that its function might be the actualization of this evidence, in itself supralogical, apparently never crosses the minds of pure logicians.

This brings us to a point that is overlooked by every form of rationalism insofar as it replaces Intellection with mere logic: namely that in regard to Intellection the rational faculty has two functions to fulfill, the one descending or communicating and the other ascending or actualizing. In the first case, the task of reason is to formulate direct intellectual perceptions dialectically, availing itself for this purpose of symbolical expressions or logical demonstrations on which, however, those perceptions themselves are in no wise dependent. In the second case, the reason of the hearer or reader for whom the teaching is intended participates in the intellection that is being communicated, not only to the extent that the logical process appears irrefutable, but first and foremost, even if only *a posteriori*, because this process actualizes through the instrumentality of the reason the intellection in question, however partial the actualization may be.

A rationalist is a person who upholds the primacy, or rather the exclusive worth, of reason as compared with Intellection on the one hand and Revelation on the other, both of which he accuses of being "irrational". He will claim, for example, that a miracle is irrational because it is contrary to reason, which is an inept argument, since there is nothing to be found in any religion which is opposed to reason as such; the most one can say is that the supernatural is contrary to common experience and also to certain subjective tendencies which have been systematized and then given the name of logic . . .[6]

• • •

Agnostics and other relativists contest the value of metaphysical certitude; in order to demonstrate the illusory character of the *de jure* certitude of truth, they oppose to it the *de facto* certitude of error, as though the psychological phenomenon of false certitudes could prevent true certitudes from being what they are and from having all their effectiveness, and as though the very existence of false certitudes did not prove in its own way the existence of true ones. The fact that a lunatic feels certain that he is something he is not does not prevent our being certain of what he is and of what we ourselves are; and the fact that we are unable to prove to him that he is mistaken does not prevent our being right. Or again, the fact that an unbalanced person may possibly have misgivings about his condition does not oblige us to have them about our own, even if we find it impossible to prove to him that our certitude is well founded. It is absurd to demand absolute proofs of suprasensorial realities that one thinks one ought to question, while refusing in the name of reason to consider metaphysical arguments that are sufficient in themselves; for (as has been said already) outside of these arguments the only proof of hidden realities that remains are these realities themselves. One cannot ask the dawn to be the sun, or a shadow to be the tree that casts it; it is the very existence of our intelligence that proves the reality of the relationships of causality, those same relationships which allow us to admit the Invisible and by the same token oblige us to do so; if the world did not prove God, the human intelligence would be deprived of its sufficient reason. First and foremost, leaving aside any question of intellectual intuition, we should infer Pure Being from the very fact of our existence; instead of starting with the idea that "I think, therefore, I am," one should say, "I am, therefore, Being is" (*sum ergo est Esse,* and not *cogito ergo sum*).[7] What counts in our eyes is most definitely not some more or less correct reasoning, but intrinsic certitude itself. Reasoning is able to convey this certitude after its fashion by describing it with a view to making its evidence manifest on the plane of discursive thought, thus furnishing a key to the actualization by others of this same certitude.[8] . . .

Letter on Existentialism[1]*

The Western mentality has given rise to four metaphysical perspectives which are either perfect or at least satisfactory as the case may be, namely: Platonism, including Neo-Platonism; Aristotelianism; Scholasticism; Palamism.

A question: Why was Kierkegaard neither Platonist, nor Aristotelian, nor Scholastic, nor Palamite? Is it because he was a Vedantist or a Mahayanist? Certainly not. Consequence: His doctrine is null and void. The proof of this is that he rejects "organized" Christianity, hence the traditional theology which upholds it, and he does so in favour of a subjectivism which is not intellectual (for in that case he would have acknowledged objective metaphysics whose mode of expression perforce is rational and abstract) but voluntaristic and sentimental; whence comes his subjectivistic or individualistic moralism, his insistence on thinking "existentially", his nullity from the point of view of the real and efficacious spirituality which saves.

The same remarks — *mutatis mutandis* — apply to Heidegger, with the aggravating circumstance that this decadent philosopher is no longer even Christian in any degree, being in fact, to put it briefly, an atheist; and what about the concept — completely antimetaphysical and hysterical — of anguish?

Pascal cannot be ranked among the existentialists; he was simply a believing rationalist unaware that the strict data for a metaphysical science pre-exist in pure Intellect; if Pascal is existentialist, then all fideism is existentialism, which is certainly not the case.

At no degree is existentialism constructive, for it has no right

*From *SCR*, Winter 1975, pp. 66-69.

to criticise the abuse of a rationality whose nature it does not even perceive. If the existentialists' criticism of reason — or of rationalism — is justified, why do they not become Platonists or Vedantists? In fact, existentialism does not bring us one bit nearer the truth; to the rationalist error, which consists in reasoning about metaphysical or even simply cosmological realities in the absence of the indispensable intellectual data, existentialism adds the inverse error and substitutes, for reasoning good or bad, true or false, an experience which is in fact infra-intellectual, a cul-de-sac. Therefore, the existentialist movement, which is a blind reaction, gets us absolutely nowhere, and there is no point in saying that "Asia, not having severed reason from intellection, did not need an existentialist movement"; apart from the fact that India has indeed known some rationalists like the Chârvâkas, who in truth does need existentialism? For one cannot need something false, something which leads to nothing.

Having in mind Kierkegaard and others like him, such as Klages, for example, who passionately opposes "life" to "thought" and paradoxically enough does so by thinking, I wrote on the subject: "What can be said of a philosopher who 'thinks' blithely about the insincerity, or the mediocrity, of 'thought' as such?" Now the word "blithely" (*allégrement*) in this case means: without scruples, without being aware of contradiction, without taking the trouble to reflect a little, without manifesting a modicum of objectivity; after all, why would an avowed subjectivist be objective? This has absolutely nothing to do with Kierkegaard's character, it being a question uniquely of the irresponsible style of his thought, his lack of a critical sense and his lack of a sense of proportion. He liquidated "organized Christianity" with a stroke of the pen; is not that enough? He had the pretension, like all philosophers, to claim to be presenting an adequate picture of the total truth and thus to be indicating a way; well he was mistaken and must therefore be rejected without pity, I will even say: with horror. For the question of knowing if he was right in some point does not come up at all; every philosopher is right in some point, and this is totally without interest. What counts is the global doctrine, its claims and its consequences.

The case which Kierkegaard makes against rational thought could never coincide with the one I myself make against the mentality of fallen man, for I make my criticism in the name of the Intellect, of which Kierkegaard had not the slightest idea. No doubt I will be told that this thinker, if he did not make his criticism in the name of intellection, at least did so in the name of faith; but he was just as ignorant as to what constitutes true faith, since in the name of his faith he attacks theology, which is precisely an indispensable objectification and a *conditio sine qua non* of the faith of the heart. Kierkegaard's faith is individualistic, not sanctifying.

Kierkegaard doubtless had a deep respect for Socrates, but this is because he understood him very imperfectly; Socratic sincerity has other foundations than existentialist sincerism. In the same manner, the *Gelassenheit* of Heidegger could have neither the meaning nor the scope of Meister Eckhart's *Gelassenheit*, of which it is merely a profane and individualistic counterfeit without any possible issue. "Ye shall know them by their fruits," said Christ.

Heidegger "seeks" a mode of knowledge which goes beyond discursive thought; this is all very well, but discursive thought is worth infinitely more in itself than anything that a Heidegger can conceive of, seek, or find.

It is obvious that Kierkegaard had to admit Revelation — namely the Bible — since he was a Protestant; he had a certain merit in being Christian, namely, in believing in Christ, in God, and in eternal life; but he had no particular intellectual merit in admitting Revelation as a principle or phenomenon, for the existence of Revelation is truly the minimum that an adversary of "organized Christianty" can admit. Not to admit the fact of Revelation is to be a deist or an atheist.

The thing which is absolutely lacking with the existentialists, and which reduces to nothing their theories as well as their moral attitudes, is an objective truth which is metaphysically integral, whether it be an orthodox theology or an authentic metaphysics. All their partial merits thus fall into a void. "He that gathereth not with me scattereth," said Christ; the "me" here is the Logos, and it is Orthodoxy in the universal as well as the particular sense.

True, Kierkegaard observed that rationality when left to itself, or rationality without faith, namely "rationalism", leads nowhere; but then neither does his altogether subjective faith — his existentialism if you prefer — lead anywhere either; and if the objection is raised that this faith nonetheless derives its inspiration from the Gospel, I can reply that rationalism likewise takes its inspiration from certain sufficient data since man lives in a world which is relatively real. What the Gospel — arbitrarily reduced to the fancies of an individual — is for Kierkegaard, so is limited experience for the rationalists; and if the Danish philosopher—who was moreover a very poor theologian—took as his basis the Gospel, then why was he so far from realising the spirit of it? For his point of view even constrains him to become neither more nor less than a saint; yet in fact he was infinitely far from the sanctity of an Albert the Great or a Thomas Aquinas, both of whom completely accepted the rationality that he, the subjectivist, rejected.

Existentialism is a pernicious substitute for intellective contemplation and sanctity. If the existentialists—so imbued with sincerism—were really sincere, they would be saints or heroes and leave rationality in peace.

Certainly truths are to be found in all the philosophers, and above all half-truths, but these truths are flanked with errors and inconsistencies, and there is moreover no need for them; hence it is pointless to dwell on them. Partial truths are only to be accepted in the domain of traditional orthodoxy, because they are only acceptable in the context of the total truth, which alone guarantees their exactitude and their efficacy. To think while denying the total Truth, which is both objective and subjective, is completely inconsistent; it is not really thinking.

The subjective can only be communicated by the objective. If Kierkegaard was right, faith would not be communicable; for in order to be communicated faith requires means which are objective, hence rational.

Truths embedded in errors are fraught indirectly with the venom of their erroneous context. Existentialism has in fact, whether it be Protestant or atheistic, promoted nothing except individualism; never the understanding of metaphysical doctrines, never sanctity!

NOTES

Modern Philosophy, Logic and Intuition

1. This is what Kant, with his rationalistic simplifications, did not foresee. According to him, every cognition which is not rational in the narrowest sense is only affectation and high-flown sentiment *(Schwärmerei)*; now if anything is an affectation, it is this very opinion. It is not on the side of the Scholastics that arbitrariness, phantasy and irrationality are to be found, but wholly on the side of the rationalists, who fling themselves with ridiculous and often pathetic arguments against everything they do not understand. With Voltaire, Rousseau and Kant bourgeois unintel-

ligence *(vaiśya* unintelligence as the Hindus would say) erects itself into a "doctrine" and becomes definitely entrenched in European "thought", giving birth, through the French Revolution, to positivist science, industry and quantitative "culture". Henceforward the mental hypertrophy of the "cultured" man ekes out the absence of intellectual penetration; all feeling for the Absolute and for principles is drowned in a commonplace empiricism, on to which is grafted a pseudo-mysticism with "positivistic" or "humanistic'' tendencies. Perhaps some people will reproach us with lack of reticence, but we would like to ask where is the reticence of the philosophers who shamelessly slash at the wisdom of countless centuries.

Rationalism Real and Apparent

1. In the course of this book it will be made sufficiently clear what is to be understood by this term. For the moment it need simply be said that Revelation is a kind of cosmic Intellection, whereas personal Intellection is comparable to a Revelation on the scale of the microcosm.

2. A liberty or illimitability of which the proof lies in the capacity to conceive the Absolute and thereby the relative as such, which also carries with it the capacity for objectivity.

3. Quantity, quality, relation, and modality; the latter no doubt replacing the Aristotelian "position".

4. Such as the principial and cosmic qualities which determine and classify phenomena, or the universal dimensions which join the world to the Supreme Essence and which include each in its own manner the qualities mentioned above. Aristotle for his part had the right not to speak of them in that he accepted God as being self-evident and his approach was in no way moralistic and empirical; since he accepted God, he did not consider his categories to be exhaustive.

5. This reservation signifies that whereas our vision cannot exhaust the nature of a visible object, the Intellect — precisely because it can reach beyond the relative — is capable in principle of becoming identified with the absolute essence of the object in question.

6. If the term "natural" is paradoxically extended to include everything which is subject to laws, then miracles are also "natural," the only difference being that in their case the laws are not psycho-physical and hence are beyond the reach of human techniques.

7. Franz von Baader, a distant disciple of Boehme, has proposed the formula *cogitor, ergo cogito et sum* (I am thought [by God], therefore I think and I am) which is a pertinent expression of the causal or ontological relationship under consideration here.

8. How well reason performs this function depends on our dialectical capacity and on the questioner's need for logical satisfaction, or on his degree of understanding.

Letter on Existentialism
1. One of our readers, Professor Huston Smith of Syracuse University, N.Y., had sent us this extract from a letter addressed to him which he considers to be of too universal an interest not to be made generally known. The author has agreed to its publication.

Criticism of Modern Science

Modern Science and the Fall of Man*

... MODERN SCIENCE, as it plunges dizzily downwards, its speed increasing in geometrical progression towards an abyss into which it hurtles like a vehicle without brakes, is another example of that loss of the "spatial" equilibrium characteristic of contemplative and still stable civilizations. This criticism of modern science — and it is by no means the first ever to be made — is made not on the grounds that it studies some fragmentary field within the limits of its competence, but on the grounds that it claims to be in a position to attain to total knowledge, and that it ventures conclusions in fields accessible only to a supra-sensible and truly intellective wisdom, the existence of which it refuses on principle to admit. In other words, the foundations of modern science are false because, from the "subject" point of view, it replaces Intellect and Revelation by reason and experiment, as if it were not contradictory to lay claim to totality on an empirical basis; and its foundations are false too because, from the "object" point of view, it replaces the universal Substance by matter alone, either denying the universal Principle or reducing it to matter or to some kind of pseudo-absolute from which all transcendence has been eliminated.

*From *LAW*, pp. 34-38.

In all epochs and in all countries there have been revelations, religions, wisdoms; tradition is a part of mankind, just as man is a part of tradition. Revelation is in one sense the infallible intellection of the total collectivity, in so far as this collectivity has providentially become the receptacle of a manifestation of the universal Intellect. The source of this intellection is not of course the collectivity as such, but the universal or divine Intellect insofar as it adapts itself to the conditions prevailing in a particular intellectual or moral collectivity, whether it be a case of an ethnic group or of one determined by more or less distinctive mental conditions. To say that Revelation is "supernatural" does not mean that it is contrary to nature insofar as nature can be taken to represent, by extension, all that is possible on any given level of reality; it means that Revelation does not originate at the level to which, rightly or wrongly, the epithet "natural" is normally applied. This "natural" level is precisely that of physical causes, and hence of sensory and psychic phenomena considered in relation to those causes.

If there are no grounds for finding fault with modern science insofar as it studies a realm within the limits of its competence — the precision and effectiveness of its results leave no room for doubt on this point — one must add this important reservation, namely, that the principle, the range and the development of a science or an art is never independent of Revelation nor of the demands of spiritual life, not forgetting those of social equilibrium; it is absurd to claim unlimited rights for something in itself contingent, such as science or art. By refusing to admit any possibility of serious knowledge outside its own domain, modern science, as has already been said, claims exclusive and total knowledge, while making itself out to be empirical and non-dogmatic, and this, it must be insisted, involves a flagrant contradiction; a rejection of all "dogmatism" and of everything that must be accepted *a priori* or not at all is simply a failure to make use of the whole of one's intelligence.

Science is supposed to inform us not only about what is in space but also about what is in time. As for the first-named category of knowledge, no one denies that Western science has accumulated an enormous quantity of observations, but as for the second category, which ought to reveal to us what the abysses of duration hold, science is more ignorant than any Siberian shaman, who can at least relate his ideas to a mythology, and thus to an adequate symbolism. There

is of course a gap between the physical knowledge — necessarily
restricted — of a primitive hunter and that of a modern physicist; but
measured against the extent of knowable things, that gap is a mere
millimetre.

Nevertheless, the very precision of modern science, or of certain of its branches, has become seriously threatened, and from a
wholly unforeseen direction, by the intrusion of psychoanalysis, not
to mention that of "surrealism" and other systematizations of the irrational; or again by the intrusion of existentialism, which indeed
belongs strictly speaking not so much to the domain of the irrational
as to that of the unintelligent. A rationality that claims self-sufficiency
cannot fail to provoke such interferences, at any rate at its vulnerable
points such as psychology or the psychological — or "psychologizing"
— interpretation of phenomena which are by definition beyond its
reach.

It is not surprising that a science arising out of the fall — or one
of the falls — and out of an illusory rediscovery of the sensory world
should also be a science of nothing but the sensory, or what is virtually sensory, and that it should deny everything which surpasses
that domain, thereby denying God, the next world and the soul, and
this presupposes a denial of the pure Intellect, which alone is capable
of knowing everything that modern science rejects. For the same
reasons, it also denies Revelation, which alone rebuilds the bridge
broken by the fall. According to the observations of experimental
science, the blue sky which stretches above us is not a world of bliss,
but an optical illusion due to the refraction of light by the atmosphere,
and from this point of view, it is obviously right to maintain that
the home of the blessed does not lie up there. Nevertheless it would
be a great mistake to assert that the association of ideas between the
visible heaven and celestial Paradise does not arise from the nature
of things, but rather from ignorance and ingenuousness mixed with
imagination and sentimentality; for the blue sky is a direct and
therefore adequate symbol of the higher — and supra-sensory —
degrees of Existence; it is indeed a distant reverberation of those
degrees, and it is necessarily so since it is truly a symbol, consecrated
by the sacred Scriptures and by the unanimous intuition of peoples.
A symbol is intrinsically so concrete and so efficacious that celestial
manifestations, when they occur in our sensory world, "descend" to
earth and "reascend" to Heaven; a symbolism accessible to the senses

takes on the function of the supra-sensible reality which it reflects. Light-years and the relativity of the space-time relationship have absolutely nothing to do with the perfectly "exact" and "positive" symbolism of appearances and its connection at once analogical and ontological with the celestial or angelic orders. The fact that the symbol itself may be no more than an optical illusion in no way impairs its precision or its efficacy, for all appearances, including those of space and of the galaxies, are strictly speaking only illusions created by relativity.

One of the effects of modern science has been to give religion a mortal wound, by posing in concrete terms problems which only esoterism can resolve; but these problems remain unresolved, because esoterism is not listened to, and is listened to less now than ever. Faced by these new problems, religion is disarmed, and it borrows clumsily and gropingly the arguments of the enemy; it is thus compelled to falsify by imperceptible degrees its own perspective, and more and more to disavow itself. Its doctrine, it is true, is not affected, but the false opinions borrowed from its repudiators corrode it cunningly "from within"; witness, for example, modernist exegesis, the demagogic levelling down of the liturgy, the Darwinism of Teilhard de Chardin, the "worker-priests", and a "sacred art" obedient to surrealist and "abstract" influences. Scientific discoveries prove nothing to contradict the traditional positions of religion, of course, but there is no one at hand to point this out; too many "believers" consider, on the contrary, that it is time that religion "shook off the dust of the centuries", which amounts to saying, that it should "liberate" itself from its very essence and from everything which manifests that essence. The absence of metaphysical or esoteric knowledge on the one hand, and the suggestive force emanating from scientific discoveries as well as from collective psychoses on the other, make religion an almost defenceless victim, a victim that even refuses more often than not to make use of the arguments at its disposal. It would nevertheless be easy, instead of slipping into the errors of others, to demonstrate that a world fabricated by scientific influences tends everywhere to turn ends into means and means into ends, and that it results either in a mystique of envy, bitterness and hatred, or in a complacent shallow materialism destructive of qualitative distinctions. It could be demonstrated too that science, although in itself neutral — for facts are facts — is none the less a seed of corruption and annihilation in the hands of man, who in general has not enough knowledge of the underlying nature of Existence to be able to integrate — and thereby to neutralize — the facts of science in a total view of the world; that the philosophical consequences of science imply fundamental contradictions; and that man has never been so ill-known and so misinterpreted as from the moment when he was subjected to the "X-rays" of a psychology founded on postulates that are radically false and contrary to his nature.

Modern science represents itself in the world as the principal, or as the only purveyor of truth; according to this style of certainty to know Charlemagne is to know his brain-weight and how tall he was. From the point of view of total truth — let it be said once more — it is a thousand times better to believe that God created this world in six days and that the world beyond lies beneath the flat surface of the earth or in the spinning heavens, than it is to know the distance from one nebula to another without knowing that phenomena merely serve to manifest a transcendent Reality which determines us in every respect and gives to our human condition its whole meaning and its whole content. The great traditions moreover, aware that a Promethean knowledge must lead to the loss of the essential and saving truth, have never prescribed nor encouraged any such accumulating of wholly external items of knowledge, for it is in fact mortal to man. It is currently asserted that such and such a scientific achievement "does honour to the human race", together with other futilities of the same kind, as if man could do honour to his nature otherwise than by surpassing himself, and as if he could surpass himself except in a consciousness of the Absolute and in sanctity.

In the opinion of most men today, experimental science is justified by its results, which are in fact dazzling from a certain fragmentary point of view, but one readily loses sight not only of the decided predominance of bad results over good, but also of the spiritual devastation inherent in the scientific outlook, *a priori* and by its very nature, a devastation which its positive results — always external and partial — can never compensate. In any event, it savours of temerity in these days to dare to recall the most forgotten of Christ's sayings: "For what shall it profit a man, if he shall gain the whole world, and lose his own soul?" (Mark viii. 36)

Modern Science and Metaphysical Reality*

Modern science, with its denial in practice or in principle of all that is really fundamental, and its subsequent rejection of the "one thing needful",[1] is like a planimetry that has no notion of the other directions. It shuts itself up entirely in physical reality or unreality, and there it accumulates an enormous mass of information, while at the same time committing itself to ever more complex conjectures. Starting out from the illusion that nature will end by yielding its ultimate secret and will allow itself to be reduced to some mathematical formula or other, this Promethean science everywhere runs up against enigmas which give the lie to its postulates and which appear as unforeseen fissures in this laboriously erected system. These fissures get plastered over with fresh hypotheses and the vicious circle goes on unchecked, with all the threats we are aware of. Some of its hypotheses, such as the theory of evolution, in practice become dogmas by reason of their usefulness, if not of their plausibility; this usefulness is not only scientific, it can just as well be philosophical or even political, according to circumstances.

In reality, the evolutionary theory, to stress this point once again, is a substitute for the traditional theory of emanation and consists in denying the periphery-center relationship.[2] Thus the very existence of the Center, source of emanation, and of the radii leading to it is denied, and an attempt is made to situate every hierarchical relationship on the curve marking the periphery. Instead of proceeding upward, starting from the corporeal level and passing through the animic sphere, then mounting toward realities at first supraformal and finally principial or metacosmic, an evolving hierarchy is imagined, advancing from matter, through vegetable and animal life, to human consciousness, itself considered as some kind of transitory accident. With a thoughtlessness that is infinitely culpable when they call themselves believers some people imagine a superman who is destined to take man's place, and who consequently would also render Christ's humanity contemptible,[3] and a certain "genius"

*From *LT*, pp. 67-71.

imagines at the end of the evolutionist and progressivist chain something he is not ashamed to call "God" and which is no more than a pseudoabsolute decked out in a pseudotranscendence; for the Eternal will always be Alpha and has always been Omega. Creatures are crystallized in the corporeal zone emanating, in a manner at once continuous and discontinuous, from the Center and from on high; they do not "evolve" by coming from matter and so from the periphery and from below. But at the same time, and beyond reach of our human point of view, creatures are all "contained" in God and do not really come out from Him; the whole play of relationships between God and the world is but a monologue of relativity.

The mystical proof of God is always, in some degree, a participation in the profound nature of things, and consequently it excludes and discredits all speculations which tend to falsify within us the image of the Real and to transfer the Divine Ideas of the Immutable onto the plane of becoming. Modern man wants to conquer space, but the least of contemplative states, or the least of intellections bearing on metaphysical realities, carries us to heights from which the nebula of Andromeda appears scarcely more than a terrestrial accident.

*   *   *

These considerations permit us to underline certain points that have already been touched on. Promethean minds believe themselves to be creatures of chance moving freely in a vacuum and capable of "self-creation", all within the framework of an existence devoid of meaning; the world, so it seems, is absurd, but no notice is taken — and this is typical — of the absurdity of admitting the appearance within an absurd world of a being regarded as capable of remarking that absurdity. Modern man is fundamentally ignorant of what the most childish of catechisms reveals, doubtless in a language that is pictorial and sentimental, yet adequate for its purpose; namely, that we are inwardly connected with a Substance which is Being, Consciousness, and Life, and of which we are contingent and transitory modalities. He is consequently unaware of being involved in a titanic drama in terms of which this world, seemingly so solid, is as tenuous as a spider's web. Existence, invisible and underlying, is concrete, not abstract; it "sleeps" and "awakes", it "breathes" and can make worlds collapse; space, time, and man are no more than minute fragments of a Being and a Movement which escapes all our measurements and all that we can imagine. The Divine Substance, however, cannot have the limiting properties of matter, nor those of an animic fluid. Its homogeneity implies a transcending discontinuity the traces of which are indeed apparent around us and within us (the body is not life and life is not intelligence), but which we cannot grasp adequately with the help of our terrestrial categories alone.

The great misconception, then, is to believe that the basis of our existence is space and that the factors which make up our individual destinies are contained in it, whereas in reality this basis — at one and the same time immutable and in movement according to the relationship envisaged — is situated in a "supra-space" which we can perceive only through the heart intellect and about which those explosions of total Consciousness, the Revelations, speak to us symbolically. The error is to believe that the causes which determine human history or which carry it to its conclusion belong to the same order as our matter or as "natural laws", whereas in fact the whole visible cosmos is resting upon an invisible volcano — but also, at a deeper ontological level, upon a formless ocean of bliss. Men imagine that this earth, these mountains, or bodies can only be destroyed by forces on their own level, by masses or energies belonging to our physical universe. What they do not see, however, is that this world, in appearance so compact, can collapse *ab intra*, that matter can flow back "inward" by a process of transmutation, and that the whole of space can shrink like a balloon emptied of air; in short, that fragility and impermanence not only affect things within a space naively supposed to be stable, they also affect existence itself with all its categories. Our nature consists precisely in the ability to escape, in our innermost core and in the "unchanging Center", from the break-up of a macrocosm that has become oversolidified, and to become reintegrated in the Immutable whence we came forth. What proves this possibility is our capacity to conceive this Immutability; it is also proved, in a concordant manner, by the fact (at once unique and multiple) of Revelation.

Modern Science-Objectivity-Subjectivity*

Believing only what one "sees": this prejudice, as crude as it is common, leads us to insert a parenthesis. Wanting to believe only what they see, scientists condemn themselves to seeing only what they believe; logic for them is their desire not to see what they do not want to believe. Scientism in fact is less interested in the real in itself—which necessarily goes beyond our limitations—than in what is non-contradictory, in what is logical therefore, or more precisely, in what is empirically logical; thus in what is logical *de facto* according to a given experience, and not in what is logical *de jure* in accordance with the nature of things. In reality the "planimetric" recording of perceptions and the elimination of the apparently contradictory only too often gives the measure of a given ignorance, even of a given stupidity; the pedants of "exact science" are moreover incapable of evaluating what is implied by the existential paradoxes in which we live, beginning with the phenomenon, contradictory in practice, of subjectivity. Subjectivity is intrinsically unique while being extrinsically multiple; now if the spectacle of a host of subjectivities other than our own causes us no great perplexity, how shall it be explained "scientifically"—that is, avoiding or eliminating all contradiction—the fact that "I alone" am "I"? So-called "exact" science can find no reason whatever for this apparent absurdity, any more than it can for that other logical and empirical contradiction which is the limitlessness of space, time and the other existential categories. Whether we like it or not we live surrounded by mysteries, which logically and existentially lead us towards transcendence.

Even if the "scientists" could observe the non-contradiction of all possible objective phenomena, there still would remain the contradictory enigma of the scission between the objective universe and the observing subject, not to speak of the "scientifically" insoluble problem of that flagrant contradiction which is the empirical uniqueness of a particular subject, to which problem we have just alluded; and even if we limit ourselves to the objective world, whose limit-

*From *FDH*, pp. 141-144 (trans. G. Polit).

lessness precisely constitutes a contradiction since it is inconceivable according to empirical logic, how can we believe for an instant that the day will finally come when we can put it into a homogeneous and exhaustive system? And how can we fail to see the fundamental and inevitable contradiction between scientistic logic — which is moreover intrinsically deficient since it lacks sufficient data — and the infinity and complexity of the real, which scientism sets itself out to explore, to exhaust and to catalog? The fundamental contradiction of scientism is to want to explain the real without the help of that first science which is metaphysics, hence not to know that only the science of the Absolute gives a meaning and a discipline to the science of the relative; and not to know at the same stroke that the science of the relative, when it is deprived of this help, can only lead to suicide, beginning with that of the intelligence, then with that of the human, and in the end, with that of humanity. The absurdity of scientism is the contradiction between the finite and the Infinite, that is to say, the impossibility of reducing the latter to the former, and the incapacity to integrate the former into the latter; and also the inability to understand that an erudition which cuts itself off from initial Unity can lead only to the innumerable, hence to the indefinite, to shattering and to nothingness.

If therefore the scientific method, or the conceptual system (*die Weltanschauung*) resulting from it, claims to have the privilege of excluding contradictions, it goes without saying that it accuses methods or systems which in its opinion are extrascientific of the defect of accepting what is contradictory; as if there could exist a human and traditional thought which accepts the contradictory *de jure* and not only *de facto*, and as if what is contradictory in religion — supposing that it is not merely in the minds of the scientists — did not imply the consciousness of an underlying non-contradiction, known by God alone! What is the significance of the theological opinion that the human mind has limits, and what is the meaning of the mysteries inasmuch as they are supposed to transcend reason, if not that man is incapable of perceiving the total and homogeneous reality behind the contradictions where his short-sightedness stops? Recourse to the Divine authority of Revelation means nothing else but that, and this is so evident that one would like to excuse oneself for pointing it out.

The man who wishes to know the visible — to know it both in

entirety and in depth — is obliged for that very reason to know the Invisible, on pain of absurdity and ineffectualness; to know it according to the principles which the very nature of the Invisible imposes on the human mind; hence to know it by being aware that the solution to the contradictions of the objective world is found ònly in the transpersonal essence of the subject, namely in the pure Intellect.

Besides — and this is another question altogether — how can the adepts of a scientism which sets out to reduce total Reality to a clockwork fail to see that the absurd — not, this time, insofar as it is simply an appearance of the unknown, but insofar as it is a manifestation of the indefinite and thereby of the unintelligible in itself — how can they fail to see that this cosmic absurdity is an integral part of the mirrorings of *Māyā* and hence of the economy of the Universe? One of the most difficult things there is morally is to concede the metaphysical right of existence to what is existentially absurd; not in theory alone, but on concrete contact with absurdity, which is almost the victory over the dragon. Now before wishing to abolish the absurd that is merely apparent, it is necessary to acknowledge the ineluctable presence of the absurd as such, which could not possibly be reabsorbed into the intelligible save in its function of being a necessary element in the equilibrium of things. For Reality does not limit itself to revealing its aspects of geometry. It also likes to conceal itself and to play hide-and-seek; it would be astonishing if it consented to unveil itself totally to mathematical minds; if it could consent to this it would not be *Maya*. Man is contingent and he is condemned to contingency, and contingency implies by definition the insoluble and the absurd.

Everything here is a question of causality: there are phenomena which seem absurd to us as long as we are ignorant of their causes, or because we are ignorant of them; and there are other phenomena which are absurd in themselves and which have no other cause than the cosmic necessity for that which has no necessity. Likewise there are possibilities which have no function other than to manifest the impossible, to the extent precisely that that is still possible; and it is possible at least in a symbolic way, which is sufficiently clear to manifest the intention of impossibility or absurdity.

Traditional and Modern Science*

The analogy between artistic naturalism and modern science permits us at this point to make a digression. We do not reproach modern science for being a fragmentary, analytical science, lacking in speculative, metaphysical and cosmological elements or for arising from the residues or debris of ancient sciences; we reproach it for being subjectively and objectively a transgression and for leading subjectively and objectively to disequilibrium and so to disaster.

Inversely, we do not have for the traditional sciences an unmixed admiration; the ancients also had their scientific curiosity, they too operated by means of conjectures and, whatever their sense of metaphysical or mystical symbolism may have been, they were sometimes — indeed often — mistaken in fields in which they wished to acquire a knowledge, not of transcendent principles, but of physical facts. It is impossible to deny that on the level of phenomena, which nevertheless is an integral part of the natural sciences, to say the least, the ancients — or the Orientals — have had certain inadequate conceptions, or that their conclusions were often most naïve; we certainly do not reproach them for having believed that the earth is flat and that the sun and the firmament revolve around it, since this appearance is natural and providential for man; but one can reproach them for certain false conclusions drawn from certain appearances, in the illusory belief that they were practising, not symbolism and spiritual speculation, but phenomenal or indeed exact science. One cannot, when all is said and done, deny that the purpose of medicine is to cure, not to speculate, and that the ancients were ignorant of many things in this field in spite of their great knowledge in certain others; in saying this, we are far from contesting that traditional medicine had, and has, the immense advantage of a perspective which includes the whole man; that it was, and is, effective in cases in which modern medicine is impotent; that modern medicine contributes to the degeneration of the human species and to overpopulation; and that an absolute medicine is neither possible nor desirable, and this

*From *EPW*, pp. 192-193.

for obvious reasons. But let no one say that traditional medicine is superior purely on account of its cosmological speculations and in the absence of particular effective remedies, and that modern medicine, which has these remedies, is merely a pitiful residue because it is ignorant of these speculations; or that the doctors of the Renaissance, such as Paracelsus, were wrong to discover the anatomical and other errors of Graeco-Arab medicine; or, in an entirely general way, that traditional sciences are marvellous in all respects and that modern sciences, chemistry for example, are no more than fragments and residues.

No piece of knowledge at the phenomenal level is bad in itself; but the important question is that of knowing, firstly, whether this knowledge is reconcilable with the ends of human intelligence, secondly, whether in the last analysis it is truly useful, and thirdly, whether man can support it spiritually; in fact there is proof in plenty that man cannot support a body of knowledge which breaks a certain natural and providential equilibrium, and that the objective consequences of this knowledge correspond exactly to its subjective anomaly. Modern science could not have developed except as the result of a forgetting of God, and of our duties towards God and towards ourselves; in an analogous manner, artistic naturalism, which first made its appearance in antiquity and was rediscovered at the beginnings of the modern era, can be explained only by the explosive birth of a passionately exteriorized and exteriorizing mentality.

NOTES

Modern Science and Metaphysical Reality

1. "Scientific" atheism is affirmed indirectly by the postulate of empty space and therefore of discontinuity, which, however, cannot be maintained with complete consistency. Now, to deny plenitude and continuity, including rhythm and necessity, or the providential element, is to deny Universal Substance with all its implications of homogeneity and transcendence.

2. This must not, of course, be confused with the emanationist heresy, which has nothing metaphysical about it and which reduces the Principle to the level of manifestation, or Substance to the level of accidents.

3. For God only manifests himself directly in a support which by definition marks the presence of the Absolute in relativity and is for this reason "relatively absolute". This "relative absoluteness" is the justification of the possibility *homo sapiens*. Man might disappear, if God so wished, but he could not change into another species; the Platonic ideas are precise possibilities and not just misty vagueness: every possibility is what it is and what it ought to be.

Criticism of Modern Art

Art—Traditional and Modern, Sacred and Profane*

. . . If we start from the idea that perfect art can be recognised by three main criteria— nobility of content, this being a spiritual condition, apart from which art has no right to exist; exactness of symbolism or at least, in the case of profane works of art, harmony of composition;[1] and purity of style or elegance of line and colour— we can discern with the help of these criteria the qualities and defects of any work of art, whether sacred or not. It goes without saying that some modern work may, as if by chance, possess these qualities; none the less it would be a mistake to see in this any justification of an art that is deprived of all positive principles; the exceptional qualities of such a work are in any case far from being characteristic of the art in question when viewed as a whole, but appear only incidentally under cover of the eclecticism which goes with anarchy. The existence of such works proves, however, that a legitimate profane art is conceivable in the West without any need to return purely and simply to the miniatures of the Middle Ages or to peasant painting,[2] for a healthy state of soul and a normal treatment of materials always guarantee the rectitude of an art devoid of pretensions. It is the nature of things— on the spiritual and on the psychological as well as on the material and technical level— which demands that

*From *LS*, pp. 122-135.

512

each of the constituent elements of art should fulfil certain elementary conditions, these being precisely the ones by which all traditional art is governed.

Here it is important to point out that one of the major errors of modern art is its confusion of art materials: people no longer know how to distinguish the cosmic significance of stone, iron or wood, just as they do not know the objective qualities of forms or colours. Stone has this in common with iron that it is cold and implacable, whereas wood is warm, live and kindly; but while the cold of stone is neutral and indifferent like that of eternity, iron is hostile, aggressive and ill-natured, and this enables us to understand the significance of the invasion of the world by iron.[3] The heavy and sinister nature of iron requires that in its use in handicrafts it should be treated lightly and with fantasy such as one sees for instance in old church screens which resemble lacework. The nature in iron ought to be neutralised by transparence in its treatment, for this does no violence to the nature of this metal but on the contrary confers legitimacy on its qualities of hardness and inflexibility by thus turning them to account; the sinister nature of iron implies that it has no right to full and direct manifestation but should be harshly treated or broken in order to be able to express its virtues. The nature of stone is quite different; in the raw state it has about it something sacred, and this is also true of the noble metals, which are like iron transfigured by cosmic light or fire or by planetary forces. It must be added that concrete — which, like iron, has invaded the whole world — is a base and quantitative sort of counterfeit stone; in it the spiritual aspect of eternity is replaced by an anonymous and brutal heaviness; if stone is implacable like death, concrete is brutal like an overwhelming destruction.

Before proceeding further we would wish to add the following reflection, not unrelated to the tyrannous expansion of the use of iron: it is easy to be astonished at the haste shown by the most artistic peoples of the East in adopting ugly things of the modern world; but it must not be overlooked that, apart from any question of aesthetics or spirituality, people have in all ages imitated those who were the strongest: before having strength people want to have at least the appearance of strength, and the ugly things of the modern world have become synonymous with power and independence. The essence of artistic beauty is spiritual, whereas material strength is "worldly", and, since the worldly regard strength as synonymous with intelligence, the beauty of the tradition becomes synonymous not merely with weakness, but also with stupidity, illusion and the ridiculous; being ashamed of weakness is almost always accompanied by hatred of what is looked on as the cause of this apparent inferiority — in this case, tradition, contemplation, truth. If most people — regardless of social level — have not enough discernment to overcome this lamentable optical illusion, some salutary reactions are none the less observable in some quarters.

It is told of Til Eulenspiegel[4] that, having been engaged as court painter to a prince, he presented to the assembled company a blank canvas, declaring that whoever was not the child of honest parents would see nothing on the canvas. Since none of the assembled lords was willing to admit he saw nothing, all pretended to admire the blank canvas. Now there was a time when this tale could pass as a pleasantry and none would have dared to foretell that it would one day enter into the manners of a "civilised" world. But in our day a nobody can in the name of "art for art's sake" show us anything he likes and, if we cry out in protest in the name of truth and intelligence, we are told we have not understood, as though some mysterious deficiency prevented us from understanding, not Chinese or Aztec art, but some inferior daub by a European living in the next street. By an abuse of language very prevalent today "to understand" means "to accept" and to reject means not to understand, as if it never happened that one refuses something precisely because one does understand it or accepts it only because one does not.

Behind all this lies a double and fundamental error but for which the pretensions of so-called artists would be inconceivable: it is the error of supposing that an originality which runs quite contrary to the hereditary collective norm is psychologically possible in one who is not insane and that a man can produce a true work of art which is not in any degree understandable to a great many intelligent and cultivated people belonging to the same civilisation, the same race and the same period as the selfstyled artist.[5] In reality the premisses of such originality or singularity do not exist in the normal human soul; still less do they exist in pure intelligence. Modern singularities, far from relating to some "mystery" of artistic creation, merely spell philosophical error and mental deformity. Everyone believes himself obliged to be a great man; novelty is taken for originality, morbid introspection for profundity, cynicism for sincerity and pretentiousness for genius, so that a point is even reached where a diagram of microbes or some zebra-like striping may be accepted as a painting. "Sincerity" is elevated to the rank of an absolute criterion, as though a work of art could not be psychologically "sincere" and at the same time spiritually false or artistically a nullity. Artists so affected make the grave mistake of deliberately ignoring the objective and qualitative value of forms and colours and of believing themselves to be sheltered in a subjectivism which they deem interesting and impenetrable, whereas in reality it is merely commonplace and ridiculous. Their very mistake forces them to have recourse to the lowest possibilities in the world of forms, just as Satan, when he wanted to be as "original" as God, had no choice open to him but the abominable.[6] In a general way cynicism seems to play an important part in a certain atheistical morality: virtue, it says, consists, not in dominating oneself and remaining silent, but in letting oneself run riot and proclaiming the fact from every housetop; every sin is good if boasted of with brutality; a struggle in silence is labelled "hypocrisy" because something remains concealed. To the same order of ideas belongs the belief that it is "sincere" or "realistic" to uncover cynically what nature keeps hidden as though nature acted without good purpose.

The modern conception of art is false in so far as it puts creative imagination — or even just the impulse to create — in the place of qualitative form, or in so far as a subjective and conjectural valuation is substituted for an objective and spiritual one; to do this is to replace by talent alone — by talent real or illusory — that skill and craftsmanship which must needs enter into the very definition of art, as if talent could have meaning quite apart from the normative constants that are its criteria. It is clear that originality has no meaning except through its content, exactly as is the case with sincerity; the originality of an error or the talent of an incompetent and subversive individual could not offer the slightest interest: a well-executed copy of a good model is worth more than an original creation which is the "sincere" manifestation of an evil genius.[7] When everyone wants to create and no one is willing to copy; when every work wants to be unique instead of inserting itself into a traditional continuity from which it draws its sap and of which it eventually becomes perhaps one of the finest flowers, it only remains for man to cry out his own nothingness in the face of the world; this nothingness will of course be viewed as synonymous with originality, since the less the artist recks of tradition or normality the greater will his talent be deemed to be. In the same order of ideas let us also mention the prejudice which would require every artist to "make himself anew", as though human life were not far too short to justify such a requirement or as though artists were not sufficiently numerous to render such a renewal on the part of each of them superfluous. After all one does not complain of the fact that a man's face remains the same from day to day, nor does one expect Persian art to turn suddenly into Maori art.

The error in the thesis of "art for art's sake" really amounts to supposing that there are relativities which bear their adequate justification within themselves, in their own relative nature, and that consequently there are criteria of value inaccessible to pure intelligence and foreign to objective truth. This error involves abolishing the primacy of the spirit and its replacement either by instinct or taste, by criteria that are either purely subjective or else arbitrary. We have already seen that the definition, laws and criteria of art cannot be derived from art itself, that is, from the competence of the artist as such; the foundations of art lie in the spirit, in metaphysical, theological and mystical knowledge, not in knowledge of the craft alone nor yet in genius, for this may be anything at all; in other words the intrinsic principles of art are essentially subordinate to extrinsic principles of a higher order. Art is an activity, an exteriorisation, and thus depends by definition on a knowledge that transcends it and gives it order; apart from such knowledge art has no justification: it is knowledge which determines action, manifestation, form, and never the reverse. It is not necessary to produce works of art oneself in order to have the right to judge an artistic production in its essentials; decisive artistic competence only comes into play in relation to an intellectual competence which must be already present.[8] No relative point of view can claim unqualified competence except in the case of innocuous activities in which competence applies anyhow in a very narrow field; now human art derives from a relative point of view; it is an application, not a principle.

Modern criticism more and more tends to put works of art into factitious categories: art is thus made out to be no more than a movement, and a point has been reached where works of art are appraised only in terms of other works and apart from any objective and stable criterion. The artist of the *"avant-garde"* is one whose vanity and cynicism impart momentum to the movement; critics seek, not for works which are good in themselves — some of them would deny that such works exist — but for works which are "novel" or "sincere" and can serve as points of reference in a movement which is in reality a downhill slide towards dissolution; the "quality" of art is then seen only in its movement and its relationships, which amounts to saying that no work has intrinsic value; everything has become fugitive and discontinuous. Artistic relativism destroys the very notion of art just as philosophic relativism destroys the notion of truth; relativism of whatever kind kills intelligence. One who despises truth cannot in sound logic propound his own contempt of it as truth.

In the same context it is significant that people are quite ready to extol some so-called artist on the ground that he "expresses his period" as though a period as such — something which may have no particular character — had rights over truth;[9] if what a "surrealist" expresses really corresponded to our times, this expression would prove only one thing, namely, that our times are not worth expressing; very fortunately, however, our times do still contain something besides surrealism. Be that as it may, to pretend that a work of art is good because "it expresses our times" amounts to affirming that a phenomenon is good simply because it expresses some thing: in that case crime is good because it expresses a criminal tendency, an error is good because it expresses a lack of knowledge and so forth. What defenders of surrealist tendencies either forget or do not know is above all that forms, whether in pictures, in sculpture, in architecture or in some other medium, arise from a hierarchy of cosmic values and translate either truths or errors so that here there is no place for adventuring; the psychological efficacy of forms, so beneficial when they are true, makes them on the contrary deadly if they are false.

In order to maintain an illusion of objectivity in an all-pervading subjectivity, quite imaginary and definitely hysterical qualities are projected into the most insignificant futilities: people discuss endlessly about "shades of contrast and balance" as if these were not to be found everywhere; in doing so they end by trampling in scorn rugs which are masterpieces of abstract art though unsigned. When almost anything may be art and anyone may be an artist, neither the word "art" nor the word "artist" retains any meaning; it is true that there exists a perversion of sensibility and intelligence ready to discover new dimensions and even "drama" in the most uncalled for extravagances, but a sane man has no need to occupy his mind with these things.[10] The great mistake of the surrealists is to believe that profundity lies in the direction of what is individual, that it is this, and not the universal, which is mysterious, and that the mystery grows more profound the more one delves into what is obscure and morbid: this is mystery turned upside down and therefore satanic, and it is at the same time a counterfeit of the "originality"—or uniqueness—of God. The error is to be found, however, also on another and seemingly opposite side: art then becomes an uninspired technique and a work of art amounts to no more than a "construction"; there it is not a case of residues of the subconscious, but only of reason and calculation, though this by no means excludes interferences from the irrational any more than intuitive surrealism, for its part, excludes calculated procedures. Pseudo-sincere affectations of simplicity do not escape from this same condemnation, for brutal compression and idiotism have no kind of connection with the simplicity of primordial things.

All that has been said above also applies in one way or another both to poetry and to music: here too some people arrogate to themselves the right to call realistic or sincere anything which, they say, "expresses the spirit of our age", when the "reality" to which they refer is only a factitious world from which they can no longer escape: they make a virtue of this incapacity and then disdainfully apply the label of "romanticism" or "nostalgia" to that innate need for harmony which is proper to every normal man. Ultramodern music—"electronic music" for example—is founded on a despising of everything that enters into the very definition of music, and, *mutatis mutandis*, the art of poetry is in similar case: it becomes no more than a system of sounds—most miserably fabricated—which violates the principle at the basis of poetry. There is no possible justification for this puerile mania for "making a clean sweep" of centuries or millennia in order to "start from scratch", coupled with the inventing of new principles, new bases, new structures—such invention is not merely senseless in itself but also incompatible with any creative sincerity. In other words some things are mutually exclusive: no one can call forth a poem from his heart while at the same time inventing *de novo* a language in which to express it. Here, as with the visual arts, the initial error is belief in a quasi-absolute originality, that is, in something which does not answer to any positive possibility, the musical sense of a racial or traditional collectivity not being capable of a modification extending to its very roots.[11] People talk about "liberating" music from this or that "prejudice", or "convention", or "constraint'"; what they really do is to "liberate" it from its own nature just as they have "liberated" painting from painting, poetry from poetry and architecture from architecture; surrealism has "freed" art from art just as by execution a corpse has been freed from life.

This allusion to music obliges us to draw attention to the fact that at the time of the Renaissance and in the following centuries the decadence of European music and poetry was incomparably less — if indeed there was any decadence or in such measure as there was — than that of the plastic arts and of architecture; there is no common measure between the sonnets of Michael-Angelo and the works for which he is more famous,[12] or between Shakespeare or Palestrina and the visual art of their day. The music of the Renaissance, like that of the Middle Ages of which it is a continuation, expresses in sound what is great and chivalrous in the European soul; it makes one think of wine or mead and of stirring legends of the past. The reason for this disproportion between the arts is that intellectual decadence — decadence of contemplative, not of inventive intelligence — is far more directly manifested in the visual arts, in which elements of intellectuality are strongly involved, than in auditive or "iterative" arts, which chiefly exteriorise the many and various states — and so in the event the beauties — of that plastic substance which is the soul.[13] In the plastic arts and in architecture the Renaissance means an art of passion and megalomania. As for baroque, it is an art that dreams, but in music baroque exteriorises what may be lovable, tender or paradisial in the dream, whereas in the visual arts it manifests the illusory and ludicrous aspects of the dream, enchantment coagulating into a nightmare. In the nineteenth century romantic poetry and music reinforced and made more acute the attachments to earth; like any sentimental individualism this was a terrible sowing of lacerations and sorrows, though in romanticism in the widest sense there are still many beauties one would wish to see integrated into a love of God.

Whilst ancient music included a spiritual value which can still be felt even in music of the end of the eighteenth century, the plane of music changed at the start of the nineteenth century so that it became in fact a kind of substitute for religion or mysticism: more than in the profane music of the preceding periods musical emotion came to assume the function of an irrational excuse for every human frailty; music grew ever more hypersensitive and grandiloquent as "everyday life" became imbued with scientific rationalism and mercantile materialism. But in general it was still real music, linked with cosmic qualities and consequently still capable of becoming, even if only rarely, the vehicle of a movement of the soul towards God.

Let us, however, return to the plastic arts and add this, which will at the same time serve as a conclusion: for contemporary artists and in so far as we are concerned with profane art there can be no question of just "going back", for one never gets back to one's starting point; rather should the valid experiments of naturalism and impressionism be combined with the principles of normal and normalising art, as is in fact done by some artists who are in general little known; modern art — starting from the Renaissance — does include some more or less isolated works which, though they fit into the style of their period, are in a deeper sense opposed to it and neutralise its errors by their own qualities.[14] In the case of sacred art resort to canonical models and treatment is called for without reservation, for, if there is in modern man an originality to which a human being may have a right, this will not fail to show itself within the framework of tradition, as indeed did happen in the Middle Ages with mentalities differing greatly in space and time. But first of all it is essential to learn to see afresh, to look and to understand that what is sacred belongs to the field of the immutable and not to that of change; it is not a question of tolerating a certain artistic stability on the basis of a pretended law of change, but on the contrary of tolerating a certain variation on the basis of the necessary and clear immutability of what is sacred; it is not sufficient that there should be genius, it must also have a right to exist. Words such as "conformism" and "immobilism" have been coined so as to be able to escape with easy conscience from everything which, since it is the clothing with form of Revelation, of necessity participates in Immutability.

In so far as profane art can be legitimate — as it can be, more than ever before, in this period of disfigurement and vulgarity — its mission is one of transmitting qualities of intelligence, beauty and nobility; and this is something which cannot be realised apart from those rules which are imposed on us, not only by the very nature of the art in question, but also by the spiritual truth flowing from the divine prototype of every human creation.

NOTES

Art—Traditional and Modern, Sacred and Profane

1. This condition equally requires right measure in regard to size; a profane work should never exceed certain dimensions; those are, for miniatures, very small—to mention one example.

2. Obviously the same cannot be said so far as sacred art is concerned; in the West this is exclusively the art of ikons and cathedrals and has by definition a character of immutability. Here let us once again mention the popular art of various European countries, which is, at any rate in a relative sense, Nordic in origin, though it is difficult to assign a precise origin to an art of immemorial antiquity This "rustic" art, preserved chiefly among the Teutons and Slavs, has also no clear geographical limits and even in Africa and Asia certain of its fundamental motifs can be traced, though in the latter case there is no need to presume any borrowing. Here is a most perfect art and one which is in principle capable of bringing health to the chaos in which what remain of our craftsmen are floundering.

3. The accumulation in Christian churches and places of pilgrimage of gross and harsh ironwork cannot but impede the radiation of spiritual forces. It always gives the impression that heaven is imprisoned.

4. A character of mediaeval legend, famous for his pranks.

5. This is singularity carried to its limit, to the point of caricature. Now it is well known that "singularity" is a defect stigmatised by every monastic discipline; its gravity is related to the sin of pride.

6. Modern art builds churches shaped like molluscs and pierces their walls with assymmetrical windows looking like the results of bursts of machine-gun fire as if by this means to betray its own true feelings. However much people may boast of the boldness of some such architectural design they cannot escape the intrinsic meaning of forms: they cannot prevent such a work from being related by the language of its forms to impish phantoms and nightmares: this is spiritualism transmuted into reinforced concrete.

7. It often happens that the value of a work is denied because someone has discovered — or thinks he has — that it had been wrongly ascribed, as if the value of a work of art lay outside itself. In traditional art the masterpiece is most often an anonymous culmination of a series of replicas; a work of genius is almost always the resultant of a long collective elaboration. For example, many Chinese masterpieces are copies of which the models are unknown.

8. This competence may, however, be limited to a particular traditional world. The competence of a brāhmin may not extend to Christian ikons, though there is here no limitation of principle. A necessary competence has the "right", though not of course the "duty", to be limited to a particular system of concordant possibilities.

9. This compliment is even paid to philosophers too; "the existential", the bare fact, everywhere crushes what is true by taking its name "The contemporary period" is a sort of false divinity in whose name everything seems permissible, whether on the plane of thought, on that of art or even on that of "religion".

10   One can find "abstract" works — though not commonly — which are neither better nor worse than some African shield, but why then make celebrities of their authors, or why not, on the other hand, count every Zulu as one of the immortals?

11. We have heard certain Asiatic music blamed for its "childish melancholy", and this is characteristic of a mental deformation which admires only what is factitious or forced: everything is shut up in a psychosis of "work", of "creation", even of "construction", factors which come to be taken as synonymous with "quality" as though the beauty of a flower or a bird's song depended on laborious and hypercritical research, on an atmosphere of laboratories and vivisection.

12. Apart from his sonnets the human greatness of Michael-Angelo appears chiefly in his sculpture, in works like the *Moses* or the *Pietà*, and that apart from any question of principles or style. In his painting and architecture this greatness seems crushed by the errors of the period; it gets lost in heaviness and pathos or in the sort of cult of the coldly gigantic which is a dominant mark of the Renaissance; his statuary, moreover, often suffers from this defect. The errors in question reach a sort of paroxysm in an artist like Rubens or, in a rather different way, in the unintelligent classicism of Ingres; on the other hand they are more or less attenuated in the case of delicate romanticists like Chasseriau and Moreau, or in the German landscape painters of the same period. With the impressionists the academic spirit fell into discredit; one would gladly believe that this was due to a slightly deeper understanding, but such is not the case, for an unforeseeable change of fashion was enough to call everything once again in question; moreover an academical spirit has already revived within surrealism, though always in the climate of oppressive ugliness characteristic of that school.

13. English architecture was less devastated by the Renaissance and by baroque than that of most continental countries. It may be that, by one of those paradoxes of which history is prodigal, Anglicanism preserved (against Rome) a certain Mediaeval heritage in matters of art, and this would seem to have been the less unlikely since the English are less creative than Italians, Germans or French. Something analogous could no doubt be said about the popular architecture of Spain and particularly of Andalusia where Arab influence seems to have played the part of a preserver.

14. Of famous or well-known painters the elder Brueghel's snow scenes may be quoted and, nearer to our day, Gauguin, some of whose canvases are almost perfect, Van Gogh's flower paintings, Douanier Rousseau with his exotic forests akin to folk painting, and, among our contemporaries, Covarrubias and his Mexican and Balinese subjects. We might perhaps also allude to certain American Indian painters whose work shows, through a naturalistic influence, a vision close to that of the ancient pictography. Conversely, equivalents of the positive experiments of modern art can be found in the most varied types of traditional art, which proves not only that these experiments are compatible with the universal principles of art, but also that — once again — "there is nothing new under the sun".

PART IX

SPIRITUAL IMPRESSIONS

Selected Poems

Mostaghanem

Star-drunken night above stony field,
White domes and sobbing sea.
The warning call of the muezzin cries out into the world
From a lofty parapet.
And the cool, far-wandering wind,
How it broods in the swaying palms;
And the desert song of the lonely flute,
How it rises and flows.
Star-drunken night above pale rocks and stones,
Arabian town, thou white grave.
Into thy magic I descend,
And into thy wonder I enter.
White domes and ever-weeping sea
And stones upon golden sand.
The voice of the muezzin falls lone and heavy
Like the howl of wolves his lamenting cry
Strays through infinite space.
Houses like graves are standing nearby
And a swaying, meditative tree.

(trans. S. H. Nasr)

Shaykh Ahmad

White stone steps, then twilight dimness;
Treading softly, we scarcely breathe.
Silence; for he sleepeth. And a wave
Of fragrance from Jannah streameth throughout the room.
Oh, he sleepeth not: his eyelids veil
The motionless light of ultimate wake.
Our steps cannot waken him;
He is Allah. And he heareth us not.
Yet his worn body lieth still adream.
His hands are like leaves,
Pale autumn leaves, not of this world —
Leaves from the Tree of Paradise;
Or stars that have come down
On the aged and sick body
And on his garment's white trim.

(trans. Martin Lings)

Laila

Laila, day kens Thee not, but only darkness
Of nights has knowledge of my deep delighting,
Of glowing wine from out Thy breasts most holy,
Or of mine eyes that in the dusk beheld
Thy body's radiance and Thy hair's star-sparkle.
Life kens Thee not —'tis the twilight alone
Of death can know Thee, whom ne'er fools approach,
For they, upon Thy love, must surely perish.
Ah, death alone knows of the wine's carbuncle
On lips that in last ecstasy have kissed Thee.

(trans. Barbara Perry)

Confession

She that I sing of is the fairest day;
I that do sing am the profoundest death.
Like lightning am I, and my Word is wine;
The world lies deep within my heart's own beat.
Thou that seekest for the Singer, ask
Neither for name, nor yet for mine and thine;
For Love is all that the world-sea contains,
And death in Love of Love the essence is.

(trans. Barbara Perry)

The Name

Thy Name is wine and honey, melody
That shapes our sacred way and destiny.
Who is the Speaker and who is the Word?
Where is the song Eternity has heard?

The liberating Word comes from the sky
Of Grace and Mercy; and we wonder why
Such gift can be; the truth is not so far:
Thy Name is That which is, and what we are.

Selections from Unpublished Letters

The Garden

A MAN SEES A BEAUTIFUL GARDEN, but he knows: he will not always see this garden, because one day he will die; and he also knows: the garden will not always be there, because this world will disappear one day. And he knows also: this kinship with the beautiful garden is the gift of destiny, because if a man were to find himself in the middle of a desert, he would not see the garden; he only sees it because destiny has put him, man, here and not elsewhere.

But in the innermost region of our soul lives the Spirit, and in it is contained the garden, as it were, like a seed; and if we love this garden — and how is it possible not to love it since it is of a heavenly beauty? — we would do well to look for it there where it has always been and always will be, that is to say in the Spirit; maintain yourself in the Spirit, in your own centre, and you will have the garden and in addition all possible gardens. Similarly: in the Spirit there is no death, because here you are immortal; and in the Spirit the relationship between the contemplator and the contemplated is not only a fragile possibility; on the contrary it is part of the very nature of the Spirit and, like it, it is eternal.

The Spirit is Consciousness and Will: Consciousness of oneself and Will towards oneself; the pure Spirit is inseparably one with the Supreme Name; this is why the Orison is the road towards the Self. Maintain your self in the Spirit through Consciousness, and approach

529

the Spirit through the Will or through Love; then neither death nor the end of the world can take away the garden from you nor destroy your vision. Whatever you are in the Spirit now, you will remain so after death; and whatever is yours now in the Spirit, will be yours after death. Before God there is neither being nor ownership except in the Spirit; whatever was outward must become inward and whatever was inward will become outward: look for the garden in yourself, in your indestructible divine Substance; then this will give you a new and imperishable garden. Whatever you love externally is to be found in the Orison, therefore attach yourself to it, dwell in it and live in it. The Orison is the seed of our eternity.

On the Holiness of the Name

When we say that the Name of God is an effect of the divine Cause, this signifies: in the domain of language, to which all words and all names pertain. Now it goes without saying that, if the word "God" is an effect of the divine Cause, it is not so in a merely general sense as is the case for example with the words "stone" or "tree"; for we call the word "God" an effect of the divine Cause because, precisely, its content is God and nothing else, and because, in consequence, the fact of thinking or of pronouncing this word has an effect other than that of thinking or pronouncing the words "tree" or "stone". When I say "tree", nothing happens; when on the other hand I say "God", God listens to me, whether I invoke Him, whether I recognize His reality, or again, whether on the contrary I abuse his Name, and it is for this reason that it is said: "Hallowed be Thy Name". Moreover, writing belongs to the domain of language as well; and here also there is a quasi-magical difference between the inscription "God" and any other inscription; for God is not indifferent towards my manner of treating the inscription "God", while He is indifferent toward my manner of treating the inscription "tree", "stone", "house" or "mountain". This is so because God is the witness at once transcendent and immanent of all that happens, whether it be in the exterior world or within the soul; to the degree that we understand this through direct knowledge, or that we apprehend it through faith, — the one does not exclude the other,—we are able to have the intimate experience of this connection between God and the word which expresses Him, therefore of His presence in His Name.

Two Unequal Heredities

When a seeker plans to pass from one religious form to another, and this in view of the *religio perennis* and not through conversion, it can happen that he comes up against his religious heredity— whether this be conceptual or psychic—due to the fact that his forefathers have practiced that religion over the centuries; and the seeker will be tempted to believe that this heredity is insurmountable, thus that it has about it something absolute; while in reality it is relative by the fact that there is, in the depths of the soul, another heredity which is absolute because it is primordial and which is, precisely, the *religio perennis*. This deep-seated heredity is like the remembrance of the lost Paradise, and it can erupt in the soul by a kind of providential atavism; we have in mind here men who, while having behind them generations of religious believers impregnated with a given religious formalism, nevertheless benefit personally from the primordial heredity.

The *religio perennis* comprises essentially the following elements:

Discernment between the Real and the illusory, the Absolute and the relative, God and the world; and, by way of consequence, Discernment of the roots or the prefigurations of the relative in the Absolute, and of the reflections of the Absolute within relativity.

Sincere and persevering Concentration on the Real, by means of the Quintessential Orison.

Conformity of the soul to the Real, that is to say beauty of soul or the virtues; the essence of this beauty being the sense of the Sacred. One could also say that beauty of soul is on the one hand Faith, with all its consequences, and on the other hand Adoration, with all its consequences.

Equally forming a part of the *religio perennis*—by way of consequence—is the sense of forms under the three-fold relationship of beauty, symbolism, and sacramentality; whether the forms be those of virgin nature, including creatures, or of sacred art, or of artisanship in the broadest sense. For art is man; and man is Devotion.

Logic or integrity of the intelligence; of the will; of the soul; of the ambience.

Against Subtle Worldliness

There is an outer man and an inner man; the first lives in the world and undergoes its influence, whereas the second looks towards God and lives from Prayer. Now it is necessary that the outer man not affirm himself to the detriment of the inner man; it is the inverse which must take place. Instead of inflating the outer man and allowing the inner man to die, it is necessary to allow the inner man to expand, and to entrust the cares of the outer to God.

Who says outer man says preoccupations of the world, or even worldliness: in effect there is in every man a tendency to attach himself too much to this or that element of passing life or to worry about it too much, and the adversary takes advantage of this in order to cause troubles for us. There is also the desire to be happier than one is, or the desire not to suffer any injustices, even harmless ones, or the desire always to understand everything, or the desire never to be disappointed; all of this is of the domain of subtle worldliness, which must be countered by serene detachment, by the principial and initial certainty of That which alone matters, then by patience and confidence. When no help comes from Heaven, this is because it is a question of a difficulty which we can and must resolve with the means which Heaven has placed at our disposal. In an absolute way, it is necessary to find our happiness in Prayer; that is to say, that it is necessary to find therein sufficient happiness so as not to allow ourselves to be excessively troubled by the things of the world, seeing that dissonances cannot but exist, the world being what it is.

There is the desire not to suffer any injustices, or even simply not to be placed at a disadvantage. Now one of two things: either the injustices are the result of our past faults, and in this case our trials exhaust this causal mass; or the injustices result from our character, and in this case our trials bear witness to it; in both cases, we must thank God and invoke Him with all the more fervor, without preoccupying ourselves with worldly chaff. One must also say to oneself that the grace of Prayer compensates infinitely for every dissonance from which we can suffer, and that in relation to this grace, the inequality of terrestrial favors is a pure nothingness. Let us never forget that an infinite grace compels us to an infinite gratitude, and that the first stage of gratitude is the sense of proportions.

Sophia Perennis*

"*PHILOSOPHIA PERENNIS*" is generally understood as referring to that metaphysical truth which has no beginning, and which remains the same in all expressions of wisdom. Perhaps it would here be better or more prudent to speak of a "*Sophia perennis*", since it is not a question of artificial mental constructions, as is all too often the case in philosophy; or again, the primordial wisdom that always remains true to itself could be called "*Religio perennis*", given that by its nature it in a sense involves worship and spiritual realization. Fundamentally we have nothing against the word "philosophy", for the ancients understood by it all manner of wisdom; in fact, however, rationalism, which has absolutely nothing to do with true spiritual contemplation, has given the word "philosophy" a limitative colouring, so that with this word one can never know what is really being spoken about. If Kant is a "philosopher", then Plotinus is not, and vice versa.

With *Sophia perennis*, it is a question of the following: there are truths innate in the human Spirit, which nevertheless in a sense lie buried in the depth of the "Heart"— in the pure Intellect — and are accessible only to the one who is spiritually contemplative; and these are the fundamental metaphysical truths. Access to them is possessed by the "gnostic", "pneumatic" or "theosopher",— in the original and not the sectarian meaning of these terms,— and access to them was also possessed by the "philosophers" in the real and still innocent sense of the word: for example, Pythagoras, Plato and to a large extent also Aristotle.

*Trans. by W. Stoddart

. . .

If there were no Intellect, no contemplative and directly knowing Spirit, no "Heart-Knowledge", there would also be no reason capable of logic; animals have no reason, for they are incapable of knowledge of God; in other words: man possesses reason or understanding — and also language — only because he is fundamentally capable of supra-rational vision, and thus of certain metaphysical truth.

The fundamental content of the Truth is the Unconditioned, the Metaphysical Absolute; the Ultimate One, which is also the Absolutely Good, the Platonic Agathon. But it lies in the nature of the Absolute to be Infinity and All-Possibility, and in this sense St. Augustine said that it is in the nature of the Good to communicate itself; if there is a sun, then there is also radiation; and therein lies the necessity of the cosmos which proclaims God.

However, to say radiation is also to say separation from the source of light: since God is the absolute and infinite Good, whatever is not God — that is to say, the world as such — cannot be absolutely good: the nondivinity of the cosmos brings with it, in its limitations, the phenomenon of evil or wickedness which, because it is a contrast, emphasizes all the more the nature of the Good. "The more he blasphemes," as Eckhart said, "the more he praises God."

The essential here is discrimination between Ātmā and Māyā, between Reality seen as "Self", and relativity seen as "cosmic play": since the Absolute is infinite, — failing which it would not be the Absolute, — it must give rise to a Māyā, a "lesser reality" and in a sense an "illusion". Ātmā is the Principle, — the Primordial Principle, one might say, — and Māyā is manifestation or effect; strictly speaking Māyā is in a sense also Ātmā, since in the last analysis there is only Ātmā, and therefore both poles must impinge on one another, and must be bound up with one another, in the sense that, in Ātmā, Māyā is in a way prefigured, whereas, contrariwise, Māyā in its own fashion represents or reflects Ātmā. In Ātmā, Māyā is Being, the Creator of the world, the Personal God, who reveals Himself to the world in all His possibilities of Manifestation; in Māyā, Ātmā is any reflection of the Divine, such as the Avatara, the Holy Scriptures, the God-transmitting symbol.

In the domain of Māyā or relativity, there is not only "space", there is also "time", to speak comparatively or metaphorically: there are not only simultaneity and gradation, but also change and succession; there are not only world, but also "ages" or "cycles". All this belongs to the "play" of Māyā, to the well-nigh "magical" unfolding of the possibilities hidden in the Primordial One.

•   •   •

But in the Universal All there is not only "that which is known", there is also "that which knows"; in Ātmā the two are undivided, the one is inseparably present in the other, whereas in Māyā this One is split into two poles, namely object and subject. Ātmā is the "Self"; but one can also call it "Being",—not in the restrictive sense,—depending on the point of view or relationship in question: it is knowable as Reality, but it is also the Knowledge, dwelling within us, of all that is real.

From this it follows that the knowledge of the One or of the All, in accordance with its nature, calls for a unifying and total knowledge; it calls, over and above our thinking, for our being. And herein is defined the goal of all spiritual life: whoever knows the Absolute — or whoever "believes in God"—cannot remain stationary with this mental knowledge or with this mental faith, he must go further and involve his whole being in this knowledge or in this faith; not in so far as knowledge and faith are purely mental, but in so far as, in accordance with their true nature and through their content, they demand more and give more than mere thinking. Man must "become what he is", precisely by "becoming that which is". This immediate spiritual necessity applies both to the simplest religion and to the profoundest metaphysics, each in its own way.

And all this proceeds from the fact that man not only knows, he also wills; to the capacity of knowing the Absolute, belongs also the capacity of willing it; to the Totality of the Spirit pertains the freedom of the will. Freedom of the will would be meaningless without a goal prefigured in the Absolute; without knowledge of God, it would be neither possible nor of any use.

•   •   •

Man consists of thinking, willing and loving: he can think the true or the false, he can will the good or the bad, he can love the beautiful or the ugly. It should be emphasized here that one loves the good that is ugly for its inner beauty, and this is immortal, whereas outward ugliness is ephemeral; on the other hand, one must not forget that outward beauty, in spite of any inward ugliness, bears witness to beauty as such, which is of a celestial nature and may not be despised in any of its manifestations.

Thinking the true — or knowing the real — demands on the one hand the willing of the good and on the other the loving of the beautiful, and thus of virtue, for this is nothing else than beauty of soul; it was not for nothing that, for the Greeks, virtue pertained to true philosophy. Without beauty of soul all willing is barren, it is trivial, selfish, vain and hypocritical; and similarly: without spiritual work, that is, without the co-operation of the will, all thinking remains, in the last analysis, superficial and of no avail. The essence of virtue is that one's sentiments or feelings should correspond to the highest truth: hence in the sage his rising above things and above himself; hence his selflessness, his greatness of soul, his nobility and his generosity; metaphysical truth as content of one's consciousness does not go hand in hand with triviality, pretentiousness, ambition and the like. "Be ye therefore perfect, even as your Father in Heaven is perfect."

Furthermore: one could not love earthly values, if these were not rooted in the Divine; in earthly things one is unconsciously loving God. The spiritual man does this consciously, the earthly good always leads him back to the Divine: on the one hand he loves nothing more than God — or loves nothing so much as God — and on the other hand he loves everything that is lovable in God.

There is something that man must know or think; something that he must will or do; and something that he must love or be. He must know that God is necessary, self-sufficient Being, that He is That which cannot not be; and he must know that the world is only the possible, namely that which may either be or not be; all other discriminations and value judgements are derived from this metaphysical distinguo. Furthermore, man must will whatever directly or indirectly leads him to God, and thus abstain from whatever removes him from God; the main content of this willing is prayer, the response to God, and therein is included all spiritual activity, including metaphysical reflection. And then, as already mentioned, man must love whatever corresponds to God; he must love the Good, and since the Good necessarily transcends his own selfhood, he must make an effort to overcome this narrow and weak selfhood. One must love the Good in itself more than one's ego, and this self-knowledge and selfless love constitute the whole nobility of the soul.

• • •

The Divine is Absoluteness, Infinitude and Perfection. Māyā is not only the radiation which manifests God and which, through this manifestation, necessarily distances itself from God, it is also the principle — or the instrument — of refraction and multiplication: it manifests the Divine not only through the one existence, but also through the innumerable forms and qualities that shimmer in existence. And since we perceive these values and recognize them as values, we know that it is not enough to call the Divinity the Absolute and the Infinite; we know that, in its Absoluteness and Infinity, it is also the Perfect, from which all cosmic perfections derive, and to which in a thousand tongues they bear witness.

• • •

Pure "dogmatism" and mere "speculation", many may say. This in fact is the problem: a metaphysical exposition appears as a purely mental phenomenon, when one does not know that its origin is not a mental elaboration or an attitude of soul, but a vision which is completely independent of opinions, conclusions and creeds, and which is realized in the pure Intellect — through the "Eye of the Heart". A metaphysical exposition is not true because it is logical, — in its form it could also not be so, — but it is in itself logical, that is to say, well-founded and consequential, because it is true. The thought-process of metaphysics is not an artificial support for an opinion that has to be proved, it is simply description that has been adapted to the rules of human thinking; its proofs are aids, not ends in themselves.

St. Thomas Aquinas said that it was impossible to prove the Divine Being, not because it was unclear, but, on the contrary, because of its "excess of clarity". Nothing is more foolish than the question as to whether the supra-sensory can be proved: for, on the one hand, one can prove everything to the one who is spiritually gifted, and, on the other, the one who is not so gifted is blind to the best of proofs. Thought is not there in order to exhaust reality in words, — if it could do this, it would itself be reality, a self-contradictory supposition, — but its role can only consist in providing keys to Reality; the key is not Reality, nor can it wish to be so, but it is a way to it for those that can and will tread that way; and in the way there is already something of the end, just as in the effect there is something of the cause.

That modern thought, still wrongly called "philosophical", distances itself more and more from a logic which is deemed to be "scholastic", and more and more seeks to be "psychologically" and even "biologically" determined, does not escape our notice, but this cannot in any way prevent us from thinking or being in the manner that the theomorphic nature of man, and hence the sufficient reason of the human state, demand. One speaks much today of the "man of our time" and one claims for him the right to determine the truth of this "time", as if man were a "time", and as if truth were not valid for man as such; what in man is mutable does not belong to man as such; what constitutes the miracle of "man" is not subject to change, for, in the image of God, there can be neither decrease nor increase. And that man is this image follows from the simple fact that he possesses the concept of the Absolute. In this one primordial concept lies the whole essence of man and therefore also his whole vocation.

Appendix—The Writings of Schuon

SINCE 1933 WHEN THE FIRST ARTICLE of Schuon appeared in *Le Voile d'Isis* in Paris, an important series of books and articles has been produced by this most creative master. Usually written in French, many of these works have been translated into various languages, including not only the main European ones such as English, Italian, Spanish, German, and Portuguese, but also Oriental tongues such as Arabic and Persian. His articles have been printed over the years mostly in the *Etudes Traditionnelles*, but also in *France-Asie*, *Studies in Comparative Religion*, *Sophia Perennis*, *Islamic Quarterly*, *Kairos*, *Antaios*, *Zeitschrift für Ganzheitsforschung*, *Rivista di Studi Iniziatici*, *Initiative*, *Triveni*, and other journals in East and West.

Since those articles of Frithjof Schuon which in his own eyes deserved to be preserved have been mostly incorporated in his books, a complete bibliography of his writings is not called for. We have therefore confined ourselves to the enumeration of his books and their translations:

Leitgedanken zur Urbesinnung, Zurich and Leipzig, Orell Füssli Verlag, 1935; second edition as *Urbesinnung—Das Denken des Eigentlichen*, Freiburg im Breisgau, Aurum Verlag, 1989.

De L'Unité transcendante des religions, Paris, Gallimard, 1948, 1958; revised edition, Paris, Le Seuil, 1979; Paris, Sulliver, 2000.
  Translations:
    The Transcendent Unity of Religions, London, Faber & Faber, 1953; New York, Harper & Row, 1975; Wheaton (Illinois), The Theosophical Publishing House, 1993.
    De la unidad transcendente de las religiones, Buenos Aires, Ediciones Anaconda, 1949; Madrid, Ediciones Heliodoro, 1980; new edition, Mallorca, José J. de Olañeta, Editor, 2004.
    De l'Unità trascendente delle religione, Bari, Gius, La terza & Figli, 1949 (new translation as *Unita trascendente...*, Rome, Editione Mediterranae, 1953).
    Da Unidade transcendente das religiones, Sao Paulo, Livraria Martins Editora, 1953.
    Von der Inneren Einheit der Religionen, Ansata, Interlaken, 1981.

L'Oeil du coeur, Paris, Gallimard, 1950; new revised edition, Paris, Dervy-Livres, 1974; Lausanne, L'Âge d'Homme, 2001.
  Translations:
    The Eye of the Heart, Bloomington (Indiana), World Wisdom Books, 1997.

El ojo del corazón, Mallorca, José J. de Olañeta, Editor, 2003.

Perspectives spirituelles et faits humains, Paris, Les Cahiers du Sud, 1953; Paris, Maisonneuve & Larose, 1989; Lausanne, L'Âge d'Homme, 2001.
Translations:
    Spiritual Perspectives and Human Facts, London, Faber & Faber, 1954; new revised edition, Bedfont, Perennial Books, 1987.
    Perspectivas espirituales y hechos humanos, Mallorca, José J. de Olañeta, Editor, 2001.

Sentiers de gnose, Paris, La Colombe, 1957; Paris, La Place Royale, 1987, 1996.
Translations:
    Gnosis—Divine Wisdom, London, John Murray, 1959; London, Perennial Books, 1978, 1990.
    Senderos de Gnosis, José J. de Olañeta, Mallorca, Editor, 2002.

Castes et races, Lyon, Paul Derain, 1957; Milano, Archè, 1979.
Translations:
    Castes and Races, London, Perennial Books, 1959, 1982.
    Castas y Razas, Mallorca, José J. de Olañeta, Editor, 1983.

Les Stations de la Sagesse, Paris, Buchet/Chastel, 1958; Paris, Maisonneuve & Larose, 1992.
Translations:
    Stations of Wisdom, London, John Murray, 1961; London, Perennial Books, 1978; new edition, Bloomington (Indiana), World Wisdom Books, 1995.
    La Stazioni della saggetta, Rome, Edizioni Mediterranae, 1981.
    Las estaciones de la sabiduría, Mallorca, José J. de Olañeta, Editor, 2001.

Language of the Self, Madras, Ganesh, 1959; Bangalore, Select Books, 1998; Bloomington (Indiana), World Wisdom Books, 1999.

Images de l'esprit, Paris, Flammarion, 1961; Le Courrier du Livre, 1982.
Translation:
    Imágenes del Espíritu: Shinto, Budismo, Yoga, Mallorca, José J. de Olañeta, Editor, 2001.

Comprendre l'Islam, Paris, Gallimard, 1961; Paris, Le Seuil, 1976.
Translations:
    Understanding Islam, London, Allen & Unwin, 1963; Baltimore, Penguin Books, 1972; revised translation, Bloomington (Indiana), World Wisdom Books, 1994, 1997.
    Comprendere l'Islam, Milano, Archè, 1976.
    Comprender el Islam, Mallorca, José J. de Olañeta, Editor, 1987.
    Hatta nafham al-islam, (Arabic), Beirut, 1980.

Regards sur les mondes anciens, Paris, Editions Traditionnelles, 1968; Falicon, Nataraj, 1997.
Translations:

Light on the Ancient Worlds, London, Perennial Books, 1965;
   Bloomington (Indiana), World Wisdom Books, 1984; new edition,
   World Wisdom, 2006.
Miradas a los mundos antiguos, Madrid, Taurus Ediciones, 1980; new
   edition, Mallorca, José J. de Olañeta, Editor, 2004.

In the Tracks of Buddhism, London, Allen & Unwin, 1968.

Dimensions of Islam, London, Allen & Unwin, 1969.

Logique et transcendance, Paris, Editions Traditionnelles, 1970.
   Translations:
   Logic and Transcendence, New York, Harper & Row, 1975; London,
      Perennial Books, 1984.
   Der Mensch und die Gewissheit, Stuttgart, Edition Axel Menges, 1996.
   Logica y transcendencia, Mallorca, José J. de Olañeta, Editor, 2000.

Das Ewige im Verganglichen, Weilheim, Oberbayern, Otto Wilhelm Barth
Verlag, 1970.

Tidols Besinning I besinninglos Tid-ur Frithjof Schuon Werk, ed. K. Almquist,
Stockholm, Natur och Kultur, 1973.

Forme et substance dans les religions, Paris, Dervy-Livres, 1975.
   Translations:
   Form and Substance in the Religions, Bloomington (Indiana), World
      Wisdom, 2002.
   Forma y substancia en las religiones, Mallorca, José J. de Olañeta, Editor,
      1998.

Islam and the Perennial Philosophy, London, World of Islam Publishing Co.,
1976.

L'Esotérisme comme principe et comme voie, Paris, Dervy-Livres, 1978, 1997.
   Translations:
   Esoterism as Principle and as Way, London, Perennial Books, 1981.
   El esoterismo como principio y como vía, Madrid, Taurus Ediciones, 1982;
      new edition, Mallorca, José J. de Olañeta, Editor, 2003.

Le Soufisme voile et quintessence, Paris, Dervy-Livres, 1980.
   Translations:
   Sufism, Veil and Quintessence, Bloomington (Indiana), World Wisdom
      Books, 1981.
   El sufismo, velo y quintaesencia, Mallorca, José J. de Olañeta, Editor,
      2000.

Du Divin à l'humain, Paris, Le Courrier du Livre, 1981.
   Translations:
   From the Divine to the Human, Bloomington (Indiana), World Wisdom
      Books, 1982.
   De lo Divino a lo humano, Mallorca, José J. de Olañeta, Editor, 1982.

Christianisme/Islam: visions d'oecuménisme ésotérique, Milan, Archè, 1981.
Translations:
    Christianity/Islam—Essays on Esoteric Ecumenism, Bloomington
    (Indiana), World Wisdom Books, 1985.
    Cristianismo—Islam. Visiones de ecumenismo esotérico, Mallorca, José J. de
    Olañeta, Editor, 2003.

Sur les traces de la Religion pérenne, Paris, Le Courrier du Livre, 1982.
Translation:
    Tras las huellas de la religión perenne, Mallorca, José J. de Olañeta, Editor,
    1982.

Approches du phénomène religieux, Paris, Le Courrier du Livre, 1982.
Translations:
    In the Face of the Absolute, Bloomington (Indiana), World Wisdom
    Books, 1989.
    Aproximaciones al fenómeno religioso, Mallorca, José J. de Olañeta, Editor,
    2000.

Resumé de métaphysique intégrale, Paris, Le Courrier du Livre, 1985.
Translations:
    Survey of Metaphysics and Esoterism, Bloomington (Indiana), World
    Wisdom Books, 1986. (including *Sur les traces de la Religion pérenne*.)
    Resumen de metafísica integral, Mallorca, José J. de Olañeta, Editor, 2000.

Avoir un centre, Paris, Maisonneuve, 1988.
Translations:
    To Have a Center, Bloomington (Indiana), World Wisdom Books, 1990.
    Tener un centro, Mallorca, José J. de Olañeta, Editor, 2001.

Racines de la condition humaine, Paris, La Table Ronde, 1990.
Translations:
    Roots of the Human Condition, Bloomington (Indiana), World Wisdom
    Books, 1991; second edition, World Wisdom, 2002.
    Raíces de la condición humana, Madrid, Grupo Libro, 1995; new edition,
    Mallorca, José J. de Olañeta, Editor, 2002.

The Feathered Sun—Plains Indians in Art and Philosophy, Bloomington
(Indiana), World Wisdom Books, 1990.
Translation:
    El sol emplumado. Los indios de las Praderas a través del arte y la filosofía,
    Mallorca, José J. de Olañeta, Editor, 1992.
    Il Sole Piumato: Religione e Arte degli Indiani delle Praterie, Roma, Edizione
    Mediterranee, 2000.

Les Perles du pèlerin, Paris, Le Seuil, 1991.
Translations:
    Echoes of Perennial Wisdom, Bloomington (Indiana), World Wisdom
    Books, 1992.

Las Perlas del Peregrino, Mallorca, José J. de Olañeta, Editor, 1990.

Images of Primordial and Mystic Beauty, Bloomington (Indiana), Abodes, 1992.

Le Jeu des Masques, Lausanne, L'Âge d'Homme, 1992.
Translations:
   The Play of Masks, Bloomington (Indiana), World Wisdom Books, 1992.
   El juego de las máscaras, Mallorca, José J. de Olañeta, Editor, 2003.

Treasures of Buddhism, Bloomington (Indiana), World Wisdom Books, 1993.
Translations:
   Trésors du Bouddhisme, Falicon, Nataraj, 1997.
   Tesoros del budismo, Barcelona, Paidós, 1998.

Road to the Heart, Bloomington (Indiana), World Wisdom Books, 1995.

La Transfiguration de l' Homme, Paris, Maisonneuve Larose, 1995.
Translations:
   The Transfiguration of Man, Bloomington (Indiana), World Wisdom
   Books, 1995.
   La transfiguración del hombre, Mallorca, José J. de Olañeta, Editor, 2003.

Liebe, Verlag Herder, 1997.

Leben, Verlag Herder, 1997.

Glück, Verlag Herder, 1997.

Sinn, Verlag Herder, 1997.

Poésies didactiques (Vol 1-10), Sottens, Les Sept Flèches, 2001.

Songs for a Spiritual Traveler: Selected Poems, Bloomington (Indiana), World Wisdom, 2002.

Adastra & Stella Maris: Poems by Frithjof Schuon, Bloomington (Indiana), World Wisdom, 2003.

Edited Writings of Frithjof Schuon

The Essential Writings of Frithjof Schuon, ed. Seyyed Hossein Nasr, New York, Amity House, 1986.

The Fullness of God: Frithjof Schuon on Christianity, ed. James S. Cutsinger, Bloomington (Indiana), World Wisdom, 2004.

Prayer Fashions Man: Frithjof Schuon on the Spiritual Life, ed. James S. Cutsinger, Bloomington (Indiana), World Wisdom, 2005.

Table of Abbreviations

CI *Christianisme/Islam*
DI *Dimensions of Islam*
EPW *Esoterism as Principle and as Way*
FDH *From the Divine to the Human*
GDW *Gnosis — Divine Wisdom*
IPP *Islam and the Perennial Philosophy*
ITB *In the Tracks of Buddhism*
LAW *Light on the Ancient Worlds*
LS *Language of the Self*
LT *Logic and Transcendence*
SCR *Studies in Comparative Religion*
SPHF *Spiritual Perspectives and Human Facts*
STRP *Sur les traces de la Religion pérenne*
SVQ *Sufism, Veil and Quintessence*
SW *Stations of Wisdom*
TUR *The Transcendent Unity of Religions*
UI *Understanding Islam*

Biographical Notes

FRITHJOF SCHUON

BORN IN BASLE, SWITZERLAND in 1907, Frithjof Schuon was the twentieth century's pre-eminent spokesman for the perennialist school of comparative religious thought.

The leitmotif of Schuon's work was foreshadowed in an encounter during his youth with a marabout who had accompanied some members of his Senegalese village to Basle for the purpose of demonstrating their African culture. When Schuon talked with him, the venerable old man drew a circle with radii on the ground and explained: "God is the center; all paths lead to Him." Until his later years Schuon traveled widely, from India and the Middle East to America, experiencing traditional cultures and establishing lifelong friendships with Hindu, Buddhist, Christian, Muslim, and American Indian spiritual leaders.

A philosopher in the tradition of Plato, Shankara, and Eckhart, Schuon was a gifted artist and poet as well as the author of over twenty books on religion, metaphysics, sacred art, and the spiritual path. Describing his first book, *The Transcendent Unity of Religions*, T. S. Eliot wrote, "I have met with no more impressive work in the comparative study of Oriental and Occidental religion", and world-renowned religion scholar Huston Smith has said of Schuon that "the man is a living wonder; intellectually apropos religion, equally in depth and breadth, the paragon of our time". Schuon's books have been translated into over a dozen languages and are respected by academic and religious authorities alike.

More than a scholar and writer, Schuon was a spiritual guide for seekers from a wide variety of religions and backgrounds throughout the world. He died in 1998.

SEYYED HOSSEIN NASR is University Professor of Islamic Studies at the George Washington University. The author of over fifty books and five hundred articles, he is one of the world's most respected writers and speakers on Islam, its arts and sciences, and its traditional mystical path, Sufism. His publications include *Sufi Essays, Knowledge and the Sacred, Religion and the Order of Nature, A Young Muslim's Guide to the Modern World, The Heart of Islam: Enduring Values for Humanity,* and *Islam: Religion, History, and Civilization.* A volume in the prestigious *Library of Living Philosophers* series has been dedicated to his thought.